Wow! 1001 Homemade Dairy-Free Recipes

(Wow! 1001 Homemade Dairy-Free Recipes - Volume 1)

Lisa Perry

Copyright: Published in the United States by Lisa Perry/ © LISA PERRY

Published on October, 13 2020

All rights reserved. No part of this publication may be reproduced, stored in retrieval system, copied in any form or by any means, electronic, mechanical, photocopying, recording or otherwise transmitted without written permission from the publisher. Please do not participate in or encourage piracy of this material in any way. You must not circulate this book in any format. LISA PERRY does not control or direct users' actions and is not responsible for the information or content shared, harm and/or actions of the book readers.

In accordance with the U.S. Copyright Act of 1976, the scanning, uploading and electronic sharing of any part of this book without the permission of the publisher constitute unlawful piracy and theft of the author's intellectual property. If you would like to use material from the book (other than just simply for reviewing the book), prior permission must be obtained by contacting the author at author@polentarecipes.com

Thank you for your support of the author's rights.

Content

CHAPTER 1: DAIRY-FREE MAIN DISH RECIPES 15

1. Alaskan Cod And Shrimp With Fresh Tomato 15
2. American Chop Suey II 15
3. Angela's Easy Breaded Chicken 16
4. Apple Radish BBQ Ribs 16
5. Asian Breakfast Stir Fry 16
6. Aunt Fannie's Dinner 17
7. BBQ Chili Pasta 17
8. BBQ Salmon Over Mixed Greens 18
9. Bachelor's Hash 19
10. Bahamian Baked Grouper 19
11. Baked Honey Mustard Chicken 20
12. Baked Slow Cooker Chicken 20
13. Baked Tilapia In Garlic And Olive Oil 20
14. Balsamic Chicken Breasts 21
15. Barbeque Pork Two Ways 21
16. Barbeque Seitan And Black Bean Burritos 22
17. Barbequed Marinated Flank Steak 23
18. Beefy Spanish Rice 23
19. Bessy's Zesty Grilled Garlic Herb Chicken 23
20. Best Burger Ever 24
21. Big M's Spicy Lime Grilled Prawns 24
22. Blackened Chicken 25
23. Blackened Tuna Steaks With Mango Salsa 25
24. Braised Balsamic Chicken 26
25. Buckwheat Tortilla Pizza 26
26. Bulgur Veggie Stir Fry 27
27. Busy Day Deer 28
28. Butternut Squash Porridge 28
29. Cabin Dinner 28
30. Carol's Arroz Con Pollo 29
31. Chicken Fried Chicken 29
32. Chicken Lo Mein 30
33. Chicken Seitan 30
34. Chicken And Lentils With Rosemary 31
35. Chicken And Sausage With Bowties 32
36. Chinese Chicken Fried Rice I 32
37. Chtitha Batata (Algerian Potato Stew) 33
38. Coal Miners Pasties 33
39. Cola Pot Roast I 34
40. Cola Basted Ham 34
41. Cold Roasted Moroccan Spiced Salmon ... 35
42. Corned Beef And Cabbage II 35
43. Cornish Game Hens With Garlic And Rosemary 36
44. County Fair Corn Dogs 37
45. Cranberry Pot Roast 37
46. Creamy Apple Cinnamon Raisin Oatmeal 37
47. Creamy Beef Tips With Mushrooms 38
48. Creamy Vegan Pumpkin Penne Pasta 38
49. Crunchy Vegan Tostadas 39
50. Cuban Black Beans I 40
51. Dad's Candied Salmon 40
52. Day Before Pay Day Fried Rice 41
53. Delicious Beef Tongue Tacos 41
54. Duck Cassoulet 42
55. Easy Cauliflower Ceviche 42
56. Easy Garlic And Rosemary Chicken 43
57. Easy Herb Roasted Turkey 43
58. Easy Pasta Fagioli 43
59. Easy Pork And Sauerkraut 44
60. Easy Tilapia 44
61. Easy Vegan Overnight Oats 45
62. Egg Foo Young 45
63. Egg Fried Rice 46
64. Eggplant, Zucchini And Sweet Red Pepper Stew 46
65. Emily's Mediterranean Pasta 47
66. Farro And Lentil Masala 47
67. Favorite Barbecue Chicken 48
68. Fennel And Mustard Seed Chicken 48
69. Filipino Style Chicken Curry 49
70. Fish In Ginger Tamarind Sauce 49
71. Flat Iron, Grilled 49
72. Flavorful Rice 50
73. Garbanzo Bean Patties 50
74. Garlic Pork Kabobs 51
75. Garlic Top Sirloin Pot Roast 51
76. Ginger Veggie Stir Fry 52
77. Grandma's Famous Salmon Cakes 52
78. Gravlox 53
79. Grecian Pork Tenderloin 53
80. Green Beans And Tofu 54
81. Grilled Fish Steaks 54
82. Grilled Rock Lobster Tails 55
83. Grilled Salmon I 55
84. Grilled Shrimp And Apple Skewers 55

85. Halibut Cheeks With Ginger Orange Sauce 56
86. Halibut With Vegetables 56
87. Ham Stir Fry With Couscous 57
88. Hamburgers And Ketchup Gravy 57
89. Hawaiian Hot Dog Surprise 58
90. Hawaiian Shrimp 58
91. Herb And Chicken Pasta 59
92. Homemade Cereal 59
93. Honey Peanut Granola 60
94. Island Chicken With Fruit Salsa 60
95. Italian Chicken Marinade 61
96. Italian One Step Casserole 61
97. JJ's Vegan Burritos 62
98. Jalapeno Steak 62
99. Jamie's Black Beans And Rice 63
100. Jay's Jerk Chicken 63
101. Kabobs 63
102. Kimbop (Korean Sushi) 64
103. Lamb Ribs With Honey And Wine 65
104. Lemon Pepper Cod 65
105. Lemony Steamed Fish 65
106. Lentils And Spinach 66
107. Light Fruit And Nut Granola 66
108. Lobster Tails Steamed In Beer 67
109. London Broil I 67
110. Loosemeat Sandwiches III 68
111. Luau Chicken 68
112. Lumpia Rolls 69
113. Man Catching Meat Loaf 69
114. Maple Glazed Ribs 70
115. Marie's Easy Slow Cooker Pot Roast 70
116. Marinated Pork Tenderloin 71
117. Marinated Tofu 71
118. Mexican Bean Burgers 72
119. Mexican Pasta 72
120. Moo Goo Gai Pan II 73
121. Moong Dal 73
122. Morgan's Grilled Fish 74
123. Moroccan Chicken Sann 74
124. Mussels Marinara Di Amore 75
125. North Carolina Style Pulled Pork 75
126. Pan Seared Salmon I 76
127. Pasta For Don And His Loves 77
128. Patsy's Best Barbeque Beef 77
129. Pesto Pasta With Chicken 78
130. Pickled And Fried Filipino Fish (Daing Na Bangus) 78
131. Poor Man's Fried Rice 78
132. Porcupines 79
133. Pork Chops In Red Sauce 79
134. Portuguese Cod Fish Casserole 80
135. Potato Crusted Scallops 80
136. Pressure Cooker Chicken With Duck Sauce 81
137. Punjabi Chicken In Thick Gravy 81
138. Quick Breakfast In A Pita 82
139. Quick Gnocchi 82
140. Quick Vegan Veggie Sandwich 83
141. Quick And Easy Vegetable Curry 83
142. RamJam Chicken 84
143. Red Beans And Spaghetti 84
144. Rice Noodles With Shiitakes, Choy, And Chiles 84
145. Rice With Black Beans 85
146. Roast Leg Of Lamb With Rosemary 85
147. Roasted Leeks With Eggs (Paleo And Keto Friendly) 86
148. Roasted Rack Of Lamb 87
149. Rosemary Braised Lamb Shanks 87
150. Salisbury Steak 88
151. Salmon With Brown Sugar Glaze 88
152. Sarma (Stuffed Cabbage) 89
153. Scott Hibb's Amazing Whisky Grilled Baby Back Ribs 89
154. Seared Ahi Tuna Steaks 90
155. Shrimp Asopao 90
156. Simple Country Ribs 91
157. Sirloin Marinara 91
158. Slow Cooked Squirrel 92
159. Slow Cooker Barbeque 92
160. Slow Cooker Barbequed Pork For Sandwiches 92
161. Slow Cooker Chicken Cacciatore 93
162. Slow Cooker Cranberry Pork 93
163. Slow Cooker Ham And Beans 94
164. Slow Cooker Honey Garlic Chicken 94
165. Slow Cooker Latin Chicken 95
166. Slow Cooker Lentils And Sausage 95
167. Slow Cooker Pork 95
168. Slow Cooker Sauerkraut And Sausage 96
169. Smoky Roll Ups 96
170. Spaetzle I 97
171. Spaghetti Al Amatraciana 97

#	Recipe	Page
172.	Spam On The Go	97
173.	Spanish Tortilla	98
174.	Spicy Burgers	98
175.	Spicy Couscous With Dates	99
176.	Spicy Grilled Chicken	99
177.	Spicy Pasta	100
178.	Spicy Shredded Beef	100
179.	Sri Lankan Chicken Curry	101
180.	Steamed Egg (Chawan Mushi)	101
181.	Stuffed Butternut Squash	102
182.	Stuffed Cabbage	102
183.	Summer Salmon Skewers	103
184.	Sweet Coconut Oatmeal	103
185.	Sweet And Sour Meatballs II	104
186.	Sweet, Sticky And Spicy Chicken	104
187.	Szechuan Spicy Eggplant	105
188.	Tequila Garlic Prawns	105
189.	Tequila Lime Burgers	106
190.	Texas Pork Ribs	106
191.	Thai Grilled Chicken With Sweet Chile Dipping Sauce	107
192.	The Best Ever Vegan Sushi	107
193.	Throw Together Mexican Casserole	108
194.	Tofu Turkey II	109
195.	Try It You'll Like It Kraut Casserole	110
196.	Tuna Steaks With Melon Salsa	110
197.	Turkey Sausage Pie	111
198.	Veal Roast Blanquette	111
199.	Vegan Enchilada Bake	112
200.	Vegan Green Lentil Curry	112
201.	Vegan Mac And No Cheese	113
202.	Vegan Mexican Casserole	113
203.	Vegan Overnight Oats	114
204.	Vegan Pasta With Spinach, Mushrooms, And Garlic	114
205.	Vegan Pumpkin Overnight Oats In The Slow Cooker	115
206.	Vegan Stuffed Peppers With Rice	115
207.	Vegan Sweet Potato Chickpea Curry	116
208.	Vegan Sweet Potato Enchiladas	116
209.	Vegan Tofu Fajitas	117
210.	Vegan Tofu Spinach Lasagna	118
211.	Vegan Tofu And Sweet Potato Curry	118
212.	Vegan Vanilla Nut Oatmeal	119
213.	Vegan Vegetable Curry	119
214.	Vegan Vegetable Double Tortilla Pizza	120
215.	Vegetable Fried Rice	120
216.	Vegetable Masala	121
217.	Vegetarian Chickpea Sandwich Filling	121
218.	Veggie Meatloaf	122
219.	Veggie Pot Pie	122
220.	Veggie Puree	123
221.	Whole Wheat And Honey Pizza Dough	123
222.	Wonton Noodle Soup	124
223.	Yakisoba Chicken	125
224.	Yuba Noodle Salad	125
225.	Yummy Honey Chicken Kabobs	126
226.	Zucchini Wrapped In Tortillas	126
227.	Zucchini And Eggs	127
228.	Zucchini With Chickpea And Mushroom Stuffing	127

CHAPTER 2: DAIRY-FREE POTATO SALAD RECIPES 128

#	Recipe	Page
229.	Alabi Potato Salad	128
230.	All Canadian Potato Salad	128
231.	Always A Winner Potato Salad	129
232.	Argentinean Potato Salad	129
233.	Asian Potato Salad	130
234.	Authentic German Potato Salad	130
235.	Baked Potato Salad With Dill	131
236.	Balsamic Glazed Roasted Potato Salad	131
237.	Balsamic Vinegar Potato Salad	132
238.	Barbeque Potato Salad	132
239.	Bea's Mashed Potato Salad	133
240.	Benny's Potato Salad	133
241.	Brian's German Potato Salad	134
242.	Brown Mustard Potato Salad	134
243.	Bud's Potato Salad	135
244.	Caramelized Onion And Bacon Potato Salad	135
245.	Chicken Potato Salad	136
246.	Dad's Potato Salad	136
247.	Deli Cious Potato Salad	137
248.	Diane's Scotch Irish Potato Salad	137
249.	Easy Potato Salad With Dill	138
250.	Easy Salad Olivieh	138
251.	English Pub Potato Salad With Cucumber And Bacon	139
252.	Ensalada Rusa	139
253.	French Potato Salad	140
254.	German Potato Salad	140
255.	Grandma Sophie's Smashed Potato Salad	141

256. Grandpa Buick's Famous Potato Salad ...141
257. Green Bean And Potato Salad 142
258. Grilled Mustard Potato Salad 142
259. Hawaiian Bruddah Potato Mac (Macaroni) Salad 143
260. Hot German Potato Salad II 143
261. Hot German Potato Salad III 144
262. Hot Red Potato Salad 144
263. Kikuchan's Potato Crab Salad 145
264. Lela's Fourth Of July Potato Salad 145
265. Lena's Potato Salad 146
266. Liege Style Salad 146
267. Mama's Potato Salad 147
268. Marinated Potato Salad With Anchovy Vinaigrette 147
269. Mediterranean Potato Salad 148
270. Mom's Italian Potato Salad 148
271. Mom's Russian Potato Salad 148
272. Mother's Potato Salad 149
273. My Mom's Good Old Potato Salad 149
274. My Sister's Favorite Potato Salad...Ever..150
275. Octoberfest German Potato Salad 150
276. Oktoberfest Potato Salad 151
277. Olivier Salad 151
278. Potato Arugula Salad 152
279. Potato Salad 152
280. Potato Salad I 153
281. Potato Salad With Bacon, Olives, And Radishes 153
282. Potato Salad With Radishes 154
283. Quick Potato Salad 154
284. Red And Sweet Potato Salad 155
285. Red's Potato Salad 155
286. Restaurant Style Potato Salad 156
287. Roasted Potato Salad With Balsamic Bacon Vinaigrette 156
288. Roasted Potato Salad With Vinaigrette ...157
289. Roasted Potato And Garlic Salad 158
290. Roasted Red Potato Salad 158
291. Roasted Sweet Potato Mango Salad 159
292. Rockin Robin's Classic Potato Salad 159
293. Russian Beet And Potato Salad 160
294. Russian Salmon And Potato Salad 160
295. Schwabischer Kartoffelsalat (German Potato Salad Schwabisch Style) 161
296. Schwabischer Kartoffelsalat (Schwabish Potato Salad) 161
297. Slow Cooker German Potato Salad 162
298. Southern Potato Salad 162
299. Spicy Black Bean Potato Salad 163
300. Spicy Dill Potato Salad 163
301. Spicy Sweet Potato Salad 164
302. Sweet Potato Potato Salad 164
303. Sweet Potato Salad 165
304. Tangy Potato Salad 165
305. Veggie Potato Salad For A Crowd 166
306. Warm Steak And Potato Salad 166
307. Warm Sweet Potato Salad 167
308. Yucatan Potato Salad 167

CHAPTER 3: AWESOME DAIRY-FREE RECIPES 168

309. Absolutely Amazing Ahi 168
310. Acai Bowl 169
311. Acapulco Margarita Grouper 169
312. Adobo Herb Salsa 170
313. Agedashi Esque Tofu 170
314. Ajo Blanco Con Uvas 170
315. Alaskan BBQ Salmon 171
316. Almond Butter And Banana Oatmeal Cookies 171
317. Almond Flour Brownies 172
318. Almond Yummies 172
319. Almost Fat Free British Tea Loaf 172
320. Aloha Chicken 173
321. Amazing Vegan Oatmeal Cookies 173
322. American Style Red Beans And Rice 174
323. Angel Food Cake III 174
324. Apple Bundt Cake 175
325. Apple Butter The Easy Way 175
326. Apple Enchilada Dessert 176
327. Apples By The Fire 176
328. Apricot Glazed Chicken 176
329. Artichoke Salsa 177
330. Asian Barbequed Steak 177
331. Asian Beef With Snow Peas 178
332. Asian Lettuce Wraps 178
333. Asian Vegetable Roll 179
334. Asparagus Wrapped In Crisp Prosciutto 179
335. Aunt Kate's Green Beans In Tomatoes . 180
336. Authentic Chinese Steamed Fish 180
337. Authentic German Lebkuchen 181
338. Avocado Black Bean Brownies 181
339. Avocado Paletas 182

340. Avocado Tacos 182
341. Awesome Green Beans 183
342. Awesome Korean Steak 183
343. BBQ Pork For Sandwiches 183
344. BBQ Teriyaki Pork Kabobs 184
345. Bacon 184
346. Bacon And Date Appetizer 185
347. Baked Beans II 185
348. Baked Beans III 186
349. Baked Beans, Texas Ranger 186
350. Baked Chicken With Peaches 186
351. Baked Cod In Foil 187
352. Baked Kale Chips 187
353. Baked Rice And Vegetables In Broth ... 188
354. Baked Stuffed Pumpkin 188
355. Baked Sweet Potatoes 189
356. Baked Tofu Stir Fry 189
357. Baked Vegetables I 190
358. Baked And Poached Tilapia 190
359. Balsamic Vinegar And Ginger Bok Choy 191
360. Banana Angel Food Cake 191
361. Banana Chocolate Creamed Cashew Cake 192
362. Banana Oatmeal Cookie 192
363. Banana Tortilla Snacks 193
364. Bandito Beans 193
365. Barbecued Beef 194
366. Barbequed Ribs 194
367. Basic Guacamole Dip 195
368. Basic Hummus 195
369. Basmati Rice 195
370. Bean And Kale Ragu 196
371. Beer Battered Onion Rings 196
372. Beetroot Hummus 197
373. Beets 197
374. Best Beef Dip Ever 198
375. Best Ever Vegan Chocolate Mug Cake ... 198
376. Best Guacamole 199
377. Best Peanut Butter Cookies Ever ... 199
378. Big Guy Strawberry Pie 199
379. Big Soft Ginger Cookies 200
380. Biscotti 200
381. Black Bean Brownies 201
382. Black Bean Hummus 201
383. Black Bean Salsa 202
384. Black Beans 202
385. Black Beans And Rice 203
386. Black Beans With Bacon 203
387. Black Eyed Peas Spicy Style 204
388. Black Eyed Peas And Ham Hocks ... 204
389. Blueberry Crisp II 204
390. Blueberry Smoothie Bowl 205
391. Boiled Raisin Cake I 205
392. Boneless Chicken Breast With Tomatoes, Coconut Milk, And Chickpeas In The Slow Cooker 206
393. Boniet 206
394. Boston Baked Beans 206
395. Braciola II 207
396. Brazilian White Rice 208
397. Breakfast Brownies 208
398. Breakfast Polenta Porridge 209
399. Breakfast Sausage 209
400. Broccoli And Rice 209
401. Broccoli And Rice Stir Fry 210
402. Brooklyn Girl's Penne Arrabiata ... 210
403. Brown Mixers 211
404. Brownies Allergy Free! 211
405. Brussels Sprouts In Mustard Sauce ... 212
406. Buffalo Chicken Fingers 212
407. Burgundy Mushrooms 213
408. Busy Day Chicken 213
409. Butternut Squash Paleo 'Porridge' ... 213
410. Cabbage Roll Casserole 214
411. Cajun Spicy Potato Wedges 214
412. Cantonese Dinner 215
413. Caribbean Beef Loin Steaks 215
414. Caribbean Holiday Shrimp 216
415. Carrot Fruit Ring 216
416. Carrot Patties 217
417. Carrot Rice Nut Burger 217
418. Carrot Souffle 218
419. Carrot Souffle With Brown Sugar ... 218
420. Carrot, Tomato, And Spinach Quinoa Pilaf 218
421. Cashew Milk 219
422. Cassie's Zucchini Brownies 219
423. Certified Angus Beef® Jalapeno Beef Poppers 220
424. Ceviche Self Portrait 220
425. Chanterelle And Caramelized Onion Bruschetta 221
426. Chap Chee Noodles 221
427. Charley's Slow Cooker Mexican Style Meat

428. Cherry Chicken Lettuce Wraps ... 222
429. Chewy Peanut Butter Brownies ... 223
430. Chewy Sugar Cookies ... 223
431. Chia Coconut Pudding With Coconut Milk 224
432. Chicken Fried Steak Cuban Style ... 224
433. Chicken Honey Nut Stir Fry ... 225
434. Chicken Piccata III ... 225
435. Chicken Wraps ... 226
436. Chicken Yum Yums ... 226
437. Chicken And Dumplings I ... 227
438. Chicken In A Pot ... 227
439. Chickpea Curry ... 228
440. Chili Lime Chicken Kabobs ... 228
441. Chinese Fried Noodles ... 229
442. Chinese Style Stuffed Mushrooms ... 229
443. Chocolate Chip Mint Vegan Nice Cream 230
444. Chocolate Coconut Overnight Oats ... 230
445. Chocolate Crinkles II ... 230
446. Chocolate Olive Oil Cake ... 231
447. Chocolate Peanut Butter Energy Balls ... 231
448. Chocolate Protein Cookies ... 232
449. Chocolate Vegan Nice Cream ... 232
450. Chocolate, Almond, And Coconut Vegan Fat Bombs ... 233
451. Christmas Casserole Cookies II ... 233
452. Cinnamon Apple Toast ... 234
453. Cinnamon Rice With Apples ... 234
454. Cocktail Meatballs ... 234
455. Cocktail Meatballs I ... 235
456. Cocktail Meatballs IV ... 235
457. Coconut Chocolate Chip Cupcakes ... 236
458. Coconut Ice ... 236
459. Coconut Rice ... 237
460. Coconut Sevai (Rice Noodles) ... 237
461. Coconut Chocolate Sugar Free Ice Pops 238
462. Cookie Mix In A Jar III ... 238
463. Coricos Sonorenses ... 239
464. Corn Fritters Southern Style ... 239
465. Corned Beef Hash ... 240
466. Corned Beef Hash (Abalos Style) ... 240
467. Corned Beef Hash Cakes ... 240
468. Corned Beef Potato Pancakes ... 241
469. Corned Beef And Cabbage I ... 241
470. Cornmeal Mush ... 241
471. Country Style Fried Potatoes ... 242
472. Couscous With Mushrooms And Sun Dried Tomatoes ... 242
473. Crab Hash With Old Bay & Basil ... 243
474. Cranberry Almond Biscotti ... 243
475. Cranberry Pistachio Biscotti ... 244
476. Crazy Crust Apple Pie ... 244
477. Creamy Coconut Carbonara (Without Milk!) 245
478. Crispy Vegetable Pakoras ... 245
479. Crust For Veggie Pot Pie ... 246
480. Cuban Beans And Rice ... 246
481. Curried Beef A La Tim ... 247
482. Curried Mango Chicken ... 247
483. Curried Peas ... 248
484. Curried Quinoa ... 248
485. Dairy Free Cinnamon Streusel Coffee Cake 248
486. Dairy , Nut , And Gluten Free Green Bean Casserole ... 249
487. Dairy Free Keto And Vegan Chocolate Fat Bombs ... 250
488. Dairy Free Persimmon Pecan Cookies ... 250
489. Dairy Free Vanilla Brownies ... 251
490. Dairy Free, Gluten Free Pumpkin Bars .. 251
491. Dark Choco Bliss ... 252
492. Date Nut And Brown Sugar Bars ... 252
493. Dave's Ultimate Guacamole ... 252
494. Dee's Mexican Rice ... 253
495. Deep Fried Oysters ... 253
496. Delicious Vegan Gnocchi ... 254
497. Deliciously Organic Carrot Spread ... 254
498. Depression Cake I ... 255
499. Dilled Green Beans ... 255
500. Dirty Rice ... 256
501. Do It Yourself Salmon Poke Bowls ... 257
502. Down Home Baked Beans ... 257
503. Down South Style Green Beans ... 258
504. Drip Beef Sandwiches ... 258
505. Dulcia Domestica ... 258
506. Easiest Pot Roast Ever ... 259
507. Easy Breaded Shrimp ... 259
508. Easy Bruschetta ... 259
509. Easy Chocolate Tofu Pie ... 260
510. Easy Creamy Vegan Macaroni And Cheese 260
511. Easy Creamy Vegan Mushroom Risotto 261
512. Easy Grilled Chicken Teriyaki ... 261

513. Easy Guacamole 262
514. Easy Marinated Pork Tenderloin 262
515. Easy Masoor Daal 263
516. Easy Mexican Rice 263
517. Easy Olive Oil, Tomato, And Basil Pasta 263
518. Easy Roasted Red Pepper Hummus 264
519. Easy Three Ingredient Gluten Free German Christmas Coconut Cookies 264
520. Easy Veggie Samosas 265
521. Edith's Stuffing 265
522. Egg In A Hole 266
523. Egg Free And Milk Free Baked Oatmeal 266
524. Egg Yolk Sponge Cake 266
525. Eggless Ginger Cookies 267
526. Eggless, Milkless, Butterless Cake III 267
527. Eggplant With Almonds 268
528. Eileen's Spicy Gingerbread Men 269
529. Espinacas Con Garbanzos (Spinach With Garbanzo Beans) 269
530. Extra Easy Hummus 270
531. Fabienne's Leeks And Monkfish 270
532. Fabulous And Easy Guacamole 270
533. Fanouropita (Vegan Greek Raisin, Walnut, And Olive Oil Cake) 271
534. Fat Free Refried Beans 271
535. Fava Bean Breakfast Spread 272
536. Favorite Peanut Butter Cookies 272
537. Fiery Pork Skewers 273
538. Fireball® Horchata Pops 273
539. Firecracker Grilled Alaska Salmon 274
540. Fish Fillets Italiano 274
541. Flourless Chocolate Mousse Cake 274
542. Flourless Peanut Butter Cookies 275
543. Fortune Cookies I 275
544. Fragrant Lemon Chicken 276
545. French Burgers 276
546. Fresh Pear Cake 277
547. Fresh Pineapple Dessert 278
548. Fresh Salsa 278
549. Fresh Tomato Salsa 278
550. Fried Cabbage II 279
551. Fried Corn With Bacon 279
552. Fried Green Tomatoes I 279
553. Fried Green Tomatoes II 280
554. Fried Okra 280
555. Fried Rice II 281

556. Fried Zucchini 281
557. Frijoles A La Charra 282
558. Fudgy Brownies I 282
559. Garlic Chicken And Grapes 282
560. Garlic Chicken Stir Fry 283
561. Garlic New Potatoes 284
562. Garlic Rice 284
563. Garlic And Ranch Turkey Burgers 284
564. German Apple Cake I 285
565. Gina's Lemon Pepper Chicken 285
566. Gingerbread Biscotti 286
567. Glazed Corned Beef 286
568. Gluten And Dairy Free Roasted Cashew Cake 287
569. Gluten Free Avocado Brownies 287
570. Gluten Free Dehydrated Rosemary And Cranberry Crisps 288
571. Gluten Free Teff Crackers 288
572. Gluten Free And Dairy Free Pumpkin Mug Cake 289
573. Gluten Free And Dairy Free Vanilla Banana Pops 289
574. Gnocchi I 290
575. Gobble Up Granola Snacks 290
576. Golden Milk Nice Cream 291
577. Gourmet Chicken Sandwich 291
578. Grandma's Gingersnap Cookies 292
579. Grandma's Taffy 292
580. Grandmother's Oatmeal Cookies 293
581. Grape Nuts® Coconut Ice Cream 293
582. Green Bean And Bacon Saute 294
583. Green Beans And Potatoes 294
584. Green Beans With Bacon Dressing 295
585. Green Beans With Hazelnuts And Lemon 295
586. Green Potatoes 296
587. Green Stuff (Cucumber Guacamole) 296
588. Green Tomato And Bell Pepper Delight 296
589. Grilled 'Fusion' Pork Chops 297
590. Grilled Asian Chicken 297
591. Grilled Asian Ginger Pork Chops 298
592. Grilled Asparagus 298
593. Grilled Brown Sugar Pork Chops 298
594. Grilled Chicken With Herbs 299
595. Grilled Lemon Pepper Zucchini 299
596. Grilled Marinated Shrimp 300
597. Grilled Mediterranean Salmon In Foil 300

598. Grilled Portobello Mushrooms 301
599. Grilled Salmon II 301
600. Grilled Shrimp Scampi 302
601. Grilled Spiced Chicken With Caribbean Citrus Mango Sauce 302
602. Grilled Tilapia With Mango Salsa 303
603. Grilled Whole Stuffed Trout 303
604. Ground Beef And Sausage In Red Beans And Rice 304
605. Grown Up Dole® Whip 304
606. Guacamole With Nopales (Mexican Cactus) 305
607. Gumdrop Squares 305
608. Gyros Burgers 306
609. Halibut Mango Ceviche 306
610. Halloween Guacamole 307
611. Halloween Vegan Yacon Syrup Cookies 307
612. Ham And Pineapple Kabobs 308
613. Hariton's 'Famous' Vegetarian Casserole 308
614. Harvard Beets 309
615. Hawaiian Style Pasta 309
616. Healthy Banana Cookies 310
617. Healthy Chocolate Pudding 310
618. Healthy Gingerbread Spice Cake With Butternut Squash Puree 310
619. Hearty Pumpkin Spice Oatmeal 311
620. Herbed Chicken Nuggets 311
621. Herbed Mushrooms With White Wine 312
622. Herbed Potatoes With Sauce 312
623. Homemade Marshmallows II 313
624. Homemade Vegan Chive And Garlic Cream Cheese 313
625. Honey Cake III 313
626. Honey Mustard BBQ Pork Chops 314
627. Honey Pork Fillets 314
628. Hot Banana Salsa 315
629. Hot Cinnamon Candy Covered Apples 315
630. House Fried Rice 316
631. Hummus I 316
632. Hummus III 317
633. Hummus IV 317
634. Hunan Kung Pao 317
635. Indian Spiced Rice 318
636. Indian Style Sheekh Kabab 319
637. Indian Style Salmon Fry 319
638. Instant Pot® Classic Hummus 320
639. Irish Boiled Dinner (Corned Beef) 320

640. Italian Chicken Spaghetti With Tequila .. 321
641. Italian Chicken With Garlic And Lemon 321
642. Italian Stewed Tomatoes 322
643. Jamaican Jerked Chicken 322
644. Jambalasta 322
645. Jeff's Sloppy Joes 323
646. Jewish Apple Cake I 324
647. Josephine's Puerto Rican Chicken And Rice 324
648. Kahlua® Brownies With Peanut Butter . 325
649. Kale And Adzuki Beans 325
650. Kasha And Bowties (Kasha Varnishkas) 326
651. Keema (Indian Style Ground Meat) 326
652. Keto Peanut Butter Fudge Fat Bomb 327
653. Kettle Corn 327
654. Key Lime Thyme Pie 327
655. Kielbasa With Honey Mustard 328
656. Killer Pumpkin Pie 329
657. Kristen's Awesome Oatmeal Cookies 329
658. Kung Pao Chicken 330
659. La Genovese 330
660. Lace's Coconut Bread 331
661. Lamb Casserole 331
662. Lamb L'Arabique 332
663. Lamb Lover's Pilaf 332
664. Lamb For Lovers 333
665. Lavonne's Scrumptious White Wine Chicken 334
666. Lemon Ginger Shrimp 334
667. Lemon Pepper Pasta 335
668. Lemon String Beans 335
669. Lemon And Almond Slices 335
670. Lemon And Thyme Lamb Chops 336
671. Lengua (Beef Tongue) 336
672. Lentil Loaf 337
673. Linguine With Chicken And Sauteed Vegetables 337
674. Linnie's Spanish Rice 338
675. Lion Veggie Tray 338
676. Liver And Bacon 339
677. Lokshin Kugel (Noodle Pudding) 339
678. Loose Meat On A Bun, Restaurant Style 340
679. Mac And 'Shews (Vegan Mac And Cheese) 340
680. Magaricz 341
681. Mamma Rita's Eggs And Tomato Sauce 341
682. Mandarin Orange Couscous 341

683. Mango Papaya Salsa 342
684. Mango Pecan Chicken 342
685. Maria's Spanish Rice 343
686. Marinated Mushrooms With Red Bell Peppers 343
687. Marinated Pork Roast 344
688. Marinated Rosemary Lemon Chicken 344
689. Marinated Tuna Steak 344
690. Marrakesh Vegetable Curry 345
691. Marzipan Candy 345
692. Mashed Potatoes And Celery Root 346
693. Maui Chicken 346
694. Mayonnaise Cake I 347
695. Mean Woman Pasta 347
696. Meatless Stuffed Peppers 348
697. Mediterranean Brown Rice Pilaf 348
698. Mediterranean Lemon Chicken 349
699. Mexican Ceviche 350
700. Mexican Hot Chocolate Cupcakes (Vegan) 350
701. Mexican Rice 351
702. Mexican Rice I 351
703. Mexican Vegetable Rice 352
704. Michelle's Soft Sugar Cookies 352
705. Microwave Caramel Popcorn 353
706. Microwave Vegetables 353
707. Middle Eastern White Beans 354
708. Mint Chip Coconut Milk Ice Cream 354
709. Mmm Mmm Better Brownies 354
710. Mock Angel Food Cake 355
711. Moist Vegan Sugar Cookies 355
712. Molasses Cookies 356
713. Molasses Sugar Cookies 356
714. Molasses Beef Curry 357
715. Molly's Chicken 357
716. Mom's Baked Beans I 358
717. Mom's Baked Beans II 358
718. Mom's Ginger Snaps 358
719. Momma's Potatoes 359
720. Moroccan Chicken 359
721. Moroccan Salmon Cakes With Garlic Mayonnaise 360
722. Moroccan Vegan Tagine 360
723. Mumze's Sticky Chicken 361
724. Mushroom Slow Cooker Roast Beef 361
725. My Amish Friend's Caramel Corn 362
726. My Own Famous Stuffed Grape Leaves 362
727. Night Before Oatmeal In A Jar 363
728. No Bake Coconut Fruit Tarts 363
729. No Bake Quinoa Bars 364
730. Nutty Granola II 364
731. Oatmeal Peanut Butter Cookies 365
732. Okra And Tomatoes 365
733. Old Fashioned Fruit Soup 366
734. One Bowl Rice 366
735. One Skillet Corned Beef Hash 366
736. Onions In Raisin Sauce 367
737. Orange, Mango, And Ginger Sorbet 367
738. Oriental Style Halibut 368
739. Orzo With Mushrooms And Walnuts 368
740. Oven Baked Vegetables 369
741. Oven Fried Potatoes II 369
742. Oven Fried Sesame Potatoes 370
743. Oven Roasted Potatoes 370
744. Paleo Spaghetti Pie (Grain, Gluten, And Dairy Free) 370
745. Paleo Tropical Ice Cream 371
746. Party Pancit 371
747. Passover Chocolate Chip Cookies 372
748. Pasta With Tuna Sauce 373
749. Pat's Baked Beans 373
750. Pea Shoots And Chicken In Garlic Sauce 374
751. Peach And Strawberry Sorbet 374
752. Peanut Butter Bliss Cookies Vegan, Gluten Free, No Sugar Added 374
753. Peanut Butter Stuffed Jalapenos 375
754. Pear Hedgehog 375
755. Pear And Almond Tart (Dairy And Gluten Free) 376
756. Pecan Pie Bars I 376
757. Peppered Elk Skillet 377
758. Pepperoncini Beef 377
759. Perfect Pita Chips 378
760. Perfect Sushi Rice 378
761. Persian Sabzi Polo (Herb Rice With Fava Beans) 378
762. Pineapple Angel Food Cake I 379
763. Pineapple Chicken 379
764. Pineapple Chicken Tenders 380
765. Pineapple Orange Sorbet 380
766. Pineapple Salsa 380
767. Pineapple And Mango Skewers With Coconut Dip 381

768. Pipirrana (Spanish Potato Salad) 381
769. Pistachio Coconut Ice Cream 382
770. Platski 383
771. Playgroup Granola Bars 383
772. Porcupine Meatballs II 383
773. Pork Chops And Sauerkraut 384
774. Pork Medallions With Port And Dried Cranberry Sauce 384
775. Pot Sticker Dumplings 385
776. Pot Stickers Traditional 386
777. Potato Chip Cookies VI 386
778. Potato Medley 387
779. Potato Squash Cakes 387
780. Potatoes And Onions 387
781. Potatoes And Peppers 388
782. Presto Vegan Pesto 388
783. Prize Winning Baby Back Ribs 389
784. Pumpkin Cake I 389
785. Pumpkin Chai Pie (Dairy Free) 390
786. Pumpkin Chocolate Coconut Oil Bars 390
787. Pumpkin Pie (Dairy, Egg, And Gluten Free) 391
788. Pumpkin Pie (Wheat Free, Egg Free, And Dairy Free) 391
789. Pumpkin Puree 392
790. Pumpkin Tart With Pecan Crust 392
791. Puttanesca I 393
792. Quick Black Beans And Rice 393
793. Quick And Easy Chicken 394
794. Quinoa And Black Beans 394
795. Raspberry Salsa 394
796. Raw Candy 395
797. Raw Chia 'Porridge' 395
798. Raw Chocolate Mousse 396
799. Raw Vegan Gingerbread Balls 396
800. Real Food Orange Cream Ice Pops 396
801. Refried Beans Without The Refry 397
802. Rich Vegan Kheer (Indian Rice Pudding) 397
803. Roast Beef With Coffee 398
804. Roast Pork With Maple And Mustard Glaze 398
805. Roasted Brussels Sprouts 398
806. Roasted Fall Vegetables 399
807. Roasted Garlic 399
808. Roasted Lemon Herb Chicken 400
809. Roasted Potatoes And Apples 400
810. Rocky Road Cake 401
811. Ronaldo's Beef Carnitas 401
812. Ruth's Grandma's Pie Crust 402
813. Salmon Croquettes 402
814. Salsa II 402
815. Salsa Steak For One 403
816. Sarah's Applesauce 403
817. Sauteed Napa Cabbage 404
818. Sauteed Sugar Snap Peas With Mushrooms 404
819. Scampi Style Scallops Over Linguine 405
820. Schweinebraten Pork Roast 405
821. Seasoned Rice 406
822. Serbian Cevapcici 406
823. Sesame Green Beans 406
824. Sesame Noodles 407
825. Sesame Raisin Cookies 407
826. Shakshooka 408
827. Shiitake Mushroom Ceviche 408
828. Short Cut Mexican Fideo (Vermicelli) 409
829. Shrimp Creole IV 409
830. Shrimp Marinaders 410
831. Shrimp And Garlic 410
832. Simple Lemon Herb Chicken 411
833. Simple Parsnip Pancakes 411
834. Simply Guacamole 412
835. Simply Delicious Tamari Almond Green Beans 412
836. Slow Cooked Corned Beef For Sandwiches 412
837. Slow Cooked Pork Barbeque 413
838. Slow Cooker Adobo Chicken 413
839. Slow Cooker Barbecue Beans 413
840. Slow Cooker Chicken Curry With Coconut Milk 414
841. Slow Cooker Chile Verde 414
842. Slow Cooker Cider Pork Roast 415
843. Slow Cooker German Style Pork Roast With Sauerkraut And Potatoes 415
844. Slow Cooker Kielbasa And Beer 416
845. Slow Cooker Roast Beef 416
846. Slow Cooker Spicy Black Eyed Peas 416
847. Slow Cooker Wieners In Wiener BBQ Sauce 417
848. Smoked Salmon Deviled Eggs 417
849. Smoked Turkey 418
850. Snappy Green Beans 418

851. Snickerdoodles I 419
852. Snow Cone Topping 419
853. Soft Peanut Butter Cookies 419
854. Southern Burgers 420
855. Southern Dirty Rice 420
856. Southern As You Can Get Collard Greens 421
857. Southwest Chicken 421
858. Spaetzle And Chicken Soup 422
859. Spaghetti Squash Pie (Gluten Free And Dairy Free) 422
860. Spaghetti With Tomato And Sausage Sauce 423
861. Spam Musubi 423
862. Spanish Rice I 424
863. Spanish Rice II 424
864. Spanish Rice In The Pressure Cooker 425
865. Spiced Air Fried Chickpeas 425
866. Spiced Nuts II 426
867. Spiced Pecans 426
868. Spicy Avocado Chocolate Pudding 427
869. Spicy Chicken Breasts 427
870. Spicy Roasted Edamame 427
871. Spinach Chickpea Curry 428
872. Spinach And Bean Casserole 428
873. Spinach And Pasta Shells 429
874. Spring Pea Medley With Edible Bowl 429
875. Steak, Onion, And Pepper Fajitas 430
876. Steamed Vegan Rice Cakes (Banh Bo Hap) 430
877. Steve's Bodacious Barbecue Ribs 431
878. Stir Fried Kale And Broccoli Florets 431
879. Strawberry Tapioca 432
880. Stuffed Boneless Quail With Wild Rice And Sage Stuffing 432
881. Stuffed Peppers 433
882. Stuffed Zucchini II 433
883. Sugar Free Cake 434
884. Sugar Snap Peas 434
885. Sugar Snap Peas With Mint 435
886. Sugar Free And Dairy Free Slow Cooker Steel Cut Oatmeal 435
887. Sugar Free And Keto Fat Bombs 435
888. Sukhothai Pad Thai 436
889. Superb Sausage Casserole 436
890. Sushi Roll 437
891. Sweet Polish Sausage 437
892. Sweet Potato And Prune Casserole 438
893. Sweet And Gooey Chicken Wings 438
894. Sweet And Sour Meatballs I 439
895. Sweet And Sour Onions 439
896. Sweet And Sour Sauce II 440
897. Swiss Chard With Garbanzo Beans And Fresh Tomatoes 440
898. Syrian Spaghetti 440
899. Tangy Chicken Breasts 441
900. Tangy Chicken Fajitas 441
901. Tart Meyer Lemon Sorbet 442
902. Tempeh Fajitas 442
903. Tequila Lime Shrimp 442
904. Tequila Steak 443
905. Teriyaki Tofu With Pineapple 443
906. Teriyaki Wraps 444
907. Texas Caviar I 444
908. Thai Basil Rolls With Hoisin Peanut Sauce 445
909. Thai Spicy Basil Chicken Fried Rice 445
910. The Best Sweet And Sour Meatballs 446
911. The Sarge's Goetta German Breakfast Treat 446
912. Thit Bo Xao Dau 447
913. Three Berry Pie 447
914. Three Ingredient Peanut Butter Cookies 448
915. Tofu Fudge Mocha Bars 448
916. Tofu Hummus 449
917. Tofu Pumpkin Pie 449
918. Tofu And Artichoke Risotto 450
919. Tofu And Vegetables Stir Fry With Couscous 450
920. Tofu And Veggies In Peanut Sauce 451
921. Tomato, Corn And Avocado Salsa 451
922. Tropical Tuna Hash 452
923. Tuna Tartare 452
924. Twice Cooked Coconut Shrimp 453
925. Ultimate Maple Snickerdoodles 453
926. Unbelievable Chicken 454
927. Unbelievable Vegan Mashed Potatoes 454
928. Unsloppy Joes 455
929. Vegan Almond Snack 455
930. Vegan Almond Truffles 456
931. Vegan Apple Pie 456
932. Vegan Apple Yogurt Parfait With Maca Powder 457
933. Vegan Avocado Brownies 457

934. Vegan Baked Oatmeal Patties 458
935. Vegan Banana Ice Cream 458
936. Vegan Bean Taco Filling 459
937. Vegan Blueberry Coconut Ice Cream 459
938. Vegan Brownies 460
939. Vegan Butternut Squash And Chickpea Curry 460
940. Vegan Cashew Ricotta 461
941. Vegan Cheesecake 461
942. Vegan Chickpea Curry Without Coconut Milk 462
943. Vegan Chocolate Cake 462
944. Vegan Chocolate Ice Cream 463
945. Vegan Coconut Brownies 463
946. Vegan Coconut Rice Pudding 463
947. Vegan Curry With Tomatoes, Cauliflower, And Lentils 464
948. Vegan Edamame 464
949. Vegan Fajitas 465
950. Vegan Homemade Plain Cream Cheese . 465
951. Vegan Indian Curry With Cauliflower And Lentils 466
952. Vegan Key Lime Pie 466
953. Vegan Mashed Potatoes 467
954. Vegan Mashed Potatoes (Low Fat) 467
955. Vegan Mug Cake With Pineapple And Mint 468
956. Vegan Oat Salted Caramel Cookies 468
957. Vegan Potato Leek Gratin 469
958. Vegan Protein Chocolate Overnight Oats 469
959. Vegan Pumpkin Brownie 469
960. Vegan Pumpkin Macaroni And Cheese .. 470
961. Vegan Pumpkin Pie 471
962. Vegan Pumpkin Spice Cake 471
963. Vegan Raspberry Chocolate Tarts 472
964. Vegan Refried Beans 473
965. Vegan Roasted Vegetable Hummus 473
966. Vegan Seitan Curry With Rice 473
967. Vegan Spanish Rice Dinner 474
968. Vegan Sweet And Sour Meatballs 475
969. Vegan Thai Pumpkin Curry 475
970. Vegan Tofu Quiche 476
971. Vegan Ube Blueberry Ice Cream 476
972. Vegan Or Lactose Intolerant Ice Cream . 477
973. Vegetable Lo Mein 477
974. Vegetable Medley II 478
975. Vegetable Paella 478
976. Vegetarian Garden Stir Fry 478
977. Vegetarian Nori Rolls 479
978. Vegetarian Shepherd's Pie II 480
979. Vegetarian Spanish Rice 480
980. Veggie Pate 481
981. Veggie Quinoa 481
982. Veneto Chicken 482
983. Very Berry And Soy Delicious Ice Pops 482
984. Vietnamese Spring Rolls 482
985. Wacky Cake VIII 483
986. War Cake 483
987. Watermelon Fruit Bowl 484
988. Western Style Baked Beans 484
989. Whipped Banana "Ice Cream" 485
990. Whipped Raspberry Instant Pudding 485
991. White Chocolate Nut Free Keto And Vegan Fat Bombs 486
992. Wild Rice Pilaf 486
993. Wild Rice And Asparagus Chicken Breasts 486
994. Williamsburg Pork Cake 487
995. World's Best Oatmeal Cookies 487
996. Yellow Squash And Zucchini Delight 488
997. Yummy Vegan Chocolate Pudding 488
998. Zesty Porcupine Meatballs 489
999. Zesty Zucchini And Squash 489
1000. Zucchini Galore 489
1001. Zucchini Saute 490

INDEX **491**

CONCLUSION **498**

Chapter 1: Dairy-Free Main Dish Recipes

***

1. Alaskan Cod And Shrimp With Fresh Tomato

Serving: 6 | Prep: 10mins | Cook: 15mins | Ready in:

Ingredients

- 2 tablespoons olive oil
- 6 cloves garlic, minced
- 5 large tomatoes, chopped
- 1 teaspoon dried oregano
- 1 pound Alaskan cod
- 1/2 pound large shrimp, peeled and deveined
- salt to taste
- 1 tablespoon dried oregano, or to taste

Direction

- On medium high heat, in a skillet, heat the olive oil; cook and stir the garlic in the oil till golden brown, avoid burning the garlic. Put in the tomatoes and stir it well till their juices are released. Mix in 1 teaspoon of oregano.
- On the tomato mixture, add shrimp and cod; use salt to season. Cover the skillet and let simmer for 3 minutes. Turn the cod and season again using 1 tablespoon of oregano and salt; cover again and cook for 3 minutes longer. Take out the cover and let cook for 2-3 minutes till the juice evaporates a bit.

Nutrition Information

- Calories: 166 calories;
- Total Carbohydrate: 7.6
- Cholesterol: 85
- Protein: 21.3
- Total Fat: 5.7
- Sodium: 128

2. American Chop Suey II

Serving: 5 | Prep: 5mins | Cook: 25mins | Ready in:

Ingredients

- 1 (16 ounce) package uncooked elbow macaroni
- 1 pound lean ground beef
- 1 onion, chopped
- 2 (10.75 ounce) cans condensed tomato soup
- salt and pepper to taste

Direction

- Cook macaroni based on the package directions.
- In the meantime, stir-fry the onion and ground beef in a separate big skillet over medium high heat for 5 to 10 minutes or until meat turns crumbly and brown. Strain well and keep the onion and meat in the skillet. Put two cans of tomato soup into the skillet and mix well to blend.
- Once noodles are done, strain well and put the noodles back into the pot. Stir the hamburger mixture from the skillet into the pot. Blend well and add pepper and salt to taste.

Nutrition Information

- Calories: 664 calories;
- Sodium: 745
- Total Carbohydrate: 85.1
- Cholesterol: 68
- Protein: 30

- Total Fat: 22

3. Angela's Easy Breaded Chicken

Serving: 4 | Prep: | Cook: |Ready in:

Ingredients

- 4 skinless, boneless chicken breasts
- 1 cup Italian-style salad dressing
- 2 cups seasoned dry bread crumbs

Direction

- Set an oven to 175°C (350°F) to preheat.
- Dredge the chicken breasts in the salad dressing and coat with the breadcrumbs completely. In a lightly greased 9x13-inch baking dish, put the coated chicken breasts and bake for approximately 30 minutes in the preheated oven or until the juices run clear and the chicken is cooked through.

Nutrition Information

- Calories: 531 calories;
- Sodium: 2104
- Total Carbohydrate: 47.2
- Cholesterol: 69
- Protein: 35.9
- Total Fat: 21.4

4. Apple Radish BBQ Ribs

Serving: 4 | Prep: 10mins | Cook: 2hours35mins |Ready in:

Ingredients

- 4 pounds pork spareribs
- 2 quarts apple juice
- 3 cups barbecue sauce
- 1/2 cup prepared horseradish
- 3 tablespoons Worcestershire sauce
- 1 teaspoon garlic salt

Direction

- In a stock pot, putt the ribs, and submerge in apple juice. Boil, lower the heat, and allow to simmer for an hour to 2 hours. Preheat the oven to 175 °C or 350 °F.
- Combine together garlic salt, Worcestershire sauce, horseradish and barbecue sauce in a medium bowl. Mix in 3 tablespoons apple juice from the ribs.
- Brush ribs underside with a third of sauce. Flip them over, and set in a roasting pan. Brush surfaces with the rest of the sauce.
- In the prepped oven, allow to bake for 25 to 35 minutes, brushing from time to time with sauce.

Nutrition Information

- Calories: 1794 calories;
- Total Carbohydrate: 131.5
- Cholesterol: 363
- Protein: 70.9
- Total Fat: 107.4
- Sodium: 3152

5. Asian Breakfast Stir Fry

Serving: 1 | Prep: 20mins | Cook: 35mins |Ready in:

Ingredients

- 1 cup water
- 1/2 cup quinoa
- 1 large carrot, peeled and chopped
- 1/2 cup broccoli florets
- 1/4 cup chopped onion
- 1 (1 inch) piece ginger, peeled, or to taste
- 1 tablespoon sesame oil
- 1 tablespoon minced garlic

- 1 cup kale
- 1 tablespoon reduced-sodium soy sauce
- 1 tablespoon water
- 1/2 cup shredded boneless, skinless baked chicken breast
- 1 cooking spray (optional)
- 2 large eggs
- 1 teaspoon chile-garlic sauce (such as Sriracha®), or to taste (optional)
- 1 teaspoon fresh cilantro, or to taste (optional)
- 1 teaspoon sesame seeds, or to taste (optional)

Direction

- In a saucepan, bring water and quinoa to a boil. Lower heat to medium-low, cover, and simmer for 15-20 mins, until the quinoa is tender.
- In the bowl of a food processor, combine onion, carrot and broccoli and chop.
- In a large skillet, heat sesame oil over medium heat and put in garlic. Whisk for a minute, until fragrant. Put in chopped vegetable mixture from the food processor. Cook and stir for 3 to 5 mins or until the onions are translucent. Put in kale. Cook for a minute or until wilted. Pour water and soy sauce over the mixture. Cook 5 more mins.
- Add 1/4 cup of cooked quinoa and chicken to the skillet with vegetable mixture. Cook and stir for 2-3 mins or until heated through. Place stir-fry to the plate.
- Coat the skillet with cooking spray. Cook eggs 3-5 mins to preference. In the plate, put cooked eggs on the top of stir-fry. Garnish with sesame seeds, cilantro and chile-garlic sauce.

Nutrition Information

- Calories: 814 calories;
- Sodium: 1015
- Total Carbohydrate: 75.4
- Cholesterol: 424
- Protein: 48.2
- Total Fat: 36.1

6. Aunt Fannie's Dinner

Serving: 6 | Prep: 20mins | Cook: 20mins | Ready in:

Ingredients

- 1/2 cup uncooked elbow macaroni
- 1 1/2 pounds ground beef
- 1/2 onion, chopped
- 1 teaspoon garlic powder
- salt and pepper to taste
- 1 (8 ounce) can tomato sauce
- 1 cup stewed, diced tomatoes
- 1 (15 ounce) can whole kernel corn, drained

Direction

- Place a lightly salted water in a large pot and make it boil. Cook pasta for 8-10 minutes or until al dente; strain.
- Stir-fry ground beef for 5 minutes in a large skillet over medium heat. Place in the onion and stir-fry for 5-10 more minutes. Add pepper, salt and garlic powder to taste. Mix in the cooked macaroni, corn, stewed or diced tomatoes and tomato sauce. Mix well and let it heat through for about 5-7 minutes.

Nutrition Information

- Calories: 318 calories;
- Cholesterol: 69
- Protein: 23.2
- Total Fat: 14.3
- Sodium: 564
- Total Carbohydrate: 25.7

7. BBQ Chili Pasta

Serving: 6 | Prep: | Cook: | Ready in:

Ingredients

- 1 (8 ounce) package rotini pasta
- 1 tablespoon olive oil
- 1 onion, chopped
- 8 ounces ground turkey
- 1 green bell pepper, chopped
- 1 (15 ounce) can whole kernel corn, drained
- 1 tablespoon chili powder
- 1 tablespoon dried oregano
- 1/2 teaspoon salt
- 1 (8 ounce) can tomato sauce
- 3/4 cup barbecue sauce

Direction

- In a large pot, in the boiling salted water, cook rotelle pasta until al dente. Drain.
- In the meantime, in a large non-stick skillet, heat oil on medium-high heat, put in onion and cook onion about 2 minutes, or until tender. Put in ground turkey and cook about 3 to 4 minutes until not pink anymore. Blend in BBQ sauce, tomato sauce, salt, dried oregano, chili powder, corn, and chopped green bell pepper. Heat mixture to a boil. Lower the heat to medium and simmer about 3 to 4 minutes until slightly thick, stirring sometimes.
- In a large serving bowl, mix pasta with the turkey mixture. Enjoy immediately.

Nutrition Information

- Calories: 340 calories;
- Protein: 14.4
- Total Fat: 7.4
- Sodium: 1000
- Total Carbohydrate: 57.5
- Cholesterol: 29

8. BBQ Salmon Over Mixed Greens

Serving: 6 | Prep: 30mins | Cook: 10mins | Ready in:

Ingredients

- 2 tablespoons chili powder
- 1 tablespoon garlic powder
- 1 tablespoon onion powder
- 3 tablespoons white sugar
- 1 tablespoon salt
- 1/2 teaspoon ground allspice
- 1/2 teaspoon ground cumin
- 1/4 teaspoon ground white pepper
- 1 tablespoon paprika
- 6 (6 ounce) fillets salmon
- olive oil
- 1 1/2 cups tomato-vegetable juice cocktail
- 1 tablespoon balsamic or cider vinegar
- 1/2 cup chopped tomatoes
- 4 tablespoons olive oil
- 1 pound mixed salad greens, rinsed and dried

Direction

- Combine the paprika, white pepper, cumin, allspice, salt, sugar, onion powder, garlic powder and chili powder in a small bowl. Set aside 1 1/2 tbsp. of the mixture for the vinaigrette, then sprinkle the leftover spice mixture on top of the salmon fillets. Put on cover and let it chill in the fridge for 6 hours.
- Set the grill to preheat to high heat.
- Oil the grill grate lightly and spread a small amount of olive oil on the salmon fillets. Let the salmon cook for 4- 5 minutes on each side or until it can be easily flaked using a fork.
- To make the vinaigrette, combine the reserved spice mixture, olive oil, tomatoes, vinegar and tomato-vegetable juice cocktail in a small bowl. In a big bowl, put the salad greens and drizzle vinaigrette on top, then toss until coated.
- Distribute the greens among individual serving plates and put salmon fillet on top of each plate, then scoop any leftover vinaigrette on top of the salmon.

Nutrition Information

- Calories: 413 calories;
- Protein: 36.1

- Total Fat: 22.8
- Sodium: 1441
- Total Carbohydrate: 16.2
- Cholesterol: 92

9. Bachelor's Hash

Serving: 6 | Prep: 30mins | Cook: 1hours10mins | Ready in:

Ingredients

- 1 pound ground beef
- 1 cup chopped onion, divided
- 3 large potatoes, grated
- salt and ground black pepper to taste
- 4 carrots, peeled and grated
- 1 (15.25 ounce) can whole kernel corn, drained
- 1 (15 ounce) can green beans, drained
- 8 slices bacon

Direction

- Preheat an oven to 375°F (190°C).
- Over medium-high heat, heat a large skillet and stir in the ground beef. Cook until the beef is evenly browned and crumbly. Drain off any excess grease; discard. Move the meat to an 8x8-inch baking dish.
- Top with a layer of about 1/4 of the onion, evenly spread over the onion the grated potatoes. Add salt and pepper to season. Spread over another quarter of the onion, top with carrots in a layer. Add another salt and pepper to season. Place one more layer of onion, cover with corn. Taste with salt and pepper, add the rest of onion on top. Over the onion, spread the green beans, and top with sliced bacon. Place aluminum foil over to cover.
- In the preheated oven, bake for 40 minutes, then take the foil out and go on baking about 20 more minutes until the potatoes are soft and the bacon is crisp.

Nutrition Information

- Calories: 542 calories;
- Cholesterol: 71
- Protein: 23.8
- Total Fat: 26.7
- Sodium: 721
- Total Carbohydrate: 54.2

10. Bahamian Baked Grouper

Serving: 4 | Prep: 20mins | Cook: 1hours | Ready in:

Ingredients

- 4 (4 ounce) fillets grouper
- 1/4 cup fresh lime juice
- 1 pinch red pepper flakes (to taste)
- salt and ground black pepper to taste
- 1 tomato, thinly sliced
- 1 onion, thinly sliced
- 1 green bell pepper, thinly sliced

Direction

- Put grouper onto a plate. Drizzle lime juice on fillets. Season with red pepper flakes, pepper and salt. Use plastic wrap to cover. Keep in the fridge for 8 hours to overnight.
- Preheat the oven to 175 degrees C/350 degrees F. Grease a baking dish lightly.
- Lay fillets in 1 layer in prepped baking dish. Put bell pepper slices, onion slices and tomato slices on fillets. Use aluminum foil to cover.
- Bake in the preheated oven for about 1 hour until fish easily flakes.

Nutrition Information

- Calories: 144 calories;
- Total Fat: 1.4
- Sodium: 52
- Total Carbohydrate: 9.6
- Cholesterol: 42
- Protein: 23.3

11. Baked Honey Mustard Chicken

Serving: 6 | Prep: 15mins | Cook: 45mins | Ready in:

Ingredients

- 6 skinless, boneless chicken breast halves
- salt and pepper to taste
- 1/2 cup honey
- 1/2 cup prepared mustard
- 1 teaspoon dried basil
- 1 teaspoon paprika
- 1/2 teaspoon dried parsley

Direction

- Preheat oven to 350°F (175°C).
- Sprinkle breasts of chicken with pepper and salt to taste, and place in a slightly greased 13x9-inch baking dish. Mix the parsley, paprika, basil, mustard, and honey in a small bowl until combined well. Over the chicken, pour half of the mixture, and brush to cover.
- In the preheated oven, bake for half an hour. Turn pieces of chicken over and brush with the rest half of the mustard honey mixture. Bake for another 10 to 15 minutes, or up to when chicken is not pink anymore and juices run clear. Before serving, allow to cool for 10 minutes.

Nutrition Information

- Calories: 232 calories;
- Protein: 25.6
- Total Fat: 3.7
- Sodium: 296
- Total Carbohydrate: 24.8
- Cholesterol: 67

12. Baked Slow Cooker Chicken

Serving: 6 | Prep: 20mins | Cook: 10hours | Ready in:

Ingredients

- 1 (2 to 3 pound) whole chicken
- salt and pepper to taste
- 1 teaspoon paprika

Direction

- Wad 3 pieces of aluminum foil into 3 to 4-inch balls and arrange them in the base of the slow cooker.
- Wash the inside and outside of the chicken under cold running water. Use paper towels to pat dry. Flavor with paprika, pepper, and salt, then put in the slow cooker on top of the crumpled aluminum foil.
- Turn the slow cooker to high for 1 hour, then decrease to low for about 8 to 10 hours until the chicken is not pink anymore and the juices run clear.

Nutrition Information

- Calories: 408 calories;
- Sodium: 133
- Total Carbohydrate: 0.2
- Cholesterol: 142
- Protein: 35.2
- Total Fat: 28.5

13. Baked Tilapia In Garlic And Olive Oil

Serving: 4 | Prep: 5mins | Cook: 30mins | Ready in:

Ingredients

- 4 (4 ounce) fillets tilapia
- 4 cloves crushed garlic
- 3 tablespoons olive oil
- 1 onion, chopped

- 1/4 teaspoon cayenne pepper

Direction

- Crush garlic, rub it on the fish fillets and put them in a shallow, non-reactive dish. Drizzle olive oil over the fish fillet until they are covered. Take some onions and put them on top of the fish. Cover the dish and put it in the fridge overnight for the fish to soak in the marinade.
- Set the oven at 175°C (350°F) and start preheating.
- If using baking method, move the fish, onion, garlic and olive oil to a 9x13 inch baking tray. Dredge cayenne or white pepper on top. If using grilling method, use aluminum foil to wrap the fish with pepper, onion, garlic and oil.
- Put in the oven and start baking at 175°C (350°F) for 30 minutes.

Nutrition Information

- Calories: 217 calories;
- Protein: 23.5
- Total Fat: 11.7
- Sodium: 74
- Total Carbohydrate: 3.6
- Cholesterol: 41

14. Balsamic Chicken Breasts

Serving: 2 | Prep: 10mins | Cook: 50mins | Ready in:

Ingredients

- 2 sweet potatoes, peeled and cut into 2-inch pieces
- 1 tablespoon olive oil
- salt and pepper to taste
- 2 skinless, boneless chicken breast halves
- 1/2 cup balsamic vinegar
- salt and ground black pepper to taste
- 1/2 cup balsamic vinegar

Direction

- Set an oven to preheat to 200°C (400°F).
- On a baking tray, put the potatoes then drizzle olive oil on top of the potatoes and sprinkle pepper and salt to season.
- In a baking dish, put the chicken breasts then pour 1/2 cup of balsamic vinegar on top of the breasts. Sprinkle pepper and salt to season, then use aluminum foil to cover.
- In the preheated oven, put the potatoes and let it bake for 10 minutes. Put the dish with the chicken in the oven and cook both the chicken and potatoes for an additional 20 minutes. Turn both the chicken and potatoes, then lower the oven heat to 175°C (350°F). Let it bake for an additional 20 minutes.
- In a small saucepan, pour 1/2 cup of balsamic vinegar and put it over medium heat. Let it cook until it reduces to approximately 1/4 cup. Put the chicken breasts on top of the potatoes, then drizzle reduced balsamic vinegar on top to serve.

Nutrition Information

- Calories: 379 calories;
- Cholesterol: 68
- Protein: 29.8
- Total Fat: 8.5
- Sodium: 179
- Total Carbohydrate: 44.7

15. Barbeque Pork Two Ways

Serving: 8 | Prep: 15mins | Cook: 8hours | Ready in:

Ingredients

- 2 1/2 pounds pork shoulder
- 1/2 cup chopped onion
- 1 clove garlic, minced

- 1/4 cup brown sugar
- 1 teaspoon dry mustard
- 1/2 teaspoon salt
- 1/4 teaspoon ground black pepper
- 2 cups ketchup
- 1/4 cup Worcestershire sauce

Direction

- Cut the boneless pork shoulder crosswise into 1/4 -inch slices. Partially freezing it will make cutting easier.
- Mix Worcestershire sauce, ketchup, pepper, salt, dry mustard, brown sugar, garlic, onion, and sliced pork in the slow cooker; combine well and cover. Cook on low, stirring from time to time, for 6 to 8 hours until the meat is softened.
- Or: Mix Worcestershire sauce, ketchup, pepper, salt, dry mustard, brown sugar, garlic, onion, and pork in a Dutch oven or large saucepan, blend well. Heat to a boil, lower the heat and cover. Simmer, stirring from time to time, for 2 1/2 to 3 hours until the pork is tender.

Nutrition Information

- Calories: 279 calories;
- Sodium: 965
- Total Carbohydrate: 24.7
- Cholesterol: 56
- Protein: 15.8
- Total Fat: 13.6

---

16. Barbeque Seitan And Black Bean Burritos

Serving: 10 | Prep: 30mins | Cook: 40mins | Ready in:

Ingredients

- 3 tablespoons olive oil
- 1 small onion, chopped
- 5 green onions, chopped
- 2 cloves garlic, minced
- 2 habanero peppers, seeded and minced
- 1 red bell pepper, chopped
- 1 1/2 (8 ounce) packages seitan
- 1 (15 ounce) can black beans, rinsed and drained
- 1 (16 ounce) can diced tomatoes
- 3 cups cooked white rice
- 3 tablespoons chopped fresh cilantro
- 1 (18 ounce) bottle barbecue sauce
- 10 (10 inch) flour tortillas

Direction

- Heat the oil in a big saucepan (wok pans will also work well) on medium-high and sauté the bell pepper, habanero, garlic, green onions and yellow onion until the onions turn translucent. Add the seitan and sauté for an additional of 5 minutes. Add the tomatoes and black beans, then heat through.
- Mixed together the 1 cup barbecue sauce, cilantro and cooked rice with the heated mixture in a medium size mixing bowl.
- On a flat surface, lay the tortillas, then scoop approximately 3/4 cup of the filling on the middle of each tortilla. Wrap the tortilla so the mixture is captured on the inside.
- Pour the barbecue sauce in a casserole dish to coat the bottom of the dish. Put the burritos in the dish and pour more barbecue sauce atop them. Let it bake for 35 minutes in a preheated 175°C (350°F) oven.

Nutrition Information

- Calories: 509 calories;
- Protein: 18.3
- Total Fat: 5.3
- Sodium: 1240
- Total Carbohydrate: 83.7
- Cholesterol: 0

17. Barbequed Marinated Flank Steak

Serving: 6 | Prep: 15mins | Cook: 10mins | Ready in:

Ingredients

- 1/4 cup soy sauce
- 3 tablespoons honey
- 2 tablespoons distilled white vinegar
- 1/2 teaspoon ground ginger
- 1/2 teaspoon garlic powder
- 1/2 cup vegetable oil
- 1 1/2 pounds flank steak

Direction

- Blend vegetable oil, garlic powder, ginger, vinegar, honey and soy sauce in a blender.
- In a ceramic or shallow glass dish, put steak. Pierce both steak sides using a sharp fork. Put marinade on steak. Flip and coat other side. Keep in fridge, covered, for 8 hours to overnight.
- Preheat grill to high heat.
- Put grate on the highest level. Lightly brush with oil. Put steaks on grill. Throw marinade. Grill steaks, flipping once, for 10 minutes or your preferred doneness.

Nutrition Information

- Calories: 388 calories;
- Total Fat: 27.8
- Sodium: 663
- Total Carbohydrate: 9.7
- Cholesterol: 47
- Protein: 24.8

18. Beefy Spanish Rice

Serving: 6 | Prep: 10mins | Cook: 20mins | Ready in:

Ingredients

- 2 tablespoons vegetable oil
- 1 cup uncooked converted white rice
- 1/2 cup chopped onion
- 1/2 cup chopped green bell pepper
- 1 pound ground beef
- 1 cup canned corn
- 1 (6 ounce) can tomato sauce
- 1/2 cup ketchup
- 1 cup water
- salt and pepper to taste
- garlic powder to taste

Direction

- Heat the oil in a big saucepan on medium heat, then add bell pepper, onion and rice and sauté for 5 minutes or until the onions become soft. Add the ground beef and sauté until it turns brown. Drain the excess fat and oil.
- Add the water, ketchup, tomato sauce and corn. Lower the heat to low, put cover on and let it simmer for 20 minutes, until the rice has cooked, stirring from time to time. Add garlic powder, pepper and salt to season to taste.

Nutrition Information

- Calories: 365 calories;
- Protein: 15.1
- Total Fat: 25
- Sodium: 496
- Total Carbohydrate: 20.9
- Cholesterol: 64

19. Bessy's Zesty Grilled Garlic Herb Chicken

Serving: 4 | Prep: 15mins | Cook: 40mins | Ready in:

Ingredients

- 4 skinless, boneless chicken breast halves
- 1 cup extra virgin olive oil
- 1/2 cup white sugar

- 1/2 tablespoon honey
- 1/2 teaspoon saffron
- 4 cloves garlic, minced
- 1 teaspoon dried basil
- 1 teaspoon dried thyme
- 1 teaspoon cayenne pepper
- 1 teaspoon salt
- 1/2 teaspoon dried oregano
- 1/4 teaspoon dried parsley
- 1 pinch dried sage

Direction

- In shallow dish, put chicken. Mix sage, parsley, oregano, salt, cayenne pepper, thyme, basil, garlic, saffron, honey, sugar and olive oil in medium bowl. Put mixture on chicken. Cover, marinate in the fridge for 20-25 minutes.
- Preheat a grill to medium heat.
- Oil grill grate lightly. Discard marinade; put chicken on grill. Cook till juices are clear and exterior is charred for 10 minutes per side.

Nutrition Information

- Calories: 748 calories;
- Total Carbohydrate: 29.1
- Cholesterol: 67
- Protein: 24.9
- Total Fat: 59
- Sodium: 641

20. Best Burger Ever

Serving: 6 | Prep: 10mins | Cook: 10mins | Ready in:

Ingredients

- 2 pounds extra-lean ground beef
- 1 (1 ounce) package dry onion soup mix
- 1 egg, lightly beaten
- 2 teaspoons hot pepper sauce
- 2 teaspoons Worcestershire sauce
- 1/4 teaspoon ground black pepper
- 3/4 cup rolled oats

Direction

- Preheat the outdoor grill on medium-high; grease the grate lightly.
- Mix oats, beef, hot sauce, egg, and onion soup mix together in a big bowl; form into six patties.
- On medium-high heat, grill patties for 10-20mins or up until the preferred doneness.

Nutrition Information

- Calories: 323 calories;
- Cholesterol: 122
- Protein: 30.2
- Total Fat: 17.3
- Sodium: 564
- Total Carbohydrate: 10.3

21. Big M's Spicy Lime Grilled Prawns

Serving: 12 | Prep: 30mins | Cook: 5mins | Ready in:

Ingredients

- 48 large tiger prawns, peeled and deveined
- 4 limes, zested and juiced
- 4 green chile peppers, seeded and chopped
- 4 cloves garlic, crushed
- 1 (2 inch) piece fresh ginger root, chopped
- 1 medium onion, coarsely chopped
- skewers

Direction

- Take a large, non-metallic bowl and put in the prawns and lime zest. In a food processor, blend garlic, onion, ginger, chile pepper, and lime juice until smooth. Add a little oil as needed to move the blending along. Pour the

mixture over the prawns and stir well. Cover and refrigerate for 4 hours.
- Set grill on medium-high to pre-heat. Skewer the prawns, poking in the tail and out of the head.
- Brush oil on the grill grate. Grill prawns, turning once, until opaque, about 5 minutes.

Nutrition Information

- Calories: 62 calories;
- Sodium: 100
- Total Carbohydrate: 5.1
- Cholesterol: 85
- Protein: 9.8
- Total Fat: 0.6

22. Blackened Chicken

Serving: 2 | Prep: 10mins | Cook: 10mins | Ready in:

Ingredients

- 1/2 teaspoon paprika
- 1/8 teaspoon salt
- 1/4 teaspoon cayenne pepper
- 1/4 teaspoon ground cumin
- 1/4 teaspoon dried thyme
- 1/8 teaspoon ground white pepper
- 1/8 teaspoon onion powder
- 2 skinless, boneless chicken breast halves

Direction

- Prepare the oven by heating to 350°F or 175°C. Apply a bit of grease to a baking sheet. Heat a cast-iron skillet until piping hot on high heat.
- Combine onion powder, white pepper, paprika, cayenne, salt, cumin and thyme. Apply cooking spray on the chicken breasts on both sides then coat with spice mixture.
- Put the chicken breasts in a hot pan and cook for about a minute on each side. Then, transfer the chicken to the baking sheet.
- Let it bake in the oven and cook the chicken for five minutes or until it is not pink.

Nutrition Information

- Calories: 135 calories;
- Cholesterol: 67
- Protein: 24.7
- Total Fat: 3
- Sodium: 205
- Total Carbohydrate: 0.9

23. Blackened Tuna Steaks With Mango Salsa

Serving: 4 | Prep: 45mins | Cook: 10mins | Ready in:

Ingredients

- 2 tablespoons olive oil
- 2 tablespoons lime juice
- 2 cloves garlic, minced
- 4 tuna steaks
- 1 fresh mango - peeled, pitted, and chopped
- 1/4 cup finely chopped red bell pepper
- 1/2 Spanish onion, finely chopped
- 1 green onion, chopped
- 2 tablespoons chopped fresh cilantro
- 1 jalapeno pepper, seeded and minced
- 2 tablespoons lime juice
- 1 1/2 teaspoons olive oil
- 2 tablespoons paprika
- 1 tablespoon cayenne pepper
- 1 tablespoon onion powder
- 2 teaspoons salt
- 1 teaspoon ground black pepper
- 1 teaspoon dried thyme
- 1 teaspoon dried basil
- 1 teaspoon dried oregano
- 1 tablespoon garlic powder
- 4 tablespoons olive oil

Direction

- In a bowl, mix garlic, lime juice and olive oil together. Use the mixture to rub all over tuna steaks. Transfer the steaks in a sealable container and leave in the fridge for 3 hours to chill.
- In a bowl, mix jalapeno pepper, cilantro, green onion, Spanish onion, bell pepper and mango together and whisk. Put in the lime juice and 1 1/2 teaspoons of olive oil, then toss to incorporate. Let chill in the fridge for 60 minutes.
- In a bowl, combine garlic powder, oregano, basil, thyme, pepper, salt, onion powder, cayenne pepper and paprika. Take the tuna steaks out of the fridge and gently wash with water, then coat each side of each steak by dipping in the spice mixture.
- In a big skillet, heat 2 tablespoons of olive oil on medium heat. Gently place the tuna steaks into the heated oil. Cook each side of the tuna for 3 minutes; transfer to a plate. Heat the rest of olive oil (2 tablespoons) in the skillet. Place tuna with the uncooked side down into the skillet and cook for an additional 3 minutes, then take off the heat right away.
- Lay half a cup of mango salsa on each 4 serving plates. Place the tuna steaks on top of the salsa, then serve while the steak are still warm.

Nutrition Information

- Calories: 458 calories;
- Sodium: 1233
- Total Carbohydrate: 18.3
- Cholesterol: 77
- Protein: 42.1
- Total Fat: 24.7

24. Braised Balsamic Chicken

Serving: 6 | Prep: 10mins | Cook: 25mins | Ready in:

Ingredients

- 6 skinless, boneless chicken breast halves
- 1 teaspoon garlic salt
- ground black pepper to taste
- 2 tablespoons olive oil
- 1 onion, thinly sliced
- 1 (14.5 ounce) can diced tomatoes
- 1/2 cup balsamic vinegar
- 1 teaspoon dried basil
- 1 teaspoon dried oregano
- 1 teaspoon dried rosemary
- 1/2 teaspoon dried thyme

Direction

- Use pepper and garlic salt to season both sides of chicken breasts.
- In a skillet over medium heat, put in oil then heat it; add seasoned chicken breasts and cook for 3-4 minutes per side until chicken turns brown. Put in onion; stir and cook for 3-4 minutes until onion turns brown.
- Pour balsamic vinegar and diced tomatoes over chicken; use thyme, rosemary, oregano, and basil for seasoning. Simmer for about 15 minutes until the juices run clear and chicken is not pink anymore. An instant-read thermometer inserted into the center should register at least 165 degrees F (74 degrees C).

Nutrition Information

- Calories: 196 calories;
- Total Fat: 7
- Sodium: 511
- Total Carbohydrate: 7.6
- Cholesterol: 61
- Protein: 23.8

25. Buckwheat Tortilla Pizza

Serving: 2 | Prep: 15mins | Cook: 28mins | Ready in:

Ingredients

- Tortilla base:
- 1/3 cup buckwheat flour
- 1/3 cup water
- 1/2 teaspoon dried oregano
- 2 teaspoons olive oil, divided
- Toppings:
- 1/2 (14.5 ounce) can diced tomatoes
- 1 clove garlic, crushed
- 1 tomato, sliced
- 5 tablespoons fresh spinach
- 1 tablespoon nutritional yeast

Direction

- Set an oven to preheat to 400°F (200°C).
- In a bowl, mix together the 1 tsp olive oil, oregano, water and buckwheat, stir until well combined.
- In a skillet, heat 1 tsp of olive oil on medium-high heat, add 1/2 of the tortilla batter and cook for about 2 minutes, until the edges become dry. Flip and cook for another 2-3 minutes, until it becomes brown on the other side. Transfer to a baking tray. Repeat with the leftover batter.
- In the same skillet, put the garlic and diced tomatoes on medium heat, boil. Lower the heat and simmer for about 5 minutes until it becomes soft. Spread the tomato mixture on top of the tortillas and put slices of tomato, spinach and nutritional yeast.
- Bake in the preheated oven for about 10 minutes until it turns golden.

Nutrition Information

- Calories: 156 calories;
- Protein: 6.3
- Total Fat: 5.9
- Sodium: 26
- Total Carbohydrate: 22.9
- Cholesterol: 0

26. Bulgur Veggie Stir Fry

Serving: 4 | Prep: 20mins | Cook: 25mins | Ready in:

Ingredients

- 1 cup dry bulgur wheat
- 2 cups water
- 1/4 teaspoon cumin seeds
- 1 teaspoon vegetable oil
- 3 cloves garlic, minced
- 1/2 onion, chopped
- 1/2 (16 ounce) package firm tofu, drained and cubed
- 1 cup chopped broccoli
- 1/2 green bell pepper, chopped
- 4 kumquats, thinly sliced
- 1/4 cup fresh basil leaves
- 1/2 lemon, juiced
- salt to taste
- cayenne pepper to taste

Direction

- Boil water and bulgur wheat in a medium saucepan. Lower heat; cover. Simmer for 15 minutes. Take off heat; use a fork to fluff.
- Cook cumin seeds for 1-2 minutes till lightly toasted in a medium skillet on medium heat. Put oil into skillet. Sauté onions and garlic till tender. Mix in tofu; cook till browned lightly.
- Mix green bell pepper and broccoli into skillet; cook till tender. Mix in basil leaves and kumquat slices; sprinkle lemon juice. Season with cayenne pepper and salt. Serve over cooked bulgur wheat.

Nutrition Information

- Calories: 188 calories;
- Total Fat: 6.7
- Sodium: 168
- Total Carbohydrate: 24.3
- Cholesterol: 0
- Protein: 12.8

27. Busy Day Deer

Serving: 4 | Prep: 20mins | Cook: 15mins | Ready in:

Ingredients

- 2 tablespoons olive oil
- 1 onion, diced
- 1/4 bell pepper, diced
- 2 (1/2 pound) venison steaks, cubed
- 1 (1 ounce) package dry onion and mushroom soup mix
- 3 1/2 cups water
- 2 tablespoons all-purpose flour

Direction

- In a big skillet, heat oil. In the hot oil, cook venison, pepper and onion until meat is cooked through. Stir in water and soup mix, then keep on cooking until pepper as well as onion is soft. Put in flour and whisk over the heat until there are not lumps anymore. Cook and stir the sauce until it is thickened.

Nutrition Information

- Calories: 221 calories;
- Total Fat: 9.6
- Sodium: 484
- Total Carbohydrate: 9.9
- Cholesterol: 79
- Protein: 22.8

28. Butternut Squash Porridge

Serving: 4 | Prep: 15mins | Cook: 35mins | Ready in:

Ingredients

- 2 cups water
- 1 cup hulled millet
- 1 butternut squash - peeled, seeded, and cut into cubes
- 1/2 teaspoon salt

Direction

- In a saucepan, bring water to a boil, then put in millet and cook for 15 minutes, or until half of the water is absorbed. Put salt and butternut squash into the millet carefully, then simmer for 15-20 minutes, or until squash and millet are soft.
- Use a potato masher to mash the squash until the mixture has the texture of porridge.

Nutrition Information

- Calories: 304 calories;
- Total Fat: 2.4
- Sodium: 307
- Total Carbohydrate: 66.3
- Cholesterol: 0
- Protein: 8.1

29. Cabin Dinner

Serving: 6 | Prep: 15mins | Cook: 1hours | Ready in:

Ingredients

- 1/4 cup vegetable oil
- 4 cloves garlic, chopped
- 1 yellow onion, diced
- 1 red bell pepper, chopped
- 2 teaspoons chopped parsley
- 1 tablespoon chili powder
- 2 teaspoons ground cumin
- 2 teaspoons paprika
- 2 teaspoons ground turmeric
- salt and pepper to taste
- 1 1/2 (16 ounce) cans kidney beans, drained with liquid reserved
- 2 tablespoons tomato paste
- hot sauce to taste

Direction

- Heat the oil in the Dutch oven on medium heat. Sauté the pepper, salt, turmeric, paprika, cumin, chili powder, parsley, bell pepper, onion and garlic till the onions soften. Whisk in the kidney beans and some reserved liquid till have the consistency that you like. Whisk in hot sauce and tomato paste.
- Lower the heat to low, keep covered and let simmer for 60 minutes, whisk once in a while. Put in extra bean liquid and/or the water if needed so that the beans do not dry out.

Nutrition Information

- Calories: 258 calories;
- Protein: 7.2
- Total Fat: 10.6
- Sodium: 498
- Total Carbohydrate: 34
- Cholesterol: 3

30. Carol's Arroz Con Pollo

Serving: 4 | Prep: 15mins | Cook: 30mins | Ready in:

Ingredients

- 4 skinless, boneless chicken breast halves
- 1/2 teaspoon salt
- 1/2 teaspoon ground black pepper
- 1/2 teaspoon paprika
- 3 tablespoons vegetable oil
- 1 green bell pepper, chopped
- 3/4 cup chopped onion
- 1 1/2 teaspoons minced garlic
- 1 cup long-grain white rice
- 1 (14.5 ounce) can chicken broth
- 1/2 cup white wine
- 1/8 teaspoon saffron
- 1 (14.5 ounce) can stewed tomatoes
- 1 tablespoon chopped fresh parsley

Direction

- Cut every breast to 1-in. pieces. Sprinkle 1/4 tsp. each of paprika, pepper and salt on chicken.
- Heat oil in big skillet on medium heat. Add chicken; cook till golden. Remove chicken; put aside.
- Put garlic, onions and green pepper in skillet. Cook for 5 minutes. Add rice; mix and cook for 1-2 minutes till rice is opaque. Mix in tomatoes, saffron, white wine and broth. Mix in leftover paprika, pepper and salt. Boil. Cover; simmer for 20 minutes.
- Put chicken in skillet; cook to reheat. Mix parsley in.

Nutrition Information

- Calories: 471 calories;
- Sodium: 1015
- Total Carbohydrate: 49.5
- Cholesterol: 69
- Protein: 30
- Total Fat: 14

31. Chicken Fried Chicken

Serving: 6 | Prep: 25mins | Cook: 20mins | Ready in:

Ingredients

- 30 saltine crackers
- 2 tablespoons all-purpose flour
- 2 tablespoons dry potato flakes
- 1 teaspoon seasoned salt
- 1/2 teaspoon ground black pepper
- 1 egg
- 6 skinless, boneless chicken breast halves
- 2 cups vegetable oil for frying

Direction

- In big resealable plastic bag, put crackers; seal bag. With rolling pin, crush crackers till

they're coarse crumbs. Add pepper, seasoned salt, potato flakes and flour; stir well.
- In shallow dish/bowl, beat egg; One by one, dredge chicken pieces in egg. Put into bag with the crumb mixture then seal bag; shake to coat.
- Heat oil to 175°C/350°F in big saucepan/deep fryer.
- Fry chicken for 15-20 minutes till juices are clear and golden brown, frequently turning.

Nutrition Information

- Calories: 887 calories;
- Protein: 29.2
- Total Fat: 79.6
- Sodium: 389
- Total Carbohydrate: 14.2
- Cholesterol: 103

32. Chicken Lo Mein

Serving: 4 | Prep: 45mins | Cook: 30mins | Ready in:

Ingredients

- 4 skinless, boneless chicken breast halves - cut into thin strips
- 5 teaspoons white sugar, divided
- 3 tablespoons rice wine vinegar
- 1/2 cup soy sauce, divided
- 1 1/4 cups chicken broth
- 1 cup water
- 1 tablespoon sesame oil
- 1/2 teaspoon ground black pepper
- 2 tablespoons cornstarch
- 1 (12 ounce) package uncooked linguine pasta
- 2 tablespoons vegetable oil, divided
- 2 tablespoons minced fresh ginger root
- 1 tablespoon minced garlic
- 1/2 pound fresh shiitake mushrooms, stemmed and sliced
- 6 green onions, sliced diagonally into 1/2 inch pieces

Direction

- Mix 1/4 cup of soy sauce, 1 1/2 tbsp. of vinegar and 2 1/2 tsp. of white sugar with chicken in a medium non-reactive bowl; mix to coat the chicken well. Cover; marinate for 1 hour minimum in the fridge.
- Mix leftover soy sauce, vinegar and sugar with ground black pepper, sesame oil, water and chicken broth in a separate medium bowl. Dissolve cornstarch with some of the mixture in another small bowl; add to the bulk of the mixture slowly, mixing well. Put aside.
- Follow package directions to cook linguine. Drain; put aside. Heat 1 tbsp. of vegetable oil in big saucepan or wok on high heat till it begins to smoke. Add chicken; stir-fry till browned or for 4-5 minutes. Put this and all juices on a warm plate.
- Heat leftover vegetable oil in the pan or wok on high heat. Add green onions, mushrooms, garlic and ginger; stir-fry for half a minute. Add reserved sauce mixture then the chicken; simmer for 2 minutes till sauce starts to thicken. Add reserved noodles; gently toss, coating all well with the sauce.

Nutrition Information

- Calories: 599 calories;
- Protein: 38
- Total Fat: 14.7
- Sodium: 1877
- Total Carbohydrate: 78.6
- Cholesterol: 61

33. Chicken Seitan

Serving: 12 | Prep: 20mins | Cook: 45mins | Ready in:

Ingredients

- 2 cups vital wheat gluten
- 1 teaspoon dried rosemary

- 1 teaspoon dried thyme
- 1 teaspoon dried sage
- 1/4 teaspoon cumin seed
- 1/4 teaspoon garlic powder
- 2 cups water
- 1/3 cup tamari or soy sauce
- 8 cups water
- 1/2 cup tamari or soy sauce
- 1/2 teaspoon onion powder
- 2 (4 inch) pieces dashi kombu (dried kelp)

Direction

- Combine garlic powder, cumin seed, sage, thyme, rosemary and vital wheat gluten together in a big glass bowl. Mix together soy sauce or tamari and water in a separate bowl. Pour liquid into the gluten mixture with a sturdy spoon, working very rapidly. The gluten will develop very quickly and become extremely elastic and rubbery. Put a little water rapidly into the mixture in case there is any dry mix remains to soak remaining dry mix up. On a flat and clean countertop, place the dough and knead it several times then form into a log with the diameter of your first. Forming the dough may be somewhat tricky because the dough is very resistant and rubbery but you have to be patient. Put aside to rest about 15 minutes while making the stock.
- Boil together dashi kombu, onion powder, 1/2 cup of soy sauce or tamari and 8 cups of water in a big stock pot. Slice gluten log into favorite shapes, at least half an inch thick. Drop gluten pieces into the boiling stock separately. Lower heat to low and simmer, covered, about 45 minutes. Now, you can coat the saitan with bread crumbs and fry, then chop up and use to make salads, or season it as preferred.

Nutrition Information

- Calories: 103 calories;
- Sodium: 1119
- Total Carbohydrate: 9.1
- Cholesterol: 0
- Protein: 14.8
- Total Fat: 0.1

34. Chicken And Lentils With Rosemary

Serving: 4 | Prep: 10mins | Cook: 40mins | Ready in:

Ingredients

- 4 bone-in chicken breast halves, with skin
- 2 teaspoons seasoned salt (eg. LAWRY'S®)
- 1 tablespoon vegetable oil
- 1 large onion, finely chopped
- 3 carrots, finely chopped
- 3 cloves garlic, minced
- 1 (2 ounce) jar pimento peppers, drained and chopped
- 2 cups chicken broth
- 1/2 cup dry red wine
- 1 (16 ounce) package steamed lentils
- 1 teaspoon chopped fresh rosemary
- 2 tablespoons white balsamic vinegar
- 1 tablespoon lemon juice

Direction

- Liberally season chicken using seasoned salt. Heat oil on medium high heat in a big skillet. Add chicken; cook for 10 minutes till all sides brown well. Remove chicken from pan; put aside.
- Reduce heat. Add onion; mix and cook for 5 minutes till translucent. Mix in pimento, carrot and garlic; mix and cook for 3 minutes. Put chicken broth into pan; boil while scraping browned food bits off bottom of pan using a wooden spoon.
- Mix in vinegar, wine, rosemary and lentils. Put chicken into pan; simmer for 20 minutes till juices are clear and chicken breasts aren't pink at bone. Take off heat; mix lemon juice into sauce. Serve.

Nutrition Information

- Calories: 538 calories;
- Cholesterol: 127
- Protein: 56.7
- Total Fat: 15.9
- Sodium: 612
- Total Carbohydrate: 36.2

35. Chicken And Sausage With Bowties

Serving: 8 | Prep: 15mins | Cook: 45mins | Ready in:

Ingredients

- 1 (16 ounce) package uncooked farfalle pasta
- 2 skinless, boneless chicken breasts
- 1 pound hot Italian turkey sausage, casings removed
- 1 tablespoon olive oil
- 2 cloves garlic, sliced
- 1 (14.5 ounce) can crushed tomatoes
- 1/2 cup red wine
- 2 tablespoons chopped fresh basil
- 1 teaspoon dried rosemary

Direction

- Boil a big pot filled with water that's slightly salted, and add the pasta, cook until they become al dente, about 8-10 minutes.
- Wash the chicken breasts, then cut into large bite-size chunks, and also cut the sausages into the big size portions. Combine garlic and oil in a big deep skillet and cook over a medium-low heat long enough to infuse oil with flavor. Remove the garlic from the oil.
- In the same skillet with the infused oil, add the sausage and chicken, gently brown both of them until opaque. Add the wine and tomatoes, then let boil then simmer for 20 minutes. Season the sauce with pepper, salt, rosemary, and basil to your taste. Add the cooked drained pasta into the skillet, toss to serve.

Nutrition Information

- Calories: 382 calories;
- Sodium: 526
- Total Carbohydrate: 47.6
- Cholesterol: 51
- Protein: 24
- Total Fat: 9.1

36. Chinese Chicken Fried Rice I

Serving: 7 | Prep: 25mins | Cook: 15mins | Ready in:

Ingredients

- 1/2 tablespoon sesame oil
- 1 onion
- 1 1/2 pounds cooked, cubed chicken meat
- 2 tablespoons soy sauce
- 2 large carrots, diced
- 2 stalks celery, chopped
- 1 large red bell pepper, diced
- 3/4 cup fresh pea pods, halved
- 1/2 large green bell pepper, diced
- 6 cups cooked white rice
- 2 eggs
- 1/3 cup soy sauce

Direction

- In a big cooking pan, heat the oil on medium heat. Sauté the onion in the hot oil until it's soft then add 2 tablespoons of soy sauce and the chicken and stir-fry it for 5-6 minutes.
- Add the celery, carrots, pea pods, green bell pepper, and red bell pepper while stirring then stir-fry for 5 more minutes. Add the rice and mix well.
- Add 1/3 soy sauce and scrambled eggs while stirring, heat it through and serve while it's hot.

Nutrition Information

- Calories: 425 calories;
- Protein: 34.7
- Total Fat: 9.5
- Sodium: 1060
- Total Carbohydrate: 47.5
- Cholesterol: 134

37. Chtitha Batata (Algerian Potato Stew)

Serving: 4 | Prep: 10mins | Cook: 45mins | Ready in:

Ingredients

- Dersa:
- 4 cloves garlic, peeled and halved
- 1 small fresh red chile pepper, seeded and chopped
- 1 teaspoon ground cumin
- 1 teaspoon paprika
- 1/2 teaspoon black pepper
- 1/2 teaspoon cayenne pepper
- 1/2 teaspoon salt
- 2 tablespoons olive oil
- Stew:
- 1 1/2 pounds new potatoes, halved
- 1 tablespoon tomato paste
- water to cover
- salt to taste

Direction

- In a mortar, mix salt, cayenne, black pepper, paprika, cumin, chile pepper and garlic; grind with a pestle till a paste forms. Put in olive oil; combine dersa properly.
- Place a large saucepan on medium heat; stir-fry the dersa for 2-4 minutes till fragrant. Put in potato halves; stir to incorporate with the dersa. Mix in tomato sauce. Transfer in enough water to just cover the potatoes; boil.
- Lower the heat; simmer for around 40 minutes, till the potatoes become tender.
- Ladle the cooked potatoes into a serving bowl. Scoop any of the remaining sauce on top of the potatoes.

Nutrition Information

- Calories: 206 calories;
- Sodium: 378
- Total Carbohydrate: 32.8
- Cholesterol: 0
- Protein: 4.1
- Total Fat: 7.2

38. Coal Miners Pasties

Serving: 6 | Prep: 30mins | Cook: 45mins | Ready in:

Ingredients

- 4 cups all-purpose flour
- 2 teaspoons salt
- 1 1/2 cups lard
- 10 tablespoons ice water
- 2 pounds top round steak, cut into 1/4 inch cubes
- 5 red potatoes, peeled and chopped
- 3 turnips, peeled and cubed
- 1 1/2 cups chopped onion
- 1 teaspoon freshly ground black pepper
- 1 tablespoon salt

Direction

- In a bowl, put lard, 2 tsp. salt and flour. Rub lard into flour quickly using your fingertips until it looks like small peas. Pour ice water in; shape into a ball. If it feels too dry, add more water. Distribute dough to 6 balls. Wrap it in plastic. Chill for an hour.
- Mix pepper, leftover 1 tbsp. salt, onions, potatoes, turnips and meat in a bowl.
- Preheat oven to 205 degrees C/400 degrees F.

- On a floured surface, roll out 1 ball to about 1/4-in. thick. Trace a 9-in. circle in the dough with a cake pan. Cut circle out. In the center of the circle, put 1 1/2 cups of meat mixture. Fold circle edges to meet above the meat filing. Crimp dough at the top to seal it. Repeat until you use all the dough. Transfer pasties with a spatula to an ungreased sheet.
- Bake pasties until golden for 45 minutes. Serve at room temperature or hot.

Nutrition Information

- Calories: 1186 calories;
- Total Carbohydrate: 98.9
- Cholesterol: 141
- Protein: 45.4
- Total Fat: 66.6
- Sodium: 2203

39. Cola Pot Roast I

Serving: 8 | Prep: 30mins | Cook: 2hours30mins | Ready in:

Ingredients

- 1 (14.5 ounce) can stewed tomatoes
- 1 cup cola-flavored carbonated beverage
- 1 packet dry spaghetti sauce mix
- 1 cup chopped onion
- 3/4 cup chopped celery
- 1 1/2 teaspoons salt
- 1/2 teaspoon garlic salt
- 3 pounds beef chuck roast
- 2 tablespoons vegetable oil

Direction

- In a big bowl, break up the tomatoes in their own juice. Mix in spaghetti sauce mix, celery, garlic salt, salt, onion, and cola. Mix until the spaghetti sauce mix dissolves.

- On medium high heat in a Dutch oven, brown the meat in the oil for about 10 minutes on every side. Drain out all the fat. Pour the tomato mixture on the meat. Cover it and bring down the heat to low. Slowly simmer for about 2 1/2 hours or until meat gets tender.

Nutrition Information

- Calories: 324 calories;
- Cholesterol: 77
- Protein: 21.1
- Total Fat: 21
- Sodium: 1166
- Total Carbohydrate: 12.2

40. Cola Basted Ham

Serving: 13 | Prep: 30mins | Cook: 3hours45mins | Ready in:

Ingredients

- 1 (10 pound) fully-cooked, bone-in ham
- 6 cups cola-flavored carbonated beverage
- 1 cup packed light brown sugar
- 1 tablespoon mustard powder
- 2 tablespoons Dijon-style prepared mustard
- 2 cups dried bread crumbs

Direction

- Set an oven at 165°C (325°F) to preheat.
- Put ham in a shallow pan with the fat side down. Add cola into the pan until 1/2 inch deep. Bake for 2-3 hours, basting with cola every 15 minutes, until the ham can be pierced easily with a fork. Insert a meat thermometer into the center of the ham and it will state 60°C (140°F). Remove the ham from the pan and let cool.
- Next, increase the temperature of the oven to 190°C (375°F).
- Use a sharp knife to cut away the rind. Mix enough cola, bread crumbs, mustard, and

sugar to make a thick paste. Then spread it over the entire ham. In the oven, arrange the ham on a roasting rack and bake for 45 minutes until the mustard paste has melted into a dark glaze, basting every 10 minutes. Before slicing, allow to sit at room temperature for a half-hour.

Nutrition Information

- Calories: 665 calories;
- Sodium: 334
- Total Carbohydrate: 41.9
- Cholesterol: 214
- Protein: 69.3
- Total Fat: 22.6

41. Cold Roasted Moroccan Spiced Salmon

Serving: 6 | Prep: 15mins | Cook: 12mins | Ready in:

Ingredients

- 3/4 teaspoon ground cinnamon
- 3/4 teaspoon ground cumin
- 1/2 teaspoon salt
- 1/2 teaspoon ground ginger
- 1/4 teaspoon mustard powder
- 1/4 teaspoon ground nutmeg
- 1/8 teaspoon cayenne pepper
- 1/8 teaspoon ground allspice
- 2 teaspoons white sugar
- 2 pounds (1-inch thick) boneless, skin-on center-cut salmon fillets
- 1 tablespoon fresh lime juice

Direction

- Mix the cinnamon, salt, cumin, ginger, nutmeg, mustard, cayenne, sugar, and allspice in a small bowl. Let it rest.
- Use a foil to line a baking sheet, then use nonstick cooking spray to coat it. Use cold water to rinse the salmon, then dry with paper towels. Sprinkle the skin lightly with some spice mix, and place the salmon on the baking sheet with its skin downward. Use the leftover spice mix to rub evenly on the salmon.
- Leave the salmon to warm to room temperature for 30 to 40 minutes.
- Prepare an oven by heating it to 220 degrees C or 425 degrees F.
- Drizzle it with some lime juice and leave in the oven for 12 minutes to roast. Remove the salmon from the oven. Let it stand for 15 minutes at room temperature. It should still be rare when taken out of the oven, but it will continue to cook as it stands. Then, after 15 minutes, use foil to wrap the fish tightly and place in the fridge for a minimum of two hours until it's time to serve.

Nutrition Information

- Calories: 225 calories;
- Sodium: 261
- Total Carbohydrate: 2.2
- Cholesterol: 84
- Protein: 30.2
- Total Fat: 9.8

42. Corned Beef And Cabbage II

Serving: 8 | Prep: 20mins | Cook: 3hours | Ready in:

Ingredients

- 4 1/2 pounds corned beef brisket
- 5 black peppercorns
- 1/2 teaspoon garlic powder
- 1 onion, peeled and left whole
- 2 bay leaves
- 1 pinch salt
- 1 small head cabbage, cored and cut into wedges
- 6 large potatoes, quartered
- 4 large carrots, peeled and sliced

- 1/4 cup chopped fresh parsley
- 2 tablespoons butter

Direction

- Put the peppercorns, beef brisket, garlic powder, bay leaves, salt and onion in a six qt. Dutch oven. Pour water into the pan until it covers 1 inch atop everything. Bring to a boil and cook for 20 minutes. Take off any residue that floats on top. Lessen heat to a simmer and cook for 2-3 hours until the meat can be pulled apart with a fork.
- When meat is done, put in potatoes, cabbage and carrots, pushing them down into the liquid. Simmer for another 15 minutes or until the potatoes are soft. Take off any oil on top. Add in the parsley and butter. Take the pot away from the heat.
- Transfer meat onto a serving dish, letting it sit for 15 minutes. Transfer vegetables to a bowl and keep it hot. Cut briskets diagonally against the grain. Serve onto platter and pour juices over vegetables and meat.

Nutrition Information

- Calories: 515 calories;
- Total Fat: 24.4
- Sodium: 1328
- Total Carbohydrate: 49.2
- Cholesterol: 117
- Protein: 25.5

43. Cornish Game Hens With Garlic And Rosemary

Serving: 4 | Prep: 20mins | Cook: 1hours | Ready in:

Ingredients

- 4 Cornish game hens
- salt and pepper to taste
- 1 lemon, quartered
- 4 sprigs fresh rosemary
- 3 tablespoons olive oil
- 24 cloves garlic
- 1/3 cup white wine
- 1/3 cup low-sodium chicken broth
- 4 sprigs fresh rosemary, for garnish

Direction

- Preheat the oven to 230 degrees C/450 degrees F.
- Use 1 tbsp. olive oil to rub hens. Season hens lightly with pepper and salt. Put 1 sprig rosemary and 1 lemon wedge in every hen's cavity. Put in a big heavy roasting pan. Surround hens with garlic cloves. Roast for 25 minutes in the preheated oven.
- Lower the oven temperature to 175 degrees C/350 degrees F. Whisk together leftover 2 tbsp. oil, chicken broth and wine in a mixing bowl. Pour on hens. Keep roasting for about 25 minutes longer until hens become golden brown and the juices are clear. Baste using the pan juices in 10- minute intervals.
- Put hens on a platter, putting any cavity juices in the roasting pan. Use aluminum foil to tent hens to retain warmth. Put garlic cloves and pan juices in a medium saucepan. Boil for about 6 minutes until liquid is reduce to become a sauce consistency. Cut hens lengthwise in half. Put on plates. Put garlic and sauce around the hens. Top with rosemary sprigs. Serve.

Nutrition Information

- Calories: 814 calories;
- Total Fat: 57.5
- Sodium: 1383
- Total Carbohydrate: 9.7
- Cholesterol: 340
- Protein: 59.4

44. County Fair Corn Dogs

Serving: 10 | Prep: 10mins | Cook: 20mins | Ready in:

Ingredients

- 10 beef frankfurters
- 1/2 cup all-purpose flour for dusting
- 2/3 cup cornmeal
- 1/3 cup all-purpose flour
- 2 tablespoons corn flour (optional)
- 1 teaspoon salt
- 1 pinch ground cayenne pepper
- 1 egg
- 2 tablespoons corn oil
- 1/2 cup water
- 1 quart vegetable oil for frying

Direction

- Insert the sticks into the franks. Dust with flour. Set aside.
- Prepare the batter by mixing cornmeal, corn flour, 1/3 cup flour, cayenne pepper, salt, 2 tablespoons oil, egg, and water in a big bowl. Whisk well.
- Put 1 quart of oil in a pan over high heat (to about 375°F / 190°C). Dip or coat the franks in the batter. Fry until browned lightly. Remove excess oil with paper towels. Serve.

Nutrition Information

- Calories: 372 calories;
- Total Fat: 29
- Sodium: 824
- Total Carbohydrate: 17.7
- Cholesterol: 56
- Protein: 9.7

45. Cranberry Pot Roast

Serving: 10 | Prep: 20mins | Cook: 4hours15mins | Ready in:

Ingredients

- 3 cups beef broth
- 1 cup water
- 2 (14.5 ounce) cans cranberry sauce
- 1 (4 pound) beef chuck roast
- salt and ground black pepper to taste
- 3 tablespoons all-purpose flour
- 2 tablespoons vegetable oil
- 1 large sweet onion, chopped

Direction

- In a saucepan over high heat, pour the water and beef broth in and bring it to a boil. Mix in the cranberry sauce and stir until it dissolves. Pour the sauce into the slow cooker set on high.
- Sprinkle salt and pepper onto the beef roast to season then coat evenly with flour. In a big skillet, heat the vegetable oil over medium heat and place the roast in. Cook it in the hot oil for about 2 minutes per side until all sides are evenly brown. Move the roast into a slow cooker together with the chopped onion.
- Leave the roast to cook for about 4 hours until the roast easily pulls apart with fork.

Nutrition Information

- Calories: 587 calories;
- Total Fat: 35.4
- Sodium: 378
- Total Carbohydrate: 33.8
- Cholesterol: 129
- Protein: 32.5

46. Creamy Apple Cinnamon Raisin Oatmeal

Serving: 2 | Prep: 5mins | Cook: 10mins | Ready in:

Ingredients

- 2 cups water
- 2 teaspoons brown sugar
- 1 teaspoon ground cinnamon
- 2 tablespoons maple syrup
- 1 cup uncooked rolled oats
- 2 tablespoons raisins
- 1 apple - peeled, cored and cubed

Direction

- Mix cinnamon, water, syrup and brown sugar in a medium saucepan. Cook mixture until it begins to boil.
- When water is boiling, lower heat and pour in oats. For 5 minutes, cook mixture until oats have completely soak up all the water. Take off heat, add raisins and apples. Serve.

Nutrition Information

- Calories: 293 calories;
- Sodium: 7
- Total Carbohydrate: 64
- Cholesterol: 0
- Protein: 5.9
- Total Fat: 2.9

47. Creamy Beef Tips With Mushrooms

Serving: 6 | Prep: 25mins | Cook: 1hours11mins | Ready in:

Ingredients

- 1 (14 ounce) can coconut milk
- 1 cup beef broth
- 8 ounces portobello mushrooms, cleaned and sliced
- 1 green bell pepper, cut into strips
- 1 yellow onion, cut into strips
- 1 teaspoon sea salt
- 1 1/2 pounds beef sirloin tips, cubed
- 1 (16 ounce) package linguine pasta

Direction

- Preheat an oven to 200°C (400°F).
- Mix sea salt, onion, green bell pepper, portobello mushrooms, beef broth and coconut milk in a 9x13-in. casserole dish; stir well. Add beef tips; mix till coated well.
- In preheated oven, bake for 1 hour till sauce is thick and beef is tender.
- Boil a big pot of lightly salted water; cook linguine at a boil for 11 minutes till tender yet firm to chew. Drain; serve sauce and beef tips on pasta.

Nutrition Information

- Calories: 594 calories;
- Sodium: 483
- Total Carbohydrate: 60.7
- Cholesterol: 60
- Protein: 31.7
- Total Fat: 26.2

48. Creamy Vegan Pumpkin Penne Pasta

Serving: 12 | Prep: 25mins | Cook: 1hours25mins | Ready in:

Ingredients

- 1 1/2 cups raw cashews
- 9 teaspoons extra-virgin olive oil, divided
- 1 small sugar pie pumpkin, halved and seeded
- 5 fresh sage leaves
- 1 yellow onion, chopped
- 5 cloves garlic, minced
- 1/2 cup unsweetened coconut milk
- 1 cup tomato sauce
- 1 teaspoon dried basil
- 1/2 teaspoon oregano
- sea salt and ground black pepper to taste
- 2 (16 ounce) packages penne pasta
- 1/4 cup fresh basil, or to taste

Direction

- In a bowl, add cashews and water to cover, then allow cashews to soak about 4 hours or overnight. Drain and rinse cashews.
- Set the oven to 175°C or 350°F to preheat.
- Drizzle 3 tbsp. of oil in a baking dish and put in pumpkin with cut-sides facing down. Use a fork to pierce several holes in the skin and use aluminum foil to cover.
- In the preheated oven, bake about 40 minutes. Put sage leaves into the baking dish of pumpkin and replace the aluminum foil. Bake for another 5 minutes, until pumpkin is extremely soft. Take out of the oven and keep covered, allow sage and pumpkin to continue to steam for 10-15 minutes longer.
- In a big skillet, heat 2 tbsp. of olive oil over moderate heat. Put in garlic and onion, then cook and stir for 3-5 minutes, until turning golden brown. Put in salt, oregano, dried basil, steamed sage leaves and tomato sauce. Cook and stir the mixture for 10 minutes, until blended. Scrape flesh of pumpkin into the skillet and put in coconut milk. Simmer about 15-20 minutes longer, then get rid of sage leaves.
- Fill tomato mixture into a blender until halfway and put in a half of the soaked cashews. Use pepper and salt to season liberally. Place a lid on blender to cover and hold the lid down using a potholder, then pulse for several times prior to leaving on to blend until the mixture is creamy and smooth. Put in leftover 4 tbsp. of olive oil and blend again. Transfer to a pot. Do the same process with leftover tomato mixture and adjust seasoning if needed.
- Bring lightly salted water in a big pot to a boil. Put in penne and cook for 11 minutes while stirring sometimes, until pasta is soft but still firm to the bite. Drain pasta and save 1/2 cup of pasta water. Bring pasta back to the pot.
- Stir half of the sauce into the pot with cooked pasta. Put in more if necessary to coat. Put in 1/4 cup of reserved pasta water at a time to thin the sauce to get desired creamy consistency. Put in leftover sauce as wanted. Put fresh basil on top and serve pasta hot.

Nutrition Information

- Calories: 441 calories;
- Total Fat: 15.3
- Sodium: 250
- Total Carbohydrate: 66.1
- Cholesterol: 0
- Protein: 13.7

49. Crunchy Vegan Tostadas

Serving: 2 | Prep: 15mins | Cook: 20mins | Ready in:

Ingredients

- 2 (8 inch) flour tortillas
- cooking spray
- 2 tablespoons vegetable oil
- 1/2 onion, chopped
- 1 (12 ounce) can pinto beans, drained
- 1 teaspoon paprika
- 1 teaspoon ground cumin
- 1 cup water
- 1 cup roasted tomato salsa
- 1/2 cup guacamole
- 1/4 cup shredded lettuce
- 2 tablespoons corn

Direction

- Start preheating the oven to 350°F (175°C). Use cooking spray to spray tortillas on both sides. Put on a cookie sheet.
- In a frying pan, heat oil over medium heat. Cook onion for 3 minutes until soft. Mix in cumin, paprika, and beans. Add water. Boil it, lower the heat and simmer for 10-15 minutes until the beans are tender. Strain the beans and move to a bowl. Put a handful of beans aside to use for garnishing. Mash the rest of the beans.

- Meanwhile, put tortillas in the preheated oven to bake for 5 minutes each side until crispy and turning golden.
- Spread over the tortillas with the mashed beans. Smooth on top with salsa. Add a big scoop of guacamole. Use corn, lettuce, and the saved beans to garnish.

Nutrition Information

- Calories: 570 calories;
- Protein: 16.8
- Total Fat: 25.5
- Sodium: 1557
- Total Carbohydrate: 73.9
- Cholesterol: 0

50. Cuban Black Beans I

Serving: 6 | Prep: 20mins | Cook: 1hours30mins | Ready in:

Ingredients

- 1 pound black beans, washed
- 1 onion, chopped
- 1 red bell pepper, chopped
- 1 green bell pepper, chopped
- 2 bay leaves
- 1 1/2 teaspoons paprika
- 1 1/2 teaspoons ground cumin
- 1 tablespoon dried oregano
- 2 minced hot green chile peppers
- 3 cloves garlic, minced
- 1/4 cup balsamic vinegar
- salt to taste
- ground black pepper to taste

Direction

- Soak the beans covered in water in a large bowl overnight.
- Rinse the beans and pour into a large stock pot. Add chile peppers, onion, oregano, bell peppers, paprika, bay leaves, and cumin along with water to cover. Heat to boil, decrease the heat and let to simmer for 1 1/2 hours.
- Check the tenderness of the beans and once tender, add balsamic vinegar and garlic. Season with pepper and salt to taste.

Nutrition Information

- Calories: 296 calories;
- Sodium: 11
- Total Carbohydrate: 55.5
- Cholesterol: 0
- Protein: 17.6
- Total Fat: 1.5

51. Dad's Candied Salmon

Serving: 4 | Prep: 10mins | Cook: 25mins | Ready in:

Ingredients

- 1 (2 pound) whole salmon fillet
- 3 tablespoons dry mustard
- 1/2 cup brown sugar
- 1/2 lemon

Direction

- Heat an oven to 220°C (425°F) beforehand.
- Line a baking sheet using aluminium foil and put the salmon on, skin-side-down. Use mustard to scrub into the salmon's flesh and then use brown sugar to evenly spread over the salmon. Squeeze lemon over the fish. Bring the foil's edges together and seal to make a packet.
- In the preheated oven, bake for 25-30 minutes till the flesh flakes easily with a fork.

Nutrition Information

- Calories: 459 calories;
- Protein: 45.3

- Total Fat: 17.1
- Sodium: 101
- Total Carbohydrate: 29.8
- Cholesterol: 112

52. Day Before Pay Day Fried Rice

Serving: 6 | Prep: 15mins | Cook: 20mins |Ready in:

Ingredients

- 3 tablespoons vegetable oil, divided
- 3 eggs, beaten
- 3 cups cold, cooked white rice
- 2 cups chopped cooked chicken
- 1/2 cup sliced celery
- 1/2 cup shredded carrot
- 1 cup frozen green peas, thawed
- 2 green onions, sliced
- 3 tablespoons soy sauce

Direction

- On medium-high heat, heat a tablespoon of oil in a big pan or wok. Cook and stir eggs in hot oil until firm and scrambled. Take the eggs out of the wok then set aside.
- Add the remaining 2 tablespoons oil in the wok then turn to high heat. Mix in rice until completely covered in oil. Mix in green onions, chicken, peas, carrot, and celery. Turn to medium heat, cover then let it steam for 5 minutes. Mix in soy sauce and scrambled eggs; cook until the eggs are completely heated.

Nutrition Information

- Calories: 315 calories;
- Total Fat: 13.1
- Sodium: 559
- Total Carbohydrate: 28.1
- Cholesterol: 128
- Protein: 20.1

53. Delicious Beef Tongue Tacos

Serving: 20 | Prep: 15mins | Cook: 8hours15mins |Ready in:

Ingredients

- 1 beef tongue
- 1/2 white onion, sliced
- 5 cloves garlic, crushed
- 1 bay leaf
- salt to taste
- 3 tablespoons vegetable oil
- 5 Roma tomatoes
- 5 serrano peppers
- salt to taste
- 1/2 onion, diced
- 2 (10 ounce) packages corn tortillas

Direction

- In a slow cooker, put the beef tongue and pour water to cover. Add the bay leaf, garlic and slices of onion, then add salt to season. Put cover on and cook for 8 hours or overnight on low. Take out the tongue and shred the meat into strands.
- In a skillet, heat the oil on medium heat. Cook the peppers and tomatoes in the hot oil until all sides become soft. Transfer the peppers and tomatoes in a blender and keep the oil on the heat, then add salt to season. Briefly blend until still a bit chunky. In the skillet, cook the diced onion until it becomes translucent; mix in the tomato mixture. Cook for an additional 5-6 minutes. Assemble the tacos by putting the shredded tongue meat into a tortilla and scooping the salsa on top of the meat.

Nutrition Information

- Calories: 227 calories;
- Total Fat: 14
- Sodium: 46
- Total Carbohydrate: 14

- Cholesterol: 66
- Protein: 11.4

54. Duck Cassoulet

Serving: 8 | Prep: 30mins | Cook: 7hours30mins | Ready in:

Ingredients

- 1 pound pork sausage links, sliced
- 1 tablespoon whole cloves
- 1 whole onion, peeled
- 3 sprigs fresh parsley
- 1 sprig fresh thyme
- 1/2 pound bacon
- 1 sprig fresh rosemary
- 1 pound dry navy beans, soaked overnight
- 1 bay leaf
- 3 carrots, peeled and sliced
- 3 cloves garlic, minced
- 1 pound skinned, boned duck breast halves, sliced into thin strips.
- 1 fresh tomato, chopped

Direction

- Brown the sliced sausage on medium heat in a big skillet
- Insert whole cloves inside the onion. Roll up the bacon then tie it using a string. Tie the rosemary, parsley, and thyme together.
- Put duck, minced garlic, carrots, bay leaf, fresh herbs, onion studded with cloves, bacon, sausage and soaked beans in a big slow cooker. Pour sufficient amount of water to cover the other ingredients. On high setting, cook for 1 hour. Adjust heat to low, keep on cooking for 6-8 hours.
- Get rid of the herbs, bacon and onion. Mix in the chopped tomatoes. Keep cooking for 30 minutes. Serve

Nutrition Information

- Calories: 548 calories;
- Total Fat: 26.8
- Sodium: 584
- Total Carbohydrate: 40.2
- Cholesterol: 104
- Protein: 36.7

55. Easy Cauliflower Ceviche

Serving: 8 | Prep: 15mins | Cook: 10mins | Ready in:

Ingredients

- 1 large head cauliflower
- 4 small carrots, peeled and finely chopped
- 3 large plum tomatoes, seeded and chopped
- 1 small white onion, finely chopped
- 8 sprigs cilantro, chopped
- 1 1/2 limes, juiced
- salt to taste
- 1 avocado - peeled, pitted, and sliced

Direction

- Put a steamer insert into a saucepan and fill with water to just below the steamer's bottom. Take to a boil. Put in cauliflower, cover, then steam for 7 minutes. Let cool then cut finely.
- In a bowl, add cilantro, onion, tomatoes, carrots and chopped cauliflower. Top with lime juice and add salt for seasoning. Cover and chill for a minimum of 30 minutes. Enjoy garnished with avocado slices.

Nutrition Information

- Calories: 89 calories;
- Sodium: 73
- Total Carbohydrate: 13.4
- Cholesterol: 0
- Protein: 3.3
- Total Fat: 3.9

56. Easy Garlic And Rosemary Chicken

Serving: 2 | Prep: | Cook: | Ready in:

Ingredients

- 2 skinless, boneless chicken breasts
- 2 cloves garlic, chopped
- 2 tablespoons dried rosemary
- 1 tablespoon lemon juice
- salt and pepper to taste

Direction

- Set the oven to 375°F (190°C).
- Coat the chicken breasts with garlic, then drizzle the lemon juice, rosemary, pepper and salt to taste. Put in a 9x13-inch baking dish and let it bake in the oven for roughly 25 minutes or until done and the juices run clear; take note that the baking time varies on how thick the chicken breasts are.

Nutrition Information

- Calories: 147 calories;
- Total Fat: 2
- Sodium: 79
- Total Carbohydrate: 3.7
- Cholesterol: 68
- Protein: 27.6

57. Easy Herb Roasted Turkey

Serving: 16 | Prep: 15mins | Cook: 3hours30mins | Ready in:

Ingredients

- 1 (12 pound) whole turkey
- 3/4 cup olive oil
- 2 tablespoons garlic powder
- 2 teaspoons dried basil
- 1 teaspoon ground sage
- 1 teaspoon salt
- 1/2 teaspoon black pepper
- 2 cups water

Direction

- Preheat the oven to 165°C or 325°F. Rinse the turkey, throw away the organs and giblets, and put in a roasting pan with a lid.
- Mix black pepper, salt, ground sage, dried basil, garlic powder and olive oil in a small bowl. Apply the mixture to outer of uncooked turkey with a basting brush. Into the base of roasting pan, add water, and place the cover.
- Allow to bake for 3 to 3 1/2 hours, or till inner temperature of the chunkiest portion of thigh reads 82°C or 180°F. Take turkey out of oven, and let sit for half an hour prior to carving.

Nutrition Information

- Calories: 597 calories;
- Total Fat: 33.7
- Sodium: 311
- Total Carbohydrate: 0.9
- Cholesterol: 198
- Protein: 68.2

58. Easy Pasta Fagioli

Serving: 4 | Prep: 10mins | Cook: 30mins | Ready in:

Ingredients

- 1 tablespoon olive oil
- 1 carrot, diced
- 1 stalk celery, diced
- 1 thin slice onion, diced
- 1/2 teaspoon chopped garlic
- 4 (8 ounce) cans tomato sauce
- 1 (14 ounce) can chicken broth
- freshly ground black pepper to taste

- 1 tablespoon dried parsley
- 1/2 tablespoon dried basil leaves
- 1 (15 ounce) can cannellini beans, drained and rinsed
- 1 1/2 cups ditalini pasta

Direction

- In a saucepan, heat olive oil on medium heat. Sauté onion, celery and carrot till soft. Add garlic. Briefly sauté. Mix basil, parsley, pepper, chicken broth and tomato sauce in. Simmer it for 20 minutes.
- Boil a big pot with lightly salted water. Add ditalini pasta. Cook till al dente for 8 minutes; drain.
- Add beans to sauce mixture. Simmer for several minutes. When pasta is done, mix into beans and sauce mixture.

Nutrition Information

- Calories: 338 calories;
- Total Fat: 5.1
- Sodium: 1882
- Total Carbohydrate: 60.7
- Cholesterol: 2
- Protein: 13.4

59. Easy Pork And Sauerkraut

Serving: 5 | Prep: 15mins | Cook: 6hours | Ready in:

Ingredients

- 1 pound pork roast, cut into 1 inch cubes
- 1 (32 ounce) jar sauerkraut with juice
- 1/2 (12 fluid ounce) can or bottle beer
- 1/2 apple, peeled and cored
- 1 tablespoon minced garlic
- 1/2 tablespoon fresh dill weed
- 1 teaspoon onion salt
- 1 teaspoon dry mustard

Direction

- In a slow cooker, mix all the ingredients and stir thoroughly. Immerse the apple below the other ingredients.
- Cook for 1 hour on High, decrease heat to Low and continue to cook for about five hours or until the pork has cooked through. Get rid of the apple and then serve.

Nutrition Information

- Calories: 139 calories;
- Total Fat: 4
- Sodium: 1567
- Total Carbohydrate: 11.7
- Cholesterol: 32
- Protein: 12.6

60. Easy Tilapia

Serving: 2 | Prep: 15mins | Cook: 15mins | Ready in:

Ingredients

- 2 (3 ounce) fillets tilapia fillets
- 2 tablespoons olive oil
- salt and pepper to taste
- 1 lemon, halved
- 1/2 cup white wine
- 2 tomatoes, seeded and chopped
- 3 tablespoons capers
- 1 cup asparagus spears, trimmed and cut in half
- 3 tablespoons butter

Direction

- On medium heat, heat a big non-stick skillet. Drizzle olive oil on fillets and use pepper and salt to season. Turn fillets into the skillet and spread half of a lemon on. Cook until fish flesh easily flakes apart with a folk, 3 minutes on each side. Turn the fillets into a platter and keep warm.

- In the skillet, put pepper, salt, capers, tomatoes, remaining 1/2 lemon, and wine. Boil on medium heat until alcohol burns off, 2 minutes. Lower the heat to low and place fillets together with asparagus back to the pan. Cover pan and bring to a boil for 2 minutes, then put asparagus and fish in a platter and keep warm.
- Heat the skillet on medium high heat again and whip in butter, boil until desired consistency. Drizzle fish with sauce and then serve.

Nutrition Information

- Calories: 462 calories;
- Total Carbohydrate: 16.3
- Cholesterol: 77
- Protein: 21.4
- Total Fat: 32.6
- Sodium: 1726

61. Easy Vegan Overnight Oats

Serving: 1 | Prep: 10mins | Cook: |Ready in:

Ingredients

- 3/4 cup soy milk
- 1/4 cup rolled oats
- 2 tablespoons chia seeds
- 1 banana, sliced
- 4 strawberries, sliced
- 1/4 cup fresh blueberries

Direction

- In a mason jar, combine chia seeds, oats, and soy milk. Layer banana, strawberries, and blueberries respectively on top of the oats mixture. Cover and chill overnight.
- Stir the mixture well, pouring in more soy milk if needed.

Nutrition Information

- Calories: 419 calories;
- Total Fat: 11.6
- Sodium: 100
- Total Carbohydrate: 70.3
- Cholesterol: 0
- Protein: 13.8

62. Egg Foo Young

Serving: 4 | Prep: 10mins | Cook: 15mins |Ready in:

Ingredients

- 1 teaspoon sesame oil
- 1 cup chopped onion
- 1/4 cup chopped green onion
- 1/2 cup chopped celery
- 1 cup bean sprouts
- 1/4 teaspoon cornstarch
- 1/2 pound shrimp, peeled, deveined and roughly chopped
- 2 tablespoons soy sauce
- 1 teaspoon salt
- 8 eggs, well beaten

Direction

- Heat the sesame oil in a cooking pan on medium heat then fry the celery, onions, and sprouts lightly in the oil. Pour in the cornstarch while stirring then add the soy sauce, salt, and shrimp. Stir them together until mixed thoroughly then take off heat and move to a bowl or dish.
- Put the pan back on the heat then fry the eggs on the pan while gently stirring.
- Put the shrimp and vegetable mixture back in the pan while the eggs have not yet set and are still like a liquid. Continue frying until the eggs have completely cooked.

Nutrition Information

- Calories: 239 calories;
- Cholesterol: 462
- Protein: 25.4
- Total Fat: 12.1
- Sodium: 1313
- Total Carbohydrate: 7.7

63. Egg Fried Rice

Serving: 4 | Prep: 5mins | Cook: 15mins | Ready in:

Ingredients

- 1 cup water
- 1/2 teaspoon salt
- 2 tablespoons soy sauce
- 1 cup uncooked instant rice
- 1 teaspoon vegetable oil
- 1/2 onion, finely chopped
- 1/2 cup green beans
- 1 egg, lightly beaten
- 1/4 teaspoon ground black pepper

Direction

- Boil soy sauce, salt and water in saucepan. Put in the rice and mix. Take it off the heat, put a cover on and let rest for 5 minutes.
- In a wok or medium-sized skillet, heat the oil over moderate heat. Sauté green beans and onions for 2 to 3 minutes. Add egg and fry for 2 minutes, scrambling the egg while cooking.
- Mix in cooked rice, combine thoroughly and scatter pepper on top.

Nutrition Information

- Calories: 145 calories;
- Total Fat: 2.7
- Sodium: 848
- Total Carbohydrate: 24.6
- Cholesterol: 46
- Protein: 4.9

64. Eggplant, Zucchini And Sweet Red Pepper Stew

Serving: 4 | Prep: 20mins | Cook: 1hours | Ready in:

Ingredients

- 1 eggplant, cut into 1 inch cubes
- 1/4 cup olive oil
- 1 cup chopped onion
- 5 cloves garlic, chopped
- 1/2 cup Basmati rice
- 1 zucchini, cut into large chunks
- 1 large red bell pepper, chopped
- 3 fresh tomatoes, diced
- 1 cup Marsala wine
- 1 1/2 cups water
- 1/2 teaspoon salt, or to taste
- 1/4 teaspoon red pepper flakes
- 1/4 cup chopped fresh basil
- 1/4 cup chopped fresh parsley
- 1 sprig fresh rosemary, chopped

Direction

- In a colander, arrange eggplant and dust salt over top.
- In a large pot or Dutch oven, heat the olive oil. Wash the eggplant, then pat it dry. Sauté until it is browned lightly. Mix in onion, sauté until it turns transparent. Mix in garlic, sauté for 2-3 minutes.
- Stir in red pepper flakes, salt, water, wine, tomatoes, red bell pepper, zucchini, and rice. Cook over medium-high heat until the mixture comes to a low boil. Turn down the heat and simmer until the vegetables become tender, 45 minutes.
- Take away from the heat, then stir in rosemary, parsley, and basil.

Nutrition Information

- Calories: 402 calories;
- Cholesterol: 0

- Protein: 5.5
- Total Fat: 14.5
- Sodium: 1054
- Total Carbohydrate: 50.7

- Total Fat: 11.7
- Sodium: 1203
- Total Carbohydrate: 54.2
- Cholesterol: 0
- Protein: 12.6

65. Emily's Mediterranean Pasta

Serving: 2 | Prep: 5mins | Cook: 20mins | Ready in:

Ingredients

- 1/2 (8 ounce) package uncooked spaghettini
- 1/2 cup sun-dried tomatoes, packed without oil
- 1 tablespoon olive oil
- 1/2 cup chopped red onion
- 3 cloves garlic, sliced
- 1/2 cup sliced fresh mushrooms
- 1/4 cup sliced green olives
- 1/4 cup Italian seasoned bread crumbs
- freshly ground black pepper to taste

Direction

- Boil a medium pot of lightly salted water, then add pasta and let it cook for 8-10 minutes or until al dente, then drain. In a small pot, put the sun-dried tomatoes and pour water to cover, then boil on medium-high heat and let it cook for around 5 minutes or until it becomes tender. Drain, chop and put aside.
- In a big skillet, heat the olive oil on medium-low heat. Fry the garlic and onion in the oil for about 5 minutes, until the onions become transparent. Add the sun-dried tomatoes and mushrooms and let it cook for about 5 minutes on low heat. Put in the spaghettini and toss until coated. Stir in the green olives. Serve it hot with lots of black pepper and bread crumbs on top.

Nutrition Information

- Calories: 360 calories;

66. Farro And Lentil Masala

Serving: 4 | Prep: 15mins | Cook: 50mins | Ready in:

Ingredients

- 1 teaspoon salt
- 2 carrots, finely chopped
- 2 stalks celery, finely chopped
- 1 small onion, finely chopped
- 2 tablespoons olive oil
- 1 tablespoon garam masala
- 4 cups vegetable broth, or more to taste
- 1/2 cup semi-pearled farro
- 1 cup red lentils

Direction

- Drizzle salt on top of onion, celery and carrots. Over medium heat, heat one tablespoon of oil in a large soup pot and then cook while stirring the veggies for about 5 minutes until the onion becomes translucent. Push the vegetables to the side to form a clear space in the middle of pot. Then heat one tablespoon of oil in the middle. Drizzle garam masala atop the oil and then toast for about 1 to 2 minutes. Mix into the veggies until coated well.
- Add the vegetable broth into pot and heat to a boil. Decrease the heat to medium-low and put in farro. Cover the pot and simmer for about 20 minutes until nearly tender. Put in the lentils. Cover pot and let it simmer while adding extra broth if necessary for about 20 minutes until lentils and farro become tender and not mushy. Add salt to taste.

Nutrition Information

- Calories: 355 calories;
- Total Carbohydrate: 54.9
- Cholesterol: 0
- Protein: 16.7
- Total Fat: 9.3
- Sodium: 1089

67. Favorite Barbecue Chicken

Serving: 2 | Prep: 5mins | Cook: 35mins | Ready in:

Ingredients

- 1 1/2 tablespoons olive oil
- 1/4 cup diced onion
- 2 cloves garlic, minced
- 5 tablespoons ketchup
- 3 tablespoons honey
- 3 tablespoons brown sugar
- 2 tablespoons apple cider vinegar
- 1 tablespoon Worcestershire sauce
- salt and pepper to taste
- 2 skinless, boneless chicken breast halves

Direction

- Prepare grill for medium-high heat.
- Heat olive oil over medium heat in a skillet. Sauté garlic and onion in heated oil until softened. Mix in pepper, salt, Worcestershire sauce, apple cider vinegar, brown sugar, honey, and ketchup. Cook until sauce is thickened, for a couple of minutes. Put off the heat; let the sauce cool.
- Lightly grease the grill grate with oil. Immerse chicken in sauce, turning to coat evenly. Grill chicken, turning one time, for 10 to 15 minutes. Transfer chicken and sauce to the skillet. Let simmer over medium heat for about 5 minutes per side.

Nutrition Information

- Calories: 452 calories;

- Sodium: 714
- Total Carbohydrate: 60.1
- Cholesterol: 67
- Protein: 25.7
- Total Fat: 13.1

68. Fennel And Mustard Seed Chicken

Serving: 4 | Prep: 10mins | Cook: 20mins | Ready in:

Ingredients

- 4 bone-in chicken breast halves, with skin
- 1/2 teaspoon salt and pepper, or to taste
- 1 tablespoon mustard seed
- 1 tablespoon fennel seed
- 2 tablespoons olive oil
- 2 cloves garlic, thinly sliced

Direction

- Sprinkle chicken to taste with pepper and salt. Grind mustard and fennel seeds in clean coffee grinder; on chicken pieces, sprinkle freshly ground spices.
- Heat olive oil in big frying pan on medium heat; in olive oil, cook garlic, frequently mixing. Put chicken in pan when garlic starts to brown. Set heat to high; brown both sides quickly. Lower heat; cover. Cook chicken till meat is tender and juices are clear.

Nutrition Information

- Calories: 377 calories;
- Cholesterol: 127
- Protein: 45.9
- Total Fat: 19.5
- Sodium: 400
- Total Carbohydrate: 2.2

69. Filipino Style Chicken Curry

Serving: 4 | Prep: 20mins | Cook: 40mins | Ready in:

Ingredients

- 1 tablespoon vegetable oil
- 1 pound skinless, boneless chicken breast halves, chopped
- 1 stalk lemongrass, sliced
- 1 onion, sliced
- 1 cup chicken stock
- 1 cube chicken bouillon
- 2 cloves garlic, minced
- 1 1/2 cups coconut milk
- 1 large potato, sliced
- 1 carrot, sliced
- 1 tablespoon curry powder
- 1 red bell pepper, chopped
- 2 tablespoons peanut butter
- salt and pepper to taste

Direction

- In a saucepan, heat the vegetable oil on medium heat, then add the chicken and let it cook for about 10 minutes, until it turns brown. Stir in the garlic, chicken bouillon, chicken stock, onion and lemongrass, then boil. Lower the heat and let it simmer for 5 minutes, then add curry powder, carrots, potatoes and coconut milk. Allow it to simmer for about 20 minutes, until the carrots and potatoes become soft. Stir in the pepper, salt, peanut butter and bell pepper.

Nutrition Information

- Calories: 495 calories;
- Total Fat: 29
- Sodium: 738
- Total Carbohydrate: 31.1
- Cholesterol: 66
- Protein: 31

70. Fish In Ginger Tamarind Sauce

Serving: 4 | Prep: 15mins | Cook: 30mins | Ready in:

Ingredients

- 1 tablespoon cooking oil
- 1 teaspoon mustard seed
- 2 tablespoons chopped fresh ginger
- 1 cup chopped onions
- 2 cups water
- 1 tablespoon tamarind paste
- 2 tablespoons coriander powder
- 1/2 teaspoon ground red pepper
- salt to taste
- 1/2 pound cod fillets, cut into 1 inch cubes
- fresh curry leaves (optional)

Direction

- In a saucepan, heat oil on medium-high heat. In hot oil, cook mustard seeds until they start to crackle. Mix in onion and ginger. Cook for 5 minutes. Put water and mix in tamarind paste. Boil. Season with salt, chile powder, and coriander. Lower heat to medium-low. Cook for 15 minutes, occasionally mixing.
- In sauce, cook fish until fish has cooked through. Top with fresh curry leaves. Serve.

Nutrition Information

- Calories: 125 calories;
- Total Fat: 4.8
- Sodium: 325
- Total Carbohydrate: 9.1
- Cholesterol: 24
- Protein: 11.5

71. Flat Iron, Grilled

Serving: 4 | Prep: 10mins | Cook: 15mins | Ready in:

Ingredients

- 4 (6 ounce) flat iron steaks
- 2 tablespoons olive oil
- 1 tablespoon ground black pepper
- 2 teaspoons kosher salt
- 1 teaspoon garlic powder
- 1 teaspoon onion powder
- 1 teaspoon cayenne pepper
- 1 teaspoon dark brown sugar
- 2 teaspoons fresh lime juice

Direction

- On a platter, lay out the steaks and let to come to room temperature, for approximately 30 minutes.
- Set an outdoor grill to high heat to preheat and oil the grate lightly.
- Set an oven to 200°C (400°F) to preheat.
- In a small bowl, whisk together the lemon juice, brown sugar, cayenne pepper, onion powder, garlic powder, salt, pepper and olive oil. Rub 1 side of each steak evenly with the mixture.
- On the hot grill, lay the steaks, seasoned side facing up, for 2 minutes. Turn and sear the seasoned side for approximately 2 minutes.
- Move the steaks to the preheated oven, then bake for 8-10 minutes for medium-well, seasoned side facing up, or bake to your preferred doneness. Let rest for 3-4 minutes prior to serving.

Nutrition Information

- Calories: 393 calories;
- Sodium: 1071
- Total Carbohydrate: 3.6
- Cholesterol: 116
- Protein: 35.3
- Total Fat: 26.5

72. Flavorful Rice

Serving: 8 | Prep: 5mins | Cook: 20mins | Ready in:

Ingredients

- 4 1/2 cups water
- 3 cups uncooked white rice
- 2 tablespoons olive oil
- 2 tablespoons distilled white vinegar
- 1/2 teaspoon dried basil
- 1/2 teaspoon dried oregano
- 1 pinch salt
- 1 pinch ground black pepper
- 1 (14.5 ounce) can diced tomatoes, drained

Direction

- Mix together tomatoes, pepper, salt, oregano, basil, vinegar, olive oil, rice and water in the rice steamer. Following the settings of steamer to cook.

Nutrition Information

- Calories: 312 calories;
- Cholesterol: 0
- Protein: 6.1
- Total Fat: 4
- Sodium: 82
- Total Carbohydrate: 60.5

73. Garbanzo Bean Patties

Serving: 12 | Prep: 15mins | Cook: 3hours40mins | Ready in:

Ingredients

- 1 (16 ounce) package dry chickpeas
- 1 onion, chopped
- 1 tablespoon dried thyme
- salt and pepper to taste
- 2 1/2 cups dry bread cubes
- 2 eggs, beaten
- 4 tablespoons vegetable oil

Direction

- Add at least 12 cups of water to cover garbanzo beans in a large pot. Cook over medium heat until tender, about 2-1/2 to 3 hours. You might need to pour in more water so check occasionally.
- Working in the small batches, set the blender to either blend or chop setting, process the garbanzo beans. Blend until becoming a paste. Put in pepper, salt, thyme and onions into the mixture; then mix well. Put in egg and bread cubes; and mix well.
- Shape garbanzo bean mixture into patties.
- In a large skillet, heat oil over medium heat. Fry the patties until each side turns golden brown.

Nutrition Information

- Calories: 84 calories;
- Protein: 2.2
- Total Fat: 5.8
- Sodium: 62
- Total Carbohydrate: 6.2
- Cholesterol: 31

74. Garlic Pork Kabobs

Serving: 4 | Prep: 15mins | Cook: 25mins | Ready in:

Ingredients

- 1 3/4 cups Swanson® Chicken Stock
- 2 tablespoons cornstarch
- 2 cloves garlic, minced
- 1 tablespoon packed brown sugar
- 1 tablespoon ketchup
- 2 teaspoons vinegar
- 1 pound boneless pork loin, cut into 1-inch cubes
- 12 medium mushrooms
- 1 large red onion, cut into 12 wedges
- 4 cherry tomatoes
- 4 cups hot cooked regular long-grain white rice

Direction

- Take a 1-quart saucepan and stir stock, vinegar, ketchup, cornstarch, and brown sugar until smooth. Cook over medium-high, with constant stirring, until the mixture boils and then thickens. Remove from heat.
- Alternately thread the pork, onions, and mushrooms onto 4 skewers.
- Oil the grill rack lightly and set the grill to medium heat. Grill for 20 minutes, until pork is cooked sufficiently. Turn and baste frequently with the stock mixture. When done grilling, thread a whole tomato at the tip of each skewer.
- Let the remaining stock mixture boil over medium heat, and serve as sauce for the kabobs. Plate with rice.

Nutrition Information

- Calories: 915 calories;
- Total Fat: 11.3
- Sodium: 321
- Total Carbohydrate: 162.8
- Cholesterol: 55
- Protein: 35.5

75. Garlic Top Sirloin Pot Roast

Serving: 8 | Prep: 30mins | Cook: 6hours | Ready in:

Ingredients

- 1 teaspoon salt
- 1 teaspoon freshly ground black pepper
- 1 teaspoon paprika
- 1 (3 pound) top sirloin roast
- 6 cloves garlic, slivered
- 6 Yukon Gold potatoes, peeled and quartered
- 4 carrots, cut into 2 inch pieces
- 2 large sweet onions, peeled and chopped
- 1/2 cup water
- 1/2 cup beef broth

- 3 cubes beef bouillon
- 1 bay leaf
- 2 large green bell peppers, cut into 2 inch pieces

Direction

- Massage paprika, pepper and salt into the meat. Use a small knife to make slits in the roast then press the garlic chips into the roast.
- Place the onions, carrots and potatoes into a big slow cooker together and lay the meat on top of all the vegetables. Pour in the beef broth and water, followed by the bay leaf and bouillon cubes.
- Cover the slow cooker with its lid. Let it cook for 6 hours on high or 8 hours on low. In the last half an hour before it's done, put the green peppers in.

Nutrition Information

- Calories: 378 calories;
- Total Fat: 16.1
- Sodium: 824
- Total Carbohydrate: 26.1
- Cholesterol: 91
- Protein: 31.5

76. Ginger Veggie Stir Fry

Serving: 6 | Prep: 25mins | Cook: 15mins | Ready in:

Ingredients

- 1 tablespoon cornstarch
- 1 1/2 cloves garlic, crushed
- 2 teaspoons chopped fresh ginger root, divided
- 1/4 cup vegetable oil, divided
- 1 small head broccoli, cut into florets
- 1/2 cup snow peas
- 3/4 cup julienned carrots
- 1/2 cup halved green beans
- 2 tablespoons soy sauce
- 2 1/2 tablespoons water
- 1/4 cup chopped onion
- 1/2 tablespoon salt

Direction

- Blend 2 tbsp. vegetable oil, 1 tsp. ginger, garlic and cornstarch in a big bowl, until the cornstarch dissolves. Stir in green beans, carrots, snow peas and broccoli, then toss until lightly coated.
- In a wok or a big skillet, heat the leftover 2 tbsp. of oil on medium heat. Cook the vegetables in oil for 2 minutes, mixing continuously, to avoid burning. Mix in water and soy sauce. Stir in the leftover 1 tsp. ginger, salt and onion. Let it cook until the vegetables become tender but still crisp.

Nutrition Information

- Calories: 119 calories;
- Protein: 2.2
- Total Fat: 9.3
- Sodium: 903
- Total Carbohydrate: 8
- Cholesterol: 0

77. Grandma's Famous Salmon Cakes

Serving: 4 | Prep: 10mins | Cook: 20mins | Ready in:

Ingredients

- 1 (14.75 ounce) can salmon, drained and flaked
- 2 eggs, beaten
- 1 small onion, diced
- 1 teaspoon ground black pepper
- 3 tablespoons vegetable oil

Direction

- Skim the salmon and discard any bones. Whisk eggs in a mixing bowl and add pepper, salmon, and diced onion. Stir well.
- Form into 7-8 patties, about 2-ounce each patty. In a big frying pan, heat oil over medium heat. Fry each patty until turning golden brown and crunchy, about 5 minutes per side.

Nutrition Information

- Calories: 307 calories;
- Cholesterol: 138
- Protein: 27.5
- Total Fat: 20.3
- Sodium: 407
- Total Carbohydrate: 2.3

78. Gravlox

Serving: 16 | Prep: 1hours | Cook: | Ready in:

Ingredients

- 2 pounds salmon fillet, bones removed
- 4 tablespoons coarse sea salt
- 3 tablespoons light brown sugar
- 1 tablespoon pepper
- 1 bunch fresh dill, chopped
- 3 tablespoons vodka

Direction

- Drape the plastic wrap atop a glass baking dish. Halve salmon in lengthwise and put one half into the dish with the skin side down. Combine together pepper, salt, and brown sugar. Drizzle half of the mixture atop the salmon in dish, add the chopped dill to cover and add vodka on top of the whole mixture.
- Drizzle remaining salt mixture atop remaining half of salmon. Put on top of the salmon in dish with the skin side up. Snuggly fold plastic wrap atop entire salmon. Put a board onto the fish and then use a heavy object to weigh it down.
- Chill the fish for about 24 to 36 hours while flipping after every 12 hours. To serve, divide the filets and then carefully brush off the dill, salt, and sugar. Use a sharp knife to chop into very thin pieces.

Nutrition Information

- Calories: 121 calories;
- Total Fat: 6.2
- Sodium: 1356
- Total Carbohydrate: 2.9
- Cholesterol: 33
- Protein: 11.4

79. Grecian Pork Tenderloin

Serving: 6 | Prep: 15mins | Cook: 30mins | Ready in:

Ingredients

- 1 1/2 cups fresh lime juice
- 3/4 cup olive oil
- 6 cloves garlic, sliced
- 2 teaspoons salt
- 6 tablespoons dried oregano
- 2 (1 pound) pork tenderloins

Direction

- In a large resealable plastic bag, combine the oregano, salt, olive oil, lime juice, and garlic. Seal the bag and shake it until the ingredients are well-combined. Taste the mixture for tartness. Add more oil if the mixture is too tart and add more lime if the mixture has not enough zing. Also, the flavors of garlic and salt should be upfront, and not overpowering. Add the tenderloins into the bag with marinade. Seal the bag and flip it until coated. Marinate it inside the fridge for 2-5 hours.
- Set the grill to medium heat for preheating.

- Oil the grill grate lightly. Discard the marinade and grill the tenderloins for 20-30 minutes, flipping only once until the desired doneness is reached.

Nutrition Information

- Calories: 404 calories;
- Cholesterol: 65
- Protein: 24.3
- Total Fat: 31.1
- Sodium: 829
- Total Carbohydrate: 9.1

80. Green Beans And Tofu

Serving: 4 | Prep: 10mins | Cook: 25mins | Ready in:

Ingredients

- 1 (12 ounce) package firm tofu, cubed
- 5 tablespoons olive oil, divided
- 1/2 teaspoon chili powder, or to taste
- salt and freshly ground black pepper to taste
- 1 pound fresh green beans, trimmed
- 1 clove garlic, minced
- 1 teaspoon seasoned salt

Direction

- In a bowl, mix together pepper, salt, chili powder, 1/4 cup olive oil, and tofu and let marinate, about 10-20 minutes.
- Boil water in a pot; add beans and cook for 15-20 minutes until soft but not mushy. Strain.
- In a skillet, heat the leftover 1 tablespoon olive oil over medium heat. Put in tofu and cook for 3 minutes until turning light brown, tossing sometimes. Add garlic and cook for another 1 minute. Add beans and use seasoned salt, pepper, and salt to season.

Nutrition Information

- Calories: 252 calories;
- Total Fat: 21.1
- Sodium: 285
- Total Carbohydrate: 10.4
- Cholesterol: 0
- Protein: 9

81. Grilled Fish Steaks

Serving: 8 | Prep: 15mins | Cook: 12mins | Ready in:

Ingredients

- 8 (3 ounce) fillets fresh tuna steaks, 1 inch thick
- 1/2 cup soy sauce
- 1/3 cup sherry
- 1/4 cup vegetable oil
- 1 tablespoon fresh lime juice
- 1 clove garlic, minced

Direction

- In a shallow baking dish, put in the tuna steaks. Combine the vegetable oil, soy sauce, fresh lime juice, garlic and sherry in a medium-sized bowl. Coat all sides of the tuna steaks with the soy sauce mixture. Cover the tuna steaks and keep in the fridge for at least an hour.
- Preheat the grill to high heat.
- Slightly grease the grill grate with oil. Put the marinated tuna steaks on the grill without the marinade. Cook the tuna steaks on the grill for 3-6 minutes each side until the desired doneness is achieved.

Nutrition Information

- Calories: 171 calories;
- Total Fat: 7.6
- Sodium: 993
- Total Carbohydrate: 3
- Cholesterol: 38
- Protein: 20.9

82. Grilled Rock Lobster Tails

Serving: 2 | Prep: 15mins | Cook: 12mins | Ready in:

Ingredients

- 1 tablespoon lemon juice
- 1/2 cup olive oil
- 1 teaspoon salt
- 1 teaspoon paprika
- 1/8 teaspoon white pepper
- 1/8 teaspoon garlic powder
- 2 (10 ounce) rock lobster tails

Direction

- Preheat the grill on high heat.
- Squeeze lemon juice in a small bowl; mix in olive oil gradually. Stir in garlic powder, salt, white pepper, and paprika. Using a big knife, break lobster tails lengthwise; slather marinade on its meat side.
- Grease the grill grate lightly with oil. Put the lobster tails on the preheated grill with its meat side down and grill for 10-12 minutes. Flip once and use the marinade to baste regularly; get rid of any leftover marinade. The lobster is cooked when it is firm to the touch and opaque.

Nutrition Information

- Calories: 742 calories;
- Protein: 44.3
- Total Fat: 60.9
- Sodium: 2036
- Total Carbohydrate: 4.3
- Cholesterol: 169

83. Grilled Salmon I

Serving: 6 | Prep: 15mins | Cook: 16mins | Ready in:

Ingredients

- 1 1/2 pounds salmon fillets
- lemon pepper to taste
- garlic powder to taste
- salt to taste
- 1/3 cup soy sauce
- 1/3 cup brown sugar
- 1/3 cup water
- 1/4 cup vegetable oil

Direction

- Use lemon pepper, garlic powder, and salt to season fillets.
- In a small bowl, mix together brown sugar, soy sauce, water, and vegetable oil until sugar dissolves. Place fish fillets and soy sauce mixture in a big resealable plastic bag seal, and coat by flipping. Put in refrigerator for 2 or more hours.
- Set grill to medium heat.
- Brush grill grate with a little oil. Put salmon on heated grill and discard the marinade. For 6 to 8 minutes a side, cook the salmon until with a fork the fish easily flakes.

Nutrition Information

- Calories: 318 calories;
- Total Carbohydrate: 13.2
- Cholesterol: 56
- Protein: 20.5
- Total Fat: 20.1
- Sodium: 1092

84. Grilled Shrimp And Apple Skewers

Serving: 4 | Prep: 20mins | Cook: 10mins | Ready in:

Ingredients

- 3 tablespoons honey
- 3 tablespoons olive oil
- 1 tablespoon chopped fresh basil
- 1 tablespoon strawberry jam
- 1/4 teaspoon crushed red pepper flakes
- 1 clove garlic, minced
- 2 tablespoons red wine vinegar
- 1 tablespoon lemon juice
- 2 teaspoons white sugar
- 2 Gala apples, cored and cut into eighths
- 16 jumbo shrimp, peeled and deveined

Direction

- In a small bowl, whisk white sugar, lemon juice, red wine vinegar, garlic, red pepper flakes, strawberry jam, basil, olive oil, and honey together. In a large plastic zip bag, add shrimp and apples. Cover shrimp and apples with the marinade, seal the bag, and shake to coat; let sit in the fridge for 30 minutes.
- Heat an outdoor grill for medium-high heat beforehand.
- On soaked wooden skewers or 4 metals, skewer alternately the shrimp and apples. Discard the remaining marinade.
- On the preheated grill, allow the skewers to cook for about 5 minutes each side until the shrimp are gets opaque.

Nutrition Information

- Calories: 307 calories;
- Total Carbohydrate: 29.1
- Cholesterol: 213
- Protein: 23.2
- Total Fat: 11.5
- Sodium: 247

85. Halibut Cheeks With Ginger Orange Sauce

Serving: 2 | Prep: 10mins | Cook: 10mins | Ready in:

Ingredients

- 1/4 cup fresh orange juice
- 2 teaspoons minced fresh cilantro
- 1 teaspoon minced fresh ginger root
- 1 clove garlic, minced
- 1 tablespoon soy sauce
- 1 teaspoon sesame oil
- 1/4 teaspoon red pepper flakes
- 1 tablespoon olive oil
- 4 (3 ounce) halibut cheeks

Direction

- Whisk red pepper flakes, sesame oil, soy sauce, garlic, ginger, cilantro and orange juice in a small bowl; put aside.
- In a skillet, heat olive oil on medium high heat. Cook halibut cheeks, 2-3 minutes per side, till golden brown on both sides. Put orange juice mixture into skillet; boil. Lower heat to medium. Simmer till sauce thickens slightly and halibut easily flakes with a fork. Put halibut cheeks onto a plate. Drizzle orange sauce on; serve.

Nutrition Information

- Calories: 293 calories;
- Total Carbohydrate: 4.7
- Cholesterol: 63
- Protein: 37.2
- Total Fat: 12.5
- Sodium: 547

86. Halibut With Vegetables

Serving: 6 | Prep: 15mins | Cook: 20mins | Ready in:

Ingredients

- 2 pounds halibut fillets
- salt and pepper to taste
- 1/4 cup olive oil
- 1/2 cup chopped fresh parsley
- 1 yellow onion, thinly sliced
- 2 stalks celery, chopped
- 1 green bell pepper, chopped
- 1 (16 ounce) can diced tomatoes
- 2 tablespoons capers
- 4 cloves garlic, minced

Direction

- Preheat an oven to 220°C/425°F.
- Wash halibut; pat dry. Slice to serving-sized pieces. Put into 9x13-in. baking pan. Sprinkle pepper and salt on. Mix garlic, capers, tomatoes, bell pepper, celery, onion, parsley and olive oil; put on halibut.
- Bake for 20 minutes till halibut is slightly opaque in the middle. Take out of the oven. Before serving, let stand for 10 minutes.

Nutrition Information

- Calories: 291 calories;
- Sodium: 304
- Total Carbohydrate: 8.5
- Cholesterol: 56
- Protein: 34
- Total Fat: 12

87. Ham Stir Fry With Couscous

Serving: 6 | Prep: 10mins | Cook: 10mins | Ready in:

Ingredients

- 1 1/2 cups water
- 1 cup couscous
- 2 cups chicken broth
- 1/4 cup cornstarch
- 3 tablespoons soy sauce
- 3 tablespoons brown sugar
- 1/8 teaspoon ground ginger
- 1 tablespoon vegetable oil
- 2 cloves garlic, minced
- 1 (16 ounce) package mixed broccoli and cauliflower florets
- 1 carrot, sliced
- 1/4 pound cooked ham, cut into strips
- 1 (8 ounce) can sliced water chestnuts, drained
- 1/2 cup sliced almonds

Direction

- For the couscous, boil water in a medium saucepan. Add the couscous and adjust the heat to medium-low. Simmer the couscous for 8-10 minutes until fluffy. Cover the pan and set it aside.
- Mix the ginger, cornstarch, broth, brown sugar, and soy sauce in a small bowl. Once the mixture is well-combined, set it aside.
- Put oil in a wok or large skillet. Add the cauliflower, carrot, garlic, and broccoli. Stir-fry the mixture for 7-8 minutes until crisp-tender. (If the mixture is too dry, add water.)
- Mix the broth mixture and pour it over the vegetable mixture. Mix in water chestnuts and ham. Cook the mixture for 2 minutes while stirring frequently. Mix in almonds. Serve the stir-fry mixture over the hot couscous.

Nutrition Information

- Calories: 318 calories;
- Total Fat: 8.9
- Sodium: 994
- Total Carbohydrate: 46.6
- Cholesterol: 11
- Protein: 12.9

88. Hamburgers And Ketchup Gravy

Serving: 4 | Prep: 10mins | Cook: 45mins | Ready in:

Ingredients

- 1 pound ground beef
- 1/2 cup ketchup
- 1/2 cup bread crumbs
- 1 teaspoon onion powder
- 1/2 teaspoon steak seasoning, or to taste
- salt and pepper to taste
- 2 teaspoons vegetable oil
- 1 large onion, cut into chunks
- 1 cup ketchup
- 1/2 cup water, or as needed

Direction

- Combine pepper, salt, steak seasoning, onion powder, bread crumbs, 1/2 cup of ketchup and ground beef in a medium bowl. Shape the mixture into small fat hamburger meatballs or patties.
- In a big heavy skillet, heat oil over moderately high heat. In the skillet, put patties and cook both sides until browned. Transfer the patties to a plate and drain the grease from skillet.
- Stir together water and leftover ketchup gradually in the same pan. If the mixture seems thick, put in more water, conversely, put in more ketchup if the mixture seems thin. Put in onion and bring to a boil. Lower heat to moderately low then bring patties back to pan and simmer, covered, about a half hour. Stir after a half hour and keep on simmering without a lid in case the gravy is still thin, until you get thickened gravy.

Nutrition Information

- Calories: 378 calories;
- Sodium: 1323
- Total Carbohydrate: 36.1
- Cholesterol: 69
- Protein: 22.8
- Total Fat: 16.6

89. Hawaiian Hot Dog Surprise

Serving: 20 | Prep: 5mins | Cook: 30mins | Ready in:

Ingredients

- 2 (16 ounce) packages hot dogs, cut into pieces
- 2 (8 ounce) cans pineapple chunks, undrained
- 2 cups brown sugar
- 1 cup white sugar
- 2 (16 ounce) cans baked beans

Direction

- In a slow cooker, put the baked beans, white and brown sugar, pineapple, and hot dog pieces. Then cook for 15 minutes on high, lower heat, and allow it to simmer for 15 more minutes, or until ready to serve. You can keep this dish on low the whole day.

Nutrition Information

- Calories: 298 calories;
- Total Fat: 13.4
- Sodium: 671
- Total Carbohydrate: 39.2
- Cholesterol: 24
- Protein: 7.3

90. Hawaiian Shrimp

Serving: 6 | Prep: 30mins | Cook: 8mins | Ready in:

Ingredients

- 2 pounds medium shrimp, peeled and deveined
- 2 (20 ounce) cans pineapple chunks, juice reserved
- 1/2 pound bacon slices, cut into 2 inch pieces
- 2 large red bell peppers, chopped
- 1/2 pound fresh mushrooms, stems removed
- 2 cups cherry tomatoes
- 1 cup sweet and sour sauce

- skewers

Direction

- Preheat grill on high.
- Alternately thread shrimp, red bell peppers, pineapple, bacon, cherry tomatoes, and mushroom caps on skewers. Arrange them in a shallow baking dish. In a small bowl, combine sweet and sour sauce with reserved pineapple juice and save a small amount for basting. Sauce over the skewers with this mixture.
- Grease the grill grates lightly. Grill for 6 to 8 minutes, or until shrimps are opaque, basting regularly with reserved sauce.

Nutrition Information

- Calories: 385 calories;
- Sodium: 714
- Total Carbohydrate: 47.1
- Cholesterol: 244
- Protein: 32.4
- Total Fat: 8.1

91. Herb And Chicken Pasta

Serving: 4 | Prep: 15mins | Cook: 15mins | Ready in:

Ingredients

- 1 (16 ounce) package angel hair pasta
- 4 skinless, boneless chicken breast halves
- salt and pepper to taste
- 1/2 teaspoon dried basil
- 1/2 teaspoon dried rosemary
- 1/2 teaspoon Cajun seasoning (optional)
- 1/2 teaspoon crushed red pepper flakes (optional)
- 1/4 cup olive oil
- 3 cloves garlic, chopped
- 1 onion, chopped
- 1 cup chicken broth

Direction

- Allow a large saucepan of lightly salted water to come to a boil and add in the pasta. Boil until cooked firm, about 8-10 minutes, then drain and set aside.
- At the same time, season the chicken with red pepper flakes, Cajun seasoning, rosemary, basil, pepper, and salt. In a large pan, heat the oil on a medium heat and add the chicken, cooking until it turns brown. Remove chicken from the pan and stirring, add in onions and garlic, and cook until clear.
- Place the chicken back onto skillet over the onion mixture and add the broth. Simmer until the chicken is completely cooked and no longer pink inside. Pour the mixture over the pasta to serve.

Nutrition Information

- Calories: 597 calories;
- Sodium: 559
- Total Carbohydrate: 66.2
- Cholesterol: 68
- Protein: 41
- Total Fat: 18.5

92. Homemade Cereal

Serving: 12 | Prep: 15mins | Cook: 1hours | Ready in:

Ingredients

- 7 cups quick cooking oats
- 1 cup wheat germ
- 1 cup wheat bran
- 1/2 cup brown sugar
- 1/2 cup vegetable oil
- 1/2 cup honey
- 1/2 cup water
- 1 tablespoon vanilla extract
- 1 teaspoon ground cinnamon (optional)
- 1 teaspoon ground nutmeg (optional)

- 1 teaspoon salt
- 1 cup chopped dates
- 1 cup chopped pecans
- 1 cup flaked coconut (optional)

Direction

- Preheat an oven to 135°C/275°F.
- Mix wheat bran, wheat germ and oats in a big bowl.
- Blend water, honey, vegetable oil and brown sugar in a medium bowl. Mix salt, nutmeg, cinnamon and vanilla extract in. Mix brown sugar mixture into oat mixture till evenly moist. Put in a shallow big baking dish.
- In the preheated oven, bake, mixing every 15 minutes, for 45 minutes till lightly brown. Mix coconut, pecans and dates into dish. Bake for 15 more minutes. Cool; keep in airtight containers.

Nutrition Information

- Calories: 525 calories;
- Cholesterol: 0
- Protein: 10.7
- Total Fat: 22.3
- Sodium: 219
- Total Carbohydrate: 76.8

93. Honey Peanut Granola

Serving: 6 | Prep: 15mins | Cook: 1hours | Ready in:

Ingredients

- 3 cups quick cooking oats
- 1/2 cup chopped peanuts
- 1/4 cup wheat germ
- 1/3 cup honey
- 1/3 cup brown sugar
- 1/4 cup vegetable oil
- 2 tablespoons warm water
- 1/2 teaspoon salt
- 1 teaspoon vanilla extract

Direction

- Set the oven to 120°C or 250°F and coat a baking sheet lightly with grease.
- Mix together wheat germ, peanuts and oats in a big bowl.
- Mix together vanilla, salt, water, vegetable oil, brown sugar and honey in a separate bowl, then stir well. Put the mixture into the oat mixture, then stir. On a cookie sheet, spread out the oat mixture.
- Bake about an hour while stirring every 15 mins. Take away from the oven and allow to cool before serving.

Nutrition Information

- Calories: 428 calories;
- Total Carbohydrate: 60.1
- Cholesterol: 0
- Protein: 9.4
- Total Fat: 18.2
- Sodium: 202

94. Island Chicken With Fruit Salsa

Serving: 8 | Prep: 15mins | Cook: 30mins | Ready in:

Ingredients

- 2 (15 ounce) cans pineapple tidbits, drained with juice reserved
- 2 mangos - peeled, seeded and diced
- 2 green chile peppers, diced
- 1/3 cup chopped fresh cilantro
- 1/2 cup freshly squeezed lime juice and pulp
- 1/2 cup fresh orange juice
- 1/4 cup dark rum
- 1/2 clove garlic, minced
- 8 skinless, boneless chicken breasts

Direction

- In a bowl, combine garlic, rum, orange juice, lime juice and pulp, cilantro, peppers, mangos, pineapple and the reserved juice from 1 can. Let rest for 1 hour before putting in chicken.
- To get the marinade, strain the juice from the salsa. For the chicken topping, put aside enough salsa without the juice. In a bowl, marinate the chicken breast halves with the leftover salsa and juice mixture for 2 to 6 hours.
- Start preheating the oven at 325°F (165°C).
- Remove the salsa used for marinating and bake the chicken in the prepared oven for 30 minutes until juices run clear. Spread reserved salsa over the top to serve.

Nutrition Information

- Calories: 261 calories;
- Cholesterol: 67
- Protein: 25.7
- Total Fat: 3.1
- Sodium: 63
- Total Carbohydrate: 29.6

95. Italian Chicken Marinade

Serving: 4 | Prep: 15mins | Cook: 15mins | Ready in:

Ingredients

- 1 (16 ounce) bottle Italian-style salad dressing
- 1 teaspoon garlic powder
- 1 teaspoon salt
- 4 skinless, boneless chicken breast halves

Direction

- Combine salt, garlic powder, and salad dressing in a shallow baking dish. Add chicken and toss until evenly coated. Chill in fridge for at least 4 hours to marinate (or overnight for the best flavor).
- Set the grill to high heat.
- Grease the grate lightly with oil. Skip marinating sauce and grill chicken until the juices run clear, 8 minutes on each side.

Nutrition Information

- Calories: 455 calories;
- Protein: 25.1
- Total Fat: 34.2
- Sodium: 2469
- Total Carbohydrate: 12
- Cholesterol: 67

96. Italian One Step Casserole

Serving: 7 | Prep: 20mins | Cook: 1hours20mins | Ready in:

Ingredients

- 1 pound sausages
- 4 potatoes, peeled and cubed
- 2 carrots, chopped
- 1 onion, chopped
- 3 (15 ounce) cans crushed tomatoes with juice
- 1 1/2 teaspoons salt
- 1 pinch ground black pepper
- 1 pinch dried oregano

Direction

- Set the oven to 190°C or 375°F to preheat.
- Take casings away from sausage and slice into pieces with 1 inch size. Put these sausage pieces into a 15"x10" roasting pan. Layer potatoes, carrots and onions on top of the sausages. Pour tomatoes overall layers, then use oregano, ground black pepper and salt to season.
- Place on a cover and bake about an hour at 190°C or 375°F, then take cover off and bake for 15-20 minutes longer.

Nutrition Information

- Calories: 424 calories;
- Total Fat: 23.7
- Sodium: 1483
- Total Carbohydrate: 38.1
- Cholesterol: 46
- Protein: 14.7

97. JJ's Vegan Burritos

Serving: 6 | Prep: 20mins | Cook: 25mins | Ready in:

Ingredients

- 1 tablespoon olive oil
- 1 (15 ounce) can black beans, drained and rinsed
- 1 red bell pepper, finely chopped
- 1 small white onion, finely chopped
- 2 jalapeno peppers, seeded and finely chopped, divided
- 1 (1 ounce) package taco seasoning
- 1 teaspoon salt
- 1 bunch green onions, finely chopped
- 1/3 cup fresh oregano leaves
- 6 flour tortillas

Direction

- Preheat an oven to 220°C/425°F. Use olive oil to grease a big pie pan.
- Cook salt, taco seasoning, 1 jalapeno pepper, onion, bell pepper and black beans for 15 minutes till juices release in a frying pan; take off heat. Mix in leftover jalapeno pepper, oregano and green onions.
- Use 1/6 black bean mixture to fill a tortilla; wrap into a burrito and repeat using leftover filling and tortillas. Put burritos into prepped pie pan.
- In the preheated oven, bake for 10 minutes till slightly brown and crisp.

Nutrition Information

- Calories: 353 calories;
- Protein: 11.4
- Total Fat: 8.3
- Sodium: 1470
- Total Carbohydrate: 57.7
- Cholesterol: 0

98. Jalapeno Steak

Serving: 6 | Prep: 5mins | Cook: 10mins | Ready in:

Ingredients

- 4 jalapeno peppers, stemmed
- 4 cloves garlic, peeled
- 1 1/2 teaspoons cracked black pepper
- 1 tablespoon coarse salt
- 1/4 cup lime juice
- 1 tablespoon dried oregano
- 1 1/2 pounds top sirloin steak

Direction

- In a blender, add oregano, lime juice, salt, pepper, garlic and jalapenos. Blend until smooth.
- Put steak into a big resealable plastic bag or a shallow pan. Pour the sauce over, flip to coat. Seal the bag or cover the pan, let marinate for 8 hours or overnight in the fridge.
- Set an outdoor grill over high heat and preheat; brush oil over the grate lightly.
- Drain the steak and dispose the marinade. Cook the steak on the grill for 5 minutes each side, or until it reaches your preferred doneness.

Nutrition Information

- Calories: 186 calories;
- Cholesterol: 60
- Protein: 19.1
- Total Fat: 10.5
- Sodium: 1206

- Total Carbohydrate: 3.1

99. Jamie's Black Beans And Rice

Serving: 4 | Prep: 15mins | Cook: 15mins | Ready in:

Ingredients

- 1 cup uncooked white rice
- 2 tablespoons vegetable oil
- 1 (10 ounce) package frozen green bell peppers and onions
- 1 (15 ounce) can black beans, undrained
- 1 (10 ounce) can enchilada sauce

Direction

- Boil 2 cups of water in a saucepan, then add rice and mix. Lower the heat, put cover on and let it simmer for 20 minutes.
- In the meantime, in a big skillet, heat the oil on medium heat; sauté the onions and peppers until becoming tender. Mix in enchilada sauce and beans, then simmer for 15 minutes. Serve on top of cooked rice.

Nutrition Information

- Calories: 350 calories;
- Protein: 5.1
- Total Fat: 16.1
- Sodium: 13
- Total Carbohydrate: 46.4
- Cholesterol: 26

100. Jay's Jerk Chicken

Serving: 4 | Prep: 15mins | Cook: 30mins | Ready in:

Ingredients

- 6 green onions, chopped
- 1 onion, chopped
- 1 jalapeno pepper, seeded and minced
- 3/4 cup soy sauce
- 1/2 cup distilled white vinegar
- 1/4 cup vegetable oil
- 2 tablespoons brown sugar
- 1 tablespoon chopped fresh thyme
- 1/2 teaspoon ground cloves
- 1/2 teaspoon ground nutmeg
- 1/2 teaspoon ground allspice
- 1 1/2 pounds skinless, boneless chicken breast halves

Direction

- Mix together brown sugar, onion, green onions, jalapeno pepper, cloves, thyme, allspice, nutmeg, vinegar, soy sauce, and vegetable oil in a blender or food processor for about 15 seconds.
- In a medium bowl, put in chicken and cover with marinade. Refrigerate overnight or 4 to 6 hours.
- Set the grill in high heat to preheat.
- Oil the grill grate lightly. On the preheated grill, cook chicken until juices run clear or for 6 to 8 minutes.

Nutrition Information

- Calories: 385 calories;
- Total Fat: 18.2
- Sodium: 2798
- Total Carbohydrate: 15.4
- Cholesterol: 97
- Protein: 39.2

101. Kabobs

Serving: 10 | Prep: 30mins | Cook: 10mins | Ready in:

Ingredients

- 1/2 cup teriyaki sauce

- 1/2 cup honey
- 1/2 teaspoon garlic powder
- 1/2 pinch ground ginger
- 2 red bell peppers, cut into 2 inch pieces
- 1 large sweet onion, peeled and cut into wedges
- 1 1/2 cups whole fresh mushrooms
- 1 pound beef sirloin, cut into 1 inch cubes
- 1 1/2 pounds skinless, boneless chicken breast halves - cut into cubes
- skewers

Direction

- Combine honey, teriyaki sauce, garlic powder, and ginger in a large re-sealable plastic bag. Put in the red bell peppers, mushrooms, onion wedges, beef, and chicken. Close the bag and let sit in the fridge for 4 hours to one day.
- Pre-heat grill on medium-high.
- Remove the meat and vegetables from the marinade and skewer them, leaving some space in between each item. Dispose of the marinade.
- Oil the grates. Grill until meat and vegetables are nicely cooked, turning as needed, about 10 minutes.

Nutrition Information

- Calories: 304 calories;
- Sodium: 623
- Total Carbohydrate: 21.2
- Cholesterol: 74
- Protein: 24.8
- Total Fat: 13.3

102. Kimbop (Korean Sushi)

Serving: 4 | Prep: 40mins | Cook: 20mins | Ready in:

Ingredients

- 1 cup uncooked glutinous white rice (sushi rice)
- 1 1/2 cups water
- 1 tablespoon sesame oil
- salt, to taste
- 2 eggs, beaten
- 4 sheets sushi nori (dry seaweed)
- 1 cucumber, cut into thin strips
- 1 carrot, cut into thin strips
- 4 slices American processed cheese, cut into thin strips
- 4 slices cooked ham, cut into thin strips
- 2 teaspoons sesame oil

Direction

- In a colander or strainer, rinse rice until water is clear. Boil combined rice and water in a saucepan. Reduce heat to low, simmer for 12-14 minutes, covered, until rice becomes tender. Place cooked rice on a baking sheet to let cool. Season using salt and 1 tablespoon of sesame oil.
- As rice simmers, pour eggs in a skillet on medium-high heat. Cook without turning or stirring to achieve a layer of cooked egg that's flat. When it's fully cooked, take out of skillet and put on a cutting board to cool. Set aside.
- Separate nori sheets on a flat surface. Distribute cooled rice on them, leaving a 1/2-inch strip of seaweed seen at the top of every sheet. Place strips of ham, cheese, carrot, cucumber, and egg in thin layers on rice. Starting with the bottom of every nori, firmly roll every piece using a bamboo sushi mat to a cylindrical shape. Brush every roll using 1/2 teaspoon sesame oil. Slice to 6 equal pieces.

Nutrition Information

- Calories: 354 calories;
- Total Fat: 15.2
- Sodium: 510
- Total Carbohydrate: 41.2
- Cholesterol: 113
- Protein: 11.9

103. Lamb Ribs With Honey And Wine

Serving: 6 | Prep: 10mins | Cook: 1hours10mins | Ready in:

Ingredients

- 3 1/2 pounds lamb ribs
- 2 onions, chopped
- 1 cup dry white wine
- 1/4 cup soy sauce
- 1/4 cup fresh lemon juice
- 1 tablespoon honey
- 1 tablespoon olive oil
- 2 teaspoons minced garlic
- 1 teaspoon ground cinnamon
- 1 teaspoon salt
- 1 teaspoon ground black pepper

Direction

- Place the lamb in a baking dish, 9x13-inch in size.
- In a small bowl, mix pepper, salt, cinnamon, garlic, olive oil, honey, lemon juice, soy sauce, white wine and onions. Combine thoroughly and put the mixture on the entire lamb. Cover using plastic wrap and refrigerate to marinate for an hour.
- Preheat the oven to 200 °C or 400 °F.
- In the prepped oven, let the lamb roast for an hour and 10 minutes till soft and browned.

Nutrition Information

- Calories: 507 calories;
- Total Carbohydrate: 10.2
- Cholesterol: 112
- Protein: 25.8
- Total Fat: 36.8
- Sodium: 1077

104. Lemon Pepper Cod

Serving: 4 | Prep: 5mins | Cook: 10mins | Ready in:

Ingredients

- 3 tablespoons vegetable oil
- 1 1/2 pounds cod fillets
- 1 lemon, juiced
- ground black pepper to taste

Direction

- Set heat to medium-high and heat oil in a large skillet until hot. Fry fillets and drizzle 1/2 lemon juice over the tops. Season with pepper. Fry for 4 minutes then flip. Drizzle the rest of the lemon juice and season with pepper. Continue to fry until fillets easily flake using fork.

Nutrition Information

- Calories: 236 calories;
- Total Carbohydrate: 2.9
- Cholesterol: 73
- Protein: 30.7
- Total Fat: 11.5
- Sodium: 105

105. Lemony Steamed Fish

Serving: 6 | Prep: 15mins | Cook: 30mins | Ready in:

Ingredients

- 6 (6 ounce) halibut fillets
- 1 tablespoon dried dill weed
- 1 tablespoon onion powder
- 2 teaspoons dried parsley
- 1/4 teaspoon paprika
- 1 pinch seasoned salt, or more to taste
- 1 pinch lemon pepper
- 1 pinch garlic powder
- 2 tablespoons lemon juice

Direction

- Prepare oven for preheating at 375 degrees F (190 degrees C).
- Prepare foil and cut into 6 squares. It must be large enough for each fillet.
- Place fillet at the middle of the foil square. Drizzle onion powder, paprika, dill weed, lemon pepper, garlic powder, seasoned salt and parsley on each fillet. Squeeze lemon juice on each fillet and wrap over with foil to create a pocket. Seal edges by folding foil. Prepare baking sheets and transfer sealed packets.
- Place in preheated oven. For 30 minutes, cook until fish flakes easily with a fork.

Nutrition Information

- Calories: 142 calories;
- Total Fat: 1.1
- Sodium: 184
- Total Carbohydrate: 1.9
- Cholesterol: 61
- Protein: 29.7

106. Lentils And Spinach

Serving: 4 | Prep: 10mins | Cook: 55mins | Ready in:

Ingredients

- 1 tablespoon vegetable oil
- 2 white onions, halved and sliced into 1/2 rings
- 3 cloves garlic, minced
- 1/2 cup lentils
- 2 cups water
- 1 (10 ounce) package frozen spinach
- 1 teaspoon salt
- 1 teaspoon ground cumin
- freshly ground black pepper to taste
- 2 cloves garlic, crushed

Direction

- Heat oil on medium heat in a heavy pan; sauté onion till it starts to be golden for around 10 minutes. Add minced garlic; sauté for around 1 minute.
- Put water and lentils in saucepan; boil. Cover; reduce heat. Simmer till lentils are soft for 35 minutes. Depending on lentils and water, it might take less time.
- Meanwhile, follow package directions to cook spinach in microwave. Put cumin, salt and spinach in saucepan; cover. Simmer for 10 minutes till all is heated. Grind in lots of pepper; to taste, press in extra garlic.

Nutrition Information

- Calories: 165 calories;
- Cholesterol: 0
- Protein: 9.7
- Total Fat: 4.3
- Sodium: 639
- Total Carbohydrate: 24

107. Light Fruit And Nut Granola

Serving: 6 | Prep: 10mins | Cook: 35mins | Ready in:

Ingredients

- 2 cups rolled oats
- 1/2 cup spelt flour
- 1/2 cup packed brown sugar
- 1 teaspoon ground cinnamon
- 3/4 teaspoon ground ginger
- 3 tablespoons canola oil
- 1/4 cup applesauce
- 3 tablespoons maple syrup
- 1/4 cup diced dried apricots
- 1/4 cup chopped pecans
- 3 tablespoons flax seeds, ground

Direction

- Turn the oven to 150° C (300° F). Use parchment paper to line a baking tray.
- Mix the spelt flour, rolled oats, cinnamon, brown sugar, canola oil, ginger, maple syrup, applesauce, pecans, ground flax seed and dried apricots together in a mixing bowl; blend completely. Put the granola mixture on the baking tray.
- Bake granola for 20 minutes, mix and then bake again for 15 minutes longer until dry. Serve it fully cooled.

Nutrition Information

- Calories: 379 calories;
- Cholesterol: 0
- Protein: 6.7
- Total Fat: 15.1
- Sodium: 11
- Total Carbohydrate: 57.4

108. Lobster Tails Steamed In Beer

Serving: 2 | Prep: 5mins | Cook: 8mins | Ready in:

Ingredients

- 2 whole lobster tail
- 1/2 (12 fluid ounce) can beer

Direction

- Put beer in a medium-sized saucepan and let it boil over medium to high heat.
- Cut first a slit at the back of the lobster shell along its length if the lobster tails are still in the shell.
- Put a steamer basket over the saucepan with boiling beer. Put the thawed lobster tails in the steamer basket and place a cover on top. Lower the heat and let it simmer for 8 minutes.

Nutrition Information

- Calories: 209 calories;
- Total Fat: 1.7
- Sodium: 566
- Total Carbohydrate: 4.1
- Cholesterol: 180
- Protein: 36.1

109. London Broil I

Serving: 6 | Prep: 15mins | Cook: 15mins | Ready in:

Ingredients

- 3 cloves garlic, minced
- 1/2 cup soy sauce
- 2 tablespoons vegetable oil
- 2 tablespoons ketchup
- 1 teaspoon dried oregano
- 1 teaspoon ground black pepper
- 1 (2 pound) flank steak or round steak

Direction

- Combine black pepper, oregano, ketchup, oil, soy sauce and garlic together in a small bowl. Use a fork to poke the meat on both sides, then put the meat and marinade into a big resealable plastic bag. Marinate it in the fridge for 8 hours or overnight.
- Preheat the grill to medium-high heat and oil the grate lightly. Set the steak on top of the grill and throw the marinade away. Cook the meat on each side for 5 to 8 minutes, depending on how thick it is. Be careful not to overcook, as the meat tastes better on the rare side.

Nutrition Information

- Calories: 222 calories;
- Total Fat: 9.1
- Sodium: 1313
- Total Carbohydrate: 3.8

- Cholesterol: 75
- Protein: 30.1

110. Loosemeat Sandwiches III

Serving: 8 | Prep: | Cook: 40mins | Ready in:

Ingredients

- 2 pounds lean ground beef
- 1 teaspoon salt
- 1/2 teaspoon ground black pepper
- 1 1/2 cups water
- 1 onion, chopped
- 24 slices dill pickle slices
- 4 ounces prepared mustard
- 8 hamburger buns

Direction

- Cook ground beef in a big skillet over moderate heat until browned, then drain. Bring back to pan together with pepper, salt and cover with water. Lower heat to low and simmer the beef without a cover for 15-30 minutes, until water has gone.
- Serve meat on buns with chopped onion, dill pickle slices as well as mustard on top.

Nutrition Information

- Calories: 356 calories;
- Sodium: 995
- Total Carbohydrate: 24.2
- Cholesterol: 74
- Protein: 26.6
- Total Fat: 16.3

111. Luau Chicken

Serving: 6 | Prep: 15mins | Cook: 1hours | Ready in:

Ingredients

- 1 cup unsweetened pineapple juice
- 2 tablespoons brown sugar
- 2 tablespoons ketchup
- 1/4 teaspoon ground ginger
- 1/4 teaspoon garlic salt
- 1 tablespoon cornstarch
- 1 tablespoon soy sauce
- 6 cooked boneless, skinless chicken breasts, cut into 1-inch pieces
- 1 green bell pepper, cut into 1 inch pieces
- 1 onion, cut into 1 inch pieces
- 1 (8 ounce) can sliced water chestnuts

Direction

- Prepare the oven by preheating to 350°F (175°C).
- Mix soy sauce, cornstarch, garlic salt, ginger, ketchup, brown sugar, and pineapple juice in a big skillet. Simmer for 5 minutes on low heat.
- In a 9x13-inch baking dish, put the cooked chicken, water chestnuts, onion, and bell pepper. The put the skillet sauce/mixture on the top. Use aluminum foil to cover the dish then place in the preheated oven and bake for 1 hour.

Nutrition Information

- Calories: 283 calories;
- Total Carbohydrate: 19.8
- Cholesterol: 82
- Protein: 31.3
- Total Fat: 8.3
- Sodium: 356

112. Lumpia Rolls

Serving: 40 | Prep: 1hours | Cook: 20mins |Ready in:

Ingredients

- 2 pounds ground beef
- 2 pounds ground pork
- vegetable oil
- 1 1/2 cups carrots, finely chopped
- soy sauce to taste
- 3 cups bean sprouts
- 1 cup sugar snap peas, chopped
- 1 cup fresh mushrooms, finely chopped
- 1 cup green onions, finely chopped
- salt to taste
- garlic powder to taste
- black pepper to taste
- 1 (14 ounce) package Lumpia Wrappers
- 1 egg white, beaten
- canola oil for frying

Direction

- In a large frying pan, pour a small amount of oil on medium heat and cook beef and pork until brown. Remove from pan, drain, and set aside in a large mixing bowl. Pour soy sauce in pan and cook the carrots in it until tender. Stir in snap peas, mushrooms, green onions and bean sprouts with a drizzle of each soy sauce, garlic powder, black pepper, and salt; stir and cook for 5 minutes, or until vegetables soften. Add to pork and beef and toss to mix.
- Cover spring roll wrappers with damp cloth to avoid drying them out and work in batches of about 5 or so at a time. On a clean work surface, position the wrapper in a way that one corner is facing you; put small amount of filling mixture on the closest corner to you. Fold over and fold the two outside corners inward. Roll it with the top corner open like a burrito. Using a brush, apply a small amount of egg white on top corner, roll it up and then seal. Do the same with the rest of the wrappers and filling.
- Fry rolls until golden brown, about 5 minutes in a deep skillet or a deep-fryer with vegetable oil heated to 190 degrees C or 375 degrees F, and then rest on paper towels to drain.

Nutrition Information

- Calories: 313 calories;
- Sodium: 170
- Total Carbohydrate: 7.2
- Cholesterol: 37
- Protein: 9.1
- Total Fat: 27.6

113. Man Catching Meat Loaf

Serving: 6 | Prep: 25mins | Cook: 55mins |Ready in:

Ingredients

- 1 tablespoon butter
- 1 yellow onion, minced
- 1 green bell pepper, diced
- 6 crimini mushrooms, chopped
- 1 tablespoon minced garlic
- 1 (12 ounce) can diced tomatoes
- 1/2 teaspoon dried oregano
- 1 teaspoon dried basil
- 1/2 teaspoon ground mustard
- 1/2 teaspoon curry powder
- 1/2 teaspoon crushed red pepper flakes
- 1/2 pound ground beef
- 1/2 pound ground veal
- 1/4 pound bulk hot Italian sausage
- 1 egg
- 3 tablespoons Worcestershire sauce
- 1/4 cup ketchup
- 3 tablespoons prepared spicy mustard
- 3 tablespoons teriyaki sauce
- 1 cup Italian-style bread crumbs
- 4 slices thick sliced bacon
- 1/3 cup ketchup
- 1/4 cup Worcestershire sauce

- 1 tablespoon yellow mustard

Direction

- Preheat an oven to 175°C/350°F.
- Melt butter in skillet on medium heat; mix and cook mushrooms, bell pepper and onion for 2-3 minutes in butter. Mix red pepper, curry powder, ground mustard, basil, oregano, diced tomatoes and garlic in; cook for 5 minutes till mushrooms are golden brown and onions are translucent. Put aside.
- With your hands, gently mix teriyaki, mustard, 1/4 cup ketchup, 3 tablespoons Worcestershire sauce, egg, veal, sausage and beef in bowl; fold breadcrumbs and mushroom mixture in. Shape mixture to loaf; put on baking dish then lay bacon slices over loaf.
- In preheated oven, bake for 45 minutes.
- As meat loaf bakes, prep glaze: Whisk yellow mustard, 1/4 cup Worcestershire sauce and 1/3 cup ketchup in bowl; put glaze on loaf. Put in oven for 10 minutes more; before serving, rest meat loaf for 5 minutes.

Nutrition Information

- Calories: 516 calories;
- Total Carbohydrate: 31.7
- Cholesterol: 127
- Protein: 25.7
- Total Fat: 31.5
- Sodium: 1742

114. Maple Glazed Ribs

Serving: 6 | Prep: 15mins | Cook: 1hours25mins | Ready in:

Ingredients

- 3 pounds baby back pork ribs
- 3/4 cup maple syrup
- 2 tablespoons packed brown sugar
- 2 tablespoons ketchup
- 1 tablespoon cider vinegar
- 1 tablespoon Worcestershire sauce
- 1/2 teaspoon salt
- 1/2 teaspoon mustard powder

Direction

- Put the ribs in big pot, and submerge in water. Place cover, and allow to simmer till meat is soft for an hour. Let drain, and turn ribs onto a shallow dish.
- Mix together the mustard powder, salt, Worcestershire sauce, vinegar, ketchup, brown sugar and maple syrup in a small saucepan. Allow to come to a gentle boil, and let cook for 5 minutes, mixing often. Cool partially, then add on top of ribs, and refrigerate to marinate for 2 hours.
- Have grill ready for indirect heat cooking. Take the ribs off marinade. Turn the marinade onto a small saucepan, and allow to boil for a few minutes.
- Grease grate lightly. Allow to cook for approximately 20 minutes, basting with cooked marinade often, till well glazed.

Nutrition Information

- Calories: 485 calories;
- Sodium: 411
- Total Carbohydrate: 30.5
- Cholesterol: 117
- Protein: 24.2
- Total Fat: 29.5

115. Marie's Easy Slow Cooker Pot Roast

Serving: 8 | Prep: 40mins | Cook: 9hours | Ready in:

Ingredients

- 4 pounds chuck roast

- salt and pepper to taste
- 1 packet dry onion soup mix
- 1 cup water
- 3 carrots, chopped
- 1 onion, chopped
- 3 potatoes, peeled and cubed
- 1 stalk celery, chopped

Direction

- Sprinkle salt and pepper onto the roast. Season to taste. In a big skillet, cook the roast on high heat for approximately 4 minutes per side until all sides have browned.
- Put the roast into the slow cooker then mix in the celery, potatoes, onion, carrots, water and soup mix then cover. On a low setting, cook it for 8 to 10 hours.

Nutrition Information

- Calories: 540 calories;
- Sodium: 272
- Total Carbohydrate: 18.2
- Cholesterol: 147
- Protein: 45.7
- Total Fat: 30.6

116. Marinated Pork Tenderloin

Serving: 4 | Prep: 10mins | Cook: 20mins | Ready in:

Ingredients

- 1/4 cup soy sauce
- 1/4 cup packed brown sugar
- 2 tablespoons sherry
- 1 1/2 teaspoons dried minced onion
- 1 teaspoon ground cinnamon
- 2 tablespoons olive oil
- 1 pinch garlic powder
- 2 (3/4 pound) pork tenderloins

Direction

- In a large resealable plastic bag, mix the sherry, olive oil, a touch of garlic powder, cinnamon, dried onion, soy sauce, and brown sugar. Seal the bag and shake it until well-mixed. Add the pork into the bag with marinade and seal. Refrigerate the sealed bag for 6-12 hours.
- Set the grill to high heat for preheating.
- Put oil onto the grate lightly. Arrange the tenderloins onto the grill, discarding the marinade. Cook the pork for 20 minutes until the desired doneness reaches. Slice the pork into medallions to serve.

Nutrition Information

- Calories: 278 calories;
- Total Fat: 10.7
- Sodium: 1008
- Total Carbohydrate: 16.9
- Cholesterol: 73
- Protein: 27

117. Marinated Tofu

Serving: 3 | Prep: 10mins | Cook: 20mins | Ready in:

Ingredients

- 1 pound tofu, plain or seasoned
- 1 (12 ounce) bottle barbecue sauce
- 1 tablespoon olive oil

Direction

- Drain tofu and slice into cubes or slices; according to your recipe. In a shallow dish, put the tofu and add barbeque sauce to coat. Put a cover on and refrigerate for 3 hours to overnight, flipping sometimes.
- Turn the oven to 350°F (175°C) to preheat.
- In a non-stick skillet, heat oil over medium-high heat. Cook with a little sauce until all

sides are brown, flipping sometimes. Put the tofu back into the baking dish.
- Bake for approximately 10 minutes in the preheated oven.

Nutrition Information

- Calories: 323 calories;
- Total Carbohydrate: 43.4
- Cholesterol: 0
- Protein: 12.2
- Total Fat: 12.1
- Sodium: 1264

118. Mexican Bean Burgers

Serving: 8 | Prep: | Cook: | Ready in:

Ingredients

- 1 carrot, sliced
- 1 (15 ounce) can kidney beans
- 1/2 cup chopped green bell pepper
- 1/2 cup chopped onion
- 2 cups salsa
- 1 cup dried bread crumbs
- 1/2 cup whole wheat flour
- 1/2 teaspoon ground black pepper
- salt to taste
- 1 pinch chili powder

Direction

- Fill the bowl with a 1/4 inch of water and submerge the carrot inside. Seal it with a plastic wrap and cook in the microwave for 2 minutes until the carrot is soft. Let it drain.
- In a large bowl, pound the steamed carrot and beans, and then mix in onion, whole wheat flour, green pepper, bread crumbs, and salsa. Flavor it with chili powder, salt, and black pepper. Add flour to create a firmer mixture, or add more salsa if the mixture is too stiff.

Form the mixture into eight patties and arrange it on a greased baking pan.
- Heat a large skillet over medium heat and coat it with cooking spray. Cook the patties for 8 minutes on each side until firm and browned all over.

Nutrition Information

- Calories: 151 calories;
- Total Fat: 1.2
- Sodium: 609
- Total Carbohydrate: 29.7
- Cholesterol: 0
- Protein: 7

119. Mexican Pasta

Serving: 4 | Prep: 5mins | Cook: 15mins | Ready in:

Ingredients

- 1/2 pound seashell pasta
- 2 tablespoons olive oil
- 2 onions, chopped
- 1 green bell pepper, chopped
- 1/2 cup sweet corn kernels
- 1 (15 ounce) can black beans, drained
- 1 (14.5 ounce) can peeled and diced tomatoes
- 1/4 cup salsa
- 1/4 cup sliced black olives
- 1 1/2 tablespoons taco seasoning mix
- salt and pepper to taste

Direction

- Boil a big pot of slightly salted water. Put in the pasta and cook until al dente, about 8 to 10 minutes; let drain.
- Meanwhile, over moderate heat, heat the olive oil in a big skillet. In oil, cook pepper and onions for 10 minutes till slightly browned. Mix in corn and heat completely. Mix in salt and pepper, taco seasoning, olives, salsa,

tomatoes and black beans and let cook for 5 minutes till well heated.
- Toss cooked pasta and sauce, serve.

Nutrition Information

- Calories: 358 calories;
- Total Fat: 9.4
- Sodium: 589
- Total Carbohydrate: 59.5
- Cholesterol: 0
- Protein: 10.3

120. Moo Goo Gai Pan II

Serving: 4 | Prep: 30mins | Cook: 15mins | Ready in:

Ingredients

- 1 tablespoon vegetable oil
- 1/4 pound sliced fresh mushrooms
- 1/4 pound snow peas
- 1 (8 ounce) can sliced water chestnuts, drained
- 1/4 pound sliced bok choy
- salt and black pepper to taste
- 1 tablespoon vegetable oil
- 1 teaspoon minced garlic
- 1 teaspoon minced fresh ginger root
- 3/4 cup skinless, boneless chicken breast meat - thinly sliced
- 1 teaspoon white wine
- 1/4 teaspoon white sugar
- 1/4 cup chicken broth
- 1 tablespoon cornstarch
- 2 tablespoons water

Direction

- In a large pan or wok set over high heat, heat a tablespoon of vegetable oil. Add water chestnuts, bok choy, mushrooms, and snow peas then season with pepper and salt. Cook for 5 minutes or until the vegetables are tender. Take the vegetables off the wok or pan then wipe clean.
- Add the remaining a tablespoon of oil in the pan or wok, then cook ginger and garlic. Stir for a few seconds until garlic begins to golden brown. Add the chicken and cook for 5 minutes or until it is no longer pink. Mix in chicken broth, wine, and sugar, then allow mixture to boil. Make a slurry with water and cornstarch, then add to the sauce. Once the sauce simmers, stir for 30 seconds or until the sauce turns clear and thick. Put the vegetables back into the pan then toss until well coated with sauce and hot.

Nutrition Information

- Calories: 174 calories;
- Cholesterol: 25
- Protein: 12
- Total Fat: 8.4
- Sodium: 48
- Total Carbohydrate: 13.2

121. Moong Dal

Serving: 6 | Prep: 30mins | Cook: 30mins | Ready in:

Ingredients

- 2 1/2 cups dried yellow split peas
- 2 1/2 cups water
- 1 1/2 teaspoons salt
- 1/2 teaspoon grated fresh ginger root
- 1 teaspoon diced jalapeno chile pepper
- 1/2 cup diced tomatoes
- 3 teaspoons lemon juice
- 1/2 teaspoon ground turmeric
- 2 teaspoons vegetable oil
- 1 teaspoon cumin seed
- 1/2 dried red chile pepper
- 1 pinch Asafoetida
- 2 cloves garlic, finely chopped
- 1/4 cup chopped fresh cilantro

Direction

- Rinse split peas; put in a saucepan with 2 1/2 cups of water. Soak split peas for 30 minutes.
- Heat salt, water and split peas till boiling; lower heat to medium low. Cook for 15-20 minutes till thick and tender; if needed, add more water to avoid drying out. Mix in turmeric, lemon juice, tomato, jalapeno pepper and ginger.
- Heat oil inside a small saucepan. Add red chile pepper and cumin seed; add garlic and Asafoetida powder when pepper is heated. Mix the mixture into the split peas. Add cilantro; stir well.

Nutrition Information

- Calories: 127 calories;
- Total Fat: 2.4
- Sodium: 656
- Total Carbohydrate: 20.4
- Cholesterol: 0
- Protein: 7.3

122. Morgan's Grilled Fish

Serving: 4 | Prep: 10mins | Cook: 10mins | Ready in:

Ingredients

- 1/4 cup olive oil
- 1 tablespoon dried parsley
- 2 tablespoons dried thyme
- 1 tablespoon dried rosemary
- 1 clove garlic, minced
- 4 (6 ounce) fillets salmon
- 1 lemon, juiced

Direction

- Prepare the grill by preheating to medium heat.
- Combine the garlic, rosemary, thyme, parsley, and olive oil in a shallow glass dish. Add the salmon in the dish, flipping to coat. Squeeze lemon juice over each fillet. Cover and refrigerate for 30 minutes to marinate.
- Put oil lightly on the grill grate. Place salmon on the grill and get rid of any left marinade. Cook salmon on the preheated grill for 8-10 minutes over medium heat, flipping once. Fish is cooked once it flakes easily using a fork.

Nutrition Information

- Calories: 405 calories;
- Sodium: 84
- Total Carbohydrate: 5.2
- Cholesterol: 83
- Protein: 29.6
- Total Fat: 30.1

123. Moroccan Chicken Sann

Serving: 6 | Prep: 15mins | Cook: 45mins | Ready in:

Ingredients

- 1/2 cup soy sauce
- 1/2 cup fresh lemon juice
- 1/2 cup sherry
- 1/2 cup honey
- 1/2 teaspoon ground thyme
- 2 teaspoons curry powder
- 1/2 teaspoon dried oregano
- 1/2 teaspoon ground ginger
- 1/2 teaspoon ground black pepper
- 1 clove garlic, pressed
- 3 pounds cut up chicken pieces
- 1 1/2 cups uncooked brown rice
- 3 cups water
- 2 tablespoons olive oil
- 8 pitted prunes
- 8 dried apricot halves

Direction

- Whisk the garlic, ground black pepper, ground ginger, dried oregano, curry powder, thyme, honey, sherry, lemon juice and soy sauce together. In a resealable bag, put the chicken with the marinade and let it marinate for a minimum of 30 minutes to a maximum of 24 hours.
- Boil the water and brown rice in a pan on high heat. Lower the heat to medium-low, then simmer for 45-50 minutes with cover, until the liquid was absorbed, and the rice is soft.
- In a big pan, heat the olive oil on medium-high heat and brown the chicken pieces on all sides. Sprinkle apricots and prunes on the chicken and pour the marinade into the pan. Let it simmer with cover, then cook for 30 minutes. Take out he cover and let it simmer for about 15 minutes, until the juices run clear, chicken loses its pink color at the bone and the sauce thickens a bit. In inserted instant-read thermometer near the bone should register 74°C (165°F). Serve on top of brown rice.

Nutrition Information

- Calories: 681 calories;
- Total Fat: 23.1
- Sodium: 1425
- Total Carbohydrate: 82.2
- Cholesterol: 97
- Protein: 36.6

124. Mussels Marinara Di Amore

Serving: 4 | Prep: 5mins | Cook: 15mins | Ready in:

Ingredients

- 1 tablespoon olive oil
- 1 clove garlic, minced
- 1 (14.5 ounce) can crushed tomatoes
- 1/2 teaspoon dried oregano
- 1/2 teaspoon dried basil
- 1 pinch crushed red pepper flakes
- 1/4 cup white wine
- 1 pound mussels, cleaned and debearded
- 8 ounces linguini pasta
- 1 lemon - cut into wedges, for garnish

Direction

- Heat oil in a large skillet over medium heat and sauté garlic until it turns transparent.
- Put red pepper flakes, basil, oregano and tomatoes into skillet; lower the heat to low and let it simmer in 5 minutes.
- At the same time, boil lightly salted water in a large pot. Cook pasta in boiling water until al dente, about 8-10 minutes. Drain; set aside.
- Put mussels and wine into the skillet. Cover, higher the heat to high, and continue cooking until the mussel shells open, about 3-5 minutes.
- Combine with hot pasta. Top with parsley and squeeze lemon wedge on top. Use leftover lemon for decoration. Serve.

Nutrition Information

- Calories: 304 calories;
- Total Fat: 5.4
- Sodium: 188
- Total Carbohydrate: 52.8
- Cholesterol: 9
- Protein: 13

125. North Carolina Style Pulled Pork

Serving: 10 | Prep: 1hours | Cook: 6hours | Ready in:

Ingredients

- 1 tablespoon mild paprika
- 2 teaspoons light brown sugar
- 1 1/2 teaspoons hot paprika
- 1/2 teaspoon celery salt

- 1/2 teaspoon garlic salt
- 1/2 teaspoon dry mustard
- 1/2 teaspoon ground black pepper
- 1/2 teaspoon onion powder
- 1/4 teaspoon salt
- 8 pounds pork butt roast
- 2 cups cider vinegar
- 1 1/3 cups water
- 5/8 cup ketchup
- 1/4 cup firmly packed brown sugar
- 5 teaspoons salt
- 4 teaspoons crushed red pepper flakes
- 1 teaspoon ground black pepper
- 1 teaspoon ground white pepper
- 2 pounds hickory wood chips, soaked

Direction

- Combine salt, onion powder, ground black pepper, dry mustard, garlic salt, celery salt, hot paprika, light brown sugar and mild paprika in a small bowl. Rub all sides of roast with spice mixture. Wrap using plastic wrap, and chill for 8 hours or overnight.
- Have a grill ready for indirect heat.
- On top of coals, scatter a handful of submerged wood, or put in the gas grill smoker box. On the grate on top of a drip pan, put the pork butt roast. Put on the grill cover, and let pork cook for about 6 hours till pork is soft and shreds effortlessly. Monitor every hour, putting in fresh coals and hickory chips as necessary to keep smoke and heat.
- Take pork off the heat and put on a cutting board. Cool meat for about 15 minutes, then with 2 forks, shred into bite-sized portions. This needs patience.
- Mix together white pepper, black pepper, red pepper flakes, salt, brown sugar, ketchup, water and cider vinegar in a medium bowl. Keep mixing till salt and brown sugar have dissolved. In a big roasting pan, put vinegar sauce and shredded pork, and coat pork by mixing. Serve right away, or place on the cover and retain warm on grill for 1 hour maximum till serving.

Nutrition Information

- Calories: 426 calories;
- Cholesterol: 135
- Protein: 39.1
- Total Fat: 23.1
- Sodium: 1698
- Total Carbohydrate: 12.1

126. Pan Seared Salmon I

Serving: 4 | Prep: 10mins | Cook: 10mins | Ready in:

Ingredients

- 4 (6 ounce) fillets salmon
- 2 tablespoons olive oil
- 2 tablespoons capers
- 1/8 teaspoon salt
- 1/8 teaspoon ground black pepper
- 4 slices lemon

Direction

- Set a big heavy skillet to preheat for 3 minutes on medium heat.
- Coat olive oil on the salmon. Put in the skillet and turn up the heat to high. Let it cook for 3 minutes. Sprinkle it with pepper, salt and capers. Flip over the salmon and let it cook for 5 minutes or until it becomes brown. When it flakes easily by a fork, it means that the salmon is done.
- Place the salmon to individual plates and put slices of lemon on top to garnish.

Nutrition Information

- Calories: 371 calories;
- Protein: 33.7
- Total Fat: 25.1
- Sodium: 300
- Total Carbohydrate: 1.7
- Cholesterol: 99

127. Pasta For Don And His Loves

Serving: 4 | Prep: 30mins | Cook: 5mins | Ready in:

Ingredients

- 1/3 cup soy flour
- 1 cup whole wheat flour
- 1/2 cup spelt flour
- 3/4 teaspoon salt
- 1/2 cup water, or as needed

Direction

- In a medium-sized bowl, whisk the salt, spelt flour, whole wheat flour and soy flour together. Pour in the water, and combine using hand or in a stand mixer with dough hook attachment. Pour in additional water as necessary to shape a stiff but pliable dough. Mix or knead using hand for roughly 10 minutes. Keep covered, and allow dough to stand for half an hour, or if no pasta machine is available, allow to stand for no less than 60 minutes.
- Split the dough into four pieces to roll easier. Run the dough through a pasta machine if available, or use the rolling pin to roll the dough out into very thin but not transparent onto a floured surface.
- If you make noodles, let pasta sheet dry for several minutes. Dust using the flour, and roll into a loose tube. Slide tube into a-quarter in. slices for the linguine, or to the size that you want.
- To cook: Boil a big pot of lightly-salted water. Put in the pasta, and cook for 1-5 minutes till al dente (based on the thickness). The cooked pasta would float to water surface.

Nutrition Information

- Calories: 182 calories;
- Sodium: 439
- Total Carbohydrate: 34.7
- Cholesterol: 0
- Protein: 8.5
- Total Fat: 2.3

128. Patsy's Best Barbeque Beef

Serving: 12 | Prep: 30mins | Cook: 12hours | Ready in:

Ingredients

- 1 bunch celery, chopped
- 3 large onions, chopped
- 1 medium green bell pepper, chopped
- 1 1/4 cups ketchup
- 1/2 cup water
- 3 tablespoons barbeque sauce
- 3 tablespoons cider vinegar
- 1/8 teaspoon hot pepper sauce
- 2 teaspoons chili powder
- 2 tablespoons salt
- 1 teaspoon pepper
- 6 pounds boneless beef chuck roast, trimmed and chopped

Direction

- Combine hot pepper sauce, vinegar, barbeque sauce, water, ketchup, green pepper, onions and celery in a large bowl. Use pepper, salt and chili powder to season.
- In a slow cooker, put the roast; use sauce mixture to cover. Cook on Low with a cover for about 12 hours.
- Use a fork to shred the meat. Raise the cooking temperature to High; continue cooking until the most of liquid reduces.

Nutrition Information

- Calories: 381 calories;
- Protein: 28.2
- Total Fat: 23.5

- Sodium: 1701
- Total Carbohydrate: 13.7
- Cholesterol: 103

129. Pesto Pasta With Chicken

Serving: 8 | Prep: 10mins | Cook: 20mins | Ready in:

Ingredients

- 1 (16 ounce) package bow tie pasta
- 1 teaspoon olive oil
- 2 cloves garlic, minced
- 2 boneless skinless chicken breasts, cut into bite-size pieces
- crushed red pepper flakes to taste
- 1/3 cup oil-packed sun-dried tomatoes, drained and cut into strips
- 1/2 cup pesto sauce

Direction

- Boil a big pot of lightly salted water. Put in pasta and cook till al dente for 8 to 10 minutes; drain.
- In a big skillet over medium heat, heat oil. Sauté garlic till soft, then mix in chicken. Put red pepper flakes to season. Cook till chicken is golden and cooked through.
- Put together pesto, sun-dried tomatoes, chicken and pasta in a big bowl. Coat equally by tossing.

Nutrition Information

- Calories: 328 calories;
- Total Carbohydrate: 43.3
- Cholesterol: 22
- Protein: 17.4
- Total Fat: 10.1
- Sodium: 154

130. Pickled And Fried Filipino Fish (Daing Na Bangus)

Serving: 4 | Prep: 20mins | Cook: 10mins | Ready in:

Ingredients

- 1 (6 ounce) whole milkfish (bangus), or to taste
- salt and ground black pepper to taste
- 5 cloves garlic, minced
- 1/2 cup white vinegar
- vegetable oil for frying

Direction

- Take off the scales from bangus. Then slice a lengthwise slit in the fish along the back to get rid of innards, intestines, and gills. Scatter open the fish to expose the flesh; then pat dry completely.
- On a ridged plate, lay the fish flat then dust with pepper and salt. Scatter garlic on the flesh then put vinegar on it. Use plastic wrap to cover then keep in the refrigerator for 1 hour up to overnight to marinate.
- Get rid of the marinade and use paper towels to pat dry the fish.
- In a big skillet set on medium-high heat, add oil. Fry in the fish for 7-10 minutes until crispy and golden brown.

Nutrition Information

- Calories: 129 calories;
- Total Fat: 9.6
- Sodium: 70
- Total Carbohydrate: 1.2
- Cholesterol: 22
- Protein: 8.9

131. Poor Man's Fried Rice

Serving: 4 | Prep: 10mins | Cook: 20mins | Ready in:

Ingredients

- 1 1/2 cups uncooked instant rice
- 1 tablespoon sesame oil
- soy sauce to taste
- 2 eggs, beaten
- 1 teaspoon finely chopped fresh ginger root
- 1/4 cup finely chopped green onions

Direction

- In a medium saucepan, boil water. Mix in rice and put on the cover. Take off the heat and rest for 5 minutes. Fluff using a fork and let any excess water drain.
- In a big skillet, heat the oil on medium heat. Mix in soy sauce and rice; heat briefly then turn out the rice onto a bowl.
- In the same skillet, scramble the eggs, then mix in the rice. Mix in green onions and ginger; heat thoroughly and serve.

Nutrition Information

- Calories: 214 calories;
- Sodium: 41
- Total Carbohydrate: 32
- Cholesterol: 93
- Protein: 6
- Total Fat: 6.5

132. Porcupines

Serving: 5 | Prep: 30mins | Cook: 1hours | Ready in:

Ingredients

- 1 pound lean ground beef
- 1/2 cup uncooked white rice
- 1/2 cup water
- 1/2 cup chopped onion
- 1 teaspoon salt
- 1/2 teaspoon celery salt
- 1/8 teaspoon garlic powder
- 1/8 teaspoon ground black pepper
- 1 (15 ounce) can tomato sauce
- 1 cup water

Direction

- Mix together the onion, 1/2 cup of water, rice and ground beef in a big bowl. Blend in pepper, garlic powder, celery salt and salt, then stir well. Form into 1 1/2-inch balls.
- Set an oven to 175°C (350°F) to preheat. Brown the meatballs in a big skillet on medium heat, then drain the fat.
- Mix together the 1 cup of water and tomato sauce in an 11x7-inch baking dish. Put the brown meatballs into the tomato sauce, flipping to coat well.
- Put cover on and bake for 45 minutes in a preheated oven. Take off the cover and cook for another 15 minutes.

Nutrition Information

- Calories: 275 calories;
- Protein: 18.5
- Total Fat: 12.8
- Sodium: 1107
- Total Carbohydrate: 21.1
- Cholesterol: 55

133. Pork Chops In Red Sauce

Serving: 4 | Prep: 10mins | Cook: 1hours | Ready in:

Ingredients

- 4 center cut pork chops
- 1 onion, sliced
- 1 to taste salt and pepper to taste
- 1 cube beef bouillon
- 1/2 cup hot water
- 1 (10.75 ounce) can condensed tomato soup

Direction

- Set the oven to 190°C or 375°F to preheat.

- Heat a big skillet coated lightly with oil on moderately high heat. In the hot skillet, brown both sides of pork chops.
- Put in a casserole dish with pork chops and arrange sliced onions on top to cover. In hot water, dissolve bouillon cube and mix with tomato soup. Add over pork chops with soup mixture.
- Cover the casserole. In the preheated oven, bake for an hour.

Nutrition Information

- Calories: 150 calories;
- Sodium: 862
- Total Carbohydrate: 12.9
- Cholesterol: 35
- Protein: 15.4
- Total Fat: 4.2

134. Portuguese Cod Fish Casserole

Serving: 6 | Prep: 20mins | Cook: 45mins | Ready in:

Ingredients

- 2 pounds salted cod fish
- 5 large potatoes, peeled and sliced
- 3 large onions, sliced
- 3/4 cup olive oil
- 2 cloves garlic, minced
- 1 tablespoon chopped fresh parsley
- 1 1/2 teaspoons crushed red pepper flakes
- 1 teaspoon paprika
- 3 tablespoons tomato sauce

Direction

- Steep salted cod in cold water overnight or for several hours. Drain water, repeat the step. Heat a big pot of water till boiling. Cook cod for 5 minutes; drain and let it cool down, leaving cod in big pieces. Put aside.
- Preheat oven to 190 degrees C (375 degrees F).
- Layer 1/2 of the potato slices, all of the cod, and all of the onions in one 11x8 casserole dish. Add the leftover slices of potato on top. Whisk tomato sauce, paprika, pepper flakes, parsley, garlic, and olive oil in a small-sized bowl. Add equally on top of casserole.
- Bake in preheated oven till potatoes are soft for 45 minutes.

Nutrition Information

- Calories: 953 calories;
- Protein: 101
- Total Fat: 31.1
- Sodium: 10693
- Total Carbohydrate: 63.8
- Cholesterol: 230

135. Potato Crusted Scallops

Serving: 4 | Prep: 5mins | Cook: 15mins | Ready in:

Ingredients

- 4 cups potato chips, crushed
- 1 pound sea scallops (12-15 per pound)

Direction

- Set the oven to 190°C or 375°F to preheat. Use cooking spray to coat a baking sheet slightly.
- In a shallow dish, arrange potato chips, then roll the scallops into potato chips until covered. On the prepped baking sheet, arrange coated scallops.
- Bake for 15-20 minutes, until cooked through.

Nutrition Information

- Calories: 476 calories;
- Total Carbohydrate: 35.1
- Cholesterol: 68
- Protein: 32.4

- Total Fat: 23.5
- Sodium: 642

136. Pressure Cooker Chicken With Duck Sauce

Serving: 4 | Prep: 10mins | Cook: 20mins | Ready in:

Ingredients

- 1 tablespoon olive oil
- 1 (3 pound) whole chicken, cut into pieces
- salt and pepper to taste
- 1/2 teaspoon paprika
- 1/2 teaspoon dried marjoram
- 1/4 cup white wine
- 1/4 cup chicken broth
- DUCK SAUCE:
- 1/4 cup apricot preserves
- 2 tablespoons white vinegar
- 1 1/2 teaspoons minced fresh ginger root
- 2 tablespoons honey

Direction

- Without covering, heat olive oil in the pressure cooker over medium-high heat. Put in chicken and fry until evenly brown on all sides as equally as possible. Take chicken out from the cooker and sprinkle with marjoram, paprika, salt and pepper to season. Drain and remove fat from the cooker. Pour in wine and chicken broth, scraping any bits of food that are stuck to the bottom and return chicken back to the cooker.
- Seal the lid and set cooker over medium-high heat. Bring to high pressure until the chicken is tender, about 8 minutes. Decrease pressure then open the lid. Chicken meat should have an internal temperature of 180°F (82°C).
- Transfer chicken to a serving plate. In the pot, combine vinegar, ginger, honey and the apricot preserves. Bring to a boil and cook for about 10 minutes, without covering, until sauce is reduced into a syrupy and thick consistency. Serve chicken topped with the prepared sauce.

Nutrition Information

- Calories: 552 calories;
- Protein: 46.1
- Total Fat: 29.1
- Sodium: 295
- Total Carbohydrate: 22.3
- Cholesterol: 146

137. Punjabi Chicken In Thick Gravy

Serving: 8 | Prep: 25mins | Cook: 1hours5mins | Ready in:

Ingredients

- 2 tablespoons vegetable oil
- 2 tablespoons ghee (clarified butter)
- 8 chicken legs, skin removed
- 1 teaspoon cumin seeds
- 1 onion, finely chopped
- 5 cloves garlic, minced
- 2 tablespoons minced fresh ginger root
- 1 small tomato, coarsely chopped
- 1 tablespoon tomato paste
- 1 tablespoon garam masala
- 1 tablespoon ground turmeric
- 1 teaspoon salt, or to taste
- 1 serrano chile pepper, seeded and minced
- 1 cup water
- 1/4 cup chopped fresh cilantro

Direction

- In a big pot, heat ghee and oil on medium heat. Cook cumin seeds in oil till seeds start to change in color.
- Mix chopped onion in; stir and cook for 5 minutes till onion is translucent and soft. Add

ginger and garlic; cook for 5 more minutes till onions brown.
- Mix water, serrano pepper, salt, turmeric, garam masala, tomato paste and chopped tomato in; simmer for 5 minutes. Put chicken in sauce. Gently mix to coat legs; cover pan. Lower heat to medium-low. Cook for 40 minutes till chicken isn't pink near the bone. Use cilantro to garnish; serve.

Nutrition Information

- Calories: 325 calories;
- Total Fat: 21.5
- Sodium: 394
- Total Carbohydrate: 4.3
- Cholesterol: 102
- Protein: 27.7

138. Quick Breakfast In A Pita

Serving: 2 | Prep: 1mins | Cook: 6mins | Ready in:

Ingredients

- 1 pita bread, cut in half
- 2 eggs
- salt and pepper to taste
- 1/2 cup cooked and diced potatoes

Direction

- Set oven to 350°F (175°C) to preheat. Warm pita bread in the oven.
- Heat a medium skillet over high heat. Coat the skillet with cooking spray. Add potatoes and sauté for about 5 minutes until lightly browned. Lower heat to medium and add eggs. Gently stir for about 45 seconds until eggs are firm. Add pepper and salt for seasoning. Take pita out of the oven. Fill egg and potato mixture into pita bread. Serve right away.

Nutrition Information

- Calories: 184 calories;
- Cholesterol: 186
- Protein: 9.7
- Total Fat: 5.4
- Sodium: 232
- Total Carbohydrate: 24

139. Quick Gnocchi

Serving: 2 | Prep: 10mins | Cook: 5mins | Ready in:

Ingredients

- 1 cup dry potato flakes
- 1 cup boiling water
- 1 egg, beaten
- 1 teaspoon salt
- 1/8 teaspoon ground black pepper
- 1 1/2 cups all-purpose flour

Direction

- Transfer potato flakes into a medium-size bowl. Add in boiling water and mix until well blend. Leave the potato to cool.
- Mix in pepper, egg, and salt. Mix in right amount of flour to form a fairly stiff dough. Flip out the dough onto a well-floured board and then knead gently.
- Separate the dough in half. Fold each half into a long thin roll to the thickness of a breadstick. Chop into bite-size pieces with a floured knife.
- Put several gnocchi into boiling water. When gnocchi floats to the surface of the pot, remove them using a slotted spoon. Repeat this until all of them are cooked.

Nutrition Information

- Calories: 462 calories;
- Sodium: 1225
- Total Carbohydrate: 91.3
- Cholesterol: 93

- Protein: 14.8
- Total Fat: 3.5

140. Quick Vegan Veggie Sandwich

Serving: 1 | Prep: 20mins | Cook: 5mins | Ready in:

Ingredients

- 1 tablespoon extra-virgin olive oil
- 1 small garlic clove, finely chopped
- 1/2 small tomato, finely chopped
- 1/4 green bell pepper, finely chopped
- 1/4 red onion, finely chopped
- salt and ground black pepper to taste
- 2 slices multigrain bread
- 1 tablespoon hummus spread
- 1 tablespoon vegan mayonnaise (such as Follow Your Heart® Vegenaise)
- salt and ground black pepper to taste
- 4 sun-dried tomatoes packed in oil, drained and chopped
- 2 leaves lettuce, or more to taste

Direction

- In a frying pan, heat garlic and olive oil on medium for a minute. Put in onion, bell pepper and tomato. Cook for 4 minutes until soft. Flavor with pepper and salt, then take away from the heat.
- Toast the bread slices while cooking the vegetables. Spread hummus over one slice. Spread the vegan mayonnaise over the other, the flavor lightly with pepper and salt.
- Arrange the cooked vegetables, lettuce, and sun-dried tomatoes on a slice, then put the remaining slice on top. Halve the sandwich.

Nutrition Information

- Calories: 293 calories;
- Sodium: 661

- Total Carbohydrate: 38.2
- Cholesterol: 0
- Protein: 10.7
- Total Fat: 12.3

141. Quick And Easy Vegetable Curry

Serving: 5 | Prep: | Cook: | Ready in:

Ingredients

- 1 tablespoon olive oil
- 1 onion, chopped
- 2 cloves crushed garlic
- 2 1/2 tablespoons curry powder
- 2 tablespoons tomato paste
- 1 (14.5 ounce) can diced tomatoes
- 1 cube vegetable bouillon
- 1 (10 ounce) package frozen mixed vegetables
- 1 1/2 cups water
- salt and pepper to taste
- 2 tablespoons chopped fresh cilantro

Direction

- In the big sauce pan on medium high, heat the oil and sauté the garlic and onion till golden. Mix in the tomato paste and curry powder, cook 2-3 minutes.
- Whisk in the pepper and salt to taste, water, mixed vegetables, vegetable bouillon cube and tomatoes. Cook about half an hour till the veggies cooked well yet not crunchy. Drizzle with the fresh cilantro before serving.

Nutrition Information

- Calories: 103 calories;
- Sodium: 267
- Total Carbohydrate: 15.7
- Cholesterol: 0
- Protein: 3.5
- Total Fat: 3.5

142. RamJam Chicken

Serving: 8 | Prep: 20mins | Cook: 15mins | Ready in:

Ingredients

- 1/4 cup soy sauce
- 3 tablespoons dry white wine
- 2 tablespoons lemon juice
- 2 tablespoons vegetable oil
- 3/4 teaspoon dried Italian-style seasoning
- 1 teaspoon grated fresh ginger root
- 1 clove garlic, crushed
- 1/4 teaspoon onion powder
- 1 pinch ground black pepper
- 8 skinless, boneless chicken breast halves - cut into strips

Direction

- Mix together ground black pepper, onion powder, garlic, ginger, Italian-style seasoning, oil, lemon juice, wine and soy sauce in a big resealable plastic bag. In the bag, put chicken and seal. Allow chicken to marinate in the fridge for a minimum of 3 hours to overnight.
- Preheat an outdoor grill for moderately-high heat.
- Thread chicken onto skewers and put aside. In a small saucepan, add marinade and bring to a boil over high heat.
- Coat the grill grate slightly with oil and cook the chicken on prepped grill while basting with the sauce for a few times, about 8 minutes on each side. Chicken is done once juices run clear.

Nutrition Information

- Calories: 303 calories;
- Total Fat: 9.1
- Sodium: 568
- Total Carbohydrate: 1.5
- Cholesterol: 134
- Protein: 49.6

143. Red Beans And Spaghetti

Serving: 8 | Prep: 12hours | Cook: 1hours30mins | Ready in:

Ingredients

- 1/2 pound dry kidney beans, soaked overnight
- 1 (16 ounce) package uncooked spaghetti
- salt to taste

Direction

- Wash the beans and place them in a large pot. Immerse the beans with water and let it boil over medium-high heat. Adjust the heat to medium-low and bring to simmer for 1 hour. Cover the pot partially and simmer until the beans are soft. To prevent it from drying out and scorching, add more water in the pot as necessary.
- Add spaghetti once the beans are soft and let it cook until al dente. Add salt according to your taste.

Nutrition Information

- Calories: 303 calories;
- Total Fat: 1.1
- Sodium: 7
- Total Carbohydrate: 59.2
- Cholesterol: 0
- Protein: 13.7

144. Rice Noodles With Shiitakes, Choy, And Chiles

Serving: 4 | Prep: | Cook: | Ready in:

Ingredients

- 2 1/2 tablespoons soy sauce
- 3 tablespoons sake
- 2 tablespoons balsamic vinegar
- 2 teaspoons white sugar
- 3 tablespoons water
- 2 teaspoons cornstarch
- 1 tablespoon canola oil
- 2 tablespoons dark sesame oil
- 2 cloves garlic, sliced
- 6 whole dried red chile peppers, seeded and diced
- 1 tablespoon minced fresh ginger root
- 1 medium head bok choy, cut into 1 1/2 inch strips
- 20 fresh shiitake mushrooms, stemmed and quartered
- 8 green onions, halved lengthwise
- 2 (9 ounce) packages fresh rice noodles
- 2 tablespoons sesame seeds, toasted

Direction

- Mix cornstarch, water, sugar, vinegar, sherry or sake, and soy sauce in a small bowl. In a wok or big skillet, heat oils on high heat. When oil is almost smoking. Add hot peppers and garlic. Take wok or skillet off heat once 10 seconds pass.
- Bring heat down to medium-high then put wok or skillet back on heat. Add green onions, shiitakes, bok choy, and ginger. Cook on high heat for 3 minutes, constantly stirring. Add soaked or fresh rice noodles and soy sauce mixture together. Cook for another 2 minutes or until noodles are tender and hot. Immediately serve noodles with toasted sesame seeds on top.

Nutrition Information

- Calories: 486 calories;
- Sodium: 728
- Total Carbohydrate: 77.5
- Cholesterol: 0
- Protein: 10.5
- Total Fat: 13.3

145. Rice With Black Beans

Serving: 8 | Prep: 5mins | Cook: 15mins | Ready in:

Ingredients

- 1 onion, chopped
- 1 tablespoon vegetable oil
- 1 (14.5 ounce) can stewed tomatoes
- 1 (15 ounce) can black beans, undrained
- 1/2 teaspoon dried oregano
- 1/2 teaspoon garlic powder
- 1 cup instant white rice

Direction

- In a large saucepan, cook and stir onion in oil until translucent and tender, but not brown. Put in garlic powder, oregano, beans and tomatoes. Heat to a boil. Mix in rice, bring the mixture to a boil. Lower the heat to simmer, and cover.
- Allow the mixture to simmer for 5 minutes. Take off from heat and rest for 5 minutes to serve.

Nutrition Information

- Calories: 80 calories;
- Total Fat: 2
- Sodium: 114
- Total Carbohydrate: 14.4
- Cholesterol: 0
- Protein: 1.6

146. Roast Leg Of Lamb With Rosemary

Serving: 6 | Prep: 15mins | Cook: 1hours20mins | Ready in:

Ingredients

- 1/4 cup honey
- 2 tablespoons prepared Dijon-style mustard
- 2 tablespoons chopped fresh rosemary
- 1 teaspoon freshly ground black pepper
- 1 teaspoon lemon zest
- 3 cloves garlic, minced
- 5 pounds whole leg of lamb
- 1 teaspoon coarse sea salt

Direction

- Mix garlic, lemon zest, ground black pepper, rosemary, mustard and honey well in a small bowl; apply to lamb. Cover; marinate overnight in the fridge.
- Preheat an oven to 230°C/450°F.
- Put lamb onto a rack in a roasting pan; sprinkle salt to taste.
- Bake for 20 minutes at 230°C/450°F; lower heat to 200°C/400°F. Roast to get medium-rare for 55-60 minutes; internal temperature should be at least 63°C/145°F using a meat thermometer. Rest roast for 10 minutes; carve.

Nutrition Information

- Calories: 922 calories;
- Total Fat: 64.6
- Sodium: 631
- Total Carbohydrate: 13.6
- Cholesterol: 261
- Protein: 67.9

147. Roasted Leeks With Eggs (Paleo And Keto Friendly)

Serving: 2 | Prep: 25mins | Cook: 15mins | Ready in:

Ingredients

- 2 leeks
- 3 green onions
- 2 tablespoons ghee (clarified butter), melted
- 1/2 teaspoon sea salt
- 1/4 teaspoon ground black pepper
- Avocado Vinaigrette:
- 1 ripe avocado, pitted, flesh scooped from skin
- 3/4 cup light olive oil
- 1 lemon, juiced
- 1/4 cup red wine vinegar
- salt and ground black pepper to taste
- 1 teaspoon olive oil
- 2 eggs
- 1/4 cup sliced almonds, toasted
- 1/8 teaspoon red pepper flakes

Direction

- Set an oven to 200°C (400°F) to preheat.
- Get rid of the bottom 1/2 inch and green tops of the leeks. Halve the leeks lengthwise.
- On a sheet pan, put the green onions and leeks and drizzle ghee on top. Add pepper and sea salt.
- Roast for 15-20 minutes in the preheated oven until brown.
- Prepare the vinaigrette: In a food processor, thoroughly blend the pepper, salt, vinegar, lemon juice, 3/4 cup olive oil and avocado.
- In a skillet, heat 1 tsp. of oil on medium-low heat. Break the eggs into the opposite sides of the skillet and cook for 2-3 minutes, until the yolks are still runny, and the whites barely set.
- Take out the onions and leeks from the oven and put the sunny side up eggs on top. Sprinkle with red pepper flakes and almonds, then drizzle avocado vinaigrette on top to finish.

Nutrition Information

- Calories: 1219 calories;
- Sodium: 608
- Total Carbohydrate: 27.8
- Cholesterol: 196
- Protein: 11.8
- Total Fat: 124.6

148. Roasted Rack Of Lamb

Serving: 4 | Prep: 20mins | Cook: 20mins | Ready in:

Ingredients

- 1/2 cup fresh bread crumbs
- 2 tablespoons minced garlic
- 2 tablespoons chopped fresh rosemary
- 1 teaspoon salt
- 1/4 teaspoon black pepper
- 2 tablespoons olive oil
- 1 (7 bone) rack of lamb, trimmed and frenched
- 1 teaspoon salt
- 1 teaspoon black pepper
- 2 tablespoons olive oil
- 1 tablespoon Dijon mustard

Direction

- Preheat an oven to 230 degrees C (450 degrees F). Set the oven rack into the middle position.
- Mix 1/4 teaspoon pepper, 1 teaspoon salt, rosemary, garlic and bread crumbs in a large bowl. Toss in two tablespoons of olive oil in order to moisten the mixture. Reserve.
- Season all over the rack with pepper and salt. Over high heat, heat two tablespoons of olive oil in a large heavy oven proof skillet, then sear the rack of lamb for 1 to 2 minutes on all sides. Reserve for several minutes. Use mustard to brush the rack of lamb, then roll in bread crumb mixture until coated evenly. To prevent charring, cover the ends of bones with foil.
- Arrange the rack in the skillet with bone side down, then roast lamb in the preheated oven for 12 to 18 minutes depending on your desired doneness. Measure the temperature in the middle of meat using a meat thermometer after 10 to 12 minutes and take out the meat or cook for longer to suit your taste. Leave it to rest for 5 to 7 minutes while loosely covered, prior to carving in between the ribs.

Nutrition Information

- Calories: 481 calories;
- Total Fat: 40.8
- Sodium: 1369
- Total Carbohydrate: 5.6
- Cholesterol: 94
- Protein: 22.2

149. Rosemary Braised Lamb Shanks

Serving: 6 | Prep: 30mins | Cook: 2hours | Ready in:

Ingredients

- 6 lamb shanks
- salt and pepper to taste
- 2 tablespoons olive oil
- 2 onions, chopped
- 3 large carrots, cut into 1/4 inch rounds
- 10 cloves garlic, minced
- 1 (750 milliliter) bottle red wine
- 1 (28 ounce) can whole peeled tomatoes with juice
- 1 (10.5 ounce) can condensed chicken broth
- 1 (10.5 ounce) can beef broth
- 5 teaspoons chopped fresh rosemary
- 2 teaspoons chopped fresh thyme

Direction

- Scatter pepper and salt on shanks. In Dutch oven or heavy big pot, heat the oil over medium-high heat. Let the shanks cook in batches for 8 minutes till all sides are brown. Put shanks to a plate.
- To pot, put garlic, carrots and onions, and sauté for 10 minutes till golden brown. Mix in beef broth, chicken broth, tomatoes and wine. Put thyme and rosemary to season. Put shanks back to pot, forcing down to soak. Boil, then lower heat to medium-low. Put cover, and allow to simmer for 2 hours till meat is soft.

- Uncover pot. Let simmer for 20 minutes more. To a platter, put the shanks, put in a warm oven. Allow juices in pot to boil for 15 minutes till thickened. Scoop on top of shanks.

Nutrition Information

- Calories: 481 calories;
- Total Fat: 21.8
- Sodium: 759
- Total Carbohydrate: 17.6
- Cholesterol: 93
- Protein: 30.3

150. Salisbury Steak

Serving: 6 | Prep: 20mins | Cook: 20mins | Ready in:

Ingredients

- 1 (10.5 ounce) can condensed French onion soup
- 1 1/2 pounds ground beef
- 1/2 cup dry bread crumbs
- 1 egg
- 1/4 teaspoon salt
- 1/8 teaspoon ground black pepper
- 1 tablespoon all-purpose flour
- 1/4 cup ketchup
- 1/4 cup water
- 1 tablespoon Worcestershire sauce
- 1/2 teaspoon mustard powder

Direction

- In a big bowl, mix together 1/3 cup of condensed French onion soup with bread crumbs, egg, black pepper, salt and ground beef. Form into 6 patties in an oval shape.
- In a big skillet on medium-high heat, brown each side of the patties. Get rid of excess fat.
- Mix the rest of the soup and flour until smooth in a small bowl. Mix in water, mustard powder, Worcestershire sauce and ketchup. Put on the meat in the skillet. Cover and cook for 20 minutes with occasional stirring.

Nutrition Information

- Calories: 440 calories;
- Cholesterol: 127
- Protein: 23
- Total Fat: 32.3
- Sodium: 818
- Total Carbohydrate: 14.1

151. Salmon With Brown Sugar Glaze

Serving: 4 | Prep: 5mins | Cook: 10mins | Ready in:

Ingredients

- 1/4 cup packed light brown sugar
- 2 tablespoons Dijon mustard
- 4 (6 ounce) boneless salmon fillets
- salt and ground black pepper to taste

Direction

- Turn on the oven's broiler to preheat; position the oven rack at about 6 inches apart from direct heat. Spray the broiler pan rack with cooking spray.
- Use pepper and salt to season the salmon; place it onto the broiler pan. In a small bowl, whisk Dijon mustard and brown sugar together. Use a spoon to spread mixture on top of the salmon fillets evenly.
- Cook for 10-15 minutes under preheated broiler until the fish can be easily flaked using a fork.

Nutrition Information

- Calories: 330 calories;
- Protein: 29
- Total Fat: 16.2

- Sodium: 310
- Total Carbohydrate: 15
- Cholesterol: 83

152. Sarma (Stuffed Cabbage)

Serving: 6 | Prep: 15mins | Cook: 3hours | Ready in:

Ingredients

- 1 large head cabbage
- 1 pound lean ground beef
- 1/2 pound ground pork
- 1/2 pound ground ham
- 1 cup uncooked long-grain white rice
- 1 onion, finely chopped
- 1 egg
- 1/2 teaspoon garlic powder
- 1 teaspoon salt
- 1 teaspoon coarse ground black pepper
- 1 pound sauerkraut
- 1 cup tomato juice
- water to cover

Direction

- In the freezer, keep cabbage for several days. Take cabbage out of the freezer to thaw on the night prior to making rolls.
- Mix well together pepper, salt, garlic powder, egg, onion, rice, ham, pork and beef in a big bowl. Shape the meat mixture into oblong balls with 1/2 cup of the mixture at a time. Then wrap each ball with cabbage leaf.
- In the bottom of a big pot, spread the sauerkraut and top with cabbage rolls, seam-side facing down. Drizzle rolls with tomato juice and put in enough amount of water to cover. Bring to a boil then lower heat to low and simmer about 3 hours while putting in additional water as needed.

Nutrition Information

- Calories: 532 calories;
- Total Fat: 22.7
- Sodium: 1135
- Total Carbohydrate: 43.8
- Cholesterol: 141
- Protein: 38.4

153. Scott Hibb's Amazing Whisky Grilled Baby Back Ribs

Serving: 4 | Prep: 20mins | Cook: 2hours40mins | Ready in:

Ingredients

- 2 (2 pound) slabs baby back pork ribs
- coarsely ground black pepper
- 1 tablespoon ground red chile pepper
- 2 1/4 tablespoons vegetable oil
- 1/2 cup minced onion
- 1 1/2 cups water
- 1/2 cup tomato paste
- 1/2 cup white vinegar
- 1/2 cup brown sugar
- 2 1/2 tablespoons honey
- 2 tablespoons Worcestershire sauce
- 2 teaspoons salt
- 1/4 teaspoon coarsely ground black pepper
- 1 1/4 teaspoons liquid smoke flavoring
- 2 teaspoons whiskey
- 2 teaspoons garlic powder
- 1/4 teaspoon paprika
- 1/2 teaspoon onion powder
- 1 tablespoon dark molasses
- 1/2 tablespoon ground red chile pepper

Direction

- Set the oven to 300°F (150°C) to preheat.
- Chop each rack of ribs in half, so you've got 4 half racks. Sprinkle the ribs with salt, 1 tbsp. of chili pepper, and pepper (more pepper than salt). Use an aluminum foil to wrap each of the half racks. Let them bake for 2 1/2 hours.

- In the meantime, put oil in a medium saucepan and heat it over medium heat. Stir in onions and cook for 5 minutes. Mix in honey, Worcestershire sauce, water, brown sugar, tomato paste, and vinegar. Season the mixture with liquid smoke, onion powder, 2 tsp. of salt, whiskey, 1/2 tbsp. of ground chile pepper, garlic powder, 1/4 tsp. of black pepper, paprika, and dark molasses. Boil the mixture; reduce the heat. Simmer the mixture for 1 1/4 hours, uncovered, until thickened. Remove it from the heat; put aside.
- Set an outdoor grill over high heat to preheat.
- Get the ribs from the oven and let them stand for 10 minutes. Remove the racks from the aluminum foil and place them into the grill. Grill each side of the ribs for 3-4 minutes. Brush them with the sauce while grilling, just before serving them (make sure not to add the sauce too early to prevent it from burning).

Nutrition Information

- Calories: 1043 calories;
- Total Fat: 68.5
- Sodium: 1720
- Total Carbohydrate: 54.7
- Cholesterol: 234
- Protein: 50.7

154. Seared Ahi Tuna Steaks

Serving: 2 | Prep: 5mins | Cook: 12mins | Ready in:

Ingredients

- 2 (5 ounce) ahi tuna steaks
- 1 teaspoon kosher salt
- 1/4 teaspoon cayenne pepper
- 1/2 tablespoon butter
- 2 tablespoons olive oil
- 1 teaspoon whole peppercorns

Direction

- Sprinkle cayenne pepper and salt on the tuna steaks to taste.
- Put the butter and olive oil in a skillet and let the butter melt over medium-high heat. Let the peppercorns cook for about 5 minutes until the peppercorns pop and become soft. Put the seasoned tuna steaks carefully into the skillet and let it cook until the desired doneness is achieved (1 1/2 minutes each side if you want it rare).

Nutrition Information

- Calories: 301 calories;
- Sodium: 1034
- Total Carbohydrate: 0.7
- Cholesterol: 71
- Protein: 33.3
- Total Fat: 17.8

155. Shrimp Asopao

Serving: 8 | Prep: 35mins | Cook: 35mins | Ready in:

Ingredients

- 1 pound shrimp, peeled and deveined
- 1/2 teaspoon salt
- 1/2 teaspoon ground black pepper
- 1 tablespoon adobo seasoning
- 3 tablespoons olive oil
- 1/2 green bell pepper, diced
- 1/2 red bell pepper, diced
- 1 small tomato, seeded and diced
- 1 small onion, diced
- 3 cloves garlic, minced
- 1 tablespoon tomato paste
- 1 1/2 cups short-grain rice
- 7 cups water
- 1 bay leaf
- crushed red pepper to taste
- 3/4 cup frozen petite peas

Direction

- Season shrimp with adobo seasoning, salt, and pepper and reserve.
- Over medium-high heat, heat olive oil in a large, deep pot, add the onion, tomato, green bell pepper, and red bell pepper and then cook in the hot oil until onion becomes soft. Stir in the tomato paste and garlic. Mix in rice until it's coated. Add in the water. Place in the bay leaf. Heat the mixture to a boil, decrease the heat to medium-low and let to simmer for about 20 minutes. Place in the peas and the seasoned shrimp. Let cook for about 5 minutes until the shrimp turns pink. Remove from the heat source immediately.

Nutrition Information

- Calories: 263 calories;
- Protein: 15.1
- Total Fat: 6.5
- Sodium: 265
- Total Carbohydrate: 35.2
- Cholesterol: 86

156. Simple Country Ribs

Serving: 4 | Prep: 10mins | Cook: 1hours | Ready in:

Ingredients

- 2 1/2 pounds pork spareribs
- 2 (18 ounce) bottles barbeque sauce
- 1 onion, quartered
- 1 teaspoon salt
- 1/2 teaspoon ground black pepper

Direction

- In a big stock pot, put the spareribs together with pepper, salt, onion and barbeque sauce. Add in sufficient water to submerge. Let come to a gentle boil, and allow to cook for about 40 minutes.
- Preheat the grill for high heat.
- Grease grate lightly. Take the spareribs off the stock pot, and put on prepped grill. Baste ribs with barbeque sauce in the saucepan as it cooks. Let the ribs grill for 20 minutes, basting and flipping often, or till well browned.

Nutrition Information

- Calories: 882 calories;
- Protein: 36.4
- Total Fat: 38.3
- Sodium: 3518
- Total Carbohydrate: 94.1
- Cholesterol: 150

157. Sirloin Marinara

Serving: 8 | Prep: 15mins | Cook: 15mins | Ready in:

Ingredients

- 2 tablespoons olive oil
- 1 onion, thinly sliced
- 2 pounds top sirloin steak, sliced
- 2 cups chunky pasta sauce
- 2 cloves garlic, minced
- 1/2 cup red wine

Direction

- In a 10-inch skillet, heat the oil on medium-high heat; add the onions and sauté for about 5 minutes until becoming tender. Add the steak strips, then flip so that they get brown on all sides, approximately 10 minutes.
- Add the red wine, garlic and tomato sauce. Lower the heat to low and let it simmer for 10-15 minutes or until the steak becomes cooked through.

Nutrition Information

- Calories: 276 calories;
- Total Fat: 15.4

- Sodium: 300
- Total Carbohydrate: 10.5
- Cholesterol: 62
- Protein: 20

158. Slow Cooked Squirrel

Serving: 6 | Prep: 20mins | Cook: 8hours | Ready in:

Ingredients

- 2 squirrels - skinned, gutted, and cut into pieces
- 4 large potatoes, quartered
- 1 pound carrots, chopped
- 1 green bell pepper, chopped
- 4 onions, sliced
- 2 cups water
- 1/4 medium head cabbage
- 1 teaspoon salt
- 1 teaspoon ground black pepper

Direction

- Put the ground black pepper, salt, cabbage, water, onions, green bell pepper, carrots, potatoes and squirrel meat in a slow cooker.
- Put on cover and let it cook for 8 hours on low setting.

Nutrition Information

- Calories: 314 calories;
- Sodium: 500
- Total Carbohydrate: 59.1
- Cholesterol: 42
- Protein: 16.4
- Total Fat: 2.2

159. Slow Cooker Barbeque

Serving: 8 | Prep: 10mins | Cook: 9hours | Ready in:

Ingredients

- 1 (3 pound) boneless chuck roast
- 1 teaspoon garlic powder
- 1 teaspoon onion powder
- salt and pepper to taste
- 1 (18 ounce) bottle barbeque sauce

Direction

- In the slow cooker, place the roast. Dust with onion powder and garlic powder, then flavor with pepper and salt. Spread barbeque sauce over. Cook on Low for 6 - 8 hours.
- Take the meat out of the slow cooker, shred, then put it back. Cook for 1 hour more. Serve hot.

Nutrition Information

- Calories: 343 calories;
- Protein: 20.5
- Total Fat: 17.9
- Sodium: 895
- Total Carbohydrate: 23.3
- Cholesterol: 74

160. Slow Cooker Barbequed Pork For Sandwiches

Serving: 12 | Prep: 10mins | Cook: 7hours | Ready in:

Ingredients

- 2 1/2 pounds boneless pork roast
- salt and ground black pepper to taste
- 2 cups strong brewed coffee
- 2 tablespoons Worcestershire sauce
- 2 tablespoons bourbon whiskey
- 10 cloves garlic
- 3 cups beef broth
- 1 cup water
- 1 small onion, diced
- 1 pinch crushed red pepper flakes

- 2 (12 ounce) bottles barbeque sauce

Direction

- Use pepper and salt to season roast. In a slow cooker, put seasoned roast, Worcestershire sauce, coffee, red pepper flakes, onion, water, beef broth, garlic and bourbon whiskey, then set to low setting. Cook for 3-4 hours. Take garlic cloves out of the cooker and use a fork to mash them, then bring mashed garlic back to the slow cooker. Cook for 3-4 hours more.
- Remove roast to a big cutting board and get rid of liquid. Use 2 forks to shred the roast into strands, then bring the meat back to slow cooker. Stir in barbecue sauce and keep on cooking for 1-3 hours on low setting.

Nutrition Information

- Calories: 224 calories;
- Total Fat: 9.2
- Sodium: 914
- Total Carbohydrate: 22.3
- Cholesterol: 37
- Protein: 10.6

161. Slow Cooker Chicken Cacciatore

Serving: 6 | Prep: 15mins | Cook: 9hours | Ready in:

Ingredients

- 6 skinless, boneless chicken breast halves
- 1 (28 ounce) jar spaghetti sauce
- 2 green bell pepper, seeded and cubed
- 8 ounces fresh mushrooms, sliced
- 1 onion, finely diced
- 2 tablespoons minced garlic

Direction

- Place chicken into a slow cooker. Add garlic, onion, mushrooms, green bell peppers and spaghetti sauce on top.
- Cook, covered, for 7-9 hours on Low.

Nutrition Information

- Calories: 261 calories;
- Total Fat: 6.1
- Sodium: 590
- Total Carbohydrate: 23.7
- Cholesterol: 63
- Protein: 27.1

162. Slow Cooker Cranberry Pork

Serving: 6 | Prep: 10mins | Cook: 4hours | Ready in:

Ingredients

- 1 (16 ounce) can cranberry sauce
- 1/3 cup French salad dressing
- 1 onion, sliced
- 1 (3 pound) boneless pork loin roast

Direction

- Stir together the onion, salad dressing and cranberry sauce in a medium bowl. In a slow cooker, put the pork and pour the sauce mixture to cover.
- Put cover and let it cook for 8 hours on Low or 4 hours on High. The pork is done once the internal temperature reaches 63°C (145°F).

Nutrition Information

- Calories: 374 calories;
- Total Carbohydrate: 32.9
- Cholesterol: 80
- Protein: 26.8
- Total Fat: 15.1
- Sodium: 184

163. Slow Cooker Ham And Beans

Serving: 8 | Prep: 10mins | Cook: 12hours | Ready in:

Ingredients

- 1 pound dried great Northern beans, soaked overnight
- 1/2 pound cooked ham, chopped
- 1/2 cup brown sugar
- 1 tablespoon onion powder
- 1 tablespoon dried parsley
- 1/2 teaspoon garlic salt
- 1/2 teaspoon black pepper
- 1/4 teaspoon cayenne pepper
- water to cover

Direction

- In a slow cooker, mix together the cayenne pepper, black pepper, garlic salt, parsley, onion powder, brown sugar, ham and beans. In the slow cooker, pour enough water to cover the mixture by approximately 2 inches. Set the slow cooker to low, then simmer for 12 hours, mixing from time to time.

Nutrition Information

- Calories: 318 calories;
- Cholesterol: 16
- Protein: 17.8
- Total Fat: 5.9
- Sodium: 492
- Total Carbohydrate: 49.8

164. Slow Cooker Honey Garlic Chicken

Serving: 10 | Prep: 20mins | Cook: 4hours | Ready in:

Ingredients

- 1 tablespoon vegetable oil
- 10 boneless, skinless chicken thighs
- 3/4 cup honey
- 3/4 cup lite soy sauce
- 3 tablespoons ketchup
- 2 cloves garlic, crushed
- 1 tablespoon minced fresh ginger root
- 1 (20 ounce) can pineapple tidbits, drained with juice reserved
- 2 tablespoons cornstarch
- 1/4 cup water

Direction

- In a skillet, heat oil on medium heat, then cook chicken thighs in hot oil until just browned evenly on every sides. Transfer thighs into a slow cooker.
- Combine reserved pineapple juice, ginger, garlic, ketchup, soy sauce and honey in a bowl. Add into slow cooker.
- Cook, covered, over high heat, about 4 hours. Mix in pineapple tidbits, then serve.
- In a small bowl, combine water and cornstarch. Take thighs out of the slow cooker. Combine the rest of the sauce in the slow cooker with cornstarch mixture until thickened. Pour sauce on top of the chicken to serve.

Nutrition Information

- Calories: 235 calories;
- Total Fat: 6
- Sodium: 724
- Total Carbohydrate: 34.4
- Cholesterol: 42
- Protein: 13

165. Slow Cooker Latin Chicken

Serving: 6 | Prep: 25mins | Cook: 4hours10mins | Ready in:

Ingredients

- 1 tablespoon olive oil
- 3 pounds skinless chicken thighs
- salt and ground black pepper to taste
- 1/4 cup loosely packed cilantro leaves
- 2 large sweet potatoes, cut into chunks
- 1 red bell pepper, cut into strips
- 2 (15.5 ounce) cans black beans, rinsed and drained
- 1/2 cup chicken broth
- 1/4 cup loosely packed cilantro leaves
- 1 cup hot salsa
- 2 teaspoons ground cumin
- 1/2 teaspoon ground allspice
- 3 large cloves garlic, chopped
- lime wedges, for garnish

Direction

- In a big skillet, heat olive oil and use pepper and salt to season chicken thighs. Sprinkle chicken thigh with 1/4 cup of cilantro, then brown chicken for 3-5 minutes per side in the frying pan.
- In the bottom of a slow cooker, arrange chicken. On top of chicken, put black beans, red bell pepper and sweet potatoes. In a bowl, combine garlic, allspice, cumin, salsa, 1/4 cup of cilantro leaves and chicken broth, then put into the slow cooker. Set the slow cooker to low setting and cook about 4 hours. Use lime wedges to decorate to serve.

Nutrition Information

- Calories: 591 calories;
- Total Fat: 18.1
- Sodium: 980
- Total Carbohydrate: 56.9
- Cholesterol: 137
- Protein: 50.2

166. Slow Cooker Lentils And Sausage

Serving: 12 | Prep: 15mins | Cook: 3hours | Ready in:

Ingredients

- 1 (16 ounce) package dry lentils
- 1 (16 ounce) can diced tomatoes, drained
- 2 (14 ounce) cans beef broth
- 3 cups water
- 1 carrot, chopped
- 2 pounds kielbasa (Polish) sausage, cut into 1/2 inch pieces
- 1 stalk celery, chopped

Direction

- Wash lentils (do not soak) then drain. Combine celery, sausage, carrot, water, tomatoes, broth and lentils in a slow cooker.
- Put on cover and cook for 6-7 hours on Low, or 3 hours on High. Mix thoroughly then serve.

Nutrition Information

- Calories: 357 calories;
- Sodium: 966
- Total Carbohydrate: 22.8
- Cholesterol: 50
- Protein: 18.8
- Total Fat: 21.2

167. Slow Cooker Pork

Serving: 8 | Prep: 5mins | Cook: 8hours | Ready in:

Ingredients

- 3 pounds pork shoulder
- 2 (1 ounce) packages taco seasoning mix
- chili powder to taste
- crushed red pepper to taste

Direction

- Put the pork shoulder and taco seasoning into a slow cooker. Put chili powder and/or red pepper flakes, if desired. Put in water until the meat is covered. Put the lid over the pot then cook for 8 hours on low.
- Discard pork shoulder from pot then shred.

Nutrition Information

- Calories: 195 calories;
- Protein: 18.8
- Total Fat: 10.1
- Sodium: 573
- Total Carbohydrate: 4.8
- Cholesterol: 67

168. Slow Cooker Sauerkraut And Sausage

Serving: 5 | Prep: 15mins | Cook: 4hours | Ready in:

Ingredients

- 1 (20 ounce) can sauerkraut
- 1/4 cup brown sugar
- 1 1/2 pounds ground pork sausage
- 1 onion, sliced

Direction

- Mix the brown sugar and sauerkraut in a medium bowl and then transfer to a slow cooker. Spread the onion and sausage on top of the sauerkraut.
- Cook for 2 hours on high, checking for dryness, and adding more water if need be.
- Switch to low setting and then cook for 2 more hours on low.

Nutrition Information

- Calories: 640 calories;
- Total Fat: 55.1
- Sodium: 1653
- Total Carbohydrate: 19
- Cholesterol: 93
- Protein: 17.2

169. Smoky Roll Ups

Serving: 6 | Prep: 10mins | Cook: 25mins | Ready in:

Ingredients

- 3 skinless, boneless chicken breast halves - pounded thin
- 12 slices smoked beef
- 1/2 cup ketchup
- 1/2 cup mayonnaise
- 1/2 cup apricot jam

Direction

- Start preheating the oven at 350°F (175°C).
- Remove the fat from the smoked meat, put a piece on each chicken breast slice and roll. Secure with toothpicks and arrange with seam side down in a 9x13-inch baking dish.
- Combine jam, mayonnaise, and ketchup. Spread the mixture over chicken and bake, without covering, in the prepared oven for 20 to 25 minutes.

Nutrition Information

- Calories: 358 calories;
- Sodium: 1177
- Total Carbohydrate: 23.1
- Cholesterol: 79
- Protein: 25.1

- Total Fat: 19

170. Spaetzle I

Serving: 4 | Prep: 5mins | Cook: 3mins | Ready in:

Ingredients

- 4 cups all-purpose flour
- 5 eggs
- 1 teaspoon salt
- 3/4 cup water

Direction

- Combine salt, eggs, and flour in a big bowl. Add a little bit of water at a time until forming a soft dough.
- In a big pot, boil 2 quarts water and squeeze out the dough into the water by pressing through a large-holed colander or using a fruit/noodle press. Once the noodles float up, about 3 - 4 minutes, they are done. Serve this as a side or a main dish.

Nutrition Information

- Calories: 544 calories;
- Cholesterol: 231
- Protein: 20.7
- Total Fat: 7.4
- Sodium: 769
- Total Carbohydrate: 95.9

171. Spaghetti Al Amatraciana

Serving: 2 | Prep: 15mins | Cook: 15mins | Ready in:

Ingredients

- 1/4 pound thinly sliced pancetta bacon, chopped
- 1 onion, chopped
- 1 teaspoon crushed red pepper flakes
- 1 (14.5 ounce) can crushed tomatoes
- 1/4 cup white wine
- 1/2 pound uncooked spaghetti
- salt and pepper to taste

Direction

- Cook red pepper flakes, onion and bacon in a large skillet on medium heat until onion is soft but not browned.
- Mix in wine and tomatoes; simmer for about 20 minutes. At the same time, boil a large pot of mildly salted water. Put in pasta and cook until firm to the bite, about 8-10 minutes; strain.
- Put pasta into the sauce and toss evenly; simmer for 2-3 more minutes (this will blend the pasta and the sauce). Sprinkle black ground pepper and salt to season; serve right away.

Nutrition Information

- Calories: 798 calories;
- Cholesterol: 39
- Protein: 25.5
- Total Fat: 28.2
- Sodium: 752
- Total Carbohydrate: 106.7

172. Spam On The Go

Serving: 6 | Prep: 10mins | Cook: 10mins | Ready in:

Ingredients

- 1 (8 ounce) package uncooked spaghetti
- 1 tablespoon vegetable oil
- 1 (12 ounce) container fully cooked luncheon meat (e.g. Spam), cubed
- 1/2 green onion, chopped
- 1 clove garlic, chopped

- 1 tablespoon soy sauce
- 1/2 cup water
- 1/2 tablespoon sesame oil
- 1 teaspoon freshly ground black pepper

Direction

- Bring lightly salted water in a large pot to a boil. Cook pasta in boiling water until al dente, for 8 to 10 minutes; drain off water.
- In the meantime, heat vegetable oil over medium heat in a medium saucepan. Sauté garlic, green onion, and luncheon meat in the heated oil until lightly browned. Mix in cooked spaghetti, then mix in pepper, sesame oil, water, and soy sauce. Stir everything well to combine; cook until thoroughly heated and serve right away.

Nutrition Information

- Calories: 346 calories;
- Sodium: 920
- Total Carbohydrate: 30.3
- Cholesterol: 39
- Protein: 12.5
- Total Fat: 19.3

173. Spanish Tortilla

Serving: 4 | Prep: 10mins | Cook: 10mins | Ready in:

Ingredients

- 1/4 cup olive oil
- 2 potatoes, peeled
- 4 slices bacon
- 2 slices cooked ham, diced
- 1/2 onion, thinly sliced
- 1/2 red bell pepper, sliced
- 4 eggs
- 1/4 teaspoon Spanish seasoning

Direction

- Cut edges off of potatoes so that potatoes are roughly square; slice thinly. Over medium heat, heat olive oil in a medium-sized skillet. Put in potatoes and lightly fry. Take potatoes out using a slotted spoon and put aside.
- Add bacon to a big, deep skillet. Cook till browned equally over medium-high heat. Take the bacon out, crumble and put aside. Reserve 1 tablespoon bacon grease and cook red pepper, onion and ham. Take out of the heat.
- Whip Spanish seasoning and eggs together. Add eggs to the skillet along with vegetables. Put in potatoes and bacon. Cook but do not mix over medium heat till the bottom starts to brown. Flip the omelet over and let the both sides brown. Serve while still warm.

Nutrition Information

- Calories: 447 calories;
- Protein: 14.3
- Total Fat: 33.9
- Sodium: 558
- Total Carbohydrate: 22.1
- Cholesterol: 213

174. Spicy Burgers

Serving: 8 | Prep: 15mins | Cook: 10mins | Ready in:

Ingredients

- 2 pounds ground beef
- 2 teaspoons minced garlic
- 2 fresh jalapeno peppers, seeded and minced
- 1 small fresh poblano chile pepper, seeded and minced
- 1 fresh habanero pepper, seeded and minced (optional)
- 1 teaspoon crushed red pepper flakes
- 2 tablespoons chopped fresh cilantro
- 1 teaspoon ground cumin

Direction

- Heat the grill on high heat.
- Mix the beef, jalapeno peppers, garlic, red pepper flakes, habanero pepper, poblano pepper, cumin and cilantro. Shape to burger patties.
- Apply oil to the grate lightly then place the burger on the grill. Cook for 5 minutes on each side or until it's well done.

Nutrition Information

- Calories: 232 calories;
- Sodium: 67
- Total Carbohydrate: 1.1
- Cholesterol: 70
- Protein: 19.1
- Total Fat: 16.4

175. Spicy Couscous With Dates

Serving: 2 | Prep: 10mins | Cook: 20mins | Ready in:

Ingredients

- 1 tablespoon olive oil
- 1 medium onion, chopped
- 2 whole star anise pods
- salt to taste
- 3 cloves garlic, peeled and chopped
- 1/2 red bell pepper, chopped
- 2 dried hot red peppers, diced
- 1/2 teaspoon ground black pepper
- 4 large fresh mushrooms, chopped
- 1 tablespoon lemon juice
- 1/4 cup chopped dates
- 1 teaspoon ground cinnamon
- 1 cup uncooked couscous
- 1 1/2 cups vegetable stock

Direction

- Take a medium-sized saucepan and heat on medium heat. Stir fry onion until it becomes tender. Season using salt and anise pods. Add in black pepper, dried hot red peppers, red bell pepper and garlic. Cook while stirring until vegetables become tender.
- Add lemon juice and mushrooms to the vegetables. Add in cinnamon and dates. Let it simmer for 10 minutes on low heat.
- Put couscous in a saucepan and pour in vegetable stock to cover. Let it boil. Lower heat to low and simmer for 3-5 minutes while covered until all the moisture is absorbed.
- Use fork to fluff couscous then mix in vegetables before serving.

Nutrition Information

- Calories: 594 calories;
- Total Fat: 10.6
- Sodium: 315
- Total Carbohydrate: 111.9
- Cholesterol: 0
- Protein: 18

176. Spicy Grilled Chicken

Serving: 6 | Prep: 15mins | Cook: 15mins | Ready in:

Ingredients

- 1/3 cup vegetable oil
- 2 tablespoons lime juice
- 1/2 teaspoon grated lime zest
- 2 cloves crushed garlic
- 1 1/2 teaspoons fresh oregano
- 1/4 teaspoon red pepper flakes
- 1 teaspoon salt
- 1/4 teaspoon ground black pepper
- 6 skinless, boneless chicken breast halves

Direction

- In a shallow glass dish, blend black pepper, salt, red pepper flakes, oregano, garlic, lime zest, lime juice, and oil. Put in chicken, and shake to coat. Marinate, covered, in the refrigerator for about 1 hour, flipping on occasion.
- Start preheating grill for medium-high heat.
- Grease the grill grate lightly with oil. Drain chicken, discard marinade. Grill chicken about 6 to 8 minutes per side, until juices run out clear.

Nutrition Information

- Calories: 242 calories;
- Cholesterol: 67
- Protein: 24.6
- Total Fat: 15.1
- Sodium: 446
- Total Carbohydrate: 1

177. Spicy Pasta

Serving: 6 | Prep: 10mins | Cook: 20mins | Ready in:

Ingredients

- 1 (12 ounce) package rotini pasta
- 1 tablespoon vegetable oil
- 1 clove garlic, crushed
- 1 teaspoon dried basil
- 1 teaspoon Italian seasoning
- 1 onion, diced
- 2 red chile peppers, seeded and chopped
- 1 (14.5 ounce) can diced tomatoes
- 3 drops hot pepper sauce
- salt and ground black pepper to taste

Direction

- Boil the lightly salted water in a large pot. In the boiling water, cook pasta until al dente or for 8-10 mins, then drain.
- In the meantime, in a saucepan, heat oil over medium heat. Sauté basil with garlic and the Italian seasoning for 2-3 mins. Mix in chiles and onion, then cook until the onion becomes tender. Mix in the hot sauce and tomatoes, then simmer until heated through or for 5 mins. Toss with cooked pasta. Add pepper and salt to season.

Nutrition Information

- Calories: 134 calories;
- Sodium: 117
- Total Carbohydrate: 22.5
- Cholesterol: 0
- Protein: 4.4
- Total Fat: 2.8

178. Spicy Shredded Beef

Serving: 4 | Prep: 30mins | Cook: 2hours | Ready in:

Ingredients

- 2 tablespoons vegetable oil
- 1 pound lean beef chuck, trimmed and cut into 1 inch cubes
- 1 clove garlic, minced
- 1/2 teaspoon salt
- 1/2 teaspoon ground cumin
- 1 (16 ounce) can diced tomatoes

Direction

- In a big skillet, heat oil. Let beef cubes brown for 10 to 12 minutes. Lower heat, put in cumin, salt and garlic. Cook for 15 minutes longer.
- Put in can of tomatoes and warm to boil. Lower the heat to simmer, put on cover and let cook for 90 to 120 minutes. To skillet, put water as necessary to prevent the mixture from dry out.

- Once cooked extremely tender, let cool, then pull meat apart with 2 forks. Return on heat and mix till most of liquid has vaporized.
- In case preparing to freeze, cool prior to placing in freezer bags and putting in freezer.
- For soft burritos, put warm flour tortilla with grated cheese, salsa and mixture of meat.

Nutrition Information

- Calories: 352 calories;
- Sodium: 630
- Total Carbohydrate: 4
- Cholesterol: 81
- Protein: 20.6
- Total Fat: 27.3

179. Sri Lankan Chicken Curry

Serving: 4 | Prep: 25mins | Cook: 35mins | Ready in:

Ingredients

- 3 (6 ounce) boneless skinless chicken breasts
- 2 tablespoons white vinegar
- 1 teaspoon tamarind juice (optional)
- 1/4 cup Madras curry powder
- 1 tablespoon salt, or to taste
- 1 teaspoon ground black pepper
- 2 tablespoons coconut oil
- 1 red onion, sliced
- 4 green chile peppers, halved lengthwise
- 8 green cardamom pods
- 6 whole cloves
- 12 curry leaves
- 1 teaspoon fresh ginger root, crushed
- 1 (2 inch) cinnamon stick, broken in half
- 3 cloves garlic, minced
- 1/2 cup water
- 1 1/2 tablespoons tomato paste
- 3 tablespoons roasted Madras curry powder
- 1/2 (14 ounce) can coconut milk

Direction

- Chop chicken into the bite-size pieces. In the bowl, mix the pepper, salt, a quarter cup of curry powder, tamarind juice and vinegar. Put in the chicken and coat by tossing.
- Heat coconut oil in the frying pan or wok on medium heat. Cook cinnamon stick, ginger, curry leaves cloves, cardamom pods, green chiles, and sliced onion roughly 5 minutes or till onion becomes tender and translucent. Lower the heat to medium low, keep cooking and mixing for 15-20 minutes longer or till onion becomes soft and dark brown. Mix in garlic and cook for 1 more minute.
- Put in tomato paste, water, and chicken mixture. Mix and let simmer roughly 10 minutes or till chicken become thoroughly cooked. Put in roasted curry powder and mix till evenly dissolved.
- Slowly mix in coconut milk and let simmer for 2 to 3 minutes longer. The coconut milk may curdle if you cook overheat.

Nutrition Information

- Calories: 393 calories;
- Total Carbohydrate: 20.9
- Cholesterol: 73
- Protein: 31.4
- Total Fat: 22.4
- Sodium: 1878

180. Steamed Egg (Chawan Mushi)

Serving: 2 | Prep: 5mins | Cook: 12mins | Ready in:

Ingredients

- 2 eggs
- 1 cup cooled chicken or fish stock
- 1 dash sake
- 1/2 teaspoon soy sauce
- 1/2 cup chopped cooked chicken breast meat
- 1 shiitake mushroom, sliced into strips

- 2 sprigs fresh parsley, for garnish

Direction

- Gently beat the eggs in a medium-sized bowl as you gradually add the sake, soy sauce and chicken stock. In each of the 2 small tea cups, split an even amount of the chicken and mushroom then fill it up with the prepared egg mixture.
- Fill a saucepan or a steamer with about 1 inch of water and let it boil. Lower the heat to a simmer, then put the filled tea cups in the steamer. Cover the steamer and allow the mixture to steam for 12 minutes or until the egg has the silky consistency like tofu and it is already firm but soft in texture. Put a sprig of parsley to garnish on top of each cup and serve.

Nutrition Information

- Calories: 157 calories;
- Total Fat: 8.1
- Sodium: 527
- Total Carbohydrate: 3.3
- Cholesterol: 213
- Protein: 17.3

181. Stuffed Butternut Squash

Serving: 2 | Prep: 30mins | Cook: 1hours25mins | Ready in:

Ingredients

- 1 butternut squash, halved and seeded
- 1/2 cup basmati rice
- 6 Brussels sprouts, trimmed and quartered lengthwise
- 1 medium carrot, peeled, sliced and julienned
- 1/3 (15.5 ounce) can garbanzo beans
- 1/4 cup soy milk
- 3 tablespoons tamari
- 1/2 teaspoon ground turmeric
- 2 cloves garlic, minced

Direction

- Preheat the oven to 400°F (205°C). Pour in an inch of water into the baking dish then insert the squash. Use foil to cover the dish up and put it into the preheated oven. Leave it baking until the squash becomes fork tender, about an hour. Maintain its warmth.
- Fill a saucepan up with water and lead it to boiling point then insert rice and start stirring. Lower the heat. For the next 20 minutes, leave it simmering with a cover on. In a skillet, add the garbanzo beans, carrots and Brussels sprouts at medium high heat. Combine garlic, turmeric, tamari and soymilk then pour this mixture into the skillet. Toss to coat. Leave it simmering with a cover on until the contents tenderize, about 20 minutes. If needed, insert additional soy-tamari mixture or a little bit of water in order to keep it from drying out. Mix vegetable mixture together with rice and add it to the squash by scooping. Before serving, add extra tamari and season to your liking. If desired, serve with a green salad.

Nutrition Information

- Calories: 714 calories;
- Cholesterol: 0
- Protein: 21.5
- Total Fat: 3
- Sodium: 1812
- Total Carbohydrate: 166.2

182. Stuffed Cabbage

Serving: 8 | Prep: 10mins | Cook: 1hours | Ready in:

Ingredients

- 1 large head cabbage
- 1 pound lean ground beef
- 1 egg, beaten

- 1 onion, finely diced
- 3/4 cup cooked white rice
- salt and pepper to taste
- 1 (10.75 ounce) can condensed tomato soup

Direction

- Freeze cabbage in freezer overnight. Take out of freezer. Thaw. Peel leaves away.
- Preheat an oven to 175°C/350°F.
- Mix pepper, salt, onion, egg, rice and beef. Stir together well. Form a small handful to a small ball/roll. In middle of cabbage leaf, put it on. Fold leaves sides over. Roll ball up into leaf. In baking dish, put them, seam side down. Continue till you use all the filling.
- Mix 1/2 can water and soup. Put over stuffed cabbage.
- Bake for 1 hour at 175°C/350°F, uncovered. Baste frequently with sauce.

Nutrition Information

- Calories: 248 calories;
- Total Fat: 13.1
- Sodium: 288
- Total Carbohydrate: 19.6
- Cholesterol: 66
- Protein: 14

183. Summer Salmon Skewers

Serving: 2 | Prep: 30mins | Cook: 8mins | Ready in:

Ingredients

- 2 (6 ounce) skinless salmon fillets, about 1-inch thick, cut into 2-inch strips
- 1/3 cup lemon juice
- 1/4 cup white wine
- 1 tablespoon chopped fresh mint
- 1 tablespoon chopped fresh dill
- 2 tablespoons chopped fresh parsley
- 2 tablespoons minced garlic
- 1 pinch crushed red pepper flakes
- 1/4 cup olive oil

Direction

- Set grill on medium-low to pre-heat.
- Place the salmon in a baking dish. Take a bowl and whisk together wine, lemon juice, garlic, dill, mint, red pepper flakes, and parsley. Continue whisking as you drizzle in olive oil into the same bowl. Pour the marinade over the salmon and let it soak in the fridge for a maximum of 30 minutes.
- Lengthwise thread the salmon onto metal or water-soaked wooden skewers. Grill until cooked through and opaque in middle, about 4 minutes per side. Serve as soon as it's off the grill.

Nutrition Information

- Calories: 561 calories;
- Cholesterol: 83
- Protein: 30
- Total Fat: 43.4
- Sodium: 87
- Total Carbohydrate: 7.8

184. Sweet Coconut Oatmeal

Serving: 3 | Prep: 5mins | Cook: 20mins | Ready in:

Ingredients

- 1 (14 ounce) can coconut milk
- 1 cup rolled oats
- 2 tablespoons honey
- 1/4 cup coconut flakes (optional)
- 2 tablespoons brown sugar, or more to taste
- 1 teaspoon ground cinnamon

Direction

- Bring coconut milk in a small saucepan to a gentle boil over medium-low heat. Mix in

honey and oats; reduce heat and simmer for about 15 minutes until milk has been mostly absorbed.
- Sprinkle cinnamon, brown sugar, and coconut flakes into the oatmeal. Cook for about 5 more minutes until oats are creamy and flavors are blended well.

Nutrition Information

- Calories: 490 calories;
- Total Fat: 34.6
- Sodium: 25
- Total Carbohydrate: 44.8
- Cholesterol: 0
- Protein: 6.8

185. Sweet And Sour Meatballs II

Serving: 5 | Prep: 5mins | Cook: 15mins | Ready in:

Ingredients

- 1 pound ground beef
- 1 egg
- 1 onion, chopped
- 1 cup dry bread crumbs
- salt and pepper to taste
- 1 cup water
- 1/2 cup cider vinegar
- 1/2 cup ketchup
- 2 tablespoons cornstarch
- 1 cup brown sugar
- 2 tablespoons soy sauce

Direction

- In a big bowl, mix together pepper, salt, bread crumbs, onion, egg, and beef. Shape into 1 – 1 1/2 -inch meatballs.
- In a big skillet, sauté meatballs over medium heat till all sides are browned.
- In another medium bowl, combine soy sauce, sugar, cornstarch, ketchup, vinegar, and water. Spread over meatballs, let sauce thicken. Keep heating till the sauce has just begun to bubble.

Nutrition Information

- Calories: 601 calories;
- Total Fat: 26.3
- Sodium: 878
- Total Carbohydrate: 70.5
- Cholesterol: 114
- Protein: 20.4

186. Sweet, Sticky And Spicy Chicken

Serving: 4 | Prep: 10mins | Cook: 12mins | Ready in:

Ingredients

- 1 tablespoon brown sugar
- 2 tablespoons honey
- 1/4 cup soy sauce
- 2 teaspoons chopped fresh ginger root
- 2 teaspoons chopped garlic
- 2 tablespoons hot sauce
- salt and pepper to taste
- 4 skinless, boneless chicken breast halves - cut into 1/2 inch strips
- 1 tablespoon vegetable oil

Direction

- In a small bowl, combine hot sauce, garlic, ginger, soy sauce, honey, and brown sugar.
- Lightly season the chicken strips with pepper and salt.
- In a big skillet, heat oil over medium heat. Add chicken strips and brown both sides for 1 minute per side. Pour the sauce over the chicken. Simmer without a cover for 8-10 minutes until the sauce is thick.

Nutrition Information

- Calories: 232 calories;
- Total Carbohydrate: 13.9
- Cholesterol: 59
- Protein: 22.8
- Total Fat: 9.3
- Sodium: 1176

187.   Szechuan Spicy Eggplant

Serving: 4 | Prep: 25mins | Cook: 20mins | Ready in:

Ingredients

- 1 (1 1/2 pound) eggplant
- 4 tablespoons soy sauce
- 1/4 cup chicken stock
- 1 teaspoon chili sauce
- 1 teaspoon white sugar
- 1/2 teaspoon ground black pepper
- 2 tablespoons oyster sauce (optional)
- 1 tablespoon cornstarch
- 4 tablespoons water
- 2 cloves garlic, minced
- 4 large green onions, finely chopped
- 1 tablespoon chopped fresh ginger root
- 1/4 pound fresh shrimp - peeled, deveined, and diced
- 1/3 pound lean ground beef
- 1 tablespoon sesame oil
- 4 cups hot cooked rice

Direction

- Cut the eggplant into 1-inch cubes, and discard the stem. Whisk oyster sauce, sugar, chili sauce, ground black pepper, soy sauce, and chicken stock together in a medium bowl. Mix well and set aside. Combine water and cornstarch on a separate small bowl then put aside.
- Spread a large and deep pan over high heat with cooking spray; wait a few minutes until it becomes very hot. Cook dried shrimp (if choosing), garlic, half of the green onions, and ginger for 3 to 5 minutes or until they begin to turn brown. Make sure to stir continuously. Add in the ground pork or beef and stir constantly for another 3 minutes or until browned.
- Place the eggplant in the pan and mix all the ingredients. Add the reserved soy sauce mixture, then cover the pan. Lower the heat to medium-low; leave to simmer for about 15 minutes while stirring sometimes. If using fresh shrimp, put it in during the last few minutes of cooking process. Mix in the remaining cornstarch mixture and allow to heat until the mixture thickens. Lastly, mix in sesame oil and the remaining green onions.
- Pour over hot rice for serving.

Nutrition Information

- Calories: 441 calories;
- Total Fat: 12.6
- Sodium: 1079
- Total Carbohydrate: 61.6
- Cholesterol: 71
- Protein: 20

188.   Tequila Garlic Prawns

Serving: 4 | Prep: 20mins | Cook: 10mins | Ready in:

Ingredients

- 2 tablespoons olive oil
- 10 cloves garlic, crushed
- 1 pound large shrimp, deveined
- 1/4 cup best-quality white tequila
- 2 tablespoons fresh lime juice
- 1/2 bunch cilantro, finely chopped

Direction

- In a skillet, heat olive oil on moderate heat, then cook in the hot oil with garlic for 2-3 minutes, until turning light golden. Put in lime juice, tequila and shrimp, then cook for 3-5 minutes, until shrimp are pink. Take away from the heat and use cilantro to sprinkle over shrimp. Toss to mix, then peel and eat.

Nutrition Information

- Calories: 195 calories;
- Sodium: 203
- Total Carbohydrate: 3.4
- Cholesterol: 173
- Protein: 19.2
- Total Fat: 7.8

189. Tequila Lime Burgers

Serving: 8 | Prep: 10mins | Cook: 20mins | Ready in:

Ingredients

- 2 pounds ground beef
- 1/4 cup steak sauce
- 1/4 cup Worcestershire sauce
- 2 tablespoons Montreal steak seasoning
- 2 tablespoons tequila
- 2 tablespoons fresh lime juice
- 1 teaspoon lime zest

Direction

- Preheat outdoor grill to high heat; oil grate lightly.
- Mix lime zest, lime juice, tequila, Montreal seasoning, Worcestershire sauce, steak sauce and ground beef till evenly combined in big bowl; from mixture, shape 8 patties.
- On preheated grill, cook patties, 7-10 minutes per side for well done or to desired doneness.

Nutrition Information

- Calories: 225 calories;
- Total Fat: 13.4
- Sodium: 951
- Total Carbohydrate: 4
- Cholesterol: 69
- Protein: 19.2

190. Texas Pork Ribs

Serving: 12 | Prep: 30mins | Cook: 5hours | Ready in:

Ingredients

- 6 pounds pork spareribs
- 1 1/2 cups white sugar
- 1/4 cup salt
- 2 1/2 tablespoons ground black pepper
- 3 tablespoons sweet paprika
- 1 teaspoon cayenne pepper, or to taste
- 2 tablespoons garlic powder
- 5 tablespoons pan drippings
- 1/2 cup chopped onion
- 4 cups ketchup
- 3 cups hot water
- 4 tablespoons brown sugar
- cayenne pepper to taste
- salt and pepper to taste
- 1 cup wood chips, soaked

Direction

- Rinse the ribs and remove any excess fats. Mix ground black pepper, garlic powder, a 1/4 cup of salt, sugar, 1 tsp. of cayenne pepper, and paprika in a medium bowl. Coat the ribs into the spice mix generously. Pile two racks of ribs into each of the two 10x15-inch roasting pans. Cover the pan and refrigerate it for at least 8 hours.
- Set the oven to 275°F (135°C) to preheat. Bake the ribs, uncovered, for 3-4 hours until the ribs almost fall apart from the bones and tender.
- Get 5 tbsp. of the drippings from the bottom of the roasting pans and pour it into the skillet that is set over medium heat. Cook the onion

into the pan with drippings until tender and lightly browned. Mix in ketchup; heat and stir constantly for 3-4 minutes longer. Stir in brown sugar and water; season the mixture with salt, pepper, and cayenne pepper to taste. Adjust the heat to low; cover the pan and simmer the mixture for 1 hour, pouring in more water as needed to achieve the desired thickness.
- Set the grill to medium-low heat to preheat.
- Once the ribs are ready to grill, add the soaked wood chips into the coals or the gas grill's smoker box. Put a small amount of oil into the grill grate. Arrange the ribs into the grill, two racks at a time to avoid crowding. Let them cook for 20 minutes while flipping from time to time. During the last 10 minutes of grilling, baste the ribs with the sauce so that the sauce won't burn.

Nutrition Information

- Calories: 614 calories;
- Protein: 33.4
- Total Fat: 30.9
- Sodium: 991
- Total Carbohydrate: 53.1
- Cholesterol: 127

191. Thai Grilled Chicken With Sweet Chile Dipping Sauce

Serving: 4 | Prep: 15mins | Cook: 30mins | Ready in:

Ingredients

- 1/2 cup coconut milk
- 2 tablespoons fish sauce
- 2 tablespoons minced garlic
- 2 tablespoons chopped cilantro
- 1 teaspoon ground turmeric
- 1 teaspoon curry powder
- 1/2 teaspoon white pepper
- 1/2 (3 pound) chicken, cut into pieces
- 6 tablespoons rice vinegar
- 4 tablespoons water
- 4 tablespoons white sugar
- 1 teaspoon minced garlic
- 1/2 teaspoon minced bird's eye chile
- 1/4 teaspoon salt

Direction

- Combine together white pepper, curry powder, turmeric, cilantro, 2 tablespoons minced garlic, fish sauce and coconut milk in a shallow dish. Add the chicken and flip to coat. Cover the dish and chill for about 4 hours or overnight.
- Preheat the grill to high heat.
- Mix salt, bird's eye chile, 1 teaspoon minced garlic, sugar, water and vinegar in a saucepan. Heat to boil. Decrease the heat to low and let to simmer for about 5 minutes until the liquid is reduced. Mix the sauce occasionally. Take out from the heat and let to cool prior to use.
- Coat the grill grate lightly with oil. Get rid of marinade and put the chicken onto the grill. Let cook for 10 minutes on each side or until juices run clear and chicken is slightly charred. Brush with the sauce prior to serving. Then serve the rest of the sauce on the side for dipping.

Nutrition Information

- Calories: 332 calories;
- Sodium: 769
- Total Carbohydrate: 16.1
- Cholesterol: 73
- Protein: 24.4
- Total Fat: 19

192. The Best Ever Vegan Sushi

Serving: 6 | Prep: 30mins | Cook: 38mins | Ready in:

Ingredients

- 1 cup short-grain sushi rice
- 2 cups water
- 1 pinch salt
- 1 1/2 teaspoons vegetable oil
- 1/4 cup rice vinegar
- 2 tablespoons white sugar
- 1/8 teaspoon salt
- 1 (16 ounce) package extra-firm tofu
- 1 tablespoon olive oil, or more as needed
- 1/4 small onion, minced (optional)
- 1 teaspoon garlic, minced (optional)
- 1/4 cup vegan mayonnaise (such as Follow Your Heart® Vegenaise®)
- 2 tablespoons sriracha sauce, or to taste
- 2 sheets nori, or as needed
- 1/2 avocado - peeled, pitted, and sliced
- 1/2 cup matchstick-sliced Savoy cabbage
- 1/4 cup matchstick-cut carrots
- 1/4 cup matchstick-cut seeded cucumber

Direction

- In a saucepan, mix together the water, a pinch of salt and rice and let it boil. Use a thin wooden spoon or a bamboo rice spatula to mix the mixture once. Lower the heat setting to low heat then cover the pan. Let the mixture cook for about 20 minutes until the rice has softened and all of the cooking water has been absorbed. Allow the cooked rice to cool down.
- In a small saucepan, put the vegetable oil and let it heat up over medium heat setting. Put in the sugar, 1/8 teaspoon of salt and rice vinegar. Allow the mixture to heat up until all of the sugar has fully dissolved and the cooking liquid has started to simmer. Remove the pan away from the heat and allow the mixture to cool down for a minimum of 10 minutes until the mixture is cool enough to the touch safely. Slowly fold small amount of the cooled liquid into the cooled down rice until the texture of the rice mixture is slightly sticky and wet but is not gooey (it may not be necessary to add in all of the liquid).
- Use a paper towel to press any excess liquid out of the tofu then slice it into strips.
- In a small skillet, put the olive oil and let it heat up over medium heat setting. Put in the onion, garlic and tofu strips and let it cook for about 4 minutes on each side while stirring it until the tofu turns golden brown in color.
- In a small bowl, combine the sriracha and vegan mayonnaise.
- Put a sheet of nori onto a sushi mat with its rough side facing up. Use your wet fingers to firmly pat a thick, even layer of the prepared rice on top of the entire nori sheet, covering it fully. Line the cabbage, cooked tofu strips, cucumber, avocado and carrots over the rice along the bottom side of the nori sheet.
- Roll the sushi mat and the nori sheet over the filling. Remove the sushi mat and use plastic wrap to wrap the roll, tightly twisting both ends of the plastic wrap to compress the sushi roll together. Keep it in the fridge for 5-10 minutes until it has set. Do the whole process again for the rest of the filling and nori sheet.
- Take out the sushi roll from the plastic wrap, then cut it into pieces and put the sriracha-mayonnaise mixture on top.

Nutrition Information

- Calories: 299 calories;
- Sodium: 338
- Total Carbohydrate: 36.8
- Cholesterol: 0
- Protein: 8.9
- Total Fat: 13.6

193. Throw Together Mexican Casserole

Serving: 4 | Prep: 5mins | Cook: 30mins | Ready in:

Ingredients

- 1 pound ground beef

- 1 (15 ounce) can sweet corn, drained
- 1 cup mild, chunky salsa
- 1/4 cup sliced black olives
- 3 1/2 cups cooked egg noodles
- 1 (15.25 ounce) can kidney beans, drained and rinsed
- 1/4 cup taco sauce
- 1 (1.25 ounce) package taco seasoning mix
- 1/2 cup tomato sauce

Direction

- Start preheating the oven to 325°F (165°C).
- In a skillet, cook ground beef over medium heat until brown evenly; drain.
- Combine tomato sauce, seasoning mix, taco sauce, beans, cooked noodles, olives, salsa, corn and beef in a baking dish (about 9x13 inches).
- Bake in prepared oven until cooked through, about 30 minutes.

Nutrition Information

- Calories: 663 calories;
- Total Fat: 21.8
- Sodium: 1960
- Total Carbohydrate: 84.7
- Cholesterol: 109
- Protein: 34.4

194. Tofu Turkey II

Serving: 4 | Prep: 15mins | Cook: 50mins | Ready in:

Ingredients

- 1 pound firm tofu
- 1 teaspoon salt
- 1/4 teaspoon dried marjoram
- 1/4 teaspoon dried savory
- 1/4 teaspoon pepper
- 1 (12 ounce) package dry bread stuffing mix
- 2/3 cup water
- 1/4 cup soy margarine
- 1 slice bread, cubed
- 1/2 teaspoon sage
- 2 tablespoons water
- 5 tablespoons vegetable oil, divided
- 1 teaspoon barbeque sauce
- 1/2 teaspoon prepared mustard
- 1 tablespoon orange jam
- 1 teaspoon orange juice
- 1 tablespoon sesame seeds

Direction

- Drain and wash tofu; place tofu in a blender or food processor, blend until smooth. Mix in pepper, savory, marjoram, and salt. Use 2 sheets of paper towel to line a sieve and put over an empty bowl. Transfer tofu to lined sieve and press against sides to make a deep well in the center. Put 2 more sheets of paper towel over tofu and keep in the refrigerator for 2 hours.
- In the meantime, mix together margarine, 2/3 cup water, and stuffing mix in a medium saucepan over medium-high heat. Bring to a boil; lower the heat to low, simmer for 5 minutes, covered. Take away from heat; allow it to stand for 5 minutes and use a fork to fluff it. Add 2 tablespoons water, sage, and bread cubes to the stuffing.
- After the tofu has chilled for 2 hours, prepare the oven by preheating to 350°F (175°C). Use 2 tablespoons of the vegetable oil to grease a baking sheet.
- Take the top layer of paper towels away from the tofu. Press the tofu again against the sides of the sieve to make a well, if needed. Scoop the stuffing mixture into the well and use a spoon to smooth the surface. Flip the tofu mold over onto the prepared baking sheet. Take off the rest of the paper towel layer and use your hands to form the tofu if it has lost its shape or cracked.
- Place in the preheated oven and bake for 30 minutes.
- In the meantime, mix together the rest 3 tablespoons oil, sesame seeds, orange juice,

orange jam, mustard, and barbecue sauce to make a glaze. After the tofu has baked for 30 minutes, spoon or brush the glaze over it. Place back into the oven and bake for 20 more minutes.
- Broil for 3 to 5 minutes, or until the tofu is crispy and browned.

Nutrition Information

- Calories: 787 calories;
- Total Fat: 42.4
- Sodium: 2124
- Total Carbohydrate: 76.9
- Cholesterol: < 1
- Protein: 28.2

195. Try It You'll Like It Kraut Casserole

Serving: 8 | Prep: 20mins | Cook: 2hours45mins | Ready in:

Ingredients

- 1 pound country style pork ribs
- salt and pepper to taste
- 1/4 cup dry white wine (optional)
- 1/2 cup water
- 1 tablespoon caraway seed
- 1 tablespoon brown sugar
- 1 pound sauerkraut, drained
- 1 medium red apple - cored and diced
- 1 pound carrots, peeled and cut into large chunks

Direction

- Preheat an oven to 175°C/350°F.
- Use pepper and salt to season ribs. In a big skillet, heat 1 tsp. oil on medium high heat. Cook ribs, occasionally turning, till all sides are browned well. If using, add wine, then brown sugar, caraway seeds and water. Mix to melt sugar. Mix carrots, apple and drained sauerkraut in. Put into big casserole dish.
- In preheated oven, bake for 2 1/2 hours, covered, adding water if needed to avoid drying out.

Nutrition Information

- Calories: 140 calories;
- Total Fat: 6.7
- Sodium: 719
- Total Carbohydrate: 12.5
- Cholesterol: 23
- Protein: 7.1

196. Tuna Steaks With Melon Salsa

Serving: 2 | Prep: 20mins | Cook: 6mins | Ready in:

Ingredients

- 1 small cantaloupe, flesh removed and finely diced
- 1/2 red chile pepper, seeded and chopped
- 10 fresh basil leaves, cut into thin strips
- 2 tablespoons extra-virgin olive oil
- 2 tablespoons fresh lime juice
- 1 pinch salt
- 1 pinch white sugar
- 2 tablespoons extra-virgin olive oil
- 2 (5 ounce) tuna steaks
- salt and ground black pepper to taste

Direction

- In a bowl, combine sugar, salt, lime juice, 2 tablespoons of olive oil, basil, chile pepper and the cantaloupe.
- In a skillet, heat 2 tablespoons olive oil. Use pepper and salt to season tuna steaks. Cook tuna for 3 minutes each side in oil. For serving, pour cantaloupe mixture over every steak.

Nutrition Information

- Calories: 482 calories;
- Total Fat: 28.8
- Sodium: 89
- Total Carbohydrate: 20.8
- Cholesterol: 64
- Protein: 35.3

197. Turkey Sausage Pie

Serving: 4 | Prep: 20mins | Cook: 15mins | Ready in:

Ingredients

- 2 (10 ounce) cans refrigerated pizza dough
- 1 tablespoon olive oil
- 1 pound turkey sausage links, without casings
- 1 onion, diced
- 1 green bell pepper, diced
- 1 (8 ounce) can tomato sauce

Direction

- Set the oven to 190°C or 375°F to preheat. Coat one 10-inch quiche dish or pie pan lightly with oil.
- In the greased pan, put 1 sheet of pizza dough. Trim the edges of dough to fit the pan, if needed. In the preheated oven, bake dough about 7 minutes, then take out and put aside.
- While baking dough in the oven, heat oil in a big skillet over moderately high heat. Crumble sausage into the skillet and sauté about 2 minutes. Put in green peppers and onions, then sauté until onion is browned slightly and sausage is cooked through, about 5-7 more minutes. Put in tomato sauce and stir well.
- Put sausage mixture into the baked crust and place another sheet of pizza dough on top to cover. Trim the edges as needed and seal gently 2 crusts together. Cut steam vents in top.
- Bake at 190°C or 375°F until turning golden brown, about 15 minutes.

Nutrition Information

- Calories: 617 calories;
- Total Fat: 19.8
- Sodium: 2238
- Total Carbohydrate: 73.9
- Cholesterol: 86
- Protein: 34.8

198. Veal Roast Blanquette

Serving: 8 | Prep: 1hours | Cook: 1hours30mins | Ready in:

Ingredients

- 4 pounds veal shoulder roast
- 1/4 teaspoon dried thyme
- 4 carrots, halved
- 1 pound small potatoes
- 1/2 pound small white onions
- 1/2 pound mushrooms
- 2 tablespoons all-purpose flour
- 1 (10 ounce) package frozen green peas
- 2 egg yolks

Direction

- Brown all sides of roast in 8-quart Dutch oven on medium high heat. Add 2 cups water and thyme; boil. Lower heat to low and cover; simmer for 30 minutes.
- Add onions, potatoes and carrots to pot; cover. Simmer for 30 minutes. Toss mushrooms in; cover. Simmer till veal and veggies are tender for 15 minutes. Remove veggies and roast; keep warm.
- Mix 2 tablespoons water and flour till blended without lumps in cup; mix into liquid inside Dutch oven slowly. Cook till gravy is slightly thick, constantly mixing. Mix peas in; heat through.

- Beat egg yolks in small bowl; mix small amount hot gravy in. Put egg yolk mixture into gravy slowly; whisk till thick. Don't boil. Serve: Put some gravy on veggies and veal; serve leftover gravy in gravy boat.

Nutrition Information

- Calories: 414 calories;
- Total Fat: 13.3
- Sodium: 284
- Total Carbohydrate: 23
- Cholesterol: 255
- Protein: 48.9

199. Vegan Enchilada Bake

Serving: 6 | Prep: 15mins | Cook: 45mins | Ready in:

Ingredients

- 1 cup crushed tomatoes
- 2 cups cooked white rice
- 1 (15 ounce) can vegetarian refried beans
- 1/2 (16 ounce) can diced tomatoes and green chiles (such as RO*TEL®)
- 8 ounces sliced seitan
- 1/2 (8 ounce) package shredded mozzarella-style vegan cheese (such as Daiya®)
- 9 (6 inch) corn tortillas
- 1 (15 ounce) can green enchilada sauce

Direction

- Set the oven to 175°C or 350°F to preheat.
- Add crushed tomatoes to the bottom of a casserole dish, then layer a third of the rice, a third of the beans, a third of the diced tomatoes, a third of the seitan, a third of vegan cheese, a third of tortillas and a third of enchilada sauce, respectively in that order, into the dish. Repeat layering two times to make 2 more layers.
- In the preheated oven, bake for 45 minutes, until casserole is heated through and vegan cheese is melted.

Nutrition Information

- Calories: 395 calories;
- Total Carbohydrate: 57.5
- Cholesterol: 0
- Protein: 21.9
- Total Fat: 8.4
- Sodium: 1158

200. Vegan Green Lentil Curry

Serving: 3 | Prep: 10mins | Cook: 25mins | Ready in:

Ingredients

- 1 tablespoon cooking oil
- 1 onion, finely chopped
- 1 green bell pepper, finely chopped
- 1 clove garlic, finely chopped
- 1 tablespoon garam masala
- 1 tablespoon mild curry powder
- 2 teaspoons ground cumin
- 1 teaspoon ground turmeric
- 1 (14.5 ounce) can diced tomatoes
- 1 (15 ounce) can cooked green lentils

Direction

- In a large skillet, heat oil over medium-high heat. Add garlic, bell pepper, and onion; cook for about 5 minutes until soft. Mix in turmeric, cumin, curry powder, and garam masala and cook for 1 to 2 minutes until aromatic. Add tomatoes, bring to simmer and keep cooking for 5 minutes. Stir in lentils well. Simmer the mixture for 10 minutes, no boiling.

Nutrition Information

- Calories: 273 calories;

- Total Carbohydrate: 43.2
- Cholesterol: 0
- Protein: 15.3
- Total Fat: 6.5
- Sodium: 28

201. Vegan Mac And No Cheese

Serving: 4 | Prep: 15mins | Cook: 45mins | Ready in:

Ingredients

- 1 (8 ounce) package uncooked elbow macaroni
- 1 tablespoon vegetable oil
- 1 medium onion, chopped
- 1 cup cashews
- 1/3 cup lemon juice
- 1 1/3 cups water
- salt to taste
- 1/3 cup canola oil
- 4 ounces roasted red peppers, drained
- 3 tablespoons nutritional yeast
- 1 teaspoon garlic powder
- 1 teaspoon onion powder

Direction

- Prepare the oven by preheating to 350°F (175°C).
- Place a lightly salted water in a large pot and make it boil. Put in the macaroni and cook for 8-10 minutes or until al dente; strain. Place in a medium-sized baking dish.
- In a medium-sized saucepan over medium heat, put vegetable oil to heat. Add in onion and cook until lightly browned and tender. Carefully combine with macaroni. Combine salt, water, lemon juice and cashews in a food processor or blender. Slowly mix in onion powder, garlic powder, nutritional yeast, roasted red peppers and canola oil. Process until smooth. Blend well with the onions and macaroni.
- Place in the preheated oven and bake for 45 minutes until lightly browned. Let it cool for 10-15 minutes prior to serving.

Nutrition Information

- Calories: 648 calories;
- Cholesterol: 0
- Protein: 16.5
- Total Fat: 39.2
- Sodium: 329
- Total Carbohydrate: 61.6

202. Vegan Mexican Casserole

Serving: 8 | Prep: 30mins | Cook: 36mins | Ready in:

Ingredients

- 1 tablespoon vegetable oil
- 1/2 yellow onion, diced
- 3 cloves garlic, diced
- 18 ounces soy chorizo
- 1 (15 ounce) can black beans
- 1 (15 ounce) can tomato sauce
- 3 tomatoes, diced
- 1 (4 ounce) can diced jalapeno peppers
- 1 (4 ounce) can diced green chilies
- 1 package chicken taco seasoning mix
- 1/2 bunch cilantro
- 4 (8-inch) wheat soft taco shells
- 1 (8 ounce) package vegan Cheddar cheese

Direction

- Set oven to 350°F (175°C) to preheat.
- In a skillet over medium-high heat, combine garlic and onion. Sauté for about 1 minute until aromatic. Add green chiles, jalapeno peppers, diced tomatoes, tomato sauce, black beans, and chorizo. Cook for 5 to 7 minutes until mixture is bubbly. Mix in cilantro and taco seasoning; put off the heat.

- Distribute 1 cup of chorizo mixture all over the bottom of a 9x13-inch baking pan. Cover with 2 tortillas. Top tortillas with 1/2 of the remaining chorizo mixture, and sprinkle top with vegan Cheddar cheese. Add the rest of tortilla shells and chorizo mixture.
- Bake for about half an hour in the preheated oven until mixture is bubbling hot.

Nutrition Information

- Calories: 432 calories;
- Total Fat: 20.2
- Sodium: 2413
- Total Carbohydrate: 42.4
- Cholesterol: 0
- Protein: 19.8

203. Vegan Overnight Oats

Serving: 1 | Prep: 5mins | Cook: | Ready in:

Ingredients

- 5 tablespoons rolled oats
- 5 tablespoons unsweetened almond milk, or more to taste
- 1 tablespoon shredded unsweetened coconut
- 2 teaspoons chia seeds
- 1 teaspoon maple syrup
- 1/2 teaspoon ground cinnamon
- 1 pinch salt
- 1/2 banana, chopped

Direction

- Combine salt, cinnamon, maple syrup, chia seeds, coconut, almond milk, and oats in a jar; mix well. Stir in chopped banana. Chill with a cover for 8 hours to overnight. Add more almond milk if necessary, then enjoy.

Nutrition Information

- Calories: 252 calories;
- Total Fat: 8
- Sodium: 211
- Total Carbohydrate: 42.4
- Cholesterol: 0
- Protein: 5.6

204. Vegan Pasta With Spinach, Mushrooms, And Garlic

Serving: 2 | Prep: 15mins | Cook: 15mins | Ready in:

Ingredients

- 1/2 (16 ounce) box penne pasta
- 3 tablespoons olive oil, divided
- 1 (8 ounce) package sliced fresh mushrooms
- 1 bunch spinach, roughly chopped
- 2 cloves garlic, chopped
- 2 tablespoons balsamic vinegar
- salt and ground black pepper to taste

Direction

- Boil a big pot of lightly salted water, then add penne and cook for about 11 minutes, stirring from time to time, until it becomes tender yet firm to the bite; drain.
- In a skillet, heat 1 tbsp. of olive oil on medium heat and cook the mushrooms for 3-5 minutes, until light brown. Mix in garlic and spinach. Cook for about 3 minutes until the spinach becomes wilted. Add the drained pasta and mix to blend. Stir in balsamic vinegar and leftover 2 tbsp. of olive oil, then add pepper and salt to season.

Nutrition Information

- Calories: 658 calories;
- Total Carbohydrate: 94.7
- Cholesterol: 0
- Protein: 23.5

- Total Fat: 23.9
- Sodium: 228

205. Vegan Pumpkin Overnight Oats In The Slow Cooker

Serving: 4 | Prep: 5mins | Cook: 8hours | Ready in:

Ingredients

- 2 1/2 cups water
- 1 cup steel-cut oats
- 1 cup almond milk
- 1 cup canned pumpkin puree
- 1 teaspoon vanilla extract
- 1 teaspoon pumpkin pie spice
- 1/4 teaspoon salt

Direction

- In a slow cooker, combine salt, pumpkin pie spice, vanilla extract, pumpkin puree, almond milk, and steel-cut oats, and water.
- Cook on low setting for 8 hours.

Nutrition Information

- Calories: 209 calories;
- Sodium: 338
- Total Carbohydrate: 35.8
- Cholesterol: 0
- Protein: 7.3
- Total Fat: 4

206. Vegan Stuffed Peppers With Rice

Serving: 4 | Prep: 15mins | Cook: 50mins | Ready in:

Ingredients

- 4 red bell peppers, tops and seeds removed
- salt to taste
- 1 cup vegan "ground beef," frozen (such as Beyond Meat®)
- 1 cup diced onion
- 1 cup diced tomatoes
- 1 (14 ounce) can vegetable broth, divided
- 1 teaspoon garlic powder
- 1 teaspoon chili powder
- 1/2 teaspoon ground black pepper
- 1 cup water
- 1 (8 ounce) package Spanish rice mix
- 1 cup black beans, rinsed and drained
- 1 cup corn, drained
- 1 tablespoon nutritional yeast (optional)
- 4 ounces tomato sauce

Direction

- Bring a large pot of water to a boil. Add bell peppers; cook for 8-10 minutes until soft. Drain; sprinkle salts to the insides. Put aside for 10 minutes.
- Set the oven to 350°F (175°C) and start preheating. Using aluminum foil, line a baking dish.
- In a large skillet, over medium-high heat, combine salt, black pepper, chili powder, garlic powder, 2/3 cup broth, diced tomatoes, onion and vegan ground beef; bring to a high simmer. Cook while stirring occasionally for 5-10 minutes until 2/3 cup of liquid has steamed off or been absorbed. Remove from heat.
- In a saucepan, over medium heat, combine Spanish rice package, a cup broth and water. Bring to boiling; lower the heat to simmer; cook for 8 minutes. Add corn and black beans; stir to combine. To keep rice stuffing moist, add "ground beef" mixture with enough liquid. Combine in nutritional yeast; stir until well mixed.
- Drain excess water from peppers. With a spoon, stuff with rice mixture, tightly packing filling down. Transfer stuffed peppers to the lined baking pan; scoop more rice mixture around them. Top over rice and peppers with tomato sauce. Use aluminum foil to cover.

- Bake in the prepared oven for 20 minutes. Get rid of foil and bake without a cover for 10 more minutes. Allow peppers to rest for 5 minutes; serve.

Nutrition Information

- Calories: 295 calories;
- Sodium: 1116
- Total Carbohydrate: 51.8
- Cholesterol: 0
- Protein: 19.2
- Total Fat: 2.6

207. Vegan Sweet Potato Chickpea Curry

Serving: 6 | Prep: 10mins | Cook: 20mins | Ready in:

Ingredients

- 3 tablespoons olive oil
- 1 onion, chopped
- 2 cloves garlic, minced
- 2 teaspoons minced fresh ginger root
- 1 (15 ounce) can chickpeas, drained
- 1 (14.5 ounce) can diced tomatoes
- 1 (14 ounce) can coconut milk
- 1 sweet potato, cubed
- 1 tablespoon garam masala
- 1 teaspoon ground cumin
- 1 teaspoon ground turmeric
- 1/2 teaspoon salt
- 1/4 teaspoon red chile flakes
- 1 cup baby spinach

Direction

- In a skillet, heat the oil on medium heat and cook the ginger, garlic and onion for about 5 minutes until softened. Add sweet potato, coconut milk, tomatoes and chickpeas, then boil. Lower the heat to low and let it simmer for around 15 minutes until it becomes tender.
- Sprinkle salt, chile flakes, turmeric, cumin and garam masala to season, then add spinach right before serving.

Nutrition Information

- Calories: 293 calories;
- Total Carbohydrate: 22.3
- Cholesterol: 0
- Total Fat: 21.6
- Protein: 5.1
- Sodium: 515

208. Vegan Sweet Potato Enchiladas

Serving: 8 | Prep: 20mins | Cook: 44mins | Ready in:

Ingredients

- 1 large sweet potato, chopped
- 2 tablespoons olive oil
- 1 onion, chopped
- 3 cloves garlic, minced, or more to taste
- 2 (15.5 ounce) cans black beans, drained and rinsed
- 1 green bell pepper, chopped
- 1 (16 ounce) bag frozen chopped spinach, thawed and drained
- 1 tablespoon lime juice, or to taste
- 1 teaspoon ground cumin, or more to taste
- 1 teaspoon cayenne pepper
- salt to taste
- 3 cups enchilada sauce, divided
- 8 (8 inch) flour tortillas

Direction

- Turn oven to 350°F (175°C) to preheat.
- Position a steamer insert into a saucepan and pour in water to just below the bottom of the steamer. Boil the water. Put sweet potatoes into the steamer; steam, covered, for 2 to 6 minutes until tender.

- Heat olive oil over medium heat in a skillet. Sauté onion in heated oil for about 5 minutes until transparent. Add garlic; sauté for 2 to 4 minutes until aromatic. Add salt, cayenne pepper, cumin, lime juice, spinach, green bell pepper, black beans, and steamed sweet potato. Sauté for about 5 minutes until flavors meld. Pour in 2 cups enchilada sauce; cook for about 5 minutes longer until liquid is slightly absorbed.
- Ladle 1 to 2 cups of enchilada mixture into a 9x13-inch baking dish's bottom and approximately 1 cup into each tortilla. Place filled tortillas in the baking dish. Stream the remaining 1 cup of enchilada sauce over tortillas in the baking dish.
- Bake for 20 minutes in the preheated oven until enchiladas are thoroughly heated and sauce has a deep red color.

Nutrition Information

- Calories: 407 calories;
- Protein: 14
- Total Fat: 9.6
- Sodium: 999
- Total Carbohydrate: 67.2
- Cholesterol: 0

209. Vegan Tofu Fajitas

Serving: 4 | Prep: 30mins | Cook: 15mins | Ready in:

Ingredients

- 1 (16 ounce) package extra-firm tofu
- 1/2 lime, juiced
- 1 tablespoon ground cumin
- 1 tablespoon liquid amino acid (such as Bragg®)
- 1 pinch cayenne pepper
- 1 large red onion, thinly sliced
- 1/2 green bell pepper, sliced
- 1/2 red bell pepper, sliced
- 1 small jalapeno pepper, seeded and diced
- cooking spray
- 4 (8 inch) whole wheat tortillas
- 1 avocado, sliced
- 1 Roma tomato, diced
- 1/2 cup chopped cilantro

Direction

- Press tofu firmly with paper towels to dry. Cut into strips; transfer to a wide dish.
- In a small bowl, mix cayenne pepper, liquid amino acid, cumin and lime juice. Top half of the mixture over tofu; gently toss. Marinate, covered, for 20 minutes to overnight in the fridge.
- In a large bowl, combine jalapeno, red bell pepper, green bell pepper, red onion and the rest of lime juice mixture. Toss well. Marinate, covered, for 20 minutes to overnight in the fridge.
- Using cooking spray, spray a large non-stick skillet; place over high heat. Cook while stirring tofu for 8-10 minutes until all sides turn brown. Place onto a plate.
- Using cooking spray to spray the skillet again; return to high heat. Add onion-pepper mixture; cook while stirring for 8-10 minutes until browned. Transfer tofu back to the skillet.
- Warm tortillas; place tofu mixture, avocado, tomato and cilantro on top.

Nutrition Information

- Calories: 313 calories;
- Total Fat: 15.1
- Sodium: 411
- Total Carbohydrate: 39.9
- Cholesterol: 0
- Protein: 17.7

210. Vegan Tofu Spinach Lasagna

Serving: 8 | Prep: 15mins | Cook: 1hours40mins | Ready in:

Ingredients

- 1 (12 ounce) package fresh mushrooms, sliced
- 1 onion, chopped
- 1 (28 ounce) can tomato sauce
- 1 (28 ounce) can diced tomatoes
- 1 tablespoon Italian seasoning
- 1 (8 ounce) package whole wheat lasagna noodles, dry
- 1 (16 ounce) package frozen chopped spinach, thawed and drained
- 1 (16 ounce) package soft tofu
- 1 (16 ounce) package firm tofu
- 1/4 cup unsweetened almond milk
- 1/4 cup lemon juice, or to taste
- 1/2 teaspoon garlic powder

Direction

- Put a frying pan over medium-high heat. Cook the onion and mushrooms until tender. Mix in the Italian seasoning, tomato sauce and diced tomatoes into the sautéed onion and mushrooms. Simmer the mixture for at least an hour or until the sauce is thick and all the flavors have combined.
- Put water in a big pot with a little bit of salt and boil. Put in the lasagna noodles and cook for about 8 minutes while occasionally stirring until pasta firm to chew but tender. Drain the noodles.
- Preheat oven at 350°F (175°C).
- Remove excess liquid from the spinach by squeezing it.
- In a food processor or blender, put the almond milk, lemon juice, garlic powder, firm tofu and soft tofu. Blend the mixture until the texture resembles ricotta cheese. In a big bowl, put the tofu mixture and mix in the spinach.
- In a 9x13-inch pan, put in a thin layer of sauce evenly on bottom and add a layer of lasagna noodles and 1/2 of tofu mixture on top. Do the whole layering process again with the remaining ingredients finishing with left sauce, lasagna noodles, tofu, more noodles, and a little sauce on top. Use aluminum foil to cover the baking pan.
- Put in heated oven and bake for 40-50 minutes or until the top is bubbling and hot.

Nutrition Information

- Calories: 289 calories;
- Sodium: 692
- Total Carbohydrate: 37.3
- Cholesterol: 0
- Protein: 21.5
- Total Fat: 8.6

211. Vegan Tofu And Sweet Potato Curry

Serving: 4 | Prep: 15mins | Cook: 30mins | Ready in:

Ingredients

- 1 tablespoon sunflower oil
- 1 onion, chopped
- 2 cloves garlic, minced
- 1 tablespoon grated fresh ginger root
- 4 cups peeled and cubed sweet potatoes
- 1 tablespoon mild curry powder
- 1 (14.5 ounce) can diced tomatoes
- 1/2 cup warm vegetable stock
- 1/2 (10 ounce) package frozen peas
- salt and freshly ground black pepper to taste
- 9 ounces firm tofu, cubed
- 1 sprig fresh mint, leaves picked

Direction

- In a large saucepan, heat oil over medium heat and cook ginger, garlic, and onion, stirring frequently for 5 minutes, until translucent and soft. Put in sweet potatoes and cook for 3 more

minutes. Sprinkle with curry powder and cook for 30 seconds.
- In the pot, mix tomatoes and their juices. Pour in vegetable stock and bring it to boil. Turn to medium-low heat, cook with a cover for 12 to 15 minutes until sweet potatoes are tender. Put in peas and simmer for 5 more minutes. Sprinkle with pepper and salt to season. Mix in tofu and gently stir together. Heat for 3 minutes. Decorate with fresh mint leaves.

Nutrition Information

- Calories: 277 calories;
- Sodium: 376
- Total Carbohydrate: 43.8
- Cholesterol: 0
- Protein: 11
- Total Fat: 7.1

212. Vegan Vanilla Nut Oatmeal

Serving: 1 | Prep: 5mins | Cook: 10mins | Ready in:

Ingredients

- 3/4 cup vanilla soy milk
- 1/2 cup rolled oats
- 2 teaspoons white sugar
- 2 teaspoons chia seeds (optional)
- 2 teaspoons chopped almonds
- 1 teaspoon vanilla bean powder
- 1/4 teaspoon sea salt
- 1/4 teaspoon ground cinnamon

Direction

- In a saucepan, stir together cinnamon, salt, vanilla bean powder, almonds, chia seeds, sugar, oats, and soy milk over medium heat. Cook, stirring often for 5-7 minutes until the mixture reaches your desired thickness.

Nutrition Information

- Calories: 352 calories;
- Protein: 12.9
- Total Fat: 9.4
- Sodium: 536
- Total Carbohydrate: 55.3
- Cholesterol: 0

213. Vegan Vegetable Curry

Serving: 6 | Prep: 20mins | Cook: 35mins | Ready in:

Ingredients

- Curry Paste:
- 4 green chile peppers
- 3 tablespoons grated fresh coconut
- 1 (1 inch) piece ginger root, minced
- 4 cloves garlic
- Curry:
- 2 tablespoons vegetable oil
- 3 onions, chopped
- 1 small head cauliflower, cut into florets
- 3 small potatoes, peeled and cubed
- 1 1/2 (10 ounce) packages frozen peas
- 1 teaspoon ground turmeric
- 1 teaspoon ground coriander
- salt to taste
- water to cover
- 1/4 cup chopped fresh cilantro
- 1 teaspoon garam masala

Direction

- In the bowl of a food processor, mix garlic, coconut, and green chile peppers and then grind to form a paste.
- Over medium-high heat, heat oil in a large skillet and then add curry paste. Cook while stirring for about 1 to 2 minutes. Add coriander, turmeric, peas, potatoes, cauliflower and onions. Add salt to taste. Cook for about 5 minutes until the veggies soften slightly. Add water to cover and raise the heat

to high. Heat to a boil, decrease the heat and let it simmer for 25 to 30 minutes until vegetables are tender and water is reduced.
- Drizzle with garam masala and fresh cilantro prior to serving.

Nutrition Information

- Calories: 245 calories;
- Cholesterol: 0
- Protein: 8.5
- Total Fat: 6.1
- Sodium: 134
- Total Carbohydrate: 42.2

214. Vegan Vegetable Double Tortilla Pizza

Serving: 4 | Prep: 15mins | Cook: 20mins | Ready in:

Ingredients

- 1 tablespoon vegetable oil
- 2 (12 inch) flour tortillas
- 1/2 cup tomato sauce, or more to taste
- 5 mushrooms, sliced
- 1/2 green bell pepper, chopped
- 1/2 red onion, chopped
- 1/2 white onion, chopped
- 5 black olives, sliced
- 3 pieces sun-dried tomatoes, chopped
- 1/2 jalapeno pepper, chopped

Direction

- Set the oven to 400°F (200°C) and start preheating. Use parchment paper to line a baking sheet; brush olive oil over.
- Place a tortilla on the lined baking sheet; add 1/4 cup tomato sauce. Place another tortilla on top; spread 1/4 cup tomato sauce more on top of tortilla. Garnish the pizza with jalapeno pepper, sun-dried tomatoes, black olives, white onion, red onion, green bell pepper and mushrooms.
- Bake in the prepared oven for about 20 minutes until toppings become softened.

Nutrition Information

- Calories: 245 calories;
- Protein: 6.5
- Total Fat: 8.8
- Sodium: 621
- Total Carbohydrate: 35.7
- Cholesterol: 0

215. Vegetable Fried Rice

Serving: 4 | Prep: 15mins | Cook: 40mins | Ready in:

Ingredients

- 3 cups water
- 1 1/2 cups quick-cooking brown rice
- 2 tablespoons peanut oil
- 1 small yellow onion, chopped
- 1 small green bell pepper, chopped
- 1 teaspoon minced garlic
- 1/4 teaspoon red pepper flakes
- 3 green onions, thinly sliced
- 3 tablespoons soy sauce
- 1 cup frozen petite peas
- 2 teaspoons sesame oil
- 1/4 cup roasted peanuts (optional)

Direction

- Boil water in a cooking pan then add the rice while stirring. Lower the heat, cover the pan and leave it for 20 minutes, simmering.
- While the rice is cooking, put the peanut oil in a large cooking pan or wok and heat it over medium heat. Cook the onions, garlic, bell pepper and pepper flakes in the oil for 3 minutes with occasional stirring.

- Turn the heat up to medium high heat and stir-fry the cooked rice, soy sauce, and green onions for 1 minute. Mix in the peas and cook for a minute more. Turn the heat off then pour the sesame oil in and blend well. If you prefer, you can add peanuts for garnishing.

Nutrition Information

- Calories: 299 calories;
- Sodium: 731
- Total Carbohydrate: 36.7
- Cholesterol: 0
- Protein: 8.5
- Total Fat: 14.7

216. Vegetable Masala

Serving: 4 | Prep: 10mins | Cook: 20mins | Ready in:

Ingredients

- 2 potatoes, peeled and cubed
- 1 carrot, chopped
- 10 French-style green beans, chopped
- 1 quart cold water
- 1/2 cup frozen green peas, thawed
- 1 teaspoon salt
- 1/2 teaspoon ground turmeric
- 1 tablespoon vegetable oil
- 1 teaspoon mustard seed
- 1 teaspoon ground cumin
- 1 onion, finely chopped
- 2 tomatoes - blanched, peeled and chopped
- 1 teaspoon garam masala
- 1/2 teaspoon ground ginger
- 1/2 teaspoon garlic powder
- 1/2 teaspoon chili powder
- 1 sprig cilantro leaves, for garnish

Direction

- Place green beans, carrots and potatoes in the cold water. Let them soak while you prepare other vegetables; drain.
- Place the turmeric, salt, peas, green beans, carrots, and potatoes in a microwave-safe dish. Cook for 8 minutes.
- Place a large skillet over medium heat, heat oil. Cook cumin and mustard seeds; once seeds start to pop and sputter, put in the onion and sauté until transparent. Whisk in the chili powder, garlic, ginger, garam masala, and tomatoes; sauté in 3 minutes. Pour over the tomato mixture with the cooked vegetables and sauté 1 minute. Serve with cilantro leaves as garnish.

Nutrition Information

- Calories: 167 calories;
- Sodium: 641
- Total Carbohydrate: 29.8
- Cholesterol: 0
- Protein: 4.2
- Total Fat: 4.3

217. Vegetarian Chickpea Sandwich Filling

Serving: 3 | Prep: 20mins | Cook: | Ready in:

Ingredients

- 1 (19 ounce) can garbanzo beans, drained and rinsed
- 1 stalk celery, chopped
- 1/2 onion, chopped
- 1 tablespoon mayonnaise
- 1 tablespoon lemon juice
- 1 teaspoon dried dill weed
- salt and pepper to taste

Direction

- Dry and rinse the chickpeas with water; transfer to medium bowl. Mash the chickpeas using a fork. Stir in dill, celery, lemon juice, onion, and mayonnaise to taste. Season with pepper and salt.

Nutrition Information

- Calories: 259 calories;
- Total Carbohydrate: 43.5
- Cholesterol: 2
- Protein: 9.3
- Total Fat: 5.8
- Sodium: 576

218. Veggie Meatloaf

Serving: 4 | Prep: 15mins | Cook: 1hours5mins | Ready in:

Ingredients

- 1 cup uncooked white rice
- 2 tablespoons vegetable oil
- 1 onion, finely chopped
- 1 cup cooked lentils
- 1 cup chopped fresh mushrooms
- 1 tablespoon vegetarian Worcestershire sauce
- salt and pepper to taste
- 1 egg, beaten
- 1 tablespoon garlic powder
- 1 tablespoon Italian seasoning
- 1 tablespoon dried parsley
- 1/2 cup ketchup

Direction

- Set the oven to 175°C (350°F) and begin preheating.
- Boil 2 cups of water in a saucepan. Put in rice and stir occasionally. Lower the heat, let simmer with a cover for 20 minutes.
- In a small skillet, heat oil on medium heat. Sauté onions until soft and put aside.

- Mix cooked onions, parsley, Italian seasoning, garlic powder, egg, pepper, salt, Worcestershire sauce, mushrooms, lentils and cooked rice in a big bowl and blend well. Pat into a prepared pan and coat the surface with ketchup.
- Bake for 45 minutes in the prepared oven.

Nutrition Information

- Calories: 373 calories;
- Total Fat: 9
- Sodium: 440
- Total Carbohydrate: 62.7
- Cholesterol: 46
- Protein: 11.5

219. Veggie Pot Pie

Serving: 6 | Prep: 30mins | Cook: 1hours | Ready in:

Ingredients

- 2 tablespoons olive oil
- 1 onion, chopped
- 8 ounces mushrooms
- 1 clove garlic, minced
- 2 large carrots, diced
- 2 potatoes, peeled and diced
- 2 stalks celery, sliced 1/4 inch wide
- 2 cups cauliflower florets
- 1 cup fresh green beans, trimmed and snapped into 1/2 inch pieces
- 3 cups vegetable broth
- 1 teaspoon kosher salt
- 1 teaspoon ground black pepper
- 2 tablespoons cornstarch
- 2 tablespoons soy sauce
- 1 recipe pastry for double-crust pie

Direction

- Set an oven to preheat to 220°C (425°F).

- Heat the oil in a saucepan or a big skillet. Cook the garlic, mushrooms and onions in oil for 3-5 minutes, mixing often. Stir in celery, potatoes and carrots. Stir in vegetable broth, green beans and cauliflower, then boil. Lower the heat down to a simmer. Let it cook for about 5 minutes until the vegetables become barely tender. Sprinkle pepper and salt to season.
- Combine 1/4 cup of water, soy sauce and cornstarch in a small bowl, until the cornstarch becomes fully dissolved. Mix into the vegetables and let it cook for about 3 minutes until the sauce becomes thick.
- Roll out half of the dough to line an 11x7-inch baking dish. Pour the filling into the dish lined with pastry. Roll out the leftover dough, lay out on top the filling, then seal and flute the edges.
- Let it bake for 30 minutes in the preheated oven or until the crust turns brown.

Nutrition Information

- Calories: 469 calories;
- Sodium: 1198
- Total Carbohydrate: 54.4
- Cholesterol: 0
- Protein: 8.4
- Total Fat: 25

220. Veggie Puree

Serving: 8 | Prep: 15mins | Cook: 45mins | Ready in:

Ingredients

- 3 (10.5 ounce) cans vegetable broth
- 1 potato, peeled and cubed
- 1 carrot, peeled and sliced
- 1/2 cup frozen green peas, thawed
- 1/2 cup frozen corn kernels, thawed
- 1 turnip, peeled and cubed
- 1/4 cup shredded cabbage
- 1 (6 ounce) can sliced mushrooms, drained
- 1/2 teaspoon salt
- 1 1/2 teaspoons brown sugar

Direction

- Boil vegetable broth in a big saucepan over medium-high heat.
- Add salt, mushrooms, cabbage, turnip, corn, peas, carrots, and potatoes to the boiling broth. Boil until the vegetables have fully cooked, about 40 minutes. Strain.
- Put the vegetables in a blender or food processor and puree. Sprinkle brown sugar over the puree and mix lightly. Put a cover on tightly and preserve in the fridge.

Nutrition Information

- Calories: 67 calories;
- Sodium: 485
- Total Carbohydrate: 14.1
- Cholesterol: 0
- Protein: 2.3
- Total Fat: 0.5

221. Whole Wheat And Honey Pizza Dough

Serving: 12 | Prep: 10mins | Cook: 10mins | Ready in:

Ingredients

- 1 (.25 ounce) package active dry yeast
- 1 cup warm water
- 2 cups whole wheat flour
- 1/4 cup wheat germ
- 1 teaspoon salt
- 1 tablespoon honey

Direction

- Preheat oven to 175 degrees C or 350 degrees F
- Melt yeast in a small bowl with warm water. Let stand for 10 minutes until creamy.

- Mix salt, wheat germ, and flour in a big bowl. Create a well in the center then put in the yeast mixture and honey. Mix well until combined. Cover it and put in a warm area to rise for several minutes.
- Roll out dough on a pizza pan that's been floured and pierce several holes on it using a fork.
- Bake in the preheated oven for 5-10 minutes or until it reaches your preferred crispiness is achieved

Nutrition Information

- Calories: 83 calories;
- Total Carbohydrate: 17.4
- Cholesterol: 0
- Protein: 3.5
- Total Fat: 0.6
- Sodium: 196

222. Wonton Noodle Soup

Serving: 4 | Prep: 30mins | Cook: 15mins | Ready in:

Ingredients

- 1/2 pound shrimp, shelled and deveined
- 1 tablespoon minced celery
- 1 tablespoon minced green onion
- 1 egg white
- 1/2 teaspoon sesame oil
- 1/2 teaspoon salt
- 2 teaspoons cornstarch, divided
- 24 round wonton wrappers
- 2 tablespoons water
- 1 pound dry Chinese noodles
- 1 quart chicken stock
- 4 tablespoons minced green onion

Direction

- Pulse shrimp in a food processor several times to chop roughly. Mix 1 teaspoon of cornstarch, salt, sesame oil, egg white, 1 tablespoon of green onion and celery with the shrimp and pulse several more times to get a chunky paste. Take the mixture to a bowl, mix rapidly to get elastic mixture.
- Add a scant teaspoon of the shrimp mixture in the middle of each wonton wrapper on a flat surface. Mix leftover 1 teaspoon of cornstarch with 2 tablespoons of water to get a paste. Brush some cornstarch mixture one at a time around the wonton wrapper and fold in half to get a half circle, press edges to seal. Place the wonton with its straight edge facing you, curve the straight edge and seal the tips with extra cornstarch paste. Do the same with the rest of wontons.
- Boil water in a big pot and cook noodles in boiling water for 8 to 10 minutes until tender but firm enough to bite. Drain and distribute into 4 serving bowls.
- In the meantime, let the chicken broth simmer over moderate-low heat.
- Boil water in another big pot and add the wontons to the boiling water. When the wontons float on the surface, keep cooking for 60 more seconds. Use a slotted spoon to take them out when finished and distribute into 4 bowls.
- Ladle the hot chicken broth into the bowls with wontons and noodles and use the rest of chopped green onions for decoration then serve.

Nutrition Information

- Calories: 590 calories;
- Sodium: 1363
- Total Carbohydrate: 116.5
- Cholesterol: 91
- Protein: 28.2
- Total Fat: 4.9

223. Yakisoba Chicken

Serving: 6 | Prep: 15mins | Cook: 15mins | Ready in:

Ingredients

- 1/2 teaspoon sesame oil
- 1 tablespoon canola oil
- 2 tablespoons chile paste
- 2 cloves garlic, chopped
- 4 skinless, boneless chicken breast halves - cut into 1 inch cubes
- 1/2 cup soy sauce
- 1 onion, sliced lengthwise into eighths
- 1/2 medium head cabbage, coarsely chopped
- 2 carrots, coarsely chopped
- 8 ounces soba noodles, cooked and drained

Direction

- Combine chili paste, canola oil and sesame oil in a large skillet; stir-fry for half a minute. Put in garlic. Stir fry 30 seconds more. Put in a quarter cup of the soy sauce and chicken. Stir fry for about 5 mins until chicken is no longer pink. Take off the mixture from the pan. Put aside, keep it warm.
- Combine carrots, cabbage, and onion in emptied pan. Stir-fry for 2-3 mins until the cabbage starts to wilt. Stir in chicken mixture, cooked noodles, and remaining soy sauce to pan; blend by mixing. Enjoy!

Nutrition Information

- Calories: 295 calories;
- Total Carbohydrate: 40.7
- Cholesterol: 46
- Protein: 26.3
- Total Fat: 4.8
- Sodium: 1621

224. Yuba Noodle Salad

Serving: 2 | Prep: 20mins | Cook: | Ready in:

Ingredients

- 1/2 cup vegetable oil
- 1/3 cup warm rice wine vinegar
- 2 tablespoons peanut butter
- 1 tablespoon honey
- 1 tablespoon finely grated fresh ginger
- 1 teaspoon hot chili sauce (such as sambal)
- 1 teaspoon soy sauce
- 1/2 teaspoon toasted sesame oil
- 1 (5 ounce) package yuba (tofu skins), cut into 1-inch wide strips
- 1/2 cup chopped fresh cilantro
- 1/4 cup shaved carrot strips, or to taste
- 1/4 cup thinly sliced cabbage, or to taste
- 1/4 cup sliced green onions
- 1/2 teaspoon black sesame seeds, or to taste

Direction

- In a bowl, whisk together the sesame oil, soy sauce, chili sauce, ginger, honey, peanut butter, vinegar and vegetable oil until the dressing becomes creamy and smooth.
- In a bowl, toss together the green onions, cabbage, carrots, cilantro and yuba strips. Pour approximately 1/2 of the dressing on top of the salad and mix until coated. Mix the leftover dressing into the salad until the salad is dressed to your preference. Put black sesame seeds on top.

Nutrition Information

- Calories: 775 calories;
- Sodium: 384
- Total Carbohydrate: 22.4
- Cholesterol: 0
- Protein: 22.8
- Total Fat: 67.8

225. Yummy Honey Chicken Kabobs

Serving: 12 | Prep: 15mins | Cook: 15mins | Ready in:

Ingredients

- 1/4 cup vegetable oil
- 1/3 cup honey
- 1/3 cup soy sauce
- 1/4 teaspoon ground black pepper
- 8 skinless, boneless chicken breast halves - cut into 1 inch cubes
- 2 cloves garlic
- 5 small onions, cut into 2 inch pieces
- 2 red bell peppers, cut into 2 inch pieces
- skewers

Direction

- Whisk pepper, soy sauce, honey and oil together in a big bowl. Prior to putting in chicken, save a little marinade to brush on kabobs while cooking. Put in the bowl with peppers, onions, garlic and chicken, then marinate in the fridge for a minimum of 2 hours (longer will be better).
- Preheat the grill for high heat.
- Drain marinade from vegetables and chicken; get rid of marinade. Thread onto skewers with vegetables and chicken, alternately.
- Coat the grill grate lightly with oil and put on the grill with skewers. Cook until juices run clear, about 12-15 minutes. Turn and use reserved marinade to brush over often.

Nutrition Information

- Calories: 178 calories;
- Sodium: 442
- Total Carbohydrate: 12.4
- Cholesterol: 45
- Protein: 17.4
- Total Fat: 6.6

226. Zucchini Wrapped In Tortillas

Serving: 4 | Prep: 20mins | Cook: 20mins | Ready in:

Ingredients

- 1 tablespoon vegetable oil
- 1 teaspoon mustard seed (optional)
- 1 teaspoon cumin seeds
- 1 small red onion, thinly sliced
- 1 tablespoon grated fresh ginger
- 4 cups grated zucchini
- 1/2 teaspoon chili powder
- 1/4 teaspoon ground black pepper
- 1/4 teaspoon ground cloves
- 1/4 teaspoon ground cinnamon
- salt to taste
- 4 (10 inch) flour tortillas
- 4 fresh chives
- 1/2 cup sour cream (optional)

Direction

- Heat the oil in a medium size sauté pan or wok on medium-high heat, then add cumin seeds and mustard. Once they start to pop, reduce the heat and add the ginger and onion. Sauté until the onions turn light pink in color and tender.
- Add the shredded zucchini, then turn up the heat a bit. Mix often for about 5 to 10 minutes, until the zucchini is well cooked and soft. Stir in the salt, cinnamon, clove, pepper and chili powder.
- Warm the tortillas and put on a flat surface. In the center of each tortilla, put 1/4 of the zucchini filling. Roll up each tortilla and use chive to tie it closed. You may serve the wrap with a dollop of sour cream alongside to make a well-rounded wrap.

Nutrition Information

- Calories: 361 calories;
- Total Fat: 10.2
- Sodium: 376

- Total Carbohydrate: 48
- Cholesterol: 13
- Protein: 9.2

227. Zucchini And Eggs

Serving: 1 | Prep: 5mins | Cook: 5mins | Ready in:

Ingredients

- 2 teaspoons olive oil
- 1 small zucchini, sliced
- 1 egg, beaten
- salt and pepper to taste

Direction

- Heat a small skillet on medium heat. Add oil and sauté zucchini until softened. Arrange zucchini in a level layer and spread beaten egg evenly over the top. Cook until egg is set. Flavor with pepper and salt.

Nutrition Information

- Calories: 184 calories;
- Cholesterol: 138
- Protein: 6.9
- Total Fat: 15.8
- Sodium: 76
- Total Carbohydrate: 4.5

228. Zucchini With Chickpea And Mushroom Stuffing

Serving: 8 | Prep: 30mins | Cook: 30mins | Ready in:

Ingredients

- 4 zucchini, halved
- 1 tablespoon olive oil
- 1 onion, chopped
- 2 cloves garlic, crushed
- 1/2 (8 ounce) package button mushrooms, sliced
- 1 teaspoon ground coriander
- 1 1/2 teaspoons ground cumin, or to taste
- 1 (15.5 ounce) can chickpeas, rinsed and drained
- 1/2 lemon, juiced
- 2 tablespoons chopped fresh parsley
- sea salt to taste
- ground black pepper to taste

Direction

- Set an oven to preheat to 175°C (350°F), then grease a shallow baking dish.
- Scoop out the flesh from the zucchini and chop the flesh, then put it aside. Put the shells in the prepped dish.
- In a big skillet, heat the oil on medium heat. Sauté the onions for 5 minutes, then add the garlic and sauté for another 2 minutes. Stir in the mushrooms and chopped zucchini and sauté for 5 minutes. Stir in the pepper, salt, parsley, lemon juice, chickpeas, cumin and coriander. Scoop the mixture into the zucchini shells.
- Let it bake for 30-40 minutes in the preheated oven or until the zucchini becomes tender.

Nutrition Information

- Calories: 107 calories;
- Total Fat: 2.7
- Sodium: 170
- Total Carbohydrate: 18.4
- Cholesterol: 0
- Protein: 4.5

Chapter 2: Dairy-Free Potato Salad Recipes

***

229. Alabi Potato Salad

Serving: 20 | Prep: 15mins | Cook: 20mins | Ready in:

Ingredients

- 5 pounds potatoes
- 1 cup mayonnaise
- 1 cup dill pickle relish
- 1/4 cup prepared yellow mustard, or to taste
- 12 hard-cooked eggs, peeled and chopped
- 2 cups chopped celery (optional)
- 2 teaspoons paprika
- 20 buttery round crackers

Direction

- Cover potatoes with enough water in a large pot. Boil then cook till a fork can pierce easily into the potatoes, for about 20 minutes. Let drain and put aside to cool.
- Combine celery, hard-cooked eggs, mustard, relish and mayonnaise together in a big bowl. Chop the potatoes into cubes then place in the bowl. Gently mix to coat. Add a drizzling of paprika to garnish and position crackers around the edge.

Nutrition Information

- Calories: 159 calories;
- Total Fat: 13.1
- Sodium: 283
- Total Carbohydrate: 5.7
- Cholesterol: 131
- Protein: 4.7

230. All Canadian Potato Salad

Serving: 12 | Prep: 20mins | Cook: 30mins | Ready in:

Ingredients

- 4 pounds russet potatoes
- 3 tablespoons cider vinegar
- 3 large eggs
- 2/3 cup mayonnaise, or more to taste
- 2 teaspoons salt
- 1 teaspoon dry mustard
- 1/2 teaspoon celery seed
- 1/2 teaspoon ground black pepper
- 2 tablespoons hot water, or as needed
- 3 stalks celery, diced
- 1 red bell pepper, seeded and diced
- 1 onion, finely diced
- 3 green onions, thinly sliced
- 1/4 cup diced dill pickles
- 2 tablespoons chopped fresh parsley
- 1 teaspoon paprika

Direction

- Cover potatoes with salted water in a large pot then boil. Lower heat to medium-low then simmer for 25 minutes till tender. Drain and cut the unpeeled potatoes into 1-inch cubes. Sprinkle with vinegar while the potatoes are still warm. Put aside for 20 minutes to let completely cool.
- Cover eggs with water in a saucepan then boil. Take away from the heat and allow eggs to stand for 15 minutes in hot water. Take the eggs away from the hot water. Place under cold running water to cool then peel. Slice 2 eggs into dices with 1/4-inch size. Cut the leftover egg into slices with 1/4-inch size. Put aside to garnish.
- In a large bowl, stir together black pepper, celery seed, dry mustard, salt, mayonnaise and 2 diced eggs. Add in hot water and stir. Stir

parsley, pickles, green onions, onion, red bell pepper, celery and potatoes in the mayonnaise mixture. Store in the fridge, covered, for 30 minutes to chill. Drizzle paprika over the salad and top with reserved egg slices before serving.

Nutrition Information

- Calories: 238 calories;
- Protein: 4.7
- Total Fat: 11.3
- Sodium: 850
- Total Carbohydrate: 30.4
- Cholesterol: 51

231. Always A Winner Potato Salad

Serving: 12 | Prep: 20mins | Cook: 35mins | Ready in:

Ingredients

- 10 large baking potatoes, scrubbed
- 12 eggs
- 3 bunches green onions, chopped
- 6 dill pickles, chopped
- 1 (4 ounce) can shrimp
- 1 (4 ounce) can small shrimp, drained
- 2 cups low-fat mayonnaise
- salt and pepper to taste
- 2 tablespoons celery salt
- 2 tablespoons paprika

Direction

- Cover potatoes with water in a big pot. Bring to a boil till soft. Take away from the water and put aside to cool. Peel the potatoes and slice into chunks with bite size.
- Completely cover eggs with cold water in a saucepan. Boil for 1 minute. Cover then take away from the heat. Allow eggs to stand for 10-12 minutes in hot water. Take away from

the hot water; let cool then peel and chop the eggs.
- Combine cans of shrimp, dill pickles, green onions, eggs and potatoes together in a big bowl. Mix in paprika, celery salt and mayonnaise. Add ground black pepper and salt to taste. Let chill for 2 hours then serve.

Nutrition Information

- Calories: 359 calories;
- Total Fat: 6
- Sodium: 1288
- Total Carbohydrate: 60.5
- Cholesterol: 218
- Protein: 18.3

232. Argentinean Potato Salad

Serving: 6 | Prep: 20mins | Cook: 30mins | Ready in:

Ingredients

- 4 russet potatoes - peeled, boiled, and cubed
- 3 hard cooked eggs, chopped
- 1 (10 ounce) can mixed vegetables
- 1/2 cup mayonnaise
- 1/2 teaspoon black pepper
- 1/2 teaspoon ground mustard
- 1/2 tablespoon fresh lemon juice
- 1/2 teaspoon dried dill weed
- 5 tablespoons chopped pimiento-stuffed olives
- salt and black pepper to taste

Direction

- Boil lightly salted water in a big pot. Add peeled potatoes and cook for about 15 minutes till tender but still firm. Drain, let cool then cube.
- Cover eggs with cold water in a saucepan. Boil and immediately take away from heat. Allow eggs to stand in hot water, covered, for 10-12 minutes. Take away from the hot water and let

cool. Peel, slice and toss the eggs with vegetables and potatoes in a large serving or mixing bowl.
- Combine green olives, dill weed, lemon juice, ground mustard, 1/2 tsp of black pepper and mayonnaise together in a separate bowl. Stir till blended. Spread over the potato mixture with the dressing. Add pepper and salt to taste; toss till coated. Store in the fridge, cover for 1 hour or overnight.

Nutrition Information

- Calories: 271 calories;
- Protein: 5.6
- Total Fat: 18.4
- Sodium: 862
- Total Carbohydrate: 22.1
- Cholesterol: 99

233. Asian Potato Salad

Serving: 12 | Prep: 25mins | Cook: 20mins | Ready in:

Ingredients

- 4 slices bacon, crisply cooked and crumbled
- 6 new red potatoes
- 1 1/3 cups mayonnaise
- 1 teaspoon sugar
- 1 tablespoon soy sauce
- 1 teaspoon sesame oil
- 1/8 teaspoon dry hot mustard
- 1/8 teaspoon salt
- 3/4 cup chopped bok choy
- 1 red bell pepper, seeded and diced
- 1/2 cup chopped green onion
- 1/4 cup chopped fresh cilantro

Direction

- Cook bacon in a large and deep skillet over medium-high heat till evenly brown. Let drain, crumble and put aside.
- In the meantime, boil salted water in a big pot. Add and cook potatoes for about 15 minutes till tender but firm. Drain, let cool then chop into chunks with bite size.
- For the dressing, combine salt, mustard powder, sesame oil, soy sauce, sugar and mayonnaise together.
- In a big bowl, combine cilantro, green onion, red pepper, bok choy, bacon and potatoes together. Spread over the dressing and stir well. Store in the fridge for at least 1 hour to let flavors blend. Serve.

Nutrition Information

- Calories: 282 calories;
- Total Fat: 21.2
- Sodium: 320
- Total Carbohydrate: 20.3
- Cholesterol: 13
- Protein: 3.8

234. Authentic German Potato Salad

Serving: 4 | Prep: 30mins | Cook: 20mins | Ready in:

Ingredients

- 3 cups diced peeled potatoes
- 4 slices bacon
- 1 small onion, diced
- 1/4 cup white vinegar
- 2 tablespoons water
- 3 tablespoons white sugar
- 1 teaspoon salt
- 1/8 teaspoon ground black pepper
- 1 tablespoon chopped fresh parsley

Direction

- Put the potatoes in a pot and fill with sufficient amount of water to immerse the potatoes. Allow the water to boil and let the

potatoes cook in the boiling water for about 10 minutes until you can prick the potatoes with ease using a fork. Drain the cooked potatoes and put aside to let it cool down.
- In a big and deep skillet placed over medium-high heat setting, put in the bacon and let it cook while flipping the bacon if need be until it becomes crispy and turns brown in color. Take the cooked bacon from the skillet and put it aside.
- Sauté the onion in the bacon drippings over medium heat setting until it turns brown in color. Put in the sugar, vinegar, pepper, water and salt. Let the mixture boil, then put in the parsley and cooked potatoes. Break 1/2 of the cooked bacon to smaller pieces and add it into the potato mixture. Let the mixture cook until fully heated, then place it in a serving dish. Break the remaining 1/2 of the cooked bacon to smaller pieces directly on top of the potato mixture; serve it while still warm.

Nutrition Information

- Calories: 183 calories;
- Total Carbohydrate: 32.2
- Cholesterol: 10
- Protein: 5.4
- Total Fat: 3.9
- Sodium: 796

235. Baked Potato Salad With Dill

Serving: 6 | Prep: 20mins | Cook: | Ready in:

Ingredients

- 4 baking potatoes
- 4 ounces fresh bean sprouts
- 1/4 cup coarsely chopped walnuts
- 4 celery, thinly sliced
- 4 radishes, sliced
- 3 tablespoons chopped fresh dill weed
- 2 tablespoons chopped fresh parsley
- 1/3 cup mayonnaise
- 2 tablespoons lemon juice
- 4 teaspoons Dijon-style prepared mustard
- 1/4 teaspoon curry powder

Direction

- Preheat oven to 400°F or 200°C. Use a fork to pierce the potatoes then bake in the preheated oven till tender, for 1 hour. Take away from the oven. Allow to cool and chill till cold.
- Peel, cube and add the potatoes along with parsley, dill weed, radishes, celery, walnuts and bean sprouts in a large bowl.
- Whisk together curry powder, mustard, lemon juice and mayonnaise.
- Spread over the potato mixture with dressing. Toss till coated. Store in the fridge, covered, till ready to serve.

Nutrition Information

- Calories: 227 calories;
- Total Fat: 13.2
- Sodium: 208
- Total Carbohydrate: 25.3
- Cholesterol: 5
- Protein: 3.8

236. Balsamic Glazed Roasted Potato Salad

Serving: 8 | Prep: 30mins | Cook: 30mins | Ready in:

Ingredients

- 1/3 cup olive oil
- 3 tablespoons balsamic vinegar
- 1 tablespoon honey
- 1 tablespoon paprika
- 1 clove garlic, minced
- salt and ground black pepper to taste

- 2 pounds baby Yukon Gold potatoes, quartered
- 1/2 pound cremini mushrooms, quartered
- 1 large sweet onion, chopped
- 2 slices bacon
- 2 green onions, sliced (optional)
- 1/3 cup chopped fresh parsley (optional)
- 2 tablespoons balsamic vinegar

Direction

- Preheat the oven to 400°F or 200°C. Line aluminum foil on a baking sheet.
- In a large bowl, whisk together black pepper, salt, garlic, paprika, honey, 3 tbsp. of balsamic vinegar and olive oil. Add sweet onion, mushrooms and potatoes in the vinegar mixture and stir. Toss till coated. Spread over the prepped baking sheet with vegetables.
- Bake in the preheated oven for 30-40 minutes till it's easy to pierce potatoes using a fork.
- In a large and deep skillet, cook the bacon over medium-high heat for about 10 minutes while turning occasionally till evenly browned. Place bacon slices on a plate lined with paper towel to drain; crumble bacon.
- In a large bowl, place the potato mixture then toss with the leftover 2 tbsp. of balsamic vinegar, parsley, green onions and bacon.

Nutrition Information

- Calories: 234 calories;
- Cholesterol: 5
- Protein: 4.6
- Total Fat: 12.5
- Sodium: 72
- Total Carbohydrate: 27.8

237. Balsamic Vinegar Potato Salad

Serving: 8 | Prep: 15mins | Cook: 20mins | Ready in:

Ingredients

- 10 medium red potatoes, diced
- 1 small onion, chopped
- 1/2 cup diced roasted red peppers
- 1 (4 ounce) can sliced black olives, drained
- 1 (10 ounce) can quartered artichoke hearts, drained
- 1/2 cup balsamic vinegar
- 3 teaspoons olive oil
- 1 teaspoon dried oregano
- 1 teaspoon dried basil
- 1/2 teaspoon mustard powder
- 2 tablespoons chopped fresh parsley

Direction

- Cover potatoes with enough water in a saucepan. Boil then cook till tender, for 5-10 minutes. Let drain and move to a large bowl.
- Add artichokes, olives, red peppers and onion to the potatoes bowl. Whisk together parsley, mustard powder, basil, oregano, olive oil and balsamic vinegar in a separate bowl. Spread over the vegetables and stir till coated. Before serving, let chill for at least 4 hours to overnight.

Nutrition Information

- Calories: 257 calories;
- Total Fat: 3.9
- Sodium: 407
- Total Carbohydrate: 51.1
- Cholesterol: 0
- Protein: 6.9

238. Barbeque Potato Salad

Serving: 12 | Prep: 25mins | Cook: 20mins | Ready in:

Ingredients

- 5 pounds unpeeled potatoes, cubed
- 1 small red onion, diced

- 6 hard-cooked eggs, peeled and finely diced
- 1 1/2 cups mayonnaise
- 1/2 cup barbeque sauce
- 1/2 teaspoon garlic powder
- salt and ground black pepper to taste
- 1 teaspoon paprika (optional)

Direction

- Cover cubed potatoes with water in a big kettle. Boil over medium-high heat then lower to medium-low heat. Cover then simmer for 15-20 minutes till just tender. Drain the potatoes and place them as a single layer on the baking sheets. Store in the fridge to chill for 2 hours till cold.
- In a large bowl, combine pepper, salt, garlic powder, barbeque sauce, mayonnaise, egg, red onion and cooled potatoes. Drizzle with paprika if preferred.

Nutrition Information

- Calories: 398 calories;
- Total Fat: 24.5
- Sodium: 319
- Total Carbohydrate: 38.6
- Cholesterol: 103
- Protein: 7.3

239. Bea's Mashed Potato Salad

Serving: 4 | Prep: 20mins | Cook: | Ready in:

Ingredients

- 1 (4 ounce) package Idahoan® Baby Reds® Flavored Mashed Potatoes
- 1 dill pickle, finely chopped
- 3 radishes, thinly sliced
- 1 hard-boiled egg, sliced
- 2 celery stalks, finely chopped
- 2 tablespoons red onion, finely chopped
- 3 tablespoons mayonnaise*
- 1 tablespoon stone ground mustard
- 1 teaspoon yellow mustard
- Salt and pepper to taste
- 1/4 teaspoon celery seed (optional)

Direction

- Ready Idahoan Baby Reds based on the package directions.
- Mix in red onion, celery, hard-boiled egg, radishes, and pickles.
- In another bowl, mix mustard and mayo then stir in mashed potato mixture.
- Add pepper and salt to season and taste and celery seed if desired.

Nutrition Information

- Calories: 153 calories;
- Total Fat: 10.6
- Sodium: 377
- Total Carbohydrate: 11.7
- Cholesterol: 57
- Protein: 3.4

240. Benny's Potato Salad

Serving: 10 | Prep: 15mins | Cook: 10mins | Ready in:

Ingredients

- 2 1/2 pounds potatoes, cubed
- 4 hard-cooked eggs, peeled and chopped
- 1/3 cup chopped green olives
- 1/3 cup dill pickle relish
- 1/4 cup sweet pickle relish
- 1/4 cup chopped green onion
- 1/2 cup mayonnaise
- 3 teaspoons yellow mustard
- 3 teaspoons brown mustard
- 1 teaspoon white wine vinegar
- 1 teaspoon garlic powder
- 1 teaspoon ground black pepper

- 1 teaspoon ground white pepper
- 1/2 teaspoon salt
- 2 teaspoons celery seed
- 1/2 teaspoon dill seed
- 1 teaspoon chopped fresh dill

Direction

- Cover potatoes with enough water in a big pot. Boil then cook till tender but not mushy, for about 5 minutes. Place in a colander to drain and let cold water run over to cool. Put aside.
- Combine wine vinegar, brown and yellow mustards, mayonnaise, green onion, sweet and dill pickle relishes, green olives and eggs together in a big serving bowl. Add dill, dill seed, celery seed, salt, white and black pepper and garlic powder to taste. Mix well; add in potatoes and stir to coat. Let chill to let flavors blend, for at least 2 hours.

Nutrition Information

- Calories: 217 calories;
- Total Fat: 11.6
- Sodium: 501
- Total Carbohydrate: 24
- Cholesterol: 78
- Protein: 5.4

241. Brian's German Potato Salad

Serving: 12 | Prep: 35mins | Cook: 20mins | Ready in:

Ingredients

- 4 pounds red potatoes, halved
- 1 pound Bacon, cut into 1/2-inch pieces
- 1 cup chopped onion
- 1/4 cup all-purpose flour
- 1/4 cup white sugar
- 1 1/2 teaspoons salt

- 1 cup apple cider vinegar
- 2 teaspoons celery seed
- 2 tablespoons chopped fresh parsley

Direction

- Cover the potatoes with salted water in a large pot. Boil then lower to medium-low heat. Cover and simmer for 10 minutes till just tender. Drain and let steam dry for 1-2 minutes. Cut into 1/2-inch pieces then transfer into a big mixing bowl.
- In the meantime, in a large skillet, stir onion and bacon together over medium heat for 15 minutes till the onion is very tender but hasn't turned brown and the bacon fat has rendered. Stir in salt, sugar and flour then cook for 1 minute. Add in vinegar; simmer and cook for 5 minutes till slightly thick.
- Spread over the potatoes with the dressing and drizzle with parsley and celery seed. Gently stir till combined. Serve while hot.

Nutrition Information

- Calories: 316 calories;
- Total Fat: 17.4
- Sodium: 617
- Total Carbohydrate: 32.1
- Cholesterol: 26
- Protein: 7.8

242. Brown Mustard Potato Salad

Serving: 8 | Prep: 20mins | Cook: 20mins | Ready in:

Ingredients

- 8 red potatoes, diced
- 3 hard-boiled eggs, chopped
- 1 cup mayonnaise, or to taste
- 1/2 red onion, minced
- 1/4 cup spicy brown mustard

- 4 teaspoons sweet pickle relish
- 1 teaspoon chopped fresh parsley
- 1 teaspoon chopped fresh dill
- 1 pinch ground black pepper
- 1 pinch paprika

Direction

- Salt water and pour over potatoes in a large pot, then boil. Lower the heat to medium-low and simmer for about 20 minutes until tender. Drain and cool potatoes by rinsing in running cold water.
- Combine paprika, black pepper, dill, parsley, pickle relish, brown mustard, onion, mayonnaise, eggs and potatoes in a bowl, toss to coat completely.

Nutrition Information

- Calories: 389 calories;
- Total Fat: 24.6
- Sodium: 311
- Total Carbohydrate: 37.1
- Cholesterol: 90
- Protein: 7.2

243. Bud's Potato Salad

Serving: 20 | Prep: 15mins | Cook: 20mins | Ready in:

Ingredients

- 10 pounds potatoes
- 1 cup water
- 1 cup white wine vinegar
- 1 cup white sugar
- 2 onions, diced
- salt and pepper to taste
- 1 tablespoon celery seed
- 2 cups mayonnaise

Direction

- Boil salted water in a big pot. Add and cook potatoes for about 15 minutes till tender but still firm. Let drain and let cool.
- When the potatoes are cooled, slice then place as a layer in a large dish or bowl.
- Combine sugar, vinegar and water together in a saucepan. Boil then cook for 1 minute. Take away from the heat and spread over the potatoes. Chill, covered, for at least 12 hours.
- Remove the excess marinade then add mayonnaise, celery seed, pepper, salt and onions. Stir well then serve chilled.

Nutrition Information

- Calories: 377 calories;
- Total Carbohydrate: 51.5
- Cholesterol: 8
- Protein: 5
- Total Fat: 17.8
- Sodium: 141

244. Caramelized Onion And Bacon Potato Salad

Serving: 10 | Prep: 10mins | Cook: 35mins | Ready in:

Ingredients

- 30 small small potatoes, or more as needed
- 1 large red onion, sliced into 1/8-inch pieces
- 1 teaspoon dried tarragon
- 3 fluid ounces white wine
- 4 slices bacon, cut into 1/2-inch pieces
- 1/2 cup tzatziki sauce, or more to taste
- 5 tablespoons chopped fresh chives
- salt and ground black pepper to taste

Direction

- Use a big pot and place the potatoes in with salted water. Let it boil then turn the heat down to medium low. Let it simmer between

10 to 15 minutes until the potatoes are tender. Drain and cool then cut potatoes in half.
- Heat a frying pan over medium heat and cook onions for about 20 minutes or until it becomes golden brown and softened. Add in tarragon then pour white wine to deglaze the pan. Let it simmer between 2 to 3 minutes until the wine evaporates.
- Cook the bacon in a big skillet over medium high heat for ten minutes, turning occasionally until evenly browned. Drain the bacon slices using paper towels.
- Mix together the potatoes, bacon and onion in a big bowl. Fold tzatziki sauce, chives, black pepper and salt into the potato mixture.

Nutrition Information

- Calories: 403 calories;
- Total Fat: 12.3
- Sodium: 125
- Total Carbohydrate: 83.7
- Cholesterol: 4
- Protein: 11.6

245. Chicken Potato Salad

Serving: 7 | Prep: | Cook: |Ready in:

Ingredients

- 2 boneless chicken breast halves, cooked
- 2 hard-cooked eggs
- 3 potatoes, cooked
- 1 1/4 cups pickled cucumbers
- 1/4 teaspoon salt
- 2 tablespoons olive oil
- 2/3 cup mayonnaise

Direction

- Chop pickled cucumbers, potatoes, eggs and chicken into very small pieces. Combine all together. Add mayonnaise, salt then olive oil.

Toss till coated. Store in the fridge for 2-3 hours then serve.

Nutrition Information

- Calories: 340 calories;
- Protein: 12.6
- Total Fat: 24.5
- Sodium: 600
- Total Carbohydrate: 17.9
- Cholesterol: 92

246. Dad's Potato Salad

Serving: 15 | Prep: 45mins | Cook: 45mins |Ready in:

Ingredients

- 5 pounds potatoes, unpeeled
- 12 eggs
- 1 (16 ounce) package uncooked spiral pasta
- 1 (16 ounce) jar dill pickles, chopped (reserve juice)
- 2 bunches green onions, chopped
- 3 cups mayonnaise, or to taste
- 2 tablespoons Worcestershire sauce
- 1/4 cup dill pickle juice, or as needed
- salt and pepper to taste

Direction

- Cover the potatoes with salted water in a large pot. Boil over high heat then lower to medium-low heat. Simmer, covered for 20 minutes till tender. Drain and let steam dry for 1-2 minutes. Let the potatoes cool.
- Meanwhile, place a single layer of the eggs in a saucepan and cover the eggs by 1 inch with water. Cover and boil over high heat. Take the eggs away from the heat while the water is boiling. Allow eggs to stand for 15 minutes in hot water. Discard the hot water then place eggs under cold running water in the sink to cool. Peel once they're cold.

- Bring lightly salted water to a rolling boil in a large pot over high heat. When the water is boiling, add in the spiral pasta, stir then bring back to a boil. Uncover and cook while stirring occasionally for 8 minutes till the pasta is cooked through yet firm to bite. Place onto a colander positioned in the sink to drain well. Use cold water to rinse the salad then allow to cool.
- Peel the potatoes. In a large bowl, chop hard-cooked eggs and potatoes into pieces with bite size. Mix in green onions, dill pickles and cooked pasta. Stir together pepper and salt to taste, enough dill pickle juice to make the dressing creamy, Worcestershire sauce and mayonnaise in a bowl. Spread over the potato mixture with the dressing. Toss lightly till all the ingredients are coated with dressing. Let the salad chill for at least 30 minutes till cold.

Nutrition Information

- Calories: 613 calories;
- Total Fat: 39.8
- Sodium: 726
- Total Carbohydrate: 53.8
- Cholesterol: 166
- Protein: 13.2

247. Deli Cious Potato Salad

Serving: 8 | Prep: 35mins | Cook: 25mins | Ready in:

Ingredients

- 8 potatoes
- 1/2 pound salami, cubed
- 3 hard-cooked eggs, chopped
- 2 apples, cored and chopped
- 1 onion, chopped
- 3 dill pickles, chopped
- 3 tablespoons mayonnaise
- 3 tablespoons red wine vinegar
- salt and ground black pepper to taste
- 1 pinch paprika, or to taste

Direction

- Cover potatoes with salted water in a large pot then boil. Lower to medium-low heat for 20 minutes till tender. Drain, let cool and cut the potatoes into chunks.
- In a skillet, cook salami over medium heat for 5 minutes till heated through. Discard excess fat and let cool.
- In a large bowl, mix pickles, onion, apples, eggs and potatoes.
- Add paprika, black pepper, salt, red wine vinegar, mayonnaise and salami in the potato mixture then stir. Before serving, let chill for at least 2 hours.

Nutrition Information

- Calories: 371 calories;
- Total Fat: 14.9
- Sodium: 671
- Total Carbohydrate: 46.7
- Cholesterol: 110
- Protein: 13.7

248. Diane's Scotch Irish Potato Salad

Serving: 20 | Prep: 30mins | Cook: 20mins | Ready in:

Ingredients

- 10 pounds red potatoes
- 2 cups chopped celery
- 2 cups chopped red onion
- 6 hard-boiled eggs, peeled and coarsely chopped
- 1 cup sliced black olives
- 1 cup sliced green olives with pimentos
- 1 cup dill pickle relish
- 1/2 cup sweet pickle relish
- 1 teaspoon smoked paprika

- 1/4 cup prepared mustard, or as needed
- 1/4 cup apple cider vinegar, or as needed
- 1/2 cup mayonnaise, or as needed
- salt and ground black pepper to taste

Direction

- Cover potatoes with water in a large pot then boil. Lower heat to medium-low then cover and simmer for 20 minutes till tender. Let drain and cool.
- Discard the potatoes' skins and slice into chunks. Transfer into a large bowl.
- Lightly stir potatoes together with paprika, sweet pickle relish, dill pickle relish, green olives, black olives, eggs, red onion and celery till combined thoroughly.
- Stir in mayonnaise, vinegar and mustard. Mix lightly to coat and moisten all the ingredients. Add up to 1/2 cup more of mayonnaise to the salad and stir if it's not moist enough.
- Add ground black pepper and salt to taste. Prepare the salad one day ahead then store in the fridge overnight to get the best flavor.

Nutrition Information

- Calories: 259 calories;
- Cholesterol: 66
- Protein: 6.9
- Total Fat: 8
- Sodium: 388
- Total Carbohydrate: 42

249. Easy Potato Salad With Dill

Serving: 5 | Prep: 18mins | Cook: 12mins | Ready in:

Ingredients

- 1 pound red potatoes, cut into 3/4-inch cubes
- 1/4 cup mayonnaise
- 2 tablespoons cider vinegar
- 2 sprigs chopped fresh dill, or to taste
- salt and pepper to taste
- 1/2 cucumber - peeled, seeded, and finely chopped
- 4 green onions, sliced

Direction

- Cover potatoes with salted water in a large pot. Boil over high heat then lower to medium-low heat. Cover then simmer for 12 minutes till tender. Drain and let steam dry while making the dressing.
- Whisk together pepper, salt, dill, apple cider vinegar and mayonnaise. Add in green onions and cucumber then stir. Gently toss warm potatoes with the dressing till the potatoes are coated. Store in the fridge, covered, for at least 2 hours then serve.

Nutrition Information

- Calories: 150 calories;
- Total Fat: 8.9
- Sodium: 71
- Total Carbohydrate: 16.2
- Cholesterol: 4
- Protein: 2.2

250. Easy Salad Olivieh

Serving: 24 | Prep: 35mins | Cook: 35mins | Ready in:

Ingredients

- 6 large potatoes
- 2 cups mayonnaise
- 1 stalk celery, diced
- 8 hard-cooked eggs, chopped
- 1 whole rotisserie roast chicken, pulled and diced
- 2 tablespoons mustard
- 1/4 cup chopped pitted green olives
- 1 tablespoon salt

- 3 large dill pickles, chopped

Direction

- Cover potatoes with salted water in a large pot. Boil then lower to medium-low heat. Cover then simmer for 30 minutes till fork-tender. Drain and let cool. Peel the potatoes then dice. In a large mixing bowl, place the diced potatoes then store in the fridge till cold. When the potatoes are cold, fold in pickles, salt, olives, mustard, chicken, eggs, celery and mayonnaise. Store in the fridge for 2 hours then serve.

Nutrition Information

- Calories: 324 calories;
- Protein: 13.9
- Total Fat: 22.1
- Sodium: 725
- Total Carbohydrate: 17.7
- Cholesterol: 108

251. English Pub Potato Salad With Cucumber And Bacon

Serving: 8 | Prep: 30mins | Cook: 20mins | Ready in:

Ingredients

- 8 red potatoes
- 6 slices bacon
- 1 cup mayonnaise
- 1 cucumber, chopped
- 1/2 cup chopped red onion
- 3 hard-cooked eggs, chopped
- 1 cup celery, chopped
- 1/2 cup chopped fresh parsley
- 1 tablespoon paprika
- salt and pepper to taste
- 1 hard-cooked egg, sliced
- 3 sprigs fresh parsley, or as desired
- 1 pinch paprika, for garnish

Direction

- Cover potatoes with salted water in a big pot; boil. Lower the heat to medium-low then simmer for about 20 minutes till tender. Drain and let cool. Chop potatoes then move to a big salad bowl.
- Cook the bacon over medium-high heat in a big skillet while occasionally stirring for about 10 minutes till browned evenly. Place bacon slices on paper towels to drain. Crumble the bacon once cool.
- Stir 1 tbsp. of paprika, 1/2 cup of parsley, celery, 3 chopped eggs, red onion, cucumber, crumbled bacon and mayonnaise together with the potatoes till combined thoroughly. Add black pepper and salt to taste. Add a pinch of paprika, 3 sprigs of fresh parsley and slices of hard-cooked egg to garnish the salad.

Nutrition Information

- Calories: 441 calories;
- Cholesterol: 124
- Protein: 10.9
- Total Fat: 28
- Sodium: 380
- Total Carbohydrate: 38.9

252. Ensalada Rusa

Serving: 4 | Prep: 20mins | Cook: 20mins | Ready in:

Ingredients

- 3 beets, trimmed
- 4 potatoes, peeled and cubed
- 1 teaspoon salt
- 4 eggs
- 1/2 cup mayonnaise, or to taste

Direction

- Cover the beets with water in a saucepan; boil. Lower heat to medium then gently boil for

about 20 minutes till tender. Take away from the boiling water and cool. Peel, dice then chill the beets.
- In a separate saucepan, cover the potatoes with water; add in salt and stir. Bring the potato cubes to boil for about 15 minutes till tender but not mushy. Place the potatoes in a colander positioned in the sink to drain and chill.
- Boil a saucepan of water then lower heat to medium. Add in 1-2 more tsp of salt and stir. Lower the eggs very gently into the boiling water and simmer for 15 minutes, ensure that they don't hit the pan's bottom and crack. Transfer eggs to a bowl full of ice water and ice; chill the eggs till thoroughly cold. Peed the eggs then dice.
- In a salad bowl, combine eggs, potato cubes and chilled beets together. Add in mayonnaise and stir gently to taste.

Nutrition Information

- Calories: 459 calories;
- Total Fat: 27.1
- Sodium: 868
- Total Carbohydrate: 44.3
- Cholesterol: 196
- Protein: 11.8

253. French Potato Salad

Serving: 5 | Prep: 15mins | Cook: 15mins | Ready in:

Ingredients

- 9 potatoes
- 1/2 cup vegetable oil
- 1/4 cup tarragon vinegar
- 1/4 cup beef consomme
- 1/4 cup chopped green onions
- 2 tablespoons chopped fresh parsley
- 1 teaspoon salt
- 1 teaspoon ground black pepper

Direction

- Boil salted water in a big pot; put in potatoes. Cook for about 15mins until the potatoes are tender but still firm; drain. Place potatoes in a big bowl and allow them to cool for a bit. Skin and cut potatoes onto a big bowl.
- Mix pepper, oil, salt, vinegar, parsley, green onion, and consommé together in a small bowl.
- Toss dressing and warm potatoes together; cover. Chill for a few hours to overnight.

Nutrition Information

- Calories: 500 calories;
- Cholesterol: < 1
- Protein: 9.3
- Total Fat: 22.4
- Sodium: 1474
- Total Carbohydrate: 68

254. German Potato Salad

Serving: 4 | Prep: 10mins | Cook: 45mins | Ready in:

Ingredients

- 4 potatoes
- 4 slices bacon
- 1 tablespoon all-purpose flour
- 2 tablespoons white sugar
- 1/3 cup water
- 1/4 cup white wine vinegar
- 1/2 cup chopped green onions
- salt and pepper to taste

Direction

- Boil salted water in a big pot. Add and cook potatoes for about 15 minutes till tender but still firm. Drain, let the potatoes cool then chop.
- Cook bacon in a big and deep skillet over medium high heat till evenly brown. Let drain

then crumble and put aside. Save up the bacon fat.
- Add vinegar, water, sugar and flour to the skillet then cook over medium heat in the reserved bacon fat till the dressing is thickened.
- Add in green onions, potatoes and bacon then stir to coat. Cook till heated then add pepper and salt to taste. Serve while still warm.

Nutrition Information

- Calories: 328 calories;
- Sodium: 250
- Total Carbohydrate: 46.1
- Cholesterol: 19
- Protein: 8
- Total Fat: 12.8

255. Grandma Sophie's Smashed Potato Salad

Serving: 8 | Prep: 15mins | Cook: 30mins | Ready in:

Ingredients

- 5 pounds potatoes, peeled, cut into 2 inch chunks
- 3 hard-cooked eggs, peeled and finely diced
- 1/2 cup finely chopped dill pickle
- 2 cups mayonnaise
- salt to taste

Direction

- Boil potatoes for about 25-30 minutes till soft. Transfer potatoes into a big bowl.
- While the potatoes are no longer steaming but still warm, use a fork to stir in hard-cooked eggs. Stir in dill pickle then mix in mayonnaise. Add salt to taste. Keep stirring till there're not many big chunks remaining and potatoes are mashed.

Nutrition Information

- Calories: 642 calories;
- Sodium: 1352
- Total Carbohydrate: 51.9
- Cholesterol: 91
- Protein: 8.6
- Total Fat: 45.8

256. Grandpa Buick's Famous Potato Salad

Serving: 12 | Prep: 30mins | Cook: 20mins | Ready in:

Ingredients

- 3 pounds red potatoes
- 3 (4.5 ounce) cans small shrimp, drained
- 2 sweet onions, finely diced
- 6 hard-cooked eggs, sliced 1/8-inch thick
- 1 (16 ounce) jar sweet pickles, drained and finely diced
- 1/2 cup mayonnaise
- salt and ground black pepper to taste
- 1 pinch paprika, or to taste

Direction

- Cover red potatoes with salted water in a large pot then boil. Lower heat to medium-low then simmer for 20 minutes till tender and cracks begin to appear on the peels. Drain and cool. Peel and the cooled potatoes into 1/8-inch dices.
- In a large salad bowl, place mayonnaise, sweet pickles, hard-cooked eggs, onions, shrimp and potatoes then stir till combined. Add black pepper and salt to taste. Drizzle with paprika. Let the salad chill for at least 3 hours then serve.

Nutrition Information

- Calories: 272 calories;

- Total Fat: 10.9
- Sodium: 318
- Total Carbohydrate: 30.5
- Cholesterol: 165
- Protein: 13.4

- Calories: 176 calories;
- Sodium: 97
- Total Carbohydrate: 17.3
- Cholesterol: 0
- Protein: 1.9
- Total Fat: 11.3

257. Green Bean And Potato Salad

Serving: 10 | Prep: 15mins | Cook: 30mins | Ready in:

Ingredients

- 1 1/2 pounds red potatoes
- 3/4 pound fresh green beans, trimmed and snapped
- 1/4 cup chopped fresh basil
- 1 small red onion, chopped
- salt and pepper to taste
- 1/4 cup balsamic vinegar
- 2 tablespoons Dijon mustard
- 2 tablespoons fresh lemon juice
- 1 clove garlic, minced
- 1 dash Worcestershire sauce
- 1/2 cup extra virgin olive oil

Direction

- In a big pot filled with about 1 in. of water, place the potatoes; boil and cook till potatoes are tender, for about 15 minutes. After the first 10 minutes, add in the green beans to steam. Drain the potatoes, let cool and slice into quarters. Move into a big bowl then toss with pepper, salt, red onion and fresh basil. Put aside.
- Whisk together olive oil, Worcestershire sauce, garlic, lemon juice, mustard and balsamic vinegar in a medium bowl. Spread over the salad then stir till coated. Add pepper and salt to taste if desired.

Nutrition Information

258. Grilled Mustard Potato Salad

Serving: 4 | Prep: 20mins | Cook: 25mins | Ready in:

Ingredients

- 3 Yukon Gold potatoes, cubed
- 3 red potatoes, cubed
- 1/4 cup canola oil
- 3 tablespoons distilled white vinegar
- 1 tablespoon Dijon mustard
- 1/2 teaspoon celery salt
- 1/4 teaspoon pepper

Direction

- Preheat an outdoor grill for high heat.
- Boil salted water in a large pot. Cook potatoes till tender but firm, for 10-15 minutes till tender but firm. Drain then place in a medium bowl.
- Mix pepper, celery salt, Dijon mustard, vinegar and canola oil in a small bowl. Toss the potatoes with 1/2 of the mixture.
- Place a single layer of potatoes on a sheet of foil and put on the prepared grill. Cook while turning occasionally till browned lightly, for 7-9 minutes. Take away from the heat and let cool. Toss with the leftover oil mixture then serve.

Nutrition Information

- Calories: 316 calories;
- Total Fat: 14.3
- Sodium: 295

- Total Carbohydrate: 42.7
- Cholesterol: 0
- Protein: 4.9

259. Hawaiian Bruddah Potato Mac (Macaroni) Salad

Serving: 20 | Prep: 30mins | Cook: 20mins | Ready in:

Ingredients

- 5 eggs
- 7 large potatoes, peeled and cubed
- 1 cup elbow macaroni
- 3 cups mayonnaise
- 1 tablespoon sherry vinegar (optional)
- 1 1/2 teaspoons curry powder
- 1 teaspoon celery seed
- salt and black pepper to taste
- 2 cups grated carrots
- 1 cup frozen green peas, cooked, drained
- 1 small sweet onion, finely chopped

Direction

- In a saucepan, place a single layer of eggs and cover them by 1 inch with water. Cover then boil over high heat. When the water is boiling, take away from the heat and allow eggs to stand for 15 minutes in hot water. Discard hot water and leave eggs under cold running water in the sink to cool. Once the eggs are cooled, peel then chop.
- Boil salted water in a large pot. Add and cook potatoes for 15 minutes till tender but firm. Let drain and refrigerate till cooled.
- Boil a large pot of lightly salted water over high heat to a rolling boil. Add macaroni in the boiling water, stir and let boil again. Uncover, cook the pasta while stirring occasionally for 8 minutes till the pasta is firm to bite but has cooked through. Place pasta in a colander positioned in a sink to drain. Use cold water to rinse.
- In a bowl, whisk together pepper, salt, celery seed, curry powder, vinegar and mayonnaise. In a large bowl, combine onion, peas, carrots, chopped eggs, macaroni and cooled potatoes. Carefully add in the dressing and stir. Store in the fridge, covered, overnight.

Nutrition Information

- Calories: 387 calories;
- Total Carbohydrate: 30.2
- Cholesterol: 59
- Protein: 5.7
- Total Fat: 27.7
- Sodium: 346

260. Hot German Potato Salad II

Serving: 6 | Prep: 10mins | Cook: 30mins | Ready in:

Ingredients

- 3 pounds potatoes
- 1 pound bacon, cubed
- 1 onion, diced
- 2 cups white sugar
- 2 cups white wine vinegar

Direction

- Boil salted water in a large pot. Add and cook potatoes for 15 minutes till tender but firm. Drain, let the potatoes cool and chop.
- In a large and deep skillet, cook onion and bacon over medium heat till bacon is browned evenly. Discard excess grease from the skillet.
- Add vinegar and sugar into the onion mixture and bacon. Boil then spread the mixture over the potatoes. Stir.

Nutrition Information

- Calories: 575 calories;

- Sodium: 596
- Total Carbohydrate: 108.2
- Cholesterol: 27
- Protein: 14.1
- Total Fat: 10.6

261. Hot German Potato Salad III

Serving: 12 | Prep: 10mins | Cook: 50mins | Ready in:

Ingredients

- 9 potatoes, peeled
- 6 slices bacon
- 3/4 cup chopped onions
- 2 tablespoons all-purpose flour
- 2 tablespoons white sugar
- 2 teaspoons salt
- 1/2 teaspoon celery seed
- 1/8 teaspoon ground black pepper
- 3/4 cup water
- 1/3 cup distilled white vinegar

Direction

- In a large pot, salt the water then bring to a boil. Pour potatoes and cook for about 30 minutes until tender, but still firm. Drain off the water, allow to cool then cut into thin slices.
- Fry bacon in a large, deep skillet over medium-high heat until evenly browned. Drain, chop into small pieces and set aside, reserve the bacon fat.
- Use bacon drippings to stir-fry onions until golden brown.
- Combine pepper, celery seed, salt, sugar, and flour in a small bowl, mix well. Pour the dried combination to the sautéed onions and keep stirring until the bubbles appear, turn off the heat. Pour vinegar and water and stir gently. Bring back to the stove and boil, stirring continuously. Remain the process for 1 minute. Lightly mix sliced potatoes and bacon into the vinegar-water compound, keep stirring gently until the potatoes are thoroughly heated.

Nutrition Information

- Calories: 205 calories;
- Total Fat: 6.5
- Sodium: 512
- Total Carbohydrate: 32.9
- Cholesterol: 10
- Protein: 4.3

262. Hot Red Potato Salad

Serving: 8 | Prep: 15mins | Cook: 45mins | Ready in:

Ingredients

- 6 red potatoes
- 6 slices bacon, diced
- 1 onion, diced
- 1/2 cup chopped celery
- 1 cube chicken bouillon
- 1/2 cup boiling water
- 1 cup vinegar
- 2 teaspoons salt
- 1/4 teaspoon ground black pepper
- 1 egg, beaten
- 1/4 cup chopped fresh parsley

Direction

- Clean then scrub baking the potatoes. Boil salted water in a large pot. Add and cook potatoes for 15 minutes till tender but firm. Drain and cool the potatoes then cut them into thick slices. Transfer the slices to a large bowl.
- In a large and deep skillet, cook bacon over medium high heat till crisp. Add celery and onion into the skillet; stir and cook gently till the vegetables are yellow in color.
- Let the bouillon cube dissolve in the boiling water. Add in pepper, salt and vinegar then

stir. Transfer the broth mixture to the skillet of the onion and bacon mixture then boil.
- Gradually stir in the egg till the mixture is slightly thick. Spread over the potatoes with the vegetable mixture. Lightly toss in parsley.

Nutrition Information

- Calories: 240 calories;
- Protein: 6.3
- Total Fat: 10.3
- Sodium: 922
- Total Carbohydrate: 31
- Cholesterol: 38

263. Kikuchan's Potato Crab Salad

Serving: 8 | Prep: 20mins | Cook: 30mins | Ready in:

Ingredients

- 6 small russet potatoes
- 3 hard-cooked eggs, chopped
- 1 (6 ounce) can lump crabmeat, drained
- 1 (2.25 ounce) can sliced black olives, drained
- 1/2 carrot, grated
- 1/2 cup mayonnaise, or to taste
- 1/2 teaspoon white sugar
- salt and pepper to taste

Direction

- In a big saucepan, pour enough water to submerge potatoes. Boil. Cook for 30 minutes till tender on medium high heat. Drain. Peel then dice while hot. This makes the salad fluffy. Refrigerate, covered, till cold.
- Toss carrot, black olives, crabmeat, eggs and potatoes in a big serving bowl. Sprinkle sugar. Mix enough mayonnaise in to moisten. Use pepper and salt to season to taste. Chill till serving time.

Nutrition Information

- Calories: 215 calories;
- Total Carbohydrate: 27
- Cholesterol: 92
- Protein: 9.5
- Total Fat: 8
- Sodium: 316

264. Lela's Fourth Of July Potato Salad

Serving: 30 | Prep: 30mins | Cook: 1hours | Ready in:

Ingredients

- 10 pounds potatoes, peeled
- 2 (6 ounce) cans black olives, diced
- 2 (6 ounce) jars green olives, diced
- 1 cup dill pickle chips, diced
- 1 cup sweet onion (such as Vidalia®), finely chopped
- 16 hard-cooked eggs, chopped
- 1/4 cup prepared yellow mustard
- 7 cups Hellmann's® or Best Foods® Canola Cholesterol Free Mayonnaise

Direction

- Cover potatoes with salted water in a large pot then boil. It may require two pots. Lower to medium-low heat and simmer for 1 to 1 1/2 hours till fork-tender. After 1 hour, check the doneness. Drain the potatoes and let rinse under cold water.
- In a big heavy-duty disposable foil pan, place hard-cooked eggs, onion, pickle chips, green and black olives. Chop the potatoes into small pieces once they're cooled. Gently combine with the olive-egg mixture.
- Combine yellow mustard and mayonnaise together. Mix the salad ingredients well with the dressing. Let chill for at least 2 hours then serve.

Nutrition Information

- Calories: 356 calories;
- Sodium: 839
- Total Carbohydrate: 28.4
- Cholesterol: 113
- Protein: 6.8
- Total Fat: 22.5

265. Lena's Potato Salad

Serving: 8 | Prep: 15mins | Cook: 25mins | Ready in:

Ingredients

- 8 extra large eggs
- 8 large potatoes, peeled and chopped
- 1 (3 ounce) jar pitted and sliced green olives
- 1/2 cup mayonnaise
- 2 tablespoons Dijon mustard
- salt and pepper to taste

Direction

- Cover eggs with enough cold water in a saucepan. Boil and immediately take away from the heat. Cover and allow eggs to stand for 10-12 minutes in hot water. Take the eggs away from the hot water. Let cool and peel. Don't chop.
- Add enough water to cover in a pot then bring the potatoes to a boil till tender, for 15 minutes. Take away from the heat then let stand for 10 minutes in the hot water. Drain then allow to cool.
- In a large bowl, place the eggs and potatoes. Using your hands to mix mustard, mayonnaise and olives; then mash potatoes and eggs. Add pepper and salt to taste. Store in the fridge, covered, till serve.

Nutrition Information

- Calories: 482 calories;
- Sodium: 531
- Total Carbohydrate: 66.3
- Cholesterol: 221
- Protein: 15
- Total Fat: 18.4

266. Liege Style Salad

Serving: 12 | Prep: 20mins | Cook: 25mins | Ready in:

Ingredients

- 2 pounds potatoes, peeled and cubed
- 2 pounds fresh green beans, trimmed and snapped into 1 1/2 inch pieces
- 1 pound thick cut bacon
- 3 small onions, sliced
- 2 cups balsamic vinegar
- salt and pepper to taste

Direction

- Cover potatoes with enough water in a pot. Boil and cook for 10 minutes till tender. Boil water in a separate pot. Add and cook green beans for 5 minutes. Let drain.
- In a large skillet, fry the bacon over medium heat till crisp. Discard bacon and put aside. In the bacon droppings, fry onions till browned and tender. Discard and put aside. Stir balsamic vinegar into the skillet to get all of the browned bits removed from the pan's bottom.
- Combine bacon, onions, potatoes and green beans in a large bowl. Spread over them with the balsamic vinegar and toss till coated. Add pepper and salt to taste.

Nutrition Information

- Calories: 288 calories;
- Protein: 7.6
- Total Fat: 17.3
- Sodium: 335
- Total Carbohydrate: 26.7

- Cholesterol: 26

267. Mama's Potato Salad

Serving: 20 | Prep: 20mins | Cook: 10mins | Ready in:

Ingredients

- 5 pounds potatoes, peeled and cubed
- 2 cups mayonnaise
- 1/2 cup yellow mustard
- 1 cup chopped onion
- 2 tablespoons prepared horseradish
- sea salt to taste
- 8 hard-cooked eggs, chopped
- 3 dill pickles, chopped (optional)
- freshly ground black pepper to taste

Direction

- Cover the potatoes with enough water in a big pot. Boil and cook till tender, for about 10 minutes. Let drain and add in a serving bowl.
- Add in pepper, salt and onion in and stir while the potatoes are still hot to let them absorb the flavor. Let cool for about 20 minutes.
- Stir horseradish, mustard and mayonnaise into the salad. Add in dill pickles and eggs then stir gently. Generously grind black pepper on top to finish off. Let chill for about 30 minutes then serve.

Nutrition Information

- Calories: 285 calories;
- Sodium: 370
- Total Carbohydrate: 23
- Cholesterol: 83
- Protein: 4.9
- Total Fat: 19.8

268. Marinated Potato Salad With Anchovy Vinaigrette

Serving: 7 | Prep: 15mins | Cook: 30mins | Ready in:

Ingredients

- 1 1/2 cups vegetable oil
- 1/2 cup white wine vinegar
- 1/4 cup chopped parsley
- 1 1/2 teaspoons salt
- 1 teaspoon white sugar
- 1 (2 ounce) can anchovy filets
- 2 cloves garlic, minced
- 3 pounds red potatoes
- 1 pound Italian sausage
- 2 cups chopped green onions
- 1/3 cup chopped parsley
- 6 ounces black olives, pitted and halved
- salt and pepper to taste

Direction

- Blend vinegar, sugar, garlic, anchovy fillets, parsley, oil, and salt in a blender until smooth.
- Boil a large pot of salted water. Gently add the potatoes and cook for 15 minutes until tender and firm. Drain once done and slice it into cubes. Pour the prepared vinaigrette over the potatoes. Allow it to marinate overnight.
- Cook the sausage in a large deep skillet over medium-high heat until browned all over. Drain and crumble. Put aside.
- Mix green onions, olives, parsley, sausage, and the potatoes together with its dressing. Season the mixture with pepper and salt to taste and toss together. Serve.

Nutrition Information

- Calories: 833 calories;
- Sodium: 1439
- Total Carbohydrate: 36.2
- Cholesterol: 55
- Protein: 15.7
- Total Fat: 71

269. Mediterranean Potato Salad

Serving: 16 | Prep: 15mins | Cook: 45mins | Ready in:

Ingredients

- 2 pounds potatoes
- 1 green bell pepper, minced
- 1 cucumber, sliced and quartered
- 1/2 cup sliced red onion
- 8 ounces crumbled feta cheese
- 1 lemon, juiced
- 1/2 cup Italian-style salad dressing
- salt and pepper to taste
- 3 pita breads, cut into wedges

Direction

- Boil salted water in a large pot. Add and cook potatoes for 15 minutes till tender but firm. Drain, let the potatoes cool then chop.
- Combine cheese, red onion, cucumbers, green peppers and potatoes in a large bowl.
- Whisk together pepper, salt, salad dressing and lemon juice. Spread over the salad and toss till coated. Serve along with pita bread wedges if preferred.

Nutrition Information

- Calories: 139 calories;
- Cholesterol: 13
- Protein: 4.5
- Total Fat: 5.3
- Sodium: 344
- Total Carbohydrate: 19.2

270. Mom's Italian Potato Salad

Serving: 6 | Prep: 15mins | Cook: 25mins | Ready in:

Ingredients

- 5 large Yukon Gold potatoes
- 1 large cucumber, chopped
- 5 stalks celery, chopped
- 1 large red onion, chopped
- 3/4 cup green olives with pimento, chopped
- 1/4 cup olive oil
- 1/2 cup red wine vinegar
- 1/4 teaspoon garlic powder
- salt and ground black pepper to taste

Direction

- Cover potatoes with water in a large saucepan then boil over high heat. Lower heat to medium-low and simmer for 15 minutes till tender. Drain, cool and cut the potatoes into 1-inch cubes.
- In a large bowl, combine olives, onion, celery, cucumber and potatoes.
- In a small bowl, whisk together garlic powder, red wine vinegar and olive oil. Spread over the vegetables and potatoes with the dressing then mix well. Add pepper and salt to taste then let chill. Stir the salad again then serve.

Nutrition Information

- Calories: 249 calories;
- Sodium: 458
- Total Carbohydrate: 34.3
- Cholesterol: 0
- Protein: 4.2
- Total Fat: 11.5

271. Mom's Russian Potato Salad

Serving: 6 | Prep: 20mins | Cook: 20mins | Ready in:

Ingredients

- 5 small beets

- 2 potatoes
- 1 carrot, peeled
- 1/4 cup chopped onion
- 1 dill pickle, chopped
- 1/2 cup sauerkraut, drained
- 3 tablespoons olive oil
- salt to taste

Direction

- In a saucepan, place carrot, potatoes and beets then fill with water and boil. Lower heat and simmer for 20 minutes till tender. Discard the vegetables and let cool. Peel potatoes and beets. Dice and place carrot, potatoes and beets in a salad bowl. Add in salt, olive oil, sauerkraut, pickle and onion then stir. Let the salad chill for 2-3 hours. Serve while still cold.

Nutrition Information

- Calories: 95 calories;
- Total Fat: 6.9
- Sodium: 262
- Total Carbohydrate: 8
- Cholesterol: 0
- Protein: 1.3

272. Mother's Potato Salad

Serving: 10 | Prep: 45mins | Cook: 20mins | Ready in:

Ingredients

- 5 pounds whole russet potatoes
- 5 eggs
- 1 1/2 cups mayonnaise (such as Hellman's®)
- 2 tablespoons prepared yellow mustard (such as French's®)
- 1 small onion, chopped
- 3 stalks celery, chopped
- 7 sweet gherkins, chopped
- 25 pimento-stuffed green olives, sliced
- 1 pinch salt to taste
- 1 green bell pepper, sliced (optional)

Direction

- Cover potatoes with salted water in a large pot. Boil over high heat and lower to medium-low. Cover then simmer for 20 minutes till tender. Drain and let steam dry for 1-2 minutes. Let cool then peel and cut potatoes into cubes.
- Place a single layer of the eggs in a saucepan and cover the eggs by 1 inch with water. Cover and boil over high heat. When the water is boiling, take away from the heat and allow eggs to stand for 15 minutes in hot water. Discard the hot water then place the eggs under cold running water in the sink to cool. Once they're cold, peel and slice. Save up 1 attractive slice to garnish.
- In a bowl, mix mustard and mayonnaise together. Lightly combine together olives, sweet gherkins, celery, onion, eggs and potatoes in a large salad bowl till combined thoroughly. Spread over the salad with mayonnaise dressing. Toss gently till all the ingredients are coated with dressing. Add salt to taste, place green pepper slices on top of the salad and add the remaining egg slice in the middle to garnish. Let chill till ready to serve.

Nutrition Information

- Calories: 501 calories;
- Total Fat: 30.1
- Sodium: 613
- Total Carbohydrate: 51.6
- Cholesterol: 106
- Protein: 8.8

273. My Mom's Good Old Potato Salad

Serving: 8 | Prep: 25mins | Cook: 12mins | Ready in:

Ingredients

- 5 pounds potatoes, peeled and chopped
- 10 eggs
- 1 large onion, chopped
- 1 (24 ounce) jar sweet pickles, drained and chopped
- 2 cups mayonnaise

Direction

- Boil potatoes in water in a large pan over medium-low heat for about 12 minutes till tender. Drain and refrigerate the potatoes till cooled.
- Bring eggs in a saucepan of cold water to a full boil over medium heat. Turn off the heat and cover. Let the eggs sit for about 15 minutes in the hot water. Place the eggs under cold running water to cool thoroughly then shell them. Chop and place the cooled eggs in a big salad bowl.
- Add mayonnaise, sweet pickles and onion in the eggs then stir. Chill the mixture for at least 1/2 hour in the fridge for the flavors to blend. Stir in the chopped potatoes that have been chilled and store in the fridge for at least half an hour. Serve cold.

Nutrition Information

- Calories: 788 calories;
- Total Fat: 50.5
- Sodium: 806
- Total Carbohydrate: 71.5
- Cholesterol: 253
- Protein: 14.8

274. My Sister's Favorite Potato Salad...Ever

Serving: 6 | Prep: 15mins | Cook: 15mins | Ready in:

Ingredients

- 6 red potatoes, cut into chunks
- 3/4 cup mayonnaise
- 1/4 cup red wine vinegar
- 1 tablespoon Dijon mustard
- 1 tablespoon dried dill weed
- 1 teaspoon celery salt
- salt and pepper to taste

Direction

- Cover potatoes with enough water in a pot then boil. Cook till tender, for 15 minutes. Drain and let cool.
- Gently combine pepper, salt, celery salt, dill, Dijon mustard, red wine vinegar, mayonnaise and potatoes in a bowl. Store in the fridge, covered, for at least 30 minutes then serve.

Nutrition Information

- Calories: 354 calories;
- Total Fat: 22.2
- Sodium: 480
- Total Carbohydrate: 36.3
- Cholesterol: 10
- Protein: 4.4

275. Octoberfest German Potato Salad

Serving: 7 | Prep: 15mins | Cook: 15mins | Ready in:

Ingredients

- 3 pounds potatoes, peeled and sliced
- 1/2 cup chopped onion
- 2 teaspoons salt
- 1/2 cup mayonnaise
- 1/4 cup vegetable oil
- 1/2 cup cider vinegar
- 2 tablespoons white sugar
- 2 tablespoons dried parsley
- ground black pepper to taste

Direction

- In a big pot, let salted water boil. Put in the peeled and sliced potatoes and allow them to cook in boiling salted water for about 15 minutes until the potatoes have softened but are still firm. Drain the cooked potatoes and place them in a big bowl. Put in the onions.
- Mix the vinegar, mayonnaise, sugar, pepper, parsley, oil and salt together in a big bowl then slowly mix in the potato-and-onion mixture. Before serving, allow the mixture to rest for 1 hour first to let the flavors seep through.

Nutrition Information

- Calories: 355 calories;
- Total Fat: 20.5
- Sodium: 768
- Total Carbohydrate: 39.5
- Cholesterol: 6
- Protein: 4.3

276. Oktoberfest Potato Salad

Serving: 6 | Prep: 20mins | Cook: 30mins | Ready in:

Ingredients

- 6 potatoes
- 1 teaspoon dry mustard powder
- 1 teaspoon water
- 4 slices bacon
- 1/4 cup chopped onion
- 1/4 cup white sugar
- 1/4 cup water
- 1/2 cup cider vinegar
- 1 cup diced celery, divided
- 3 tablespoons chopped fresh parsley, divided
- salt and ground black pepper to taste

Direction

- Cover potatoes with salted water in a big pot then boil. Lower heat to medium-low then simmer for about 20 minutes till tender. Let drain and cool.
- In a small bowl, combine 1 tsp of water with mustard and allow to stand for flavor to develop, for 10 minutes.
- Cook bacon while occasionally turning in a big skillet over medium-high heat for about 10 minutes till evenly browned. Place bacon slices on paper towels to drain. Keep the bacon drippings in skillet. Cool then crumble bacon.
- Cook onion over medium heat in the reserved bacon drippings for about 5 minutes till onion is soft and translucent. Add cider vinegar, 1/4 cup of water, sugar and mustard paste in the onion and stir; boil. Lower heat to low then let the vinegar dressing simmer for 2 minutes.
- Peel (if preferred), cut 3 potatoes and place in a salad bowl in a layer. Drizzle parsley, celery and 1/2 of the crumbled bacon over the potatoes; add black pepper and salt to taste. Pour over the layer with a little of the vinegar. Make the layer again with the 3 leftover potatoes, bacon, celery, parsley, salt, and black pepper. Spread over salad with the leftover dressing. Before serving, allow to stand at room temperature, covered, before 30 minutes.

Nutrition Information

- Calories: 242 calories;
- Protein: 6.9
- Total Fat: 2.9
- Sodium: 170
- Total Carbohydrate: 47.3
- Cholesterol: 7

277. Olivier Salad

Serving: 6 | Prep: 30mins | Cook: 20mins | Ready in:

Ingredients

- 5 potatoes, peeled
- 3 eggs

- 1 (16 ounce) jar dill pickles
- 1 (15 ounce) can peas, drained
- 3/4 pound cooked chicken breast meat, very finely chopped
- 1/2 cup mayonnaise
- ground black pepper to taste
- 1/2 cup mayonnaise
- 2 tomatoes, sliced

Direction

- Cover potatoes with salted water in a large pot. Boil over high heat then lower heat to medium-low. Cover then simmer for 20 minutes till tender. Drain and let steam dry for 1-2 minutes. Refrigerate the potatoes till cooled. Grate the cooled potatoes into a large bowl.
- Meanwhile, place a single layer of the eggs in a saucepan and cover the eggs by 1 inch with water. Cover and boil over high heat. When the water is boiling, take away from the heat and allow eggs to stand for 15 minutes in the hot water. Discard the hot water and place the eggs under cold running water in the sink to cool. Once they're cold, peel.
- Dice the dill pickles and cooked eggs. In the salad bowl of potatoes, place 2/3 of the dill pickles and the eggs; save up the rest of the pickles. Add 3/4 of the peas in the bowl and save up the remaining. Add chicken breast meat into bowl. Add in black pepper and 1/2 cup of mayonnaise. Stir the mixture very lightly to well coat all the ingredients while the peas stay as a whole. Transfer the salad to an attractive mound set on a platter. Pour over the salad with a layer of 1/2 cup of mayonnaise. Top the salad with tomato slices then add the remaining peas and diced pickle to decorate.

Nutrition Information

- Calories: 588 calories;
- Total Fat: 34.2
- Sodium: 1387
- Total Carbohydrate: 44
- Cholesterol: 155
- Protein: 27.9

278. Potato Arugula Salad

Serving: 6 | Prep: 20mins | Cook: 15mins | Ready in:

Ingredients

- 1 1/2 pounds red potatoes, cubed
- 3 tablespoons white vinegar
- 2 cloves garlic, minced (optional)
- 1/2 teaspoon salt
- 1/4 teaspoon black pepper
- 1/4 cup olive oil
- 1 bunch arugula - rinsed, dried and torn

Direction

- Boil salted water in a big pot. Add and cook potatoes for about 15 minutes till tender but still firm. Drain and let cool. Move to a big bowl.
- In the meantime, combine pepper, salt, garlic and vinegar in a mixing bowl. Sprinkle in olive oil then whisk till thick.
- Toss arugula, oil mixture and vinegar together with potatoes. Serve at room temperature.

Nutrition Information

- Calories: 181 calories;
- Total Fat: 9.4
- Sodium: 210
- Total Carbohydrate: 22.5
- Cholesterol: 0
- Protein: 3.1

279. Potato Salad

Serving: 20 | Prep: 20mins | Cook: 10mins | Ready in:

Ingredients

- 5 pounds red potatoes, chopped
- 3 cups mayonnaise
- 2 cups finely chopped pickles
- 5 hard-cooked eggs, chopped
- 1/2 cup chopped red onion
- 1/2 cup chopped celery
- 3 tablespoons prepared mustard
- 1 tablespoon apple cider vinegar
- 1 teaspoon salt, or to taste
- 1/2 teaspoon ground black pepper

Direction

- Cover potatoes with salted water in a big pot then boil. Lower heat to medium-low then simmer for about 10 minutes till tender. Let drain then bring the potatoes back to the empty pot. Let dry while preparing the dressing. Drizzle with salt.
- In a large bowl, combine pepper, 1 tsp salt, cider vinegar, mustard, celery, red onion, hard-cooked eggs, pickles and mayonnaise together. Add potatoes in the mayonnaise mixture then fold. Before serving, let chill for at least 6 hours or overnight.

Nutrition Information

- Calories: 339 calories;
- Total Carbohydrate: 20.4
- Cholesterol: 53
- Protein: 4.1
- Total Fat: 27.6
- Sodium: 538

280. Potato Salad I

Serving: 12 | Prep: 15mins | Cook: 30mins | Ready in:

Ingredients

- 5 pounds red potatoes, diced
- 4 eggs
- 4 stalks celery, chopped
- 1 green bell pepper, chopped
- 1 (16 ounce) jar sweet pickles, cubed
- 3/4 tablespoon prepared mustard
- 3/4 cup mayonnaise
- 1 onion, finely chopped
- 1 teaspoon white sugar
- salt and pepper to taste

Direction

- Boil salted water in a large pot. Add and cook potatoes for 15 minutes till tender but firm. Let drain and move to a large bowl.
- Cover eggs completely with cold water in a medium saucepan then boil. Cover and take away from the heat. Allow eggs to stand for 10-12 minutes in hot water. Take away from the hot water. Peel while placing under the cold running water. Chop then put aside.
- Add white sugar, onion, mayonnaise, prepared mustard, sweet pickle cubes, green bell pepper, celery and eggs in the potatoes and stir. Add pepper and salt to taste. Store in the fridge, covered, to chill for at least 3 hours then serve.

Nutrition Information

- Calories: 299 calories;
- Sodium: 308
- Total Carbohydrate: 40.8
- Cholesterol: 67
- Protein: 6.3
- Total Fat: 13.1

281. Potato Salad With Bacon, Olives, And Radishes

Serving: 5 | Prep: 20mins | Cook: 25mins | Ready in:

Ingredients

- 5 potatoes

- 1 pound bacon
- 2 stalks celery
- 4 small green onions
- 12 stuffed green olives
- 5 radishes
- 1/4 cup mayonnaise
- 1 tablespoon lemon juice

Direction

- Wash, peel and cut the potatoes into 1/2 to 3/4-inch pieces. Boil salted water in a large pot. Add and cook the potatoes for 10 minutes till tender but firm.
- Cut bacon into small pieces then cook in a large, deep skillet over medium high heat till evenly brown. Don't overcook.
- Chop radishes, stuffed olives, green onions and celery into small pieces then place into a big bowl. Mix in bacon and potatoes together. Stir in lemon juice and mayonnaise to taste. Refrigerate to chill for a few hours before serving. Top with a few sliced of hard-boiled eggs if desired.

Nutrition Information

- Calories: 677 calories;
- Cholesterol: 66
- Protein: 14.6
- Total Fat: 50.9
- Sodium: 1040
- Total Carbohydrate: 40.9

282. Potato Salad With Radishes

Serving: 4 | Prep: 15mins | Cook: 25mins | Ready in:

Ingredients

- 1 3/4 pounds Yukon Gold potatoes
- 1 white onion, chopped
- 2 bunches radishes, sliced
- Dressing:
- 4 tablespoons red wine vinegar
- 1 teaspoon Dijon mustard
- salt and freshly ground black pepper
- 1/2 cup extra-virgin olive oil
- 2 tablespoons chopped fresh chives

Direction

- Cover potatoes with salted water in a large pot then boil. Lower to medium-low heat then simmer for 20-25 minutes till tender. Drain.
- Let the potatoes cool till it can be handled easily. Peel then slice the potatoes in a big bowl. Let completely cool for 30 minutes. Add radishes and onion.
- In a cup or a bowl, whisk pepper, salt, mustard and red wine vinegar. Sprinkle in olive oil and whisk till well combined. Add in chives and stir. Sprinkle over the potato mixture and carefully stir in. Put aside for 15 minutes. Add pepper and salt to season.

Nutrition Information

- Calories: 422 calories;
- Cholesterol: 0
- Protein: 4.4
- Total Fat: 28.3
- Sodium: 98
- Total Carbohydrate: 38.5

283. Quick Potato Salad

Serving: 6 | Prep: 20mins | Cook: 5mins | Ready in:

Ingredients

- 2 potatoes, peeled and diced
- 3 hard-cooked eggs, peeled and diced
- 1/2 cucumber, peeled and diced
- 1 tomato, diced
- 1 celery stalk, diced
- 1/4 onion, diced

- 1/4 cup chopped green onion
- 3/4 cup low-fat mayonnaise
- 1 tablespoon prepared yellow mustard
- salt and ground black pepper to taste

Direction

- Boil lightly salted water in a large pot. Add and cook potatoes for 5-7 minutes till soft. Drain and rinse the potatoes in cold water.
- In a large bowl, combine mustard, mayonnaise, green onion, onion, celery, tomato, cucumber, eggs and potatoes. Stir to combine evenly. Add pepper and salt to taste.

Nutrition Information

- Calories: 160 calories;
- Total Fat: 4.8
- Sodium: 391
- Total Carbohydrate: 24.5
- Cholesterol: 93
- Protein: 5.5

284. Red And Sweet Potato Salad

Serving: 12 | Prep: 10mins | Cook: 15mins | Ready in:

Ingredients

- 6 red potatoes, diced
- 3 large sweet potatoes, diced
- 3/4 cup mayonnaise
- 1/2 red onion, diced
- 1 tablespoon prepared horseradish
- 1 tablespoon spicy brown mustard
- 1 tablespoon roasted garlic-flavored olive oil
- 1/4 pound crumbled cooked bacon
- 1 pinch garlic powder
- 1 pinch sea salt
- 1 pinch ground white pepper
- 1 pinch paprika

Direction

- Cover sweet potatoes and red potatoes with salted water in a large pot then boil. Lower heat to medium-low then simmer for 15-20 minutes till tender. Drain.
- Place the potato mixture in a large bowl then store in the fridge for 30 minutes till cooled.
- Respectively mix mayonnaise, red onion, horseradish, mustard, olive oil, bacon, garlic powder, sea salt, and white pepper into the potato mixture. Add paprika to garnish.

Nutrition Information

- Calories: 336 calories;
- Total Carbohydrate: 41.1
- Cholesterol: 16
- Protein: 7.6
- Total Fat: 16.3
- Sodium: 411

285. Red's Potato Salad

Serving: 50 | Prep: 30mins | Cook: 20mins | Ready in:

Ingredients

- 40 baby russet potatoes
- 6 large hard-boiled eggs - whites diced, yolks whole
- 3 stalks celery with leaves, diced
- 5 green onions, sliced
- 4 radishes, minced
- 2 cups mayonnaise
- 3 tablespoons sweet pickle relish
- 3 tablespoons whole grain mustard
- 2 tablespoons dried chives
- 2 tablespoons mustard-mayonnaise sandwich sauce (such as Durkee® Famous Sauce®)
- 1 tablespoon dried parsley
- 1 teaspoon kosher salt
- 1/2 teaspoon dried basil
- 1/4 teaspoon ground white pepper

- 6 radishes, cut into roses
- 3 large hard-boiled eggs, sliced

Direction

- Cover potatoes with salted water in a large pot then boil. Lower to medium-low heat then simmer for 20 minutes till tender enough to pierce with a fork. Drain, let cool and quarter the potatoes.
- In a large bowl, stir together minced radishes, green onions, celery, whole egg yolk, diced egg whites and potatoes. Carefully stir in white pepper, basil, kosher salt, parsley, mustard-mayonnaise sandwich sauce, chives, mustard, pickle relish and mayonnaise till coated and well-combined. Use plastic wrap to cover the bowl and store in the fridge for 8 hours to overnight till flavors blend.
- Add egg slices and radish roses to garnish the potato salad.

Nutrition Information

- Calories: 214 calories;
- Sodium: 152
- Total Carbohydrate: 30.9
- Cholesterol: 42
- Protein: 4.8
- Total Fat: 8.4

286. Restaurant Style Potato Salad

Serving: 8 | Prep: 15mins | Cook: 15mins | Ready in:

Ingredients

- 2 pounds russet potatoes
- 1 cup mayonnaise
- 4 teaspoons sweet pickle relish
- 4 teaspoons white sugar
- 2 teaspoons chopped white onion
- 2 teaspoons prepared mustard
- 1 teaspoon white wine vinegar
- 1 tablespoon minced celery
- 1 teaspoon minced pimento
- 1/2 teaspoon shredded carrot
- 1/4 teaspoon dried parsley
- 1/4 teaspoon ground black pepper
- salt to taste

Direction

- Boil salted water in a large pot. Add and cook potatoes for 15 minutes till tender but firm. Drain, let cool then chop the potatoes.
- Combine salt, pepper, parsley, carrot, pimentos, celery, vinegar, mustard, onion, sugar, sweet pickle relish, mayonnaise and potatoes in a large bowl. Mix well then chill till serve.

Nutrition Information

- Calories: 298 calories;
- Total Fat: 22
- Sodium: 200
- Total Carbohydrate: 23.9
- Cholesterol: 10
- Protein: 2.6

287. Roasted Potato Salad With Balsamic Bacon Vinaigrette

Serving: 8 | Prep: 45mins | Cook: 30mins | Ready in:

Ingredients

- 3 pounds baby red potatoes, cut in half
- 1/2 cup olive oil
- 1/2 cup minced garlic
- 1 tablespoon seafood seasoning
- 8 ounces bacon
- 1/4 cup balsamic vinegar
- 1/2 cup minced garlic
- salt and pepper to taste

- 1/2 cup olive oil
- 1 large red onion, cut into 1/2-inch dice
- 1 bunch parsley, minced
- 5 hard boiled eggs, roughly chopped

Direction

- Start preheating oven to 175 degrees C (350 degrees F).
- Add seafood seasoning, 1/2 cup garlic, and 1/2 cup olive oil to halved potatoes and toss. In a single layer onto baking sheets, place and take to preheated oven, bake for 30 to 40 minutes (it depends on the size of potatoes), until tender and golden brown. Take out of the oven once cooked and cool slightly.
- At the same time, cook bacon in a large, deep skillet over medium heat until crispy and evenly browned. Drain bacon grease and reserve. Cool the bacon slice, crumble and set aside.
- In a large bowl, beat together balsamic vinegar, pepper, garlic and salt. To make a vinaigrette, pour the oil slowly with steady stream into the bowl while whisking vigorously. Use the vinaigrette and reserved bacon grease to toss the roasted potatoes together. Fold red onion, eggs and parsley into the mixture. Let stand for 20 minutes, before serving, at room temperature.

Nutrition Information

- Calories: 573 calories;
- Total Fat: 43.3
- Sodium: 490
- Total Carbohydrate: 36.5
- Cholesterol: 136
- Protein: 12

288. Roasted Potato Salad With Vinaigrette

Serving: 8 | Prep: 20mins | Cook: 25mins | Ready in:

Ingredients

- 2 pounds cubed red potatoes
- 10 tablespoons vegetable oil
- 2 teaspoons paprika
- 1 tablespoon dried dill weed
- 2 tablespoons vegetable oil
- 1 banana pepper, sliced into 1/4 inch rings
- 1 red bell pepper, thinly sliced
- 2 large stalks celery, sliced 1/4 inch wide
- 1 small red onion, thinly sliced
- 1/4 cup red wine vinegar
- 1/2 cup olive oil
- 1/2 teaspoon kosher salt

Direction

- Preheat an oven to 450°F or 230°C.
- Toss 10 tablespoons of vegetable oil with potatoes. Drizzle with dill and paprika. Toss to evenly coat the potatoes with spices and pour over a baking sheet. Bake in the preheated oven for 25 minutes till a fork can easily pierce into the potatoes.
- Meanwhile, heat 2 tablespoons of vegetable oil over medium heat in a big skillet. Stir in onion, celery, bell pepper and banana pepper. Cook while stirring for 10 minutes till the vegetables are soft. In a bowl, toss the roasted potatoes with the pepper mixture. Store in the fridge for 1 hour till cold.
- Whisk together kosher salt, olive oil and red wine vinegar while the potatoes are still cooling. Toss the salad dressing in the potatoes right before serving.

Nutrition Information

- Calories: 397 calories;
- Sodium: 143
- Total Carbohydrate: 21.6
- Cholesterol: 0
- Protein: 2.8
- Total Fat: 34.3

289. Roasted Potato And Garlic Salad

Serving: 6 | Prep: 15mins | Cook: 30mins | Ready in:

Ingredients

- 8 red potatoes - unpeeled, scrubbed and cubed
- 2 red bell peppers
- 2 medium heads garlic
- 1/2 cup olive oil
- salt and pepper to taste
- 1/3 cup balsamic vinegar
- 1/3 cup olive oil
- 1 teaspoon dried oregano

Direction

- Preheat the oven to 400°F or 200°C.
- In a large bowl, place 1/2 cup of olive oil. Toss oil with the cubed potatoes till coated. Evenly spread on a baking sheet.
- Pass the red peppers through oil in the bowl till coated evenly. Transfer into another baking sheet.
- Cut about 1/2 inch off the garlic's top and sprinkle with the leftover oil from the bowl. Lay on the baking sheet together with the red peppers. Drizzle pepper and salt over garlic, peppers and potatoes. Leave both sheets for 20 minutes in the oven.
- Make sure the potatoes are crispy, brown and soft. If not, bring the potatoes back to the oven till done, for 10 minutes more. The garlic and peppers will be done once garlic is dark brown and the peppers turn black. They will take longer than the potatoes but the total won't be more than 40 minutes.
- Once finished roasting everything, add the potatoes in a bowl and place the peppers in a plastic bag, seal and allow them to steam for 10 minutes so that their skins will be loosened.
- Take out the peppers; discard their skins and seeds then chop the peppers. Stir in the bowl of potatoes.
- In a separate small bowl, place the garlic heads upside down then squeeze the softened garlic past. Mix in oregano, 1/3 cup of olive oil and balsamic vinegar till smooth. Spread over the peppers and potatoes with dressing and toss till coated. Add pepper and additional salt to taste. Best when served at room temperature or while warm. If you want to prepare beforehand, store in the fridge and place in the microwave to reheat till just warmed through.

Nutrition Information

- Calories: 520 calories;
- Total Fat: 30.6
- Sodium: 27
- Total Carbohydrate: 55.9
- Cholesterol: 0
- Protein: 7

290. Roasted Red Potato Salad

Serving: 8 | Prep: 25mins | Cook: 45mins | Ready in:

Ingredients

- 10 red potatoes, cut into bite-size pieces
- olive oil, or as needed
- 3 hard-cooked eggs, chopped
- 1/2 stalk celery, chopped
- 1/4 cup chopped green onion
- 3 slices cooked bacon, chopped
- 1 cup mayonnaise
- salt and ground black pepper to taste

Direction

- Preheat the oven to 375°F or 190°C.
- Spread over a baking sheet with potato pieces and sprinkle with olive oil.
- Roast in the preheated oven for 45 minutes till tender. Discard from the oven and leave to cool for at least 15 minutes.
- In a large salad bowl, place roasted potatoes and combine with bacon, green onion, celery and hard-cooked eggs. Add in mayonnaise

and stir. Add black pepper and salt to taste. Store in the fridge, covered, for 60 minutes for the flavors to blend.

Nutrition Information

- Calories: 456 calories;
- Total Fat: 28.5
- Sodium: 250
- Total Carbohydrate: 43.8
- Cholesterol: 92
- Protein: 8.5

291. Roasted Sweet Potato Mango Salad

Serving: 6 | Prep: 20mins | Cook: 20mins | Ready in:

Ingredients

- Potatoes:
- 4 large sweet potatoes, cut into cubes
- cooking spray
- 1/2 teaspoon salt
- 1/2 teaspoon ground black pepper
- Dressing:
- 1 lemon, juiced
- 3 tablespoons olive oil
- 2 tablespoons brown sugar
- 1 teaspoon sea salt
- 1/2 teaspoon ground black pepper
- Salad:
- 2 large mangoes - peeled, seeded, and chopped
- 3/4 cup minced onion
- 3/4 cup chopped fresh cilantro
- 1 large avocado - peeled, pitted, and chopped
- 1 green onion, chopped
- 1/2 habanero pepper, seeded and minced

Direction

- Preheat the oven to 400°F or 200°C.
- On a baking sheet, spread the sweet potatoes. Use cooking spray to coat then add 1/2 teaspoon of black pepper and 1/2 teaspoon of salt to taste.
- In the preheated oven, roast potatoes for 20 minutes till soft. Move potatoes into a plate and store in the fridge till completely cool.
- In a bowl, whisk 1/2 teaspoon of black pepper, sea salt, brown sugar, olive oil and lemon juice then allow to rest for at least 5 minutes.
- In a large bowl, mix together habareno pepper, green onion, avocado, cilantro, onion, mangoes and chilled sweet potatoes. Sprinkle over potato mixture with dressing and toss till coated.

Nutrition Information

- Calories: 495 calories;
- Sodium: 666
- Total Carbohydrate: 91.4
- Cholesterol: 0
- Protein: 6.9
- Total Fat: 14.2

292. Rockin Robin's Classic Potato Salad

Serving: 10 | Prep: 20mins | Cook: 25mins | Ready in:

Ingredients

- 2 1/2 pounds potatoes, peeled
- 4 eggs
- 1 cup diced celery
- 3/4 cup chopped green onions
- 1 1/2 cups mayonnaise
- 2 tablespoons prepared yellow mustard
- salt and ground black pepper to taste

Direction

- Cover potatoes with salted water in a large pot then boil. Lower to medium-low heat then simmer for 20 minutes till tender but firm. Drain and store in the fridge for 30 minutes till cool.
- Cover eggs with water in a saucepan. Boil then take away from the heat. Allow eggs to stand for 15 minutes in hot water. Take the eggs away from the hot water then place under cold running water to cool. Peel eggs and dice.
- In a large bowl, place chopped potatoes. Add in green onions, celery and eggs; stir then mix in mustard and mayonnaise. Add pepper and salt to taste.

Nutrition Information

- Calories: 359 calories;
- Cholesterol: 87
- Protein: 5.5
- Total Fat: 28.4
- Sodium: 284
- Total Carbohydrate: 22.1

293. Russian Beet And Potato Salad

Serving: 8 | Prep: 20mins | Cook: 30mins | Ready in:

Ingredients

- 2 beets
- 4 small potatoes
- 2 small carrots
- 3 small dill pickles, diced
- 1/4 cup vegetable oil
- 2 tablespoons champagne vinegar
- salt to taste
- 3 green onions, chopped

Direction

- Boil water in a large pot then cook beets for 30 minutes till tender. Boil water in another pot then cook carrots and potatoes for 20 minutes till tender. Drain, cool and remove the vegetables' skins. Dice then place vegetables in a big bowl.
- In the bowl, place diced pickles together with carrots, potatoes and beets. Sprinkle over the mixture with vinegar and olive oil then toss till coated. Add salt to taste. Drizzle with green onions. Let completely chill before serving.

Nutrition Information

- Calories: 145 calories;
- Cholesterol: 0
- Protein: 2
- Total Fat: 7
- Sodium: 384
- Total Carbohydrate: 19.6

294. Russian Salmon And Potato Salad

Serving: 6 | Prep: 25mins | Cook: 15mins | Ready in:

Ingredients

- 2 eggs
- 3 medium baking potatoes, peeled and cubed
- 1 tablespoon olive oil
- 1 large onion, chopped
- 1 (16 ounce) can salmon, drained
- 1 cup mayonnaise, or as needed
- 1 tablespoon chopped fresh parsley, for garnish

Direction

- Cover eggs with cold water in a saucepan. Boil then immediately take away from the heat. Cover then allow eggs to stand for 10-12 minutes in hot water. Take away from hot water. Let cool then peel.
- Meanwhile, cover potatoes with enough water in a saucepan. Boil then cook till tender, for 10-

15 minutes. Take away from the heat; let drain and put aside.
- Heat oil over medium heat in a skillet. Add and sauté onions for 10 minutes till translucent and lightly browned.
- Spread flaked salmon over the bottom of a serving dish or a glass baking dish. Spread over the salmon with the sautéed onions. Gently spread over the layer of onions with a little bit of mayonnaise. Place potatoes on top and moisten the layer with just enough mayonnaise. Lastly, cover the potato layer with sliced eggs. Spread over the eggs with mayonnaise and add chopped parsley to garnish. Save up some egg to chop and drizzle over the top if desired. Let chill for 1 hour then serve.

Nutrition Information

- Calories: 523 calories;
- Cholesterol: 109
- Protein: 22.3
- Total Fat: 38.6
- Sodium: 508
- Total Carbohydrate: 22.1

295. Schwabischer Kartoffelsalat (German Potato Salad Schwabisch Style)

Serving: 8 | Prep: 15mins | Cook: 25mins | Ready in:

Ingredients

- 2 pounds potatoes, unpeeled
- 1/2 small onion, diced
- 1/2 teaspoon prepared yellow mustard
- salt and ground black pepper to taste
- 1 cup vegetable stock
- 3 tablespoons vinegar, or more to taste
- 2 tablespoons vegetable oil

Direction

- Cover potatoes with salted water in a large pot then boil. Lower to medium-low heat then simmer for 20 minutes till tender. Drain and let potatoes slightly cool. Peel the potatoes then slice. In a bowl, mix onions and potatoes. Add in black pepper, salt and mustard then stir.
- Boil vegetable stock in a small saucepan. Spread over the potato mixture then stir till combined. Add in vinegar, stir and allow to rest for 10 minutes. Add in vegetable oil; stir. Add black pepper and salt to taste if preferred.

Nutrition Information

- Calories: 121 calories;
- Total Fat: 3.6
- Sodium: 45
- Total Carbohydrate: 20.4
- Cholesterol: 0
- Protein: 2.4

296. Schwabischer Kartoffelsalat (Schwabish Potato Salad)

Serving: 12 | Prep: 30mins | Cook: 15mins | Ready in:

Ingredients

- 5 pounds white potatoes with skin
- 2 cubes chicken bouillon
- 3/4 cup boiling water
- 1/4 cup balsamic vinegar
- 1 hard-cooked egg, diced
- freshly ground black pepper to taste
- 1 tablespoon chopped fresh parsley
- 2 teaspoons mayonnaise
- 1 cup olive oil

Direction

- Cover potatoes with enough water in a large pot then boil. Cook till a fork can easily pierce

into the potatoes, for 20 minutes. Let drain and slightly cool. It's easy to peel them (if desired) while still hot. Let completely cool then slice into thin pieces.
- In a large bowl, place the potatoes. Let the chicken bouillon dissolve in boiling water then add in the potatoes. Add in parsley, mayonnaise, pepper, egg and vinegar then stir gently. Lastly, mix in the olive oil. Before serving, allow to stand for 15 minutes at room temperature. It's best to serve this salad at room temperature.

Nutrition Information

- Calories: 307 calories;
- Protein: 3.9
- Total Fat: 19.3
- Sodium: 215
- Total Carbohydrate: 30.8
- Cholesterol: 18

297. Slow Cooker German Potato Salad

Serving: 8 | Prep: 15mins | Cook: 5hours | Ready in:

Ingredients

- 2 pounds potatoes, peeled and sliced
- 1 cup chopped onion
- 1 cup sliced celery
- 1/2 cup chopped green bell pepper
- 1/2 cup cooking oil
- 1/2 cup vinegar
- salt and ground black pepper to taste
- 6 slices cooked bacon, crumbled
- 2 tablespoons chopped fresh parsley

Direction

- In a slow cooker, combine pepper, salt, vinegar, oil, green bell pepper, celery, onion and potatoes.
- Cook for 5-6 hours on Low. Add parsley and bacon for garnish.

Nutrition Information

- Calories: 246 calories;
- Total Fat: 15.7
- Sodium: 125
- Total Carbohydrate: 22.8
- Cholesterol: 5
- Protein: 4.4

298. Southern Potato Salad

Serving: 4 | Prep: 30mins | Cook: 30mins | Ready in:

Ingredients

- 4 potatoes
- 4 eggs
- 1/2 stalk celery, chopped
- 1/4 cup sweet relish
- 1 clove garlic, minced
- 2 tablespoons prepared mustard
- 1/2 cup mayonnaise
- salt and pepper to taste

Direction

- Boil salted water in a big pot. Add and cook potatoes for about 15 minutes till tender but still firm. Let drain then chop.
- Cover eggs with cold water in a saucepan. Boil then cover and take away from the heat. Allow eggs to stand for 10-12 minutes in hot water. Take away from hot water. Peel the eggs then chop.
- Mix pepper, salt, mayonnaise, mustard, garlic, sweet relish, celery, eggs and potatoes together in a big bowl. Gently combine then serve while still warm.

Nutrition Information

- Calories: 460 calories;
- Sodium: 455
- Total Carbohydrate: 44.6
- Cholesterol: 196
- Protein: 11.3
- Total Fat: 27.4

299. Spicy Black Bean Potato Salad

Serving: 12 | Prep: 15mins | Cook: 25mins | Ready in:

Ingredients

- 8 medium red potatoes
- 4 eggs
- 8 slices bacon
- 1 (15 ounce) can black beans, drained and rinsed
- 3 green onions, diced
- 3 fresh jalapeno peppers, diced
- 1/2 green bell pepper, diced
- 2 1/2 cups mayonnaise
- 2 tablespoons brown mustard
- 1 teaspoon Cajun seasoning
- salt and pepper to taste

Direction

- Cover potatoes with enough water in a pot. Boil then cook till tender. Let drain then dice the potatoes; let cool.
- Cover eggs with enough cold water in a pot. Boil and immediately take away from the heat. Cover then allow eggs to stand for 10-12 minutes in hot water. Drain, let cool then peel the eggs and chop.
- Cook bacon over medium-high heat in a skillet till brown evenly. Drain, crumble the bacon then put aside.
- Combine Cajun seasoning, mustard, mayonnaise, bell peppers, jalapeno peppers, green onions, black beans, 1/2 of the bacon and chopped eggs in a large bowl. Add in cooled potatoes that have been diced; mix gently. Add pepper and salt to taste; drizzle with the leftover bacon. Store in the fridge, covered, till ready to serve.

Nutrition Information

- Calories: 503 calories;
- Cholesterol: 86
- Protein: 7.5
- Total Fat: 40.9
- Sodium: 502
- Total Carbohydrate: 28.3

300. Spicy Dill Potato Salad

Serving: 12 | Prep: 30mins | Cook: 35mins | Ready in:

Ingredients

- 3 pounds russet potatoes, peeled and cubed
- 4 eggs
- 2 red bell peppers
- 2 green bell peppers
- 1 red onion
- 2 cups reduced-fat mayonnaise
- 1/2 cup horseradish mustard
- 4 chipotle peppers in adobo sauce, chopped
- 1/4 cup adobo sauce from chipotle peppers
- 8 sprigs fresh dill, chopped
- 1 clove garlic, minced, or to taste
- 1 pinch ground cumin, or to taste
- salt and ground black pepper to taste

Direction

- Cover potatoes with salted water in a big pot. Boil over high heat then lower to medium-low. Cover then simmer for 10-15 minutes till tender. Drain and let steam dry for 1-2 minutes. Transfer to a large bowl and store in the fridge to chill for 1 hour till cold.
- Meanwhile, place a single layer of the eggs in a saucepan and cover the eggs by 1 inch with water. Cover then boil over high heat. When

the water is boiling, take away from the heat and allow eggs to stand for 15 minutes in hot water. Discard the hot water and place the eggs under cold running water in the sink to cool. Peel the cold eggs. Chop then add in the bowl of potatoes.

- Preheat the oven to 425°F or 220°C. Halve the bell peppers then discard the stems, core and seeds. On a baking sheet, place the peppers with the cut sides facing down. Halve the onion. On a baking sheet, place the onion with the cut sides facing down.
- In the preheated oven, roast the onion and peppers for 25 minutes till the vegetables' skin chars in places. Discard large pieces of burned skin then chop onions and peppers. Place into the bowl of eggs and potatoes.
- Stir pepper and salt together with cumin, garlic, dill, adobo sauce, chipotle peppers, horseradish mustard and mayonnaise in a bowl to combine thoroughly. Spread over the potato mixture with the dressing then toss lightly till vegetables, eggs and potatoes are coated thoroughly with dressing. Let chill then serve.

Nutrition Information

- Calories: 153 calories;
- Protein: 5.5
- Total Fat: 3.9
- Sodium: 190
- Total Carbohydrate: 25.8
- Cholesterol: 63

301. Spicy Sweet Potato Salad

Serving: 8 | Prep: 30mins | Cook: 20mins | Ready in:

Ingredients

- 2 sweet potatoes
- 1 pound red potatoes
- 1 pound Yukon Gold potatoes
- 1 large red onion
- 2 teaspoons salt
- 1 clove garlic, minced
- 1 jalapeno pepper, seeded and minced
- 1/4 cup fresh lemon juice
- 1 cup mayonnaise
- 1 tablespoon curry powder
- 1/4 cup chopped fresh parsley
- 1/4 teaspoon freshly ground black pepper

Direction

- Wash and pierce Yukon Gold potatoes and sweet potatoes with a fork then microwave till tender. Bring the red potatoes to a boil in salted water till tender. For the potatoes to hold up in the salad, don't overcook. Drain the red potatoes and let all 3 types of potatoes chill overnight.
- Peel and dice Yukon Golds and sweet potatoes into 1/2-in. cubes. Quarter the red potatoes. Transfer all the potatoes to a large bowl.
- Thinly slice the red onion and put on a colander. Drizzle the onion with salt and drain by allowing it to sit for 30 minutes in the colander. Squeeze onion to discard excess water then place to the bowl of potatoes. Combine pepper, parsley, curry powder, mayonnaise, lemon juice, jalapeno and garlic. Let chill till ready to serve.

Nutrition Information

- Calories: 333 calories;
- Total Fat: 22.1
- Sodium: 757
- Total Carbohydrate: 32.3
- Cholesterol: 10
- Protein: 3.3

302. Sweet Potato Potato Salad

Serving: 8 | Prep: 10mins | Cook: 45mins | Ready in:

Ingredients

- 2 potatoes
- 1 sweet potato
- 4 eggs
- 2 stalks celery, chopped
- 1/2 onion, chopped
- 3/4 cup mayonnaise
- 1 tablespoon prepared mustard
- 1 teaspoon salt
- 1 1/2 teaspoons ground black pepper

Direction

- Boil salted water in a large pot. Add and cook potatoes for 30 minutes till tender but firm. Let the potatoes drain and cool then peel and chop.
- Cover eggs with cold water in a saucepan. Boil then cover and take away from the heat. Allow eggs to stand for 10-12 minutes in hot water. Take away from the hot water. Let cool then peel the eggs and chop.
- Combine onion, celery, eggs and potatoes.
- Whisk together pepper, salt, mustard and mayonnaise. Place into the potato mixture then toss well till coated. Store in the fridge. Serve chilled.

Nutrition Information

- Calories: 244 calories;
- Sodium: 481
- Total Carbohydrate: 14.3
- Cholesterol: 101
- Protein: 4.9
- Total Fat: 19

303. Sweet Potato Salad

Serving: 12 | Prep: 15mins | Cook: 15mins | Ready in:

Ingredients

- 3 pounds red potatoes
- 2 1/2 pounds sweet potatoes
- 1/4 cup white wine vinegar
- 1/4 cup olive oil
- 1 clove garlic, minced
- 1/4 cup dill pickle relish
- 1/2 cup chopped red onion
- 1/3 cup mayonnaise
- 1 pinch ground black pepper
- 1/3 cup sour cream
- 1/2 cup chopped parsley

Direction

- Boil a big pot of salted water, then add potatoes. Cook for about 15 minutes until soft yet still firm. Drain and let it cool; slice.
- Mix the onion, dill pickle relish, garlic, olive oil and vinegar in a big bowl. Stir and cover with sliced potatoes.
- Beat parsley, sour cream, pepper and mayonnaise together. Pour on top of the potatoes and let it chill for a minimum of 8 hours.

Nutrition Information

- Calories: 267 calories;
- Total Fat: 11
- Sodium: 153
- Total Carbohydrate: 39.6
- Cholesterol: 5
- Protein: 4.1

304. Tangy Potato Salad

Serving: 8 | Prep: 20mins | Cook: 20mins | Ready in:

Ingredients

- 4 potatoes
- 4 eggs
- 1/4 cup diced red onion
- 1/4 cup diced dill pickles
- 1/2 cup mayonnaise

- 1/4 cup spicy mustard
- 2 tablespoons chopped fresh chives
- 1 teaspoon ground black pepper

Direction

- Boil 2 pots of water. Cook eggs in one pot and potatoes in the other one for 20 minutes till potatoes are semi-soft. Move eggs and potatoes into a bowl of cold water till they're both cooled.
- Dice then place potatoes in a big bowl. Halve the eggs; discard yolks then put in another bowl. Dice and add egg whites in potatoes. Combine pickles and red onion into the potato mixture.
- Whisk egg yolk, black pepper, chives, mustard and mayonnaise together till smooth. Gently stir mayonnaise mixture into the potato mixture to evenly coat. Store in the fridge for 10-15 minutes.

Nutrition Information

- Calories: 228 calories;
- Total Fat: 13.5
- Sodium: 369
- Total Carbohydrate: 21.7
- Cholesterol: 98
- Protein: 5.6

305. Veggie Potato Salad For A Crowd

Serving: 24 | Prep: 40mins | Cook: 15mins | Ready in:

Ingredients

- 3 pounds small red potatoes, unpeeled
- 2 cups chopped red onions
- 12 ounces fresh green beans, trimmed, cooked al dente
- 3 1/2 cups roughly chopped red cabbage
- 1 pint grape tomatoes, halved
- 3 tablespoons capers, drained
- 2 ounces basil leaves, trimmed and torn in large pieces
- salt and freshly ground black pepper to taste
- Mustard Dressing:
- 2/3 cup extra virgin olive oil
- 3 tablespoons white balsamic or rice vinegar
- 1 teaspoon salt
- 1 1/2 teaspoons Dijon mustard
- 3 cloves garlic, crushed

Direction

- Cook potatoes in a whole in a big pot till done. Let cool then slice into pieces with bite size. Mix all the ingredients from potatoes through basil in a very big bowl. Combine the dressing ingredients together. Toss with vegetables then season with pepper and salt. Let chill then serve.

Nutrition Information

- Calories: 119 calories;
- Total Fat: 6.4
- Sodium: 147
- Total Carbohydrate: 14.4
- Cholesterol: 0
- Protein: 2

306. Warm Steak And Potato Salad

Serving: 4 | Prep: 10mins | Cook: 17mins | Ready in:

Ingredients

- 1 pound new potatoes
- 1 pound beef sirloin steak
- 1/2 teaspoon salt
- 1/4 teaspoon ground black pepper
- 8 cups mixed baby salad greens
- 1 pint cherry tomatoes, halved
- 2 tablespoons minced shallot

- 2 tablespoons olive oil
- 1 tablespoon red wine vinegar
- 1 teaspoon Dijon mustard
- 1/4 teaspoon dried tarragon

Direction

- Cover potatoes with enough water in a pot. Boil then cook for 10 minutes till tender but firm. Let drain then cover to keep the potatoes warm.
- Preheat a grill for medium-high heat or preheat oven to broil. Add pepper and salt on both steak's sides to taste. Grill or broil till it reaches the desired doneness, for 6-8 minutes each side.
- In the meantime, whisk together tarragon, mustard, vinegar and oil to make the dressing. Add pepper and salt to the dressing to taste.
- Place shallots, tomatoes and greens in 4 plates. While the unpeeled potatoes are still warm, quarter and slice steak in strips with 1/4-in. thickness. Place potatoes and steak on top of the salad greens. Sprinkle over salads with dressing. Serve while still warm.

Nutrition Information

- Calories: 359 calories;
- Total Fat: 17.6
- Sodium: 409
- Total Carbohydrate: 27.9
- Cholesterol: 60
- Protein: 23.2

307. Warm Sweet Potato Salad

Serving: 12 | Prep: 20mins | Cook: 25mins | Ready in:

Ingredients

- 6 large sweet potatoes, peeled and diced
- 4 large baking potatoes, peeled and diced
- 1/2 cup mayonnaise
- 1/4 cup Dijon mustard
- 1/3 cup balsamic vinegar
- 1 teaspoon ground turmeric
- 1 tablespoon chopped chives
- salt and ground black pepper to taste
- 2 slices crisply cooked bacon, crumbled
- 2 green onions, finely chopped
- 1 red onion, finely chopped

Direction

- Cover potatoes and diced sweet potatoes in a Dutch oven then boil for 20 minutes till tender enough to pierce with a fork but not mushy. Drain and let the cooked potatoes slightly cool.
- In the meantime, in a large bowl, mix together pepper, salt, chives, turmeric, balsamic vinegar, mustard and mayonnaise. Toss in cooked potatoes, red and green onions and bacon till coated. Add green onion or extra chives as garnish to serve.

Nutrition Information

- Calories: 376 calories;
- Total Fat: 8
- Sodium: 367
- Total Carbohydrate: 70.7
- Cholesterol: 5
- Protein: 6.7

308. Yucatan Potato Salad

Serving: 8 | Prep: 15mins | Cook: 15mins | Ready in:

Ingredients

- 6 russet potatoes, peeled and cubed
- 2 fresh poblano chile peppers
- 3 hard cooked eggs, chopped
- 1/2 cup chopped celery
- 1/2 cup chopped white onion
- 3 medium sweet pickles, chopped
- 12 green olives, sliced

- 1/4 cup lime juice
- 1 cup vegetable oil
- 1 teaspoon salt
- 1/2 teaspoon ground black pepper
- 1 teaspoon mustard powder

Direction

- Heat oven to 400°F or 200°C. Boil potatoes in a saucepan full of water to cover the potatoes for 10 minutes until they become tender. Drain cooked potatoes.
- Place the peppers directly on the oven rack and roast until they become charred. Turn every 10 minutes. Put the peppers inside a paper bag and let it sweat. Once cooled, peel off the skins then remove the stem and seeds. Chop the peppers into pieces.
- Use a big bowl to combine the warm potatoes, eggs, peppers, celery, olives, sweet pickles and onion. In a separate bowl, whisk the lime juice, pepper, salt, vegetable oil, and mustard powder. You may use a high-speed mixer to emulsify it quickly. Pour the mixture on the potato salad then mix well. Add more seasoning if needed then serve.

Nutrition Information

- Calories: 419 calories;
- Total Fat: 30.3
- Sodium: 518
- Total Carbohydrate: 32.7
- Cholesterol: 70
- Protein: 6.2

Chapter 3: Awesome Dairy-Free Recipes

***

309. Absolutely Amazing Ahi

Serving: 6 | Prep: 10mins | Cook: 15mins | Ready in:

Ingredients

- 3/4 pound sashimi grade tuna steak, diced
- 1/2 cup diced cucumber
- 1 avocados - peeled, pitted and diced
- 1/4 cup chopped green onion
- 1 1/2 teaspoons red pepper flakes
- 1 tablespoon toasted sesame seeds
- 1 1/2 teaspoons lemon juice
- 2 teaspoons sesame oil
- 1/2 cup soy sauce

Direction

- Mix together sesame seeds, red pepper flakes, green onion, avocado, cucumber, and tuna in a medium bowl. Add the soy sauce, sesame oil, and lemon juice and mix cautiously to combine so as not to mash the avocado. Put this bowl into a large bowl that has been filled with ice. Keep in the refrigerator to chill for 15 minutes, but no longer - or you will lose the excellent freshness of the fish.
- When it is chilled, take the bowl away from the ice, and invert onto a serving plate. Pair with your favorite crackers or toasted bread to serve.

Nutrition Information

- Calories: 155 calories;
- Total Fat: 8
- Sodium: 1227
- Total Carbohydrate: 6.1
- Cholesterol: 26
- Protein: 15.8

310. Acai Bowl

Serving: 1 | Prep: 10mins | Cook: | Ready in:

Ingredients

- 1 cup acai berry sorbet
- 2 tablespoons granola, or as desired
- 4 strawberries, sliced
- 1 banana
- 2 teaspoons unsweetened coconut flakes, or as desired
- 1 teaspoon honey, or as desired

Direction

- In a bowl, add acai sorbet and put a layer of granola on top. Arrange bananas and strawberry over granola layer. Add coconut over mixture and drizzle some honey on top.

Nutrition Information

- Calories: 551 calories;
- Sodium: 27
- Total Carbohydrate: 107.7
- Cholesterol: 0
- Protein: 4.3
- Total Fat: 12.8

311. Acapulco Margarita Grouper

Serving: 4 | Prep: 20mins | Cook: 12mins | Ready in:

Ingredients

- 4 (6 ounce) grouper fillets
- 1/3 cup tequila
- 1/2 cup orange liqueur
- 3/4 cup fresh lime juice
- 1 teaspoon salt
- 3 large cloves garlic, peeled
- 4 tablespoons olive oil
- 3 medium tomatoes, diced
- 1 medium onion, chopped
- 1 small jalapeno, seeded and minced
- 4 tablespoons chopped fresh cilantro
- 1 pinch white sugar
- salt to taste
- 1 tablespoon olive oil
- ground black pepper to taste

Direction

- Put the fish into a shallow baking dish. Mix the orange liqueur, olive oil, 1 tsp. of salt, tequila, lime juice, and garlic in a bowl. Spread the mixture all over the fillets, pressing it into the fish. Cover the dish and place it inside the fridge for 30 minutes, flipping the fillets only once.
- Set the grill to high heat for preheating.
- Mix the jalapeno, sugar, tomatoes, cilantro, and onion in a medium bowl. Season the mixture with salt to taste; put aside.
- Take the fillets out of the marinade, patting the fillets until dry. Brush the fillets with oil and sprinkle them with ground black pepper. Boil the remaining marinade in a small saucepan for a few minutes. Remove it from the heat and strain, removing the garlic cloves. Put the marinade aside to cool.
- Grill each side of the fish for 4 minutes until it can be flaked easily using a fork. Place the fillets into a serving dish. Spread the salsa all over the fish. Drizzle the cooked marinade over before serving.

Nutrition Information

- Calories: 511 calories;
- Total Fat: 19
- Sodium: 1245
- Total Carbohydrate: 26.3
- Cholesterol: 62
- Protein: 34.7

312. Adobo Herb Salsa

Serving: 4 | Prep: 15mins | Cook: | Ready in:

Ingredients

- 1 (28 ounce) can diced tomatoes
- 1 green bell pepper, diced
- 1/4 cup minced red onion
- 1/4 cup minced fresh cilantro
- 1 tablespoon adobo sauce from canned chipotle peppers
- 1 tablespoon chopped fresh tarragon
- 1/2 teaspoon salt
- 2 tablespoons balsamic vinegar

Direction

- Toss together vinegar, tarragon, adobo sauce, cilantro, onion, bell pepper and tomatoes in a bowl, then season with salt to taste. Cover and chill for a minimum of a half hour.

Nutrition Information

- Calories: 59 calories;
- Cholesterol: 0
- Protein: 2.1
- Total Fat: 0.2
- Sodium: 621
- Total Carbohydrate: 10.4

313. Agedashi Esque Tofu

Serving: 2 | Prep: 10mins | Cook: 5mins | Ready in:

Ingredients

- 1 (12 ounce) package extra firm tofu
- 3 tablespoons cornstarch
- oil for frying
- 2 green onions, chopped
- 2 tablespoons hoisin sauce

Direction

- Slice the tofu, making 12 cubes. Put cornstarch in a shallow bowl or on a plate, dredge the tofu in it until thoroughly coated.
- Heat enough oil to submerge the tofu halfway through. Fry the tofu in the hot oil until crispy, about 3 to 5 minutes per side. Drain them on paper towels.
- Sprinkle green onions on top of tofu. Drizzle hoisin sauce on top. Immediately serve.

Nutrition Information

- Calories: 433 calories;
- Total Fat: 32.4
- Sodium: 275
- Total Carbohydrate: 22.5
- Cholesterol: < 1
- Protein: 17.5

314. Ajo Blanco Con Uvas

Serving: 6 | Prep: 30mins | Cook: | Ready in:

Ingredients

- 1/8 cup ground almonds
- 1/2 cup toasted bread crumbs
- 5 cloves garlic
- sea salt to taste
- 2 tablespoons olive oil
- 1 tablespoon white wine vinegar
- 2 cups water
- 6 cubes ice
- 1 pound seedless green grapes, skinned

Direction

- In a mortar, grind salt, almonds, garlic, and bread crumbs until it forms into a paste; stir in oil gradually. Mix in vinegar and put the mixture in a soup tureen. Toss in grapes, ice, and water. Set aside for half hour in a cool place. Serve.

Nutrition Information

- Calories: 153 calories;
- Protein: 2.6
- Total Fat: 7.2
- Sodium: 69
- Total Carbohydrate: 21.4
- Cholesterol: 0

315. Alaskan BBQ Salmon

Serving: 16 | Prep: 10mins | Cook: 17mins | Ready in:

Ingredients

- 1 cup brown sugar
- 1/2 cup honey
- 1 dash liquid smoke flavoring
- 1/2 cup apple cider vinegar
- 1 (4 pound) whole salmon fillet

Direction

- Set grill to high heat.
- Mix together honey, liquid smoke, vinegar and brown sugar in a small bowl.
- Baste one side of salmon with the prepared sauce then place the fillet on the grill, side basted down. Cook for 7 minutes while generously basting top. Turn the fish over and cook for another 8 minutes. Brush basting sauce on some more. Turn one last time and let it cook for 2 minutes longer. Watch the salmon to avoid overcooking as it will lose flavor and juiciness if overcooked.

Nutrition Information

- Calories: 269 calories;
- Sodium: 59
- Total Carbohydrate: 22.3
- Cholesterol: 56
- Protein: 19.6
- Total Fat: 11

316. Almond Butter And Banana Oatmeal Cookies

Serving: 18 | Prep: 15mins | Cook: 12mins | Ready in:

Ingredients

- cooking spray
- 3 ripe bananas
- 2 cups rolled oats
- 1/3 cup unsweetened vanilla-flavored almond milk
- 2 tablespoons almond butter
- 1 teaspoon vanilla extract
- 1/8 teaspoon pumpkin pie spice
- 1 pinch salt
- 2 tablespoons sliced almonds, or to taste (optional)
- 1 1/2 tablespoons turbinado sugar, or to taste (optional)

Direction

- Set the oven to 325°F (165°C) and start preheating. Use cooking spray to grease a baking sheet.
- In a large bowl, mash bananas. Mix in salt, pumpkin pie spice, vanilla extract, almond butter, almond milk and oats.
- Spoon banana and oat mixture by spoonfuls onto baking sheet. Scatter almond slices over cookies; top with turbinado sugar.
- Bake cookies for 12-14 minutes in the prepared oven until set and the bottom turn browned.

Nutrition Information

- Calories: 73 calories;
- Cholesterol: 0
- Protein: 1.8
- Total Fat: 2.1
- Sodium: 21
- Total Carbohydrate: 12.4

317. Almond Flour Brownies

Serving: 8 | Prep: 10mins | Cook: 30mins | Ready in:

Ingredients

- 3/4 cup blanched almond flour
- 2/3 cup agave nectar
- 1/2 cup chopped walnuts (optional)
- 2 eggs
- 5 tablespoons unsweetened cocoa powder
- 1/4 cup coconut oil
- 1 teaspoon vanilla extract

Direction

- Preheat an oven to 175°C or 350°F.
- Mix vanilla extract, coconut oil, cocoa powder, eggs, walnuts, agave nectar and almond flour in a bowl; spread in an 8-in. square baking dish.
- In preheated oven, bake for 30 minutes till brownie edges start to pull from dish's sides; slightly cool brownies for 5 minutes before slicing.

Nutrition Information

- Calories: 215 calories;
- Total Fat: 13.5
- Sodium: 18
- Total Carbohydrate: 24.3
- Cholesterol: 46
- Protein: 3.3

318. Almond Yummies

Serving: 12 | Prep: | Cook: | Ready in:

Ingredients

- 1 1/2 cups all-purpose flour
- 1 cup white sugar
- 2 teaspoons almond extract
- 2 eggs
- 1/4 cup sliced almonds

Direction

- Configure oven to 175 degrees C (350 degrees F) for preheating.
- Mix the eggs, almond extract, sugar and flour in a medium bowl until well blended. Shape dough into balls of an inch. Transfer to a cookie sheet, top each with an almond slice. Bake until golden brown, for 8 to 10 minutes.

Nutrition Information

- Calories: 147 calories;
- Total Fat: 2
- Sodium: 12
- Total Carbohydrate: 29
- Cholesterol: 31
- Protein: 3.1

319. Almost Fat Free British Tea Loaf

Serving: 8 | Prep: 5mins | Cook: 1hours | Ready in:

Ingredients

- 1 teaspoon vegetable oil
- 10 ounces raisins
- 10 fluid ounces strong hot tea
- 12 ounces self-rising flour
- 4 ounces white sugar
- 1 teaspoon ground allspice
- 1 egg, beaten

Direction

- Prepare the oven by preheating to 350°F (175°C). Prepare an oiled loaf pan.
- In a bowl, mix tea and raisins. Soak for about 30 minutes.

- In another bowl, combine allspice, sugar, and flour. Put in egg and raisin-tea mixture. Use a rubber spatula to carefully mix; avoid over mixing. Transfer the mixture to the prepared loaf pan.
- Bake for about 1 hour in the preheated oven until a toothpick poked into the center comes out clean.

Nutrition Information

- Calories: 322 calories;
- Sodium: 547
- Total Carbohydrate: 73.2
- Cholesterol: 23
- Protein: 6
- Total Fat: 1.8

320. Aloha Chicken

Serving: 8 | Prep: 20mins | Cook: 1hours | Ready in:

Ingredients

- 4 pounds chicken thighs
- 1 teaspoon ground ginger
- 1 teaspoon paprika
- 1 tablespoon onion powder
- 2 tablespoons garlic salt
- 3 tablespoons cider vinegar
- 1 cup ketchup
- 1/4 cup soy sauce
- 1 (20 ounce) can crushed pineapple with juice
- 1/4 cup packed brown sugar

Direction

- Prepare the oven by preheating to 400°F (200°C).
- Pile chicken pieces in one layer in a 9x3-inch baking dish that is well greased. Combine garlic salt, onion powder, paprika, and ginger in a small bowl. Mix in vinegar. Split this mixture. Then sweep 1/2 on chicken pieces and place in preheated oven to bake for 15 minutes. Flip the chicken pieces, baste with the rest of 1/2 of the vinegar mixture the bake for 15 more minutes. In the meantime, mix brown sugar, pineapple, soy sauce, and ketchup in a medium bowl. Once chicken baking time is up, scoop the pineapple/soy mixture on the chicken. Then bake for 30 more minutes. And serve immediately.

Nutrition Information

- Calories: 485 calories;
- Total Fat: 23.8
- Sodium: 2276
- Total Carbohydrate: 27.4
- Cholesterol: 141
- Protein: 39.7

321. Amazing Vegan Oatmeal Cookies

Serving: 40 | Prep: 20mins | Cook: 15mins | Ready in:

Ingredients

- 1 cup non-dairy margarine
- 1/2 cup brown sugar
- 1/2 cup confectioners' sugar
- 1/2 cup lukewarm water
- 2 tablespoons ground flax seeds
- 1 teaspoon vanilla extract
- 2 cups all-purpose flour
- 2 teaspoons baking powder
- 2 cups rolled oats
- 1/4 cup shredded coconut
- 2 1/2 teaspoons ground cinnamon
- 1/2 teaspoon ground cloves
- 1/2 cup vegan chocolate chips (optional)
- 1/2 cup dried apricots, quartered (optional)

Direction

- Set an oven to preheat to 190°C (375°F).

- In a big bowl, mix together the confectioner's sugar, brown sugar and margarine, then beat it using an electric mixer until it becomes creamy. Mix in the vanilla extract, flax seeds and water, then add the baking powder and flour. Fold in the cloves, cinnamon, coconut and oats, then add the apricots and chocolate chips.
- Shape the dough into small balls and lay it out on the baking sheets. Use the palm of your hand to flatten slightly.
- Let it bake in the preheated oven for about 15 minutes, until the edges turn golden.

Nutrition Information

- Calories: 106 calories;
- Total Carbohydrate: 13.2
- Cholesterol: 0
- Protein: 1.3
- Total Fat: 5.3
- Sodium: 71

322. American Style Red Beans And Rice

Serving: 4 | Prep: 5mins | Cook: 30mins | Ready in:

Ingredients

- 1 tablespoon olive oil
- 1 (15 ounce) can kidney beans
- 1 1/2 cups tomato sauce
- 4 1/2 cups water, divided
- 1/2 teaspoon dried oregano
- 1/2 teaspoon dried basil
- 1 pinch dried thyme
- salt and pepper to taste
- 5 teaspoons adobo seasoning, divided
- 2 cups uncooked white rice

Direction

- Mix a half cup of water, thyme, olive oil, tomato sauce, basil, pepper, 2 tsp. of adobo, salt, oregano, and kidney beans in a large saucepan and simmer it over low heat.
- While waiting, boil 4 cups of water. Stir in rice and reduce the heat. Cover the pot and simmer for 20 minutes until the liquid is all absorbed and the rice is cooked. Add the remaining 3 tsp. of adobo. Serve the cooked beans over the hot rice.

Nutrition Information

- Calories: 511 calories;
- Total Carbohydrate: 101.1
- Cholesterol: 0
- Protein: 14.7
- Total Fat: 5.1
- Sodium: 712

323. Angel Food Cake III

Serving: 14 | Prep: 30mins | Cook: 45mins | Ready in:

Ingredients

- 1 cup cake flour
- 1 1/2 cups white sugar
- 12 egg whites
- 1 1/2 teaspoons vanilla extract
- 1 1/2 teaspoons cream of tartar
- 1/2 teaspoon salt

Direction

- Set the oven to preheat at 375°F (190°C). Make sure that you're using a dry and clean 10-inch tube pan. Having oils and dirt can deflate the egg whites. In a bowl, sift flour and 3/4 of the sugar together. Set it aside.
- Beat egg whites with salt, vanilla, and cream of tartar, until you form medium stiff peaks. Slowly add the rest of the sugar until you get stiff peaks. Once you reach this volume,

slowly fold the sifted flour mixture, 1/3 at a time. Avoid overmixing. Pour the batter into the tube pan.
- In the oven, bake for 40-45. It's done when it springs back after you touch it. Place the pan upside down, balance it on top of a bottle. This avoids decompressing as it cools. Once cooled, run a knife through the edges to loosen it up. Flip and transfer to a plate.

Nutrition Information

- Calories: 136 calories;
- Total Fat: 0.1
- Sodium: 131
- Total Carbohydrate: 29.9
- Cholesterol: 0
- Protein: 4

324. Apple Bundt Cake

Serving: 12 | Prep: 30mins | Cook: 1hours | Ready in:

Ingredients

- 2 cups apples - peeled, cored and diced
- 1 tablespoon white sugar
- 1 teaspoon ground cinnamon
- 3 cups all-purpose flour
- 3 teaspoons baking powder
- 1/2 teaspoon salt
- 2 cups white sugar
- 1 cup vegetable oil
- 1/4 cup orange juice
- 2 1/2 teaspoons vanilla extract
- 4 eggs
- 1 cup chopped walnuts
- 1/4 cup confectioners' sugar for dusting

Direction

- Set an oven to preheat to 175°C (350°F), then grease and flour a 10-inch Bundt or tube pan. Mix together the 1 tsp cinnamon, 1 tbsp. white sugar and diced apples in a medium bowl, then put aside. Sift together the salt, baking powder and flour, then put aside.
- Mix together the eggs, vanilla, orange juice, oil and 2 cups of white sugar in a big bowl, then beat at high speed until it becomes smooth. Mix in the flour mixture and fold in the chopped walnuts.
- Pour 1/3 of the batter into the prepped pan, then sprinkle 1/2 of the apple mixture on top. Alternate the layers of the batter and filling and end it with the batter.
- Let it bake for 55-60 minutes in the preheated oven or until the top bounces back once touch lightly. Allow it to cool for 10 minutes in the pan, then flip out onto a wire rack and completely cool. Dust with confectioner's sugar.

Nutrition Information

- Calories: 523 calories;
- Total Carbohydrate: 66.3
- Cholesterol: 62
- Protein: 6.9
- Total Fat: 26.7
- Sodium: 243

325. Apple Butter The Easy Way

Serving: 16 | Prep: 10mins | Cook: 20mins | Ready in:

Ingredients

- 2 pounds chopped apples
- 1/3 cup maple syrup
- 1/2 teaspoon ground cinnamon

Direction

- Mix together the cinnamon, maple syrup and apples in a microwaveable bowl. Microwave for 15 minutes on high, then move the mixture to a blender and process it until it has a smooth consistency. Put the mixture back into the bowl and microwave for another 5 minutes. Allow it to cool and move to a jar. Store it in the fridge.

Nutrition Information

- Calories: 47 calories;
- Total Fat: 0.1
- Sodium: 1
- Total Carbohydrate: 12.3
- Cholesterol: 0
- Protein: 0.2

326. Apple Enchilada Dessert

Serving: 6 | Prep: 15mins | Cook: 20mins | Ready in:

Ingredients

- 1 (21 ounce) can apple pie filling
- 6 (8 inch) flour tortillas
- 1 teaspoon ground cinnamon
- 1/3 cup margarine
- 1/2 cup white sugar
- 1/2 cup packed brown sugar
- 1/2 cup water

Direction

- Preheat an oven to 175°C/350°F.
- Evenly put fruit on all tortillas; sprinkle with cinnamon. Roll up tortillas; put on an 8x8-in. lightly greased baking pan, seam side down.
- Boil water, sugars and margarine in a medium saucepan; lower the heat. Simmer for 3 minutes, constantly mixing.
- Evenly put sauce on tortillas; if desired, sprinkle with extra cinnamon on top. In the preheated oven, bake for 20 minutes.
- Creates 6 big tortillas; to serve 12, you can cut in half.

Nutrition Information

- Calories: 484 calories;
- Sodium: 400
- Total Carbohydrate: 88.3
- Cholesterol: 0
- Protein: 4.5
- Total Fat: 13.5

327. Apples By The Fire

Serving: 1 | Prep: 5mins | Cook: 10mins | Ready in:

Ingredients

- 1 Granny Smith apple, cored
- 1 tablespoon brown sugar
- 1/4 teaspoon ground cinnamon

Direction

- Fill apple core with cinnamon and brown sugar; wrap apple in big heavy foil piece, twisting extra foil into tail for handle. Put apple in campfire coals/barbeque; cook till soft for 5-10 minutes. Remove then unwrap; be careful with hot sugar.

Nutrition Information

- Calories: 114 calories;
- Total Fat: 0
- Sodium: 5
- Total Carbohydrate: 30.9
- Cholesterol: 0
- Protein: 0.5

328. Apricot Glazed Chicken

Serving: 5 | Prep: | Cook: | Ready in:

Ingredients

- 6 skinless, boneless chicken breasts
- 1 (10.75 ounce) can low-sodium chicken broth
- 3/4 cup apricot preserves
- 1 tablespoon light soy sauce
- 1 tablespoon cornstarch
- 1 tablespoon water

Direction

- Use the nonstick cooking spray to spray a big skillet. Brown the chicken in the preheated skillet.
- Put in the soy sauce, jam and chicken broth. Let it simmer till the chicken is done and not pink anymore inside or for 20 minutes.
- Take the chicken out of the skillet. Put 1 tbsp. of water and 1 tbsp. of cornstarch into the sauce to thicken. If you want it to be thicker, add the same amounts more of each. Bring the chicken back to the skillet and completely coat with sauce by flipping.

Nutrition Information

- Calories: 296 calories;
- Sodium: 227
- Total Carbohydrate: 35.1
- Cholesterol: 83
- Protein: 33.7
- Total Fat: 1.9

329. Artichoke Salsa

Serving: 5 | Prep: 10mins | Cook: | Ready in:

Ingredients

- 1 (6.5 ounce) jar marinated artichoke hearts, drained and chopped
- 3 roma (plum) tomatoes, chopped
- 2 tablespoons chopped red onion
- 1/4 cup chopped black olives
- 1 tablespoon chopped garlic
- 2 tablespoons chopped fresh basil
- salt and pepper to taste

Direction

- Combine tomatoes, olives, artichoke hearts, onion, pepper, garlic, and salt in a medium bowl. Best served with tortilla chips chilled or at room temperature.

Nutrition Information

- Calories: 52 calories;
- Sodium: 278
- Total Carbohydrate: 6.8
- Cholesterol: 0
- Protein: 1.9
- Total Fat: 2.8

330. Asian Barbequed Steak

Serving: 8 | Prep: 15mins | Cook: 10mins | Ready in:

Ingredients

- 1/4 cup chili sauce
- 1/4 cup fish sauce
- 1 1/2 tablespoons dark sesame oil
- 1 tablespoon grated fresh ginger root
- 3 cloves garlic, peeled and crushed
- 2 pounds flank steak

Direction

- Whisk garlic, ginger, sesame oil, fish sauce and chili sauce together in a medium bowl. Reserve several tablespoons of the mixture for brushing steaks when grilling. Then score the flank steak and transfer into a shallow dish. Add the remaining marinade on top of the steak and then flip to coat. Cover the dish and place in fridge to marinate for at least three hours.
- Preheat the outdoor grill over high heat.
- Brush the grilling surface lightly with oil. Then grill the steak for about five minutes on each

side or to the doneness desired. Be sure to brush often with reserved marinade mixture.

Nutrition Information

- Calories: 160 calories;
- Total Fat: 10.7
- Sodium: 582
- Total Carbohydrate: 1.1
- Cholesterol: 36
- Protein: 14

331. Asian Beef With Snow Peas

Serving: 4 | Prep: 5mins | Cook: 10mins | Ready in:

Ingredients

- 3 tablespoons soy sauce
- 2 tablespoons rice wine
- 1 tablespoon brown sugar
- 1/2 teaspoon cornstarch
- 1 tablespoon vegetable oil
- 1 tablespoon minced fresh ginger root
- 1 tablespoon minced garlic
- 1 pound beef round steak, cut into thin strips
- 8 ounces snow peas

Direction

- Put together the rice wine, soy sauce, cornstarch, and brown sugar in a small bowl then put aside.
- Pour oil in a cooking pan or wok and heat it on medium-high heat. Add the garlic and ginger to the oil and stir-fry for 30 seconds. Add the steak and stir-fry until it's browned evenly for 2 minutes. Add the snow peas in then stir-fry for 3 more minutes. Pour in the soy sauce mixture and boil with constant stirring. Reduce the heat and allow to simmer until the sauce has become smooth and thick. Serve right away.

Nutrition Information

- Calories: 203 calories;
- Total Carbohydrate: 9.7
- Cholesterol: 39
- Protein: 16
- Total Fat: 10
- Sodium: 711

332. Asian Lettuce Wraps

Serving: 4 | Prep: 20mins | Cook: 15mins | Ready in:

Ingredients

- 16 Boston Bibb or butter lettuce leaves
- 1 pound lean ground beef
- 1 tablespoon cooking oil
- 1 large onion, chopped
- 1/4 cup hoisin sauce
- 2 cloves fresh garlic, minced
- 1 tablespoon soy sauce
- 1 tablespoon rice wine vinegar
- 2 teaspoons minced pickled ginger
- 1 dash Asian chile pepper sauce, or to taste (optional)
- 1 (8 ounce) can water chestnuts, drained and finely chopped
- 1 bunch green onions, chopped
- 2 teaspoons Asian (dark) sesame oil

Direction

- Wash the entire lettuce leaves and pat dry, be cautious not damage them. Reserve.
- Over moderately-high heat, heat a big skillet. In hot skillet, cook and mix cooking oil and beef for 5 to 7 minutes till crumbly and browned. Let drain and throw the grease; turn beef onto a bowl. In the same skillet used for beef, cook and mix the onion for 5 to 10 minutes till slightly soft. Into the onions, mix chili pepper sauce, ginger, vinegar, soy sauce,

garlic and hoisin sauce. Put cooked beef, sesame oil, green onions and water chestnuts; cook and mix for 2 minutes till onions barely start to wilt.
- Place the leaves of lettuce around outer edge of a big serving platter and stack the meat mixture in the middle.

Nutrition Information

- Calories: 388 calories;
- Total Fat: 22.3
- Sodium: 580
- Total Carbohydrate: 24.3
- Cholesterol: 69
- Protein: 23.4

333. Asian Vegetable Roll

Serving: 4 | Prep: 20mins | Cook: 1hours15mins | Ready in:

Ingredients

- cooking spray
- 1/2 spaghetti squash, halved and seeded
- 1/4 cup broccoli florets, chopped
- 1 1/2 cups spinach leaves
- 4 (10 inch) flour tortillas
- 1 teaspoon miso paste
- 1/4 cup olive oil, or as needed

Direction

- Preheat an oven to 175°C/350°F. Use cooking spray to coat baking sheet.
- Put spaghetti squash half on prepped baking dish, cut side down.
- Bake for 40 minutes till squash flesh easily shreds and is tender. Shred flesh strands from rind; put in bowl.
- In steamer basket above a pan of boiling water, put broccoli. Steam for 8 minutes till tender. Put spinach in steamer basket at final 2 minutes. Put spinach and broccoli in different bowls.
- Down middle of each tortilla, spread 1/4 tsp. miso paste. Put 1 tbsp. broccoli florets, 1 tbsp. spinach and 2 tbsp. spaghetti squash on miso paste down middle of tortillas. Fold tortilla sides up around filling; fold ends up to enclose filling.
- In skillet, heat 1/4 cup olive oil on high heat.
- Put 1 rolled tortilla in frying pan, seam side down. Use spatula to press tortilla gently. Cook, 2-3 minutes per side, till tortilla is golden brown, flipping once. Fry leftover tortillas the same way, adding extra olive oil if needed.

Nutrition Information

- Calories: 373 calories;
- Total Fat: 19.6
- Sodium: 525
- Total Carbohydrate: 43.2
- Cholesterol: 0
- Protein: 7

334. Asparagus Wrapped In Crisp Prosciutto

Serving: 16 | Prep: 5mins | Cook: 15mins | Ready in:

Ingredients

- 1 tablespoon olive oil
- 16 spears fresh asparagus, trimmed
- 16 slices prosciutto

Direction

- Set an oven to preheat to 220°C (450°F). Use aluminum foil to line a baking sheet and coat it using olive oil.
- Wrap each asparagus spear with 1 slice of prosciutto, beginning at the bottom and spiral

it up to the tip. Put the wrapped spares on the prepped baking sheet.
- Let it bake in the preheated oven for 5 minutes. Take it out and shake the pan back and forth to roll over the spears. Put it back into the oven for an additional of 5 minutes or until the prosciutto becomes crisp and the asparagus becomes tender. Serve it right away.

Nutrition Information

- Calories: 64 calories;
- Total Fat: 5.4
- Sodium: 279
- Total Carbohydrate: 0.6
- Cholesterol: 13
- Protein: 3.1

335. Aunt Kate's Green Beans In Tomatoes

Serving: 4 | Prep: 10mins | Cook: 1hours | Ready in:

Ingredients

- 2 cloves garlic, chopped
- 2 tablespoons vegetable oil
- 1 (14.25 ounce) can diced tomatoes with basil and oregano
- 1 (8 ounce) can tomato sauce
- 1 pound fresh green beans, trimmed and snapped
- salt and pepper to taste

Direction

- Sauté garlic in oil in a big saucepan on moderately low heat, until garlic is browned lightly. Stir in tomato sauce and diced tomatoes, then cover and cook about 30 to 45 minutes.
- Stir into the tomatoes with green beans and cook until softened. Season to taste with pepper and salt.

Nutrition Information

- Calories: 134 calories;
- Total Fat: 7.1
- Sodium: 792
- Total Carbohydrate: 15.2
- Cholesterol: 0
- Protein: 3.8

336. Authentic Chinese Steamed Fish

Serving: 6 | Prep: 15mins | Cook: 15mins | Ready in:

Ingredients

- 1 (4 pound) whole rockfish, dressed
- 1/4 cup vegetable oil
- 1 green onion, thinly sliced diagonally
- 1 (1 inch) piece fresh ginger, peeled and cut into matchstick strips
- 1/2 cup soy sauce

Direction

- Pour water in a big pot, filling it 1/2 full then on top of the pot, put a bamboo steamer with a lid. Bring the water to a rolling boil. Clean the fish by scouring off its scales then wash it off using cold water. Move the fish to a small metal plate with its belly side down.
- Place it in the steamer then cover and cook for 10-12 minutes until the fish is already flaky and not opaque. Avoid taking the pot lid off until it is finished steaming to make sure that the fish is completely tender and cooked.
- While steaming the fish, put together the vegetable oil, ginger, and green onions in a small cooking pan. Cook them on medium-high heat until the ginger starts to bubble. Pour the hot oil carefully on the steamed fish then dribble with soy sauce and serve.

Nutrition Information

- Calories: 379 calories;
- Protein: 58.1
- Total Fat: 13.8
- Sodium: 1385
- Total Carbohydrate: 2
- Cholesterol: 104

337. Authentic German Lebkuchen

Serving: 25 | Prep: 20mins | Cook: 20mins | Ready in:

Ingredients

- 25 backoblaten (German baking wafers)
- 2 cups blanched almond flour
- 1 1/4 cups white sugar
- 3 eggs
- 1/2 cup ground hazelnuts
- 7 tablespoons finely chopped candied lemon and orange peel
- 2 teaspoons ground cinnamon
- 1 teaspoon vanilla sugar
- 1 pinch ground cloves
- 2 cups chopped dark chocolate

Direction

- Set an oven to preheat to 175°C (350°F). Use parchment paper to line a baking sheet and lay out the backoblaten or German baking wafers on top and leave a 1-inch of space in between them.
- Mix together the ground cloves, vanilla sugar, ground cinnamon, candied orange and lemon peel, ground hazelnuts, eggs, sugar and almond flour and mix into a firm dough.
- Form the mixture into balls. Lay out the balls on the prepped wafers, then gently press to flatten it into 1/2-inch high rounds.
- Let it bake in the preheated oven for 15-20 minutes until it turns light brown in color. Allow it to fully cool for about 30 minutes.
- Put the chocolate over a double boiler on top of simmering water. Mix often and scrape down the sides using a rubber spatula to prevent it from scorching, until the chocolate melts for around 5 minutes. Use chocolate to cover the top of each lebkuchen.

Nutrition Information

- Calories: 211 calories;
- Cholesterol: 23
- Protein: 4.1
- Total Fat: 11.7
- Sodium: 9
- Total Carbohydrate: 24.8

338. Avocado Black Bean Brownies

Serving: 16 | Prep: 10mins | Cook: 25mins | Ready in:

Ingredients

- 1 tablespoon coconut oil
- 2 1/2 tablespoons water
- 1 tablespoon flaxseed meal
- 1 (15 ounce) can no-salt-added black beans, drained and rinsed
- 1/2 cup coconut sugar
- 1/2 avocado, peeled
- 2 teaspoons coconut oil
- 2/3 cup cocoa powder
- 1/4 teaspoon baking soda
- 1/4 teaspoon baking powder
- 1/3 cup vegan chocolate chips, plus more for topping

Direction

- Set an oven to preheat to 175°C (350°F). Use 1 tbsp. of coconut oil to grease one 8-inch square baking dish.

- In a small bowl, mix together the flaxseed meal and water to make a flax egg, then put aside for about 5 minutes to let it thicken.
- In a food processor, put 2 tsp of coconut oil, avocado, coconut sugar, black beans and flax egg and puree until well blended. Add baking powder, baking soda and cocoa powder, then blend it for 3-4 minutes until the batter becomes smooth.
- Move the batter to a big bowl and fold in the chocolate chips. Pour it into the baking dish and smoothen the top.
- Let it bake in the preheated oven for about 25 minutes, until an inserted toothpick in the middle exits clean. Slice it into 16 bars and put additional chocolate chips on top.

Nutrition Information

- Calories: 79 calories;
- Sodium: 34
- Total Carbohydrate: 13.1
- Cholesterol: 0
- Protein: 2.3
- Total Fat: 3

339. Avocado Paletas

Serving: 10 | Prep: 20mins | Cook: 5mins | Ready in:

Ingredients

- 1 cup water
- 1/2 cup white sugar
- 3 avocados, peeled and pitted
- 1 lime, juiced
- 1/4 teaspoon salt

Direction

- In a saucepan, bring water and sugar to a boil. Stir constantly until the sugar has dissolved. Reserve to cool.
- Transfer the sugar-water mixture to a blender along with salt, avocados and lime juice. Blend until the mixture is smooth. Transfer the mixture to 10 ice pop molds.
- Chill for about 2 hours until solid but still soft. Insert wooden sticks and continue to freeze for about 12 to 24 hours until firm.

Nutrition Information

- Calories: 137 calories;
- Cholesterol: 0
- Protein: 1.3
- Total Fat: 8.9
- Sodium: 63
- Total Carbohydrate: 15.8

340. Avocado Tacos

Serving: 6 | Prep: 20mins | Cook: 5mins | Ready in:

Ingredients

- 3 avocados - peeled, pitted, and mashed
- 1/4 cup onions, diced
- 1/4 teaspoon garlic salt
- 12 (6 inch) corn tortillas
- 1 bunch fresh cilantro leaves, finely chopped
- jalapeno pepper sauce, to taste

Direction

- Prepare the oven by preheating to 325°F (165°C).
- Combine in a medium bowl the garlic salt, onions and avocados.
- Lay out corn tortillas in one layer on a large baking sheet, and put in the preheated oven for 2 to 5 minutes until warmed through.
- Spread avocado mixture on tortillas. Decorate with cilantro and drizzle with jalapeno pepper sauce.

Nutrition Information

- Calories: 279 calories;
- Protein: 5.3
- Total Fat: 16.3
- Sodium: 111
- Total Carbohydrate: 32.8
- Cholesterol: 0

341. Awesome Green Beans

Serving: 8 | Prep: 15mins | Cook: 45mins | Ready in:

Ingredients

- 1 tablespoon olive oil
- 1 onion, finely chopped
- 6 cloves garlic, finely chopped
- 6 links spicy pork sausage, sliced
- 1 cup water
- 2 pounds frozen green beans
- seasoning salt to taste

Direction

- In a big saucepan, heat oil on moderate heat. Sauté garlic and onion until softened, then stir in sausage and cook until browned evenly.
- Add in water and bring to a boil. Stir in green beans, then lower heat to moderately low. Cover and simmer about a half hour, until softened. Check the water level often and put in more as necessary to prevent scorching. Season to taste with salt.

Nutrition Information

- Calories: 108 calories;
- Total Fat: 5.6
- Sodium: 107
- Total Carbohydrate: 9.2
- Cholesterol: 15
- Protein: 4.9

342. Awesome Korean Steak

Serving: 6 | Prep: 20mins | Cook: 10mins | Ready in:

Ingredients

- 2 pounds thinly sliced Scotch fillet (chuck eye steaks)
- 1/2 cup soy sauce
- 5 tablespoons white sugar
- 2 1/2 tablespoons sesame seeds
- 2 tablespoons sesame oil
- 3 shallots, thinly sliced
- 2 cloves garlic, crushed
- 5 tablespoons mirin (Japanese sweet wine)

Direction

- Mix mirin, garlic, shallots, sesame oil, sesame seeds, sugar, and soy sauce in a big bowl. Add meat, mixing to coat. Cover then keep in fridge for 12-24 hours.
- Heat a big skillet on medium heat. Fry meat until it's not pink for 5-10 minutes. Serve with fried rice or salad.

Nutrition Information

- Calories: 376 calories;
- Sodium: 1249
- Total Carbohydrate: 21.4
- Cholesterol: 69
- Protein: 20.6
- Total Fat: 21.9

343. BBQ Pork For Sandwiches

Serving: 12 | Prep: 15mins | Cook: 4hours30mins | Ready in:

Ingredients

- 1 (14 ounce) can beef broth
- 3 pounds boneless pork ribs
- 1 (18 ounce) bottle barbeque sauce

Direction

- Add a can of beef broth into the slow cooker, then put in boneless pork ribs. Cook on high heat for 4 hours until meat can be shredded easily. Transfer the meat and shred with 2 forks. It may seem that it's not successful right away, but it will.
- Start preheating the oven at 350°F (175°C). Place the shredded pork to a Dutch oven or iron skillet and blend in barbeque sauce.
- Bake in the prepared oven for 30 minutes until heated thoroughly.

Nutrition Information

- Calories: 355 calories;
- Total Fat: 18.1
- Sodium: 623
- Total Carbohydrate: 15.2
- Cholesterol: 83
- Protein: 30.2

344. BBQ Teriyaki Pork Kabobs

Serving: 6 | Prep: 30mins | Cook: 20mins | Ready in:

Ingredients

- 3 tablespoons soy sauce
- 3 tablespoons olive oil
- 1 clove garlic, minced
- 1/2 teaspoon crushed red pepper flakes
- salt and pepper to taste
- 1 pound boneless pork loin, cut into 1 inch cubes
- 1 (14.5 ounce) can low-sodium beef broth
- 2 tablespoons cornstarch
- 2 tablespoons soy sauce
- 1 tablespoon brown sugar
- 2 cloves garlic, minced
- 1/4 teaspoon ground ginger
- 3 portobello mushrooms, cut into quarters
- 1 large red onion, cut into 12 wedges
- 12 cherry tomatoes
- 12 bite-size chunks fresh pineapple

Direction

- Mix 3 tbsp. of soy sauce, red pepper flakes, pepper, salt, a clove of minced garlic, and olive oil in a shallow dish. Add the pork cubes, flipping them until coated evenly with the marinade. Cover the dish and chill inside the fridge for 3 hours.
- Mix beef broth, brown sugar, ginger, 2 cloves of minced garlic, 2 tbsp. of soy sauce, and cornstarch in a saucepan. Bring the mixture to a boil while constantly stirring it. Lower the heat and simmer for 5 minutes.
- Set the outdoor grill over high heat for preheating. Oil the grate lightly. Use skewers to thread the pork cubes, making sure you arrange them alternately with mushrooms, onion, tomatoes, and chunks of pineapple.
- Cook the pork on the grill for 15 minutes until cooked through. Flip the skewers over and baste them with the sauce while cooking.

Nutrition Information

- Calories: 297 calories;
- Protein: 19.4
- Total Fat: 17
- Sodium: 867
- Total Carbohydrate: 17.6
- Cholesterol: 48

345. Bacon

Serving: 16 | Prep: 10mins | Cook: 6hours | Ready in:

Ingredients

- 4 pounds raw pork belly
- 1/2 cup packed brown sugar
- 1/4 cup sugar-based curing mixture (such as Morton® Tender Quick®)
- 1 gallon cold water, or as needed
- 1 (10 pound) bag charcoal briquettes
- hickory or apple wood chips

Direction

- Mix water, curing mixture and brown sugar in 2-gallon container. Submerge pork belly in mixture till completely covered. You may weight down meat with dinner plate/similar object if it floats. Refrigerate for 6 days, covered.
- In outdoor smoker, light charcoal. In bowl of water, soak wood chips. Coals are ready when temperature of smoker is at 140-150°. Smoke pork belly, throwing handful of wood chips on coals once an hour, for 6 hours. Keep in fridge; cut and fry with store-bought bacon as you would.

Nutrition Information

- Calories: 614 calories;
- Total Fat: 60.1
- Sodium: 1814
- Total Carbohydrate: 6.7
- Cholesterol: 82
- Protein: 10.6

346. Bacon And Date Appetizer

Serving: 6 | Prep: 30mins | Cook: 5mins | Ready in:

Ingredients

- 1 (8 ounce) package pitted dates
- 4 ounces almonds
- 1 pound sliced bacon

Direction

- Set broiler to preheat.
- Cut dates in the center to form slits. Put an almond inside every date. Use bacon to wrap dates, hold in place with toothpicks.
- Broil until bacon is crisp and evenly brown for 10 minutes.

Nutrition Information

- Calories: 560 calories;
- Total Fat: 43.7
- Sodium: 631
- Total Carbohydrate: 32.2
- Cholesterol: 51
- Protein: 13.7

347. Baked Beans II

Serving: 6 | Prep: 20mins | Cook: 1hours | Ready in:

Ingredients

- 2 (15 ounce) cans baked beans with pork
- 1/2 cup packed brown sugar
- 1/2 onion, chopped
- 1/2 cup ketchup
- 1 tablespoon prepared mustard
- 1 teaspoon Worcestershire sauce
- 1 teaspoon red wine vinegar
- salt and pepper to taste
- 2 slices bacon

Direction

- Preheat the oven to 175 degrees C (350 degrees F).
- Mix pork and beans, Worcestershire sauce, brown sugar, mustard, onion, vinegar and ketchup in a 9x9 inch baking dish. Add pepper and salt to taste. Add bacon slices on top.
- Bake for about 1 hour at 175 degrees C (350 degrees F) or until the bacon is cooked and the sauce is thickened.

Nutrition Information

- Calories: 287 calories;
- Total Fat: 6.5
- Sodium: 924
- Total Carbohydrate: 52.3
- Cholesterol: 16
- Protein: 8.9

348. Baked Beans III

Serving: 5 | Prep: 5mins | Cook: 1hours | Ready in:

Ingredients

- 1 (28 ounce) can baked beans
- 1/2 pound bacon, cut into small pieces
- 8 ounces brown sugar

Direction

- Set an oven to 200°C (400°F) to preheat.
- Pour the beans into a 2-qt. casserole dish.
- In a 9-inch skillet, put the bacon, fully covering the bottom of the pan. Spread the brown sugar on top of the bacon and cook on medium heat. Move to the casserole dish once the bacon grease begins to bubble up through the sugar, then mix with the beans.
- Bake for 45 minutes in the preheated oven.

Nutrition Information

- Calories: 526 calories;
- Total Fat: 21
- Sodium: 929
- Total Carbohydrate: 77.4
- Cholesterol: 31
- Protein: 12.8

349. Baked Beans, Texas Ranger

Serving: 6 | Prep: 15mins | Cook: 1hours | Ready in:

Ingredients

- 1 (28 ounce) can baked beans with pork
- 1 medium onion, diced
- 1 medium bell pepper, diced
- 4 links spicy pork sausage, cut into chunks
- 2 tablespoons chili powder
- 3 tablespoons Worcestershire sauce
- 4 tablespoons vinegar
- 1/2 cup packed brown sugar
- 1/2 cup ketchup
- 1 teaspoon garlic powder
- salt to taste
- 1 dash cayenne pepper (optional)

Direction

- Set the oven to 175°C or 350°F to preheat.
- Mix together sausage, bell pepper, onion and baked beans in a Dutch oven, then season with salt, garlic powder, ketchup, brown sugar, vinegar, Worcestershire sauce and chili powder. Put in a dash of cayenne, if wanted.
- In the preheated oven, cover and bake for an hour.

Nutrition Information

- Calories: 301 calories;
- Total Fat: 6.1
- Sodium: 1031
- Total Carbohydrate: 55.7
- Cholesterol: 23
- Protein: 10.8

350. Baked Chicken With Peaches

Serving: 8 | Prep: 15mins | Cook: 30mins | Ready in:

Ingredients

- 8 skinless, boneless chicken breast halves
- 1 cup brown sugar
- 4 fresh peaches - peeled, pitted, and sliced
- 1/8 teaspoon ground ginger
- 1/8 teaspoon ground cloves
- 2 tablespoons fresh lemon juice

Direction

- Set an oven to 175°C (350°F) to preheat, then grease a 9x13-inch baking dish lightly.
- In the prepped baking dish, put the chicken and sprinkle 1/2 cup of brown sugar on top. Put slices of peach on top of the chicken and sprinkle with lemon juice, cloves, ginger and the leftover 1/2 cup of brown sugar.
- Bake in the preheated oven for about 30 minutes and baste it with juices frequently, until the juices run clear and the chicken is cooked through.

Nutrition Information

- Calories: 248 calories;
- Cholesterol: 67
- Protein: 24.6
- Total Fat: 2.8
- Sodium: 68
- Total Carbohydrate: 30.3

351. Baked Cod In Foil

Serving: 4 | Prep: 25mins | Cook: 20mins | Ready in:

Ingredients

- 2 tomatoes, cubed
- 1 red bell pepper, seeded and cubed
- 1 onion, minced
- 2 tablespoons olive oil
- 2 tablespoons chopped fresh basil
- 1 clove garlic, minced
- aluminum foil
- 4 (5 ounce) cod fillets
- lemon, juiced
- salt and ground black pepper to taste

Direction

- Preheat the oven to 200 degrees C (400 degrees F).
- In a bowl, mix garlic and basil, olive oil, onion, bell pepper, and tomatoes well.
- On a working surface, lay 4 aluminum foil sheets and add 1 cod fillet in the middle of each. Scoop tomato mixture equally on top of the 4 fillets. Sprinkle with lemon juice and use pepper and salt to season. Place a second foil sheet over and seal the edges to form a parcel. Repeat with the leftover fillets and tomato mixture.
- Bake in the preheated oven for roughly 20 minutes till cod could be flaked easily using a fork. Take out of the oven and gently unwrap the parcels. Scoop onto warmed plates and serve right away.

Nutrition Information

- Calories: 216 calories;
- Sodium: 146
- Total Carbohydrate: 10.4
- Cholesterol: 52
- Protein: 27
- Total Fat: 8

352. Baked Kale Chips

Serving: 6 | Prep: 10mins | Cook: 10mins | Ready in:

Ingredients

- 1 bunch kale
- 1 tablespoon olive oil
- 1 teaspoon seasoned salt

Direction

- Heat oven to 175 degrees Celsius or 350 degrees Fahrenheit. Place parchment paper on a non-insulted cookie sheet.
- Use kitchen shears or knife to carefully remove leaves from thick stems. Tear to small pieces. Thoroughly wash and dry kale using a salad spinner. Drizzle olive oil on kale and sprinkle seasoning salt on top.
- Bake until edges brown for 10-15 minutes but aren't burnt.

Nutrition Information

- Calories: 58 calories;
- Protein: 2.5
- Total Fat: 2.8
- Sodium: 185
- Total Carbohydrate: 7.6
- Cholesterol: 0

353. Baked Rice And Vegetables In Broth

Serving: 4 | Prep: 15mins | Cook: 30mins | Ready in:

Ingredients

- 3/4 cup uncooked long-grain rice
- 1 tablespoon uncooked wild rice
- 1/4 cup uncooked brown rice
- 1/4 cup sliced fresh mushrooms
- 1/4 chopped fresh broccoli
- 1/4 cup chopped carrots
- 1/4 cup chopped red bell pepper
- 1/4 cup finely chopped onion
- 1 teaspoon salt
- 1 teaspoon dried onion flakes
- 1 teaspoon paprika
- 1/4 teaspoon black pepper
- 2 1/2 cups vegetable broth

Direction

- Set the oven to 425°F (220°C) and start preheating.
- Combine broth, black pepper, paprika, onion flakes, salt, onion, bell pepper, carrots, broccoli, mushrooms, brown rice, wild rice and white rice in a 9 x 13-inch baking dish. Combine well; cover.
- Bake in the prepared oven until cooked through or for half an hour; stir once during baking.

Nutrition Information

- Calories: 210 calories;
- Protein: 5.1
- Total Fat: 1
- Sodium: 877
- Total Carbohydrate: 44.3
- Cholesterol: 0

354. Baked Stuffed Pumpkin

Serving: 6 | Prep: 30mins | Cook: 1hours | Ready in:

Ingredients

- 1 medium sugar pumpkin
- 6 Granny Smith apples - peeled, cored and chopped
- 1 cup chopped walnuts
- 1 (16 ounce) can whole berry cranberry sauce
- 1 (20 ounce) can pineapple chunks, drained
- 3/4 cup packed brown sugar
- 1/2 cup golden raisins
- 1/2 cup dark rum (optional)
- 2 teaspoons minced fresh ginger root
- 1 tablespoon freshly grated nutmeg
- 1 tablespoon ground cinnamon

Direction

- Set the oven to 175°C or 350°F. Place a rack in the middle of the oven.

- Slice the top of the pumpkin off then set aside. Use a metal spoon to scoop the seeds out.
- Combine rum, apples, raisins, walnuts, brown sugar, pineapple, and cranberry sauce in a big bowl. Mix in cinnamon, nutmeg, and ginger to season. Transfer the mixture in the cleaned pumpkin then place the top back on.
- Directly place the pumpkin on a thick baking sheet or baking stone. Bake in the preheated oven for an hour until the pumpkin starts to soften. Take the pumpkin out of the oven then stir. Gently scrape the sides to let pumpkin pieces fall in the apple mixture.

Nutrition Information

- Calories: 617 calories;
- Total Fat: 13.7
- Sodium: 31
- Total Carbohydrate: 117.7
- Cholesterol: 0
- Protein: 7

355. Baked Sweet Potatoes

Serving: 4 | Prep: 10mins | Cook: 1hours5mins | Ready in:

Ingredients

- 2 tablespoons olive oil
- 3 large sweet potatoes
- 2 pinches dried oregano
- 2 pinches salt
- 2 pinches ground black pepper

Direction

- Heat the oven beforehand to 175 °C or 350 °F. Use just enough olive oil to coat the bottom of a glass or non-stick baking dish.
- Wash and peel the sweet potatoes then slice them into medium size pieces. Put them in the baking sheet and coat them with the olive oil by turning them. Moderately sprinkle with pepper, salt and oregano to taste.
- Bake in the preheated oven until soft, about 60 minutes.

Nutrition Information

- Calories: 321 calories;
- Total Carbohydrate: 61
- Cholesterol: 0
- Protein: 4.8
- Total Fat: 7.3
- Sodium: 92

356. Baked Tofu Stir Fry

Serving: 4 | Prep: 15mins | Cook: 30mins | Ready in:

Ingredients

- 1 (12 ounce) package extra-firm tofu, cubed
- 6 tablespoons soy sauce
- 2 tablespoons grated fresh ginger
- 1 tablespoon sesame oil, divided
- 2 teaspoons honey
- 2 teaspoons rice wine vinegar
- 1 teaspoon minced garlic
- 1 cup frozen sugar snap peas
- 1 cup shredded carrots
- 1 cup fresh bean sprouts
- 1 bell pepper, cut into strips
- 6 green onions, chopped

Direction

- Turn on the oven at 400°F (200°C). Line aluminum foil on a baking sheet; arrange tofu on top.
- In a bowl, combine garlic, rice wine vinegar, honey, 1 teaspoon of sesame oil, ginger, and soy sauce. Transfer 1/2 the mixture over the tofu.
- Bake tofu in the prepared oven until equally browned, for 30 minutes.

- In a large skillet (or wok), heat 1 teaspoon sesame oil after 15 minutes of baking time. Put in carrots and sugar snap peas; stir-fry until slightly tender, for 5 minutes. Place to a plate. Heat the 1 teaspoon sesame oil left in the skillet. Add in green onions, bell pepper, and bean sprouts; stir-fry until slightly tender, for 5 minutes.
- Pour carrots and sugar snap peas back in the skillets. Add in the remaining soy sauce mixture. Stir-fry until flavors are well-combined, for additional 5 minutes. Be careful when combining in tofu.

Nutrition Information

- Calories: 185 calories;
- Total Carbohydrate: 17.8
- Cholesterol: 0
- Protein: 12.4
- Total Fat: 8.5
- Sodium: 1385

357. Baked Vegetables I

Serving: 4 | Prep: 15mins | Cook: 45mins | Ready in:

Ingredients

- 2 potatoes, peeled and cubed
- 4 carrots, cut into 1 inch pieces
- 1 head fresh broccoli, cut into florets
- 4 zucchini, thickly sliced
- salt to taste
- 1/4 cup olive oil
- 1 (1 ounce) package dry onion soup mix

Direction

- Heat the oven beforehand to 200 °C or 400 °F. Lightly grease oil on a big, shallow baking dish.
- In the prepared baking dish, mix the vegetables then sprinkle lightly with salt. Spread olive oil over the mixture and use the dry soup mix to sprinkle over top.
- Bake it in the preheated oven until vegetables become fork-tender, about 30 to 45 minutes.

Nutrition Information

- Calories: 306 calories;
- Sodium: 719
- Total Carbohydrate: 41.4
- Cholesterol: 0
- Protein: 7.8
- Total Fat: 14.5

358. Baked And Poached Tilapia

Serving: 4 | Prep: 10mins | Cook: 20mins | Ready in:

Ingredients

- 4 (4 ounce) fillets tilapia
- 1/4 cup fresh lemon juice
- 2 1/2 teaspoons ground coriander
- 1 1/2 teaspoons dried parsley
- 1 roma (plum) tomato, diced

Direction

- In a bowl, put parsley, coriander, tilapia, and lemon juice. Mix until the fillets are coated evenly. Chill at least 2 hours.
- Preheat an oven to 175 degrees C (350 degrees F). Coat a baking dish lightly with grease.
- Spread the fillets at the bottom of the baking dish prepared and place tomato on top of each fillet. Sprinkle the remaining marinade atop fillets. Cover using aluminum foil.
- Bake 15 minutes in the preheated oven. Remove the foil and then bake while uncovered for 5 minutes.

Nutrition Information

- Calories: 125 calories;
- Protein: 23.4
- Total Fat: 1.8
- Sodium: 74
- Total Carbohydrate: 2.7
- Cholesterol: 41

359. Balsamic Vinegar And Ginger Bok Choy

Serving: 4 | Prep: 15mins | Cook: 15mins | Ready in:

Ingredients

- 4 heads baby bok choy
- 3 tablespoons olive oil
- 1/4 cup water
- 2 tablespoons capers
- 1 1/2 teaspoons minced garlic
- 1 1/2 teaspoons minced fresh ginger root
- 2 tablespoons balsamic vinegar
- 1 dash fresh lemon juice, or to taste

Direction

- Separate the leaves from the stems of the bok choy. Slice the stems into bite sized chunks and cut up the leaves.
- To heat the olive oil, set a large skillet over medium heat.
- In the oil, cook the bok choy stems for 3 minutes or until they become slightly tender. Mix and cook the leaves for 10 more minutes in water until it evaporates. Combine the garlic, ginger, and capers and stir for another minute to cook. Drizzle lemon juice and vinegar on top of the bok choy and set aside from the heat. Serve right after.

Nutrition Information

- Calories: 111 calories;
- Cholesterol: 0
- Protein: 1.7

- Total Fat: 10.4
- Sodium: 195
- Total Carbohydrate: 4.1

360. Banana Angel Food Cake

Serving: 12 | Prep: 30mins | Cook: 1hours | Ready in:

Ingredients

- 1 1/2 cups egg whites
- 1/2 teaspoon cream of tartar
- 1/4 teaspoon baking powder
- 1 teaspoon vanilla extract
- 1/2 teaspoon ground cinnamon
- 1/4 cup rolled oats
- 3 ripe bananas, mashed
- 1 cup cake flour
- 2 cups confectioners' sugar
- 1/4 teaspoon salt

Direction

- Turn on the oven to 325°F (165°C) to preheat.
- Beat egg whites until it forms stiff peaks but not dry.
- Mix together mashed bananas, oats, cinnamon, vanilla, baking powder and cream of tartar.
- Mix together the salt, confectioners' sugar and flour in a separate bowl.
- Add banana mixture into egg whites by folding in. Add flour mixture into the banana/egg white mixture by folding. Transfer the batter into a non-stick cooking-spray coated 9 or 10 inch round cake pan.
- Put into the oven to bake at 325°F (165°C) until the cake is lightly golden in color and firm, about 1 hour. Let it cook for 5 minutes; then slip out of the pan to transfer it onto a serving dish. Use a light dusting of confectioners' sugar to garnish.

Nutrition Information

- Calories: 170 calories;
- Total Fat: 0.3
- Sodium: 110
- Total Carbohydrate: 37.6
- Cholesterol: 0
- Protein: 4.8

361. Banana Chocolate Creamed Cashew Cake

Serving: 12 | Prep: 20mins | Cook: | Ready in:

Ingredients

- 3 cups raw cashews
- Crust:
- 1 cup almonds
- 1 cup pecans
- 4 Medjool dates, pitted
- 2 teaspoons coconut oil, melted
- 2 teaspoons cocoa powder
- 1/4 teaspoon salt
- Filling:
- 4 cups banana, coarsely chopped
- 2 teaspoons ground cinnamon
- 1 teaspoon ground nutmeg
- 1 teaspoon vanilla extract
- 3/4 cup coconut oil, melted
- Topping:
- 1/2 cup chopped vegan dark chocolate
- 1/4 cup coconut milk

Direction

- In a bowl, cover cashews with water to soak, allow 3 hours to overnight; drain.
- In the bowl of a food processor, mix pecans, almonds, 2 teaspoons coconut oil, dates, salt and cocoa powder together for around 1 to 3 minutes till ground finely and start to form a paste. In a springform pan of 9-inch in size, press mixture to the bottom. Let crust refrigerate till ready to use.
- In the bowl of a food processor, process cashews until ground finely. Put in cinnamon, banana, vanilla extract and nutmeg; blend till combined. In a thin stream through the feed tube, add 3/4 cup coconut oil while processor is running until smooth, thin filling forms. Pour filling into crust and place in the refrigerator for at least 4 hours till set.
- In a heatproof bowl, place chopped chocolate. In a saucepan, heat coconut milk till near boiling; pour over chocolate. Whisk until smooth glaze forms. Pour over cake and allow to refrigerate for at least 30 minutes longer till set.

Nutrition Information

- Calories: 584 calories;
- Cholesterol: < 1
- Protein: 10.1
- Total Fat: 47.1
- Sodium: 270
- Total Carbohydrate: 39.2

362. Banana Oatmeal Cookie

Serving: 24 | Prep: | Cook: | Ready in:

Ingredients

- 1 1/2 cups sifted all-purpose flour
- 1/2 teaspoon baking soda
- 1 teaspoon salt
- 1/4 teaspoon ground nutmeg
- 3/4 teaspoon ground cinnamon
- 3/4 cup shortening
- 1 cup white sugar
- 1 egg
- 1 cup mashed bananas
- 1 3/4 cups quick cooking oats
- 1/2 cup chopped nuts

Direction

- Preheat the oven to 400°F (200°C).
- Sieve the baking soda, nutmeg, flour, cinnamon and salt together.
- Cream the sugar and shortening together and whisk it until it has a light and fluffy texture. Put in the oatmeal, egg, nuts and banana. Mix the mixture thoroughly.
- Put the dry mixture into the oatmeal mixture and stir the two mixtures thoroughly; put teaspoonfuls of the mixture onto an ungreased cookie sheet.
- Put it in preheated oven and let it bake for 15 minutes until the edges are slightly browned. Let the baked cookies cool down on a wire rack. Keep it in a covered container.

Nutrition Information

- Calories: 170 calories;
- Cholesterol: 8
- Protein: 2.4
- Total Fat: 8.8
- Sodium: 127
- Total Carbohydrate: 21.2

363. Banana Tortilla Snacks

Serving: 1 | Prep: 5mins | Cook: |Ready in:

Ingredients

- 1 (6 inch) flour tortilla
- 2 tablespoons peanut butter
- 1 tablespoon honey
- 1 banana
- 2 tablespoons raisins

Direction

- Place tortilla flat on a surface. Put honey and peanut butter on tortilla. Arrange banana in the center and spread raisins all over. Wrap up and serve.

Nutrition Information

- Calories: 520 calories;
- Cholesterol: 0
- Protein: 12.8
- Total Fat: 19.3
- Sodium: 357
- Total Carbohydrate: 82.9

364. Bandito Beans

Serving: 24 | Prep: 15mins | Cook: 5hours |Ready in:

Ingredients

- 1 pound mild pork sausage
- 1 (15 ounce) can wax beans, drained
- 1 (15 ounce) can cut green beans, drained
- 1 (15 ounce) can lima beans, drained
- 1 (15 ounce) can black beans, drained
- 1/2 (28 ounce) can barbeque baked beans, with liquid
- 1 (15 ounce) can chili beans, with liquid
- 1 (6 ounce) can tomato paste
- 1 cup packed light brown sugar
- 1/4 cup barbeque sauce
- 1 small green bell pepper, diced
- 1 small yellow onion, diced
- 1 teaspoon fennel seed

Direction

- Cook sausage till evenly brown in skillet on medium heat; drain grease. Put sausage in slow cooker.
- Mix black beans, lima beans, green beans and wax beans into slow cooker with sausage; mix chili beans with liquid and baked beans with liquid in. Mix fennel seed, onion, green bell pepper, barbeque sauce, brown sugar and tomato paste in.
- Cover slow cooker; cook for a minimum of 5 hours on Low.

Nutrition Information

- Calories: 169 calories;
- Total Fat: 4.4
- Sodium: 591
- Total Carbohydrate: 26.5
- Cholesterol: 11
- Protein: 7.1

365. Barbecued Beef

Serving: 12 | Prep: 20mins | Cook: 10hours | Ready in:

Ingredients

- 1 1/2 cups ketchup
- 1/4 cup packed brown sugar
- 1/4 cup red wine vinegar
- 2 tablespoons prepared Dijon-style mustard
- 2 tablespoons Worcestershire sauce
- 1 teaspoon liquid smoke flavoring
- 1/2 teaspoon salt
- 1/4 teaspoon ground black pepper
- 1/4 teaspoon garlic powder
- 1 (4 pound) boneless chuck roast

Direction

- Mix together liquid smoke, Worcestershire sauce, Dijon-style mustard, red wine vinegar, brown sugar and ketchup in a big bowl; mix in garlic powder, pepper and salt.
- Put chuck roast into the slow cooker; put ketchup mixture on chuck roast. Cover; cook for 8-10 hours on Low.
- Take chuck roast out of the slow cooker; use a fork to shred. Put back into the slow cooker; mix meat to coat in sauce evenly. Keep cooking for about 1 hour.

Nutrition Information

- Calories: 276 calories;
- Total Carbohydrate: 13.5
- Cholesterol: 65
- Protein: 18.7
- Total Fat: 16.2
- Sodium: 562

366. Barbequed Ribs

Serving: 8 | Prep: 30mins | Cook: 3hours | Ready in:

Ingredients

- 4 pounds baby back pork ribs
- 4 cloves garlic, sliced
- 1 tablespoon white sugar
- 1 tablespoon paprika
- 2 teaspoons salt
- 2 teaspoons ground black pepper
- 2 teaspoons chili powder
- 2 teaspoons ground cumin
- 1/2 cup dark brown sugar
- 1/2 cup cider vinegar
- 1/2 cup ketchup
- 1/4 cup chili sauce
- 1/4 cup Worcestershire sauce
- 1 tablespoon lemon juice
- 2 tablespoons onion, chopped
- 1/2 teaspoon dry mustard
- 1 clove crushed garlic

Direction

- Preheat an oven to 150 °C or 300 °F. In a shallow roasting pan, put the ribs on a rack. Spread 4 sliced garlic cloves on top of ribs. Place cover, and let bake for 2 1/2 hours. Allow to slightly cool.
- Combine together ground cumin, chili powder, black pepper, salt, paprika and white sugar in a small bowl. Massage the spices on cooled ribs. Place cover, and chill overnight.
- Combine together 1 clove garlic, dry mustard, onion, lemon juice, Worcestershire sauce, chili sauce, ketchup, cider vinegar and brown sugar in a small saucepan. Allow to simmer without cover over moderately-low heat for an hour.

Set aside a bit amount for basting; the rest will be a dipping sauce.
- Preheat the grill for moderate heat.
- On grill, put the ribs. Grill with cover for approximately 12 minutes, basting with reserved sauce, till well glazed and browned. Serve together with leftover dipping sauce.

Nutrition Information

- Calories: 588 calories;
- Total Carbohydrate: 18.9
- Cholesterol: 170
- Protein: 44.2
- Total Fat: 37.5
- Sodium: 1041

367. Basic Guacamole Dip

Serving: 28 | Prep: 20mins | Cook: | Ready in:

Ingredients

- 4 ripe avocados - peeled, pitted, and mashed
- 2 tomatoes, diced
- 2 tablespoons minced onion
- 1 tablespoon lemon juice

Direction

- Combine together the lemon juice, onion, tomato and avocado in a bowl then gently mix. Present right away. Place the left portions inside the refrigerator.

Nutrition Information

- Calories: 48 calories;
- Sodium: 2
- Total Carbohydrate: 2.9
- Cholesterol: 0
- Protein: 0.7
- Total Fat: 4.2

368. Basic Hummus

Serving: 12 | Prep: 15mins | Cook: 5mins | Ready in:

Ingredients

- 2 cloves garlic, peeled and crushed
- 2 tablespoons olive oil
- 1 (15 ounce) can garbanzo beans, drained, liquid reserved
- 1 tablespoon sesame seeds
- salt and pepper to taste

Direction

- On medium heat, cook and stir the garlic in olive oil for about 3 minutes in a medium pan, until it becomes soft.
- In a food processor or blender, put the garbanzo beans and around 1 teaspoon of reserved liquid, then blend until it becomes smooth. Stir in the pepper, salt, sesame seeds and garlic and blend to your preferred consistency, putting more reserved garbanzo bean liquid as desired. Put in the refrigerator to chill until ready to serve.

Nutrition Information

- Calories: 53 calories;
- Total Fat: 2.9
- Sodium: 70
- Total Carbohydrate: 5.6
- Cholesterol: 0
- Protein: 1.3

369. Basmati Rice

Serving: 4 | Prep: | Cook: 20mins | Ready in:

Ingredients

- 1 3/4 cups water

- 1 cup basmati rice
- 1/4 cup frozen green peas
- 1 teaspoon cumin seeds

Direction

- Bring water in a saucepan to a boil, then put in rice and stir. Lower heat, then cover and simmer about 20 minutes.
- Once rice is cooked, mix in cumin and peas, then cover and allow to stand about 5 minutes.

Nutrition Information

- Calories: 175 calories;
- Total Fat: 0.7
- Sodium: 15
- Total Carbohydrate: 38.3
- Cholesterol: 0
- Protein: 4.1

370. Bean And Kale Ragu

Serving: 6 | Prep: 10mins | Cook: 1hours15mins | Ready in:

Ingredients

- 2 tablespoons olive oil
- 1 onion, chopped
- 1 pound kale, stems removed and leaves coarsely chopped
- 1 (14 ounce) can diced tomatoes with green chile peppers
- 2 cloves garlic, minced
- 1 1/2 cups water
- 2 bay leaves
- 1/4 teaspoon ground cumin
- 1 teaspoon onion powder
- 2 (15 ounce) cans canned cannellini beans, drained and rinsed
- 1 tablespoon chopped fresh oregano
- 1 teaspoon chopped fresh basil
- salt and ground black pepper to taste

Direction

- In a big deep skillet, heat olive oil on medium high heat. Add kale and onions. Stir and cook for 5-7 minutes till kale wilts and lessens in volume and onion is transparent.
- Lower heat to medium. Mix onion powder, cumin, bay leaves, garlic, water, green chiles and tomatoes into kale mixture. Simmer veggie mixture for 1 hour till kale is soft. Mix cannellini beans in. Keep simmering for 10 minutes till beans heat through. Mix basil and oregano in. To taste, put pepper and salt.

Nutrition Information

- Calories: 206 calories;
- Cholesterol: 0
- Protein: 8.7
- Total Fat: 5.7
- Sodium: 592
- Total Carbohydrate: 31.9

371. Beer Battered Onion Rings

Serving: 6 | Prep: 10mins | Cook: 15mins | Ready in:

Ingredients

- 2 cups all-purpose flour
- 1 egg, beaten
- 2 teaspoons dried parsley
- 2 teaspoons garlic powder
- 2 teaspoons dried oregano
- salt and pepper to taste
- 1 cup beer
- 3 large onions, sliced into rings
- 1 cup oil for frying

Direction

- Combine pepper, salt, oregano, garlic powder, parsley, egg and flour in a shallow bowl. Put

in beer gradually until it forms a thick batter, stirring. Pour in less or more beer depending on preferred consistency of batter.
- Heat oil in a heavy frying pan over medium-high heat (adjust the amount, depending on the pan size to have a couple of inches of the oil). Dip the onions in the batter once the oil is hot and fry, flipping once to evenly brown both sides. Place on paper towels to drain.

Nutrition Information

- Calories: 248 calories;
- Sodium: 17
- Total Carbohydrate: 40.9
- Cholesterol: 31
- Protein: 6.7
- Total Fat: 5.1

372. Beetroot Hummus

Serving: 8 | Prep: 25mins | Cook: 1hours20mins | Ready in:

Ingredients

- 8 ounces chickpeas
- 1 large onion, chopped
- 1 pound beets
- 1/2 cup tahini
- 3 cloves garlic, crushed
- 1/4 cup fresh lemon juice
- 1 tablespoon ground cumin
- 1/4 cup olive oil

Direction

- Cover the chickpeas with cold water in a big bowl, then soak overnight.
- Let the chickpeas drain and put it in a heavy, big pan. Put onion and water to cover, then boil it on medium heat. Cook until the chickpeas become very soft or for 1 hour. Let it drain, then set aside 1 cup of cooking liquid; let it cool.
- In the meantime, put beets in a big pan and cover it with water. Boil it on medium heat and cook until it becomes soft. Drain it and let the beets cool prior to chopping and peeling.
- In a food processor, process the beets until pureed. Stir in cumin, lemon juice, garlic, tahini, onions and chickpeas, then blend until it becomes smooth. While the motor is running, gradually pour in the olive oil and cooking liquid that you have set aside. Keep on blending until the mixture is incorporated well. Trickle with a bit of olive oil.

Nutrition Information

- Calories: 219 calories;
- Protein: 5.3
- Total Fat: 15.4
- Sodium: 142
- Total Carbohydrate: 17.8
- Cholesterol: 0

373. Beets

Serving: 4 | Prep: 10mins | Cook: 15mins | Ready in:

Ingredients

- 1 (16 ounce) can sliced beets, drained with liquid reserved
- 2 teaspoons lemon juice
- 1/2 teaspoon salt
- 1 tablespoon brown sugar
- 1 teaspoon cornstarch
- 1 tart green apple, peeled and sliced

Direction

- Mix well together cornstarch, brown sugar, salt, lemon juice and 1/2 cup of beet liquid in a big skillet on moderate heat. Cook and stir until the mixture is clear and thickened, then stir in apple and beets. Lower heat to low and simmer gently for 15 minutes.

Nutrition Information

- Calories: 66 calories;
- Cholesterol: 0
- Protein: 1.2
- Total Fat: 0.2
- Sodium: 512
- Total Carbohydrate: 16.6

374. Best Beef Dip Ever

Serving: 10 | Prep: 10mins | Cook: 6hours | Ready in:

Ingredients

- 4 pounds beef chuck roast
- 1 tablespoon minced garlic
- 1 tablespoon dried rosemary
- 3 bay leaves
- 1 cup soy sauce
- 6 cups water

Direction

- In slow cooker, put in roast. Add rosemary and garlic to season. Put in bay leaves. Pour in water and soy sauce. Cook for 6 to 10 hours on Low setting. It is unlike most roasts; the longer it cooks the better it is.

Nutrition Information

- Calories: 290 calories;
- Cholesterol: 82
- Protein: 22.8
- Total Fat: 20.4
- Sodium: 1498
- Total Carbohydrate: 2.5

375. Best Ever Vegan Chocolate Mug Cake

Serving: 1 | Prep: 5mins | Cook: 2mins | Ready in:

Ingredients

- 1/4 cup whole wheat flour
- 1/4 cup white sugar
- 1 tablespoon unsweetened cocoa powder
- 1/4 teaspoon baking powder
- 1/8 teaspoon baking soda
- 1 pinch salt
- 1 tablespoon unsweetened applesauce
- 1 tablespoon water, or more as needed
- 2 teaspoons white vinegar
- 1 teaspoon vanilla extract
- 1 tablespoon vegan chocolate chips
- 1 tablespoon chopped walnuts (optional)

Direction

- In a mug, combine whole wheat flour, baking powder, cocoa powder, baking soda, sugar, and salt and whisk them together. Add the applesauce, vanilla extract, vinegar, and 1 tablespoon of water to the mug and stir. If needed, add more water to achieve the consistency of a cake batter. Lastly, mix in walnuts and chocolate chips.
- Pop the mug in the microwave oven for 1.5 minutes on high power. Test is mug cake is set; otherwise, microwave for another 30 seconds.

Nutrition Information

- Calories: 376 calories;
- Cholesterol: 0
- Protein: 6.3
- Total Fat: 6.1
- Sodium: 438
- Total Carbohydrate: 78.3

376. Best Guacamole

Serving: 16 | Prep: 5mins | Cook: | Ready in:

Ingredients

- 2 avocados
- 1/2 lemon, juiced
- 2 tablespoons chopped onion
- 1/2 teaspoon salt
- 2 tablespoons olive oil

Direction

- Slice the avocados into two. Get seeds out then discard, and get the flesh of avocados and put into a small bowl. Crush the avocado using a fork. Add in salt, olive oil, onion and lemon juice. Use a plastic wrap to cover the bowl, and place inside the refrigerator for 1 hour until serving time.

Nutrition Information

- Calories: 56 calories;
- Sodium: 75
- Total Carbohydrate: 2.6
- Cholesterol: 0
- Protein: 0.6
- Total Fat: 5.4

377. Best Peanut Butter Cookies Ever

Serving: 36 | Prep: 30mins | Cook: 10mins | Ready in:

Ingredients

- 2 cups peanut butter
- 2 cups white sugar
- 2 eggs
- 2 teaspoons baking soda
- 1 pinch salt
- 1 teaspoon vanilla extract

Direction

- Set the oven to 175°C or 350°F to preheat and coat cookie sheets with grease.
- In a medium bowl, stir together sugar and peanut butter until smooth, then beat in one egg at a time. Stir in vanilla, salt and baking soda, then roll the dough into balls with 1 inch size. Arrange balls on the prepped cookie sheet with 2 inches apart. Use the back of a fork to press into the top with a criss-cross.
- In the preheated oven, bake about 8-10 minutes. Let cookies cool on baking sheet about 5 minutes prior to transferring to a wire rack to cool thoroughly.

Nutrition Information

- Calories: 132 calories;
- Total Fat: 7.5
- Sodium: 140
- Total Carbohydrate: 13.9
- Cholesterol: 10
- Protein: 3.9

378. Big Guy Strawberry Pie

Serving: 8 | Prep: 30mins | Cook: 30mins | Ready in:

Ingredients

- 1 cup water
- 3/4 cup white sugar
- 1/4 teaspoon salt
- 2 tablespoons cornstarch
- 1/4 teaspoon red food coloring (optional)
- 1 cup all-purpose flour
- 1/2 cup butter
- 3 tablespoons confectioners' sugar
- 1 teaspoon vanilla extract
- 1 quart fresh strawberries, hulled

Direction

- Mix together the food coloring (if using), cornstarch, salt, white sugar and water in a saucepan, then boil. Let it cook for around 5 minutes or until it becomes thick, then put aside to cool. Set an oven to preheat to 175°C (350°F).
- Mix together the vanilla, confectioner's sugar and flour in a big bowl. Slice in butter until the mixture looks like small crumbs. Press it into a 9-inch pie pan. Use a fork to prick all over and let it bake for 8-10 minutes in the preheated oven or until it turns light brown.
- Put the berries in the shell when the crust is cool and pour the thickened mixture on top. Let it chill in the fridge.

Nutrition Information

- Calories: 277 calories;
- Total Carbohydrate: 41.5
- Cholesterol: 31
- Protein: 2.3
- Total Fat: 11.9
- Sodium: 157

379. Big Soft Ginger Cookies

Serving: 24 | Prep: 15mins | Cook: 10mins | Ready in:

Ingredients

- 2 1/4 cups all-purpose flour
- 2 teaspoons ground ginger
- 1 teaspoon baking soda
- 3/4 teaspoon ground cinnamon
- 1/2 teaspoon ground cloves
- 1/4 teaspoon salt
- 3/4 cup margarine, softened
- 1 cup white sugar
- 1 egg
- 1 tablespoon water
- 1/4 cup molasses
- 2 tablespoons white sugar

Direction

- Preheat an oven to 175°C/350°F. Sift salt, cloves, cinnamon, baking soda, ginger and flour; put aside.
- Cream 1 cup sugar and margarine till fluffy and light in a big bowl; beat in egg. Mix in molasses and water. Mix sifted ingredients slowly into the molasses mixture. Form dough to walnut-sized balls; roll in leftover 2 tbsp. sugar. Put cookies onto ungreased cookie sheet, 2-in. apart; slightly flatten.
- In the preheated oven, bake for 8-10 minutes; cool cookies for 5 minutes on a baking sheet. Transfer to a wire rack; fully cool. Keep in airtight container.

Nutrition Information

- Calories: 143 calories;
- Total Fat: 6
- Sodium: 147
- Total Carbohydrate: 21.1
- Cholesterol: 8
- Protein: 1.6

380. Biscotti

Serving: 42 | Prep: 15mins | Cook: 25mins | Ready in:

Ingredients

- 1/2 cup vegetable oil
- 1 cup white sugar
- 3 1/4 cups all-purpose flour
- 3 eggs
- 1 tablespoon baking powder
- 1 tablespoon anise extract, or 3 drops anise oil

Direction

- Set the oven to 375°F (190°C), and start preheating. Coat cookie sheets with oil or line with parchment paper.

- Beat together anise flavoring, sugar, eggs and oil in a medium bowl till well combined. Mix baking powder and flour together, stir into the egg mixture to create a heavy dough. Separate the dough into two pieces. Shape each piece into a roll equaling the length of your cookie sheet. Arrange on the prepped cookie sheet, and press down to the thickness of 1/2 inch.
- Bake in the preheated oven until golden brown, for about 25 to 30 minutes. Take away from the baking sheet and let it cool on a wire rack. Once the cookies are cool enough to handle, cut each one into slices of 1/2 inch crosswise. On the baking sheet, arrange the slices with cut side up. Bake for 6 - 10 minutes longer per side, until lightly toasted.

Nutrition Information

- Calories: 83 calories;
- Cholesterol: 13
- Protein: 1.4
- Total Fat: 3.1
- Sodium: 40
- Total Carbohydrate: 12.3

381. Black Bean Brownies

Serving: 16 | Prep: 10mins | Cook: 30mins | Ready in:

Ingredients

- 1 (15.5 ounce) can black beans, rinsed and drained
- 3 eggs
- 3 tablespoons vegetable oil
- 1/4 cup cocoa powder
- 1 pinch salt
- 1 teaspoon vanilla extract
- 3/4 cup white sugar
- 1 teaspoon instant coffee (optional)
- 1/2 cup milk chocolate chips (optional)

Direction

- Set an oven to preheat to 175°C (350°F). Grease an 8x8 square baking dish lightly.
- In a blender, mix together the instant coffee, sugar, vanilla extract, salt, cocoa powder, oil, eggs and black beans, then blend until it becomes smooth. Pour the mixture in the prepped baking dish. Sprinkle chocolate chips on top of the mixture.
- Let it bake for about half an hour in the preheated oven, until the edges begin to pull away from the pan's sides and the surface becomes dry.

Nutrition Information

- Calories: 126 calories;
- Sodium: 129
- Total Carbohydrate: 18.1
- Cholesterol: 35
- Protein: 3.3
- Total Fat: 5.3

382. Black Bean Hummus

Serving: 8 | Prep: 5mins | Cook: | Ready in:

Ingredients

- 1 clove garlic
- 1 (15 ounce) can black beans; drain and reserve liquid
- 2 tablespoons lemon juice
- 1 1/2 tablespoons tahini
- 3/4 teaspoon ground cumin
- 1/2 teaspoon salt
- 1/4 teaspoon cayenne pepper
- 1/4 teaspoon paprika
- 10 Greek olives

Direction

- In the bowl of a food processor, mince the garlic. Stir in the 1/8 teaspoon of cayenne pepper, 1/2 teaspoon of salt, 1/2 teaspoon of cumin, tahini, 2 tablespoons of lemon juice, 2 tablespoons of reserved liquid and black beans, then blend until it become smooth. Scrape down the sides as needed. Stir in additional liquid and seasoning to taste. Decorate with Greek olives and paprika.

Nutrition Information

- Calories: 81 calories;
- Total Fat: 3.1
- Sodium: 427
- Total Carbohydrate: 10.3
- Cholesterol: 0
- Protein: 3.9

383. Black Bean Salsa

Serving: 40 | Prep: 15mins | Cook: |Ready in:

Ingredients

- 3 (15 ounce) cans black beans, drained and rinsed
- 1 (11 ounce) can Mexican-style corn, drained
- 2 (10 ounce) cans diced tomatoes with green chile peppers, partially drained
- 2 tomatoes, diced
- 2 bunches green onions, chopped
- cilantro leaves, for garnish

Direction

- Mix green onion stalks, tomatoes, diced tomatoes with green chile peppers, Mexican-style corn and black beans in a big bowl. Put the desired amount of cilantro leaves on top as a garnish. Chill for at least 8 hours to overnight in the fridge; serve.

Nutrition Information

- Calories: 42 calories;
- Cholesterol: 0
- Protein: 2.5
- Total Fat: 0.2
- Sodium: 207
- Total Carbohydrate: 8.3

384. Black Beans

Serving: 12 | Prep: 15mins | Cook: 1hours | Ready in:

Ingredients

- 2 cups dry black beans, soaked overnight
- 1 quart cold water, or as needed
- 1 onion, chopped
- 1 green bell pepper, chopped
- 5 cloves garlic, chopped
- 2 bay leaves
- 1 tablespoon salt
- 1 tablespoon ground cumin
- 1 tablespoon dried oregano
- 1/2 cup white cooking wine
- 1/4 cup distilled white vinegar
- 1/4 cup olive oil

Direction

- Mix together the oregano, cumin, salt, bay leaves, garlic, green pepper, onion, water and soaked beans in a medium stockpot, then boil on medium-high heat. Lower the heat to low and let it simmer for about an hour with a cover, until the beans become tender. Stir occasionally and pour water as needed to avoid the beans from scorching or drying out.
- Stir in olive oil, vinegar and wine once the beans become tender.

Nutrition Information

- Calories: 158 calories;
- Protein: 7
- Total Fat: 5.1
- Sodium: 784
- Total Carbohydrate: 20.3

- Cholesterol: 0

385. Black Beans And Rice

Serving: 10 | Prep: 5mins | Cook: 25mins | Ready in:

Ingredients

- 1 teaspoon olive oil
- 1 onion, chopped
- 2 cloves garlic, minced
- 3/4 cup uncooked white rice
- 1 1/2 cups low sodium, low fat vegetable broth
- 1 teaspoon ground cumin
- 1/4 teaspoon cayenne pepper
- 3 1/2 cups canned black beans, drained

Direction

- Heat the oil in a stockpot on medium-high heat, then add the garlic and onion and sauté for 4 minutes. Add the rice and sauté for two minutes.
- Add the vegetable broth, then boil. Put cover and lower the heat, then cook for 20 minutes. Add the black beans and spices.

Nutrition Information

- Calories: 140 calories;
- Total Carbohydrate: 27.1
- Cholesterol: 0
- Protein: 6.3
- Total Fat: 0.9
- Sodium: 354

386. Black Beans With Bacon

Serving: 6 | Prep: 30mins | Cook: 40mins | Ready in:

Ingredients

- 1 (8 ounce) package dry black beans
- 2 1/2 quarts water
- 3 tablespoons olive oil
- 3 cloves garlic, peeled and minced
- 1 large onion, chopped
- 1 tomato, cubed
- 1 carrot, cubed
- 1/2 pound bacon strips, diced
- 1 tablespoon chopped fresh parsley
- salt and pepper to taste

Direction

- Put the beans in a pressure cooker along with enough water to cover. Soak for 12 hours or overnight.
- Pour 2 1/2 quarts of water into the beans or enough it to fill the pressure cooker to about 2/3 full. Cover the cooker and let to cook at 10 pounds pressure for 30 minutes. Take out from the heat and reserve.
- Over medium heat, heat oil in a medium saucepan and then sauté the onion and garlic until tender. Mix in the carrot and tomato. Cook for about 5 minutes and stir in bacon. Cook while stirring until the bacon browned evenly and crisp.
- Combine the bacon and vegetable mixture into the pressure cooker containing the black beans. Cover the cooker and continue to cook at 10 pounds pressure for about 10 minutes. Decorate with parsley and then season with pepper and salt to serve.

Nutrition Information

- Calories: 381 calories;
- Total Fat: 24.4
- Sodium: 339
- Total Carbohydrate: 28.2
- Cholesterol: 26
- Protein: 13.1

387. Black Eyed Peas Spicy Style

Serving: 3 | Prep: 10mins | Cook: 30mins | Ready in:

Ingredients

- 1 (15.5 ounce) can black-eyed peas with liquid
- 1/2 onion, chopped
- minced jalapeno pepper to taste
- ground black pepper to taste

Direction

- Mix together the black pepper (to taste), jalapeno peppers, onion and black-eyed peas in a medium-size pot. Heat all the ingredients until it simmers, then cook for 30 minutes. Serve.

Nutrition Information

- Calories: 119 calories;
- Protein: 7.1
- Total Fat: 0.8
- Sodium: 433
- Total Carbohydrate: 21.4
- Cholesterol: 0

388. Black Eyed Peas And Ham Hocks

Serving: 5 | Prep: 10mins | Cook: 1hours30mins | Ready in:

Ingredients

- 3 cups water
- 1 pound dry black-eyed peas
- 2 smoked ham hocks
- salt to taste
- 1/2 teaspoon black pepper
- 1 bay leaf

Direction

- Thoroughly rinse dried peas, sorting out any small pebbles or other debris.
- In a large stockpot, fill with 3 cups of water, ham hocks, bay leaf, black-eyed peas, salt, and pepper. Allow to boil. Lower to a simmer and cook while uncovered for 1 hour and a half, or until peas and ham hocks are tender. Simmer in a separate pot in water if ham hocks require further cooking, until meat is easily separated from the bone.
- Cool and remove from the bone all meat. Stir into the peas the ham, add salt and pepper to season as needed, then serve.

Nutrition Information

- Calories: 516 calories;
- Total Fat: 18
- Sodium: 59
- Total Carbohydrate: 54.7
- Cholesterol: 54
- Protein: 35

389. Blueberry Crisp II

Serving: 9 | Prep: | Cook: 40mins | Ready in:

Ingredients

- 4 cups fresh blueberries
- 1 cup all-purpose flour
- 3/4 cup white sugar
- 1/2 teaspoon ground cinnamon
- 1/2 cup mayonnaise

Direction

- Set the oven to 350°F or 175°C for preheating.
- Arrange blueberries into the 8-inches square baking dish. Mix the flour, cinnamon, and sugar in a medium bowl. Mix in the mayonnaise until the mixture looks like coarse crumbs. Sprinkle the mixture all over the top of the berries.

- Let it bake inside the preheated oven for 35-40 minutes until the top is browned lightly.

Nutrition Information

- Calories: 240 calories;
- Total Fat: 10.1
- Sodium: 70
- Total Carbohydrate: 37.1
- Cholesterol: 5
- Protein: 2

390. Blueberry Smoothie Bowl

Serving: 1 | Prep: 10mins | Cook: | Ready in:

Ingredients

- Smoothie:
- 1 cup frozen blueberries
- 1/2 banana
- 2 tablespoons water
- 1 tablespoon cashew butter
- 1 teaspoon vanilla extract
- Toppings:
- 1/2 banana, sliced
- 1 tablespoon sliced almonds
- 1 tablespoon unsweetened shredded coconut

Direction

- In a blender, combine blueberries, cashew butter, 1/2 banana, water, and vanilla extract together. Puree until smooth. Transfer to a bowl.
- Add almonds, sliced banana, and coconut for toppings.

Nutrition Information

- Calories: 368 calories;
- Total Carbohydrate: 55.4
- Cholesterol: 0
- Protein: 6.8

- Total Fat: 15.6
- Sodium: 8

391. Boiled Raisin Cake I

Serving: 12 | Prep: 30mins | Cook: 1hours | Ready in:

Ingredients

- 2 cups raisins
- 2 cups water
- 1/2 cup vegetable oil
- 1 cup cold water
- 2 cups white sugar
- 4 cups all-purpose flour
- 1 teaspoon ground cinnamon
- 1 teaspoon ground cloves
- 1 teaspoon ground nutmeg
- 1 teaspoon baking soda
- 1/2 teaspoon salt

Direction

- Boil the raisins for 15 minutes in two cups of water. Take it out of the heat.
- Add cold water and vegetable oil into the raisins.
- In a big bowl, mix the salt, baking soda, spices, flour and sugar.
- Add the raisin mixture and mix until just combined.
- Pour it into a greased and floured 9x13-inch baking pan and let it bake in the preheated 175°C (350°F) oven for 1 hour. If a toothpick exits clean, it is done.

Nutrition Information

- Calories: 436 calories;
- Total Fat: 9.8
- Sodium: 206
- Total Carbohydrate: 84.6
- Cholesterol: 0
- Protein: 5.1

392. Boneless Chicken Breast With Tomatoes, Coconut Milk, And Chickpeas In The Slow Cooker

Serving: 4 | Prep: 15mins | Cook: 4hours5mins | Ready in:

Ingredients

- 1 (14 ounce) can tomato sauce
- 5 fluid ounces coconut milk
- 5 fluid ounces chicken broth
- 2 tablespoons curry powder
- 1 teaspoon salt, or more to taste
- 1 pinch cayenne pepper
- 1 pound skinless, boneless chicken breasts, cubed
- 1 (15 ounce) can chickpeas, drained and rinsed
- 2 potatoes, peeled and cut into small cubes
- 2 carrots, chopped
- 1 onion, thinly sliced
- 3/4 cup frozen peas
- 2 tablespoons lemon juice
- 1 bunch cilantro, chopped
- ground black pepper

Direction

- In a slow cooker, combine cayenne pepper, salt, curry powder, chicken broth, coconut milk and tomato sauce. Put in onion, carrots, potatoes, chickpeas and chicken. Stir well with liquid in slow cooker.
- Cook for 8 hours on Low or 4 hours on High, until the chicken is cooked through. Put in lemon juice and peas. Add pepper and salt to season. Cook for 5 more minutes. Distribute amongst plates. Top with cilantro.

Nutrition Information

- Calories: 454 calories;
- Sodium: 1550
- Total Carbohydrate: 52.4
- Cholesterol: 58
- Protein: 30.3
- Total Fat: 15.2

393. Boniet

Serving: 8 | Prep: 15mins | Cook: | Ready in:

Ingredients

- 2 bunches fresh parsley, finely chopped
- 1 (2 ounce) can anchovy fillets, chopped
- 3 cloves garlic, minced
- 1 1/2 tablespoons tomato paste
- 4 tablespoons distilled white vinegar
- 1/2 cup extra virgin olive oil

Direction

- Toss together in a medium bowl the garlic, anchovies, and parsley. Mix in the olive oil, vinegar and tomato paste. Present at a room temperature.

Nutrition Information

- Calories: 148 calories;
- Total Fat: 14.7
- Sodium: 239
- Total Carbohydrate: 1.9
- Cholesterol: 5
- Protein: 2.3

394. Boston Baked Beans

Serving: 6 | Prep: 30mins | Cook: 4hours | Ready in:

Ingredients

- 2 cups navy beans

- 1/2 pound bacon
- 1 onion, finely diced
- 3 tablespoons molasses
- 2 teaspoons salt
- 1/4 teaspoon ground black pepper
- 1/4 teaspoon dry mustard
- 1/2 cup ketchup
- 1 tablespoon Worcestershire sauce
- 1/4 cup brown sugar

Direction

- Start by soaking the beans in cold water overnight. Let the beans simmer in the same water for about 1 to 2 hours until tender. Drain off the water and save the liquid.
- Preheat the oven to 165 degrees C (325 degrees F).
- Spread beans on a two quart bean pot or casserole dish by putting some beans in the bottom of the dish and layering them with onion and bacon.
- Mix together Worcestershire sauce, molasses, brown sugar, salt, dry mustard, pepper and ketchup in a saucepan. Heat the mixture to boil and then spread on top of the beans. Add enough reserved bean water just to cover beans. Use aluminum foil or a lid to cover the dish.
- Bake in the preheated oven for about 3 to 4 hours until the beans become tender. Take out the lid when about halfway through the cooking process and pour in extra liquid if need be to stop beans from becoming too dry.

Nutrition Information

- Calories: 382 calories;
- Sodium: 1320
- Total Carbohydrate: 63.1
- Cholesterol: 14
- Protein: 20.7
- Total Fat: 6.3

395. Braciola II

Serving: 6 | Prep: 30mins | Cook: 2hours | Ready in:

Ingredients

- 2 pounds top sirloin
- 2 medium heads garlic, minced
- 1 cup chopped fresh parsley
- 1 tablespoon ground black pepper
- 1 teaspoon salt
- 1/4 cup olive oil
- 1 cup red wine
- 1 (28 ounce) can whole peeled tomatoes, chopped
- 1 (6 ounce) can tomato paste
- 3/4 cup water
- 1 (28 ounce) can crushed tomatoes
- 32 ounces tomato sauce
- 1 tablespoon anise seed
- 1 tablespoon dried oregano
- 2 tablespoons white sugar
- 3 tablespoons dried basil

Direction

- Cut the sirloin into 6 3/16-inch thick oblong pieces. Arrange on a waxed paper and sprinkle each with parsley, garlic, salt and pepper. Starting with the narrow end, roll up each piece and secure tightly with a kitchen twine.
- In a large Dutch oven, heat oil over medium high heat. Put rolls in the pot and brown for 1-2 minutes per side. Pour in 1/2 cup of red wine then reduce heat to low. Simmer for 10 minutes and put half of the chopped, peeled tomatoes. Cover and simmer for 15 minutes.
- Mix water and tomato paste together. Mix together with remaining peeled tomatoes, tomato sauce and crushed tomatoes. Add this in the pot in small increments, allowing to cook slightly after each addition, for 30 minutes in total. Sprinkle oregano, anise seed and sugar, then simmer for another 1 hour.

- Pour remaining wine and basil 30 minutes prior to serving. Let it simmer until ready to serve.

Nutrition Information

- Calories: 488 calories;
- Sodium: 1820
- Total Carbohydrate: 43.2
- Cholesterol: 65
- Protein: 34.8
- Total Fat: 19.1

396. Brazilian White Rice

Serving: 8 | Prep: 15mins | Cook: 30mins | Ready in:

Ingredients

- 2 cups long-grain white rice
- 2 tablespoons minced onion
- 2 cloves garlic, minced
- 2 tablespoons vegetable oil
- 1 teaspoon salt
- 4 cups hot water

Direction

- Rinse thoroughly the rice with cold water in a colander; set aside.
- In a saucepan, heat the oil over medium heat. Add the onion, and cook for one minute. Stir the garlic into the pan and cook until the golden brown. Pour in salt and the rice, cook and stir until the rice starts to brown. Add hot water over the rice mixture; stir. Lower the heat, take a cover to the saucepan, and let the mixture simmer for 20 to 25 minutes, until the water has been absorbed.

Nutrition Information

- Calories: 201 calories;
- Total Fat: 3.7
- Sodium: 297
- Total Carbohydrate: 37.5
- Cholesterol: 0
- Protein: 3.4

397. Breakfast Brownies

Serving: 12 | Prep: 15mins | Cook: 20mins | Ready in:

Ingredients

- 1 1/2 cups quick-cooking oats
- 3/4 cup brown sugar
- 3/4 cup flax seed meal
- 1/2 cup gluten-free all purpose baking flour
- 1 teaspoon baking powder
- 1/2 teaspoon ground cinnamon
- 1/4 teaspoon salt
- 1 banana, mashed
- 1/4 cup rice milk
- 1 egg
- 1 teaspoon vanilla extract

Direction

- Preheat the oven to 175°C or 350°Fahrenheit. Grease an 8-inch by 10-inch baking pan lightly.
- In a bowl, combine salt, oats, cinnamon, brown sugar, baking powder, flax seed meal, and flour. In another bowl, combine vanilla extract, banana, egg, and rice milk; mix with the flour mixture until well combined. Transfer batter in the greased baking pan.
- Bake brownies for 20 mins in the 350°Fahrenheit oven until an inserted skewer comes out without residue. Use a towel to cover the pan so the moisture stays in. Let the brownies cool for a minimum of five minutes; serve.

Nutrition Information

- Calories: 129 calories;

- Total Fat: 4.1
- Sodium: 102
- Total Carbohydrate: 20.9
- Cholesterol: 16
- Protein: 3.3

398. Breakfast Polenta Porridge

Serving: 2 | Prep: 5mins | Cook: 20mins | Ready in:

Ingredients

- 2 cups water
- 2 cups almond milk
- 3/4 cup dry polenta
- 1/4 cup almond meal
- 1 tablespoon brown sugar
- 1 teaspoon vanilla extract
- 1 cup mixed berries, sliced
- 2 pinches ground cinnamon

Direction

- Boil almond milk and water in a medium saucepan. Add almond meal and polenta in a slow stream, constantly whisking to avoid lumps. Bring down heat to low and frequently stir the porridge for 15 minutes until thick. Stir in vanilla extract and brown sugar.
- Ladle the porridge into bowls and top with a dash of cinnamon and berries.

Nutrition Information

- Calories: 465 calories;
- Sodium: 725
- Total Carbohydrate: 71.6
- Cholesterol: 5
- Protein: 12.7
- Total Fat: 14.9

399. Breakfast Sausage

Serving: 6 | Prep: 10mins | Cook: 15mins | Ready in:

Ingredients

- 2 teaspoons dried sage
- 2 teaspoons salt
- 1 teaspoon ground black pepper
- 1/4 teaspoon dried marjoram
- 1 tablespoon brown sugar
- 1/8 teaspoon crushed red pepper flakes
- 1 pinch ground cloves
- 2 pounds ground pork

Direction

- Mix the brown sugar, cloves, sage, marjoram, crushed red pepper, ground black pepper and salt together in a small bowl. Mix everything together thoroughly.
- In a big bowl, put in the pork and the prepared mixed spices. Use your hands to mix everything thoroughly and shape the mixture into patties.
- In a big skillet, put in the patties and let it cook over medium-high heat setting for 5 minutes on every side until the inside temperature of the pork is at 160°F (73°C).

Nutrition Information

- Calories: 409 calories;
- Total Fat: 32.2
- Sodium: 861
- Total Carbohydrate: 2.7
- Cholesterol: 109
- Protein: 25.6

400. Broccoli And Rice

Serving: 4 | Prep: 15mins | Cook: 25mins | Ready in:

Ingredients

- 1 head broccoli, stalk and florets chopped separately
- 2 cups water
- 2 tablespoons olive oil
- 1 tablespoon minced garlic
- 1/2 cup uncooked white rice
- salt to taste
- 1 squeeze lemon juice

Direction

- In a blender, mix together 1 cup water and broccoli stack then blend until pureed. Put in the remaining cup of water for a total of 2 cups of green water to cook the rice in.
- In a saucepan, heat olive oil on moderate heat, then cook garlic in the hot oil for 1-2 minutes, until tangy. Put in rice and cook and stir about 3 minutes. Put in salt, green water and chopped broccoli florets then bring the mixture to a boil. Lower heat to low and simmer for 15-20 minutes, until rice is softened.
- Use a fork to fluff cooked rice and squeeze on top with lemon juice before serving.

Nutrition Information

- Calories: 173 calories;
- Total Fat: 7.2
- Sodium: 69
- Total Carbohydrate: 24.3
- Cholesterol: 0
- Protein: 3.9

401. Broccoli And Rice Stir Fry

Serving: 8 | Prep: 5mins | Cook: 25mins | Ready in:

Ingredients

- 1 1/2 cups uncooked long-grain rice
- 1 tablespoon vegetable oil
- 1 (16 ounce) package frozen broccoli florets, thawed
- 3 green onions, diced
- 2 eggs, beaten
- 2 tablespoons soy sauce
- 1/2 teaspoon salt
- 1/4 teaspoon ground black pepper

Direction

- Boil 3 cups of water in a saucepan. Mix in rice. Reduce the heat and put cover on the saucepan then allow it to simmer for 20 minutes.
- In a big skillet, heat the oil over medium heat. Sauté the broccoli until it becomes crisp tender. Put in the scallions then remove from the skillet. Scramble the eggs then put the broccoli mixture back into the pan. Mix in pepper, salt, soy sauce and cooked rice.

Nutrition Information

- Calories: 187 calories;
- Total Fat: 3.4
- Sodium: 404
- Total Carbohydrate: 32.9
- Cholesterol: 46
- Protein: 6.3

402. Brooklyn Girl's Penne Arrabiata

Serving: 6 | Prep: 20mins | Cook: 25mins | Ready in:

Ingredients

- 1/2 cup olive oil, divided
- 6 cloves garlic, sliced
- 1 teaspoon red pepper flakes
- 1 (28 ounce) can diced tomatoes with garlic and olive oil
- 1/2 cup tomato sauce
- 1 bunch fresh basil, chopped

- 1 (12 ounce) package dried penne pasta
- 2 eggs
- 2 cups bread crumbs
- 1 teaspoon garlic powder
- 1 teaspoon salt
- 1 teaspoon pepper
- 1 pound thin chicken breast cutlets

Direction

- Set heat to medium, then, heat 1/4 cup of olive oil in a large skillet. Sauté the garlic in the skillet for a few minutes. Add the red pepper flakes and sauté for one more minute. Mix in the tomato sauce along with the diced tomatoes, then add in basil. Occasionally stir while letting it simmer for 20 minutes.
- While that is simmering, boil a large pot of lightly salted water. Pour in the penne, and let it cook until it softens. Drain after 8 minutes.
- Use a fork to whisk some eggs in a small bowl. Use a separate bowl to place the bread crumbs in. Mix the garlic powder, salt, and pepper with the bread crumbs. Take each cutlet and dip into the egg, then, coat completely with the bread crumbs.
- At medium heat, use a large skillet to heat the leftover olive oil. Fry each side of the chicken for 5 minutes until the coating turns into a deep brown color.
- Take the chicken and slice them into pieces. Add each chicken slice into the sauce and leave it for 10 minutes to simmer. Mix the cooked penne in, then let it simmer for another few minutes to let it absorb the flavor. Serve warm.

Nutrition Information

- Calories: 588 calories;
- Total Fat: 16.5
- Sodium: 1034
- Total Carbohydrate: 75.3
- Cholesterol: 108
- Protein: 33.6

403. Brown Mixers

Serving: 4 | Prep: 5mins | Cook: 7mins | Ready in:

Ingredients

- 2 eggs
- 1/2 cup white sugar
- 1/2 cup all-purpose flour
- 1/2 cup hazelnuts, finely chopped

Direction

- Set an oven to 190°C (375°F) to preheat, then butter a baking tray.
- Beat the sugar and eggs in a medium bowl until it becomes smooth and thick. Fold in the hazelnuts and flour. Shape the dough into balls using 2 spoons and put them onto the prepped baking tray, 2 inches apart.
- Bake in the preheated oven for 6-7 minutes or until it becomes toasted.

Nutrition Information

- Calories: 280 calories;
- Total Fat: 11.4
- Sodium: 35
- Total Carbohydrate: 39.5
- Cholesterol: 93
- Protein: 6.9

404. Brownies Allergy Free!

Serving: 20 | Prep: | Cook: |Ready in:

Ingredients

- 2 ripe bananas, mashed
- 1 1/2 cups vegetable oil
- 1 cup potato flour
- 1 cup brown rice flour
- 2 cups white sugar

- 1/2 cup unsweetened cocoa powder
- 1/2 teaspoon baking soda
- 5/8 teaspoon cream of tartar
- 1 1/2 teaspoons sea salt

Direction

- Set oven to 165°C (325°F) and start preheating. Prepare a 13x9-in. baking dish by greasing.
- Combine salt, cream of tartar, baking soda, cocoa powder, sugar, rice flour and potato flour in a big bowl. In another bowl, beat oil and bananas together. Mix into dry mixture until well combined. Transfer to the bottom of the prepared pan and spread out.
- Bake at 165°C (325°F) until the top is dry, about 20-25 minutes. Cool fully before slicing into square pieces.

Nutrition Information

- Calories: 295 calories;
- Total Fat: 16.9
- Sodium: 169
- Total Carbohydrate: 36.6
- Cholesterol: 0
- Protein: 1.7

405. Brussels Sprouts In Mustard Sauce

Serving: 6 | Prep: 10mins | Cook: 20mins | Ready in:

Ingredients

- 2 tablespoons cornstarch
- 1/4 cup water
- 1 (14.5 ounce) can chicken broth
- 1 pound Brussels sprouts
- 2 teaspoons prepared Dijon-style mustard
- 2 teaspoons lemon juice

Direction

- In a 1/4 cup of water, stir in corn-starch until dissolved. Put it to one side.
- At moderate heat, pour chicken broth into a midsized saucepan then lead it to boiling point. Insert the Brussels sprouts, cooking until they tenderize. After straining, keep the chicken broth. Move the Brussels sprouts into a warm serving dish. Move the chicken broth back to stove, stirring lemon juice and mustard in before returning the mixture back to boiling point. Insert the corn-starch mixture, cooking and stirring until it thickens. Before serving, empty the liquid mixture over Brussels sprouts.

Nutrition Information

- Calories: 41 calories;
- Cholesterol: 0
- Protein: 1.9
- Total Fat: 0.4
- Sodium: 58
- Total Carbohydrate: 9.4

406. Buffalo Chicken Fingers

Serving: 8 | Prep: 20mins | Cook: 20mins | Ready in:

Ingredients

- 4 skinless, boneless chicken breast halves - cut into finger-sized pieces
- 1/4 cup all-purpose flour
- 1 teaspoon garlic powder
- 1 teaspoon cayenne pepper
- 1/2 teaspoon salt
- 3/4 cup bread crumbs
- 2 egg whites, beaten
- 1 tablespoon water

Direction

- Set the oven to 205°C or 400°F to preheat. Use cooking spray to grease a baking sheet.

- Combine together 1/4 tsp. of salt, 1/2 tsp. of cayenne pepper, 1/2 tsp. of garlic powder and flour in a bag. Combine together remaining salt, cayenne pepper, garlic powder and bread crumbs on a plate.
- Put chicken pieces into bag and shake together with seasoned flour. Beat 1 tbsp. of water and egg whites together then transfer into a shallow bowl or dish. Dip seasoned chicken into egg mixture then roll them into seasoned bread crumb mixture to coat well. Arrange breaded chicken on prepped baking sheet.
- In the preheated oven, bake for 8 minutes. Turn chicken pieces over with tongs and bake for 8 minutes longer, until juices run clear.

Nutrition Information

- Calories: 125 calories;
- Sodium: 263
- Total Carbohydrate: 10.7
- Cholesterol: 34
- Protein: 15
- Total Fat: 2

407. Burgundy Mushrooms

Serving: 4 | Prep: 10mins | Cook: 30mins | Ready in:

Ingredients

- 1/2 cup diced onion
- 1 (10.5 ounce) can beef broth
- 2 (8 ounce) cans whole mushrooms, drained, liquid reserved from one can
- 1/3 cup Burgundy wine

Direction

- Simmer the onion in beef broth in a small saucepan for 15 minutes. Put in wine, reserved liquid and mushrooms, then simmer for another 15 minutes, or until the liquid is reduced by half. Serve warm.

Nutrition Information

- Calories: 59 calories;
- Protein: 3.2
- Total Fat: 0.5
- Sodium: 721
- Total Carbohydrate: 8.2
- Cholesterol: 0

408. Busy Day Chicken

Serving: 8 | Prep: 5mins | Cook: 9hours | Ready in:

Ingredients

- 1 (4 pound) whole chicken
- 1 1/2 cups prepared barbecue sauce

Direction

- Put chicken into the slow cooker, legs up. Put sauce inside and over the chicken; cover.
- Cook on low setting for 8-10 hours; don't check it. Steam will escape and takes quite a while to reheat.

Nutrition Information

- Calories: 375 calories;
- Sodium: 629
- Total Carbohydrate: 17
- Cholesterol: 112
- Protein: 34.8
- Total Fat: 17.5

409. Butternut Squash Paleo 'Porridge'

Serving: 3 | Prep: 10mins | Cook: 50mins | Ready in:

Ingredients

- 1 butternut squash, halved and seeded
- water as needed
- 1/4 cup coconut milk, or to taste
- 1/2 teaspoon ground cinnamon
- 1 tablespoon chopped walnuts

Direction

- Set the oven to 175°C or 350°F.
- Put in a baking dish with butternut squash halves, cut-side up, then fill 1/4 inch of water into the dish.
- In the preheated oven, bake for 50-60 minutes, until tender, then allow squash to cool.
- Spoon the squash flesh into a bowl and use a potato smash or fork to mash until smooth. Stir cinnamon and coconut milk into the squash, then place walnuts on top.

Nutrition Information

- Calories: 242 calories;
- Sodium: 22
- Total Carbohydrate: 49.9
- Cholesterol: 0
- Protein: 4.9
- Total Fat: 6

410. Cabbage Roll Casserole

Serving: 12 | Prep: 10mins | Cook: 1hours30mins | Ready in:

Ingredients

- 2 pounds ground beef
- 1 cup chopped onion
- 1 (29 ounce) can tomato sauce
- 3 1/2 pounds chopped cabbage
- 1 cup uncooked white rice
- 1 teaspoon salt
- 2 (14 ounce) cans beef broth

Direction

- Preheat an oven to 175°C/350°F.
- Brown beef in oil in a big skillet on medium high heat till redness goes away. Drain fat.
- Mix salt, rice, cabbage, tomato sauce and onion in a big mixing bowl. Add meat; mix everything together. Put mixture into a 9x13-in. baking dish. Put broth on meat mixture. In preheated oven, bake for 1 hour, covered. Mix. Replace cover. Bake for 30 more minutes.

Nutrition Information

- Calories: 352 calories;
- Sodium: 840
- Total Carbohydrate: 25.5
- Cholesterol: 64
- Protein: 17.1
- Total Fat: 20.6

411. Cajun Spicy Potato Wedges

Serving: 4 | Prep: 20mins | Cook: 40mins | Ready in:

Ingredients

- 2 tablespoons olive oil
- 2 teaspoons ground cumin
- 1 teaspoon ground coriander
- 1 teaspoon hot paprika
- 1 teaspoon ground turmeric
- 1/2 teaspoon dried oregano
- 1/2 teaspoon ground black pepper
- 1/4 teaspoon chili powder
- 2 egg whites, slightly beaten
- 2 pounds potatoes, cut into wedges

Direction

- Set an oven to preheat to 190°C (375°F). Prepare a big baking pan and spritz it with cooking spray.
- In a big bowl, whisk together the chili powder, pepper, oregano, turmeric, paprika, coriander,

cumin and olive oil. In another big bowl, put the egg whites.
- Toast the potato wedges first in the egg whites and then followed by the olive oil mixture. On the prepped baking pan, lay out the seasoned wedges in a single layer.
- Let it bake in the preheated oven for about 40 minutes, flipping from time to time, until it becomes crispy.

Nutrition Information

- Calories: 248 calories;
- Total Fat: 7.5
- Sodium: 50
- Total Carbohydrate: 40.3
- Cholesterol: 0
- Protein: 6.8

412. Cantonese Dinner

Serving: 5 | Prep: 15mins | Cook: 8hours | Ready in:

Ingredients

- 2 pounds pork steak, cut into strips
- 2 tablespoons vegetable oil
- 1 onion, thinly sliced
- 1 (4.5 ounce) can mushrooms, drained
- 1 (8 ounce) can tomato sauce
- 3 tablespoons brown sugar
- 1 1/2 teaspoons distilled white vinegar
- 1 1/2 teaspoons salt
- 2 tablespoons Worcestershire sauce

Direction

- Heat oil over medium-high heat in a large heavy skillet. Brown the pork in oil. Drain off the excess grease.
- Put Worcestershire sauce, salt, vinegar, brown sugar, tomato sauce, mushrooms, onion, and pork in a slow cooker. Cook on low for 6 to 8 hours or on high for 4 hours.

Nutrition Information

- Calories: 272 calories;
- Total Fat: 13.2
- Sodium: 1156
- Total Carbohydrate: 15.1
- Cholesterol: 70
- Protein: 23.3

413. Caribbean Beef Loin Steaks

Serving: 6 | Prep: 10mins | Cook: 6mins | Ready in:

Ingredients

- 1 fluid ounce coconut-flavored rum
- 1/4 teaspoon salt
- 1/4 teaspoon ground black pepper
- 1/8 teaspoon ground cinnamon
- 1/2 teaspoon garlic powder
- 1/2 teaspoon dried oregano
- 1/4 teaspoon dried sage
- 1/2 teaspoon white vinegar
- 1 tablespoon fresh lemon juice
- 4 slices onion
- 6 (8 ounce) beef top sirloin steaks
- 1 tablespoon olive oil

Direction

- In a bowl, mix together rum, cinnamon, powder, salt, pepper, sage, oregano, lemon juice, and vinegar; transfer mixture into a gallon-sized, resealable plastic bag. Put onion and steaks inside the marinade. Seal the bag and squeeze to release as much air as possible. Marinate for 2 and a half hours inside the refrigerator.
- Over medium heat, warm olive oil in a large skillet. Place steaks in the skillet with cover and cook for about 3 minutes each side (for

medium rare) until desired doneness is achieved.

Nutrition Information

- Calories: 381 calories;
- Cholesterol: 122
- Protein: 37.3
- Total Fat: 23.1
- Sodium: 184
- Total Carbohydrate: 2.3

414. Caribbean Holiday Shrimp

Serving: 8 | Prep: 10mins | Cook: |Ready in:

Ingredients

- 1 tablespoon vegetable oil
- 2 tablespoons minced fresh ginger root
- 2 limes, juiced
- 2 cloves garlic, minced
- 1 tablespoon soy sauce
- 1/2 teaspoon white sugar
- 1/2 teaspoon crushed red pepper flakes
- 2 pounds large cooked shrimp, peeled, tails on
- 1/2 cup chopped fresh cilantro

Direction

- Mix red pepper, sugar, soy sauce, garlic, lime juice, ginger, and oil together in a big bowl, toss thoroughly. Mix in cilantro and shrimp. Put a cover on and chill for 1-4 hours before eating. While refrigerating, toss sometimes.

Nutrition Information

- Calories: 138 calories;
- Cholesterol: 221
- Protein: 24.1
- Total Fat: 3.1
- Sodium: 369
- Total Carbohydrate: 2.9

415. Carrot Fruit Ring

Serving: 14 | Prep: | Cook: |Ready in:

Ingredients

- 1 cup vegetable oil
- 1 cup white sugar
- 1 cup packed brown sugar
- 4 eggs
- 3 cups finely grated carrots
- 2 1/2 cups all-purpose flour
- 2 teaspoons baking powder
- 1 teaspoon baking soda
- 2 teaspoons ground cinnamon
- 1 teaspoon salt
- 1 cup raisins
- 1 cup candied cherries, halved
- 1 cup candied mixed fruit
- 1 cup dates, pitted and chopped
- 1 cup coarsely chopped walnuts
- 1/2 cup all-purpose flour

Direction

- Preheat the oven to 165 degrees C (325 degrees F). Grease and flour the 10 in. tube pan.
- Whip the brown sugars and white sugar with vegetable oil. Whip in eggs one at a time. Mix in grated carrots. Put in salt, ground cinnamon, baking powder, baking soda, 2/12 cups of flour. Mix just till becoming moistened.
- Toss rest half cup of flour along with chopped walnuts, chopped dates, candied mixed fruit, candied cherries and raisins. Coat by mixing. Put in the nut mixture and fruit into the batter and mix till becoming combined. Add the batter to the prepped pan.
- Bake at 165 degrees C (325 degrees F) for 1.5 hours.

Nutrition Information

- Calories: 582 calories;
- Total Fat: 23
- Sodium: 426
- Total Carbohydrate: 91.4
- Cholesterol: 53
- Protein: 6.7

416. Carrot Patties

Serving: 4 | Prep: | Cook: | Ready in:

Ingredients

- 1 pound carrots, grated
- 1 clove garlic, minced
- 4 eggs
- 1/4 cup all-purpose flour
- 1/4 cup bread crumbs or matzo meal
- 1/2 teaspoon salt
- 1 pinch ground black pepper
- 2 tablespoons vegetable oil

Direction

- Mix well together black pepper, salt, bread crumbs, flour, eggs, garlic and grated carrots in a moderate-sized mixing bowl.
- In a frying pan, heat oil on moderately high heat. Make the mixture into patties and fry until all sides turn golden brown.

Nutrition Information

- Calories: 236 calories;
- Protein: 9.1
- Total Fat: 12.6
- Sodium: 489
- Total Carbohydrate: 22.5
- Cholesterol: 186

417. Carrot Rice Nut Burger

Serving: 20 | Prep: 1hours | Cook: 1hours30mins | Ready in:

Ingredients

- 3 cups uncooked brown rice
- 6 cups water
- 1 cup toasted cashews
- 1 pound toasted unsalted sunflower seeds
- 1 sweet onion, chopped
- 6 carrots, chopped
- 1 tablespoon extra virgin olive oil
- salt to taste

Direction

- Boil rice and water in a large pot. Decrease the heat to low, cover the pot and let it simmer for 45 minutes.
- Preheat a grill over high heat.
- Grind the sunflower seeds and toasted cashews into a fine meal using a food processor. Pour into a large bowl. In the food processor, pulse carrots and onion until finely shredded and then combine with ground nuts. Add olive oil and the cooked rice in the food processor and pulse until smooth. Combine into the bowl. Add salt to taste. Shape the mixture into patties.
- Coat the grill grate with oil. Grill patties for 6 to 8 minutes per side until browned nicely.

Nutrition Information

- Calories: 270 calories;
- Cholesterol: 0
- Protein: 7.7
- Total Fat: 16.2
- Sodium: 53
- Total Carbohydrate: 26.3

418. Carrot Souffle

Serving: 8 | Prep: 15mins | Cook: 1hours15mins | Ready in:

Ingredients

- 1 3/4 pounds carrots, peeled and chopped
- 1 cup white sugar
- 1 1/2 teaspoons baking powder
- 1 1/2 teaspoons vanilla extract
- 2 tablespoons all-purpose flour
- 3 eggs, beaten
- 1/2 cup margarine, softened
- 2 teaspoons confectioners' sugar

Direction

- Preheat an oven to 175°C/350°F.
- Cook carrots in big pot of boiling water till very tender. Drain; put in big mixing bowl.
- Use electric mixer to beat vanilla extract, baking powder and sugar till smooth while carrots are warm. Stir in margarine, eggs and flour. Put in 2-qt. baking dish.
- In preheated oven, bake for 1 hour till top is golden brown. Lightly sprinkle confectioners' sugar; serve.

Nutrition Information

- Calories: 271 calories;
- Total Fat: 13.3
- Sodium: 307
- Total Carbohydrate: 35.9
- Cholesterol: 70
- Protein: 3.4

419. Carrot Souffle With Brown Sugar

Serving: 8 | Prep: 15mins | Cook: 1hours15mins | Ready in:

Ingredients

- 2 pounds carrots, peeled and chopped
- 1/2 cup margarine
- 3 eggs
- 3/4 cup brown sugar
- 1/4 cup flour
- 1 1/2 teaspoons baking powder
- 3/4 teaspoon baking soda

Direction

- Preheat an oven to 175°C/350°F.
- Boil a stockpot of salted water; cook carrots for 10-15 minutes till tender. Take off from the heat; drain well.
- Pulse margarine and carrots to puree in a food processor. Add baking soda, baking powder, flour, brown sugar and eggs; process till smooth.
- Put carrot mixture into a round 1-qt. baking dish; put the dish inside a bigger dish with 1-in. water to avoid burning casserole's bottom.
- In the preheated oven, bake for 1 hour till firm, uncovered.

Nutrition Information

- Calories: 240 calories;
- Protein: 4
- Total Fat: 13.4
- Sodium: 425
- Total Carbohydrate: 27.6
- Cholesterol: 70

420. Carrot, Tomato, And Spinach Quinoa Pilaf

Serving: 5 | Prep: 10mins | Cook: 25mins | Ready in:

Ingredients

- 2 teaspoons olive oil
- 1/2 onion, chopped

- 1 cup quinoa
- 2 cups water
- 2 tablespoons vegetarian chicken-flavored bouillon granules
- 1 teaspoon ground black pepper
- 1 teaspoon thyme
- 1 carrot, chopped
- 1 tomato, chopped
- 1 cup baby spinach

Direction

- In a saucepan, heat the olive oil over medium heat. Cook and mix the onion in the hot oil for about 5 minutes until it becomes translucent. Decrease the heat then mix in quinoa. Toast it for 2 minutes, occasionally stirring. Mix in thyme, black pepper, bouillon granules and water. Turn the heat up to high and boil. Cover the saucepan then turn the heat down to low. Let it simmer for 5 minutes.
- Mix in the carrots. Cover and simmer for about 10 minutes more until all water is absorbed. Turn the heat off then put in the spinach and tomatoes. Stir for about 2 minutes until the tomatoes have given off their moisture and the spinach is wilted.

Nutrition Information

- Calories: 165 calories;
- Cholesterol: 0
- Protein: 5.7
- Total Fat: 4.1
- Sodium: 52
- Total Carbohydrate: 27

421. Cashew Milk

Serving: 12 | Prep: 10mins | Cook: | Ready in:

Ingredients

- 3 cups raw cashews
- 10 cups water, divided
- 1/4 cup honey

Direction

- In a bowl, add cashews and cover with enough amount of water, approximately 2 cups. Chill about 12-16 hours.
- Add to a high-speed blender with soaking water as well as cashews. Put in honey and leftover 8 cups of water, then blend on high speed until smooth.

Nutrition Information

- Calories: 209 calories;
- Cholesterol: 0
- Protein: 6.2
- Total Fat: 14.9
- Sodium: 10
- Total Carbohydrate: 16.1

422. Cassie's Zucchini Brownies

Serving: 24 | Prep: 25mins | Cook: 20mins | Ready in:

Ingredients

- 2 cups all-purpose flour
- 1 teaspoon salt
- 1 1/2 teaspoons baking soda
- 1/3 cup unsweetened cocoa powder
- 1 cup white sugar
- 2 eggs
- 2 cups grated zucchini
- 1/2 cup vegetable oil
- 1 teaspoon vanilla extract
- 1/2 cup chopped walnuts

Direction

- Set the oven at 350°F (175°C) and start preheating. Coat a 10x15 jellyroll pan with grease.

- Sift sugar, cocoa, soda, salt and flour into a large mixing bowl. Mix together vanilla, oil, zucchini and eggs; blend into the dry ingredients. Mix in walnuts.
- Bake in the preheated oven for 20 minutes. Allow to cool in the pan; cut into bars.

Nutrition Information

- Calories: 137 calories;
- Total Fat: 6.9
- Sodium: 183
- Total Carbohydrate: 17.7
- Cholesterol: 16
- Protein: 2.3

423. Certified Angus Beef® Jalapeno Beef Poppers

Serving: 42 | Prep: 15mins | Cook: 40mins | Ready in:

Ingredients

- 2 pounds Certified Angus Beef® ground chuck
- 12 ounces Food Club® Shredded Sharp Cheddar cheese
- 6 jalapenos, seeded and minced
- 1 tablespoon Food Club® Salt
- 1 tablespoon Food Club® Pure Ground Black Pepper
- 1 teaspoon whole mustard seeds
- 12 Food Club® eggs
- 1 cup Food Club® Plain Bread Crumbs
- 1 cup Food Club® Plain Panko Bread Crumbs
- oil for frying

Direction

- In a big mixing bowl, mix together the mustard seeds, pepper, salt, jalapenos, cheese and ground beef. Portion into 42 popper-shaped balls using your hand, about 1 ounce each.
- Break and whisk the eggs, then put in a shallow dish. Mix breadcrumbs and place in the 2nd shallow dish.
- Prepare a pot with frying oil and heat it to 325°F. Roll the poppers in the egg mix, 6-8 at a time, then roll in the breadcrumbs; redo the process. Deep fry for 4 minutes in batches, then allow to dry on the paper towels.

Nutrition Information

- Calories: 134 calories;
- Protein: 8.2
- Total Fat: 9.7
- Sodium: 282
- Total Carbohydrate: 4.1
- Cholesterol: 77

424. Ceviche Self Portrait

Serving: 6 | Prep: 15mins | Cook: | Ready in:

Ingredients

- 1 pound shrimp, peeled and deveined
- 4 limes, juiced
- 4 roma tomatoes, seeded and diced
- 1/2 yellow onion, finely diced
- 1 cucumber, peeled, seeded, and diced
- 4 serrano peppers, seeded and minced
- salt and pepper to taste
- 12 tostada shells
- hot pepper sauce (optional)

Direction

- Dice the shrimp and put in a mixing bowl. Squeeze the lime juice on top of the shrimp until they are fully covered, approximately 4 limes. Stir in the pepper, salt, serrano peppers, cucumber, onion and tomatoes. Put cover on and chill in the fridge for an hour.
- Modify the seasoning with pepper and salt as necessary once ready to serve. Place over the

tostada shells with a splash of hot sauce if preferred, then serve.

Nutrition Information

- Calories: 190 calories;
- Cholesterol: 115
- Protein: 14.8
- Total Fat: 5.6
- Sodium: 629
- Total Carbohydrate: 22

425. Chanterelle And Caramelized Onion Bruschetta

Serving: 8 | Prep: 10mins | Cook: 40mins | Ready in:

Ingredients

- 2 pounds onion, chopped
- 1 pound chanterelle mushrooms, halved and very thinly sliced
- 4 tablespoons olive oil, divided
- 1 teaspoon white sugar
- salt to taste
- 1 French baguette, sliced into 1/2-inch rounds

Direction

- Prepare the oven by preheating to 350°F (175°C).
- Place a skillet on the stove and turn on medium heat then put in 2 tablespoons of olive oil. Stir and cook onions for 25 minutes until they start to turn golden in color and soft. Sprinkle on sugar and keep on cooking for 10 to 15 minutes, whisking as needed, until dark brown in color and soft, but not at all crispy. Lower heat if onions are crisping.
- Place another skillet on the stove and turn on medium heat then put in the 2 tablespoons left olive oil. Cook the chanterelle mushrooms for 15 to 20 minutes until golden in color and soft.
- Put baguette rounds in one layer on a baking sheet.
- Place inside the preheated oven and bake for 3 to 5 minutes until toasted.
- On top of each piece of toast, pile a small amount of onions. Place a few mushrooms slices on top and serve hot.

Nutrition Information

- Calories: 293 calories;
- Total Fat: 7.9
- Protein: 9.2
- Sodium: 405
- Total Carbohydrate: 46.3
- Cholesterol: 0

426. Chap Chee Noodles

Serving: 4 | Prep: 35mins | Cook: 20mins | Ready in:

Ingredients

- 1 tablespoon soy sauce
- 1 tablespoon sesame oil
- 2 green onions, finely chopped
- 1 clove garlic, minced
- 1 teaspoon sesame seeds
- 1 teaspoon sugar
- 1/4 teaspoon black pepper
- 1/3 pound beef top sirloin, thinly sliced
- 2 tablespoons vegetable oil
- 1/2 cup thinly sliced carrots
- 1/2 cup sliced bamboo shoots, drained
- 1/4 pound napa cabbage, sliced
- 2 cups chopped fresh spinach
- 3 ounces cellophane noodles, soaked in warm water
- 2 tablespoons soy sauce
- 1 tablespoon sugar
- 1/2 teaspoon salt
- 1/4 teaspoon black pepper

Direction

- Mix 1/4 teaspoon pepper, 1 teaspoon sugar, sesame seeds, garlic, green onion, sesame oil and 1 tablespoon soy sauce in a big bowl. Mix in sliced beef. Marinate for 15 minutes in room temperature.
- Heat a big skillet or wok on medium-high heat. Drizzle on oil. Cook beef until it browns evenly. Mix in spinach, napa cabbage, bamboo shoots, and carrots. Add 1/4 teaspoon pepper, 1/2 teaspoon salt, 1 tablespoon sugar, 2 tablespoons soy sauce, and cellophane noodles. Bring heat to medium and cook until it is heated through.

Nutrition Information

- Calories: 264 calories;
- Sodium: 1025
- Total Carbohydrate: 27.9
- Cholesterol: 23
- Protein: 10.6
- Total Fat: 12.5

427. Charley's Slow Cooker Mexican Style Meat

Serving: 12 | Prep: 30mins | Cook: 8hours | Ready in:

Ingredients

- 1 (4 pound) chuck roast
- 1 teaspoon salt
- 1 teaspoon ground black pepper
- 2 tablespoons olive oil
- 1 large onion, chopped
- 1 1/4 cups diced green chile pepper
- 1 teaspoon chili powder
- 1 teaspoon ground cayenne pepper
- 1 (5 ounce) bottle hot pepper sauce
- 1 teaspoon garlic powder

Direction

- Clip roast of any extra fat, and put in pepper and salt to season. In big skillet, heat the olive oil on moderately-high heat. In hot skillet, put beef, and quickly brown it on every side.
- Turn roast onto slow cooker and put chopped onion on top. Add garlic powder, hot pepper sauce, cayenne pepper, chili powder and chile peppers to season. Put in sufficient water to soak a third of roast.
- Place cover, and cook for 6 hours on High, monitoring to ensure there is at least a bit of liquid in cooker bottom. Lower the heat to Low, and keep cooking till meat is completely soft and separates for 2 or up to 4 hours.
- Turn roast onto bowl and pull it apart with 2 forks, set 2 cups cooking liquid aside, if wished. Serve in burritos or tacos.

Nutrition Information

- Calories: 260 calories;
- Total Fat: 19.1
- Sodium: 315
- Total Carbohydrate: 3.3
- Cholesterol: 69
- Protein: 18.4

428. Cherry Chicken Lettuce Wraps

Serving: 6 | Prep: 15mins | Cook: 10mins | Ready in:

Ingredients

- 2 tablespoons canola oil, divided
- 1 1/4 pounds skinless, boneless chicken breast halves, cut into bite-size pieces
- 1 tablespoon minced fresh ginger root
- 2 tablespoons rice vinegar
- 2 tablespoons teriyaki sauce
- 1 tablespoon honey
- 1 pound dark sweet cherries, pitted and halved
- 1 1/2 cups shredded carrots

- 1/2 cup chopped green onion
- 1/3 cup toasted and sliced almonds
- 12 lettuce leaves

Direction

- In a big skillet, heat a tablespoon of oil over medium-high heat. In hot oil, sauté the ginger and chicken for 7 to 10 minutes till chicken is cooked completely. Reserve.
- In a bowl, mix honey, remaining 1 tablespoon oil, teriyaki sauce and vinegar together. Put the almonds, green onion, carrots, cherries and chicken mixture; mix by tossing.
- Onto the middle of every lettuce leaf, scoop 1/12 of the chicken/cherry mixture; roll leaf up surrounding the filling, serve.

Nutrition Information

- Calories: 297 calories;
- Total Fat: 12.7
- Sodium: 129
- Total Carbohydrate: 22.8
- Cholesterol: 58
- Protein: 24.4

429. Chewy Peanut Butter Brownies

Serving: 16 | Prep: 15mins | Cook: 25mins | Ready in:

Ingredients

- 1/2 cup peanut butter
- 1/3 cup margarine, softened
- 2/3 cup white sugar
- 1/2 cup packed brown sugar
- 2 egg
- 1/2 teaspoon vanilla extract
- 1 cup all-purpose flour
- 1 teaspoon baking powder
- 1/4 teaspoon salt

Direction

- Preheat the oven to 175 degrees C (350 degrees F). Grease the 9x9 inch baking pan.
- In a medium-sized bowl, cream margarine and peanut butter together. Slowly blend in vanilla, eggs, white sugar and brown sugar; stir till fluffy. Mix salt, baking powder and flour; whisk to peanut butter mixture till well-blended.
- Bake in the preheated oven till the top springs back once touched or for 30 - 35 minutes. Let cool down, and slice into 16 square pieces.

Nutrition Information

- Calories: 177 calories;
- Cholesterol: 23
- Protein: 3.7
- Total Fat: 8.5
- Sodium: 158
- Total Carbohydrate: 22.8

430. Chewy Sugar Cookies

Serving: 30 | Prep: 10mins | Cook: 15mins | Ready in:

Ingredients

- 2 3/4 cups all-purpose flour
- 1 teaspoon baking soda
- 1/2 teaspoon salt
- 1 1/4 cups margarine
- 2 cups white sugar
- 2 eggs
- 2 teaspoons vanilla extract
- 1/4 cup white sugar for decoration

Direction

- Set an oven to 175°C (350°F) to preheat. Stir together the salt, baking soda and flour in a medium bowl, then put aside.
- Cream together the 2 cups of sugar and margarine in a big bowl, until becoming fluffy

and light. Beat in the eggs, one by one, followed by the vanilla. Slowly stir in the dry ingredients until just combined. Roll the dough into walnut-sized balls, then roll the balls in the leftover 1/4 cup of sugar. Put the cookies onto the ungreased cookie sheets, placing 2 inches apart; flatten a bit.
- Bake in the preheated oven for 8-10 minutes, until the edges turn a bit brown. Let the cookies cool for 5 minutes on the baking tray prior to transferring to a wire rack to fully cool.

Nutrition Information

- Calories: 172 calories;
- Sodium: 173
- Total Carbohydrate: 23.9
- Cholesterol: 12
- Protein: 1.7
- Total Fat: 7.9

431. Chia Coconut Pudding With Coconut Milk

Serving: 6 | Prep: 10mins | Cook: | Ready in:

Ingredients

- 1/2 cup chia seeds
- 2 cups coconut milk
- 6 tablespoons unsweetened coconut milk
- 1 tablespoon agave nectar, or more to taste
- 1/2 teaspoon vanilla extract
- 1/4 teaspoon ground cinnamon
- 1 pinch salt
- 1/2 cup diced fresh strawberries (optional)

Direction

- In a bowl, put chia seeds.
- In a bowl, combine salt, cinnamon, vanilla extract, agave nectar, unsweetened coconut milk, and coconut milk. Pour over chia seeds; stir well. Allow chia seeds to steep in the coconut milk mixture for at least 20 minutes until thickened, or cover the bowl with plastic wrap and chill overnight in the fridge.
- Stir the pudding and garnish with strawberries before serving.

Nutrition Information

- Calories: 243 calories;
- Total Fat: 22.4
- Sodium: 14
- Total Carbohydrate: 10.8
- Cholesterol: 0
- Protein: 3.5

432. Chicken Fried Steak Cuban Style

Serving: 4 | Prep: 15mins | Cook: 30mins | Ready in:

Ingredients

- 4 (4 ounce) cube steaks
- 2 eggs
- 3 cups dry bread crumbs
- 1 tablespoon dried oregano
- 1 teaspoon ground cumin
- salt and pepper to taste
- 1 lemon, sliced
- 2 cups vegetable oil for frying

Direction

- Mix breadcrumbs with the pepper, salt, oregano, and cumin in a shallow dish. In another shallow dish, beat the eggs. Immerse each steak in the beaten eggs and then dip in the breadcrumb mixture. Ensure to cover every steak thoroughly with the breadcrumb mixture.
- Over medium high heat, heat one inch of oil in a large, deep skillet.

- Put the steaks in the oil when it becomes hot (this will ensure the breading does not stick to the pan). Cook the steaks, flip once, until they are browned well and golden brown for medium. You can serve together with lemon slices.

Nutrition Information

- Calories: 577 calories;
- Sodium: 661
- Total Carbohydrate: 62.3
- Cholesterol: 121
- Protein: 28.4
- Total Fat: 24

433. Chicken Honey Nut Stir Fry

Serving: 6 | Prep: 10mins | Cook: 10mins | Ready in:

Ingredients

- 2 teaspoons peanut oil
- 2 stalks celery, chopped
- 2 carrots, peeled and diagonally sliced
- 1 1/2 pounds skinless, boneless chicken breast halves - cut into strips
- 1 tablespoon cornstarch
- 3/4 cup orange juice
- 3 tablespoons light soy sauce
- 1 tablespoon honey
- 1 teaspoon minced fresh ginger root
- 1/4 cup cashews
- 1/4 cup minced green onions

Direction

- In a wok, heat 1 tsp. of oil over high heat. Put in celery and carrots, then stir fry about 3 minutes. Put in chicken and leftover 1 tsp. of oil, then stir fry about 5 minutes longer.
- Dissolve cornstarch into the orange juice in a small bowl. Mix in ginger, honey and soy sauce, then put this sauce into the wok and cook over moderate heat until thickened. Put green onions and cashews on top.

Nutrition Information

- Calories: 235 calories;
- Sodium: 529
- Total Carbohydrate: 12.9
- Cholesterol: 69
- Protein: 27.4
- Total Fat: 7.9

434. Chicken Piccata III

Serving: 4 | Prep: 15mins | Cook: 15mins | Ready in:

Ingredients

- 1 cup all-purpose flour
- 1/2 teaspoon paprika
- salt and pepper to taste
- 1 pound skinless, boneless chicken breast halves - cut into thin strips
- 1/4 cup vegetable oil
- 4 ounces fresh mushrooms, sliced
- 1/4 cup lemon juice
- 3/4 cup chicken stock
- 1/2 teaspoon garlic powder
- 1 (14 ounce) can artichoke hearts, drained and quartered

Direction

- Combine pepper, salt, paprika, and flour in a shallow mixing bowl. Press pieces of chicken into the seasoned flour to coat.
- Heat oil over medium heat in a large skillet; sauté chicken in heated oil, approximately 45 seconds per side, until light golden brown. Take chicken out of the skillet, and put to one side.
- Add chicken stock, lemon juice, and mushrooms to the skillet. Let simmer until

mixture becomes a smooth and light sauce. Sprinkle with garlic powder to season. Place chicken back into the skillet; simmer until juice runs clear and no longer pink inside. Mix in artichoke hearts, and take away from the heat.

Nutrition Information

- Calories: 444 calories;
- Protein: 33.3
- Total Fat: 17.9
- Sodium: 786
- Total Carbohydrate: 37.6
- Cholesterol: 69

435. Chicken Wraps

Serving: 10 | Prep: 4hours5mins | Cook: 20mins | Ready in:

Ingredients

- 1 pound skinless, boneless chicken breast halves
- 1/2 pound bacon
- 1 (20 ounce) can pineapple chunks
- 18 fluid ounces teriyaki sauce

Direction

- Slice the chicken into bite-size pieces and wrap it with approximately 1/3 slice of bacon, thread onto a toothpick and put pineapple chuck on top. Let it marinate for 4 hours or more in teriyaki sauce.
- Set an oven to preheat to 190°C (375°F).
- Put the marinated appetizers onto baking sheets lined with parchment. Let it bake for 20 minutes or until the bacon turns golden brown in color and the chicken is done. Let it drain on paper towels, then serve hot.

Nutrition Information

- Calories: 245 calories;
- Sodium: 2703
- Total Carbohydrate: 19
- Cholesterol: 42
- Protein: 17.2
- Total Fat: 10.8

436. Chicken Yum Yums

Serving: 6 | Prep: 15mins | Cook: 20mins | Ready in:

Ingredients

- 2 tablespoons olive oil
- 6 boned and skinned chicken breast halves
- 1 pinch salt
- 1/2 cup duck sauce
- 1/4 cup dried apricots, sliced
- 1/4 cup raisins
- 1 small apple - peeled, cored and thinly sliced

Direction

- Put oil in a large skillet and heat it over medium-high heat. Use a paper towel to pat dry chicken breasts. Season the chicken with salt and place it into the heated skillet. Reduce the heat to medium and cook each side for 3 minutes, flipping once.
- Adjust the heat to medium-low and stir in duck sauce, apples, apricots, apples and raisins. Coat each side of the chicken evenly and cook until the chicken is no longer pink in the center and the juices run clear. Add more duck sauce if preferred.

Nutrition Information

- Calories: 240 calories;
- Sodium: 134
- Total Carbohydrate: 17.7
- Cholesterol: 67
- Protein: 24.8
- Total Fat: 7.5

437. Chicken And Dumplings I

Serving: 6 | Prep: 20mins | Cook: 2hours | Ready in:

Ingredients

- 1 (2 to 3 pound) whole chicken
- 2 cups all-purpose flour
- 1 teaspoon baking powder
- 1 cup hot chicken broth
- 1 egg

Direction

- Pour salted water over chicken to cover in a Dutch oven or large stockpot and simmer until thoroughly cooked. Once chicken is tender, take out from the pot. Remove chicken bones and keep warm when preparing dumplings.
- For dumplings: sieve 1 teaspoon baking powder and 2 cups of flour into a large mixing bowl. Make a well in the center of flour/powder mixture; add 1 cup of hot chicken broth, stirring with a fork first, then with your fingers. Pour in egg and mix to combine.
- Transfer the dough to a floured work surface or board and knead for a few seconds. Cut the dough into 4 or 5 portions and roll as thin as they can be. Cut each into 1.5 or 2 inches-wide pieces. Break these pieces of dough into 2-inch-long strips. Transfer dough strips into boiling chicken broth and simmer for 10-15 minutes. Enjoy with cooked chicken.

Nutrition Information

- Calories: 349 calories;
- Sodium: 141
- Total Carbohydrate: 32.1
- Cholesterol: 82
- Protein: 22.8
- Total Fat: 13.5

438. Chicken In A Pot

Serving: 4 | Prep: 20mins | Cook: 20mins | Ready in:

Ingredients

- 3/4 cup chicken broth
- 1 1/2 tablespoons tomato paste
- 1/4 teaspoon ground black pepper
- 1/2 teaspoon dried oregano
- 1/8 teaspoon salt
- 1 clove garlic, minced
- 4 boneless, skinless chicken breast halves
- 3 tablespoons dry bread crumbs
- 2 teaspoons olive oil
- 2 cups fresh sliced mushrooms

Direction

- Mix garlic, salt, oregano, ground black pepper, tomato paste, and broth in a medium bowl. Combine thoroughly and put aside.
- Dredge the chicken into the breadcrumbs to coat thoroughly. In a large skillet, heat the oil over medium-high heat. In the oil, sauté chicken until it is browned lightly, 2 minutes on each side.
- Put the mushrooms and the saved broth mixture into the skillet, then boil. Put on a cover, turn down the heat to low and simmer for 20 minutes. Take the chicken out, then put it aside and cover to keep warm.
- Boil the broth mixture and cook until it reduces to the desired thickness, 4 minutes. Spread the sauce onto the chicken to serve.

Nutrition Information

- Calories: 206 calories;
- Protein: 28.7
- Total Fat: 6.6
- Sodium: 402

- Total Carbohydrate: 6.9
- Cholesterol: 73

439. Chickpea Curry

Serving: 8 | Prep: 10mins | Cook: 30mins | Ready in:

Ingredients

- 2 tablespoons vegetable oil
- 2 onions, minced
- 2 cloves garlic, minced
- 2 teaspoons fresh ginger root, finely chopped
- 6 whole cloves
- 2 (2 inch) sticks cinnamon, crushed
- 1 teaspoon ground cumin
- 1 teaspoon ground coriander
- salt
- 1 teaspoon cayenne pepper
- 1 teaspoon ground turmeric
- 2 (15 ounce) cans garbanzo beans
- 1 cup chopped fresh cilantro

Direction

- In a big frying pan, heat the oil on medium heat and fry the onions until it becomes tender.
- Stir in turmeric, cayenne, salt, coriander, cumin, cinnamon, cloves, ginger and garlic. Let it cook for a minute on medium heat, stirring continuously. Mix in garbanzo beans with its liquid. Keep on cooking and stirring until all the ingredients are heated through and combined well. Take it out of the heat. Mix in cilantro just prior to serving, then set aside 1 tbsp. for the garnish.

Nutrition Information

- Calories: 135 calories;
- Total Carbohydrate: 20.5
- Cholesterol: 0
- Protein: 4.1

- Total Fat: 4.5
- Sodium: 289

440. Chili Lime Chicken Kabobs

Serving: 4 | Prep: 15mins | Cook: 15mins | Ready in:

Ingredients

- 3 tablespoons olive oil
- 1 1/2 tablespoons red wine vinegar
- 1 lime, juiced
- 1 teaspoon chili powder
- 1/2 teaspoon paprika
- 1/2 teaspoon onion powder
- 1/2 teaspoon garlic powder
- cayenne pepper to taste
- salt and freshly ground black pepper to taste
- 1 pound skinless, boneless chicken breast halves - cut into 1 1/2 inch pieces
- skewers

Direction

- Whisk lime juice, olive oil, and vinegar in a small bowl. Sprinkle with salt, black pepper, paprika, chili powder, garlic powder, onion powder, and cayenne pepper. In a shallow baking dish, put the chicken and pour the sauce, stirring to coat the chicken. Put on the lid and refrigerate for at least an hour.
- Preheat grill on medium-high. Skewer chicken. Dispose of the marinade.
- Lightly great the grates. Grill chicken until juices run clear, about 10 to 15 minutes.

Nutrition Information

- Calories: 227 calories;
- Total Fat: 13
- Sodium: 64
- Total Carbohydrate: 3.2
- Cholesterol: 65

- Protein: 23.9

441. Chinese Fried Noodles

Serving: 6 | Prep: 15mins | Cook: 25mins | Ready in:

Ingredients

- 2 (3 ounce) packages Oriental flavored ramen noodles
- 3 eggs, beaten
- vegetable oil
- 4 green onions, thinly sliced
- 1 small carrot, peeled and grated
- 1/2 cup green peas
- 1/4 cup red bell pepper, minced
- 2 tablespoons sesame oil
- soy sauce

Direction

- Boil ramen noodles, without flavor packets, for 3 minutes till soft. Keep flavor packets. Drain noodles then put aside.
- In a small skillet, heat 1 tbsp. oil. In a bowl, scramble eggs. Stir and cook in hot oil till firm. Put aside.
- Heat 1 tsp. oil in another skillet on medium heat. Stir and cook green onions in the oil till soft or for 2-3 minutes. Put into another dish; put aside. In same skillet, heat another tsp. cooking oil. Stir and cook bell peppers, peas and carrots separately in the same way, putting each one aside when finished.
- In another skillet/wok, mix 1 tbsp. vegetable oil and 2 tbsp. sesame oil. Fry noodles in the oil on medium heat, regularly turning, for 3-5 minutes. Sprinkle preferred amount reserved ramen seasoning packets, sesame oil and soy sauce on noodles; toss till coated. Add veggies. Cook for another 5 minutes, frequently turning.

Nutrition Information

- Calories: 161 calories;
- Total Fat: 13
- Sodium: 294
- Total Carbohydrate: 6.9
- Cholesterol: 69
- Protein: 4.3

442. Chinese Style Stuffed Mushrooms

Serving: 4 | Prep: 15mins | Cook: 30mins | Ready in:

Ingredients

- 15 large fresh mushrooms, stems removed
- 1/2 pound ground pork
- 1/4 slice Chinese salted turnip (chung choi), rinsed and chopped
- 1 tablespoon soy sauce
- 3 tablespoons finely chopped canned water chestnuts
- 1/4 teaspoon salt
- 1/4 teaspoon white sugar

Direction

- Cut the stems off the mushrooms. You can either save it for a different use or discard. Clean the mushroom caps by wiping with a dry towel.
- Mix together the turnip, pork, water chestnuts, soy sauce, sugar, and salt in a bowl until they are well blended. Scoop the filling and stuff it in the mushroom caps tightly. Place the stuffed mushrooms with the stuffing side up in a steamer basket and place it on top of boiling water Cover and cook the mushrooms for 30 minutes then serve while it's hot.

Nutrition Information

- Calories: 142 calories;
- Cholesterol: 37
- Protein: 12

- Total Fat: 8.5
- Sodium: 403
- Total Carbohydrate: 5

443. Chocolate Chip Mint Vegan Nice Cream

Serving: 1 | Prep: 10mins | Cook: | Ready in:

Ingredients

- 1/4 cup raw cashews
- 1 ripe banana
- 1 cup ice cubes
- 3 ounces extra-firm tofu, pressed to remove water
- 2 Medjool dates, pitted
- 1 teaspoon mint extract
- 1 teaspoon soy milk, or more as needed
- 1/4 cup vegan chocolate chips

Direction

- In a bowl, put cashews and add water to cover. Let soak for 1-3 hours. Strain.
- In a blender, mix together 1 teaspoon soy milk, mint extract, dates, tofu, ice cubes, banana, and soaked cashews. Blend until smooth. If necessary, to keep the mixture as thick as possible, add additional teaspoon soy milk.
- Mix in chocolate chips and add to a bowl and enjoy.

Nutrition Information

- Calories: 433 calories;
- Total Fat: 20.2
- Sodium: 236
- Total Carbohydrate: 55.7
- Cholesterol: 0
- Protein: 13.6

444. Chocolate Coconut Overnight Oats

Serving: 1 | Prep: 5mins | Cook: | Ready in:

Ingredients

- 1 cup chocolate-flavored almond milk
- 3/4 cup old-fashioned rolled oats (such a Quaker®)
- 1 tablespoon chia seeds
- 1 tablespoon packed shredded sweetened coconut
- 1 tablespoon maple syrup
- 1 tablespoon unsweetened cocoa powder
- 1 splash vanilla extract

Direction

- In a 12-ounce mason jar, combine vanilla extract, cocoa powder, maple syrup, coconut, chia seeds, oats, and almond milk. Keep covered in the refrigerator for a minimum of 8 hours to overnight. Stir and serve cool.

Nutrition Information

- Calories: 488 calories;
- Total Fat: 11.6
- Sodium: 183
- Total Carbohydrate: 87.1
- Cholesterol: 0
- Protein: 12.5

445. Chocolate Crinkles II

Serving: 72 | Prep: 20mins | Cook: 12mins | Ready in:

Ingredients

- 1 cup unsweetened cocoa powder
- 2 cups white sugar
- 1/2 cup vegetable oil
- 4 eggs
- 2 teaspoons vanilla extract

- 2 cups all-purpose flour
- 2 teaspoons baking powder
- 1/2 teaspoon salt
- 1/2 cup confectioners' sugar

Direction

- Mix vegetable oil, white sugar and cocoa in a medium bowl. One by one, beat in eggs; mix in vanilla. Mix salt, baking powder and flour; mix into the cocoa mixture. Cover the dough; chill for at least 4 hours.
- Preheat an oven to 175°C/350°F. Line parchment paper on cookie sheets. Roll dough to 1-in. balls. I use number 50 size scoop. In confectioners' sugar, coat each ball then put onto prepped cookie sheets.
- In the preheated oven, bake for 10-12 minutes; stand for 1 minute on cookie sheet. Put on wire racks; cool.

Nutrition Information

- Calories: 58 calories;
- Total Fat: 2
- Sodium: 34
- Total Carbohydrate: 9.8
- Cholesterol: 10
- Protein: 0.9

446. Chocolate Olive Oil Cake

Serving: 8 | Prep: 15mins | Cook: 25mins | Ready in:

Ingredients

- 3 1/2 ounces 70% dark chocolate, chopped
- 2 eggs
- 1/2 cup white sugar
- 6 tablespoons olive oil
- 1 cup chopped almonds
- 1/2 cup all-purpose flour
- 1 teaspoon ground cinnamon

Direction

- Set the oven to 350°F (175°C) to preheat. Grease a 7-inch baking tray and line with parchment paper.
- Into the top of a double boiler over simmering water, put chocolate. Mix constantly for about 5 minutes, scraping down the sides using a rubber spatula to prevent scorching until chocolate has melted. Take it off the heat.
- In a big bowl, mix sugar and eggs; whip with an electric mixer until pale. Using a spatula, mix in olive oil and melted chocolate until well blended. In another bowl, stir cinnamon, flour, and almonds and put into chocolate mixture. Mix until well blended. Add to the greased baking pan.
- Bake in the prepared oven 25 to 30 minutes until a toothpick inserted in the middle exits clean. Let cool completely before cutting and serving.

Nutrition Information

- Calories: 317 calories;
- Total Fat: 21.3
- Sodium: 17
- Total Carbohydrate: 28.5
- Cholesterol: 42
- Protein: 5.4

447. Chocolate Peanut Butter Energy Balls

Serving: 34 | Prep: 15mins | Cook: | Ready in:

Ingredients

- 4 cups quick cooking oats
- 2 1/2 cups natural peanut butter
- 2 cups dry unsweetened shredded coconut
- 1 cup chocolate chips
- 1 cup dried cranberries
- 1 cup almond milk

- 1/2 cup honey, melted

Direction

- In a mixing bowl, combine honey, almond milk, cranberries, chocolate chips, shredded coconut, peanut butter, and oats; stir well.
- Shape mixture into bite-sized balls and place on a baking sheet. Chill for at least 15 minutes in the fridge until firm.

Nutrition Information

- Calories: 240 calories;
- Total Carbohydrate: 22.4
- Cholesterol: 0
- Protein: 6.7
- Total Fat: 15.7
- Sodium: 58

448. Chocolate Protein Cookies

Serving: 6 | Prep: 10mins | Cook: 8mins | Ready in:

Ingredients

- 1 small ripe banana
- 1/4 cup golden flax seeds
- 2 teaspoons chia seeds
- 2 scoops vanilla protein powder
- 1 tablespoon powdered peanut butter
- 2 tablespoons dairy-free mini chocolate chips

Direction

- Set the oven to 350°F (175°C) and start preheating. Line parchment paper on a baking sheet.
- Place banana in a bowl, use an electric mixture to mash until creamy. Blend in chia seeds and flax seeds. Mix in powdered peanut butter and protein powder. Using a spatula to fold in chocolate chips.
- Scoop dough into 6 cookies with an ice cream scoop and drop onto prepared baking sheet. Press each cookie with the palm of your hand to flatten.
- Bake in the preheated oven for 8 to 9 minutes until firm and browned in center and at all edges.
- Cool for 10 minutes on a wire rack.

Nutrition Information

- Calories: 116 calories;
- Total Carbohydrate: 7.8
- Cholesterol: 4
- Protein: 14.3
- Total Fat: 3.5
- Sodium: 79

449. Chocolate Vegan Nice Cream

Serving: 1 | Prep: 10mins | Cook: | Ready in:

Ingredients

- 1 ripe banana
- 1 cup ice cubes
- 3 ounces extra-firm tofu, pressed to remove water
- 1/3 cup cacao powder
- 1/4 cup raw cashews
- 2 Medjool dates, pitted
- 2 teaspoons vanilla extract
- 1 teaspoon soy milk, or more as needed

Direction

- Add the cashews in the bowl and cover with water. Steep for 1 - 3 hours. Drain.
- In the blender, mix 1 tsp. of soy milk, vanilla extract, dates, cacao powder, tofu, ice cubes, banana, and steeped cashews. Blend till becoming smooth. Pour in additional tsp. of

soy milk only when necessary, so that the mixture can be thick as possible.
- Add to the bowl to serve.

Nutrition Information

- Calories: 493 calories;
- Total Carbohydrate: 37.5
- Cholesterol: 0
- Protein: 16.6
- Total Fat: 30.9
- Sodium: 236

450. Chocolate, Almond, And Coconut Vegan Fat Bombs

Serving: 20 | Prep: 10mins | Cook: | Ready in:

Ingredients

- 1 cup shredded unsweetened coconut, divided
- 1/2 cup melted coconut oil
- 1/2 cup almonds, finely chopped
- 1/2 cup coconut milk
- 1/2 cup chopped Medjool dates
- 1 tablespoon low-calorie natural sweetener (such as Swerve®)

Direction

- In the bowl of a food processor, blend sweetener, half cup of shredded coconut, coconut milk, coconut oil, dates, and almonds for about 2 minutes until the resulting mixture is creamy. Place in a freezer for about 15 minutes until set.
- Form the mixture into one-inch balls and then roll into the remaining half cup of shredded coconut.

Nutrition Information

- Calories: 122 calories;
- Protein: 1.3

- Total Fat: 11.5
- Sodium: 3
- Total Carbohydrate: 5.8
- Cholesterol: 0

451. Christmas Casserole Cookies II

Serving: 60 | Prep: 20mins | Cook: 30mins | Ready in:

Ingredients

- 2 eggs
- 1/2 cup white sugar
- 1 cup chopped dates
- 1 cup flaked coconut
- 1 cup chopped walnuts
- 1 teaspoon vanilla extract
- 1/4 teaspoon almond extract

Direction

- Turn on the oven to 350°F (175°C) to preheat.
- Use an electric mixer to beat eggs in a medium bowl. Beat in sugar. Mix in almond extract, vanilla, walnuts, coconut and dates. Transfer the mixture with a spoon to a 2-quart casserole dish.
- Put into the oven to bake for 30 minutes.
- Take it out of the oven; use a wooden spoon to beat well while it is still hot.
- When the mixture is cool enough to handle, shape into small balls and roll into granulated sugar.

Nutrition Information

- Calories: 39 calories;
- Total Fat: 2.4
- Sodium: 3
- Total Carbohydrate: 4.2
- Cholesterol: 6
- Protein: 0.7

452. Cinnamon Apple Toast

Serving: 2 | Prep: 15mins | Cook: 12mins | Ready in:

Ingredients

- 1 tablespoon cornstarch
- 1 dash cinnamon
- 1/4 teaspoon nutmeg
- 1 1/4 cups unsweetened apple juice
- 1 apple - peeled, cored and thinly sliced
- 2 slices whole wheat bread
- 1 tablespoon apple syrup
- 1/4 teaspoon cinnamon
- 2 teaspoons light brown sugar

Direction

- Mix apple juice, nutmeg, cinnamon, and cornstarch together in a small saucepan, beat well combined. Boil it, lower to simmer. Stir and cook until slightly thickened, about 5 minutes. Put in an airtight container and chill to store until ready to use.
- Start preheating the oven to 500°F (260°C).
- In a microwave-safe plate, put apples and use apple syrup to sprinkle. Microwave on high until soft, about 1 minute. Put aside. Toast the bread and top with apple slices. Use the syrup to sprinkle.
- Put in the preheated oven and bake for 5 minutes, watching closely to make sure it doesn't burn. Use cinnamon to drizzle if you want. Enjoy immediately.

Nutrition Information

- Calories: 238 calories;
- Total Fat: 1.5
- Sodium: 142
- Total Carbohydrate: 53.9
- Cholesterol: 0
- Protein: 4

453. Cinnamon Rice With Apples

Serving: 4 | Prep: 10mins | Cook: 20mins | Ready in:

Ingredients

- 3/4 cup uncooked white rice
- 1 1/2 cups apple juice
- 1 apple, cored and chopped
- 1/3 cup raisins
- 1/2 teaspoon ground cinnamon
- 1/4 teaspoon salt, or to taste
- 1/4 cup chopped fresh parsley

Direction

- In a pan, combine raisins, chopped apple, apple juice, and rice, then season with salt and cinnamon. Set to boil, turn the heat down to low, then cover for 17 minutes. Lift the lid and see if the rice is moist enough to reach your taste. If not, continue cooking for another couple of minutes.
- Mix in fresh parsley and serve right away.

Nutrition Information

- Calories: 240 calories;
- Sodium: 153
- Total Carbohydrate: 56.3
- Cholesterol: 0
- Protein: 3.5
- Total Fat: 0.5

454. Cocktail Meatballs

Serving: 10 | Prep: 20mins | Cook: 1hours25mins | Ready in:

Ingredients

- 1 pound lean ground beef

- 1 egg
- 2 tablespoons water
- 1/2 cup bread crumbs
- 3 tablespoons minced onion
- 1 (8 ounce) can jellied cranberry sauce
- 3/4 cup chili sauce
- 1 tablespoon brown sugar
- 1 1/2 teaspoons lemon juice

Direction

- Turn oven to 350°F (175°C) to preheat.
- Combine minced onion, breadcrumbs, water, egg, and ground beef in a large bowl. Shape mixture into small meatballs.
- Bake for 20 to 25 minutes in the preheated oven, flipping once.
- Blend lemon juice, brown sugar, chili sauce, and cranberry sauce over low heat in a large saucepan or slow cooker. Add in meatballs; simmer for 60 minutes or until ready to serve.

Nutrition Information

- Calories: 193 calories;
- Total Fat: 10.2
- Sodium: 85
- Total Carbohydrate: 15.2
- Cholesterol: 53
- Protein: 9.8

455. Cocktail Meatballs I

Serving: 8 | Prep: 25mins | Cook: 40mins | Ready in:

Ingredients

- 1 pound ground beef
- 1/2 cup dried bread crumbs
- 1/3 cup chopped onion
- 1/4 cup milk
- 1 egg
- 1 teaspoon salt
- 1/2 teaspoon Worcestershire sauce
- 1/8 teaspoon ground black pepper
- 1/4 cup shortening
- 12 fluid ounces tomato-based chili sauce
- 1 1/4 cups grape jelly

Direction

- Blend ground black pepper, Worcestershire sauce, salt, egg, milk, onion, breadcrumbs, and ground beef in a large bowl. Combine them together and form into meatballs.
- Heat shortening in a large skillet on medium heat. Put meatballs and cook for 5-7 minutes until they are browned. Take out from the skillet and transfer to paper towels to drain.
- Place jelly and chili sauce into the skillet; heat and stir until the jelly melts. Bring the meatballs back to the skillet and stir until they are coated. Turn down the heat to low. Remove the cover and bring to a simmer for half an hour.

Nutrition Information

- Calories: 458 calories;
- Cholesterol: 72
- Protein: 12.7
- Total Fat: 22.8
- Sodium: 1038
- Total Carbohydrate: 52.5

456. Cocktail Meatballs IV

Serving: 6 | Prep: 30mins | Cook: 30mins | Ready in:

Ingredients

- 2 pounds ground beef
- 10 ounces grape jelly
- 1/4 cup chili sauce
- 2 tablespoons prepared mustard

Direction

- Set an oven to 175°C (350°F) and start preheating. Use aluminum foil to line a large roasting pan.
- Form the ground beef into golf-size balls. On the lined roasting pan, arrange them until finished, 20-25 minutes.
- At the same time, in a 2-quart Dutch oven, heat together the mustard, chili sauce, and jelly. Drain the meatballs and place into the Dutch oven. Put a cover on and bring to a simmer on low for 30 minutes. Then serve hot with toothpicks in a chaffing dish.

Nutrition Information

- Calories: 601 calories;
- Cholesterol: 129
- Protein: 25.7
- Total Fat: 40.4
- Sodium: 313
- Total Carbohydrate: 33.4

457. Coconut Chocolate Chip Cupcakes

Serving: 12 | Prep: 15mins | Cook: 20mins | Ready in:

Ingredients

- 3/4 cup gluten-free all purpose baking flour, like Bell® brand
- 1/4 cup coconut flour
- 3/4 teaspoon baking powder
- 1 teaspoon baking soda
- 1/4 teaspoon salt
- 2 tablespoons chia seeds (mixed with water)*
- 2/3 cup water
- 1 1/3 cups So Delicious® Dairy Free Vanilla Coconut Milk
- 1/2 cup coconut oil, warmed to liquefy
- 1/4 cup agave nectar
- 1 teaspoon apple cider vinegar
- 1 teaspoon vanilla extract
- 1/2 cup mini chocolate chips

Direction

- Preheat oven to 350°.
- Sift dry ingredients together, Gf flour through salt; put aside.
- Make chia seed mixture; put aside.
- Mix all leftover liquid ingredients, water to vanilla extract.
- Put wet ingredients in dry ingredients while rapidly mixing; add chocolate chips and chia seed mixture.
- Rest batter for 15 minutes.
- Put cupcake liners in muffin tin.
- Scoop batter in each liner.
- Bake the cupcakes for 15-20 minutes.

Nutrition Information

- Calories: 180 calories;
- Protein: 1.5
- Total Fat: 12.7
- Sodium: 187
- Total Carbohydrate: 17.8
- Cholesterol: 0

458. Coconut Ice

Serving: 20 | Prep: 5mins | Cook: 30mins | Ready in:

Ingredients

- 2 cups white sugar
- 2/3 cup water
- 1 teaspoon vanilla extract
- 1 1/3 cups flaked coconut
- 2 drops red food coloring

Direction

- Line waxed paper/parchment on 7x7-in. pan. Gently heat water and sugar without boiling till sugar dissolves in heavy-bottomed medium saucepan. Boil; cook till small syrup dropped into glass with cold water makes soft

ball and candy thermometer reads 120°C/240°F.
- Take off heat; mix in coconut and vanilla immediately. Mix for 5-10 minutes till it starts to thicken.
- Put 1/2 of it into prepped pan; use a spatula/knife to level surface. Mix in food coloring to tint other 1/2 of mixture. Put pink mixture over other layer; level surface. Use back of spoon to firmly press all down; let harden. Turn out of pan when firm; remove paper. Use a sharp knife to cut to squares.

Nutrition Information

- Calories: 119 calories;
- Total Fat: 4
- Sodium: 2
- Total Carbohydrate: 21.5
- Cholesterol: 0
- Protein: 0.4

459. Coconut Rice

Serving: 7 | Prep: 5mins | Cook: 25mins | Ready in:

Ingredients

- 2 1/2 cups Basmati rice
- 4 (10 ounce) cans coconut milk
- 1 pinch salt

Direction

- On high heat, boil salt, coconut milk, and rice together in a big saucepan.
- Lower heat; let it simmer for 20-25 minutes, covered, or until the rice is tender and the liquid is absorbed.

Nutrition Information

- Calories: 535 calories;
- Cholesterol: 0
- Protein: 8.1
- Total Fat: 33.2
- Sodium: 20
- Total Carbohydrate: 56.8

460. Coconut Sevai (Rice Noodles)

Serving: 6 | Prep: 5mins | Cook: 15mins | Ready in:

Ingredients

- 14 ounces rice noodles
- 1 teaspoon salt
- 3 tablespoons vegetable oil
- 1 teaspoon black mustard seed
- 2 dried red chile peppers, chopped
- 3 tablespoons brown lentils
- 4 tablespoons roasted peanuts
- 3/4 cup shredded or flaked coconut
- 1/4 cup water
- fresh cilantro, for garnish

Direction

- Put noodles in a medium sized pot then cover with enough water. Put in salt then boil. After 1-2 minutes of boiling, put noodles in a colander then run cold water through it for about 3 seconds. Drain then put aside.
- In a wok, heat oil then add lentils, chile peppers, and mustard seed when warm. Stir-fry until lentils begin to turn light brown. Add peanuts then stir-fry for 10 seconds. Mix in coconut then fry until light brown. Put in 1/4 cup of water and cooked noodles. Continue stirring everything together on heat for 10-20 seconds until well combined. Top with cilantro. Serve.

Nutrition Information

- Calories: 370 calories;
- Protein: 5.2

- Total Fat: 17.9
- Sodium: 424
- Total Carbohydrate: 48.1
- Cholesterol: 0

461. Coconut Chocolate Sugar Free Ice Pops

Serving: 8 | Prep: 15mins | Cook: | Ready in:

Ingredients

- 6 pitted dates
- 3 ripe bananas
- 3/4 (13.5 ounce) can light coconut milk
- 1/4 cup almond milk
- 2 teaspoons vanilla extract
- 1/4 cup unsweetened cocoa powder
- dash salt

Direction

- In a bowl, put the dates, pour hot water to cover and let it soak for around 6-10 minutes until it becomes soft, then drain.
- In a blender, puree the salt, cocoa powder, vanilla, almond milk, coconut milk, bananas and dates together for about 2-3 minutes, until it becomes smooth, then pour into the popsicle molds.
- Let it freeze for about 6 hours until it becomes solid throughout.

Nutrition Information

- Calories: 139 calories;
- Protein: 1.9
- Total Fat: 8.3
- Sodium: 59
- Total Carbohydrate: 17.7
- Cholesterol: 0

462. Cookie Mix In A Jar III

Serving: 36 | Prep: 20mins | Cook: | Ready in:

Ingredients

- 1 cup all-purpose flour
- 1 teaspoon ground cinnamon
- 1/2 teaspoon ground nutmeg
- 1 teaspoon baking soda
- 1/2 teaspoon salt
- 3/4 cup raisins
- 2 cups rolled oats
- 3/4 cup packed brown sugar
- 1/2 cup white sugar

Direction

- Mix salt, baking soda, ground nutmeg, ground cinnamon and flour; put aside.
- In a 1-qt. wide mouth canning jar, layer ingredients in the following order; flour mixture, the raisins, rolled oats, the brown sugar then white sugar. Firmly pack down every layer before adding the next layer; it'll be a tight fit.
- With the following instructions, attach a tag: Oatmeal Raisin Spice Cookies. Preheat an oven to 175°C/350°F. Line parchment paper on cookie sheets. Into a big mixing bowl, empty cookie mix jar; thoroughly mix with your hands. Mix in softened 3/4 cup margarine/butter. Mix in 1 tsp. vanilla and 1 slightly beaten egg till fully blended. To finish mixing, you need to use your hands. Form to walnut-sized balls; put onto parchment lined cookie sheets, 2-in. apart. In the preheated oven, bake till edges are lightly browned for 11-13 minutes; cool on cookie sheet for 5 minutes. Put onto wire racks; finish cooling.

Nutrition Information

- Calories: 67 calories;
- Cholesterol: 0
- Protein: 1.1
- Total Fat: 0.4

- Sodium: 69
- Total Carbohydrate: 15.4

463. Coricos Sonorenses

Serving: 100 | Prep: 35mins | Cook: 45mins | Ready in:

Ingredients

- 1 pound vegetable shortening
- 1 3/4 cups white sugar
- 4 eggs
- 2 oranges, zested (optional)
- 1 tablespoon vanilla extract
- 2 pounds white masa harina (corn flour)
- 3 tablespoons baking powder
- 1 1/2 teaspoons ground cinnamon (optional)
- 1 teaspoon all-purpose flour

Direction

- Whip together the sugar and shortening in a big bowl with an electric mixer until creamy. Put in the vanilla extract, orange zest and eggs.
- In a separate bowl, mix the flour, cinnamon, baking powder and corn flour. Whisk and put half of mixture into shortening mixture. Whip on the low speed till mixed. Put in the rest of flour mixture and knead using hands till the dough is mixed.
- Preheat oven to 175 degrees C (350 degrees F).
- Roll a small portion of dough out into one thin log; pinch the ends together to shape a small ring. Arrange onto a baking sheet. Repeat the process with the remaining dough. Arrange the coricos as closely together onto baking sheets as desired; they don't spread.
- Bake in preheated oven for roughly 45 minutes till the coricos turn golden-brown all over. Take out and allow it to cool down.

Nutrition Information

- Calories: 90 calories;

- Total Carbohydrate: 10.7
- Cholesterol: 7
- Total Fat: 5.1
- Protein: 1.1
- Sodium: 47

464. Corn Fritters Southern Style

Serving: 10 | Prep: 20mins | Cook: 30mins | Ready in:

Ingredients

- 6 ears freshly shucked corn
- 4 eggs
- 1/2 cup all-purpose flour
- 1/2 teaspoon salt
- 2 cups vegetable oil for frying

Direction

- Get rid of all silk from corn and cut raw corn from the cob over a big bowl. Scrape the cobs to draw out juice into the bowl, then get rid of the cobs. Stir in salt, flour and eggs to make a batter the consistency of thin pancake batter.
- In an electric skillet, heat oil to 165°C or 325°F. If you use a big skillet on the stove, preheat the oil to moderately high heat. There should be sufficient oil in the pan to cover the fritter.
- Make 4 pancake sized fritters at the same time with a big serving spoon, then fry for 5 minutes per side, or until they turn golden brown. Drain on paper towels and serve warm.

Nutrition Information

- Calories: 164 calories;
- Total Carbohydrate: 21.2
- Cholesterol: 74
- Protein: 5.9
- Total Fat: 7.5
- Sodium: 157

465. Corned Beef Hash

Serving: 6 | Prep: 10mins | Cook: 30mins | Ready in:

Ingredients

- 6 large potatoes, peeled and diced
- 1 (12 ounce) can corned beef, cut into chunks
- 1 medium onion, chopped
- 1 cup beef broth

Direction

- Simmer beef broth, onion, corned beef and potatoes, covered, in big deep skillet on medium heat till liquid is nearly gone and potatoes are at mashing consistency; stir well then serve.

Nutrition Information

- Calories: 434 calories;
- Total Fat: 8.8
- Sodium: 718
- Total Carbohydrate: 66.2
- Cholesterol: 48
- Protein: 23.3

466. Corned Beef Hash (Abalos Style)

Serving: 4 | Prep: 15mins | Cook: 30mins | Ready in:

Ingredients

- 1 tablespoon vegetable oil
- 4 cloves garlic, chopped
- 1 onion, diced
- 1 tomato, chopped
- 1 large potato, diced
- 1 (12 ounce) can corned beef
- salt and pepper to taste

Direction

- In a large skillet set on medium-high heat, add oil. Add garlic and onion then cook until scented. Mix in the potatoes and tomatoes, then cook for 7-10 minutes until potatoes are tender. Add in the corned beef, and flake into pieces. And cook for 10 more minutes, frequently stirring. Add pepper and salt to taste, then serve.

Nutrition Information

- Calories: 333 calories;
- Total Fat: 16.2
- Sodium: 853
- Total Carbohydrate: 21.1
- Cholesterol: 72
- Protein: 25.5

467. Corned Beef Hash Cakes

Serving: 8 | Prep: 10mins | Cook: 15mins | Ready in:

Ingredients

- 1 tablespoon vegetable oil
- 1 small onion, chopped
- 2 cups leftover mashed potatoes
- salt and pepper to taste
- 1 cup shredded cooked corned beef

Direction

- Heat oil in big skillet on medium heat; in oil, fry onion till translucent. Put in medium bowl; mix with corned beef and mashed potatoes. Season with pepper and salt; shape to 8 patties. Fry patties in skillet on medium high heat till both sides are golden brown.

Nutrition Information

- Calories: 114 calories;
- Total Fat: 6.1
- Sodium: 320
- Total Carbohydrate: 9.7
- Cholesterol: 13
- Protein: 5

468. Corned Beef Potato Pancakes

Serving: 4 | Prep: 15mins | Cook: 15mins |Ready in:

Ingredients

- 3 medium potatoes, shredded
- 2 green onions, chopped
- 1/2 (12 ounce) can corned beef, broken into very small chunks
- 1 egg
- salt and pepper to taste
- 1/4 cup vegetable oil

Direction

- Combine egg, corned beef, green onions and potatoes in a large mixing bowl. Add pepper and salt to taste. Shape potato mixture into golf ball-sized balls.
- In a skillet, heat oil over medium heat. Put a few potato balls at a time into the skillet, press with a spatula, and fry until they are golden brown and crispy, 7 minutes on each side. Transfer to paper towels to drain.

Nutrition Information

- Calories: 260 calories;
- Protein: 16.3
- Total Fat: 9
- Sodium: 451
- Total Carbohydrate: 28.6
- Cholesterol: 83

469. Corned Beef And Cabbage I

Serving: 5 | Prep: 10mins | Cook: 2hours25mins |Ready in:

Ingredients

- 3 pounds corned beef brisket with spice packet
- 10 small red potatoes
- 5 carrots, peeled and cut into 3-inch pieces
- 1 large head cabbage, cut into small wedges

Direction

- Cover corned beef with water in big pot/Dutch oven. Add spice packet from corned beef. Cover pot; boil. Lower to simmer; simmer till tender for 50 minutes per pound.
- Add carrots and whole potatoes; cook till veggies are nearly tender. Add cabbage; cook for 15 minutes. Remove meat; rest for 15 minutes.
- Put veggies in bowl; cover. Add as much cooking liquid kept in big pot/Dutch oven (broth) as you prefer. Across grain, slice meat.

470. Cornmeal Mush

Serving: 8 | Prep: 5mins | Cook: 7mins |Ready in:

Ingredients

- 1 1/4 cups cornmeal
- 2 1/2 cups water
- 1/2 teaspoon salt

Direction

- In a medium pan, mix salt, water, and cornmeal, cooking them on medium heat, stirring often, for 5-7 minutes until thickened.
- If you are using this as a cereal, spoon into bowls and serve with sugar and milk, if

preferred. If you are frying them, pour into a loaf pan and completely chill; take out from pan then cut into slices. Fry them in a bit of oil on medium-high heat until both sides are brown, then serve with your choice of sauce.

Nutrition Information

- Calories: 80 calories;
- Sodium: 147
- Total Carbohydrate: 17.1
- Cholesterol: 0
- Protein: 1.6
- Total Fat: 0.4

471. Country Style Fried Potatoes

Serving: 6 | Prep: 10mins | Cook: 15mins | Ready in:

Ingredients

- 1/3 cup shortening
- 6 large potatoes, peeled and cubed
- 1 teaspoon salt
- 1/2 teaspoon ground black pepper
- 1/2 teaspoon garlic powder
- 1/2 teaspoon paprika

Direction

- Heat the shortening in a big cast iron skillet on medium-high heat. Add the potatoes and cook, stirring from time to time, until the potatoes turn golden brown in color. Add paprika, garlic powder, pepper and salt to season, then serve it hot.

Nutrition Information

- Calories: 326 calories;
- Cholesterol: 0
- Protein: 4.8
- Total Fat: 11.7
- Sodium: 400
- Total Carbohydrate: 52.1

472. Couscous With Mushrooms And Sun Dried Tomatoes

Serving: 4 | Prep: 30mins | Cook: 15mins | Ready in:

Ingredients

- 1 cup dehydrated sun-dried tomatoes
- 1 1/2 cups water
- 1/2 (10 ounce) package couscous
- 1 teaspoon olive oil
- 3 cloves garlic, pressed
- 1 bunch green onions, chopped
- 1/3 cup fresh basil leaves
- 1/4 cup fresh cilantro, chopped
- 1/2 lemon, juiced
- salt and pepper to taste
- 4 ounces portobello mushroom caps, sliced

Direction

- Transfer the sun-dried tomatoes into a bowl containing one cup of water. Let it soak for 30 minutes until rehydrated. Drain the tomatoes, save the water, and then chop them.
- Mix the reserved sun-dried tomato water with enough water to yield 1 1/2 cups in a medium saucepan. Heat to a boil. Mix in couscous. Cover the pan, take out from the heat source and let it stand for 5 minutes until the liquid has been absorbed. Carefully fluff with a fork.
- Heat olive oil in a skillet and then mix in the green onions, sun-dried tomatoes, and garlic. Cook while stirring for about 5 minutes until the green onions become tender. Stir in the lemon juice, basil, and cilantro. Season with pepper and salt. Stir in mushrooms and continue to cook for 3 to 5 minutes. Mix with the cooked couscous and serve.

Nutrition Information

- Calories: 178 calories;
- Sodium: 300
- Total Carbohydrate: 36.1
- Cholesterol: 0
- Protein: 7.5
- Total Fat: 2

473. Crab Hash With Old Bay & Basil

Serving: 4 | Prep: | Cook: |Ready in:

Ingredients

- 2 tablespoons vegetable or olive oil
- 1 large onion, cut into 1/2-inch dice
- 1 (16 ounce) can crab (preferably claw), picked over
- 1 1/2 pounds starchy potatoes (such as Idaho), cut into 1/2-inch dice
- 2 tablespoons vegetable or olive oil
- 2 tablespoons ketchup
- 1 tablespoon Dijon mustard
- 1/2 teaspoon Old Bay ™ Seasoning
- 2 tablespoons chopped fresh basil (or parsley)
- 2 tablespoons water
- Salt and freshly ground black pepper

Direction

- In a 12-inch nonstick skillet set on low heat, put 2 tablespoons oil (to prevent potatoes from sticking). While heating skillet, ready the crab and onion as instructed above. A few minutes before cooking, change heat to medium-high. Once the oil begins to send up wisps of smoke, place crab and onion; cook for 4-6 minutes, stirring often, until golden brown. In the meantime, dice potatoes and toss with the rest of the oil. Place crab mixture to a bowl then set aside.
- Place potatoes to empty skillet; cook for about 10 minutes, stirring only occasionally so they make a golden-brown crust. While cooking potatoes, combine 2 tablespoons of water, fresh basil, Old Bay ™ Seasoning, mustard, and ketchup. (Recipe can be ready to this point up to 2 hours in advance. Place hot potatoes on a large lipped cookie sheet and spread; then cover once cool. Put back to the skillet to medium-high; put potatoes and re-crisp.)
- Put back the reserved crab mixture to skillet; mix in ketchup mixture, and add pepper and salt to season. Cook for about 5 minutes longer, stirring frequently until hash has nicely browned.

Nutrition Information

- Calories: 360 calories;
- Cholesterol: 62
- Protein: 21.7
- Total Fat: 14.9
- Sodium: 863
- Total Carbohydrate: 36.6

474. Cranberry Almond Biscotti

Serving: 15 | Prep: 30mins | Cook: 50mins |Ready in:

Ingredients

- 2 1/4 cups all-purpose flour
- 1 cup white sugar
- 1 teaspoon baking powder
- 1/2 teaspoon baking soda
- 2 egg whites
- 2 eggs
- 1 tablespoon vanilla extract
- 3/4 cup sliced almonds
- 1 cup sweetened-dried cranberries

Direction

- Heat the oven beforehand to 170°C or 325°F.

- In a medium sized mixing bowl, mix the dry ingredients. In another mixing bowl, whisk almond extract or vanilla, egg whites and eggs together.
- Pour egg mixture to the dry ingredients, stirring just till moist, with an electric mixer on medium speed. Put almonds and dried cranberries in then thoroughly mix.
- Divide the batter into 2 parts on a floured surface then pat each part into a log with a size of approximately 1 1/2 inch thick and 14 inches long. Put on a cookie sheet. Bake until firm or for 30 minutes. Allow it to cool until cool enough to handle or for about 10 minutes by putting on a wire rack.
- Slice the biscotti diagonally into half inch slices. Turn the temperature of the oven down to 150°C or 300°F. Put the sliced biscotti on a cookie sheet on an upright position, leaving about 1 inch space apart. Bake for another 20 minutes. Allow to cool and keep in a container with a loose cover.

Nutrition Information

- Calories: 189 calories;
- Total Fat: 3.2
- Sodium: 92
- Total Carbohydrate: 35.5
- Cholesterol: 25
- Protein: 4.2

475. Cranberry Pistachio Biscotti

Serving: 36 | Prep: 25mins | Cook: 45mins | Ready in:

Ingredients

- 1/4 cup light olive oil
- 3/4 cup white sugar
- 2 teaspoons vanilla extract
- 1/2 teaspoon almond extract
- 2 eggs
- 1 3/4 cups all-purpose flour
- 1/4 teaspoon salt
- 1 teaspoon baking powder
- 1/2 cup dried cranberries
- 1 1/2 cups pistachio nuts

Direction

- Preheat the oven to 150°C or 300°Fahrenheit.
- Combine sugar and oil together in a big bowl until thoroughly blended. Stir in almond extracts and vanilla; whisk in eggs. Mix baking powder, salt, and flour; whisk gradually into the egg mixture. Use your hands to fold in nuts and cranberries.
- Halve the dough. On a cookie sheet lined with parchment paper, shape two 12x2-in logs. To easily handle the sticky dough, dampen your hands with cold water.
- Bake in the preheated oven for 35 minutes until the logs are pale brown; take them out of the oven. Set aside for 10 minutes to cool. Lower the oven's heat to 135°C or 275°Fahrenheit.
- Diagonally slice the logs into 3/4-in thick portions; place on their sides on a parchment-covered cookie sheet. Bake for 8-10 minutes until dry; completely cool.

Nutrition Information

- Calories: 92 calories;
- Protein: 2.1
- Total Fat: 4.3
- Sodium: 55
- Total Carbohydrate: 11.7
- Cholesterol: 10

476. Crazy Crust Apple Pie

Serving: 8 | Prep: 15mins | Cook: 45mins | Ready in:

Ingredients

- 1 cup all-purpose flour
- 2 tablespoons white sugar
- 1 teaspoon baking powder
- 1/2 teaspoon salt
- 3/4 cup water
- 2/3 cup shortening
- 1 egg
- 1 (21 ounce) can apple pie filling
- 1 tablespoon lemon juice
- 1/2 teaspoon apple pie spice

Direction

- Set an oven to preheat to 220°C (425°F).
- Mix together the salt, baking powder, sugar and flour in a medium mixing bowl. Stir well, then add egg, shortening and water. Mix on low speed until the ingredients are blended and beat for 2 minutes on medium speed, then spread it into the pie pan.
- Combine the apple pie spice, lemon juice and pie filling in a medium bowl. Spread it on top of the crust but don't stir.
- Let it bake for 40-45 minutes in the preheated oven until the crust turns brown.

Nutrition Information

- Calories: 308 calories;
- Total Fat: 17.9
- Sodium: 249
- Total Carbohydrate: 35
- Cholesterol: 33
- Protein: 2.5

477. Creamy Coconut Carbonara (Without Milk!)

Serving: 2 | Prep: 20mins | Cook: 20mins | Ready in:

Ingredients

- 4 ounces fettuccine pasta
- 1 tablespoon vegetable oil
- 2 onions, coarsely chopped, or to taste
- 1 tablespoon minced garlic
- 1 cup coconut milk, divided
- 1/2 cup fresh oyster mushrooms, diced small
- 1/3 cup thinly sliced red bell pepper
- 1/3 cup thinly sliced green bell pepper
- salt and ground black pepper to taste
- 2 spring onions, sliced, or more to taste
- 1 tablespoon chopped fresh basil

Direction

- Put big pot of lightly salted water on rolling boil. Mix fettuccine in and boil again. Cook on medium heat for 8 minutest till tender yet firm to bite; drain.
- Heat oil in big saucepan on high heat. Add garlic and onion; cook for 2-4 minutes till slightly browned, constantly mixing. Add green and red bell pepper, oyster mushrooms and 1/2 cup coconut milk. Mix and cook for 3-5 minutes till just tender.
- Mix leftover 1/2 cup coconut milk and fettuccine into saucepan; season with pepper and salt. Mix basil and spring onions in. Cook for 2-3 minutes longer till sauce coats fettuccine and is creamy, uncovered.

Nutrition Information

- Calories: 601 calories;
- Total Fat: 32.6
- Sodium: 112
- Total Carbohydrate: 70.4
- Cholesterol: 0
- Protein: 13.7

478. Crispy Vegetable Pakoras

Serving: 6 | Prep: 15mins | Cook: 10mins | Ready in:

Ingredients

- 1 cup chickpea flour

- 1/2 teaspoon ground coriander
- 1 teaspoon salt
- 1/2 teaspoon ground turmeric
- 1/2 teaspoon chili powder
- 1/2 teaspoon garam masala
- 2 cloves garlic, crushed
- 3/4 cup water
- 1 quart oil for deep frying
- 1/2 head cauliflower florets
- 2 onions, sliced into rings

Direction

- Sift chickpea flour into a medium mixing bowl. Stir in garlic, garam masala, chili powder, turmeric, salt, and coriander.
- Create a well in the center of the flour. Slowly pour water into the well and mix until a thick and smooth batter forms.
- In a large heavy saucepan, heat oil to 375°F (190°C) over medium-high heat.
- Coat onions and cauliflower in the batter and fry in small batches for about 4 to 5 minutes until golden brown. Transfer to paper towels to drain before serving.

Nutrition Information

- Calories: 217 calories;
- Sodium: 406
- Total Carbohydrate: 15.9
- Cholesterol: 0
- Protein: 4.6
- Total Fat: 15.9

479. Crust For Veggie Pot Pie

Serving: 8 | Prep: | Cook: | Ready in:

Ingredients

- 2 cups all-purpose flour
- 1 teaspoon salt
- 2/3 cup shortening
- 8 tablespoons ice water

Direction

- Start preheating the oven to 220°C (425°F).
- Use a pastry blender to combine vegetable shortening with 2 cups of flour and salt. Stir in 6-8 tbsp. of ice water and mix until the mixture forms a ball. Split the ball in half.
- Roll 1 half of the ball to fit the sides and bottom of an 11x7-inch baking dish with a rolling pin. Roll out the other half to shape the top crust.
- You can use this pie crust directly with your favorite pie dish.

Nutrition Information

- Calories: 265 calories;
- Sodium: 292
- Total Carbohydrate: 23.8
- Cholesterol: 0
- Protein: 3.2
- Total Fat: 17.4

480. Cuban Beans And Rice

Serving: 6 | Prep: 10mins | Cook: 50mins | Ready in:

Ingredients

- 1 tablespoon olive oil
- 1 cup chopped onion
- 1 green bell pepper, chopped
- 2 cloves garlic, minced
- 1 teaspoon salt
- 4 tablespoons tomato paste
- 1 (15.25 ounce) can kidney beans, drained with liquid reserved
- 1 cup uncooked white rice

Direction

- In a large saucepan, warm the oil over medium heat. Cook garlic, bell pepper, and

onion until the onion is translucent. Stir in tomato paste and salt. Adjust the heat to low and simmer for 2 minutes. Mix in rice and beans.
- Transfer its liquid into a large measuring cup and add enough water until the cup reads a volume of 2 1/2 cup. Pour it back to the beans and allow it to cook covered. Cook for 45-50 minutes over low heat until the rice is cooked and the liquid is absorbed.

Nutrition Information

- Calories: 258 calories;
- Protein: 7.3
- Total Fat: 3.2
- Sodium: 750
- Total Carbohydrate: 49.3
- Cholesterol: 2

481. Curried Beef A La Tim

Serving: 4 | Prep: 10mins | Cook: 35mins | Ready in:

Ingredients

- 2 tablespoons vegetable oil
- 1 pound stew beef, cubed
- 1 1/2 teaspoons curry powder
- 1/2 teaspoon salt
- 1/2 teaspoon ground black pepper
- 2 tablespoons tomato paste
- 1/4 cup water
- 1 onion, chopped
- 2 stalks celery, chopped
- 1/2 cup raisins
- 1 apple - peeled, cored, and chopped

Direction

- Heat the oil in a large skillet over medium heat. Place the meat in the hot oil and sauté until well browned on all sides. Sprinkle the curry powder, salt, and ground black pepper over the meat and stir well.
- Beat water and tomato paste together in a small bowl, then mix the mixture into the skillet. Stir in raisins, celery, and onion, turn down the heat to low and simmer until the beef becomes tender, half an hour.
- Mix the apple into the skillet and simmer until the sauce becomes thick and the apple becomes tender, 5 minutes longer.

Nutrition Information

- Calories: 393 calories;
- Total Carbohydrate: 24.4
- Cholesterol: 73
- Protein: 24.5
- Total Fat: 22.5
- Sodium: 437

482. Curried Mango Chicken

Serving: 6 | Prep: 15mins | Cook: 20mins | Ready in:

Ingredients

- 1 tablespoon butter
- 1 onion, chopped
- 3 cloves garlic, minced
- 2 pounds skinless, boneless chicken breast meat - cut into bite-size pieces
- 3 tablespoons curry paste
- 1/2 cup mango chutney
- 1 (28 ounce) can diced tomatoes, drained

Direction

- In a skillet, melt the butter over a medium-high heat. Sauté the onions and the garlic for 2 to 3 minutes or until onions become translucent. Add in the chicken and allow to cook while stirring for about 30 seconds. Mix in the curry paste until the flavor incorporates the chicken. Pour in the tomatoes as well as the chutney, then cook for 10 more minutes or until chicken breasts center is no longer pink and the juices run clear.

Nutrition Information

- Calories: 261 calories;
- Total Fat: 5.7
- Sodium: 443
- Total Carbohydrate: 16.5
- Cholesterol: 91
- Protein: 33.1

483. Curried Peas

Serving: 4 | Prep: 10mins | Cook: 20mins | Ready in:

Ingredients

- 4 teaspoons coconut milk
- 1 teaspoon chili powder
- 1 1/2 teaspoons ground coriander seed
- 1 pinch ground turmeric
- salt to taste
- 2 teaspoons ginger oil
- 1 onion, chopped
- 1 small cinnamon stick
- 1/2 teaspoon cumin seeds
- 4 tomatoes, chopped
- 1 pound fresh pea pods, shelled

Direction

- Combine the salt, turmeric, coriander, chili powder and coconut milk in a small bowl.
- Heat the oil in a medium sauté pan on medium heat, then add cumin seeds, cinnamon stick and onion and sauté until the onions become tender.
- Stir in coconut milk mixture, peas and tomatoes. Lower the heat and let it simmer until the peas become tender.

484. Curried Quinoa

Serving: 2 | Prep: 5mins | Cook: 35mins | Ready in:

Ingredients

- 2 tablespoons olive oil, or as needed
- 1 small onion, diced
- 2 cloves garlic, minced
- 1 cup quinoa
- 2 cups chicken broth
- 1 tablespoon curry powder, or to taste
- 1 tablespoon ancho chile powder
- salt and pepper to taste

Direction

- In a big skillet, heat the oil on medium heat; add garlic and onion and cook and stir for 2 minutes. Add quinoa and cook and stir for about 5 minutes until it becomes a bit toasted.
- Pour the broth into the pan, then boil. Lower the heat and add the chile powders and curry. Put cover on and let simmer for about 25 minutes, until it becomes tender. Season pepper and salt to taste.

Nutrition Information

- Calories: 473 calories;
- Sodium: 48
- Total Carbohydrate: 62.8
- Cholesterol: 0
- Protein: 13.5
- Total Fat: 19.8

485. Dairy Free Cinnamon Streusel Coffee Cake

Serving: 8 | Prep: 10mins | Cook: 25mins | Ready in:

Ingredients

- 1/3 cup dairy free pancake mix (such as Bisquick®)
- 1/3 cup packed brown sugar
- 1/2 teaspoon ground cinnamon
- 3 tablespoons unsalted margarine
- 2 cups dairy free pancake mix (such as Bisquick®)
- 2/3 cup soy milk
- 2 tablespoons white sugar
- 1 egg, lightly beaten

Direction

- Preheat the oven to 190 ° C or 375 ° F. Oil a square, 8-inch baking pan and put aside.
- To prepare streusel, mix in mixing bowl with the brown sugar, cinnamon and 1/3 cup of pancake mix. Mash in margarine till mixture becomes crumbly. You may also do this using food processor: pulse the mixture to incorporate, about twice to thrice.
- Mix egg, sugar, soy milk and 2 cups of pancake mix barely till blended. Scatter to prepped pan. Scatter cinnamon streusel on top.
- Bake for 20 to 25 minutes in prepped oven, or till an inserted toothpick in the middle of cake gets out clean. Cool down prior to serving.

Nutrition Information

- Calories: 242 calories;
- Total Fat: 5.6
- Sodium: 631
- Total Carbohydrate: 43.4
- Cholesterol: 20
- Protein: 4.8

486. Dairy, Nut, And Gluten Free Green Bean Casserole

Serving: 10 | Prep: 20mins | Cook: 57mins | Ready in:

Ingredients

- 2 tablespoons olive oil
- 12 small shallots, thinly sliced, divided
- 1 (8 ounce) package thinly sliced baby bella mushrooms
- 6 cloves garlic, minced
- 1/4 cup dried porcini mushrooms, or to taste
- 1 1/2 cups white wine
- 1 teaspoon salt
- 2 cups chicken broth
- 1 (14 ounce) can coconut milk
- 3 (12 ounce) packages fresh green beans, trimmed
- 3 tablespoons cold water
- 3 tablespoons cornstarch
- salt and ground black pepper to taste
- 2 tablespoons gluten-free all-purpose flour, or to taste
- 1/4 cup olive oil

Direction

- Set the oven to 175°C or 350°F.
- In a big saucepan or Dutch oven, heat 2 tbsp. olive oil on medium heat. Put in garlic, mushrooms and 6 shallots, then cook and stir for around 5 minutes, until shallots and garlic are softened. Put in salt and white wine. Allow to simmer for 2-4 minutes, until flavors begin to meld. Put in coconut milk and chicken broth, then stir to mix. Put in green beans and bring the mixture to a boil.
- In a bowl, combine cornstarch and water, then add the mixture into the saucepan. Cook and stir for 3-5 minutes, until the mixture is thickened. Season with pepper and salt, then transfer the mixture into a 13"x9" baking dish.
- Bake for 35-40 minutes until it is nearly set.
- In a bowl, toss together gluten-free flour and the remaining 6 shallots to coat well.
- In a skillet, heat 1/4 cup olive oil on medium heat, then put in coated shallots, cook and stir for 4-5 minutes, until golden. Turn out the fried shallots to a paper towel to drain, then sprinkle on top of the casserole.
- Preheat the oven's broiler and place an oven rack approximately 6 inches from the source of

heat. Bring the casserole back to the oven and broil for 3-5 minutes, until shallots are crispy.

Nutrition Information

- Calories: 239 calories;
- Total Fat: 14.3
- Sodium: 500
- Total Carbohydrate: 19.6
- Cholesterol: 1
- Protein: 5.2

487. Dairy Free Keto And Vegan Chocolate Fat Bombs

Serving: 16 | Prep: 5mins | Cook: |Ready in:

Ingredients

- 1/2 cup melted coconut oil
- 1/2 cup almond butter
- 1/2 cup unsweetened cocoa powder

Direction

- In a food processor, blend the cocoa powder, almond butter and coconut oil for about 2 minutes, until it becomes creamy. Fill the mini muffin cups with the mixture and let it chill in the refrigerator for approximately 30 minutes, until set.

Nutrition Information

- Calories: 116 calories;
- Total Carbohydrate: 3.1
- Cholesterol: 0
- Protein: 1.7
- Total Fat: 12
- Sodium: 36

488. Dairy Free Persimmon Pecan Cookies

Serving: 30 | Prep: 15mins | Cook: 15mins | Ready in:

Ingredients

- 1 teaspoon baking soda
- 4 very ripe persimmons, peeled and pureed
- 2 cups whole wheat flour
- 1 tablespoon ground cinnamon
- 1 teaspoon ground nutmeg
- 1/2 teaspoon ground cloves
- 1/2 teaspoon salt
- 1/2 cup margarine
- 1/2 cup honey
- 1/2 cup agave nectar
- 1/4 cup applesauce
- 1 cup chopped dates
- 1 cup chopped pecans
- 1/4 teaspoon lemon zest

Direction

- Heat oven to 175 degrees C or 350 degrees F. Line parchment paper on baking sheets.
- In the persimmon puree, mix baking soda into it in a small bowl, put aside.
- Mix salt, cloves, nutmeg, cinnamon, and flour in a bowl.
- Beat applesauce, agave nectar, honey, and margarine in a big bowl. Slowly beat persimmon mixture in the margarine mixture. Slowly mix flour mixture in the persimmon mixture. Fold lemon zest, pecans, and dates in the mixture.
- Drop spoonsful of cookie dough on prepared baking sheets.
- Bake in the oven for 15-17n minutes until the edges become golden. Let cookies cool for a minute on the baking sheet then cool completely on a wire rack.

Nutrition Information

- Calories: 135 calories;
- Sodium: 117

- Total Carbohydrate: 21.3
- Cholesterol: 0
- Protein: 1.7
- Total Fat: 5.8

489. Dairy Free Vanilla Brownies

Serving: 6 | Prep: 10mins | Cook: 20mins | Ready in:

Ingredients

- 2 eggs, beaten
- 1/4 cup vegetable oil
- 1 tablespoon vanilla extract
- 1 cup barley flour
- 3/4 cup white sugar
- 2 teaspoons baking powder
- 3/4 teaspoon salt

Direction

- Set oven to preheat at 200°C (400°F). Prepare a small baking dish by greasing it.
- Beat together vanilla extract, vegetable oil, and eggs in a large bowl. Mix together salt, baking powder, sugar, and barley flour in another bowl; put into the eggs mixture and mix till smooth. Transfer batter to the prepared baking dish.
- Bake for 20 to 30 minutes in preheated oven until set in the center and brown on top.

Nutrition Information

- Calories: 293 calories;
- Sodium: 478
- Total Carbohydrate: 44.2
- Cholesterol: 62
- Protein: 4.7
- Total Fat: 11.1

490. Dairy Free, Gluten Free Pumpkin Bars

Serving: 24 | Prep: 15mins | Cook: 30mins | Ready in:

Ingredients

- 1 cup rice flour
- 3/4 cup soy flour
- 1/4 cup tapioca starch
- 2 teaspoons ground cinnamon
- 1 teaspoon baking soda
- 1 teaspoon baking powder
- 3/4 teaspoon ground nutmeg
- 1/2 teaspoon ground ginger
- 1/2 cup dairy-free margarine, softened
- 2 cups packed brown sugar
- 3 eggs, beaten
- 1 (15 ounce) can pumpkin puree
- 2 teaspoons vanilla extract

Direction

- Pre heat the oven to 175 degrees C (350 degrees F). Grease the 13x9-in. baking plate.
- Whisk together the ginger, nutmeg, baking powder, baking soda, cinnamon, tapioca starch, soy flour and rice flour in a bowl.
- Whip the margarine in a big bowl using the electric mixer till creamy. Whip the brown sugar into margarine till incorporated and mixture becomes lighter in color. Put in the eggs, one at a time, whipping completely each egg into mixture prior to putting in next one; put in the vanilla and pumpkin along with the third egg. Slowly blend dry mixture into wet mixture till forming the batter; add to prepped baking plate.
- Bake in preheated oven for roughly half an hour or till the toothpick inserted in middle runs out clean.

Nutrition Information

- Calories: 161 calories;
- Sodium: 174
- Total Carbohydrate: 27.2

- Cholesterol: 23
- Protein: 2.4
- Total Fat: 5.1

491. Dark Choco Bliss

Serving: 8 | Prep: 10mins | Cook: 10mins | Ready in:

Ingredients

- 1/3 cup small pearl tapioca
- 2 tablespoons chia seeds
- 1 1/2 cups water
- 4 cups coconut milk
- 1 cup palm sugar
- 1/2 cup cocoa powder
- 3 tablespoons arrowroot powder
- 1/2 teaspoon salt
- 1 teaspoon vanilla extract

Direction

- In a pot, mix together chia seeds and tapioca, then fill with water; allow to soak for 60 minutes minimum until gelatinous and thick.
- Blend salt, arrowroot powder, cocoa powder, palm sugar and coconut milk with tapioca mixture; cook, stirring, for 10-15 minutes on medium heat until it reaches desired consistency. Turn off the heat and whisk vanilla into pudding.

Nutrition Information

- Calories: 347 calories;
- Total Fat: 25.4
- Sodium: 168
- Total Carbohydrate: 32.9
- Cholesterol: 0
- Protein: 3.7

492. Date Nut And Brown Sugar Bars

Serving: 16 | Prep: 15mins | Cook: 45mins | Ready in:

Ingredients

- 2/3 cup unbleached all-purpose flour
- 2/3 cup packed brown sugar
- 1/4 cup finely chopped walnuts
- 1 teaspoon ground cinnamon
- 1/4 teaspoon ground cardamom
- 1/4 teaspoon salt
- 1/2 teaspoon baking powder
- 1 cup dates, pitted and chopped
- 2 eggs, beaten

Direction

- Preheat an oven to 180°C/3560°F; oil the 8-in. square baking pan lightly.
- Mix dates, baking powder, salt, cardamom, cinnamon, chopped walnuts, brown sugar and flour well.
- Add eggs; mix till dry ingredients get moist.
- Put batter into prepped pan; in preheated oven, bake for 25 minutes till inserted toothpick in middle exits clean. Slightly cool then cut to squares or bars.

Nutrition Information

- Calories: 101 calories;
- Sodium: 63
- Total Carbohydrate: 20.3
- Cholesterol: 23
- Protein: 1.8
- Total Fat: 1.9

493. Dave's Ultimate Guacamole

Serving: 8 | Prep: 25mins | Cook: | Ready in:

Ingredients

- 4 avocados - peeled, pitted and sliced
- 1/2 cup salsa
- 1/4 tablespoon garlic powder
- 1/2 teaspoon hot pepper sauce
- 1 pinch salt (optional)

Direction

- Get a food processor and put in the chopped avocados. Turn the processor on to medium and gently stir in the salsa until texture becomes lumpy. Mix in the hot sauce and garlic powder. Keep on blending until becomes smooth but not watery. Add salt to taste.

Nutrition Information

- Calories: 166 calories;
- Total Fat: 14.8
- Sodium: 106
- Total Carbohydrate: 9.8
- Cholesterol: 0
- Protein: 2.3

494. Dee's Mexican Rice

Serving: 4 | Prep: 10mins | Cook: 10mins | Ready in:

Ingredients

- 1 tablespoon vegetable oil
- 1 teaspoon ground turmeric
- 1 teaspoon garlic powder
- 1/2 teaspoon ground cumin
- 1/2 teaspoon ground coriander seed
- 2 teaspoons paprika
- 1 pinch red pepper flakes
- 1 pinch cayenne pepper
- 3 green onions
- 1 green bell pepper, chopped
- 1 cup pre-cooked corn kernels
- 2 small tomatoes, diced
- 1/4 cup ketchup
- 2 cups cooked rice
- salt to taste

Direction

- In a wok-style pan, heat oil together with cayenne pepper, chili flakes, paprika, coriander, cumin, garlic powder and turmeric. Put in green peppers and green onions, then sauté about 1-2 minutes on moderately high heat.
- Put in tomatoes and corn, then sauté until tomatoes draw out their juices. Put in ketchup and stir until blended.
- Put in rice and stir until heated thoroughly, then season to taste with salt.

Nutrition Information

- Calories: 209 calories;
- Total Carbohydrate: 39.6
- Cholesterol: 0
- Protein: 4.8
- Total Fat: 4.6
- Sodium: 296

495. Deep Fried Oysters

Serving: 4 | Prep: 10mins | Cook: 10mins | Ready in:

Ingredients

- 2 quarts vegetable oil for deep frying
- 1/2 cup all-purpose flour
- 1 teaspoon salt
- 1/2 teaspoon ground black pepper
- 12 ounces shucked oysters, drained
- 2 eggs, lightly beaten
- 3/4 cup fine bread crumbs

Direction

- Heat a deep fryer to 190°C/375°F.

- Mix black pepper, salt and flour; dredge oysters into flour mixture, dip into egg then roll in breadcrumbs.
- Slide oysters carefully in hot oil; cook for about 2 minutes, 5 at a time, till golden brown. Briefly drain over paper towels. Serve hot.

Nutrition Information

- Calories: 577 calories;
- Total Fat: 47.9
- Sodium: 776
- Total Carbohydrate: 27.4
- Cholesterol: 100
- Protein: 10

496. Delicious Vegan Gnocchi

Serving: 4 | Prep: 10mins | Cook: 45mins | Ready in:

Ingredients

- 2 pounds potatoes
- 3 cups whole wheat flour
- salt to taste
- 2 cloves garlic, finely chopped
- 2 (10.75 ounce) cans tomato puree
- 1 green onion, chopped
- 4 cherry tomatoes
- 2 sun-dried tomatoes
- 1 teaspoon paprika
- 1 teaspoon dried oregano
- 1 teaspoon dried basil
- 3/4 teaspoon salt
- 1 dash ground black pepper to taste

Direction

- In a big pot, put the potatoes and pour water to cover, then boil. Turn down the heat to medium-low and let it simmer for around 30 minutes until it becomes tender, then drain.
- Allow the potatoes to cool shortly for 5-10 minutes. In a bowl, peel and put the potatoes, then mash until it becomes smooth. Add the flour and knead it just until the dough becomes smooth, but do not overwork the potatoes. Sprinkle with salt to season. Use a towel to cover the bowl and allow the dough to rest for around 10 minutes.
- Split the dough into 4 portions. Roll each into a long rope, approximately one inch in diameter. Slice each rope into 1-inch-long pieces, then use a fork or your thumb to press into the center of each piece to form the gnocchi.
- Boil a big pot of water. Add the gnocchi and let them boil for 2-3 minutes, until they floats to the top. Move the cooked gnocchi to a plate or bowl.
- Heat a nonstick saucepan on medium heat, then add the garlic and let it cook for around 2 minutes, until it becomes toasted and light brown in color. Add the green onion and tomato puree and simmer for around 5 minutes, until it turns a bit thick. Add the pepper, 3/4 tsp salt, basil, oregano, paprika, sun-dried tomatoes and cherry tomatoes. Allow the sauce to simmer for around 10 more minutes, until the flavors combine. Serve it with the gnocchi.

Nutrition Information

- Calories: 585 calories;
- Total Fat: 2.8
- Sodium: 1393
- Total Carbohydrate: 128.9
- Cholesterol: 0
- Protein: 21.9

497. Deliciously Organic Carrot Spread

Serving: 10 | Prep: 15mins | Cook: 22mins | Ready in:

Ingredients

- 1 tablespoon canola oil
- 2 1/2 cups chopped carrots
- 3/4 cup chopped onion
- 1/2 cup filtered or spring water
- 1/4 cup soy milk
- 1 tablespoon miso paste
- 1/2 cup roasted cashews
- 3/4 teaspoon fine sea salt
- 1 1/2 tablespoons real maple syrup
- 1 1/2 teaspoons Chinese five-spice powder

Direction

- In a large saucepan on medium-high heat, heat canola oil. Cook onion and carrots, stirring occasionally, till the onions turn translucent and the carrots become tender. Do not brown the onions. Include in water; boil the mixture. Simmer with a cover for 15 minutes; set aside to cool.
- Transfer into a food processor or a blender when the mixture is cool enough to process safely. Include in Chinese five-spice powder, maple syrup, salt, cashew, miso paste and soy milk. Blend till smooth. Refrigerate with a cover till ready to use.

Nutrition Information

- Calories: 84 calories;
- Protein: 1.9
- Total Fat: 4.9
- Sodium: 291
- Total Carbohydrate: 9.2
- Cholesterol: 0

498. Depression Cake I

Serving: 24 | Prep: | Cook: | Ready in:

Ingredients

- 1 cup shortening
- 2 cups water
- 2 cups raisins
- 1 teaspoon ground cinnamon
- 1 teaspoon ground nutmeg
- 1 teaspoon ground allspice
- 1/2 teaspoon ground cloves
- 2 cups white sugar
- 3 cups all-purpose flour
- 1 teaspoon baking soda

Direction

- Mix together the sugar, cloves, allspice, nutmeg, cinnamon, raisins, water and shortening in a saucepan. Let it simmer for 10 minutes, then take it out of the heat and allow it to stand until cool.
- Set an oven to preheat to 175°C (350°F), then grease a 9x13-inch baking pan.
- Stir the baking soda and flour into the cooled raisin mixture and stir until just blended. Pour the batter into the prepped pan.
- Let it bake for 45 minutes at 175°C (350°F).

Nutrition Information

- Calories: 234 calories;
- Protein: 2
- Total Fat: 8.8
- Sodium: 55
- Total Carbohydrate: 38.4
- Cholesterol: 0

499. Dilled Green Beans

Serving: 5 | Prep: | Cook: | Ready in:

Ingredients

- 2 quarts water
- 2 pounds fresh green beans, washed and trimmed
- 1 teaspoon salt
- 2 teaspoons mustard seed
- 2 teaspoons dried dill weed

- 1 teaspoon red pepper flakes
- 1 teaspoon dill seed
- 4 cloves garlic, minced
- 2 cups distilled white vinegar
- 2/3 cup white sugar
- 2 cups water

Direction

- Boil 2 quarts of water. Pour in green beans and boil just until tender, about 5 minutes. Lightly soak the beans in cold water to maintain color, drain thoroughly.
- Combine garlic, dill seed, chiles, dill weed, mustard seed, and salt in a large mixing bowl, mix well. Stir in cooled beans.
- Bring 2 cups water, vinegar, salt, and sugar (to taste) in a small saucepan to a boil. Pour over beans and spice mixture. Stir to combine.
- Transfer the mixture into an airtight container and put into the fridge to chill at least overnight before serving. Keeping beans marinated 1-week in advance in refrigerator gives the best flavor.

Nutrition Information

- Calories: 176 calories;
- Total Carbohydrate: 41.7
- Cholesterol: 0
- Protein: 4
- Total Fat: 0.8
- Sodium: 489

500. Dirty Rice

Serving: 6 | Prep: 20mins | Cook: 25mins | Ready in:

Ingredients

- 2 tablespoons olive oil
- 3 cloves garlic, minced
- 1 cup chopped onion
- 1 green bell pepper, chopped
- 1 tablespoon chili powder
- 2 teaspoons annatto or achiote powder (optional)
- 1/4 teaspoon crushed red pepper
- 1 teaspoon ground cumin
- 1/4 teaspoon ground cinnamon
- 1 1/3 cups uncooked white rice
- 2 3/4 cups water
- 1 teaspoon salt
- 3 roma (plum) tomatoes, chopped
- 1 1/3 cups whole corn kernels, blanched
- 1 cup black beans, cooked and drained
- 1/4 cup toasted pine nuts
- freshly ground black pepper
- 1 red onion, thinly sliced
- 1 tablespoon fresh lime juice
- 2 tablespoons chopped fresh cilantro
- 1 lime, cut into wedges
- 2 teaspoons annatto powder

Direction

- Heat 1 tbsp. olive oil in a heavy saucepan on medium heat. Add chopped onions and garlic. Sauté, frequently stir, for 5 minutes. Mix in cinnamon, cumin, chili flakes, ground annatto, chili powder and bell pepper. Sauté the mixture for 2 minutes.
- Put rice in the saucepan. Mix to coat. Add 1 tsp. salt and water. Boil rice on high heat. Cover pan. Turn heat down to low. Simmer rice for 25 minutes.
- When rice is cooked, mix in pine nuts, black beans, corn and tomatoes. Mix in lime juice, pepper and salt. Spoon onto plates when mixture heats through. Put cilantro and sliced red onion on top. Serve with 1-2 lime wedges on each plate to squeeze it on the rice.

Nutrition Information

- Calories: 409 calories;
- Total Carbohydrate: 71.4
- Cholesterol: 0
- Protein: 13.7
- Total Fat: 9

- Sodium: 421

501. Do It Yourself Salmon Poke Bowls

Serving: 4 | Prep: 25mins | Cook: |Ready in:

Ingredients

- 4 cups cooked rice
- 4 tablespoons soy sauce
- 4 teaspoons rice vinegar
- 4 teaspoons sesame oil
- 1/4 teaspoon chile oil (optional)
- 3/4 pound sashimi-grade salmon, cut into small cubes
- Toppings:
- 1 avocado, sliced, or to taste
- 1 red bell pepper, sliced, or more to taste
- 1/4 cup shelled edamame, or more to taste
- 4 sheets dried seaweed, cut into strips, or to taste
- 1 tablespoon pickled ginger, or to taste
- 1 tablespoon furikake (Japanese nori seasoning), or to taste
- 2 tablespoons chopped green onion, or to taste
- 1 tablespoon sesame seeds, or to taste

Direction

- Separate rice into four bowls.
- In a bowl, combine chile oil, sesame oil, soy sauce, and rice vinegar to make the dressing. Combine the salmon together with the dressing. Subdivide into the 4 bowls.
- Add pickled ginger, avocado, furikake seasoning, red bell pepper, seaweed, and edamame on top of the bowls. Stud with a sprinkling of sesame seeds and chopped green onion.

Nutrition Information

- Calories: 535 calories;
- Total Carbohydrate: 59.2
- Cholesterol: 47
- Protein: 26.1
- Total Fat: 20.9
- Sodium: 1080

502. Down Home Baked Beans

Serving: 11 | Prep: 10mins | Cook: 1hours15mins |Ready in:

Ingredients

- 1 pound bacon
- 2 (28 ounce) cans baked beans
- 1 (12 ounce) bottle chili sauce
- 1 large sweet onion, chopped
- 2 cups packed brown sugar

Direction

- Preheat the oven to 175 degrees C (350 degrees F).
- Put the bacon in a large, deep skillet and then let cook over medium-high heat until browned evenly. Drain the bacon, then crumble and reserve.
- Mix together bacon, brown sugar, onion, beans, and chili sauce in a large bowl. Transfer to a 9x13 inch casserole dish.
- Bake for about 45 minutes to 1 hour in the preheated oven.

Nutrition Information

- Calories: 484 calories;
- Total Fat: 19.1
- Sodium: 884
- Total Carbohydrate: 71.6
- Cholesterol: 28
- Protein: 11.8

503. Down South Style Green Beans

Serving: 6 | Prep: 1hours | Cook: 2hours | Ready in:

Ingredients

- 6 cups water
- 1 ham hock
- 2 tablespoons lard or other cooking fat
- 1 teaspoon seasoning salt
- 1/2 teaspoon salt
- 1/2 teaspoon black pepper
- 1/2 teaspoon garlic powder
- 1/2 teaspoon onion powder
- 1 pound fresh green beans - rinsed, trimmed and snapped into bite size pieces

Direction

- In a big pot, mix together lard, ham hock and water on moderately-high heat. Season with onion powder, garlic powder, pepper, salt and seasoning salt, then bring the mixture to a boil. Lower heat to moderately low and put in green beans. Simmer with a cover for 2 hours.

Nutrition Information

- Calories: 152 calories;
- Cholesterol: 27
- Protein: 7.2
- Total Fat: 11.4
- Sodium: 370
- Total Carbohydrate: 6

504. Drip Beef Sandwiches

Serving: 5 | Prep: 20mins | Cook: 7hours | Ready in:

Ingredients

- 5 pounds chuck roast
- 2 cubes beef bouillon
- 2 tablespoons salt
- 2 teaspoons garlic salt
- 2 bay leaves
- 2 tablespoons whole black peppercorns
- 2 teaspoons dried oregano
- 1 1/2 teaspoons dried rosemary

Direction

- In a large pot, put roast and cover with water. Mix in garlic salt, salt and bouillon. In a coffee filter, place rosemary, oregano, peppercorns and bay leaves. Using a rubber band, secure tightly. Put into pot.
- Boil over high heat. Lower the heat to low, close the lid, simmer for 6 to 8 hours. Discard coffee filter and remove. Take the roast out of the pot. Use 2 forks to shred. Save the remaining broth, if desired, for dipping.

Nutrition Information

- Calories: 934 calories;
- Sodium: 4110
- Total Carbohydrate: 2.5
- Cholesterol: 295
- Protein: 87.9
- Total Fat: 61.1

505. Dulcia Domestica

Serving: 4 | Prep: 10mins | Cook: 15mins | Ready in:

Ingredients

- 12 pitted dates
- 1/4 cup chopped, toasted pine nuts
- 3 tablespoons red wine
- 1/8 teaspoon ground black pepper (optional)
- 1/4 cup honey

Direction

- Stuff the chopped nuts on the dates. Insert the nuts into the space left by the pit.
- In a small pan, place the dates and sprinkle pepper on top, if preferred. Add wine, then drizzle honey on top of the dates. Let it cook on medium heat until the skin starts to peel off from the fruit. Move the dates to a serving dish and let it cool a bit prior to serving.

Nutrition Information

- Calories: 192 calories;
- Total Fat: 4.4
- Sodium: 2
- Total Carbohydrate: 37.7
- Cholesterol: 0
- Protein: 2.7

506. Easiest Pot Roast Ever

Serving: 6 | Prep: 10mins | Cook: 5hours | Ready in:

Ingredients

- 3 pounds beef roast
- 6 potatoes
- 1 1/2 cups baby carrots
- 1 yellow onion
- 2 stalks celery
- 3 cubes beef bouillon
- 1/2 cup water

Direction

- Slice the celery, potatoes and onions in big chunky pieces and put it in a slow cooker. Place the roast over the vegetables. Throw in 3 bouillon cubes anywhere on top of the roast and add in water.
- Put the lid on and let the mixture cook on low setting for 6-8 hours or on high setting for 4-5 hours.

Nutrition Information

- Calories: 526 calories;
- Sodium: 547
- Total Carbohydrate: 42.4
- Cholesterol: 103
- Protein: 31.7
- Total Fat: 25.3

507. Easy Breaded Shrimp

Serving: 8 | Prep: 5mins | Cook: 10mins | Ready in:

Ingredients

- 1 quart vegetable oil for frying
- 4 cups shrimp, peeled and deveined
- 1 egg, beaten
- 2 cups dry bread crumbs

Direction

- In a large skillet, heat oil. Dip the shrimp into egg and transfer them to bread crumbs to coat. Add shrimp to hot oil and fry.

Nutrition Information

- Calories: 281 calories;
- Protein: 17.4
- Total Fat: 14.2
- Sodium: 301
- Total Carbohydrate: 20.1
- Cholesterol: 121

508. Easy Bruschetta

Serving: 16 | Prep: 10mins | Cook: 5mins | Ready in:

Ingredients

- 1 French baguette, cut into 1/2 inch thick circles
- 8 plum tomatoes, diced

- 1 cup chopped fresh basil
- 1/2 red onion, minced
- freshly ground black pepper
- 3 cloves garlic

Direction

- Heat the oven to 200°C or 400°F.
- In one small mixing bowl, mix basil, red onion and tomato; combine thoroughly. Add freshly ground black pepper to season. Put aside.
- On baking sheet, place the bread. Put inside the oven, and bake for about 5 minutes, till nicely toasted.
- Take bread out of oven, and turn on one big serving platter. Cool bread for 3 to 5 minutes. Rub top of every toast slice with garlic; toast must glisten with garlic. Scoop mixture of tomato liberally on every slice to serve.

Nutrition Information

- Calories: 90 calories;
- Sodium: 186
- Total Carbohydrate: 17.8
- Cholesterol: 0
- Protein: 3.8
- Total Fat: 0.6

509. Easy Chocolate Tofu Pie

Serving: 8 | Prep: 15mins | Cook: 25mins | Ready in:

Ingredients

- 1 pound silken tofu
- 1/2 cup unsweetened cocoa powder
- 1 cup white sugar
- 1 tablespoon vanilla extract
- 1/2 teaspoon cider vinegar
- 1 (9 inch) prepared graham cracker crust

Direction

- Set an oven to preheat to 190°C (375°F).
- In a food processor or an electric mixer, blend the tofu until it becomes smooth. Blend in vinegar, vanilla, sugar and cocoa, then pour it into the prepped crust.
- Let it bake for 25 minutes in the preheated oven.
- Let it chill in the fridge for an hour prior to serving.

Nutrition Information

- Calories: 293 calories;
- Total Fat: 9.7
- Sodium: 175
- Total Carbohydrate: 49.2
- Cholesterol: 0
- Protein: 5

510. Easy Creamy Vegan Macaroni And Cheese

Serving: 8 | Prep: 10mins | Cook: 33mins | Ready in:

Ingredients

- 1 (8 ounce) package elbow macaroni
- 2/3 cup rice bran oil, divided
- 2 cups unsweetened soy milk
- 1 cup nutritional yeast
- 4 cloves garlic, minced
- 2 teaspoons yellow mustard
- 1 teaspoon ground paprika

Direction

- Prepare the oven by preheating to 375°F (190°C). Ready an 8-inch baking dish, greased.
- Add the lightly salted water in a large pot and let it boil. Add elbow macaroni in the boiling water and cook for about 8 minutes, stir occasionally, until tender but firm to the bite. Strain and move to a large bowl. Add 1 tablespoon rice bran oil and toss.

- In a high-powered food processor or blender, mix together paprika, mustard, garlic, nutritional yeast, soy milk and remaining rice bran oil; process until mixture turns creamy and smooth.
- Put soy milk mixture over elbow macaroni in the bowl; toss to mix. Place into the prepared baking dish. Use aluminum foil to cover.
- Place in the preheated oven and bake for about 20 minutes until center is bubbling.

Nutrition Information

- Calories: 349 calories;
- Total Fat: 20.2
- Sodium: 53
- Total Carbohydrate: 30.4
- Cholesterol: 0
- Protein: 13.8

511. Easy Creamy Vegan Mushroom Risotto

Serving: 4 | Prep: 20mins | Cook: 25mins | Ready in:

Ingredients

- 1 onion, chopped
- 2 cloves garlic, minced
- 2 teaspoons herbes de Provence
- 2 1/4 cups vegetable broth, or as needed, divided
- 2 cups white mushrooms, sliced
- 1/2 cup chopped leek
- 1 cup Arborio rice
- 1 cup soy milk
- 1 tablespoon white wine vinegar
- 1 cup frozen peas
- 2 tablespoons lemon juice
- 2 tablespoons nutritional yeast
- 1 teaspoon salt
- 1/2 teaspoon ground black pepper

Direction

- Heat a big saucepan on medium-high heat. Sauté the herbes de Provence, garlic and onion. If the mixture is too dry, add some vegetable broth. Add leeks and mushrooms and let it cook for 3-4 minutes until heated through.
- Pour the rice and the leftover vegetable broth into the mushroom mixture, then add vinegar and soy milk. Allow it to simmer for 15-20 minutes until the liquid has been absorbed, stirring from time to time.
- Stir nutritional yeast, lemon juice and peas into the rice mixture. Let it cook for about 3 minutes until the peas are warmed through. Turn off the heat and sprinkle pepper and salt to season.

Nutrition Information

- Calories: 327 calories;
- Total Fat: 1.9
- Sodium: 921
- Total Carbohydrate: 65.7
- Cholesterol: 0
- Protein: 12.4

512. Easy Grilled Chicken Teriyaki

Serving: 4 | Prep: 15mins | Cook: 15mins | Ready in:

Ingredients

- 4 skinless, boneless chicken breast halves
- 1 cup teriyaki sauce
- 1/4 cup lemon juice
- 2 teaspoons minced fresh garlic
- 2 teaspoons sesame oil

Direction

- In a large resealable plastic bag, place chicken, sesame oil, garlic, lemon juice, and teriyaki

sauce. Seal up the bag and shake to coat. Put in the fridge for 24 hours, flipping every so often.
- Set a grill to high heat to preheat.
- Lightly grease the grill grate. Remove the chicken from the bag and discard any leftover marinade. Grill until the juices run clear when pierced with a fork, 6-8 minutes per side.

Nutrition Information

- Calories: 240 calories;
- Total Fat: 7.5
- Sodium: 691
- Total Carbohydrate: 16.6
- Cholesterol: 67
- Protein: 25.2

513. Easy Guacamole

Serving: 16 | Prep: 10mins | Cook: | Ready in:

Ingredients

- 2 avocados
- 1 small onion, finely chopped
- 1 clove garlic, minced
- 1 ripe tomato, chopped
- 1 lime, juiced
- salt and pepper to taste

Direction

- Prepare a medium size serving bowl and put in the peeled avocados then crush it. Add in the pepper, salt, lime juice, tomato, garlic and onion the mix well. Add salt, pepper and left lime juice to taste. Let it chill for 1 hour to enhance the flavors.

Nutrition Information

- Calories: 45 calories;
- Total Carbohydrate: 3.4
- Cholesterol: 0
- Protein: 0.7
- Total Fat: 3.7
- Sodium: 2

514. Easy Marinated Pork Tenderloin

Serving: 3 | Prep: 10mins | Cook: 45mins | Ready in:

Ingredients

- 1/4 cup olive oil
- 1/4 cup soy sauce
- 1 clove garlic, minced
- 3 tablespoons dijon honey mustard
- salt and ground black pepper to taste
- 2 pounds pork tenderloin

Direction

- In a bowl, mix together pepper, olive oil, salt, soy sauce, mustard, and garlic. In a big ziploc/resealable plastic bag, put in pork loin and the marinade; seal. Refrigerate for at least an hour to marinate before cooking.
- Preheat oven to 175°Celsius or 350°F.
- Move the pork loin to a baking dish, and spread the marinade over the pork loin.
- Cook in the oven for 45-60 minutes until the center of the pork is not pink anymore. An inserted instant-read thermometer in the middle of the pork should register 63°C or 145°F.

Nutrition Information

- Calories: 485 calories;
- Total Carbohydrate: 9
- Cholesterol: 169
- Protein: 55.5
- Total Fat: 24.7
- Sodium: 1492

515. Easy Masoor Daal

Serving: 4 | Prep: 5mins | Cook: 30mins |Ready in:

Ingredients

- 1 cup red lentils
- 1 slice ginger, 1 inch piece, peeled
- 1/4 teaspoon ground turmeric
- 1 teaspoon salt
- 1/2 teaspoon cayenne pepper, or to taste
- 4 teaspoons vegetable oil
- 4 teaspoons dried minced onion
- 1 teaspoon cumin seeds

Direction

- Wash the lentils well and transfer to a medium saucepan with the turmeric, ginger, cayenne pepper and salt. Fill with about an inch of water enough to cover the lentils and let the mixture boil. Scoop off any foam on top of the lentils. Lessen the heat and let it simmer while occasionally stirring until beans becomes soupy and tender.
- Meanwhile, in a microwavable dish, mix together the oil, cumin seeds and dried onion. Set the microwave on high for 45 seconds up to 1 minute until the onions are browned yet avoiding them to get burnt. Mix in the lentil mixture.

Nutrition Information

- Calories: 185 calories;
- Protein: 11.1
- Total Fat: 5.2
- Sodium: 868
- Total Carbohydrate: 25
- Cholesterol: 0

516. Easy Mexican Rice

Serving: 4 | Prep: 5mins | Cook: 1hours |Ready in:

Ingredients

- 1 1/2 cups uncooked brown rice
- 3 cups water
- 1 (1 ounce) package taco seasoning mix
- 1 (15.25 ounce) can kidney beans, drained
- 1 (15 ounce) can tomato sauce
- 1 (14.5 ounce) can diced tomatoes, drained
- salt and pepper to taste
- 1/2 cup shredded lettuce

Direction

- Bring 3 cups of water in a saucepan to a boil. Put in rice and stir. Lower heat, then cover and simmer about 45 minutes. Take away from the heat and allow to stand about 15 minutes.
- Stir in lettuce, pepper, salt, diced tomatoes, tomato sauce, kidney beans and taco seasoning, then cook on moderate heat until heated through.

Nutrition Information

- Calories: 361 calories;
- Sodium: 1459
- Total Carbohydrate: 72.3
- Cholesterol: 0
- Protein: 12.2
- Total Fat: 2.1

517. Easy Olive Oil, Tomato, And Basil Pasta

Serving: 8 | Prep: 15mins | Cook: 10mins |Ready in:

Ingredients

- 1 (16 ounce) package farfalle pasta
- 2 roma (plum) tomatoes, seeded and diced
- 1/2 cup olive oil

- 2 cloves garlic, minced
- 1/2 cup fresh basil leaves, cut into thin strips
- salt and pepper to taste

Direction

- Boil lightly salted water in a big pot. Add pasta and cook until al dente, about 8-10 minutes; drain.
- Gently combine basil, garlic, olive oil, tomatoes, and the cooked pasta in a big bowl. Use pepper and salt to season.

Nutrition Information

- Calories: 345 calories;
- Total Fat: 14.9
- Sodium: 3
- Total Carbohydrate: 44.1
- Cholesterol: 0
- Protein: 8.4

518. Easy Roasted Red Pepper Hummus

Serving: 2 | Prep: | Cook: | Ready in:

Ingredients

- 2 cloves garlic, minced
- 1 (15 ounce) can garbanzo beans, drained
- 1/3 cup tahini
- 1/3 cup lemon juice
- 1/2 cup roasted red peppers
- 1/4 teaspoon dried basil

Direction

- Process the lemon juice, tahini, garbanzo beans and garlic in an electric food processor until the mixture becomes smooth. Stir in basil and roasted peppers then blend until the peppers are chopped finely. Sprinkle pepper and salt to season, then move it into a small bowl, cover, and let it chill in the fridge until it's time to serve.

Nutrition Information

- Calories: 445 calories;
- Cholesterol: 0
- Protein: 15.9
- Total Fat: 26.9
- Sodium: 908
- Total Carbohydrate: 44.1

519. Easy Three Ingredient Gluten Free German Christmas Coconut Cookies

Serving: 45 | Prep: 25mins | Cook: 15mins | Ready in:

Ingredients

- 4 egg whites
- 1 cup white sugar
- 2 cups unsweetened coconut flakes

Direction

- Set oven to 300 0 F (150 0C) and preheat. Use parchment paper to line 2 baking sheets.
- In a glass, metal, or ceramic bowl, whisk egg whites until forming stiff peaks. Slowly combine in sugar, one tablespoon at a time, and keep beating. Use a spatula to fold in coconut flakes.
- Place onto the baking sheets little mounds of coconut mixture by 2 inches apart using 2 teaspoons.
- Put into the prepared oven and bake for 15 to 20 minutes, until lightly browned, depending on the size of the cookies. Let them cool on baking sheet for a few minutes, then carefully move onto a wire rack to cool completely.

Nutrition Information

- Calories: 46 calories;
- Total Carbohydrate: 5.4
- Cholesterol: 0
- Protein: 0.6
- Total Fat: 2.7
- Sodium: 6

520. Easy Veggie Samosas

Serving: 9 | Prep: 20mins | Cook: 25mins | Ready in:

Ingredients

- 1 tablespoon vegetable oil
- 1/2 cup chopped onion
- 3 (19 ounce) cans garbanzo beans, drained
- 2 tablespoons curry paste
- 1/2 cup apple juice
- 3 sheets frozen puff pastry, thawed
- 1/4 cup all-purpose flour for dusting

Direction

- Set the oven for preheating to 350 °F or 175 °C.
- In a big skillet, heat oil over medium-high heat. Sauté the onion for about 5 minutes or until browned. Lower the heat and add the garbanzo beans. Mix in the curry paste and apple juice till smooth and put into the skillet. Allow mixture to simmer for 10 minutes, stir occasionally. Add water or more apple juice if needed to moisten the dish as it cooks.
- Cut each pastry sheets into 3 equal rectangular sizes then cut each rectangle in half, to make 18 pieces. In a flat and lightly floured surface, roll each piece until it becomes double in size. Dust with flour as needed to prevent from sticking into the rolling pin. Take a spoonful amount of filling into the center of each pastry sheets, then fold in half. Press all edges to seal and then put on a non-stick baking sheet. Bake them in the preheated oven for about 25 minutes or until golden brown.

Nutrition Information

- Calories: 696 calories;
- Sodium: 803
- Total Carbohydrate: 82.5
- Cholesterol: 0
- Protein: 15.3
- Total Fat: 34.3

521. Edith's Stuffing

Serving: 8 | Prep: 20mins | Cook: 2hours | Ready in:

Ingredients

- 1/4 cup vegetable oil
- 3 onions, diced
- 3 (4 ounce) packets unsalted saltine crackers
- 1 (12 ounce) package coarsley crushed cornflakes
- 1 carrot, shredded
- 1 tablespoon salt
- 1 teaspoon ground black pepper
- 1 teaspoon garlic powder
- 2 eggs, lightly beaten
- 1 cup margarine
- 1/4 cup water

Direction

- On medium heat, heat oil in a pan; add onion then cook until pale brown. Set aside to cool.
- In a food processor, pulse cornflakes and crackers into crumbs; move to a big bowl. Add in garlic powder, carrots, pepper, and salt. Add in water, eggs, margarine, and onions. Mix with your hands until well combined.
- Lightly stuff inside an uncooked turkey then roast as specified.

Nutrition Information

- Calories: 654 calories;
- Total Fat: 35.8
- Sodium: 1792

- Total Carbohydrate: 76.7
- Cholesterol: 46
- Protein: 9.6

522. Egg In A Hole

Serving: 1 | Prep: 1mins | Cook: 4mins | Ready in:

Ingredients

- 1 1/2 teaspoons bacon grease
- 1 slice bread
- 1 egg
- salt and ground black pepper to taste

Direction

- In a nonstick pan, melt bacon grease over low heat.
- Cut a 1 1/2 to 2-in. hole from the center of each slice of bread with, then place in the hot skillet. Once the side facing down is toasted slightly, about 2 minutes, turn the slice over and crack the egg into hole then use pepper and salt to season. Keep on cooking until egg is nearly firm and cooked. Flip the bread again and cook for another minute to make sure both sides are done. Serve instantly.

Nutrition Information

- Calories: 231 calories;
- Sodium: 285
- Total Carbohydrate: 13.1
- Cholesterol: 208
- Protein: 8.7
- Total Fat: 15.9

523. Egg Free And Milk Free Baked Oatmeal

Serving: 6 | Prep: 15mins | Cook: 35mins | Ready in:

Ingredients

- 1 cup unsweetened applesauce
- 3/4 cup white sugar
- 3 cups oats
- 1 cup plain soy milk
- 1 tablespoon baking powder
- 1/4 teaspoon baking powder
- 1 teaspoon vegetable oil
- 1/2 teaspoon sea salt
- 1/2 cup raisins
- 1 tablespoon brown sugar, or more to taste
- 1/2 teaspoon ground cinnamon

Direction

- Grease a pie pan lightly.
- In a bowl, beat white sugar and applesauce together. Mix in soy milk, oats, 1 tablespoon plus 1/4 teaspoon baking powder, sea salt, and vegetable oil; mix well. Fold raisins into oat mixture; in the prepared pie pan, pour mixture, then place brown sugar and cinnamon on top. Allow to refrigerate for 8 hours to overnight.
- Preheat oven to 350 °F (175 °C).
- In the preheated oven, bake for around 35 to 50 minutes till oatmeal is firm.

Nutrition Information

- Calories: 348 calories;
- Sodium: 437
- Total Carbohydrate: 73.5
- Cholesterol: 0
- Protein: 7.2
- Total Fat: 4.2

524. Egg Yolk Sponge Cake

Serving: 14 | Prep: | Cook: | Ready in:

Ingredients

- 1 2/3 cups all-purpose flour

- 1 1/2 teaspoons baking powder
- 1/2 teaspoon salt
- 3/4 cup egg yolks
- 1 egg
- 1 1/2 cups white sugar
- 1 tablespoon orange zest
- 1 tablespoon orange juice, strained
- 1/2 teaspoon lemon extract
- 3/4 cup boiling water

Direction

- Start preheating the oven to 325°F (165°C).
- Sift together twice: salt, baking powder, and flour. Put back into the sifter.
- Whisk whole eggs and egg yolks together in a big mixing bowl using an electric mixer for 5 minutes until thick and turning lemon colored. Slowly add sugar, whisking after each adding. This process will take approximately 10 minutes.
- Fold in lemon extract, orange juice, and orange rind. Sift the dry ingredients into the sugar and egg mixture and fold in. Do not beat or stir. Add hot water and fold in quickly, until the liquid is just mixed. Put the batter on 1 non-oiled 10" tube pan.
- Put in the preheated oven and bake at 325°F (165°C) for 60-65 minutes. Invert the cake in the pan onto a wire rack and allow the cake to rest until cool, about 1 hour. Using a spatula to loosen cake sides from the pan and shake from the pan. Frost the cake using Orange Butter Frosting or lightly dust confectioner's sugar on top.

Nutrition Information

- Calories: 185 calories;
- Sodium: 147
- Total Carbohydrate: 33.6
- Cholesterol: 174
- Protein: 4.1
- Total Fat: 4

525. Eggless Ginger Cookies

Serving: 12 | Prep: | Cook: | Ready in:

Ingredients

- 1 cup white sugar
- 1 cup shortening
- 1 cup dark molasses
- 2 teaspoons baking soda
- 1 teaspoon ground ginger
- 1 teaspoon ground cinnamon
- 4 cups all-purpose flour

Direction

- Set an oven to 220°C (425°F) to preheat, then grease the cookie sheets lightly.
- Cream together the shortening and sugar in a big bowl until it becomes smooth; mix in the molasses. Mix together the 3 3/4 cups of the flour, cinnamon, ginger and baking soda, then blend into the molasses mixture. Add more flour if needed to make the dough stiff enough to roll out. Use the leftover flour to dust the rolling surface. Roll out the dough to 1/4-inch thick and cut it using cookie cutters.
- Bake in the preheated oven for 5-7 minutes. Take it out of the baking trays to cool on the wire racks.

Nutrition Information

- Calories: 447 calories;
- Sodium: 221
- Total Carbohydrate: 69.1
- Cholesterol: 0
- Protein: 4.3
- Total Fat: 17.5

526. Eggless, Milkless, Butterless Cake III

Serving: 12 | Prep: | Cook: | Ready in:

Ingredients

- 1 cup white sugar
- 2 tablespoons shortening
- 1/2 teaspoon ground cinnamon
- 1/2 teaspoon ground nutmeg
- 1/2 teaspoon ground allspice
- 1/2 teaspoon salt
- 1 (10.75 ounce) can condensed tomato soup
- 1 cup raisins
- 1 1/2 cups boiling water
- 1 teaspoon baking soda
- 2 cups all-purpose flour
- 1 teaspoon baking powder

Direction

- Set an oven to 175°C (350°F) to preheat, then grease an 8-inch square pan lightly.
- Mix together the raisins, soup, salt, spices, shortening and sugar in a big bowl, then mix in boiling water. Allow it to cool.
- Sift together the baking soda, baking powder and flour; add to the cooled raisin mixture and mix until just blended. Pour the batter into the prepped pan.
- Bake for 20-25 minutes, then serve it warm.

Nutrition Information

- Calories: 214 calories;
- Total Fat: 2.8
- Sodium: 385
- Total Carbohydrate: 45.8
- Cholesterol: 0
- Protein: 3

527. Eggplant With Almonds

Serving: 4 | Prep: 40mins | Cook: 35mins | Ready in:

Ingredients

- 2 large eggplants, cut into cubes
- salt
- 1/4 cup olive oil
- 1 large onion, minced
- 2 cloves garlic, minced
- 1 cup whole almonds, skin removed
- 2 cups cherry tomatoes, halved and seeded
- 4 mint leaves, sliced
- 2 tablespoons white wine
- 2 tablespoons white sugar
- 1 pinch salt
- 1/2 teaspoon chili powder
- 1/2 cup chopped fresh parsley

Direction

- In a colander, put the eggplant and sprinkle salt on top. Put the colander in the sink and drain off the liquid, approximately 20 minutes. Use paper towel to pat the cubes to remove extra salt.
- In a big frying pan, heat the olive oil on medium-high heat. Cook the onion in the oil until it turns translucent. Add the garlic and let it cook and stir for 2 minutes more. Stir in the almonds and eggplant, then cook and stir for about 20 minutes, until the eggplant becomes soft, yet not mushy.
- Mix in the chili powder, salt, sugar, white wine, mint and tomatoes, once the eggplant is cooked through. Cook the mixture for 10 minutes, stirring from time to time, then take it out of the heat and put parsley on top to garnish.

Nutrition Information

- Calories: 458 calories;
- Total Carbohydrate: 37.2
- Cholesterol: 0
- Protein: 11.7
- Total Fat: 32.4
- Sodium: 22

528. Eileen's Spicy Gingerbread Men

Serving: 30 | Prep: 20mins | Cook: 10mins | Ready in:

Ingredients

- 1/2 cup margarine
- 1/2 cup sugar
- 1/2 cup molasses
- 1 egg yolk
- 2 cups sifted all-purpose flour
- 1/2 teaspoon salt
- 1/2 teaspoon baking powder
- 1/2 teaspoon baking soda
- 1/2 teaspoon ground cinnamon
- 1 teaspoon ground cloves
- 1 teaspoon ginger
- 1/2 teaspoon ground nutmeg

Direction

- Cream the margarine and sugar in a large bowl until smooth. Stir in egg yolk and molasses. Combine baking powder, cinnamon, ginger, nutmeg, cloves, baking soda, salt, and flour. Pour the dry mixture into the molasses mixture and mix until smooth. Cover and let it chill for at least 60 minutes.
- Set the oven to 350°F or 175°C to preheat. Roll the dough in a lightly floured surface to form a 1/4-inch thick dough. Use the cookie cutter to cut the dough according to your desired shape. Place the cookies into the ungreased cookie sheets, arranging them 2-inches away from each other.
- Let it bake inside the preheated oven for 8-10 minutes until the cookies are set. Transfer the cookies on wire racks and allow them to cool completely. Frost or decorate the cookies once cooled.

Nutrition Information

- Calories: 88 calories;
- Total Fat: 3.3
- Sodium: 103
- Total Carbohydrate: 14
- Cholesterol: 7
- Protein: 1

529. Espinacas Con Garbanzos (Spinach With Garbanzo Beans)

Serving: 4 | Prep: 15mins | Cook: 10mins | Ready in:

Ingredients

- 1 tablespoon extra-virgin olive oil
- 4 cloves garlic, minced
- 1/2 onion, diced
- 1 (10 ounce) box frozen chopped spinach, thawed and drained well
- 1 (12 ounce) can garbanzo beans, drained
- 1/2 teaspoon cumin
- 1/2 teaspoon salt

Direction

- On medium-low heat, heat olive oil in a pan; add onion and garlic. Sauté for 5 minutes until translucent. Mix in salt, spinach, cumin, and garbanzo beans. While the mixture cooks, gently mash the beans with a stirring spoon. Continue cooking until the mixture is heated through.

Nutrition Information

- Calories: 169 calories;
- Total Fat: 4.9
- Sodium: 600
- Total Carbohydrate: 26
- Cholesterol: 0
- Protein: 7.3

530. Extra Easy Hummus

Serving: 4 | Prep: 5mins | Cook: | Ready in:

Ingredients

- 1 (15 ounce) can garbanzo beans, drained, liquid reserved
- 1 clove garlic, crushed
- 2 teaspoons ground cumin
- 1/2 teaspoon salt
- 1 tablespoon olive oil

Direction

- Mix olive oil, salt, garlic, cumin, and garbanzo beans in a food processor or blender. Then blend on low speed while slowly adding the reserved bean liquid until the consistency desired is achieved.

Nutrition Information

- Calories: 118 calories;
- Sodium: 502
- Total Carbohydrate: 16.5
- Cholesterol: 0
- Protein: 3.7
- Total Fat: 4.4

531. Fabienne's Leeks And Monkfish

Serving: 4 | Prep: 10mins | Cook: 1hours5mins | Ready in:

Ingredients

- 2 tablespoons olive oil
- 2 cups chopped leeks, white and light green parts only
- 1/3 cup white wine
- 1 tablespoon lemon juice
- 1 teaspoon ground cumin
- 3/4 teaspoon hot Madras curry powder, or to taste
- 1/2 teaspoon ground turmeric
- 1/2 teaspoon ground paprika
- 1/4 teaspoon ground coriander
- 1/8 teaspoon ground ginger
- 1 pinch cayenne pepper, or to taste
- salt and ground black pepper to taste
- 1 (14 ounce) can coconut milk
- 1 pound monkfish fillets, cut into cubes

Direction

- In a stock pot, heat olive oil over medium heat. Add in pepper, salt, cayenne, ginger, coriander, paprika, turmeric, Madras curry powder, cumin, lemon juice, white wine, and leeks and stir well. Cover pot and lower heat to medium-low, frequently stirring till all liquid gets absorbed, about 30 minutes. Uncover pot, add coconut milk in and stir, and lower heat to low; allow to simmer, uncovered, for 30 minutes.
- In the pot, gently lay monkfish; pour leek mixture over monkfish. Cook and gently stir over low heat for about 5 minutes till fish easily flakes with a fork.

Nutrition Information

- Calories: 390 calories;
- Total Fat: 29.8
- Sodium: 83
- Total Carbohydrate: 10.8
- Cholesterol: 28
- Protein: 19.3

532. Fabulous And Easy Guacamole

Serving: 16 | Prep: 10mins | Cook: | Ready in:

Ingredients

- 2 avocados - peeled, pitted and diced
- 1 tablespoon minced shallots
- 2 cloves garlic, minced
- 3/4 cup taco sauce

Direction

- Combine together the taco sauce, garlic, shallots, and avocados in a medium size bowl then mix well. Let it sit for at least 15 minutes until serving time.

Nutrition Information

- Calories: 45 calories;
- Total Fat: 3.7
- Sodium: 69
- Total Carbohydrate: 3.1
- Cholesterol: 0
- Protein: 0.5

533. Fanouropita (Vegan Greek Raisin, Walnut, And Olive Oil Cake)

Serving: 12 | Prep: 20mins | Cook: 45mins | Ready in:

Ingredients

- 1 3/8 cups olive oil
- 1 1/2 cups freshly squeezed orange juice
- 2 tablespoons brandy
- 1 1/2 cups white sugar
- 5 1/2 cups all-purpose flour
- 1 teaspoon baking soda
- 2 teaspoons baking powder
- 1 1/4 cups chopped walnuts
- 1 cup Thompson seedless raisins
- 1 teaspoon ground cinnamon
- 1/2 teaspoon ground cloves
- 2 tablespoons sesame seeds

Direction

- Set an oven to preheat to 175°C (350°F), then grease a 12-inch round springform pan.
- In a big bowl, mix together the brandy, orange juice and olive oil, then mix in the sugar. In a separate bowl, mix together the baking powder, baking soda and flour and sift into the oil mixture. Fold in cloves, cinnamon, raisins and walnuts, then stir well. Tip the batter into the prepped springform pan and level the top. Sprinkle sesame seeds on top.
- Let it bake in the preheated oven for 45-60 minutes, until an inserted skewer in the middle exits clean.

Nutrition Information

- Calories: 678 calories;
- Sodium: 190
- Total Carbohydrate: 85.4
- Cholesterol: 0
- Protein: 8.8
- Total Fat: 34.4

534. Fat Free Refried Beans

Serving: 4 | Prep: 10mins | Cook: 15mins | Ready in:

Ingredients

- 2 cups canned black beans, divided
- 1/2 cup water
- 2 cloves garlic, minced
- 1 teaspoon pepper
- 1 teaspoon salt
- 1 teaspoon liquid smoke flavoring
- 3/4 cup diced onion

Direction

- Mash 2/3 cup beans in a small bowl until it becomes a smooth paste.
- In a medium saucepan, combine the remaining beans with water over medium heat. Heat

through, then stir in liquid smoke, salt, pepper, and garlic.
- Stir bean paste into the whole beans and blend well. Stir in onion and cook until the onions are cooked slightly, about 10 minutes.

Nutrition Information

- Calories: 134 calories;
- Sodium: 1044
- Total Carbohydrate: 23.3
- Cholesterol: 0
- Protein: 7.7
- Total Fat: 1.5

535. Fava Bean Breakfast Spread

Serving: 6 | Prep: 10mins | Cook: 10mins | Ready in:

Ingredients

- 1 (15 ounce) can fava beans
- 1 1/2 tablespoons olive oil
- 1 large onion, chopped
- 1 large tomato, diced
- 1 teaspoon ground cumin
- 1/4 cup chopped fresh parsley
- 1/4 cup fresh lemon juice
- salt and pepper to taste
- ground red pepper, to taste

Direction

- Boil beans in pot; mix well. Add red pepper, pepper, salt, lemon juice, parsley, cumin, olive oil, tomato and onion; boil again. Lower heat to medium; cook for 5 minutes. Serve while warm with grilled pita.

Nutrition Information

- Calories: 101 calories;
- Sodium: 322
- Total Carbohydrate: 13.6
- Cholesterol: 0
- Protein: 4.6
- Total Fat: 3.7

536. Favorite Peanut Butter Cookies

Serving: 54 | Prep: 30mins | Cook: 30mins | Ready in:

Ingredients

- 1 1/4 cups creamy peanut butter
- 1 cup margarine
- 3/4 cup white sugar
- 3/4 cup packed light brown sugar
- 2 eggs
- 1/2 teaspoon vanilla extract
- 2 1/4 cups all-purpose flour
- 1 teaspoon baking powder
- 1 teaspoon baking soda

Direction

- Preheat an oven to 190°C/375°F.
- Cream white sugar, brown sugar, margarine and peanut butter in big bowl; beat vanilla and eggs in. Mix baking soda, baking powder and flour; mix into peanut butter mixture. Shape dough to walnut-sized balls; put on ungreased cookie sheets, 2-in. apart. Dip fork into flour; slightly flatten each cookie with crisscross.
- In preheated oven, bake for 12-15 minutes till just lightly browned. Cool cookies for 5 minutes on baking sheet; transfer to wire rack to completely cool.

Nutrition Information

- Calories: 109 calories;
- Sodium: 100
- Total Carbohydrate: 11
- Cholesterol: 7
- Protein: 2.3

- Total Fat: 6.6

537. Fiery Pork Skewers

Serving: 4 | Prep: 15mins | Cook: 12mins |Ready in:

Ingredients

- 2 tablespoons teriyaki sauce
- 1 tablespoon red wine vinegar
- 1 tablespoon vegetable oil
- 1 teaspoon brown sugar
- 1/2 teaspoon red pepper flakes
- 3/4 pound pork tenderloin, cut into 1 inch cubes

Direction

- Combine teriyaki sauce, vegetable oil, red wine vinegar, red pepper flakes, and brown sugar in a medium bowl. Toss the pork tenderloin cubes in the marinade to coat.
- Set an outdoor grill on high to preheat. Lightly oil the grate.
- Skewer the pork and cook on the grill, turning and basting frequently with the marinade. Grill for 10 to 12 minutes or until done to liking.

Nutrition Information

- Calories: 147 calories;
- Total Fat: 6.5
- Sodium: 390
- Total Carbohydrate: 3
- Cholesterol: 55
- Protein: 18.1

538. Fireball® Horchata Pops

Serving: 8 | Prep: 20mins | Cook: |Ready in:

Ingredients

- 2/3 cup long grain white rice
- 2 cinnamon sticks
- 3 cups warm water
- 2 cups rice milk
- 3/4 cup white sugar, or to taste
- 1/2 cup cinnamon whiskey (such as Fireball®)
- 1/4 teaspoon cayenne pepper
- 1/4 teaspoon ground cinnamon
- 1 dash ground cinnamon (optional)

Direction

- Finely grind rice with a spice/coffee grinder; put in big bowl. Add cinnamon sticks. Put in warm water. Use plastic wrap to cover. Let to sit for 8 hours to overnight.
- Through sieve above a bowl, strain rice mixture. Use a wooden spoon to squeeze out as much liquid as you can by pressing against rice. Discard the rice. Mix sugar and rice milk into strained liquid to create horchata.
- In another bowl, measure 2 1/2 cups horchata. Add 1/4 teaspoon ground cinnamon, cayenne pepper and cinnamon whiskey. Put in ice pop molds.
- Freeze for 12 hours minimum till solid.
- Under warm water, run molds to release ice pops. Before serving, sprinkle an extra dash of cinnamon.

Nutrition Information

- Calories: 207 calories;
- Total Fat: 0.6
- Sodium: 25
- Total Carbohydrate: 38.9
- Cholesterol: 0
- Protein: 1.9

539. Firecracker Grilled Alaska Salmon

Serving: 8 | Prep: 20mins | Cook: 20mins | Ready in:

Ingredients

- 8 (4 ounce) fillets salmon
- 1/2 cup peanut oil
- 4 tablespoons soy sauce
- 4 tablespoons balsamic vinegar
- 4 tablespoons green onions, chopped
- 3 teaspoons brown sugar
- 2 cloves garlic, minced
- 1 1/2 teaspoons ground ginger
- 2 teaspoons crushed red pepper flakes
- 1 teaspoon sesame oil
- 1/2 teaspoon salt

Direction

- Put the salmon filets into a medium and nonporous glass dish. Mix the green onions, vinegar, peanut oil, ginger, soy sauce, salt, brown sugar, sesame oil, garlic, and red pepper flakes in a separate medium bowl. Whisk together thoroughly and spread on top the fish. Cover and then marinate the fish for about 4 to 6 hours in the fridge.
- Prepare the outdoor grill with coals approximately five inches from grate, and coat the grate lightly with oil.
- Grill fillets at five inches away from the coals for ten minutes per inch of thickness, which is measured at the thickest section or until the fish flakes with a fork. Flip over when halfway through cooking.

Nutrition Information

- Calories: 307 calories;
- Total Fat: 21.5
- Sodium: 649
- Total Carbohydrate: 4.6
- Cholesterol: 63
- Protein: 23.3

540. Fish Fillets Italiano

Serving: 4 | Prep: 10mins | Cook: 15mins | Ready in:

Ingredients

- 2 tablespoons olive oil
- 1 onion, thinly sliced
- 2 cloves garlic, minced
- 1 (14.5 ounce) can diced tomatoes
- 1/2 cup black olives, pitted and sliced
- 1 tablespoon chopped fresh parsley
- 1/2 cup dry white wine
- 1 pound cod fillets

Direction

- On medium heat, heat oil in a big frying pan. Sauté garlic and onions in olive oil till tender.
- Mix in wine, parsley, olives and tomatoes. Let it simmer for 5 minutes.
- Add fillets into sauce. Let it simmer till fish becomes white in color for about 5 minutes longer.

Nutrition Information

- Calories: 230 calories;
- Protein: 21.2
- Total Fat: 9.4
- Sodium: 459
- Total Carbohydrate: 8.2
- Cholesterol: 41

541. Flourless Chocolate Mousse Cake

Serving: 12 | Prep: 20mins | Cook: 25mins | Ready in:

Ingredients

- 7 ounces bittersweet chocolate, chopped
- 7/8 cup margarine

- 7/8 cup white sugar, separated
- 6 eggs, separated

Direction

- Set an oven to 165°C (325°F) to preheat.
- In a saucepan, melt together the margarine and chocolate on low heat. Take out of the heat and allow it to cool to room temperature.
- In a big bowl, beat together the egg yolks and 1/2 of the sugar using an electric mixer, until it becomes fluffy and light. Mix in the chocolate mixture until just blended.
- In another bowl, beat the egg whites using an electric mixer until it becomes foamy. Slowly add the leftover sugar and keep on beating until forming stiff peaks.
- Using a rubber spatula, scoop 1/3 of the chocolate mixture onto the beaten egg whites. Run a spatula gently around the edges of the mixture and lift the bottom up and over the center, then repeat until well combined. Add the leftover chocolate mixture and fold just until the batter becomes smooth. Pour 3/4 of the batter into a 9-inch square pan.
- Bake in the preheated oven for about 25 minutes until the surface becomes firm and the edges are puffed. Place the pan on a wire rack and let the cake cool to room temperature for approximately 30 minutes. Spread the leftover batter on top of the cake. Put it in the fridge for at least 30 minutes more, until fully chilled.

Nutrition Information

- Calories: 300 calories;
- Sodium: 189
- Total Carbohydrate: 24.2
- Cholesterol: 94
- Protein: 4.4
- Total Fat: 21.1

542. Flourless Peanut Butter Cookies

Serving: 6 | Prep: | Cook: | Ready in:

Ingredients

- 1 cup peanut butter
- 1 cup white sugar
- 1 egg

Direction

- Preheat oven to 180 degrees C or 350 degrees F
- Mix the ingredients and drop by teaspoonfuls onto the cookie sheet. Bake for 8 minutes. Allow to cool down. Double the recipe as you wish because the recipe doesn't make a big amount.

Nutrition Information

- Calories: 394 calories;
- Total Fat: 22.5
- Sodium: 209
- Total Carbohydrate: 41.8
- Cholesterol: 31
- Protein: 11.8

543. Fortune Cookies I

Serving: 6 | Prep: | Cook: | Ready in:

Ingredients

- 1 egg white
- 1/8 teaspoon vanilla extract
- 1 pinch salt
- 1/4 cup unbleached all-purpose flour
- 1/4 cup white sugar

Direction

- Set oven to 400°F to preheat. Grease a cookie sheet with butter. On strips of paper about

1/2-inch-wide and 4 inches long, write fortunes. Grease 2 cookie sheets generously.

- Stir the egg white with vanilla until frothy but not stiff. Sift the sugar, salt, and flour and combine into the egg white mixture.
- Put teaspoonfuls of the batter no less than 4 inches apart on 1 greased cookie sheet. Tilt the sheet to move the batter into rounds form about 3 inches in diameter. Be careful to make batter as evenly round as possible. Don't make too many, because the cookie must be really hot to shape them so you can't do it if it's cooled. Begin with 2 or 3 to a sheet and see how many you can handle.
- Bake until cookie has a golden color half inch wide around the outer edge of the circle, or for 5 minutes. The center will still pale. While one sheet is baking, make the other.
- Take out of the oven and move cookie quickly using a wide spatula and transfer upside down on a wooden board. Put the fortune on the cookie quickly, close to the middle and fold the cookie in half. Put the folded edge across the rim of a measuring cup and pull the pointed edges down, one on the outside and one on the inside of the cup. Put folded cookies into the cups of a muffin tin (or egg carton) to keep it in shape until set.

Nutrition Information

- Calories: 54 calories;
- Protein: 1.1
- Total Fat: 0.1
- Sodium: 9
- Total Carbohydrate: 12.4
- Cholesterol: 0

544. Fragrant Lemon Chicken

Serving: 6 | Prep: 20mins | Cook: 9hours | Ready in:

Ingredients

- 1 apple - peeled, cored and quartered
- 1 stalk celery with leaves, chopped
- 1 (3 pound) whole chicken
- salt to taste
- ground black pepper to taste
- 1 onion, chopped
- 1/2 teaspoon dried rosemary, crushed
- 1 lemon, zested and juiced
- 1 cup hot water

Direction

- Rub pepper and salt on the skin of the chicken, then put celery and apple inside the chicken. Put the chicken in the slow cooker. Sprinkle chicken with lemon juice and zest, rosemary, and chopped onion. Add 1 cup of hot water into the slow cooker.
- Cook, covered, on High for 1 hour. Change to low and cook for 6 to 8 hours, basting a few times.

Nutrition Information

- Calories: 309 calories;
- Total Fat: 17.2
- Sodium: 101
- Total Carbohydrate: 7.1
- Cholesterol: 97
- Protein: 31.1

545. French Burgers

Serving: 4 | Prep: 20mins | Cook: 20mins | Ready in:

Ingredients

- 1/2 cup crumbled feta cheese
- 1/4 cup sliced green onion
- 1 teaspoon dried tarragon
- salt and ground black pepper to taste
- 1 1/2 pounds ground turkey
- 2 tablespoons olive oil
- 1 thin slice red onion

- 2 tablespoons flour
- 1/2 cup chicken broth
- 1/2 cup red wine
- 1/2 teaspoon chopped fresh parsley
- 1/2 teaspoon dried minced onion
- 1/2 teaspoon crushed bay leaf
- 1/4 teaspoon dried thyme
- salt and ground black pepper to taste

Direction

- Set the oven at 450°F (230°C) and start preheating.
- In a small bowl, combine tarragon, green onion and feta cheese; season with pepper and salt; set aside.
- Shape the ground turkey into 8 even-sized patties. Arrange four even portions of the cheese mixture on top of four of the patties. Place on top of the remaining patties on top of each. Seal by pinching the edges together.
- Bake the patties for 20-30 minutes in the preheated oven, turning once, till cooked through.
- Place a skillet on low heat; heat olive oil. Cook while stirring red onion into the hot oil till browned; take the onion away and discard. Mix in flour; cook till the mixture turns deep brown. Take the pan away from the heat; put in thyme, bay leaf, minced onion, parsley, red wine and chicken broth. Place the pan back to the heat; boil while stirring; season with pepper and salt. Spread the sauce over the prepared patties. Serve.

Nutrition Information

- Calories: 404 calories;
- Total Fat: 23.7
- Sodium: 308
- Total Carbohydrate: 5.7
- Cholesterol: 142
- Protein: 37.1

546. Fresh Pear Cake

Serving: 12 | Prep: | Cook: | Ready in:

Ingredients

- 4 cups peeled, cored and chopped pears
- 2 cups white sugar
- 3 cups sifted all-purpose flour
- 1 teaspoon salt
- 1 1/2 teaspoons baking soda
- 1 teaspoon ground nutmeg
- 1 teaspoon ground cinnamon
- 1/2 teaspoon ground cloves
- 4 egg whites
- 2/3 cup canola oil
- 1 cup chopped pecans

Direction

- Mix together sugar and pears; allow to sit for 60 minutes.
- Set oven to 165°C (325°F) and start preheating. Use non-stick cooking spray to coat a Bundt pan (10 in.).
- Blend egg whites lightly; mix with pear mixture, chopped pecans and oil.
- Combine cloves, cinnamon, nutmeg, baking soda, salt and flour. Mix in the pear mixture. Transfer to the greased Bundt pan.
- Bake for 70 minutes in preheated oven at 325°F. Take out of the oven and place on a wire rack to cool for 10 minutes, then turn out the cake.

Nutrition Information

- Calories: 455 calories;
- Sodium: 371
- Total Carbohydrate: 67.3
- Cholesterol: 0
- Protein: 5.5
- Total Fat: 19.5

547. Fresh Pineapple Dessert

Serving: 4 | Prep: 10mins | Cook: 5mins | Ready in:

Ingredients

- 1 fresh pineapple
- 1/2 cup brown sugar
- 1/2 cup flaked coconut

Direction

- Set the oven's broiler to preheat and place the oven rack approximately 6 inches from the heat source.
- Cut off the bottom and top of the pineapple. Slice it into quarters and take out the core from each piece. Place each section skin side down and separate the fruit along the skin using a sharp knife, allow the fruit to rest on the skin for the presentation. For easy eating, slice the fruit into pieces. Put it on a baking sheet and sprinkle each section with 2 tbsp. coconut and 2 tbsp. of brown sugar.
- Let it broil for about 5 minutes, until the coconut becomes toasted.

Nutrition Information

- Calories: 206 calories;
- Total Fat: 2.7
- Sodium: 35
- Total Carbohydrate: 47.3
- Cholesterol: 0
- Protein: 1

548. Fresh Salsa

Serving: 36 | Prep: 45mins | Cook: | Ready in:

Ingredients

- 6 roma tomatoes, diced
- 3 fresh jalapeno peppers, seeded and chopped
- 1/4 red onion, chopped
- 3 green onions, chopped
- 2 cloves cloves garlic, crushed
- 2 tablespoons chopped fresh cilantro
- 2 tablespoons fresh lime juice
- 2 tablespoons fresh lemon juice
- 1 1/2 teaspoons ground cumin
- 1 small jicama, peeled and chopped
- 1 (10 ounce) can diced tomatoes with green chilies, drained
- salt and ground black pepper to taste

Direction

- In a bowl, combine together chilies, diced tomatoes, jicama, cumin, lemon juice, lime juice, cilantro, garlic, green onion, red onion, jalapeno pepper and tomato, then season to taste with pepper and salt. Let the mixture sit for a minimum of an hour before serving.

Nutrition Information

- Calories: 9 calories;
- Protein: 0.3
- Total Fat: 0.1
- Sodium: 17
- Total Carbohydrate: 2.1
- Cholesterol: 0

549. Fresh Tomato Salsa

Serving: 4 | Prep: 10mins | Cook: | Ready in:

Ingredients

- 3 tomatoes, chopped
- 1/2 cup finely diced onion
- 5 serrano chiles, finely chopped
- 1/2 cup chopped fresh cilantro
- 1 teaspoon salt
- 2 teaspoons lime juice

Direction

- Stir together lime juice, salt, cilantro, chili peppers, onion and tomatoes in a medium bowl, then chill in the fridge about 1 hour before serving.

Nutrition Information

- Calories: 51 calories;
- Sodium: 592
- Total Carbohydrate: 9.7
- Cholesterol: 0
- Protein: 2.1
- Total Fat: 0.2

550. Fried Cabbage II

Serving: 6 | Prep: 20mins | Cook: 25mins | Ready in:

Ingredients

- 3 slices bacon, chopped
- 1/4 cup chopped onion
- 6 cups cabbage, cut into thin wedges
- 2 tablespoons water
- 1 pinch white sugar
- salt and pepper to taste
- 1 tablespoon cider vinegar

Direction

- In a deep, big skillet, put the bacon and let it cook on medium-high heat until it turns brown evenly. Take out the bacon and put aside.
- In the hot bacon grease, cook the onion until it becomes tender, then add the cabbage and stir in pepper, salt, sugar and water. Let it cook for about 15 minutes, until the cabbage has wilted, then mix in the bacon. Splash it with vinegar prior to serving.

Nutrition Information

- Calories: 47 calories;
- Total Fat: 2
- Sodium: 114
- Total Carbohydrate: 5.2
- Cholesterol: 5
- Protein: 2.8

551. Fried Corn With Bacon

Serving: 6 | Prep: 15mins | Cook: 10mins | Ready in:

Ingredients

- 6 ears corn, husked and cleaned
- 6 slices bacon
- 1/2 large green bell pepper, chopped

Direction

- Cut off the corn from the cob and scrape cob to release milk, then set aside.
- In a big, deep skillet, add bacon. Cook on medium high heat until browned evenly, then crumble and set aside.
- Keep 2 tbsp. bacon grease in the pan and fry pepper until just tender. Put in corn and cook until tender. Stir in the crumbled bacon and cook for 1 minute longer.

Nutrition Information

- Calories: 229 calories;
- Total Fat: 13.8
- Sodium: 234
- Total Carbohydrate: 23.7
- Cholesterol: 19
- Protein: 6.4

552. Fried Green Tomatoes I

Serving: 4 | Prep: | Cook: | Ready in:

Ingredients

- 5 tomatoes, sliced
- 1 cup cornmeal
- 1/2 cup vegetable oil
- salt and pepper to taste

Direction

- Rinse and dry each slice of tomato. Sprinkle the cornmeal on a big flat surface or on a piece of wax paper. Dunk each slice of tomato into the cornmeal and gently pat until the cornmeal covers the surface, then flip over the slice and coat the other side.
- In a big frying pan, heat the oil on medium heat, then add the slices of tomato and fry for 2-3 minutes per side, until it turns golden brown. Sprinkle pepper and salt to season, then serve it hot.

Nutrition Information

- Calories: 381 calories;
- Total Fat: 28.9
- Sodium: 18
- Total Carbohydrate: 29.5
- Cholesterol: 0
- Protein: 3.8

553. Fried Green Tomatoes II

Serving: 4 | Prep: | Cook: | Ready in:

Ingredients

- 1/3 cup bread crumbs
- 1/2 teaspoon white sugar
- 1/4 teaspoon salt
- 1/8 teaspoon ground black pepper
- 1/4 cup vegetable oil
- 1 pound green tomatoes, sliced 1/2 inch thick

Direction

- Combine together pepper, salt, bread crumbs, and sugar.
- Coat the tomatoes with the crumb mixture.
- Over medium-high heat, heat oil in a large frying pan and then fry the tomatoes for two minutes per side. Drain on paper towels.

Nutrition Information

- Calories: 185 calories;
- Total Carbohydrate: 12.8
- Cholesterol: 0
- Protein: 2.6
- Total Fat: 14.5
- Sodium: 226

554. Fried Okra

Serving: 4 | Prep: 15mins | Cook: 15mins | Ready in:

Ingredients

- 10 pods okra, sliced in 1/4 inch pieces
- 1 egg, beaten
- 1 cup cornmeal
- 1/4 teaspoon salt
- 1/4 teaspoon ground black pepper
- 1/2 cup vegetable oil

Direction

- For 5 to 10 minutes, soak the okra in egg in a small bowl. Combine pepper, salt and the cornmeal in a medium bowl.
- In a large skillet, heat oil over medium-high heat. Coat the okra evenly by dredging it in the cornmeal mixture. In hot oil put the okra carefully; continuously stirring. Turn the heat to medium once the okra starts to turn brown. Cook until it turns golden. Using paper towel, drain the okra.

Nutrition Information

- Calories: 394 calories;
- Sodium: 167

- Total Carbohydrate: 29
- Cholesterol: 46
- Protein: 4.7
- Total Fat: 29.2

555. Fried Rice II

Serving: 8 | Prep: 20mins | Cook: 10mins | Ready in:

Ingredients

- 2 cups uncooked instant rice
- 2 cubes chicken bouillon
- 1 cup snow peas
- 1 cup chopped onions
- 1 cup bean sprouts
- 3 eggs, beaten
- 2 tablespoons vegetable oil
- 2 teaspoons soy sauce, or to taste

Direction

- Boil a saucepan of 4 cups of water. Add rice and chicken bouillon, and whisk. Put a cover on; take away from heat and let sit until the liquid has absorbed, or about 5 minutes. Chill overnight.
- Add bean sprouts, onions, and snow peas to the rice.
- Scramble eggs over medium heat in a small skillet, add to the rice mixture.
- In a big wok or skillet, heat oil over medium heat. Add the rice mixture and fry with soy sauce until liquid vaporizes; make sure to not fry until crunchy.

Nutrition Information

- Calories: 170 calories;
- Total Fat: 5.8
- Sodium: 394
- Total Carbohydrate: 24.2
- Cholesterol: 70
- Protein: 5.1

556. Fried Zucchini

Serving: 4 | Prep: 15mins | Cook: 30mins | Ready in:

Ingredients

- 3 zucchini
- 1/4 cup yellow cornmeal
- 2 tablespoons olive oil
- salt and pepper to taste

Direction

- Wash and dry the zucchini then trim off ends. Cut the zucchini, making 1/8 inch thick rounds. Put the cornmeal in a medium bowl then fold in the zucchini slices and coat by thoroughly mixing.
- In a big nonstick skillet, heat oil over medium heat. Put all the zucchini slices in the hot oil and fry them over medium heat. Sprinkle with pepper and salt. If zucchini begins to brown too quickly, put in more oil. Flip it to brown the other side when it turns golden brown on one side. We want it to clump together as it cooks.
- Once zucchini turns brown evenly, reduce the heat to low then use a lid to cover the pan. Steam the zucchini until it becomes slightly tender. Flip the zucchini then replace the lid. Allow to steam until it becomes soft. Take the lid off and increase the heat to medium high. Fry the zucchini on both sides until it becomes crispy. Serve it while hot.

Nutrition Information

- Calories: 112 calories;
- Protein: 2.3
- Total Fat: 7.1
- Sodium: 5
- Total Carbohydrate: 11.1
- Cholesterol: 0

557. Frijoles A La Charra

Serving: 8 | Prep: 15mins | Cook: 5hours | Ready in:

Ingredients

- 1 pound dry pinto beans
- 5 cloves garlic, chopped
- 1 teaspoon salt
- 1/2 pound bacon, diced
- 1 onion, chopped
- 2 fresh tomatoes, diced
- 1 (3.5 ounce) can sliced jalapeno peppers
- 1 (12 fluid ounce) can beer
- 1/3 cup chopped fresh cilantro

Direction

- In a slow cooker, put pinto beans and add water until fully covered. Stir in salt and garlic. Put a cover on, and cook on high for 1 hour.
- Cook bacon on medium-high heat in a frying pan until soft and turning evenly brown. Strain approximately half of the grease. Put the onion in the frying pan, and cook until soft. Stir in jalapenos and tomatoes, and cook until cooked through. Move to the slow cooker, mixing into the beans.
- Put a lid on the slow cooker, and keep cooking on Low for 4 hours. Approximately 30 minutes before the cooking time finishes, mix in cilantro and beer.

Nutrition Information

- Calories: 353 calories;
- Cholesterol: 19
- Protein: 16
- Total Fat: 13.8
- Sodium: 741
- Total Carbohydrate: 39.8

558. Fudgy Brownies I

Serving: 24 | Prep: 15mins | Cook: 35mins | Ready in:

Ingredients

- 3/4 cup unsweetened cocoa powder
- 1/2 teaspoon baking soda
- 1/3 cup vegetable oil
- 1/2 cup boiling water
- 2 cups white sugar
- 2 eggs
- 1/3 cup vegetable oil
- 1 1/3 cups all-purpose flour
- 1 teaspoon vanilla extract
- 1/4 teaspoon salt

Direction

- Preheat an oven to 175°C/350°F and grease then flour 9x13-in. pan.
- Mix baking soda and cocoa in a big bowl. Add boiling water and 1/3 cup of vegetable oil; mix till thick and blended well. Mix in leftover 1/3 cup oil, eggs and sugar. Add salt, vanilla and flour; mix till all flour is just absorbed. Evenly spread in prepped pan.
- In preheated oven, bake till inserted toothpick in cake exits clean for 35-40 minutes; cool. Cut to squares.

Nutrition Information

- Calories: 156 calories;
- Protein: 1.8
- Total Fat: 7
- Sodium: 57
- Total Carbohydrate: 23.5
- Cholesterol: 16

559. Garlic Chicken And Grapes

Serving: 6 | Prep: 5mins | Cook: 40mins | Ready in:

Ingredients

- 3 tablespoons Dijon-style prepared mustard
- 3 tablespoons soy sauce
- 2 tablespoons honey
- 2 tablespoons white wine vinegar
- 2 cloves garlic, minced
- 2 tablespoons vegetable oil
- 3 pounds skinless, boneless chicken breast halves
- 1 tablespoon sesame seeds
- 2 cups seedless green grapes

Direction

- Mix vinegar, honey, soy sauce, and mustard. Put the sauce aside.
- In a 9 x 13 inch pan, blend garlic and oil. Put the chicken in pan and skin sides down.
- If you use thighs, cover and bake at 400°F (205°C) for 25 minutes. If you use breasts, cover and bake at 400°F (205°C) in 10 minutes. Uncover, and flip chicken pieces over. Scatter with sesame seeds. Bake until the center is no longer pink, about 15-20 minutes. Put grapes over chicken, and bake for extra 5 minutes. Take away from the oven, and place the grapes and chicken on a platter. Pour over the sauce when serving.

Nutrition Information

- Calories: 373 calories;
- Total Fat: 11.1
- Sodium: 753
- Total Carbohydrate: 18.1
- Cholesterol: 129
- Protein: 48.4

560. Garlic Chicken Stir Fry

Serving: 4 | Prep: | Cook: | Ready in:

Ingredients

- 2 tablespoons peanut oil
- 6 cloves garlic, minced
- 1 teaspoon grated fresh ginger
- 1 bunch green onions, chopped
- 1 teaspoon salt
- 1 pound boneless skinless chicken breasts, cut into strips
- 2 onions, thinly sliced
- 1 cup sliced cabbage
- 1 red bell pepper, thinly sliced
- 2 cups sugar snap peas
- 1 cup chicken broth
- 2 tablespoons soy sauce
- 2 tablespoons white sugar
- 2 tablespoons cornstarch

Direction

- In a big skillet or wok, heat the peanut oil. Once oil starts to smoke, stir in salt, green onions, ginger root and 2 cloves of minced garlic rapidly. Stir fry the onion for 2 minutes, until it is translucent. Put in chicken and stir for 3 minutes, until opaque. Put in leftover 4 cloves minced garlic and stir. Put in 1/2 cup of broth or water, peas, bell pepper, cabbage and sweet onions, then place on a cover.
- Combine cornstarch, sugar, soy sauce and leftover 1/2 cup of broth or water in a small bowl. Put the sauce mixture into the wok or skillet and stir until both vegetables and chicken are well-coated with the thickened sauce. Serve instantly on top of hot rice, if wanted.

Nutrition Information

- Calories: 337 calories;
- Sodium: 1364
- Total Carbohydrate: 32.3
- Cholesterol: 67
- Protein: 31.7
- Total Fat: 8.6

561. Garlic New Potatoes

Serving: 4 | Prep: | Cook: 20mins | Ready in:

Ingredients

- 1 (14 ounce) can Swanson® Seasoned Chicken Broth with Roasted Garlic
- 4 cups small new potatoes cut in half

Direction

- In a saucepan, put the potatoes and broth and heat to a boil, then cover.
- Let it cook for 15 minutes on low heat or until it becomes tender, then drain.

Nutrition Information

- Calories: 127 calories;
- Sodium: 402
- Total Carbohydrate: 27.9
- Cholesterol: 2
- Protein: 3.5
- Total Fat: 0.6

562. Garlic Rice

Serving: 4 | Prep: 5mins | Cook: 5mins | Ready in:

Ingredients

- 2 tablespoons vegetable oil
- 1 1/2 tablespoons chopped garlic
- 2 tablespoons ground pork
- 4 cups cooked white rice
- 1 1/2 teaspoons garlic salt
- ground black pepper to taste

Direction

- In a large skillet set on medium-high heat, add oil. Once the oil is hot, put the garlic and ground pork. Stir and cook until the garlic turns golden brown. For maximum flavor, this is the color you need, prevent it from burning, or the flavor will be bitter.
- Mix in the cooked white rice, and add pepper and garlic salt to season. Stir and cook for approximately 3 minutes until heated well and well combined. Serve and enjoy.

Nutrition Information

- Calories: 293 calories;
- Cholesterol: 6
- Protein: 5.9
- Total Fat: 9
- Sodium: 686
- Total Carbohydrate: 45.9

563. Garlic And Ranch Turkey Burgers

Serving: 4 | Prep: 20mins | Cook: 10mins | Ready in:

Ingredients

- 1 pound ground turkey
- 1 (1 ounce) package ranch dressing mix
- 1 egg
- 3 cloves garlic, minced
- 1/4 cup Worcestershire sauce
- seasoned salt and pepper to taste

Direction

- Prepare an outdoor grill by preheating it on medium-high heat and coat the grate lightly with oil.
- Combine the turkey, egg, ranch mix, garlic, seasoned salt, Worcestershire sauce, and pepper, kneading them together in a bowl until they are well blended; form into 4 patties of equal proportions.
- Grill the patties on for about 5 minutes per side to be cooked well done. Insert an instant-read thermometer into the center and it should read 165° F (74° C).

Nutrition Information

- Calories: 219 calories;
- Sodium: 796
- Total Carbohydrate: 7.7
- Cholesterol: 130
- Protein: 24.2
- Total Fat: 9.8

564. German Apple Cake I

Serving: 24 | Prep: | Cook: | Ready in:

Ingredients

- 2 eggs
- 1 cup vegetable oil
- 2 cups white sugar
- 2 teaspoons ground cinnamon
- 1/2 teaspoon salt
- 1 teaspoon vanilla extract
- 2 cups all-purpose flour
- 1 teaspoon baking soda
- 4 cups apples - peeled, cored and diced

Direction

- Heat the oven to 175°C or 350°F. Oil a cake pan, 9x13 inch in size and dust with flour.
- Use electric mixer to whip eggs and oil in mixing bowl till creamy. Put in vanilla and sugar and whip thoroughly.
- In bowl, mix baking soda, ground cinnamon and flour salt. Gently put this mixture to mixture of egg and combine till incorporated. Batter will become extremely thick. Use hand with wooden spoon to fold apples in. Scatter batter to prepped pan.
- Bake for 45 minutes at 175°C or 350°F or till cake checks done. Cool cake on wire rack. When cake cools, top with a Cream Cheese Frosting or a dust with confectioners' sugar to serve.

Nutrition Information

- Calories: 201 calories;
- Protein: 1.7
- Total Fat: 9.7
- Sodium: 107
- Total Carbohydrate: 27.7
- Cholesterol: 16

565. Gina's Lemon Pepper Chicken

Serving: 6 | Prep: | Cook: | Ready in:

Ingredients

- 6 skinless, boneless chicken breast halves
- 1 teaspoon lemon pepper
- 1 pinch garlic powder
- 1 teaspoon onion powder

Direction

- Preheat an oven to 175°C/350°F.
- Put chicken into a 9x13-in. lightly greased baking dish; season to taste with onion powder, garlic powder and lemon pepper. In the preheated oven, bake for 15 minutes.
- Flip chicken pieces; to taste, add more seasoning. Bake till juices are clear and chicken cooks through for 15 minutes more.

Nutrition Information

- Calories: 133 calories;
- Total Fat: 2.8
- Sodium: 136
- Total Carbohydrate: 0.5
- Cholesterol: 67
- Protein: 24.6

566. Gingerbread Biscotti

Serving: 48 | Prep: 25mins | Cook: 40mins | Ready in:

Ingredients

- 1/3 cup vegetable oil
- 1 cup white sugar
- 3 eggs
- 1/4 cup molasses
- 2 1/4 cups all-purpose flour
- 1 cup whole wheat flour
- 1 tablespoon baking powder
- 1 1/2 tablespoons ground ginger
- 3/4 tablespoon ground cinnamon
- 1/2 tablespoon ground cloves
- 1/4 teaspoon ground nutmeg

Direction

- Set the oven at 190 degrees C (375 degrees F) to preheat. Coat baking sheet with oil or butter.
- In a big bowl, blend together molasses, eggs, sugar, and oil. In a different bowl, mix baking powder, flours, nutmeg, cinnamon, ginger, and cloves; combine into egg mixture until a stiff dough is formed.
- Halve dough, and form each half into a cookie-sized roll. Set rolls onto baking sheet, and press down the dough until it becomes 1/2 inch thick.
- Bake for 25 minutes in the preheated oven. Take out from oven, and allow to cool completely.
- Slice diagonally to 1/2 inch thickness. Put diagonal slices on baking sheet, and bake until crispy and toasted, for another 5 to 7 minutes per side.

Nutrition Information

- Calories: 70 calories;
- Sodium: 26
- Total Carbohydrate: 12.1
- Cholesterol: 12
- Protein: 1.4
- Total Fat: 2

567. Glazed Corned Beef

Serving: 7 | Prep: 15mins | Cook: 3hours | Ready in:

Ingredients

- 4 1/2 pounds corned beef, rinsed
- 1 cup water
- 1 cup apricot preserves
- 1/4 cup brown sugar
- 2 tablespoons soy sauce

Direction

- Preheat an oven to 175°C/350°F>
- Use nonstick cooking spray to coat big pan. Put corned beef in dish; add water. Tightly cover with aluminum foil; bake for 2 hours then drain liquid.
- Mix soy sauce, brown sugar and apricot preserves in small bowl; evenly spread apricot mixture on corned beef.
- Bake for 25-30 minutes at 175°C/350°F, uncovered, till meat is tender, occasionally basting with pan drippings.
- Across grain, slice corned beef; serve.

Nutrition Information

- Calories: 463 calories;
- Total Fat: 24.3
- Sodium: 1725
- Total Carbohydrate: 38.1
- Cholesterol: 125
- Protein: 23.8

568. Gluten And Dairy Free Roasted Cashew Cake

Serving: 8 | Prep: 20mins | Cook: 28mins | Ready in:

Ingredients

- Roasted Cashew Flour:
- 1 cup coarsely chopped raw cashews
- 1 1/2 teaspoons honey
- 1/2 teaspoon coarse salt
- Cake:
- 3/4 cup oat milk
- 1/2 cup coconut oil, melted
- 2 eggs, lightly beaten
- 1 cup brown rice flour
- 1/2 cup arrowroot powder
- 1 tablespoon baking powder
- 1 1/2 teaspoons guar gum
- 1 teaspoon ground cinnamon
- 1 pinch ground nutmeg
- 1 pinch ground ginger
- 1 pinch ground cloves
- 1 pinch chili powder
- 1 pinch salt

Direction

- Preheat oven to 375 °F (190 °C).
- On a baking sheet, spread cashews. Sprinkle on top with coarse salt; use honey for drizzling over.
- In the preheated oven, roast for around 3 to 5 minutes till it has the color of golden brown. Let it cool briefly for nearly 5 minutes.
- In a blender or nut grinder, grind cashews into a meal. Sift meal through a fine sieve. Repeat grinding process till meal has a flour-like, fine consistency.
- In a bowl, mix eggs, coconut oil and oat milk together.
- In a large bowl, combine brown rice flour, 3/4 cup cashew flour, baking powder, arrowroot powder, cinnamon, guar gum, ginger, nutmeg, cloves, salt and chili powder. Create a well in the center; pour in oat milk mixture. Mix using a wooden spoon till batter is blended well.
- Use coconut oil to grease a round cake pan of 8-inch in size. Pour batter into the pan.
- In the preheated oven, bake for approximately 25 to 32 minutes till a toothpick pricked into the center comes out clean.

Nutrition Information

- Calories: 342 calories;
- Protein: 6.4
- Total Fat: 22.9
- Sodium: 354
- Total Carbohydrate: 30.4
- Cholesterol: 46

569. Gluten Free Avocado Brownies

Serving: 16 | Prep: 15mins | Cook: 36mins | Ready in:

Ingredients

- cooking spray
- 6 ounces unsweetened 70% dark chocolate
- 1 tablespoon coconut oil
- 3 avocados - peeled, pitted, and diced
- 3 eggs
- 3/4 cup honey
- 1/4 cup unsweetened cocoa powder
- 1 tablespoon coconut flour
- 1 teaspoon vanilla extract
- 1 teaspoon baking soda
- 1 teaspoon salt

Direction

- Set an oven to preheat to 175°C (350°F). Use cooking spray to grease a 9x13-inch baking pan.
- In a ceramic or microwave-safe glass bowl, melt the chocolate with coconut oil in 15-second intervals for 1-3 minutes, stirring after every melting.

- In the food processor, put diced avocado then blend it until it becomes fully smooth.
- In a bowl, whisk the salt, baking soda, vanilla extract, coconut flour, cocoa powder, honey and eggs, until well combined and add the avocado puree then mix until well incorporated. In the prepared baking pan, pour the batter.
- Let it bake in the preheated oven for 35-40 minutes, until an inserted toothpick into the middle exits clean.

Nutrition Information

- Calories: 188 calories;
- Total Fat: 13.1
- Sodium: 243
- Total Carbohydrate: 20.6
- Cholesterol: 35
- Protein: 3.7

570. Gluten Free Dehydrated Rosemary And Cranberry Crisps

Serving: 35 | Prep: 30mins | Cook: | Ready in:

Ingredients

- 1 1/2 cups almonds
- 3/4 cup chopped hemp seeds
- 1/2 cup chia seeds
- 2 tablespoons dried rosemary
- 4 packets stevia powder
- 1 tablespoon garlic and dried vegetable seasoning
- Himalayan salt and cracked black pepper to taste
- 1 cup coconut flour
- 1 cup minced dried cranberries
- 1 1/2 large bananas
- 1 Gala apple, cored and chopped
- 2 figs
- 1/2 cup finely chopped cabbage
- 1/2 cup finely chopped kale

Direction

- Use enough water to cover almonds in bowl; soak for 8 hours - overnight. Drain; mince almonds.
- Mix black pepper, salt, vegetable and garlic seasoning, stevia powder, rosemary, chia seeds, hemp seeds and almonds in big bowl.
- Pulse dried cranberries and coconut flour till evenly combined in food processor; add into seed mixture. Pulse kale, cabbage, figs, apple and bananas till pureed in food processor; add into seed mixture. Use your hands to mix seed mixture till dough is mixed well; let it stand for 30 minutes.
- Halve dough; put each half on parchment paper sheet. Put another parchment paper sheet on each roll. Use rolling pin to roll dough till thin; cut to squares. Use a spatula to transfer to food dehydrator.
- Follow manufacturer's instruction to dehydrate crackers, rotating racks if needed, for 8-10 hours till crisp. Immediately store in airtight bags.

Nutrition Information

- Calories: 85 calories;
- Total Carbohydrate: 8.2
- Cholesterol: 0
- Protein: 3
- Total Fat: 5.2
- Sodium: 23

571. Gluten Free Teff Crackers

Serving: 4 | Prep: 10mins | Cook: 40mins | Ready in:

Ingredients

- 1/2 cup water
- 1/4 cup teff flour
- 3 tablespoons tapioca flour
- 1/4 cup sunflower seed kernels

- 1/4 cup pepitas (roasted green pumpkin seeds)
- 1 tablespoon sesame seeds
- 1 tablespoon flax seeds
- 1 tablespoon teff
- 1 teaspoon black sesame seeds
- 1/4 teaspoon salt
- salt to taste

Direction

- Set an oven to preheat to 190°C (375°F), then grease a 9x12-inch baking sheet.
- In a bowl, stir together the tapioca flour, teff flour and water until it becomes smooth, then add 1/4 tsp salt, black sesame seeds, teff, flax seeds, sesame seeds, pepitas and sunflower seeds and mix until the mixture becomes soupy. Pour the mixture onto the prepped baking sheet, then tap the pan on the counter to distribute the mixture evenly in the pan.
- Let it bake in the preheated oven for about 40 minutes until the crackers become crisp, then sprinkle salt on top of the warm crackers.

Nutrition Information

- Calories: 161 calories;
- Sodium: 150
- Total Carbohydrate: 18.3
- Cholesterol: 0
- Protein: 4.9
- Total Fat: 8.5

572. Gluten Free And Dairy Free Pumpkin Mug Cake

Serving: 1 | Prep: 10mins | Cook: 2mins | Ready in:

Ingredients

- 6 tablespoons pumpkin puree
- 1 egg
- 2 tablespoons coconut oil
- 2 tablespoons honey
- 1 teaspoon vanilla extract
- 3 tablespoons blanched almond flour
- 1/2 teaspoon gluten-free baking powder
- 2 pinches ground cinnamon
- 1 pinch ground nutmeg
- 1 pinch ground ginger
- 1 pinch ground cardamom

Direction

- In a small bowl mix together coconut oil, pumpkin puree, honey, egg, and vanilla extract then put almond flour, nutmeg, cinnamon, baking powder, ginger, and cardamom and mix until well blended. Transfer mixture to a large microwaveable mug.
- On high heat, microwave for 2 minutes. Watch closely to prevent overflowing.

Nutrition Information

- Calories: 592 calories;
- Total Fat: 43.6
- Sodium: 308
- Total Carbohydrate: 44.6
- Cholesterol: 164
- Protein: 11

573. Gluten Free And Dairy Free Vanilla Banana Pops

Serving: 6 | Prep: 10mins | Cook: | Ready in:

Ingredients

- 2 large very ripe bananas
- 1 cup unsweetened vanilla-flavored almond milk (such as Almond Breeze®)
- 1 tablespoon honey

Direction

- Blend honey, almond milk and bananas till smooth in a blender. Put banana mixture in ice pop molds; freeze 8 hours to overnight till firm. Over mold, run warm water to release ice pop molds.

Nutrition Information

- Calories: 67 calories;
- Sodium: 27
- Total Carbohydrate: 16.1
- Cholesterol: 0
- Protein: 0.7
- Total Fat: 0.6

574. Gnocchi I

Serving: 4 | Prep: 30mins | Cook: 30mins | Ready in:

Ingredients

- 2 potatoes
- 2 cups all-purpose flour
- 1 egg

Direction

- Boil salted water in a large pot. Peel the potatoes and put into the pot. Cook for 15 mins until they are tender but they are still firm. Then drain. Let it cool and mash with a potato masher or fork.
- In a large bowl, combine egg, flour and one cup of the mashed potato. Knead the dough until it shapes a ball. Form the small portions of dough into the long "snakes". Slice the snakes into 1/2-in. pieces on the floured surface.
- Boil the lightly salted water in a large pot. Put in gnocchi by dropping. Cook until the gnocchi have risen to top, or about 3-5 mins. Then drain and enjoy.

Nutrition Information

- Calories: 329 calories;
- Protein: 9.7
- Total Fat: 2
- Sodium: 22
- Total Carbohydrate: 67
- Cholesterol: 53

575. Gobble Up Granola Snacks

Serving: 18 | Prep: | Cook: | Ready in:

Ingredients

- 2 1/2 cups crispy rice cereal
- 2 cups quick-cooking oats
- 1/2 cup raisins
- 1/2 cup packed brown sugar
- 1/2 cup light corn syrup
- 1/2 cup crunchy peanut butter
- 1 teaspoon vanilla extract

Direction

- Stir raisins, oats and rice cereal together in a big bowl, then put aside. Coat a 13"x9" baking dish with cooking spray.
- In a small saucepan, mix together corn syrup and brown sugar on medium heat, then heat the mixture just until boiling. Take away from the heat and stir in vanilla and peanut butter until smooth. Pour the mixture over oat and cereal mixture, mix well.
- Press the mixture into the prepped pan with the back of a big spoon, then let the mixture cool and cut into squares.

Nutrition Information

- Calories: 146 calories;
- Cholesterol: 0
- Protein: 3.3
- Total Fat: 4.2
- Sodium: 72

- Total Carbohydrate: 25.6

576. Golden Milk Nice Cream

Serving: 6 | Prep: 15mins | Cook: 5mins | Ready in:

Ingredients

- 1 (14 ounce) can coconut milk
- 2/3 (8 ounce) can coconut cream
- 1 (1 1/2 inch) piece fresh ginger, peeled and sliced
- 1 (2 inch) piece fresh turmeric root, peeled and grated
- 2 tablespoons coconut oil
- 1/2 vanilla bean, halved lengthwise
- 1/4 cinnamon stick
- 10 cardamom pods
- 1/2 teaspoon black peppercorns
- 3 tablespoons honey
- 1 (1/2 inch) piece fresh ginger, peeled and grated
- 1/8 teaspoon ground turmeric
- 1/8 teaspoon cayenne pepper (optional)

Direction

- In a bowl, split vanilla bean. Combine it with coconut oil, fresh turmeric, sliced ginger, coconut cream and coconut milk. Set aside.
- In a mortar, add peppercorns, cardamom pods and cinnamon sticks. Use pestle to grind until the cardamom pods open and cinnamon sticks turn into pieces. Smash the seeds slightly. Crush peppercorns lightly.
- In a saucepan over medium-low heat, pour in the cinnamon mixture. Release natural oils in the spices by stirring lightly. Take it off the heat.
- In a saucepan, add the coconut milk mixture. Do not leave it too hot. Stir in honey. Stir well to mix and let it sit for 15 minutes at room temperature. Put into the refrigerator to cool for 10 minutes; make sure the coconut oil is still liquid.
- Take cardamom pods and sliced ginger off the mixture and discard. Take off vanilla bean. Scrape the paste from the pod; stir it into the milk. Discard vanilla bean pod. Use an immersion blender to blend the mixture to smooth.
- In an ice cream maker, add coconut milk mixture and let it freeze for 20 minutes following the instructions of manufacturer. At the last 5 churning minutes, put in fresh grated ginger. Pour into an airtight container to freeze for 4 hours until it is firm.
- Dust ground cayenne and ground turmeric on top to serve.

Nutrition Information

- Calories: 303 calories;
- Total Fat: 22.6
- Sodium: 19
- Total Carbohydrate: 26.9
- Cholesterol: 0
- Protein: 1.9

577. Gourmet Chicken Sandwich

Serving: 4 | Prep: 10mins | Cook: 15mins | Ready in:

Ingredients

- 4 skinless, boneless chicken breast halves - pounded to 1/4 inch thickness
- ground black pepper to taste
- 1 tablespoon olive oil
- 1 teaspoon minced garlic
- 2 tablespoons mayonnaise
- 2 teaspoons prepared Dijon-style mustard
- 1 teaspoon chopped fresh rosemary
- 8 slices garlic and rosemary focaccia bread

Direction

- Add pepper on 1 side of each chicken cutlet. In a big skillet, heat the oil and cook the garlic in oil until it becomes brown, then add the chicken pepper-side facing down. Sauté the chicken for about 12-15 minutes, until the juices run clear and cooked through.
- Mix together the rosemary, mustard and mayonnaise in a small bowl. Mix together and spread the mixture on four focaccia bread slices. Put one chicken cutlet on each of the slices, then put on another slice of bread.

Nutrition Information

- Calories: 522 calories;
- Total Fat: 15.7
- Sodium: 826
- Total Carbohydrate: 58
- Cholesterol: 70
- Protein: 34.6

578. Grandma's Gingersnap Cookies

Serving: 30 | Prep: 20mins | Cook: 10mins | Ready in:

Ingredients

- 2 cups sifted all-purpose flour
- 1 tablespoon ground ginger
- 2 teaspoons baking soda
- 1 teaspoon ground cinnamon
- 1/2 teaspoon salt
- 3/4 cup shortening
- 1 cup white sugar
- 1 egg
- 1/4 cup dark molasses
- 1/3 cup cinnamon sugar

Direction

- Preheat an oven to 175°C/350°F.
- Sift salt, cinnamon, baking soda, ginger and flour into the mixing bowl; mix to evenly blend. Sift again into a separate bowl.
- Beat shortening till creamy in a mixing bowl; beat in white sugar slowly. Beat in dark molasses and egg. Sift 1/3 of flour mixture into the shortening mixture; mix to blend thoroughly. Sift in leftover flour mixture; mix together till soft dough forms. Pinch small dough amounts off; between your hands, roll to 1-in. diameter balls. Roll every ball in cinnamon sugar; put onto ungreased baking sheet, 2-in. apart.
- In the preheated oven, bake for 10 minutes till tops are slightly cracked and rounded; cool cookies on a wire rack. Keep in an airtight container.

Nutrition Information

- Calories: 121 calories;
- Total Carbohydrate: 17.5
- Cholesterol: 6
- Protein: 1.1
- Total Fat: 5.4
- Sodium: 126

579. Grandma's Taffy

Serving: 40 | Prep: 5mins | Cook: 15mins | Ready in:

Ingredients

- 2 cups sugar
- 2 tablespoons cornstarch
- 4 tablespoons butter
- 1 teaspoon salt
- 1/2 cup corn syrup
- 1 1/2 cups water
- 2 teaspoons vanilla extract
- 1 tablespoon orange, or other flavored extract
- 8 drops any color food coloring

Direction

- Combine cornstarch and sugar in a large saucepan. Include in water, corn syrup, salt, and butter; combine well. Heat to a boil on medium heat, stirring to blend in butter. Heat to 275°F (134°C), until a bit of syrup dropped from a spoon is creates hard but pliable threads.
- Take off from the heat, and blend in food coloring, flavored extract, and vanilla. Transfer into a greased 8x8-inch baking dish. When cooled enough to hold, take the candy out from the pan, and pull until it loses its gloss and turn stiff. Shape into ropes, and cut with scissors into 1-inch pieces. Encase each piece in waxed paper.

Nutrition Information

- Calories: 63 calories;
- Sodium: 69
- Total Carbohydrate: 13.5
- Cholesterol: 3
- Protein: 0
- Total Fat: 1.2

580. Grandmother's Oatmeal Cookies

Serving: 48 | Prep: 20mins | Cook: 12mins | Ready in:

Ingredients

- 3 eggs
- 1 cup raisins
- 1 teaspoon vanilla extract
- 1 cup butter flavored shortening
- 1 cup packed brown sugar
- 1 cup white sugar
- 2 1/2 cups all-purpose flour
- 2 teaspoons baking soda
- 1 teaspoon salt
- 1 teaspoon ground cinnamon
- 2 cups quick cooking oats
- 1/2 cup chopped walnuts

Direction

- Beat the eggs. Then stir in vanilla and raisins. Chill in the refrigerator for at least an hour.
- Start preheating the oven to 350°F (175°C).
- Cream white sugar, brown sugar and shortening together until fluffy and light. Combine cinnamon, salt, baking soda and flour. Then stir into sugar mixture. Mix in eggs and raisins. Stir in walnuts and oats. Form the dough into the walnut sized balls, arrange 2-inch apart on the ungreased cookie sheets.
- Bake in the prepared oven for 10-12 mins or until the edges turn golden. Place on the wire racks to cool.

Nutrition Information

- Calories: 131 calories;
- Total Carbohydrate: 18.5
- Cholesterol: 12
- Protein: 1.8
- Total Fat: 5.9
- Sodium: 107

581. Grape Nuts® Coconut Ice Cream

Serving: 14 | Prep: 10mins | Cook: | Ready in:

Ingredients

- 1/4 cup roasted flax seeds
- 2 (14 ounce) cans full-fat coconut milk, chilled
- 1 1/2 teaspoons vanilla extract
- 1 teaspoon stevia powder
- 1 teaspoon xanthan gum (optional)
- 1 teaspoon coconut oil (optional)
- 1/2 teaspoon maple extract
- 1/4 teaspoon Himalayan black salt
- 1 cup wheat and barley nugget cereal (such as Grape-Nuts®), frozen

Direction

- Pulse flax seeds in a coffee grinder until they ground finely. Remove to a blender.
- Pour coconut milk into the blender. Add black salt, maple extract, coconut oil, xanthan gum, stevia powder and vanilla extract, stir for about 2 minutes until very smooth.
- Place the blender container to the freezer to chill mixture briefly for about 15 minutes.
- Transfer mixture to an ice cream maker; churn as instructed by the manufacturer for about 25 minutes. Place into a lidded container; freeze for about half an hour until firm but still malleable. Stir in barley cereal nuggets and wheat until well-incorporated.

Nutrition Information

- Calories: 161 calories;
- Cholesterol: 0
- Protein: 2.5
- Total Fat: 13.6
- Sodium: 108
- Total Carbohydrate: 9.7

582. Green Bean And Bacon Saute

Serving: 8 | Prep: 10mins | Cook: 10mins | Ready in:

Ingredients

- 10 slices bacon, diced
- 1 tablespoon crushed garlic
- 1/2 teaspoon crushed red pepper flakes
- 2 (10 ounce) packages frozen whole green beans
- salt and pepper to taste

Direction

- Let bacon cook in a large skillet placed over medium-high heat until it becomes crispy. Remove bacon pieces with a slotted spoon and drain them on a plate lined with paper towel. Discard excess grease from the skillet, remaining about 2 tablespoons in the pan.
- Combine the red pepper flakes and the garlic with the bacon grease and let it cook over medium-high heat for 60 seconds until it releases an aroma. Add green beans, salt and pepper to season. Cook while stirring for 10 minutes, until the beans are soft but a bit crunchy. Transfer bacon back to the pan and serve after garnishing with beans.

Nutrition Information

- Calories: 83 calories;
- Cholesterol: 13
- Protein: 5.4
- Total Fat: 5
- Sodium: 269
- Total Carbohydrate: 4.8

583. Green Beans And Potatoes

Serving: 6 | Prep: 10mins | Cook: 25mins | Ready in:

Ingredients

- 3 cups thinly sliced potatoes
- 2 cups frozen green beans
- 1/2 teaspoon dried thyme
- 1/4 teaspoon ground black pepper
- 1 teaspoon vegetarian Worcestershire sauce
- 1 cup vegetable broth, divided
- 1 teaspoon cornstarch
- 1/4 cup chopped fresh parsley

Direction

- Mix together 3/4 cup of broth, Worcestershire sauce, pepper, thyme, green beans and potatoes in a big skillet on moderately high heat, then bring the mixture to a boil. Lower heat to moderately low, then cover and

simmer until vegetables are softened, about 15-20 minutes.
- Blend cornstarch with leftover broth in a small bowl, then stir in parsley and put all into potato mixture. Cook while stirring until thickened and bubbly.

Nutrition Information

- Calories: 83 calories;
- Protein: 2.1
- Total Fat: 0.2
- Sodium: 99
- Total Carbohydrate: 18.3
- Cholesterol: 0

584. Green Beans With Bacon Dressing

Serving: 8 | Prep: 5mins | Cook: 25mins | Ready in:

Ingredients

- 6 slices bacon
- 2 eggs, well beaten
- 1/3 cup vinegar
- 1/2 cup water
- 3 tablespoons white sugar
- 1/4 teaspoon salt
- 2 (15 ounce) cans green beans

Direction

- Use a large, deep skillet and cook the bacon over medium high heat until evenly brown. Drain and set aside the drippings. Crumble into pieces.
- Combine together the water, sugar, vinegar, salt and eggs in a medium bowl. Cook in the bacon drippings over low heat while stirring constantly.
- Use a saucepan to heat the green beans over medium heat. Drain and transfer the beans to a serving dish then pour the hot dressing mixture oven beans and crumbled bacon on top.

Nutrition Information

- Calories: 150 calories;
- Total Carbohydrate: 8.4
- Cholesterol: 61
- Protein: 4.9
- Total Fat: 10.7
- Sodium: 563

585. Green Beans With Hazelnuts And Lemon

Serving: 8 | Prep: 10mins | Cook: 10mins | Ready in:

Ingredients

- 1 1/2 pounds fresh green beans, washed and trimmed
- 2 tablespoons olive oil
- 1 1/2 teaspoons lemon zest
- 1/3 cup chopped toasted hazelnuts
- salt and pepper to taste

Direction

- Cook beans in a big pot of boiling salted water until tender, about 3 - 8 minutes. Drain and move to a big bowl.
- Add pepper, salt, hazelnuts, lemon zest, and olive oil. You can make the beans a day before, chill while covered. Reheat beans preferably using a microwave.

Nutrition Information

- Calories: 86 calories;
- Protein: 2.3
- Total Fat: 6.4
- Sodium: 5
- Total Carbohydrate: 6.9
- Cholesterol: 0

586. Green Potatoes

Serving: 8 | Prep: 10mins | Cook: 1hours | Ready in:

Ingredients

- 5 pounds potatoes, peeled and halved
- 3 cloves garlic, crushed
- 1/4 cup chopped parsley
- salt and pepper to taste

Direction

- Mix together the pepper, salt, parsley, garlic and potatoes in a big pot, then pour in enough water just to cover the potatoes. Put cover on and cook for 1 hour on medium heat, stirring from time to time. Allow it to stand for 10 minutes.

Nutrition Information

- Calories: 222 calories;
- Protein: 4.5
- Total Fat: 0.3
- Sodium: 14
- Total Carbohydrate: 51.6
- Cholesterol: 0

587. Green Stuff (Cucumber Guacamole)

Serving: 8 | Prep: 15mins | Cook: | Ready in:

Ingredients

- 1 large avocado, peeled and pitted
- 1 tablespoon lime juice
- 2 green onions, chopped
- 1/2 cucumber, peeled and chopped
- 1/2 teaspoon salt
- 1/2 cup cold water

Direction

- Mix together the water, salt, cucumber, green onion, lime juice and avocado in a blender; mix well until becomes smooth.

Nutrition Information

- Calories: 60 calories;
- Sodium: 149
- Total Carbohydrate: 3.8
- Cholesterol: 0
- Protein: 0.9
- Total Fat: 5.2

588. Green Tomato And Bell Pepper Delight

Serving: 6 | Prep: 5mins | Cook: 10mins | Ready in:

Ingredients

- 2 tablespoons olive oil
- 4 green tomatoes, chopped
- 1 green bell pepper, chopped
- 2 celery, chopped
- 1 bunch green onions, chopped
- 2 tablespoons apple cider vinegar

Direction

- In a big skillet, heat the olive oil on medium heat. Stir in apple cider vinegar, green onions, celery, bell pepper and green tomatoes. Sauté for around 5-10 minutes until it becomes tender-crisp.

Nutrition Information

- Calories: 127 calories;
- Protein: 2.6
- Total Fat: 6.8

- Sodium: 399
- Total Carbohydrate: 15.6
- Cholesterol: 0

589. Grilled 'Fusion' Pork Chops

Serving: 4 | Prep: 5mins | Cook: 20mins | Ready in:

Ingredients

- 1/4 cup soy sauce
- 1/4 cup lime juice
- 1 tablespoon garlic paste
- 1 tablespoon ginger paste
- 4 (1-inch-thick) pork chops
- 1 tablespoon garam masala

Direction

- Combine the ginger, lime juice, soy sauce, and garlic in a bowl.
- Arrange the pork chops onto the glass dish. Drizzle soy sauce mixture all over the chops. Cover the glass dish and chill the meat for 2-3 hours while occasionally flipping it.
- Set the outdoor grill over direct heat for preheating. Oil the grate lightly.
- Arrange the chops onto the grill. Sprinkle the chops with garam masala while cooking. Cook each side for 10 minutes.

Nutrition Information

- Calories: 194 calories;
- Sodium: 1099
- Total Carbohydrate: 3.5
- Cholesterol: 87
- Protein: 30.8
- Total Fat: 4.9

590. Grilled Asian Chicken

Serving: 4 | Prep: 15mins | Cook: 15mins | Ready in:

Ingredients

- 1/4 cup soy sauce
- 4 teaspoons sesame oil
- 2 tablespoons honey
- 3 slices fresh ginger root
- 2 cloves garlic, crushed
- 4 skinless, boneless chicken breast halves

Direction

- Using a microwave-safe bowl, mix together the soy sauce, honey, garlic, oil, and ginger root. Pop it in the microwave and heat for 1 minute on medium power, then stir. Put it back to the microwave and heat again for 30 minutes, but do not let it boil.
- On a plate or any shallow dish, place and arrange the chicken breasts. Cover the chicken with the soy sauce mixture, and marinate for 15 minutes.
- Meanwhile, preheat the grill on medium-high heat. Remove chicken from marinade, then put marinade in a saucepan. Bring it to a boil and simmer for 5 minutes over medium heat. Set the sauce aside for basting.
- Lightly brush oil onto the grill grate. Grill the marinated chicken breasts for 6 to 8 minutes per side, or until juices dry up. Frequently baste the chicken with the prepared marinade. You'll know it's done when the chicken breasts become golden brown.

Nutrition Information

- Calories: 217 calories;
- Sodium: 961
- Total Carbohydrate: 10.6
- Cholesterol: 67
- Protein: 25.7
- Total Fat: 7.6

591. Grilled Asian Ginger Pork Chops

Serving: 6 | Prep: 5mins | Cook: 10mins | Ready in:

Ingredients

- 1/2 cup orange juice
- 2 tablespoons soy sauce
- 2 tablespoons minced fresh ginger root
- 2 tablespoons grated orange zest
- 1 teaspoon minced garlic
- 1 teaspoon garlic chile paste
- 1/2 teaspoon salt
- 6 pork loin chops, 1/2 inch thick

Direction

- Combine salt, chile paste, garlic, orange zest, ginger, soy sauce and orange juice in a shallow container. Put pork chops in; coat it well by turning. Put into the refrigerator with cover overnight or for at least 2 hours with occasional turns.
- Turn on the grill to high heat to preheat; use oil to lightly grease the grate.
- Arrange pork chops on grill to cook to your desired doneness, about 5-6 minutes on each side.

Nutrition Information

- Calories: 136 calories;
- Cholesterol: 61
- Protein: 21.4
- Total Fat: 3.4
- Sodium: 548
- Total Carbohydrate: 4

592. Grilled Asparagus

Serving: 4 | Prep: 15mins | Cook: 3mins | Ready in:

Ingredients

- 1 pound fresh asparagus spears, trimmed
- 1 tablespoon olive oil
- salt and pepper to taste

Direction

- Preheat grill to high heat.
- Coat asparagus spears lightly with olive oil. Season with pepper and salt to taste.
- Grill on high heat to your desired tenderness for 2-3 minutes.

Nutrition Information

- Calories: 53 calories;
- Sodium: 2
- Total Carbohydrate: 4.4
- Cholesterol: 0
- Protein: 2.5
- Total Fat: 3.5

593. Grilled Brown Sugar Pork Chops

Serving: 6 | Prep: 20mins | Cook: 20mins | Ready in:

Ingredients

- 1/2 cup brown sugar, firmly packed
- 1/2 cup apple juice
- 4 tablespoons vegetable oil
- 1 tablespoon soy sauce
- 1/2 teaspoon ground ginger
- salt and pepper to taste
- 2 teaspoons cornstarch
- 1/2 cup water
- 6 boneless pork chops

Direction

- Set the outdoor grill to high heat for preheating.

- Mix the apple juice, salt, pepper, soy sauce, brown sugar, ginger, and oil in a small saucepan. Boil the mixture. In a small bowl, mix the cornstarch and water, and then pour the mixture into the brown sugar mixture. Whisk the mixture until thickened.
- Lightly oil the grate before arranging the pork chops onto the grill. Cook the pork chops over hot coals for 10-12 minutes, flipping the pork only once. Right before removing the chops from the grill, coat them with the sauce. Serve the pork chops together with the remaining sauce.

Nutrition Information

- Calories: 262 calories;
- Sodium: 179
- Total Carbohydrate: 21.5
- Cholesterol: 36
- Protein: 13.3
- Total Fat: 13.7

594. Grilled Chicken With Herbs

Serving: 6 | Prep: | Cook: | Ready in:

Ingredients

- 2 tablespoons chopped Italian flat leaf parsley
- 2 teaspoons fresh rosemary, minced
- 2 teaspoons chopped fresh thyme
- 1 teaspoon dried sage
- 3 cloves garlic, minced
- 1/4 cup olive oil
- 1/2 cup balsamic vinegar
- salt and pepper to taste
- 1 1/2 pounds skinless, boneless chicken breasts

Direction

- Combine pepper, salt, vinegar, oil, garlic, sage, thyme, rosemary and parsley in a blender to taste. Blend together. In a bowl or nonporous glass dish, put chicken. Add the blended marinade over. Place in the refrigerator to marinate, covered, at least 2 hours to 2 days.
- Set the oven to broil or start preheating the grill to medium high heat.
- Take the chicken away of the dish (disposing of the leftover marinade). Broil or grill until chicken is no longer pink inside and cooked through, about 6-7 minutes on each side.

Nutrition Information

- Calories: 221 calories;
- Protein: 26.5
- Total Fat: 10.5
- Sodium: 80
- Total Carbohydrate: 3.8
- Cholesterol: 66

595. Grilled Lemon Pepper Zucchini

Serving: 4 | Prep: 25mins | Cook: 30mins | Ready in:

Ingredients

- 2 small yellow squash, sliced
- 2 small zucchini, sliced
- 1 small onion, diced
- 1 red bell pepper, minced
- 1 1/2 tablespoons extra-virgin olive oil
- 1 tablespoon lemon-pepper seasoning

Direction

- Set an outdoor grill to preheat to high heat. Oil the grate lightly once it is hot.
- In a bowl, mix together the bell pepper, onion, zucchini and squash. Drizzle it with olive oil, then sprinkle lemon-pepper seasoning on top; stir until coated. Put the vegetable mixture in

the middle of a big sheet of aluminum foil. Place another big sheet of aluminum foil on top, then roll the edges of the foil sheets together to seal into a packet.
- On the preheated grill, place the packet and let it cook for about 30 minutes, until the vegetables become tender, flipping the packet every 5-10 minutes.

Nutrition Information

- Calories: 90 calories;
- Total Fat: 5.5
- Sodium: 356
- Total Carbohydrate: 9.4
- Cholesterol: 0
- Protein: 2.1

596. Grilled Marinated Shrimp

Serving: 6 | Prep: 30mins | Cook: 10mins | Ready in:

Ingredients

- 1 cup olive oil
- 1/4 cup chopped fresh parsley
- 1 lemon, juiced
- 2 tablespoons hot pepper sauce
- 3 cloves garlic, minced
- 1 tablespoon tomato paste
- 2 teaspoons dried oregano
- 1 teaspoon salt
- 1 teaspoon ground black pepper
- 2 pounds large shrimp, peeled and deveined with tails attached
- skewers

Direction

- Combine oregano, hot sauce, parsley, olive oil, garlic, black pepper, salt, tomato paste, and lemon juice in a mixing bowl. Reserve a small amount of the mixture for basting. Use the remaining marinade for the shrimp; pour in a large resealable plastic bag. Stir in shrimp. Seal the bag and store it inside the refrigerator for 2 hours to marinate.
- Set the heat of the grill to medium-low and preheat. Pierce shrimp onto the skewers, piercing near the tail and near the head once, and then discard the marinade.
- Oil the grill grate lightly. Cook each side of the shrimp for 5 minutes, basting constantly with the reserved marinade, until the shrimp is opaque.

Nutrition Information

- Calories: 447 calories;
- Total Fat: 37.5
- Sodium: 800
- Total Carbohydrate: 3.7
- Cholesterol: 230
- Protein: 25.3

597. Grilled Mediterranean Salmon In Foil

Serving: 4 | Prep: 15mins | Cook: 10mins | Ready in:

Ingredients

- 1 (10 ounce) basket cherry tomatoes, quartered
- 4 tablespoons extra-virgin olive oil
- 1 small shallot, finely chopped
- 2 tablespoons black olive tapenade
- 1/2 teaspoon salt
- 8 basil leaves
- 4 small fresh thyme sprigs
- freshly ground black pepper to taste
- 4 (12x18-inch) pieces aluminum foil
- 4 (7 ounce) salmon filets, with skin

Direction

- Set an outdoor grill to high heat to preheat and lightly grease the grate. Close the cover.

- In a bowl, combine cherry tomatoes, pepper, thyme, basil, salt, tapenade, shallot, and olive oil; mix well.
- On a work surface, lay the foil out with the shiny side-up. In the center of a piece of foil, put each salmon fillet with the skin side-down. Use 1/4 of the cherry tomato mixture to cover each piece of salmon. To make a salmon parcel, fold the edges of the foil over the salmon, make sure that the edges are sealed thoroughly.
- Lower the heat of the grill and arrange the foil parcels on the greased grate carefully. Close the cover and cook for 7-8 minutes until the center of the salmon is pale pink and easily flakes using a fork. Then remove the parcels and allow them to sit for a few minutes before opening.

Nutrition Information

- Calories: 493 calories;
- Protein: 36.2
- Total Fat: 34.4
- Sodium: 458
- Total Carbohydrate: 9.5
- Cholesterol: 98

598. Grilled Portobello Mushrooms

Serving: 3 | Prep: 10mins | Cook: 10mins | Ready in:

Ingredients

- 3 portobello mushrooms
- 1/4 cup canola oil
- 3 tablespoons chopped onion
- 4 cloves garlic, minced
- 4 tablespoons balsamic vinegar

Direction

- Clean mushrooms. Remove stems. Put aside for other use. On a plate, put caps, gill side up.
- Mix vinegar, garlic, onion and oil in a small bowl. Evenly pour mixture on mushroom caps. Let it stand for an hour.
- Grill for 10 minutes over hot grill. Immediately serve.

Nutrition Information

- Calories: 217 calories;
- Total Fat: 19
- Sodium: 13
- Total Carbohydrate: 11
- Cholesterol: 0
- Protein: 3.2

599. Grilled Salmon II

Serving: 6 | Prep: 10mins | Cook: 20mins | Ready in:

Ingredients

- 4 (4 ounce) fillets salmon
- 1/4 cup peanut oil
- 2 tablespoons soy sauce
- 2 tablespoons balsamic vinegar
- 2 tablespoons thinly sliced green onion
- 1 1/2 teaspoons brown sugar
- 1 clove garlic, minced
- 3/4 teaspoon ground ginger
- 1/2 teaspoon crushed red pepper flakes
- 1/2 teaspoon sesame oil
- 1/8 teaspoon salt

Direction

- Mix together soy sauce, brown sugar, balsamic vinegar, peanut oil, green onions, ginger, garlic, red chile flakes, salt, and sesame oil. In a glass bowl, put fish and over all pour marinade. Use plastic wrap to cover and chill in the refrigerator for 4-6 hours.
- Preheat gas grill or barbecue.

- Brush the grill rack with oil and 5 inches above coals set height. Take out salmon from the marinade and arrange on grill. Measure at thickness and grill 10 minutes per inch or until fish easily flakes when poked with a fork. Halfway through cooking, turn.

Nutrition Information

- Calories: 233 calories;
- Cholesterol: 44
- Protein: 15.3
- Total Fat: 17.6
- Sodium: 395
- Total Carbohydrate: 2.9

600. Grilled Shrimp Scampi

Serving: 6 | Prep: 30mins | Cook: 6mins | Ready in:

Ingredients

- 1/4 cup olive oil
- 1/4 cup lemon juice
- 3 tablespoons chopped fresh parsley
- 1 tablespoon minced garlic
- ground black pepper to taste
- crushed red pepper flakes to taste (optional)
- 1 1/2 pounds medium shrimp, peeled and deveined

Direction

- Mix lemon juice, olive oil, black pepper, parsley and garlic together in a non-reactive, big bowl. Put in some crushed red pepper for some spice but this is optional. Put in the shrimps and mix well to coat. Keep the marinade in the fridge for 30 minutes.
- Set the grill on high heat and preheat. Insert the marinated shrimps onto the skewers bending each shrimp so that it is pierced once near the head and tail. Throw away the remaining marinade.
- Lightly grease the grill grate. Put the shrimp skewers on the preheated grill and grill for 2 to 3 minutes per side or until the shrimp turns opaque.

Nutrition Information

- Calories: 173 calories;
- Cholesterol: 173
- Protein: 18.7
- Total Fat: 10
- Sodium: 200
- Total Carbohydrate: 1.6

601. Grilled Spiced Chicken With Caribbean Citrus Mango Sauce

Serving: 4 | Prep: 20mins | Cook: 45mins | Ready in:

Ingredients

- 1 teaspoon ground ginger
- 1/2 teaspoon ground cinnamon
- 1/4 teaspoon ground cumin
- 1/4 teaspoon ground anise seed
- 1 dash cayenne pepper
- 4 skinless, boneless chicken breast halves
- 2 cups water
- 1 cup basmati rice
- 1 mango - peeled, seeded and diced
- 1/2 cup orange juice
- 2 tablespoons fresh lime juice
- 2 tablespoons honey
- 2 teaspoons cornstarch
- 1 1/2 tablespoons water
- 2 tablespoons dark rum

Direction

- Mix cayenne pepper, anise, cumin, ginger and cinnamon in a medium bowl; rub spice mixture on chicken. Put into bowl; cover. Refrigerate for 20-30 minutes.

- Boil basmati rice and 2 cups water in a saucepan; lower heat. Cover; simmer till tender for 20 minutes.
- Boil honey, lime juice, orange juice and mango in a small saucepan. Lower heat; simmer for 5 minutes, occasionally mixing. Mix 1 1/2 tbsp. water and cornstarch till cornstarch dissolves in a small cup. Mix into mango mixture; simmer till sauce slightly thickens for 1 minutes. Mix in dark rum.
- Preheat outdoor grill to medium heat; brush oil on grate when hot.
- Grill chicken till juices are clear and not pink for 6-8 minutes per side; serve on cooked rice. Put mango sauce over.

Nutrition Information

- Calories: 418 calories;
- Sodium: 66
- Total Carbohydrate: 62.4
- Cholesterol: 67
- Protein: 28.9
- Total Fat: 3.5

602. Grilled Tilapia With Mango Salsa

Serving: 2 | Prep: 45mins | Cook: 10mins | Ready in:

Ingredients

- 1/3 cup extra-virgin olive oil
- 1 tablespoon lemon juice
- 1 tablespoon minced fresh parsley
- 1 clove garlic, minced
- 1 teaspoon dried basil
- 1 teaspoon ground black pepper
- 1/2 teaspoon salt
- 2 (6 ounce) tilapia fillets
- 1 large ripe mango, peeled, pitted and diced
- 1/2 red bell pepper, diced
- 2 tablespoons minced red onion
- 1 tablespoon chopped fresh cilantro
- 1 jalapeno pepper, seeded and minced
- 2 tablespoons lime juice
- 1 tablespoon lemon juice
- salt and pepper to taste

Direction

- In a bowl, whisk together half a teaspoon of salt, a teaspoon of pepper, basil, garlic, parsley, a tablespoon of lemon juice and extra virgin olive oil. Pour the mixture inside a resealable plastic bag. Add tilapia fillets inside the plastic bag and coat with marinade. Let the air out of the bag then seal. Let the fillets marinate in the refrigerator for an hour.
- For the mango salsa, combine jalapeno pepper, cilantro, red onion, red bell pepper and mango in a bowl. Add in a tablespoon lemon juice and the lime juice. Toss well. Sprinkle salt and pepper for added taste then place inside refrigerator until ready to serve.
- Prepare outdoor grill and preheat to medium high heat. Lightly apply oil to the grate.
- Take out the tilapia fillets from the marinade and shake the excess off. Discard remaining marinade. Cook the fillets on the preheated grill for 3-4 minutes on each side until fillets are no longer translucent in the middle and flakes easily using a fork. Serve fillets with the mango salsa.

Nutrition Information

- Calories: 634 calories;
- Sodium: 697
- Total Carbohydrate: 33.4
- Cholesterol: 62
- Protein: 36.3
- Total Fat: 40.2

603. Grilled Whole Stuffed Trout

Serving: 4 | Prep: 15mins | Cook: 10mins | Ready in:

Ingredients

- 1 lemon, halved
- 5 tablespoons olive oil
- 12 cloves garlic, chopped
- 1/4 cup chopped fresh thyme
- 1/4 cup chopped fresh rosemary
- 1 tablespoon red pepper flakes
- 4 whole trout - cleaned, rinsed, patted dry
- 1 pinch salt and freshly ground black pepper to taste

Direction

- Cut 1/2 lemon to quarts then to thin slices. Cut other half to wedges. Put aside for garnish.
- In a bowl, mix red pepper flakes, rosemary, thyme, garlic, olive oil and lemon slices.
- Generously rub trout inside and out with pepper and salt. Stuff 1/4 lemon-herb mixture in every trout cavity. Marinate in the fridge for 1 hour.
- Preheat outdoor grill to medium high heat. Oil grate lightly.
- Grill trout for 4 minutes per side until flesh easily flakes with a fork. Use lemon wedges to garnish.

Nutrition Information

- Calories: 685 calories;
- Total Carbohydrate: 8.1
- Cholesterol: 197
- Protein: 72.2
- Total Fat: 40.1
- Sodium: 221

604. Ground Beef And Sausage In Red Beans And Rice

Serving: 15 | Prep: 20mins | Cook: 40mins | Ready in:

Ingredients

- 6 cups uncooked white rice
- 1 pound kielbasa sausage
- 1 teaspoon ground cayenne pepper
- 2 pounds lean ground beef
- 1/4 onion, minced
- 2 (15 ounce) cans kidney beans, drained
- 1 (15 ounce) can pinto beans, drained
- 1 (15 ounce) can pork and beans

Direction

- Have rice in big pot ready following packaging instructions.
- Slice kielbasa into an-inch chunks and cut the chunks in quarters. Put in a big skillet for approximately 5 to 10 minutes on medium-high heat, or till slightly browned. Season to taste with cayenne pepper. Turn out this onto the pot of rice, setting aside the grease in skillet.
- Sauté the ground beef using the same skillet on medium-high heat for 5 minutes. Mix in onion and rice; lower the heat to medium and sauté for 5 minutes longer. Drain thoroughly and put into the pot. Into the pot, mix pork and beans, pinto beans and kidney beans. Put in a little of water, if needed, and let it simmer on low heat till ready to serve.

Nutrition Information

- Calories: 615 calories;
- Sodium: 621
- Total Carbohydrate: 77.1
- Cholesterol: 67
- Protein: 25.1
- Total Fat: 21.9

605. Grown Up Dole® Whip

Serving: 2 | Prep: 5mins | Cook: | Ready in:

Ingredients

- 2 cups diced frozen pineapple
- 2 (1.5 fluid ounce) jiggers coconut-flavored vodka
- 1 tablespoon chilled low-fat coconut milk, or as needed

Direction

- In a blender, mix together the vodka and pineapple. Blend it on medium speed, then add coconut milk and blend until it has a consistency of frozen yogurt and smooth. Add more coconut milk if necessary, to thin out the mixture.

Nutrition Information

- Calories: 187 calories;
- Total Fat: 0.9
- Sodium: 3
- Total Carbohydrate: 21.8
- Cholesterol: 0
- Protein: 1

606. Guacamole With Nopales (Mexican Cactus)

Serving: 4 | Prep: 5mins | Cook: 10mins | Ready in:

Ingredients

- 1/2 cup diced nopales (Mexican cactus)
- 1 large ripe avocado, halved and pitted
- 1/2 lime, juiced
- 1 tablespoon olive oil
- salt to taste
- 1 plum tomato, seeded and chopped
- 1 fresh jalapeno pepper - seeded, deveined, and minced, or to taste
- 4 sprigs fresh cilantro, chopped

Direction

- Place a small nonstick skillet pan on the stove and turn on to medium heat. Put in the nopales, stirring from time to time and cook for about 10 minutes until it becomes soft. Then let it cool.
- Crush the avocados in a bowl then add in the salt, olive oil and lime juice. Mix in the jalapeno, cilantro, tomato and cooked napoles.

Nutrition Information

- Calories: 153 calories;
- Cholesterol: 0
- Protein: 1.9
- Total Fat: 13.9
- Sodium: 49
- Total Carbohydrate: 8.3

607. Gumdrop Squares

Serving: 30 | Prep: 20mins | Cook: 25mins | Ready in:

Ingredients

- 2 tablespoons unflavored gelatin
- 1/2 cup cold water
- 3/4 cup water
- 2 cups white sugar
- 1/4 teaspoon peppermint extract
- 1/4 teaspoon lemon extract
- 1/8 teaspoon cinnamon oil
- 3 drops green food coloring
- 3 drops yellow food coloring
- 3 drops red food coloring
- 3/4 cup white sugar for decoration

Direction

- Sprinkle gelatin on cold water; put aside.
- Boil 3/4 cup water in medium saucepan on medium heat; mix 2 cups sugar in. Boil for 5 minutes; mix gelatin mixture in. Gently boil for 15 minutes.
- In cold water, dip 3 shallow small pans; remove. Take boiling mixture off heat; evenly divide to 3 heat-proof bowls. Use peppermint

to flavor one bowl, one with cinnamon and one with lemon. Tint cinnamon red, lemon yellow and peppermint green. Put each mixture in its own pan; rest to set overnight.
- Turn out gumdrops on sugared board; use sharp knife to cut to squares. In sugar, roll cut gumdrops; stand till firm.

Nutrition Information

- Calories: 71 calories;
- Protein: 0
- Total Fat: 0
- Sodium: < 1
- Total Carbohydrate: 18.3
- Cholesterol: 0

608. Gyros Burgers

Serving: 4 | Prep: 10mins | Cook: 15mins | Ready in:

Ingredients

- 1/2 pound lean ground beef
- 1/2 pound lean ground lamb
- 1/2 onion, grated
- 2 cloves garlic, pressed
- 1 slice bread, toasted and crumbled
- 1/2 teaspoon dried savory
- 1/2 teaspoon ground allspice
- 1/2 teaspoon ground coriander
- 1/2 teaspoon salt
- 1/2 teaspoon ground black pepper
- 1 dash ground cumin

Direction

- Set the outdoor grill on medium heat; preheat and oil lightly the grill grate.
- Mix together the ground lamb, garlic, ground beef, bread crumbs, and onion in a big bowl. Sprinkle on allspice, salt, cumin, pepper, savory, and coriander. Massage mixture until stiff. Mold mixture in 4 thin patties about 1/8-1/4 inch in thickness.
- For 5-7 minutes per side, cook the patties until thoroughly cooked.

Nutrition Information

- Calories: 338 calories;
- Sodium: 408
- Total Carbohydrate: 5.7
- Cholesterol: 84
- Protein: 20.3
- Total Fat: 25.4

609. Halibut Mango Ceviche

Serving: 6 | Prep: 45mins | Cook: 2hours | Ready in:

Ingredients

- 1 1/2 pounds skinless, boneless halibut, cut into 1/2 inch cubes
- 1/3 cup fresh lime juice
- 1/4 cup fresh lemon juice
- 1/4 cup tequila
- 3 jalapeno chile peppers, seeded and minced
- 1 mango - peeled, seeded and diced
- 1 green bell pepper, seeded and finely chopped
- 1/2 cup finely chopped Vidalia or other sweet onion
- 1/2 cup finely chopped red onion
- 1 mango - peeled, seeded and diced
- 1/2 bunch chopped fresh cilantro
- 1/4 cup chopped fresh parsley
- 1 teaspoon salt, or to taste

Direction

- In a non-metallic bowl, mix 1 diced mango, minced jalapeno peppers, tequila, lemon juice, lime juice and cubed halibut. Refrigerate, covered, for 1 1/2 hours.

- Add red onion, sweet onion and green pepper when ceviche sat for 1 1/2 hours. Stir well. Refrigerate, covered, for 30 more minutes.
- Fold parsley, cilantro and leftover diced mango in. Before serving, season with salt to taste.

Nutrition Information

- Calories: 217 calories;
- Total Fat: 2.9
- Sodium: 456
- Total Carbohydrate: 18
- Cholesterol: 36
- Protein: 24.8

610. Halloween Guacamole

Serving: 6 | Prep: 15mins | Cook: | Ready in:

Ingredients

- 2 ripe avocados, halved, divided
- 2 cloves garlic, minced
- 1 lemon, juiced
- 1 pinch ground cumin, or to taste
- 1 tomato, seeded and diced
- salt to taste
- 1/2 (14.5 ounce) package tortilla chips

Direction

- Set aside one avocado half with the seed.
- Get the flesh from other half of avocado and put in a blender; then blend well. Mix in the lemon juice and garlic; blend until the texture becomes smooth. Add cumin to taste. Get the flesh from remaining avocado half, then add it to the blender, mix well until you achieve the consistency you want. Place the guacamole into a bowl.
- Mix in diced tomato and add cumin, lemon juice and salt to taste.
- Get the avocado half with the seed that you set aside then sculpt a skull face, trim all the way through the flesh and skin to show the stone.
- Place the avocado skull on top of guacamole and put tortilla chips around the dish.

Nutrition Information

- Calories: 283 calories;
- Total Fat: 17.9
- Sodium: 175
- Total Carbohydrate: 31.2
- Cholesterol: 0
- Protein: 4.5

611. Halloween Vegan Yacon Syrup Cookies

Serving: 30 | Prep: 25mins | Cook: 10mins | Ready in:

Ingredients

- Cookies:
- 2 1/2 cups gluten-free flour
- 1 teaspoon baking soda
- 1/2 teaspoon ground ginger
- 1/2 teaspoon ground cinnamon
- 1/4 teaspoon ground nutmeg
- 1 dash salt
- 1/2 cup coconut oil, or more as needed
- 1/2 cup yacon syrup
- Icing:
- 1/4 cup yacon syrup
- 2 1/2 tablespoons melted dark chocolate (85% cacao)

Direction

- Turn the oven to 340°F (170°C) to preheat. Use parchment paper to line a baking sheet.
- In a big bowl, mix together salt, nutmeg, cinnamon, ginger, baking soda, and flour. In another bowl, mix together yacon syrup and

coconut oil. Pour the oil mixture into the dry ingredients and stir to form a dough.
- Roll out the dough until having approximately 1/2-in. thickness. Cut out the cookies with Halloween-themed cookie cutters; put them on the prepared baking sheet.
- Bake for 10 minutes in the preheated oven.
- As the cookies are baking, mix together melted chocolate and yacon syrup.
- Take the cookies out of the oven and put on icing while they remain hot.

Nutrition Information

- Calories: 92 calories;
- Total Carbohydrate: 13.1
- Cholesterol: < 1
- Total Fat: 4.4
- Protein: 1.2
- Sodium: 55

612. Ham And Pineapple Kabobs

Serving: 4 | Prep: 15mins | Cook: 8mins | Ready in:

Ingredients

- 3 tablespoons brown sugar
- 2 tablespoons distilled white vinegar
- 1 tablespoon vegetable oil
- 1 teaspoon prepared mustard
- 3/4 pound cooked ham, cut into 1 inch cubes
- 1 (15 ounce) can pineapple chunks, drained
- skewers

Direction

- Preheat grill on high.
- Mix together vegetable oil, vinegar, mustard, and brown sugar in a medium bowl. Cue pineapple and ham alternately onto skewers. Too similar to original text.
- Grease the grates lightly and arrange skewers on the grill, basting generously with the sauce. Grill for 6 to 8 minutes with frequent turning and brushing with sauce. Skewers are ready when the ham and pineapples are heated through and the glaze is cooked onto them.

Nutrition Information

- Calories: 342 calories;
- Protein: 16.2
- Total Fat: 19.3
- Sodium: 1097
- Total Carbohydrate: 26.8
- Cholesterol: 48

613. Hariton's 'Famous' Vegetarian Casserole

Serving: 36 | Prep: 30mins | Cook: 2hours30mins | Ready in:

Ingredients

- 8 large eggplants
- 8 large potatoes
- 8 green bell peppers
- 8 large onions
- 8 summer squash
- 6 tomatoes
- 1 pound fresh green beans
- 1 pound whole fresh mushrooms
- 2 bulbs garlic, cloves separated and peeled
- 1/4 cup chopped fresh dill weed
- 1/4 cup chopped fresh oregano
- 1/4 cup chopped fresh basil
- 1 (15 ounce) can tomato sauce
- 3/4 cup olive oil
- salt and pepper to taste

Direction

- Prep eggplant before assembling ingredients; cut to 2-in. chunks. Put into extra big bowl;

- add salted water to cover. This draws out bitterness from eggplant and let sit for 3 hours.
- Preheat an oven to 190°C/375°F.
- Cut tomatoes, squash, onion, green bell peppers and potatoes to 2-in. chunks. Cut mushrooms and green beans in half; peel garlic cloves.
- Drain then rinse eggplant; mix with other chopped veggies, basil, oregano and dill. Put into 3x13x18-in. roasting pan. Put olive oil and tomato sauce on all.
- Bake for 2 1/2 hours at 190°C/375°F, adding a bit of water halfway through cooking time to keep moist.

Nutrition Information

- Calories: 176 calories;
- Sodium: 75
- Total Carbohydrate: 30.9
- Cholesterol: 0
- Protein: 5.2
- Total Fat: 5.1

614. Harvard Beets

Serving: 3 | Prep: 5mins | Cook: 10mins | Ready in:

Ingredients

- 1 (16 ounce) can beets
- 1/2 cup white vinegar
- 3/4 cup white sugar
- 1 tablespoon cornstarch
- salt to taste

Direction

- Drain beet liquid into medium saucepan; add salt, cornstarch, sugar and vinegar to liquid. Boil on medium high heat; lower heat to medium. Mix beets in; cook till heated through.

Nutrition Information

- Calories: 207 calories;
- Total Fat: 0
- Sodium: 14
- Total Carbohydrate: 53.1
- Cholesterol: 0
- Protein: 0.1

615. Hawaiian Style Pasta

Serving: 4 | Prep: 15mins | Cook: 10mins | Ready in:

Ingredients

- 1 (8 ounce) package radiatore pasta
- 1 cup tomato pasta sauce
- 2 slices fresh pineapple, cut into pieces
- 2 cups chopped salami

Direction

- Place lightly salted water in a big pot and make it boil. Cook in pasta for 8-10 minutes or until it is al dente; strain.
- Toss cooked pasta with salami, pineapple, and tomato pasta sauce in a medium saucepan set on medium heat. Then cook for approximately 10 minutes, stirring occasionally, until the sauce starts to bubble.

Nutrition Information

- Calories: 565 calories;
- Sodium: 1767
- Total Carbohydrate: 57.7
- Cholesterol: 76
- Protein: 26.2
- Total Fat: 25.6

616. Healthy Banana Cookies

Serving: 36 | Prep: 15mins | Cook: 20mins | Ready in:

Ingredients

- 3 ripe bananas
- 2 cups rolled oats
- 1 cup dates, pitted and chopped
- 1/3 cup vegetable oil
- 1 teaspoon vanilla extract

Direction

- Set oven at 175°C (350°F) and start preheating.
- Smash bananas in a big bowl. Mix in vanilla, oil, dates and oats. Blend well, let rest for 15 minutes. Drop them by teaspoonfuls on an uncoated cookie tray.
- Put them in the preheated oven and bake until they turn light brown, or for 20 minutes.

Nutrition Information

- Calories: 56 calories;
- Total Carbohydrate: 8.4
- Cholesterol: 0
- Protein: 0.8
- Total Fat: 2.4
- Sodium: < 1

617. Healthy Chocolate Pudding

Serving: 2 | Prep: 5mins | Cook: 10mins | Ready in:

Ingredients

- 1 cup almond milk
- 1/4 cup coconut sugar
- 2 tablespoons cocoa powder
- 1 1/2 tablespoons cornstarch
- 1 teaspoon vanilla extract

Direction

- In a saucepan, put the vanilla extract, cornstarch, cocoa powder, coconut sugar and almond milk on low heat. Mix together for about 10 minutes, until it becomes smooth and thick.

Nutrition Information

- Calories: 142 calories;
- Cholesterol: 0
- Protein: 1.6
- Total Fat: 2.1
- Sodium: 87
- Total Carbohydrate: 30.7

618. Healthy Gingerbread Spice Cake With Butternut Squash Puree

Serving: 10 | Prep: 15mins | Cook: 45mins | Ready in:

Ingredients

- 1 teaspoon extra-virgin coconut oil (such as Barlean's®)
- 1/4 cup extra-virgin coconut oil (such as Barlean's®)
- 2 cups white whole wheat flour (such as King Arthur®)
- 1/4 cup ground flaxseeds (such as Barlean's®)
- 1 tablespoon freshly grated ginger
- 1 teaspoon baking soda
- 1 teaspoon ground cinnamon
- 1/4 teaspoon ground allspice
- 1/4 teaspoon sea salt
- 1/2 cup firmly packed brown sugar
- 1 egg
- 1 (10 ounce) package frozen butternut squash puree, thawed
- 1/2 cup coconut milk
- 1/4 cup molasses
- 2 teaspoons pure vanilla extract

Direction

- Preheat the oven to 190 degrees C/375 degrees F. Use 1 tsp. coconut oil to grease a 9x5-in. loaf pan.
- In a microwave-safe bowl, put 1/4 cup coconut oil. Heat in microwave for about 30 seconds until melted.
- In a big bowl, mix sea salt, allspice, cinnamon, baking soda, ginger, ground flaxseeds and flour.
- In another big bowl, mix egg, melted coconut oil and brown sugar. Add vanilla extract, molasses, coconut milk and squash puree. Mix well. Mix flour mixture into squash mixture until it's smooth. Put batter in prepped loaf pan. Smooth top out.
- Bake in preheated oven for 45-55 minutes until an inserted toothpick in the middle exits clean. Cool for 5 minutes. Turn cake out on a wire rack. Completely cool.

Nutrition Information

- Calories: 268 calories;
- Protein: 5.1
- Total Fat: 10.4
- Sodium: 186
- Total Carbohydrate: 41.7
- Cholesterol: 19

619. Hearty Pumpkin Spice Oatmeal

Serving: 2 | Prep: 5mins | Cook: 13mins | Ready in:

Ingredients

- 2 cups unsweetened almond milk
- 1/2 cup pumpkin puree
- 2 tablespoons maple syrup
- 1 teaspoon vanilla extract
- 1/4 teaspoon ground cinnamon
- 1/4 teaspoon ground nutmeg
- 1/4 teaspoon ground cloves
- 1 cup old-fashioned oats

Direction

- In a saucepan, cook cloves, nutmeg, cinnamon, vanilla extract, maple syrup, pumpkin puree, and almond milk over medium heat; bring the mixture to a boil. Add oatmeal, cook and stir often for 8-10 minutes until soft and chewy.

Nutrition Information

- Calories: 300 calories;
- Total Fat: 5.7
- Sodium: 313
- Total Carbohydrate: 55.2
- Cholesterol: 0
- Protein: 7.1

620. Herbed Chicken Nuggets

Serving: 4 | Prep: 25mins | Cook: 15mins | Ready in:

Ingredients

- 4 skinless, boneless chicken breasts
- 2 eggs, beaten
- 1 tablespoon water
- 1 teaspoon chopped fresh parsley
- 1/2 teaspoon dried thyme
- 1 pinch crushed red pepper flakes
- 1/2 cup dried bread crumbs, seasoned
- 1/2 cup wheat germ
- 1 teaspoon dried basil
- 1 teaspoon ground black pepper
- 1 tablespoon vegetable oil

Direction

- Set the oven to 220°C or 425°F. Use non-stick cooking spray to spray a baking sheet.
- Trim any fat from chicken and cube into 1-in. cubes.

- Beat eggs and water together in a bowl, then put chicken into the egg mixture.
- Mix together pepper, basil, wheat germ, bread crumbs, red pepper, thyme and parsley, then stir in the oil and blend well with a fork to distribute evenly. Transfer the seasoning mixture into a resealable plastic bag and toss the chicken cubes to coat well.
- On the prepared baking sheet, add coated chicken pieces and bake at 220°C or 425°F about 10 minutes, then turn the pieces and bake for 5 minutes longer.

Nutrition Information

- Calories: 309 calories;
- Total Fat: 9.7
- Sodium: 378
- Total Carbohydrate: 18.7
- Cholesterol: 162
- Protein: 36

621. Herbed Mushrooms With White Wine

Serving: 6 | Prep: 10mins | Cook: 15mins | Ready in:

Ingredients

- 1 tablespoon olive oil
- 1 1/2 pounds fresh mushrooms
- 1 teaspoon Italian seasoning
- 1/4 cup dry white wine
- 2 cloves garlic, minced
- salt and pepper to taste
- 2 tablespoons chopped fresh chives

Direction

- In a skillet, heat oil over medium heat and place the mushrooms, seasoning with Italian seasoning, and cook, stirring frequently, for 10 minutes.
- Mix in the garlic and the wine, and continue to cook until most of the wine evaporates. Season with a sprinkle of chives, pepper, and salt, then continue to cook for 1 minute.

Nutrition Information

- Calories: 57 calories;
- Total Carbohydrate: 5.6
- Cholesterol: 0
- Protein: 2.3
- Total Fat: 2.7
- Sodium: 5

622. Herbed Potatoes With Sauce

Serving: 4 | Prep: 10mins | Cook: 15mins | Ready in:

Ingredients

- 1 (14.5 ounce) can vegetable broth
- 1/4 teaspoon dried thyme
- 1 teaspoon dried parsley
- 7 potatoes, quartered
- 1 tablespoon cornstarch
- 2 tablespoons water

Direction

- In a medium-sized pot, mix together potatoes, parsley, thyme, and vegetable broth over medium-high heat. Boil it and lower the heat to low. Put a cover on and cook until the potatoes are soft, or about 10-20 minutes; strain, saving the broth.
- Mix water and cornstarch together in a small bowl; add to the broth and cook over medium heat until the mixture has thickened into a sauce, whisking continually. Enjoy the sauce with potatoes.

Nutrition Information

- Calories: 51 calories;
- Total Fat: 0.3
- Sodium: 215
- Total Carbohydrate: 10.6
- Cholesterol: 0
- Protein: 1.6

623. Homemade Marshmallows II

Serving: 24 | Prep: 30mins | Cook: 12mins | Ready in:

Ingredients

- 3 cups white sugar
- 1/4 cup corn syrup
- 1/4 teaspoon salt
- 3/4 cup water
- 2 teaspoons vanilla extract
- 1 cup confectioners' sugar for dusting

Direction

- Use a cooking spray to grease a 13x9-in dish generously.
- Mix water, sugar, salt, and corn syrup together in a big pot. Heat to about 112-116°C or 234-240°F until a drop of syrup into cold water forms a soft ball that turns flat when taken out of the water and placed on a flat surface. Take off heat then beat for 10-12mins using an electric mixer until it forms stiff peaks. Mix in vanilla then transfer to the greased pan.
- Refrigerate for 8hrs or overnight. Loosen the edges using a knife to cut. Dust confectioners' sugar on the surface then transfer to a surface lined with waxed paper. Dust again with confectioners' sugar then slice with a knife.

Nutrition Information

- Calories: 128 calories;
- Total Fat: 0
- Sodium: 26
- Total Carbohydrate: 32.9
- Cholesterol: 0
- Protein: 0

624. Homemade Vegan Chive And Garlic Cream Cheese

Serving: 32 | Prep: 10mins | Cook: | Ready in:

Ingredients

- 2 cups unsalted raw cashews
- 1 1/2 teaspoons nutritional yeast
- 1/2 teaspoon Himalayan salt
- 3 tablespoons plain non-dairy yogurt
- 1 tablespoon chopped fresh chives

Direction

- In a bowl with water, soak the cashews 8 hours to overnight.
- Drain water off the cashews and discard. In the bowl of a food processor, put salt, nutritional yeast, and cashews; process for 10-15 minutes until creamy and smooth. Add yogurt; combine until mixed thoroughly. Add in the chopped chives and stir. Allow to sit for an hour at room temperature, then store in the fridge.

Nutrition Information

- Calories: 48 calories;
- Total Fat: 3.8
- Sodium: 37
- Total Carbohydrate: 2.7
- Cholesterol: 0
- Protein: 1.6

625. Honey Cake III

Serving: 12 | Prep: 25mins | Cook: 45mins | Ready in:

Ingredients

- 1 cup white sugar
- 1 cup honey
- 1/2 cup vegetable oil
- 4 eggs
- 2 teaspoons grated orange zest
- 1 cup orange juice
- 2 1/2 cups all-purpose flour
- 3 teaspoons baking powder
- 1/2 teaspoon baking soda
- 1/2 teaspoon salt
- 1 teaspoon ground cinnamon

Direction

- Heat an oven to 175 ° C or 350 ° F. Oil a 9x13-inch pan and dust with flour.
- Sift cinnamon, salt, baking soda, baking powder and flour together. Put aside.
- Mix orange zest, eggs, oil, honey and sugar in a big bowl. Whip in mixture of flour and orange juice alternately, stirring barely to incorporate. Transfer the batter to prepped pan.
- Bake about 40 to 50 minutes in prepped oven for, or till an inserted toothpick in the middle of cake exits out clean. Cool down.

Nutrition Information

- Calories: 360 calories;
- Total Fat: 11
- Sodium: 264
- Total Carbohydrate: 62.6
- Cholesterol: 62
- Protein: 5

626. Honey Mustard BBQ Pork Chops

Serving: 8 | Prep: 15mins | Cook: 15mins | Ready in:

Ingredients

- 1/3 cup honey
- 3 tablespoons orange juice
- 1 tablespoon apple cider vinegar
- 1 teaspoon white wine
- 1 teaspoon Worcestershire sauce
- 2 teaspoons onion powder, or to taste
- 1/4 teaspoon dried tarragon
- 3 tablespoons Dijon mustard
- 8 thin cut pork chops

Direction

- In a large and resealable plastic bag, mix the tarragon, mustard, vinegar, honey, wine, onion powder, Worcestershire sauce, and orange juice. Slash the fatty edges of the chops, about 3 slashes, making sure you not to cut into the meat. Performing this procedure will prevent curling the meat during cooking. Add the chops into the plastic bag. Marinate inside the fridge for at least 2 hours.
- Set the grill to high heat for preheating
- Oil the grill grate lightly. Lay the chops onto the grill, discarding the marinade. Cook the chops for 6-8 minutes, flipping only once until the desired doneness is reached.

Nutrition Information

- Calories: 158 calories;
- Protein: 11.5
- Total Fat: 6.1
- Sodium: 174
- Total Carbohydrate: 14
- Cholesterol: 31

627. Honey Pork Fillets

Serving: 4 | Prep: 15mins | Cook: 40mins | Ready in:

Ingredients

- 4 pork chops
- 4 teaspoons honey

- 2 cups Worcestershire sauce
- ground black pepper to taste

Direction

- Cut each chop down the center horizontally, cutting not quite through. Open the flat to be like a butterfly. Ask the butcher to prepare the meat in this way, if possible.
- In a large shallow dish, mix Worcestershire sauce and honey. Marinate pork chops in the mixture for a maximum of 4 hours.
- Arrange the barbecue for indirect cooking.
- Flavor the chops with pepper and arrange on the well-greased grate. Cook on medium-low heat for 35 to 40 minutes.

Nutrition Information

- Calories: 273 calories;
- Total Fat: 5.1
- Sodium: 1397
- Total Carbohydrate: 32.6
- Cholesterol: 59
- Protein: 23.1

628. Hot Banana Salsa

Serving: 24 | Prep: 30mins | Cook: | Ready in:

Ingredients

- 1 large firm banana, peeled and diced
- 1/2 cup red bell pepper, seeded and diced
- 1/2 cup green bell pepper, seeded and diced
- 1/2 cup yellow bell pepper, seeded and diced
- 3 tablespoons chopped fresh cilantro
- 2 green onions, chopped
- 2 tablespoons fresh lime juice
- 1 tablespoon brown sugar
- 2 teaspoons minced fresh ginger root
- 2 teaspoons olive oil
- 1 teaspoon minced habanero pepper
- salt to taste

Direction

- Combine together the green, red, yellow and habanero peppers in a bowl together with the olive oil, banana, green onion, ginger, lime juice, cilantro, and brown sugar. Add some salt and serve within an hour.

Nutrition Information

- Calories: 14 calories;
- Total Fat: 0.4
- Sodium: < 1
- Total Carbohydrate: 2.6
- Cholesterol: 0
- Protein: 0.2

629. Hot Cinnamon Candy Covered Apples

Serving: 6 | Prep: 20mins | Cook: 1hours | Ready in:

Ingredients

- 1/2 cup confectioners' sugar
- 6 apples
- 2 cups water
- 2 cups white sugar
- 2 cups light corn syrup
- 1 tablespoon red food coloring
- 1 teaspoon cinnamon oil

Direction

- Line aluminum foil on a cookie sheet and dust it with confectioners' sugar.
- Discard stems from apples and wash them thoroughly. Use a rounded wooden craft stick to spear each apple through the bottom. Dry thoroughly and put aside.
- Heat corn syrup, sugar, and water to a boil in a large saucepan. Lower the heat to medium-high. Keep heating to boil, stirring to avoid burning, until the mixture achieves 300°F (150°C). Take away from heat, and while

stirring, put in cinnamon oil and food coloring.
- Working quickly, plunge each apple into the candy mixture, coating well. Arrange apples on the prepared cookie sheet to cool. Chill in the refrigerator for 2 hours.

Nutrition Information

- Calories: 696 calories;
- Protein: 0.3
- Total Fat: 0.5
- Sodium: 68
- Total Carbohydrate: 183.6
- Cholesterol: 0

630. House Fried Rice

Serving: 8 | Prep: 10mins | Cook: 30mins | Ready in:

Ingredients

- 1 1/2 cups uncooked white rice
- 3 tablespoons sesame oil
- 1 small onion, chopped
- 1 clove garlic, chopped
- 1 cup small shrimp - peeled and deveined
- 1/2 cup diced ham
- 1 cup chopped cooked chicken breast
- 2 stalks celery, chopped
- 2 carrots - peeled and diced
- 1 green bell pepper, chopped
- 1/2 cup green peas
- 1 egg, beaten
- 1/4 cup soy sauce

Direction

- Follow package directions to cook rice. Heat a big skillet/wok on medium high heat as rice cooks. Add sesame oil; mix in onion. Fry till golden; add garlic. Mix in chicken, ham and shrimp when garlic is browned lightly. Fry till shrimp becomes pink.
- Put heat on medium; mix in peas, green pepper, carrot and celery. Fry till veggies are crisp tender. Mix in beaten egg; cook just till egg is firm and scrambled.
- Thoroughly mix with veggies when rice is done; mix in soy sauce. To your preference, adjust seasoning; immediately serve.

Nutrition Information

- Calories: 236 calories;
- Total Fat: 8.4
- Sodium: 603
- Total Carbohydrate: 26.4
- Cholesterol: 59
- Protein: 13

631. Hummus I

Serving: 24 | Prep: 10mins | Cook: | Ready in:

Ingredients

- 2 (15 ounce) cans garbanzo beans, drained
- 1/2 cup roasted tahini
- 1/4 cup lemon juice
- 1 teaspoon grated lemon zest, minced
- 2 cloves garlic
- 1/4 cup packed flat leaf parsley
- 1/4 cup chopped green onions
- salt to taste
- ground black pepper to taste

Direction

- In the bowl of a food processor, put the green onion, parsley, garlic, lemon zest, lemon juice, tahini and garbanzo beans. Blend until it becomes smooth, then add water if the mixture seems too thick. Season pepper and salt to taste.

Nutrition Information

- Calories: 62 calories;
- Total Fat: 3.4
- Sodium: 72
- Total Carbohydrate: 6.5
- Cholesterol: 0
- Protein: 2.3

632. Hummus III

Serving: 16 | Prep: 10mins | Cook: | Ready in:

Ingredients

- 2 cups canned garbanzo beans, drained
- 1/3 cup tahini
- 1/4 cup lemon juice
- 1 teaspoon salt
- 2 cloves garlic, halved
- 1 tablespoon olive oil
- 1 pinch paprika
- 1 teaspoon minced fresh parsley

Direction

- In a food processor or blender, process the garlic, salt, lemon juice, tahini, and garbanzo beans until it becomes smooth, then move to a serving bowl.
- Trickle olive oil on top and sprinkle it with parsley and paprika.

Nutrition Information

- Calories: 77 calories;
- Sodium: 236
- Total Carbohydrate: 8.1
- Cholesterol: 0
- Protein: 2.6
- Total Fat: 4.3

633. Hummus IV

Serving: 40 | Prep: 20mins | Cook: | Ready in:

Ingredients

- 2 (15.5 ounce) cans garbanzo beans, drained
- 4 tablespoons lemon juice
- 6 cloves garlic, peeled and crushed
- 3 tablespoons tahini
- 1/4 teaspoon crushed red pepper

Direction

- In a food processor, process the garbanzo beans until it becomes a spreadable paste. Stir in crushed red pepper, tahini, garlic and lemon juice, the process until it becomes smooth. If the consistency appears too thick, use more lemon juice.

Nutrition Information

- Calories: 34 calories;
- Cholesterol: 0
- Protein: 1.3
- Total Fat: 0.9
- Sodium: 67
- Total Carbohydrate: 5.5

634. Hunan Kung Pao

Serving: 4 | Prep: 30mins | Cook: 20mins | Ready in:

Ingredients

- 4 skinless, boneless chicken breast halves - cut into 1 inch cubes
- 20 peeled and deveined large shrimp (21 to 30 per pound)
- 4 teaspoons soy sauce
- 4 teaspoons rice wine
- 2 teaspoons sesame oil
- 1 tablespoon cornstarch
- 1/2 cup vegetable oil, divided

- 4 cloves garlic, minced
- 16 dried red chile peppers, cut in half
- 2 teaspoons Szechuan peppercorns (optional)
- 1 red bell pepper, sliced
- 1 green bell pepper, sliced
- 1/4 cup dark soy sauce
- 2 tablespoons rice wine
- 2 teaspoons white sugar
- 1 cup salted peanuts
- 4 green onions, cut into 3 inch lengths
- 2 dashes sesame oil, or to taste (optional)

Direction

- In a mixing bowl, mix the shrimp and the chicken together with 4 teaspoons of rice wine, 2 teaspoons of sesame oil, and 4 teaspoons of soy sauce. Drizzle with cornstarch and mix well until they have evenly blended. Put aside for 25 minutes to marinate.
- In a wok, heat half of the vegetable oil on high heat. Cook the chicken and the shrimp in the oil while stirring for 5 minutes until the outside of the chicken has turned white yet its middle is still a little pink. Take the chicken out then clean the wok by wiping it.
- Pour the leftover vegetable oil in the same work and heat it on high heat. Cook the garlic in the oil for several seconds, stirring until garlic starts to brown. Add the Szechuan peppercorns and dried chilis while stirring and cook for several seconds until the peppers start to darken. Mix in the dark soy sauce, red and green bell peppers, 2 tablespoons of sugar, and 2 tablespoons of rice wine. Boil then add the chicken, stirring it in. Continue to cook for 5 more minutes until the peppers are almost tender and the chicken's center is not pink. Add the green onions and peanuts while stirring and cook until the green onions have gone limp. Add a few drops of sesame oil while stirring then serve.

Nutrition Information

- Calories: 790 calories;
- Total Carbohydrate: 21.1
- Cholesterol: 228
- Protein: 59
- Total Fat: 51.9
- Sodium: 1736

635. Indian Spiced Rice

Serving: 4 | Prep: | Cook: | Ready in:

Ingredients

- 1 tablespoon canola oil
- 1 cup chopped onion
- 1 tablespoon minced fresh ginger root
- 1 clove garlic, minced
- 1/2 teaspoon ground coriander seed
- 1/2 teaspoon ground cardamom
- 1/4 teaspoon ground nutmeg
- 1/2 teaspoon ground cumin
- 1 1/4 cups dry jasmine rice
- 3/4 teaspoon salt
- 1/2 cup dry lentils
- 3 cups water
- 1 potato, peeled and diced
- 1 red bell pepper, chopped
- 1/2 cup green peas
- 3 tablespoons raisins
- 1 tablespoon butter (optional)

Direction

- On medium heat, heat oil in a big saucepan or frying pan. Cook and stir onions often in hot oil until soft. Sprinkle in cumin, ginger, nutmeg, garlic, cardamom, and coriander. Cook for another 3 more minutes while mixing regularly.
- Add rice in the saucepan then sauté for 2 minutes with the spices, mix constantly. Add salt and lentils then pour in three cups of water, mix.
- Add potatoes in the pan then boil; cover. Turn to low heat then cook for 10 minutes.
- Put raisins, peas, and bell pepper into the saucepan and mix well then cover; cook for

another 10 minutes or until the lentils, potatoes, and rice are tender. If desired, mix in butter. Serve.

Nutrition Information

- Calories: 465 calories;
- Cholesterol: 8
- Protein: 13.4
- Total Fat: 7.1
- Sodium: 467
- Total Carbohydrate: 87

636. Indian Style Sheekh Kabab

Serving: 8 | Prep: 15mins | Cook: 10mins | Ready in:

Ingredients

- 2 pounds lean ground lamb
- 2 onions, finely chopped
- 1/2 cup fresh mint leaves, finely chopped
- 1/2 cup cilantro, finely chopped
- 1 tablespoon ginger paste
- 1 tablespoon green chile paste
- 2 teaspoons ground cumin
- 2 teaspoons ground coriander
- 2 teaspoons paprika
- 1 teaspoon cayenne pepper
- 2 teaspoons salt
- 1/4 cup vegetable oil
- skewers

Direction

- Mix together ground lamb, ginger paste, onions, cilantro, chile paste, and mint in a large bowl. Sprinkle with salt, cumin, cayenne, coriander, and paprika. Cover the bowl and let lamb marinate for 2 hours.
- Mold 1 cup of the lamb mixture to form sausages around the skewers. Even out the thickness all around the skewers. Keep in the fridge until ready to grill.
- Preheat grill on high.
- Generously oil the grates and arrange the kabobs, cooking for 10 minutes for well-done, and turning as necessary to cook evenly.

Nutrition Information

- Calories: 304 calories;
- Total Fat: 22.6
- Sodium: 665
- Total Carbohydrate: 4.7
- Cholesterol: 76
- Protein: 20.1

637. Indian Style Salmon Fry

Serving: 2 | Prep: 20mins | Cook: 10mins | Ready in:

Ingredients

- 2 tablespoons olive oil
- 3/4 teaspoon cumin seeds
- 1/2 teaspoon brown mustard seeds
- 1 small onion, sliced into thin half-circles
- 1 clove garlic, minced
- 1 tablespoon minced fresh ginger root
- 1 green chile pepper, chopped
- 10 fresh curry leaves, chopped (optional)
- 1 tomato, diced
- 2 (14.75 ounce) cans salmon, drained and bones removed
- 1/4 cup chopped fresh cilantro

Direction

- On medium heat, heat the olive oil in a skillet. Cook the mustard seeds and cumin until the seeds begin to pop. Stir in the ginger, curry leaves, chili pepper, onion, and garlic until it appears golden and brown. Mix the tomatoes and stir for a while; add the salmon in the pan. Use the back of the stirring spoon to break the salmon into bite-size pieces. Cook for 5-10 minutes until the salmon is heated through. Add cilantro on top before serving.

Nutrition Information

- Calories: 765 calories;
- Protein: 81.5
- Total Fat: 47.1
- Sodium: 1783
- Total Carbohydrate: 11
- Cholesterol: 262

638. Instant Pot® Classic Hummus

Serving: 8 | Prep: 10mins | Cook: 45mins | Ready in:

Ingredients

- 1 cup dry garbanzo beans
- 3 cups vegetable broth
- 1/3 cup lemon juice
- 3 tablespoons tahini
- 2 tablespoons olive oil
- 2 cloves garlic, chopped
- 1 teaspoon ground cumin
- 1/2 teaspoon salt

Direction

- In a multi-function pressure cooker like an Instant Pot®, mix together vegetable broth and garbanzo beans; secure lid. Set the pressure to high and the timer to 35 minutes as specified in the cooker's manual. Let the pressure build for 10-15 minutes.
- Use the quick-release method to relieve pressure in accordance with the cooker's manual. Uncover.
- Drain garbanzo beans and put in food processor, set aside 2/3 cup of the liquid. Add garlic, tahini, lemon juice, and olive oil in the food processor. Blend for 3 minutes until creamy and smooth. Scrape the food processor's bowl; add salt, cumin, and the reserved 2/3 cup of liquid. Blend for another minute.

Nutrition Information

- Calories: 170 calories;
- Total Carbohydrate: 19.5
- Cholesterol: 0
- Protein: 6.3
- Total Fat: 8.2
- Sodium: 331

639. Irish Boiled Dinner (Corned Beef)

Serving: 6 | Prep: 1hours | Cook: 5hours | Ready in:

Ingredients

- 1 (5 1/2 pound) corned beef brisket
- 2 large onions
- 15 small white (Irish) potatoes
- 10 carrots, cut into 1 inch pieces
- 2 heads cabbage, cored and cut into wedges

Direction

- Wash beef brisket under cold water, then transfer in a big saucepan. Pour just enough water to fill in 6 inches covering the roast. Remove skis of the onions and put them in the saucepan with the roast. Let it boil, cooking for about half an hour at a rolling boil. Lower the heat to medium-low so that the water is at a gentle boil; cover with the lid, then cook for 3 1/2 hours.
- Take out the cover from the brisket. Take out onions, slicing them into wedges. Put them back to the pot then add the carrots, then lay the cabbage over the roast. Put the potatoes over the cabbage. Seal the lid back and cook for half an hour more until potatoes are soft.

The potatoes should be submerged in the water by now, if not, return the lid on to keep on steaming.
- Take out the vegetables from the pot and transfer in another serving bowl. The corned beef dries out quickly, so let it stay on the pot until ready to slice and serve.

Nutrition Information

- Calories: 918 calories;
- Sodium: 2248
- Total Carbohydrate: 106.6
- Cholesterol: 179
- Protein: 47
- Total Fat: 35.7

640. Italian Chicken Spaghetti With Tequila

Serving: 8 | Prep: 10mins | Cook: 20mins | Ready in:

Ingredients

- 12 ounces spaghetti
- 2 tablespoons olive oil
- 4 skinless, boneless chicken breast halves - diced
- 1/4 cup Italian seasoning
- 2 teaspoons bottled minced garlic
- 1 (15.5 ounce) can diced tomatoes
- 1/2 cup tequila
- salt and ground black pepper to taste

Direction

- Bring to boil lightly-salted water in a large pot and add pasta. Cook for about 8 to 10 minutes until al dente. Drain off the water. Transfer the spaghetti into a large bowl.
- Over medium heat, heat olive oil in a skillet and then add the chicken. Cook while stirring in the hot oil until browned. Mix in garlic and Italian seasoning and then cook for about 5 minutes until chicken is cooked through. Add tequila and tomatoes and let to simmer for 5 more minutes. Add pepper and salt to taste. Transfer into the bowl containing the spaghetti and toss to combine. Serve right away.

Nutrition Information

- Calories: 311 calories;
- Cholesterol: 36
- Protein: 19.4
- Total Fat: 6.1
- Sodium: 120
- Total Carbohydrate: 35

641. Italian Chicken With Garlic And Lemon

Serving: 15 | Prep: 15mins | Cook: 1hours15mins | Ready in:

Ingredients

- 15 chicken thighs
- 8 large potatoes, peeled and quartered
- 1 cup vegetable oil, or as needed
- 1/2 cup wine vinegar
- 5 lemons, juiced
- 10 cloves crushed garlic
- 2 tablespoons dried oregano
- 2 tablespoons dried parsley
- 1 onion, minced
- salt and pepper to taste

Direction

- Preheat an oven to 175°C/350°F.
- Put chicken pieces in an enameled 10x15-in. roasting pan. Fry potatoes in 1/2-in. deep oil in a big skillet on medium-high heat till golden brown. Put in pan with chicken.
- In 1/2 cup reserved frying oil, mix pepper, salt, onion, parsley, oregano, garlic, lemon

juice and vinegar. Put mixture on potatoes and chicken.
- In preheated oven, bake for 1 1/4 hours, basting potatoes and chicken with sauce mixture. Rest for 5 minutes; serve hot.

Nutrition Information

- Calories: 275 calories;
- Total Carbohydrate: 33.3
- Cholesterol: 58
- Protein: 19.1
- Total Fat: 8.4
- Sodium: 64

642. Italian Stewed Tomatoes

Serving: 9 | Prep: 30mins | Cook: 10mins | Ready in:

Ingredients

- 24 large tomatoes - peeled, seeded and chopped
- 1 cup chopped celery
- 1/2 cup chopped onion
- 1/4 cup chopped green bell pepper
- 2 teaspoons dried basil
- 1 tablespoon white sugar

Direction

- Mix together sugar, basil, bell pepper, onion, celery and tomatoes in a big saucepan on medium heat. Cover and cook for 10 minutes while stirring from time to time to avoid sticking.

Nutrition Information

- Calories: 100 calories;
- Protein: 4.6
- Total Fat: 1
- Sodium: 34
- Total Carbohydrate: 22.2

- Cholesterol: 0

643. Jamaican Jerked Chicken

Serving: 3 | Prep: 10mins | Cook: 20mins | Ready in:

Ingredients

- 1/2 green onion, minced
- 1/4 cup orange juice
- 1 tablespoon minced fresh ginger root
- 1 tablespoon minced jalapeno peppers
- 1 tablespoon lime juice
- 1 tablespoon soy sauce
- 1 clove garlic, minced
- 1 teaspoon ground allspice
- 1/4 teaspoon ground cinnamon
- 1/2 teaspoon ground cloves
- 1 (2 to 3 pound) whole chicken, cut into pieces

Direction

- Mix together orange juice, soy sauce, lemon or lime juice, green onions, hot pepper, ginger, garlic, allspice, cloves, and cinnamon. Soak chicken in and marinate for 8 hours.
- Preheat barbecue over medium heat. After cooking chicken, boil remaining marinade for 2 to 3 minutes and spoon over chicken.

Nutrition Information

- Calories: 834 calories;
- Protein: 71.1
- Total Fat: 57.2
- Sodium: 568
- Total Carbohydrate: 4.8
- Cholesterol: 284

644. Jambalasta

Serving: 6 | Prep: 15mins | Cook: 35mins | Ready in:

Ingredients

- 3 (8 ounce) packages linguine pasta
- 2 tablespoons olive oil
- 1 onion, chopped
- 2 skinless, boneless chicken breasts, cut into strips
- 1 pound shrimp, peeled and deveined
- 1 tablespoon sugar
- 1 tablespoon Cajun seasoning
- 1 tablespoon paprika
- 1 teaspoon garlic powder
- 1 teaspoon dried oregano
- 1 teaspoon salt
- 1 tablespoon Louisiana-style hot sauce
- 1 pound kielbasa, cut into 1/4-inch slices
- 1 (28 ounce) can diced tomatoes, undrained
- 1 tablespoon cornstarch
- 2 tablespoons cold water

Direction

- Put a big pot of lightly salted water on a rolling boil on high heat. Mix in linguine when water boils; bring back to a boil. Cook pasta for 11 minutes without a cover till cooked through yet firm to chew, occasionally mixing. Drain properly in a colander set in the sink.
- Heat oil in big skillet on high heat; mix and cook onion in oil for 5 minutes till translucent. Add hot sauce, salt, oregano, garlic powder, paprika, Cajun seasoning, sugar, shrimp and chicken; cook for 8-10 minutes till juices run clear and chicken isn't pink in the middle. Mix in diced tomatoes and kielbasa. Whisk cold water and cornstarch together in a small bowl till smooth; put in skillet. Lower the heat to medium; simmer for 10 minutes till thick. Spoon over linguine.

Nutrition Information

- Calories: 860 calories;
- Total Fat: 32.1
- Sodium: 1672
- Total Carbohydrate: 94.1
- Cholesterol: 192
- Protein: 46.8

645. Jeff's Sloppy Joes

Serving: 8 | Prep: 10mins | Cook: 10mins | Ready in:

Ingredients

- 2 tablespoons olive oil
- 1 cup chopped onion
- 2 cloves garlic, minced
- 1/2 cup chopped green bell pepper
- 1 stalk celery, chopped
- 1/2 teaspoon dried oregano
- 1 pound ground beef
- 1/2 pound Italian sausage
- 1 (12 fluid ounce) can or bottle chili sauce
- 2 tablespoons red wine vinegar
- 1 tablespoon Worcestershire sauce
- 2 teaspoons brown sugar
- salt and pepper to taste

Direction

- In a large skillet, heat the oil over medium heat. Add the oregano, onion, green bell pepper, garlic and celery. Sauté for approximately 5 minutes until onion is softened. Remove to a plate and set aside.
- Combine the sausage and ground beef in the same skillet and sauté over medium high heat for around 10 minutes until browned well. Mix in chili sauce, the reserved onion mixture, brown sugar, Worcestershire sauce and vinegar, then mix well. Add pepper and salt to taste.

Nutrition Information

- Calories: 235 calories;
- Sodium: 296
- Total Carbohydrate: 8.9
- Cholesterol: 46
- Protein: 14.9

- Total Fat: 15.4

646. Jewish Apple Cake I

Serving: 14 | Prep: | Cook: | Ready in:

Ingredients

- 3 cups all-purpose flour
- 1/2 teaspoon salt
- 2 1/2 teaspoons baking powder
- 2 cups white sugar
- 1 cup vegetable oil
- 4 eggs, beaten
- 1/4 cup orange juice
- 2 teaspoons vanilla extract
- 3 apples - peeled, cored and sliced
- 2 teaspoons ground cinnamon
- 5 teaspoons white sugar

Direction

- Preheat an oven to 175°C (or 350°F). Oil and flour a 10in. tube pan. Mix together 5 teaspoons of sugar and ground cinnamon and reserve.
- Mix 2 cups of sugar, baking powder, salt and flour together in a big mixing bowl. Mix in vanilla, orange juice, beaten eggs and vegetable oil. Combine thoroughly.
- Put half of batter into greased and floured pan. Place half of sliced apples on top and scatter with half of cinnamon sugar mixture. Spread the rest of the batter on the surface and pile the rest of sliced apples and the cinnamon sugar.
- Bake at 175°C (or 350°F) for 70-90 minutes.

Nutrition Information

- Calories: 394 calories;
- Sodium: 191
- Total Carbohydrate: 55.7
- Cholesterol: 53
- Protein: 4.7

- Total Fat: 17.5

647. Josephine's Puerto Rican Chicken And Rice

Serving: 6 | Prep: 10mins | Cook: 45mins | Ready in:

Ingredients

- 1 tablespoon vegetable oil
- 5 chicken drumsticks
- 1 small onion, chopped
- 1/2 cup pitted green olives
- 2 tablespoons capers
- 1 (8 ounce) can tomato sauce
- 3 tablespoons shortening
- 2 tablespoons achiote seed
- 4 cups boiling water
- 4 cups uncooked jasmine rice

Direction

- Put capers, olives, onions and chicken into a big saucepan, sautéing at moderate heat. To have extra olive flavor, add some of the sauce. When the chicken starts browning and the onion starts turning clear, pour in the tomato sauce. Cook everything lightly by sautéing the mixture. Adjust the heat to low.
- Put shortening into a small saucepan then heat it at medium heat until melted. Insert the achiote seeds. Once the shortening becomes red, move it away from heat and start straining seeds out. Add the oil into the tomato/chicken mixture, stirring. Pour boiling water. Adjust the heat setting to moderately high level. Lead it to boiling point. Stir thoroughly.
- Insert rice, boiling for around 3 minutes. Adjust the heat to low. Cook until the rice absorbs majority of liquid and softens, about another 1/2 hour. During the process, stir from time to time. Move it away from the heat. Leave it standing for 10 minutes. Move the mixture into a big bowl. Serve at once.

Nutrition Information

- Calories: 670 calories;
- Protein: 24.8
- Total Fat: 15
- Sodium: 616
- Total Carbohydrate: 106.1
- Cholesterol: 52

648. Kahlua® Brownies With Peanut Butter

Serving: 12 | Prep: 15mins | Cook: 18mins | Ready in:

Ingredients

- 2 (4 ounce) containers applesauce
- 3/4 cup white sugar
- 1/2 cup peanut butter
- 1/4 cup water
- 1 fluid ounce coffee-flavored liqueur (such as Kahlua®), or more to taste
- 1 tablespoon egg replacer
- 1 tablespoon honey, or more to taste
- 2 teaspoons vanilla extract
- 1 1/3 cups all-purpose flour
- 3/4 cup cocoa powder
- 1/2 teaspoon baking powder
- 1/4 teaspoon salt
- 2/3 cup chopped walnuts (optional)

Direction

- Set the oven at 175°C (350°F) to preheat. Grease a 9x13-inch glass baking dish.
- In a large bowl, mix vanilla extract, honey, egg replacer, coffee-flavored liqueur, water, peanut butter, sugar, and applesauce; mix until well combined.
- Sift salt, baking powder, cocoa, and flour in another bowl. Add to the applesauce mixture and stir. Pour the batter into the greased baking dish. Scatter walnuts on top.
- In the preheated oven, bake for 18-25 minutes, or until the edges are set, and toothpick comes out with a few moist crumbs attached when inserted into the center.

Nutrition Information

- Calories: 253 calories;
- Total Fat: 10.3
- Sodium: 120
- Total Carbohydrate: 34.6
- Cholesterol: 0
- Protein: 6.2

649. Kale And Adzuki Beans

Serving: 6 | Prep: 15mins | Cook: 50mins | Ready in:

Ingredients

- 1 cup uncooked adzuki beans
- 1 tablespoon olive oil
- 2 cloves garlic, peeled and crushed
- 6 cups roughly chopped kale
- 2 tablespoons water
- 1/4 cup tamari
- 1 teaspoon ground cumin
- 1 teaspoon ground coriander
- salt and pepper to taste

Direction

- In a medium saucepan, put the adzuki beans and pour enough water to cover, then boil. Lower the heat and let it simmer for 30-45 minutes, until it becomes tender.
- In a medium skillet, heat the olive oil on medium heat and sauté garlic for around 1 minute. Stir in 2 tbsp. of water and kale. Sprinkle coriander, cumin and tamari to season. Blend in the adzuki beans thoroughly. Lower the heat to low, put on cover and let it simmer for around 20 minutes, until the kale

becomes tender. Sprinkle pepper and salt to season.

Nutrition Information

- Calories: 172 calories;
- Cholesterol: 0
- Protein: 10.1
- Total Fat: 3
- Sodium: 890
- Total Carbohydrate: 28.7

650. Kasha And Bowties (Kasha Varnishkas)

Serving: 6 | Prep: 5mins | Cook: 25mins | Ready in:

Ingredients

- 1 (13.75 ounce) can chicken broth
- 3/4 cup kasha (toasted buckwheat groats)
- 1 (12 ounce) package bow tie-shaped egg noodles
- 2 tablespoons olive oil
- 2 onions, diced
- 1 pinch salt and pepper to taste

Direction

- Boil the chicken broth with the kasha in a saucepan. Lower the heat and without cover, allow to simmer for 15 minutes.
- Boil a pot of lightly-salted water. Put pasta and allow to cook for 8 to 10 minutes till al dente; let drain and wash with cold water.
- In a skillet, put the oil over medium heat. In oil, cook and mix the onions for 7 to 10 minutes till browned lightly. Mix the kasha and drained pasta into the onions, and put salt and pepper to taste.

Nutrition Information

- Calories: 345 calories;
- Protein: 11.1
- Total Fat: 7.7
- Sodium: 331
- Total Carbohydrate: 59
- Cholesterol: 49

651. Keema (Indian Style Ground Meat)

Serving: 4 | Prep: 5mins | Cook: 20mins | Ready in:

Ingredients

- 1 1/2 pounds ground lamb
- 1 onion, finely chopped
- 2 cloves garlic, minced
- 2 tablespoons garam masala
- 1 teaspoon salt
- 4 teaspoons tomato paste
- 3/4 cup beef broth

Direction

- Cook the ground lamb in a large heavy skillet over medium heat until it turns brown evenly. Use a wooden spoon to break it apart while cooking until it is crumbled. Place the cooked lamb into a bowl, then drain off all but retain a tablespoon of fat. Sauté the onion for 5 minutes until it is translucent and soft. Mix in the garlic, sauté for a minute. Stir in salt and garam masala and cook for a minute. Place the browned lamb back into the pan, then stir in beef broth and tomato paste. Turn down the heat and simmer until the liquid evaporates and the meat is completely cooked through, about 10 - 15 minutes.

Nutrition Information

- Calories: 513 calories;
- Total Fat: 40.7
- Sodium: 885
- Total Carbohydrate: 6.4

- Cholesterol: 124
- Protein: 29.6

652. Keto Peanut Butter Fudge Fat Bomb

Serving: 10 | Prep: 10mins | Cook: | Ready in:

Ingredients

- 1 cup unsweetened peanut butter, softened
- 1 cup coconut oil
- 1/4 cup unsweetened vanilla-flavored almond milk
- 2 teaspoons vanilla liquid stevia, or as needed (optional)

Direction

- Use parchment paper to line a loaf pan.
- In the microwaveable dish, mix the coconut oil and peanut butter and then microwave it until a bit melted for 30 seconds. Add into the blender with stevia and almond milk, then blend until incorporated well. Pour it into the loaf pan and let it chill in the fridge for about 2 hours until set.

Nutrition Information

- Calories: 341 calories;
- Sodium: 122
- Total Carbohydrate: 5.3
- Cholesterol: 0
- Protein: 6.5
- Total Fat: 34.9

653. Kettle Corn

Serving: 5 | Prep: 5mins | Cook: 15mins | Ready in:

Ingredients

- 1/4 cup vegetable oil
- 1/4 cup white sugar
- 1/2 cup unpopped popcorn kernels

Direction

- On medium heat, heat vegetable oil in a big pot; mix in popcorn and sugar once the oil is hot. Cover the pot then shake constantly to avoid burning the sugar. Take off from heat when the popping is down to once every 2-3secs. Keep on shaking for a few more minutes until it stops popping. Transfer to a big bowl then cool. Mix from time to time to break the big clumps apart.

Nutrition Information

- Calories: 209 calories;
- Sodium: < 1
- Total Carbohydrate: 24.8
- Cholesterol: 0
- Protein: 2.4
- Total Fat: 11.9

654. Key Lime Thyme Pie

Serving: 8 | Prep: 15mins | Cook: 10mins | Ready in:

Ingredients

- Crust:
- 2 cups gluten-free graham crackers, blended
- 1/4 cup vegan butter, melted
- Sweetened Condensed Milk:
- 2 (11 ounce) bottles So Delicious® Culinary Coconut Milk
- 2 cups powdered sugar
- 1 pinch salt
- 1/4 teaspoon vanilla extract (optional)
- Filling:
- 2 tablespoons organic cane sugar
- 3/4 cup key lime juice, or to taste
- 1 lime, zested

- 1 (9 ounce) tub So Delicious® Dairy Free CocoWhip
- Topping:
- Candied thyme, for garnish (see directions)

Direction

- To make the crust, use the 8-oz box of gluten-free graham crackers and blend to make 2 cups of crumbs. Whisk in the melted vegan butter until blended.
- Transfer the mixture to a standard pie dish or a springform, oiled and sides lined with parchment paper then pat into bottom. Press the mixture flat to the bottom with the bottom of a drinking glass.
- Bake for 8 to 10 minutes at 350°.
- For dairy-free sweetened condensed milk: Put in the bottles of coconut culinary milk in a small/medium-size saucepan and bring to a low boil. Let it boil for 5 minutes while stirring continuously.
- Reduce the heat bringing the milk to a simmer. Put in the powdered sugar and keep on stirring until the sugar has completely dissolved. Add vanilla (if using), salt, and thyme sprigs then let it simmer for about 30 to 40 minutes until the mixture has reduced by half. Discard the sprigs from milk.
- For Candied Thyme Garnish: Boil then bring organic cane syrup and equal parts of water to a simmer until the sugar dissolves to make a simple syrup. When the mixture has cooled fully, dunk fresh sprigs of thyme into it and lay them onto parchment paper. Dust with sugar.
- To make the filling: Mix the key lime juice to the Sweetened Condensed Milk with thyme to taste.
- Add the Coco Whip into the mixture then fold and put in the lime zest to taste.
- Place the filling to the crust, cover lightly and keep in the freezer for at least 2 hours or overnight.
- Decorate with sprigs of candied thyme and key lime slices.

Nutrition Information

- Calories: 433 calories;
- Total Carbohydrate: 59.8
- Cholesterol: 0
- Protein: 2.5
- Total Fat: 22.7
- Sodium: 202

655. Kielbasa With Honey Mustard

Serving: 5 | Prep: 10mins | Cook: 5mins | Ready in:

Ingredients

- 1 pound kielbasa sausage
- 1 1/2 cups ginger ale
- 1 teaspoon brown sugar
- 8 ounces honey mustard

Direction

- Preheat oven to broil. Use aluminum foil to line a baking sheet. Cut kielbasa diagonally into quarter-inch pieces.
- In a medium-sized frying pan, sauté kielbasa in ginger ale until heated through. Drain properly. On the baking sheet, line the kielbasa, then top with brown sugar.
- Broil the kielbasa till the brown sugar melts and starts to crystallize, check after 3 - 5 minutes. For dipping, use honey mustard; serve with kielbasa.

Nutrition Information

- Calories: 400 calories;
- Total Fat: 27.9
- Sodium: 1162
- Total Carbohydrate: 28.8
- Cholesterol: 61
- Protein: 12.9

656. Killer Pumpkin Pie

Serving: 8 | Prep: 20mins | Cook: 1hours | Ready in:

Ingredients

- Crust:
- 1 1/2 cups all-purpose flour plus
- 2 tablespoons all-purpose flour
- 2 teaspoons white sugar
- 1 teaspoon salt
- 1/2 cup canola oil
- 2 tablespoons rice milk
- Filling:
- 1/2 cup white sugar
- 1/4 cup dark brown sugar
- 2 teaspoons ground cinnamon
- 1/2 teaspoon salt
- 1/2 teaspoon ground ginger
- 1/4 teaspoon ground nutmeg
- 1/4 teaspoon ground cloves
- 1 (15 ounce) can pumpkin puree
- 2 tablespoons canola oil
- 2 large eggs
- 1 teaspoon vanilla
- 1 1/4 cups rice milk

Direction

- Preheat oven to 220°C/425°F.
- Mix salt, sugar and flour in 9-in. pie pan; create well in the middle. Put rice milk and oil in the well; use fork to mix till dough forms. Evenly press mixture with hands into sides and bottom of pan; crimp crust edge.
- Mix cloves, nutmeg, ginger, salt, cinnamon, brown sugar and white sugar in big bowl; put aside. Whisk rice milk, vanilla, eggs, oil and pumpkin puree till blended evenly in another bowl. Add pumpkin mixture to dry ingredients; mix till blended fully. Put in prepped pie crust; put on cookie sheet in preheated oven.
- Bake it for 10 minutes; lower temperature to 175°C/350°F. Bake for 40-50 minutes till an inserted knife near the middle exits clean; center might wiggle a little, but it firms up out of oven. On metal rack, cool.

Nutrition Information

- Calories: 390 calories;
- Total Fat: 19.6
- Sodium: 599
- Total Carbohydrate: 49.6
- Cholesterol: 46
- Protein: 5.4

657. Kristen's Awesome Oatmeal Cookies

Serving: 30 | Prep: | Cook: | Ready in:

Ingredients

- 3/4 cup shortening
- 1 cup packed brown sugar
- 1/2 cup white sugar
- 1 egg
- 1/4 cup water
- 1 teaspoon vanilla extract
- 1 cup all-purpose flour
- 1 teaspoon salt
- 1/2 teaspoon baking soda
- 1 tablespoon ground cinnamon
- 3 cups rolled oats

Direction

- Set the oven to 3500F (1750C) and preheat. Coat cookie sheets with grease.
- Combine white sugar, brown sugar and the shortening together in a medium bowl. Mix in the vanilla, water and egg. Blend cinnamon, baking soda, salt and flour; mix into the creamed mixture. Lastly, mix in the rolled oats. By rounded spoonfuls, drop the mixture onto the greased cookie sheets.

- Put in the prepared oven and bake for 12 to 15 minutes. Leave it on baking sheets to cool down for a few minutes before transferring to wire racks to cool.

Nutrition Information

- Calories: 135 calories;
- Total Fat: 5.9
- Sodium: 103
- Total Carbohydrate: 19.4
- Cholesterol: 6
- Protein: 1.7

658. Kung Pao Chicken

Serving: 4 | Prep: 30mins | Cook: 30mins | Ready in:

Ingredients

- 1 pound skinless, boneless chicken breast halves - cut into chunks
- 2 tablespoons white wine
- 2 tablespoons soy sauce
- 2 tablespoons sesame oil, divided
- 2 tablespoons cornstarch, dissolved in 2 tablespoons water
- 1 ounce hot chile paste
- 1 teaspoon distilled white vinegar
- 2 teaspoons brown sugar
- 4 green onions, chopped
- 1 tablespoon chopped garlic
- 1 (8 ounce) can water chestnuts
- 4 ounces chopped peanuts

Direction

- For the marinade, mix a tablespoon of slurry (water and cornstarch mixture), a tablespoon of wine, a tablespoon of oil, and a tablespoon of soy sauce. In a glass dish or bowl, add in the chicken pieces and marinade then coat evenly. Cover with lid or cling wrap, then refrigerate for about half an hour.
- For the sauce, in a small bowl, mix a tablespoon of slurry (water and cornstarch mixture), chili paste, sugar, green onion, a tablespoon of soy sauce, water chestnuts, garlic, a tablespoon of oil, peanuts, vinegar, and a tablespoon of wine. Cook mixture in a medium-sized pan until it becomes aromatic.
- Drain the chicken from the marinade. Cook and stir in a large pan until the juices run clear and the meat turns white. When sauce is fragrant, add chicken to the sauce. Leave to simmer until the sauce thickens.

Nutrition Information

- Calories: 437 calories;
- Total Fat: 23.3
- Sodium: 596
- Total Carbohydrate: 25.3
- Cholesterol: 66
- Protein: 34.4

659. La Genovese

Serving: 6 | Prep: 5mins | Cook: 10mins | Ready in:

Ingredients

- 1/2 cup olive oil
- 1 pound lean ground beef
- 3 carrots, diced
- 1/2 onion, minced
- 1 teaspoon salt
- 1 pinch ground black pepper
- 3 tablespoons white wine

Direction

- Put a large skillet over medium heat to heat olive oil. Add in beef; cook and stir well to break up clumps until it starts to brown. Add pepper, salt, onion and carrots; stir well. Cook for another 5 minutes with stirs until the meat extracts clear juice and the vegetables are just tender. Put in wine; continue cooking for another 1 minute and serve.

Nutrition Information

- Calories: 332 calories;
- Protein: 13.6
- Total Fat: 28.5
- Sodium: 441
- Total Carbohydrate: 4
- Cholesterol: 46

660. Lace's Coconut Bread

Serving: 8 | Prep: 15mins | Cook: 30mins | Ready in:

Ingredients

- 1/2 cup coconut flour
- 1/2 cup unsweetened coconut flakes
- 1 lemon, zested
- 1 teaspoon baking soda
- 1 pinch salt
- 1 cup coconut yogurt
- 3 large eggs
- 1/4 cup maple syrup
- 1/2 cup chocolate chips (such as Ghirardelli®) (optional)

Direction

- Set an oven to 350 degrees F or 175 degrees C, then butter 2 4 1/2 by 2 3/4 inch mini loaf pans.
- In a bowl, combine salt, baking soda, lemon zest, flaked coconut, and coconut flour. Then, mix in maple syrup, eggs, and yogurt to create a smooth batter. Stir in the chocolate chips then pour the batter into the loaf pans.
- Bake in the oven for about 25 minutes until the tops of the bread spring back when pressed lightly. Cover with aluminum foil and bake for another 5 minutes.

- Cool in pans for 10 minutes before removing the foil and turning them out onto wire racks to completely cool.

Nutrition Information

- Calories: 161 calories;
- Cholesterol: 70
- Protein: 3.2
- Total Fat: 9.9
- Sodium: 208
- Total Carbohydrate: 17.8

661. Lamb Casserole

Serving: 6 | Prep: 20mins | Cook: 1hours30mins | Ready in:

Ingredients

- 2 sprigs fresh parsley
- 2 sprigs fresh thyme
- 2 bay leaves
- 2 pounds lamb shank, cooked and diced
- 1 pound cubed ham steak
- 10 small onions
- 5 tomatoes - blanched, peeled and chopped
- 2 cloves garlic, chopped
- 4 cups chicken stock
- 2 (15 ounce) cans cannellini beans, drained and rinsed
- 6 links pork sausage links, halved

Direction

- Tie together the sprigs of thyme and parsley with bay leaves or arrange them in a cheesecloth, then tie closed, because you can easily discard the herbs later. In a large saucepan, place stock, garlic, tomato, onion, ham, lamb and the herb bundle over medium-high heat.
- Bring to a boil. Lower the heat to low and simmer for about 60 minutes. Mix in sausage

and beans and keep simmering about 15 minutes. If you prefer thicker consistency, simmer for a few more minutes.

Nutrition Information

- Calories: 683 calories;
- Total Fat: 34.3
- Sodium: 1540
- Total Carbohydrate: 38.5
- Cholesterol: 166
- Protein: 52.7

662. Lamb L'Arabique

Serving: 5 | Prep: 20mins | Cook: 2hours | Ready in:

Ingredients

- 2 tablespoons olive oil, divided
- 2 pounds lamb shanks
- 1 large onion, quartered
- 4 cloves garlic, chopped
- 6 cups roma (plum) tomatoes, chopped
- 1 (15 ounce) can chickpeas (garbanzo beans), drained
- 1 cup cooked lentils
- 1 tablespoon ground cumin
- 1 teaspoon ground cinnamon
- 1/4 teaspoon ground nutmeg
- 1/8 teaspoon crushed red pepper flakes
- 1 teaspoon finely chopped green chile peppers
- 1 dash hot pepper sauce

Direction

- Over medium-high heat, heat one tablespoon of oil in a large skillet and add lamb shanks. Sauté until browned lightly. Take out from the skillet and put in a deep casserole dish. Sauté garlic and onion in the skillet until tender. Mix in lentils, chickpeas and tomatoes. Season the mixture with hot pepper sauce, chile peppers, red pepper flakes, nutmeg, cinnamon and cumin. Combine thoroughly and let the flavors blend for about 3 minutes on medium heat.
- Preheat an oven to 190 degrees C (375 degrees F).
- Take out the browned shanks from the casserole for a second and then place the vegetable mixture into a casserole dish. Replace the shanks atop vegetable mixture.
- Cover the dish and then bake for 2 hours at 190 degrees C (375 degrees F) or until the lamb is receding from the bone and is cooked through.

Nutrition Information

- Calories: 586 calories;
- Sodium: 292
- Total Carbohydrate: 33.8
- Cholesterol: 122
- Protein: 42.7
- Total Fat: 31.5

663. Lamb Lover's Pilaf

Serving: 6 | Prep: 10mins | Cook: 20mins | Ready in:

Ingredients

- 2 tablespoons vegetable oil, divided
- 1 1/2 pounds boneless lamb stew meat cut into 1/2 inch strips
- 1/2 teaspoon Greek-style seasoning
- 1 onion, chopped
- 2 stalks celery, minced
- 1 cup dry bulgur wheat
- 1 1/2 cups chicken broth
- 1 pinch ground cinnamon
- 1 pinch ground allspice
- 1/4 cup raisins
- 1/4 cup slivered almonds

Direction

- In a big skillet, heat 1 tbsp. of oil over moderately high heat. Use Greek seasoning to season the lamb strips and sauté them in the hot oil until browned. Take out of the skillet and put aside.
- Lower heat to moderate and heat leftover tablespoon of oil. Sauté celery and onion until soft, then put in bulgur wheat and keep on cooking for 5 more minutes, while stirring frequently.
- Stir in allspice, cinnamon, broth and reserved lamb. Lower heat to low and simmer with a cover until liquid is absorbed, about 15-20 minutes. Use raisins and almonds to decorate and serve.

Nutrition Information

- Calories: 297 calories;
- Total Fat: 12.4
- Sodium: 89
- Total Carbohydrate: 26.6
- Cholesterol: 54
- Protein: 21.4

664. Lamb For Lovers

Serving: 4 | Prep: 30mins | Cook: 8hours30mins | Ready in:

Ingredients

- 2 tablespoons olive oil
- 2 (7 bone) racks of lamb, trimmed, fat reserved
- salt and pepper to taste
- 4 cloves garlic, minced
- 1 large onion, diced
- 4 carrots, diced
- 1 cup celery tops
- 1 cup port wine
- 1 cup red wine
- 1 (14.5 ounce) can low-sodium chicken broth
- 5 sprigs fresh spearmint
- 3 sprigs fresh rosemary
- 1 cup mint apple jelly
- 2 tablespoons olive oil
- salt and pepper to taste
- 1 tablespoon garlic, minced
- 1/4 cup panko bread crumbs
- 2 tablespoons olive oil
- 4 sprigs fresh mint

Direction

- Making Demi-Glace: In a medium skillet, heat two tablespoons of olive oil on medium heat and then place in trimmings from the lamb. Season with pepper and salt, then brown the fat, lower the heat and add chicken broth, red wine, port, celery leaves, carrots, onion and 4 cloves minced garlic. Place mixture into a slow cooker and let it simmer for 8 hours or overnight on Low.
- Over medium-low heat, strain the mixture from slow cooker into saucepan. Stir in mint jelly, rosemary and spearmint. Simmer while adding extra broth, wine or port as needed, until the mixture leaves behind a coating like that of a syrup on the back of a spoon, then strain again and keep it warm as the lamb roasts.
- Roasting the Lamb: Put an oven-proof skillet or a cast iron in an oven and then preheat to 230 degrees C (450 degrees F). Rub the lamb with garlic, pepper, salt and two tablespoons of olive oil, then coat with the panko bread crumbs.
- Gently take out the heated skillet from oven. Heat two tablespoons of olive oil in skillet and then sear the lamb on each side. Place skillet containing the lamb back into the oven and continue to cook for 5 to 10 minutes, until the internal temperature is 63 degrees C (145 degrees F).
- Place a little amount of demi-glace onto a platter and then arrange the lamb crisscrossed. Drizzle with additional demi-glace and stud with fresh mint. Serve.

Nutrition Information

- Calories: 1246 calories;
- Cholesterol: 192
- Protein: 45.3
- Total Fat: 79.4
- Sodium: 422
- Total Carbohydrate: 68.4

665. Lavonne's Scrumptious White Wine Chicken

Serving: 4 | Prep: 10mins | Cook: 1hours5mins | Ready in:

Ingredients

- 4 skinless, boneless chicken breast halves
- 1 teaspoon garlic powder
- 1/4 teaspoon poultry seasoning
- 1/8 teaspoon seasoned salt
- 1/8 teaspoon ground black pepper
- 1/2 cup white wine
- 1 tablespoon Worcestershire sauce
- 1 tablespoon vegetable oil

Direction

- Heat the oven to 190°C or 375°F.
- Use pepper, salt, poultry seasoning and garlic powder to season the chicken breasts. Put breasts in baking dish, 9x13 in size. In small bowl, mix Worcestershire sauce, vegetable oil and wine; put wine mixture on chicken breasts. Use aluminum foil to cover the whole dish.
- Bake for 45 minutes, in prepped oven; remove dish's cover and scoop pan liquid on breasts. Cover with foil once more and bake till juices flow clear, for 20 minutes to half an hour.

Nutrition Information

- Calories: 187 calories;
- Total Fat: 6.1
- Sodium: 128

- Total Carbohydrate: 2.3
- Cholesterol: 65
- Protein: 23.7

666. Lemon Ginger Shrimp

Serving: 9 | Prep: 20mins | Cook: 6mins | Ready in:

Ingredients

- 3 pounds jumbo shrimp, peeled and deveined
- 1/2 cup olive oil
- 2 teaspoons sesame oil
- 1/4 cup lemon juice
- 1 onion, chopped
- 2 cloves garlic, peeled
- 2 tablespoons grated fresh ginger root
- 2 tablespoons minced fresh cilantro leaves
- 1 teaspoon paprika
- 1/2 teaspoon salt
- 1/2 teaspoon ground black pepper
- skewers

Direction

- Process pepper, salt, paprika, cilantro, ginger, garlic, onion, lemon juice, sesame oil and olive oil till smooth in a food processor/blender; put a small amount aside for basting. Put leftover mixture into the dish then add shrimp; mix to coat. Cover; refrigerate it for 2 hours.
- Preheat the grill to medium heat. Thread the shrimp onto skewers (pierce once near head and once near tail). Discard the marinade.
- Oil grill grate lightly; grill shrimp till opaque for 2-3 minutes per side. While cooking, baste using reserved sauce.

Nutrition Information

- Calories: 286 calories;
- Total Fat: 15.7
- Sodium: 355

- Total Carbohydrate: 3.8
- Cholesterol: 230
- Protein: 31

667. Lemon Pepper Pasta

Serving: 8 | Prep: 5mins | Cook: 15mins | Ready in:

Ingredients

- 1 pound spaghetti
- 2 tablespoons olive oil
- 3 tablespoons lemon juice, to taste
- 1 tablespoon dried basil
- ground black pepper to taste

Direction

- Boil a big pot of water with a little salt. Put in pasta and cook it until done, about 8 to 10 minutes. Drain it.
- Mix black pepper, basil, lemon juice and olive oil in a small bowl. Stir well then toss mixture with the pasta. You can serve it cold or hot.

Nutrition Information

- Calories: 243 calories;
- Protein: 7.5
- Total Fat: 4.2
- Sodium: 4
- Total Carbohydrate: 43
- Cholesterol: 0

668. Lemon String Beans

Serving: 5 | Prep: 15mins | Cook: 5mins | Ready in:

Ingredients

- 1 clove garlic, peeled and cut in half
- 1/4 cup fresh lemon juice
- 1/4 cup olive oil
- 1 pound fresh green beans, trimmed
- 1 teaspoon salt

Direction

- In a big bowl, combine olive oil, lemon juice and garlic then set aside.
- Bring salted water in a big pot to a boil. Cook the green beans in the water for 5-6 minutes then drain. Let the beans cool for about 10 minutes, then transfer the cooled beans into a big bowl and toss together with lemon juice mixture. Season to taste with salt. Let beans rest for 2 minutes before stirring again. Repeat 2 minutes rest and stir for one more time. Get rid of the garlic before serving.

Nutrition Information

- Calories: 128 calories;
- Total Fat: 10.9
- Sodium: 471
- Total Carbohydrate: 7.7
- Cholesterol: 0
- Protein: 1.7

669. Lemon And Almond Slices

Serving: 8 | Prep: 20mins | Cook: 30mins | Ready in:

Ingredients

- 3/4 cup cashews
- Crust:
- 1 1/2 cups ground almonds
- 2 tablespoons coconut sugar
- 2 tablespoons coconut oil, melted
- 1 teaspoon maple syrup
- Lemon Topping:
- 1 (8 ounce) can coconut cream
- 4 lemons, zested and juiced
- 1 lemon, zested

- 2 tablespoons arrowroot starch
- 1 tablespoon honey

Direction

- Soak cashews with boiling water in a bowl, about 60 minutes.
- Turn the oven to 350°F (175°C) to preheat. Use parchment paper to line an 8x10-in. baking pan.
- In a bowl, mix together coconut sugar and ground almonds. Add maple syrup and coconut oil; stir thoroughly until forming a dough. Evenly press the dough into the prepared baking pan.
- Put in the preheated oven and bake for 15-20 minutes until slightly golden.
- Drain the cashews. Put in a blender with honey, arrowroot starch, lemon zest, lemon juice, and coconut cream; pulse until having a thick cream and fully blended. Spread to the baked almond base.
- Bake for 15 minutes in the oven until turning golden. Let cool for 15 minutes, refrigerate in the fridge for 4 hours before cutting.

Nutrition Information

- Calories: 374 calories;
- Total Fat: 25.5
- Sodium: 95
- Total Carbohydrate: 37.3
- Cholesterol: 0
- Protein: 7.8

670. Lemon And Thyme Lamb Chops

Serving: 12 | Prep: 10mins | Cook: 10mins | Ready in:

Ingredients

- 1/2 cup olive oil
- 1/4 cup lemon juice
- 1 tablespoon chopped fresh thyme
- salt and pepper to taste
- 12 lamb chops

Direction

- In a small bowl, mix together the thyme, lemon juice and olive oil. Put in pepper and salt to taste. In a shallow dish, put lamb chops, and brush with olive oil mixture. Place inside the refrigerator to marinate for 1 hour.
- Prepare the grill by preheating to high heat.
- Then put oil on the grill grate lightly. Put the lamb chops on the grill and get rid of marinade. Grill for 10 minutes, flipping once or to doneness desired.

Nutrition Information

- Calories: 205 calories;
- Total Fat: 17.6
- Sodium: 34
- Total Carbohydrate: 0.5
- Cholesterol: 42
- Protein: 10.8

671. Lengua (Beef Tongue)

Serving: 10 | Prep: 15mins | Cook: 30mins | Ready in:

Ingredients

- 1 beef tongue
- 5 fresh green chile peppers
- 1 tablespoon olive oil
- 1 white onion, sliced thinly
- 4 cloves garlic, minced
- 4 small tomatoes, halved and sliced
- 2 (15 ounce) cans whole kernel corn, drained
- salt to taste

Direction

- Rinse tongue and bring into a large pot filled with water. Let simmer for about 50 minutes

each pound of tongue until not pink anymore. Take out of the water and allow to sit until cool enough to work with. Peel of the skin attached to the tongue and trim gristle. Split into 1/4" slices.
- In a skillet, bring whole peppers to medium-high heat, then roast and turn until charred on all sides. Cool, then rub off the skins. Take out seeds and stems.
- In a large skillet, bring olive oil to medium heat. Sauté garlic, onion and chile peppers until onion is translucent. Mix in tongue and keep cooking for another 5-10 minutes until tongue is browned. Mix in tomatoes and cook for 5 minutes until limp. Add in corn and cook for 2-5 minutes until heated through. Add salt to season. Serve instantly.

Nutrition Information

- Calories: 384 calories;
- Total Fat: 24.4
- Sodium: 319
- Total Carbohydrate: 20.8
- Cholesterol: 131
- Protein: 22.3

672. Lentil Loaf

Serving: 6 | Prep: 45mins | Cook: 50mins | Ready in:

Ingredients

- 1 1/8 cups green lentils
- 2 1/4 cups water
- 6 slices white bread, torn into small pieces
- 2 eggs
- 1 cup vegetable broth
- 2 tablespoons tomato paste
- 1/2 teaspoon dried basil
- 1/4 teaspoon garlic powder
- 1/2 teaspoon ground black pepper
- 1 teaspoon dried parsley
- 1 tablespoon olive oil

- 1/2 packet dry vegetable soup mix
- 1/3 cup dried bread crumbs

Direction

- In a small saucepan, combine water and lentils; heat to a boil. Lower the heat and simmer for 40 minutes until tender.
- Set oven to 205° C (400° F) and start preheating. Oil a 9x5-in. loaf pan.
- Blend dry soup mix, olive oil, parsley, black pepper, garlic powder, basil, tomato paste, broth, eggs, bread and 2 cups cooked lentils together in a big bowl. Arrange into the prepared saucepan.
- Bake 40 minutes. Sprinkle dry bread crumbs over top and keep baking for 10 more minutes. Allow to rest 10 minutes then serve.

Nutrition Information

- Calories: 272 calories;
- Protein: 14.6
- Total Fat: 5.6
- Sodium: 369
- Total Carbohydrate: 40.9
- Cholesterol: 62

673. Linguine With Chicken And Sauteed Vegetables

Serving: 6 | Prep: 30mins | Cook: 10mins | Ready in:

Ingredients

- 1/2 cup vegetable oil
- 10 cloves garlic, finely chopped
- 1 (12 ounce) package uncooked linguine pasta
- salt to taste
- 1/2 cup chopped broccoli
- 1/2 cup chopped cabbage
- 1/2 cup shredded carrots
- 1/2 cup chopped cauliflower
- 2 tablespoons diced green onions

- 1 pound chicken tenders, cut into bite-size pieces
- 3 1/2 tablespoons soy sauce
- salt and pepper to taste
- 1 cup chopped cilantro
- 4 lime wedges

Direction

- Heat oil in a skillet on medium heat. Mix in garlic; mix and cook till golden. Take off from heat; cool.
- Boil a big pot of lightly salted water. Add linguine; cook till al dente for 8-10 minutes. Drain; put in a big bowl. Put 1 tbsp. of garlic oil aside; toss leftover with pasta till coated. Season pasta using salt.
- Boil a pot of water. Immerse green onions, cauliflower, carrots, cabbage and broccoli in water for 30 seconds then drain; put aside.
- Heat saved garlic oil in skillet on medium heat. Mix in 2 tbsp. of soy sauce and chicken; cook till chicken juices are clear. Mix in leftover soy sauce and veggies; season with pepper and salt. Toss with linguine; garnish with lime and cilantro. Serve.

Nutrition Information

- Calories: 480 calories;
- Sodium: 586
- Total Carbohydrate: 45.5
- Cholesterol: 46
- Protein: 25.3
- Total Fat: 21.6

674. Linnie's Spanish Rice

Serving: 4 | Prep: | Cook: 30mins | Ready in:

Ingredients

- 1 cup uncooked white rice
- 1 teaspoon minced garlic
- 2 cups water
- 1 (16 ounce) jar salsa

Direction

- In a big saucepan, mix the rice with the garlic. Put salsa and water into the rice mixture then bring to a full boil. Reduce the temperature and simmer. Allow to simmer until the rice becomes tender, about 20 minutes. When finished, fluff the rice.

Nutrition Information

- Calories: 200 calories;
- Total Fat: 0.5
- Sodium: 674
- Total Carbohydrate: 44.2
- Cholesterol: 0
- Protein: 5.1

675. Lion Veggie Tray

Serving: 12 | Prep: 20mins | Cook: | Ready in:

Ingredients

- 1 (10 ounce) container hummus spread
- 3 black olives
- 1 red bell pepper, cut into long strips
- 3 chives, cut in half
- 2 round crackers
- 1 yellow bell pepper, cut into long strips
- 1 orange bell pepper, cut into long strips

Direction

- Into a round bowl, scoop the hummus then put in it 2 olives as eyes. For the mouth, cut the third olive into strips. For the nose, cut off a small triangle of red bell pepper. For the whiskers, slice the chives in half then stick it onto the hummus sideways, then for the ears, put 2 crackers.

- For the mane, arrange the strips of bell pepper around the lion's head.

Nutrition Information

- Calories: 47 calories;
- Cholesterol: 0
- Protein: 2
- Total Fat: 2.6
- Sodium: 106
- Total Carbohydrate: 4.4

676. Liver And Bacon

Serving: 6 | Prep: 15mins | Cook: 20mins | Ready in:

Ingredients

- 1 pound bacon
- 1 pound calves' liver, sliced
- 1 (5.5 ounce) package pork flavored seasoning coating mix (e.g. - SHAKE-N-BAKE)

Direction

- Put the bacon in large, deep skillet and then cook with medium high heat until browned evenly. Place the bacon onto a plate and save a little amount of grease in pan and the remaining aside.
- Transfer the seasoning coating mix to a large plastic bag that is resealable. Put the calves' liver into bag, 1 slice at a time. Then seal the bag and mix to coat.
- Over medium high heat, cook the liver in bacon grease and flip sometimes to brown each side. You work in batches if the skillet is small and add extra bacon grease. The liver is done if the juices run clear. Place the bacon back into skillet during the final two minutes of cooking so as to warm through. You can serve while still hot along with side dish you like.

Nutrition Information

- Calories: 320 calories;
- Total Carbohydrate: 20.8
- Cholesterol: 207
- Protein: 24.3
- Total Fat: 15.2
- Sodium: 1178

677. Lokshin Kugel (Noodle Pudding)

Serving: 8 | Prep: 30mins | Cook: 1hours | Ready in:

Ingredients

- 1 (12 ounce) package thin egg noodles
- 6 onions, diced
- 1/8 cup vegetable oil for frying
- salt and pepper to taste
- 4 eggs
- 1/4 cup dry bread crumbs
- paprika to taste

Direction

- Preheat an oven to 175 degrees C (350 degrees F). Coat a 9 x 13 baking dish with grease. Heat lightly salted water in a large pot to boil. Pour in pasta and then cook for about 8 to 10 minutes or until it is al dente. Drain the pasta.
- As the pasta cooks, over medium heat, cook the onions in oil in a medium saucepan. Season with pepper and salt. Let cook until soft and brown.
- Mix pepper and salt to taste, bread crumbs, eggs, onions and pasta in a very large mixing bowl. Combine well. Transfer to baking dish and drizzle paprika all over top. Drizzle with oil, if you like and then bake for about 50 to 60 minutes until the top is golden and crispy.

Nutrition Information

- Calories: 228 calories;

- Total Fat: 5.3
- Sodium: 107
- Total Carbohydrate: 36.2
- Cholesterol: 123
- Protein: 9.3

678. Loose Meat On A Bun, Restaurant Style

Serving: 12 | Prep: 10mins | Cook: 50mins | Ready in:

Ingredients

- 3 pounds ground beef
- 1/4 cup minced onion
- 3 tablespoons Worcestershire sauce
- 4 cups beef broth
- 1 teaspoon salt
- 1 teaspoon ground black pepper
- 2 teaspoons butter
- 12 hamburger buns, split

Direction

- Crumble onion and ground beef into a big skillet over moderately high heat. Cook the mixture until beef is not pink anymore while stirring to break up lumps. Drain off grease and bring skillet back to the stove. Put in butter, pepper, salt, beef broth and Worcestershire sauce. Bring the mixture to a boil then set the heat to low and simmer without a cover for 40 minutes, until liquid is nearly completely gone. Take away from the heat, place on a cover and allow to rest about 15 minutes prior to serving on buns.

Nutrition Information

- Calories: 341 calories;
- Total Fat: 16.4
- Sodium: 810
- Total Carbohydrate: 22.9
- Cholesterol: 71

- Protein: 23.6

679. Mac And 'Shews (Vegan Mac And Cheese)

Serving: 4 | Prep: 5mins | Cook: 15mins | Ready in:

Ingredients

- 1 cup unroasted cashews
- 1 cup vegetable broth
- 3 tablespoons nutritional yeast flakes
- 3 tablespoons fresh lemon juice
- 2 teaspoons white miso
- 2 teaspoons onion powder
- 1/2 teaspoon salt, or to taste
- black pepper to taste
- 8 ounces small shell pasta or macaroni
- 1 1/2 cups arugula (optional)

Direction

- In a high-powered blender (such as a Vitamix®), process onion powder, miso, lemon juice, yeast, broth and cashews, using spatula to scrape down sides until fully smooth. Add pepper and salt to taste, bearing in mind that it should be just a bit saltier than normal since it's going to be added to other ingredients.
- In the meantime, put a salted water in a pot and make it boil then add pasta to cook based on the package directions.
- Strain, put back into the pot, and mix in the cashew sauce. Cook over low heat for about 3 minutes, whisking until sauce thickens a bit and all is lusciously creamy. Mix in arugula (if you want), and some more salt if necessary. Serve right away.

Nutrition Information

- Calories: 430 calories;
- Protein: 17.6

- Total Fat: 16.8
- Sodium: 525
- Total Carbohydrate: 57.2
- Cholesterol: 0

680. Magaricz

Serving: 10 | Prep: 20mins | Cook: 40mins | Ready in:

Ingredients

- 1/4 cup olive oil
- 1 large eggplant, peeled and coarsely chopped
- 1 medium red bell pepper, cut into thin strips
- 1 green bell pepper, cut into thin strips
- 1 large onion, diced
- 1 cup coarsely shredded carrot
- salt to taste
- crushed red pepper flakes

Direction

- Lightly salt eggplant and place in a colander. Set aside for about 45 minutes, allowing eggplant to drain.
- Heat olive oil in a big pan over medium high heat. Toss in eggplant, onion, carrot, red and green bell peppers. Mix well to coat then turn heat down to low. Continue cooking for 40 minutes, stirring from time to time, until mixture achieves coarse jam consistency. Sprinkle with salt and red pepper flakes to taste.
- Refrigerate, covered, for at least 1 hour. Serve chilled with your preferred crackers or bread.

Nutrition Information

- Calories: 77 calories;
- Total Fat: 5.6
- Sodium: 239
- Total Carbohydrate: 6.7
- Cholesterol: 0
- Protein: 1

681. Mamma Rita's Eggs And Tomato Sauce

Serving: 4 | Prep: 5mins | Cook: 10mins | Ready in:

Ingredients

- 2 tablespoons extra virgin olive oil
- 4 ripe tomatoes, chopped
- 4 eggs
- salt and pepper to taste

Direction

- In frying pan or skillet, warm the oil over medium heat. Put tomatoes into skillet. Cook for 3-5 mins or until juices start to evaporate.
- Crack the eggs into skillet. Cook to preferred firmness, but do not break the yolks. Season to taste with pepper and salt.

Nutrition Information

- Calories: 154 calories;
- Total Fat: 11.9
- Sodium: 374
- Total Carbohydrate: 5.3
- Cholesterol: 186
- Protein: 7.5

682. Mandarin Orange Couscous

Serving: 4 | Prep: 5mins | Cook: 15mins | Ready in:

Ingredients

- 1 (10 ounce) box uncooked plain couscous
- 1 (11 ounce) can mandarin oranges, drained and liquid reserved
- 1/4 cup pine nuts, lightly toasted

Direction

- Follow the package instructions on how to prepare the couscous using the drained mandarin orange liquid as an addition to the specified amount of water. Fluff the couscous. Stir in mandarin oranges and pine nuts gently. Serve while hot.

Nutrition Information

- Calories: 344 calories;
- Protein: 11.6
- Total Fat: 4.8
- Sodium: 11
- Total Carbohydrate: 63.6
- Cholesterol: 0

683. Mango Papaya Salsa

Serving: 8 | Prep: 15mins | Cook: |Ready in:

Ingredients

- 1 mango - peeled, seeded and diced
- 1 papaya - peeled, seeded and diced
- 1 large red bell pepper, seeded and diced
- 1 avocado - peeled, pitted and diced
- 1/2 sweet onion, peeled and diced
- 2 tablespoons chopped fresh cilantro
- 2 tablespoons balsamic vinegar
- salt and pepper to taste

Direction

- Combine in a medium bowl the balsamic vinegar, cilantro, sweet onion, avocado, red bell pepper, papaya and mango. Add pepper and salt to taste. Then cover and refrigerate for at least 30 minutes until chilled then serve.

Nutrition Information

- Calories: 77 calories;
- Total Fat: 3.9
- Sodium: 5
- Total Carbohydrate: 11
- Cholesterol: 0
- Protein: 1.1

684. Mango Pecan Chicken

Serving: 4 | Prep: 15mins | Cook: 15mins |Ready in:

Ingredients

- 1 tablespoon vegetable oil
- 1 onion, halved and sliced
- 2 mangos - peeled, seeded, and cubed
- 2 tablespoons lemon juice
- 1 tablespoon white sugar
- 1/4 teaspoon ground ginger
- 1/8 teaspoon ground cinnamon
- 1/8 teaspoon ground mace
- 4 skinless, boneless chicken breast halves - cut in half lengthwise
- salt and pepper to taste
- 1 tablespoon vegetable oil
- 1/4 cup chopped pecans

Direction

- In a big saucepan, heat 1 tbsp. of vegetable oil on medium heat, then add onion and let it cook and stir for about 5 minutes, until the onion becomes translucent and soft. Add mace, cinnamon, ginger, sugar, lemon juice and mangos, then simmer and cook for 5 minutes, stirring continuously. Lower the heat to low, put on cover and let it cook for additional 5 minutes.
- Season pepper and salt to taste on the chicken breasts while the mango sauce is simmering. In a big skillet, heat the leftover 1 tbsp. of vegetable oil on medium heat. Add chicken and cook on both sides, around 8 minutes on each side, until the chicken has no visible pink color in the middle and becomes nicely browned.

- On each serving plate, put on 1-2 pieces of chicken, then scoop mango sauce on top and sprinkle it with pecans, then serve.

Nutrition Information

- Calories: 331 calories;
- Total Fat: 14.9
- Sodium: 62
- Total Carbohydrate: 25
- Cholesterol: 67
- Protein: 26

685. Maria's Spanish Rice

Serving: 6 | Prep: 10mins | Cook: 20mins | Ready in:

Ingredients

- 2 tablespoons olive oil
- 1 large yellow onion, diced
- 1 clove garlic, minced
- 1 1/2 cups uncooked white rice
- 3 cups water
- 1 (4 ounce) jar diced pimento peppers, drained

Direction

- In a medium skillet, heat oil on medium heat. Sauté garlic and onion until golden. Mix in rice, sauté until rice starts to brown. Pour in water and allow to simmer for 10 minutes.
- Mix in pimentos. Decrease the heat, cook for approximately 10-15 minutes with a cover, till all water has been absorbed.

Nutrition Information

- Calories: 235 calories;
- Total Fat: 5
- Sodium: 5
- Total Carbohydrate: 42.4
- Cholesterol: 0
- Protein: 4.3

686. Marinated Mushrooms With Red Bell Peppers

Serving: 12 | Prep: 20mins | Cook: 10mins | Ready in:

Ingredients

- 1/2 cup red wine vinegar
- 1/3 cup water
- 2 tablespoons corn oil
- 1 teaspoon white sugar
- 1 tablespoon chopped onion
- 1 tablespoon chopped fresh parsley
- 1/2 teaspoon dried basil
- 2 cloves garlic, minced
- 1/4 teaspoon salt
- 1/4 teaspoon fresh ground black pepper
- 2 (16 ounce) packages fresh mushrooms, stems removed
- 1/2 red bell pepper, diced

Direction

- Mix together pepper, salt, garlic, basil, parsley, onion, sugar, oil, water and vinegar; come to a boil. Stir in red bell pepper and mushrooms; bring the mixture to a boil again; lower the heat and allow it to simmer for 5-10 minutes, until the mushrooms are tender. Take it out of the heat and cool to room temperature. Put in a container, cover up and keep in fridge for at least 4 hours to serve.

Nutrition Information

- Calories: 44 calories;
- Total Carbohydrate: 4.2
- Cholesterol: 0
- Protein: 2.5
- Total Fat: 2.6
- Sodium: 53

687. Marinated Pork Roast

Serving: 8 | Prep: 15mins | Cook: 2hours | Ready in:

Ingredients

- 1 (4 pound) pork roast
- 1/2 cup Worcestershire sauce
- 2 tablespoons honey
- 2 tablespoons cider vinegar
- 1/2 teaspoon mustard seed
- 1/2 teaspoon mustard powder
- 1 teaspoon lemon pepper
- 1/2 teaspoon celery salt
- 1 clove garlic, minced

Direction

- Set the grill on indirect heat.
- In a large resealable plastic bag, blend garlic, celery salt, lemon pepper, mustard powder, mustard seed, vinegar, honey, and Worcestershire sauce; seal the bag and combine the ingredients. In the plastic bag, arrange the roast, then press out the air and seal the bag. Put in the fridge for 2 hours to marinate, and while marinating, turn the roast from time to time to coat.
- Oil the grill grate lightly. Arrange the roast on the grill, then discard the marinade. Put a cover on and cook until the internal heat reaches 63°C (145°F) or 1 1/2-2 hours.

688. Marinated Rosemary Lemon Chicken

Serving: 4 | Prep: 15mins | Cook: 15mins | Ready in:

Ingredients

- 1/2 cup lemon juice
- 1/8 cup olive oil
- 2 tablespoons dried rosemary
- 4 skinless, boneless chicken breast halves
- 1 lemon, sliced

Direction

- Combine rosemary, olive oil, and lemon juice in a large resealable plastic bag. Add the lemon slices and chicken in the bag. Seal then shake to coat. Keep in the refrigerator for 8 hours or overnight to marinate.
- Prepare the grill by preheating to high heat.
- Put oil lightly on the grill grate. Get rid of the marinade, and grill each side of the chicken for 8 minutes, or until juices run clear. It's ok if rosemary sticks to the chicken since the taste is great once it's grilled. Throw the stems of rosemary sprigs into the coals if using the fresh ones- they make a smoky rosemary flavor to the chicken even more.

Nutrition Information

- Calories: 209 calories;
- Total Fat: 9.9
- Sodium: 61
- Total Carbohydrate: 6.6
- Cholesterol: 67
- Protein: 25

689. Marinated Tuna Steak

Serving: 4 | Prep: 10mins | Cook: 11mins | Ready in:

Ingredients

- 1/4 cup orange juice
- 1/4 cup soy sauce
- 2 tablespoons olive oil
- 1 tablespoon lemon juice
- 2 tablespoons chopped fresh parsley
- 1 clove garlic, minced
- 1/2 teaspoon chopped fresh oregano
- 1/2 teaspoon ground black pepper
- 4 (4 ounce) tuna steaks

Direction

- Mix the soy sauce, parsley, lemon juice, orange juice, olive oil, oregano, pepper, and garlic in a large non-reactive dish. Add the tuna steaks into the marinade, flipping them well until coated. Cover the dish and refrigerate it for at least half an hour.
- Set the grill to high heat for preheating.
- Put oil onto the grate lightly. Grill the tuna steaks for 5-6 minutes. Flip the steaks over and baste them with the marinade. Cook for 5 more minutes until you reached the desired doneness. Discard the remaining marinade.

Nutrition Information

- Calories: 200 calories;
- Total Fat: 7.9
- Sodium: 945
- Total Carbohydrate: 3.7
- Cholesterol: 51
- Protein: 27.4

690. Marrakesh Vegetable Curry

Serving: 6 | Prep: 15mins | Cook: 35mins | Ready in:

Ingredients

- 1 sweet potato, peeled and cubed
- 1 medium eggplant, cubed
- 1 green bell pepper, chopped
- 1 red bell pepper, chopped
- 2 carrots, chopped
- 1 onion, chopped
- 6 tablespoons olive oil
- 3 cloves garlic, minced
- 1 teaspoon ground turmeric
- 1 tablespoon curry powder
- 1 teaspoon ground cinnamon
- 3/4 tablespoon sea salt
- 3/4 teaspoon cayenne pepper
- 1 (15 ounce) can garbanzo beans, drained
- 1/4 cup blanched almonds
- 1 zucchini, sliced
- 2 tablespoons raisins
- 1 cup orange juice
- 10 ounces spinach

Direction

- Put 3 tablespoons of oil, onion, carrots, peppers, eggplant and sweet potato in a big Dutch oven. Sauté for 5 minutes on medium heat.
- Put pepper, salt, cinnamon, curry powder, turmeric, garlic and 3 tablespoons of olive oil in a medium pan, then sauté for 3 minutes on medium heat.
- In the Dutch oven with vegetables inside, pour the spice mixture and garlic. Put orange juice, raisins, zucchini, almonds and garbanzo beans. Let it simmer for 20 minutes with cover.
- In the pot, put the spinach and cook for additional 5 minutes, then serve.

Nutrition Information

- Calories: 330 calories;
- Total Carbohydrate: 39
- Cholesterol: 0
- Protein: 8
- Total Fat: 18
- Sodium: 874

691. Marzipan Candy

Serving: 16 | Prep: | Cook: | Ready in:

Ingredients

- 8 ounces almond paste
- 2 cups confectioners' sugar
- 1/4 cup corn syrup
- 3 drops any color food coloring

Direction

- In a medium bowl, make small pieces of almond paste by breaking the paste. Put in a cup of confectioners' sugar, use your hands to work till incorporated. The mixture will be crumbly. Put in another 3/4 cup of sugar, continue working in it really well. Pour in the corn syrup, work till everything is blended evenly. Spread out the remaining sugar on a clean work surface, knead for 3-5 minutes till the dough becomes uniform and smooth. Put in more sugar and knead if the dough appears too sticky. Use plastic wrap to wrap the dough, chill the wrapped dough in the fridge for about 60 minutes. The dough should have the consistency of the modeling dough.
- Break off small pieces of marzipan for coloration. Add color and knead thoroughly till you have the desired color. Mix the colored pieces into larger portions of dough. Dust a rolling pin and work surface with confectioners' sugar, roll out dough to 1/4 inch thick. Use small cookie cutters to make candies in desire shapes.

Nutrition Information

- Calories: 138 calories;
- Sodium: 5
- Total Carbohydrate: 25.7
- Cholesterol: 0
- Protein: 1.3
- Total Fat: 3.9

692. Mashed Potatoes And Celery Root

Serving: 8 | Prep: 25mins | Cook: 27mins | Ready in:

Ingredients

- 2 1/2 pounds russet potatoes, peeled and cut into 1-inch cubes
- 1 large celery root, peeled and cut into 1-inch cubes
- 3 cloves garlic, peeled
- 1/2 cup almond milk, divided
- 1/4 cup extra-virgin olive oil, divided
- 2 tablespoons minced fresh chives
- 1/2 teaspoon salt, or to taste
- freshly ground black pepper to taste

Direction

- In a big pot, add celery root and potatoes then cover with enough water. Bring to a boil, then lower the heat and simmer for approximately 20 minutes, until softened. Drain and take back to the pot. Cook on medium high heat for 2 to 3 minutes, until dry. Take away from the heat.
- In a food processor, pulse celery root, garlic and potatoes in batches, pouring in olive oil and almond milk while pulsing to get wanted consistency. Turn out the mixture to a big bowl, then stir in black pepper, salt and chives.

Nutrition Information

- Calories: 220 calories;
- Total Fat: 7.6
- Sodium: 264
- Total Carbohydrate: 35
- Cholesterol: 0
- Protein: 4.5

693. Maui Chicken

Serving: 4 | Prep: 20mins | Cook: 30mins | Ready in:

Ingredients

- 4 skinless, boneless chicken breast halves - diced
- 2 tablespoons soy sauce
- 1 (8 ounce) can pineapple tidbits with juice
- 2 tablespoons olive oil

- 1 red bell pepper, diced
- 1 orange bell pepper, diced
- 4 crimini mushrooms, sliced
- 3 cloves garlic, minced
- 2 tablespoons fresh ginger root, minced
- 1 (8 ounce) can pineapple tidbits with juice
- 2 teaspoons black bean sauce
- 1 teaspoon crushed red pepper
- salt and ground black pepper to taste

Direction

- In a bowl, mix together 1 can of pineapple tidbits with its juice, soy sauce and chicken. Let the chicken marinate for 20 minutes. Take the chicken out of the marinade and use a colander to strain the marinade and set aside the juice. Get rid of the pineapple.
- In a big skillet, heat the olive oil on medium heat. Add the ginger, garlic, mushrooms, orange bell pepper and red bell pepper. Cook and stir the vegetable mixture until the peppers start to soften and the garlic becomes aromatic. Mix in the chicken and let it cook for about 15 minutes, until the chicken juices run clear.
- Pour in the reserved chicken marinade, crushed red pepper, black bean sauce and 1 can of pineapple tidbits with its juice, then sprinkle pepper and salt to season. Let it simmer for 5 minutes.

Nutrition Information

- Calories: 310 calories;
- Total Fat: 13.1
- Sodium: 529
- Total Carbohydrate: 24.3
- Cholesterol: 59
- Protein: 24.3

694. Mayonnaise Cake I

Serving: 24 | Prep: | Cook: | Ready in:

Ingredients

- 1 cup mayonnaise
- 1 cup white sugar
- 3/4 cup water
- 2 cups all-purpose flour
- 1 1/2 teaspoons baking soda
- 4 tablespoons unsweetened cocoa powder
- 1/2 teaspoon salt
- 2 teaspoons vanilla extract

Direction

- Set an oven to preheat to 175°C (350°F), then grease and flour two 8 or 9-inch round cake pans.
- Sift together cocoa, baking soda, salt and all-purpose flour.
- Whip together the vanilla, cold water, white sugar and mayonnaise until thoroughly mixed, then slowly add the flour mixture and beat for 2 minutes at medium speed using an electric mixer. Pour the batter into the prepped pans.
- Let it bake for 20-25 minutes at 175°C (350°F), then frost it using your favorite frosting.

Nutrition Information

- Calories: 139 calories;
- Sodium: 180
- Total Carbohydrate: 17.1
- Cholesterol: 3
- Protein: 1.3
- Total Fat: 7.5

695. Mean Woman Pasta

Serving: 4 | Prep: 20mins | Cook: 10mins | Ready in:

Ingredients

- 1 pound seashell pasta
- 3 cups chopped tomatoes
- 5 cloves garlic, minced

- 15 kalamata olives, pitted and sliced
- 1/4 cup chopped fresh basil
- 1/4 cup olive oil
- 10 pepperoncini

Direction

- Mix pepperoncinis, olive oil, basil, olives, garlic and tomatoes together. Mix together and marinate in as much time as you have; preferably overnight, however it's good to eat immediately too.
- Cook the pasta following package instructions; drain. Toss together with sauce, serve.

Nutrition Information

- Calories: 611 calories;
- Total Fat: 20.5
- Sodium: 1720
- Total Carbohydrate: 92.8
- Cholesterol: 0
- Protein: 17.4

696. Meatless Stuffed Peppers

Serving: 5 | Prep: 30mins | Cook: 1hours | Ready in:

Ingredients

- 2 tablespoons vegetable oil
- 1 large onion, chopped
- 3 cloves garlic, chopped, divided
- 4 tablespoons uncooked white rice
- 1 cup vegetable broth
- 1 pound firm tofu, crumbled
- 1/4 cup chopped fresh parsley
- 1 cup chopped fresh mushrooms
- 2 eggs
- 1/4 cup dry bread crumbs
- 1 cup finely chopped walnuts
- 1 tablespoon vegetarian Worcestershire sauce
- 1 tablespoon soy sauce
- 1 tablespoon paprika
- 6 green bell peppers
- 1 (8 ounce) can crushed tomatoes
- 1/4 cup wine
- 1 tablespoon tomato paste

Direction

- Set an oven to 175°C (350°F) and start preheating.
- In a medium skillet on medium heat, heat oil. Sauté 2 cloves of garlic and onions until the onions become translucent. Put in rice and sauté for 2 minutes. Pour in vegetable broth and stir; put a cover on and cook for 15 minutes until rice is done.
- At the same time, mix the cooked rice, paprika, soy sauce, Worcestershire, walnuts, breadcrumbs, eggs, mushrooms, parsley, and tofu in a big bowl.
- Remove the tops from the peppers and reserve tops. Core the peppers and fill them with the tofu mixture. Replace the tops on the peppers.
- Mix the remaining garlic, tomato paste, wine, and tomatoes in a shallow baking dish. In the dish, arrange the peppers and put a cover on.
- In the prepared oven, bake for an hour.

Nutrition Information

- Calories: 521 calories;
- Total Carbohydrate: 38.9
- Cholesterol: 74
- Protein: 25.6
- Total Fat: 32.2
- Sodium: 512

697. Mediterranean Brown Rice Pilaf

Serving: 6 | Prep: 30mins | Cook: 52mins | Ready in:

Ingredients

- 1 (14.5 ounce) can chicken broth

- 1 cup uncooked brown rice
- 1/2 teaspoon dried rosemary (optional)
- 2 tablespoons olive oil
- 2 cloves garlic, minced
- 1 onion, chopped
- 2 shallots
- 1/4 cup chopped green bell pepper
- 1 (15 ounce) can chickpeas, drained
- 1/4 cup drained chopped sun-dried tomatoes
- 2 eggs, slightly beaten
- salt and ground black pepper to taste
- 1/4 cup pine nuts
- 1/4 cup fresh basil

Direction

- In a saucepan, bring chicken broth to a boil, then put in rosemary and rice. Lower the heat and simmer for approximately 45 minutes, until broth is absorbed and rice is softened.
- In a big saucepan, heat olive oil on medium heat. Put in garlic then stir in shallots and onion. Cook for around 5 minutes until tender while stirring often. Put in green bell pepper and cook for approximately 1 minute until tender. Mix into the vegetable mixture with tomatoes and chickpeas, then cook for around a minute until heated through.
- Scoop cooked rice into the vegetable mixture. Add eggs and stir until whole mixture is dry. Season to taste with pepper and salt, then take away from the heat. Stir in basil and pine nuts.

Nutrition Information

- Calories: 311 calories;
- Protein: 9.7
- Total Fat: 11.3
- Sodium: 496
- Total Carbohydrate: 44
- Cholesterol: 64

698. Mediterranean Lemon Chicken

Serving: 6 | Prep: 15mins | Cook: 50mins | Ready in:

Ingredients

- 1 lemon
- 2 teaspoons dried oregano
- 3 cloves garlic, minced
- 1 tablespoon olive oil
- 1/4 teaspoon salt
- 1/4 teaspoon ground black pepper
- 6 chicken legs

Direction

- Set the oven to 425°F or 220°C for preheating.
- In a 9x13-inches baking dish, grate the peel from the lemon half. Squeeze the juice out from the lemon, about 1/4 cup of juice, and add it into the peel together with the pepper, oil, oregano, salt, and garlic. Stir the mixture until well blended.
- Remove and discard the skin from the chicken pieces. Coat the lemon mixture all over the chicken pieces. Arrange the chicken into the baking dish, bone-side up. Cover the dish and bake the chicken for 20 minutes. Flip the chicken and baste.
- Adjust the heat to 400°F or 205°C. Bake the chicken while uncovered for 30 more minutes, basting the chicken every 10 minutes. Serve the chicken together with its pan juices.

Nutrition Information

- Calories: 241 calories;
- Total Fat: 11.8
- Sodium: 200
- Total Carbohydrate: 2.8
- Cholesterol: 105
- Protein: 30.6

699. Mexican Ceviche

Serving: 8 | Prep: 30mins | Cook: 30mins | Ready in:

Ingredients

- 5 large lemons, juiced
- 1 pound jumbo shrimp, peeled and deveined
- 1/4 cup chopped fresh cilantro, or to taste
- tomato and clam juice cocktail
- 2 white onions, finely chopped
- 1 cucumber, peeled and finely chopped
- 1 large tomatoes, seeded and chopped
- 3 fresh jalapeno peppers, seeded and minced
- 1 bunch radishes, finely diced
- 2 cloves fresh garlic, minced
- tortilla chips

Direction

- Put the shrimp in a bowl. You may leave the shrimp whole or chop it coarsely; it depends on your preference. Add the lemon and cover the shrimp totally. Put cover and let it chill in the fridge for 30 minutes or until it becomes a bit firm and turns opaque.
- Add garlic, radishes, cucumber, onions and tomatoes, then toss to blend. Slowly add jalapenos and cilantro to your preferred taste (jalapeno's taste will be stronger as it marinates). Stir in the clam juices and tomato to your preferred consistency. Put cover and let it chill in the fridge for an hour, then serve chilled alongside tortilla chips.

Nutrition Information

- Calories: 387 calories;
- Total Fat: 12.4
- Sodium: 733
- Total Carbohydrate: 57.6
- Cholesterol: 86
- Protein: 17.7

700. Mexican Hot Chocolate Cupcakes (Vegan)

Serving: 12 | Prep: 20mins | Cook: 30mins | Ready in:

Ingredients

- Cupcakes:
- 1 1/2 cups all-purpose flour
- 1 cup raw cane sugar
- 1/4 cup unsweetened cocoa powder
- 1 teaspoon ground cinnamon, or to taste
- 1 teaspoon baking soda
- 1/2 teaspoon cayenne pepper, or to taste
- 1/4 teaspoon coarse kosher salt
- 1 cup water
- 1/3 cup natural unsweetened applesauce
- 1 tablespoon vegetable oil
- 1 teaspoon vanilla extract
- 1 teaspoon distilled white vinegar
- Frosting:
- 1 (6 ounce) package semisweet chocolate chips
- 2 teaspoons vegan margarine (such as Earth Balance®)
- 1 teaspoon ground cinnamon, or to taste
- 1/2 teaspoon cayenne pepper, or to taste

Direction

- Set an oven to preheat to 175°C (350°F). Lightly grease a 12-cup muffin tin or use paper liners to line the cups.
- In a big bowl, stir the salt, 1/2 tsp cayenne pepper, baking soda, 1 tsp cinnamon, cocoa powder, sugar and flour. Add the vinegar, vanilla extract, vegetable oil, applesauce and water, then stir until the batter becomes smooth.
- Scoop the batter into the prepped muffin cups and fill each 3/4 full.
- Let it bake in the preheated oven for about 25 minutes, until the tops bounce back once pressed lightly. Move to a wire rack and allow it to cool for a minimum of 15 minutes.
- Put the margarine and chocolate on top of a double boiler atop the simmering water. Mix often and use rubber spatula to scrape down

the sides to prevent it from scorching, until the chocolate melts, approximately 5 minutes. Stir 1/2 tsp cayenne pepper and 1 tsp cinnamon into the frosting.
- Spoon the frosting on top of the cupcakes and swirl it around to cover the surface.

Nutrition Information

- Calories: 209 calories;
- Total Fat: 6.3
- Sodium: 159
- Total Carbohydrate: 38.7
- Cholesterol: 0
- Protein: 2.6

701. Mexican Rice

Serving: 8 | Prep: 20mins | Cook: 30mins | Ready in:

Ingredients

- 3 tablespoons vegetable oil
- 2/3 cup diced onion
- 1 1/2 cups uncooked white rice
- 1 cup chopped green bell pepper
- 1 teaspoon ground cumin
- 1 teaspoon chili powder
- 1 1/2 (8 ounce) cans tomato sauce
- 2 teaspoons salt
- 1 clove garlic, minced
- 1/8 teaspoon powdered saffron
- 3 cups water

Direction

- Heat vegetable oil over medium-low heat in a big saucepan then put in the onions and sauté until golden.
- Put the rice into the pan and mix to coat the grains with oil. Stir in water, saffron, garlic, salt, tomato sauce, chili powder, cumin and green bell pepper. Cover and boil. Reduce the heat and simmer. Cook until rice becomes tender, about 30 to 40 minutes, occasionally stirring.

Nutrition Information

- Calories: 199 calories;
- Total Fat: 5.6
- Sodium: 809
- Total Carbohydrate: 33.8
- Cholesterol: 0
- Protein: 3.4

702. Mexican Rice I

Serving: 7 | Prep: 15mins | Cook: 30mins | Ready in:

Ingredients

- 1 1/2 teaspoons vegetable oil
- 1/2 small small onion, diced
- 2/3 cup uncooked long-grain rice
- 1/2 teaspoon ground cumin
- 1/2 teaspoon chili powder
- 3 ounces canned diced tomatoes
- 1 teaspoon salt
- 1 1/2 cups water

Direction

- In a big pan, heat oil over medium heat and stir in onion, sautéing until they are translucent.
- Pour in rice and stir to coat the grains in oil. Mix in water, salt, tomatoes, chili powder, and cumin. Set to boil, covered, then decrease the heat to low. Cook at a simmer until the rice is tender, about 20-30 minutes, occasionally stirring.

Nutrition Information

- Calories: 79 calories;
- Total Fat: 1.2
- Sodium: 364

- Total Carbohydrate: 15.1
- Cholesterol: 0
- Protein: 1.5

703. Mexican Vegetable Rice

Serving: 6 | Prep: 5mins | Cook: 10mins | Ready in:

Ingredients

- 2 tablespoons canola oil
- 1 cup diced onion
- 2 teaspoons minced garlic
- 1 1/2 cups white rice
- 1 1/2 teaspoons salt
- 3/4 teaspoon cayenne pepper
- 3 cups vegetable stock
- 1 (10 ounce) package frozen mixed peas and carrots, thawed
- 1 1/2 cups tomatoes, deseeded and diced
- 2 tablespoons chopped fresh parsley
- 2 green onions, chopped

Direction

- Sauté together rice, garlic and onion with canola oil in a big sauté pan, until rice is opaque and onion is softened. Put into the pan with vegetable stock, cayenne pepper and salt, then bring to a boil. Cover the pan and lower the heat to low, then simmer until the liquid is absorbed entirely, or for 20 minutes.
- Put in tomatoes and vegetables, then cover pan and let it sit for 5 minutes. Turn off the heat, then sprinkle on top of the rice with green onions and parsley.

Nutrition Information

- Calories: 264 calories;
- Sodium: 763
- Total Carbohydrate: 48
- Cholesterol: 0
- Protein: 6

- Total Fat: 5.7

704. Michelle's Soft Sugar Cookies

Serving: 60 | Prep: | Cook: | Ready in:

Ingredients

- 1 cup margarine
- 1 1/2 cups white sugar
- 3 eggs
- 1 teaspoon vanilla extract
- 3 1/2 cups all-purpose flour
- 2 teaspoons cream of tartar
- 1 teaspoon baking soda
- 1/2 teaspoon salt

Direction

- Cream margarine and gradually put in sugar. Beat until fluffy and light. Put in the eggs one at a time, stirring well after each of addition.
- Mix in vanilla. Gradually put in salt, baking soda, cream of tartar and flour to creamed mixture, stirring in with your hand. Chill the dough with a cover overnight.
- Start preheating the oven to 375°F (190°C). Line parchment on the paper baking sheets.
- Roll the dough out on the floured surface to 1/8 to a quarter inch thick and slice into favorite shapes. Arrange the cookies on prepared baking sheets.
- Bake for 6-8 mins at 375°F (190°C) or until the cookie is golden appearance.

Nutrition Information

- Calories: 77 calories;
- Total Fat: 3.3
- Sodium: 79
- Total Carbohydrate: 10.7
- Cholesterol: 9
- Protein: 1.1

705. Microwave Caramel Popcorn

Serving: 16 | Prep: 5mins | Cook: 10mins | Ready in:

Ingredients

- 4 quarts popped popcorn
- 1 cup brown sugar
- 1/2 cup margarine
- 1/4 cup light corn syrup
- 1/2 teaspoon salt
- 1 teaspoon vanilla extract
- 1/2 teaspoon baking soda

Direction

- Prepare a large bag of brown paper and put in popped popcorn. Put aside.
- Mix vanilla, salt, corn syrup, margarine and brown sugar in a casserole dish of 2 quarts or other heat-resistant glass plate. Put in the microwave to heat about 3 minutes. Remove and stir till the mixture is blended entirely. Bring back to the microwave and cook for another 1.5 minutes. Take out of microwave, add the baking soda and stir well.
- Put popcorn in a bag and pour syrup over popcorn. Roll the top down 1-2 times to make the bag close, then shake it to cover the corn well. Put bag in the microwave and cook it about 1 minute and 10 seconds. Take out, shake, overturn the bag, bring it back to the microwave. Cook about 1 minute and 10 seconds more. Spread the popcorn on waxed paper and allow to cool until the covering is firm. Keep in sealed container.

Nutrition Information

- Calories: 173 calories;
- Total Fat: 8.7
- Sodium: 282
- Total Carbohydrate: 23.8
- Cholesterol: 0
- Protein: 1.1

706. Microwave Vegetables

Serving: 6 | Prep: 5mins | Cook: 5mins | Ready in:

Ingredients

- 1 red bell pepper, chopped
- 1 tablespoon extra-virgin olive oil
- 7 ounces frozen peas
- 1 (12 fluid ounce) can canned sweet corn, drained
- 1 teaspoon chopped fresh cilantro (optional)
- salt and pepper to taste

Direction

- In a microwave-safe bowl, mix together the olive oil and red bell pepper. Microwave for about a minute at full power until it becomes soft. Add peas and let it cook for another 2 minutes at full power. Add corn and let it cook for an additional 1 minute. Mix the vegetables and microwave for another 30 seconds. Add cilantro and sprinkle pepper and salt to season. Mix and serve right away.

Nutrition Information

- Calories: 88 calories;
- Cholesterol: 0
- Protein: 2.8
- Total Fat: 2.7
- Sodium: 229
- Total Carbohydrate: 14

707. Middle Eastern White Beans

Serving: 6 | Prep: | Cook: 6hours | Ready in:

Ingredients

- 1 1/2 cups dried white kidney beans, soaked overnight
- 3 tablespoons tomato paste
- 1 tablespoon red pimento sauce
- 3 cloves garlic, chopped
- 3 medium onions, chopped
- 1 tablespoon lemon juice
- 1 teaspoon ground cumin
- 2 tablespoons olive oil
- salt and pepper to taste
- 1 (14.5 ounce) can beef broth

Direction

- Mix pepper, salt, olive oil, lemon juice, cumin, onions, garlic, pimento sauce, tomato paste and beans in a slow cooker until the beans are coated. Add beef broth, followed by adequate water so that the beans are entirely submerged. Put a lid on and set it to high. Cook until the liquid thickens and the beans become tender, about 6 hours. There should be not much soup at all.

Nutrition Information

- Calories: 229 calories;
- Total Fat: 5.3
- Sodium: 351
- Total Carbohydrate: 36.5
- Cholesterol: 0
- Protein: 10.6

708. Mint Chip Coconut Milk Ice Cream

Serving: 8 | Prep: 10mins | Cook: | Ready in:

Ingredients

- 24 fluid ounces canned coconut milk
- 1/3 cup agave syrup, or to taste
- 1 teaspoon peppermint extract, or to taste
- 3 ounces dark chocolate, chopped into small pieces

Direction

- Chill all the ingredients before preparing to speed up the freezing process.
- In a blender, blend the coconut milk until it becomes evenly combined and smooth. Add peppermint extract and agave syrup and blend until it has a smooth consistency. Pour the coconut milk mixture to an ice cream maker and follow the manufacturer's directions for ice cream, then add chocolate pieces when it is indicated. Let it freeze for 2 hours prior to serving.

Nutrition Information

- Calories: 269 calories;
- Protein: 2.3
- Total Fat: 22
- Sodium: 12
- Total Carbohydrate: 19.4
- Cholesterol: < 1

709. Mmm Mmm Better Brownies

Serving: 16 | Prep: 15mins | Cook: 25mins | Ready in:

Ingredients

- 1/2 cup vegetable oil
- 1 cup white sugar
- 1 teaspoon vanilla extract
- 2 eggs
- 1/2 cup all-purpose flour
- 1/3 cup unsweetened cocoa powder

- 1/4 teaspoon baking powder
- 1/4 teaspoon salt
- 1/2 cup chopped walnuts (optional)

Direction

- Preheat an oven to 175°C/350°F; grease the 9x9-in. baking pan.
- Mix vanilla, sugar and oil in a medium bowl; beat in eggs. Mix salt, baking powder, cocoa and flour; mix into egg mixture slowly till blended well. If desired, mix in walnuts; evenly spread batter in prepped pan.
- Bake till brownie starts to pull away from pan's edges for 20-25 minutes; cool on wire rack. Cut to squares.

Nutrition Information

- Calories: 161 calories;
- Cholesterol: 23
- Protein: 2.1
- Total Fat: 10.2
- Sodium: 53
- Total Carbohydrate: 17.1

710. Mock Angel Food Cake

Serving: 10 | Prep: | Cook: | Ready in:

Ingredients

- 4 1/2 cups cake flour
- 4 cups white sugar
- 2 teaspoons salt
- 2 cups boiling water
- 16 egg whites
- 2 tablespoons baking powder
- 2 teaspoons cream of tartar
- 2 teaspoons vanilla extract
- 1 teaspoon almond extract

Direction

- Set oven to preheat at 350°F (175°C).
- Sift sugar, cake flour, and salt thrice. Mix into boiling water. Let it cool.
- Whip egg whites, baking powder, cream of tartar, almond and vanilla flavorings until you see stiff peaks form. Fold this into the flour mix. Put the batter into a 12x18 inch baking pan, that hasn't been greased.
- Bake in the oven for 35 minutes at 350°F (175°C). Let it cool, inverted, in a pan. Have a tea towel underneath to absorb the steam. Add frosting as you wish when it's cooled down.

Nutrition Information

- Calories: 575 calories;
- Protein: 11.1
- Total Fat: 0.6
- Sodium: 849
- Total Carbohydrate: 131.9
- Cholesterol: 0

711. Moist Vegan Sugar Cookies

Serving: 12 | Prep: 15mins | Cook: 7mins | Ready in:

Ingredients

- cooking spray
- 1 1/2 cups all-purpose flour
- 1 teaspoon baking powder
- 1 teaspoon ground cinnamon (optional)
- 1/2 teaspoon baking soda
- 1/2 cup vegetable oil
- 1/2 cup white sugar
- 1/4 (6 ounce) container soy yogurt

Direction

- Turn the oven to 350°F (175°C) to preheat. Spray cooking spray over a baking sheet to lightly coat.
- Sift baking soda, cinnamon, baking powder, and flour into a bowl.

- In a bowl, combine soy yogurt, sugar, and vegetable oil. Mix in the flour mixture until the dough forms.
- On the prepared baking sheet, drop the dough by tablespoons, about 2 inches apart.
- Put in the preheated oven and bake for 7 minutes until turning golden.

Nutrition Information

- Calories: 173 calories;
- Cholesterol: 0
- Protein: 1.8
- Total Fat: 9.4
- Sodium: 94
- Total Carbohydrate: 20.7

712. Molasses Cookies

Serving: 30 | Prep: 10mins | Cook: 10mins | Ready in:

Ingredients

- 3/4 cup margarine, melted
- 1 cup white sugar
- 1 egg
- 1/4 cup molasses
- 2 cups all-purpose flour
- 2 teaspoons baking soda
- 1/2 teaspoon salt
- 1 teaspoon ground cinnamon
- 1/2 teaspoon ground cloves
- 1/2 teaspoon ground ginger
- 1/2 cup white sugar

Direction

- Mix egg, 1 cup sugar and melted margarine till smooth in a medium bowl; mix in molasses. Mix ginger, cloves, cinnamon, salt, baking soda and flour; blend into molasses mixture. Cover; chill for 1 hour.
- Preheat an oven to 190°C or 375°F; roll dough to walnut-size balls. Roll in leftover white sugar; put cookies on ungreased baking sheets, 2-in. apart.
- In preheated oven, bake till tops are cracked for 8-10 minutes; cool on wire racks.

Nutrition Information

- Calories: 120 calories;
- Protein: 1.1
- Total Fat: 4.7
- Sodium: 179
- Total Carbohydrate: 18.6
- Cholesterol: 6

713. Molasses Sugar Cookies

Serving: 72 | Prep: 25mins | Cook: 15mins | Ready in:

Ingredients

- 1 1/2 cups shortening
- 2 cups white sugar
- 1/2 cup molasses
- 2 eggs
- 4 cups all-purpose flour
- 4 teaspoons baking soda
- 2 teaspoons ground cinnamon
- 1 teaspoon ground cloves
- 1 teaspoon ground ginger
- 1 teaspoon salt

Direction

- In a big pan, liquify the shortening on stove, and allow to cool.
- Put the molasses, eggs and sugar, whisk thoroughly.
- Sift the dry ingredients together in another bowl and put to pan. Combine thoroughly and refrigerate for 3 hours or overnight.
- Shape into walnut-size rounds. Roll in granulated sugar. On oiled cookie sheet, put approximately 2-inch away.

- Allow to bake for 8 to 10 minutes at 190°C or 375°F.
- Keep in an airtight container to prevent from becoming too crisp. In case they lose the softness. Put a fresh bread slice in the container with cookies for a couple of hours up or overnight to make them soft once more.

Nutrition Information

- Calories: 93 calories;
- Total Fat: 4.5
- Sodium: 105
- Total Carbohydrate: 12.7
- Cholesterol: 5
- Protein: 0.9

714. Molasses Beef Curry

Serving: 4 | Prep: 20mins | Cook: 1hours45mins | Ready in:

Ingredients

- 1/2 cup all-purpose flour
- 1/4 teaspoon salt
- 1 dash ground black pepper
- 1 pound cubed beef stew meat
- 1 tablespoon olive oil
- 1 onion, diced
- 3 cups beef stock
- 2 bay leaves
- 2 tablespoons curry powder
- 2 carrots, diced
- 1/4 cup rice vinegar
- 1 tablespoon molasses
- 3 potatoes, cut into 1/4 inch cubes

Direction

- In a bowl, mix pepper, salt, and flour; add beef and toss to coat. Then, shake to get rid of the excess flour. In a large skillet, heat the olive oil over medium-high heat. Next, cook and stir beef and onions until browned. Add curry powder, bay leaves, and beef stock; stir. Boil, then lower the heat and simmer for a half-hour. Stir in potatoes, molasses, rice vinegar, and carrots; simmer for 1 hour longer until softened.

Nutrition Information

- Calories: 632 calories;
- Total Fat: 27.4
- Sodium: 319
- Total Carbohydrate: 56.4
- Cholesterol: 99
- Protein: 39.1

715. Molly's Chicken

Serving: 6 | Prep: 10mins | Cook: 8hours | Ready in:

Ingredients

- 3 1/2 pounds chicken drumsticks, skin removed
- 1/2 cup soy sauce
- 1/4 cup packed brown sugar
- 2 cloves garlic, minced
- 1 (8 ounce) can tomato sauce

Direction

- In a slow cooker, arrange drumsticks. Stir tomato sauce, garlic, brown sugar and soy sauce together in a medium bowl. Spread the sauce over the chicken.
- Cook while covered on Low heat for 8 hours.

Nutrition Information

- Calories: 356 calories;
- Protein: 50.7
- Total Fat: 10.2
- Sodium: 1543
- Total Carbohydrate: 13

- Cholesterol: 156

716. Mom's Baked Beans I

Serving: 11 | Prep: 15mins | Cook: 2hours30mins | Ready in:

Ingredients

- 2 (28 ounce) cans baked beans
- 2 onions, cut into wedges
- 1/4 cup molasses
- 1/2 cup barbeque sauce
- 1 tablespoon liquid smoke flavoring

Direction

- Preheat the oven to 165 degrees C (325 degrees F).
- Mix together beans, liquid smoke flavoring, onions, barbecue sauce and molasses in a 3-quart casserole dish.
- Bake for about 2 to 2 1/2 hours in the preheated oven while stirring each 20 minutes.

Nutrition Information

- Calories: 192 calories;
- Sodium: 619
- Total Carbohydrate: 41.9
- Cholesterol: 0
- Protein: 7
- Total Fat: 1.8

717. Mom's Baked Beans II

Serving: 9 | Prep: 15mins | Cook: 2hours20mins | Ready in:

Ingredients

- 4 slices bacon
- 1 onion, diced
- 2 (28 ounce) cans baked beans
- 3 tablespoons molasses
- 2 tablespoons prepared mustard
- 1/4 teaspoon salt
- 1/2 cup diced tomatoes
- 3/4 cup brown sugar
- 1 tablespoon dry mustard
- 1/2 cup chopped cooked ham

Direction

- Preheat the oven to 175 degrees C (350 degrees F).
- In a large and deep skillet, place onions and bacon. Then cook over medium high heat until browned evenly. Drain them and save for later use.
- Mix together beans, tomatoes, molasses, crumbled bacon, onions, mustard, dry mustard, salt, brown sugar, and ham in a large bowl. Combine thoroughly and then pour into a 2-quart casserole dish.
- Bake for an hour while covered in the preheated oven. Remove the cover and then bake for one more hour.

Nutrition Information

- Calories: 319 calories;
- Total Carbohydrate: 55.6
- Cholesterol: 13
- Protein: 11.8
- Total Fat: 8.2
- Sodium: 932

718. Mom's Ginger Snaps

Serving: 36 | Prep: 15mins | Cook: 12mins | Ready in:

Ingredients

- 1 cup packed brown sugar
- 3/4 cup vegetable oil

- 1/4 cup molasses
- 1 egg
- 2 cups all-purpose flour
- 2 teaspoons baking soda
- 1/4 teaspoon salt
- 1/2 teaspoon ground cloves
- 1 teaspoon ground cinnamon
- 1 teaspoon ground ginger
- 1/3 cup white sugar for decoration

Direction

- Set oven to 3750F (1900 C) and preheat.
- Combine egg, molasses, oil, and the brown in a large bowl. Mix together ginger, cinnamon, cloves, the flour, salt and baking soda; blend into the molasses mixture. Shape dough into 1 1/4 inch balls. Coat each ball in white sugar before putting 2 inches apart on the ungreased cookie sheets.
- Put in the prepared oven and bake until center is firm, or for 10 to 12 minutes. Let the balls cool on wire racks.

Nutrition Information

- Calories: 105 calories;
- Sodium: 91
- Total Carbohydrate: 15
- Cholesterol: 5
- Protein: 0.9
- Total Fat: 4.8

719. Momma's Potatoes

Serving: 4 | Prep: 15mins | Cook: 30mins | Ready in:

Ingredients

- 8 Yukon Gold potatoes, quartered
- 1 tablespoon dried rosemary
- 1/4 cup olive oil
- salt and pepper to taste

Direction

- Set an oven to 175°C (350°F) to preheat.
- Mix together the pepper, salt, oil, rosemary and potatoes in a big bowl, then toss well until coated.
- Evenly spread onto cookie sheet and bake for 30 minutes in the preheated oven.

Nutrition Information

- Calories: 450 calories;
- Sodium: 26
- Total Carbohydrate: 74.9
- Cholesterol: 0
- Protein: 8.6
- Total Fat: 14

720. Moroccan Chicken

Serving: 4 | Prep: 10mins | Cook: 30mins | Ready in:

Ingredients

- 1 pound skinless, boneless chicken breast meat - cubed
- 2 teaspoons salt
- 1 onion, chopped
- 2 cloves garlic, chopped
- 2 carrots, sliced
- 2 stalks celery, sliced
- 1 tablespoon minced fresh ginger root
- 1/2 teaspoon paprika
- 3/4 teaspoon ground cumin
- 1/2 teaspoon dried oregano
- 1/4 teaspoon ground cayenne pepper
- 1/4 teaspoon ground turmeric
- 1 1/2 cups chicken broth
- 1 cup crushed tomatoes
- 1 cup canned chickpeas, drained
- 1 zucchini, sliced
- 1 tablespoon lemon juice

Direction

- In a big saucepan, season the chicken with brown and salt on medium heat, until it is nearly cooked through. Take out the chicken from the pan and put it aside.
- In the same pan, sauté celery, carrots, garlic and onion till tender. Then mix in turmeric, cayenne pepper, oregano, cumin, paprika and ginger. Stir fry it for about a minute, then stir in the tomatoes and broth. Put the chicken back into the pan, minimize the heat to low and let it simmer for about 10 minutes.
- Put zucchini and chickpeas into the pan and let it simmer again. Cook until the zucchini is soft and cooked through, or for about 15 minutes with cover on. Mix in lemon juice then serve.

Nutrition Information

- Calories: 286 calories;
- Cholesterol: 67
- Protein: 36
- Total Fat: 3.7
- Sodium: 2128
- Total Carbohydrate: 27.9

721. Moroccan Salmon Cakes With Garlic Mayonnaise

Serving: 4 | Prep: 20mins | Cook: 25mins | Ready in:

Ingredients

- GARLIC MAYONNAISE:
- 1/2 cup mayonnaise
- 1 clove garlic, crushed
- 1/8 teaspoon paprika
- SALMON CAKES:
- 1/2 cup couscous
- 2/3 cup orange juice
- 1 (14.75 ounce) can red salmon, drained
- 1 (10 ounce) package frozen chopped spinach - thawed, drained and squeezed dry
- 2 egg yolks, beaten
- 2 cloves garlic, crushed
- 1 teaspoon ground cumin
- 1/2 teaspoon ground black pepper
- 1/2 teaspoon salt
- 3 tablespoons olive oil

Direction

- Mix garlic, paprika, and mayonnaise in a glass bowl or small stainless steel bowl; put aside.
- Follow the package guide on how to prepare the couscous using the 2/3 cup of orange juice instead of the water.
- Mix the drained spinach, cumin, salt, black pepper, egg yolks, red salmon, garlic, and cooked couscous in a mixing bowl. Form the mixture into patties.
- Put olive oil in a large skillet and heat it over medium heat. Fry the patties for 8-10 minutes until golden brown, flipping only once. Serve the patty with garlic mayonnaise.

Nutrition Information

- Calories: 620 calories;
- Total Fat: 46.4
- Sodium: 950
- Total Carbohydrate: 26.4
- Cholesterol: 178
- Protein: 28.8

722. Moroccan Vegan Tagine

Serving: 6 | Prep: 25mins | Cook: 1hours13mins | Ready in:

Ingredients

- 1 1/2 cups water, or as needed
- 1 cup uncooked green lentils
- 3 tablespoons olive oil
- 1 onion, chopped
- 4 cloves garlic, finely chopped
- 1 tablespoon ground turmeric

- 1 tablespoon ground coriander
- 1 teaspoon cumin seeds, finely ground
- salt and freshly ground black pepper to taste
- 3 potatoes, peeled and cubed
- 1 (14 ounce) can crushed tomatoes
- 2 sweet potatoes, peeled and cubed
- 2 large carrots, peeled and sliced
- 4 cups vegetable broth

Direction

- In a saucepan, put the lentils and water then boil. Minimize the heat to medium-low and let it simmer for about 20 minutes with cover, until the liquid was absorbed, and the lentils are soft.
- In a frypan or tagine, heat the oil on medium-high heat. Sauté the onions for about 5 minutes until it becomes translucent and brown. Put pepper, salt, cumin, coriander, turmeric and garlic and let it cook and stir for about 3 minutes until it becomes aromatic. Mix in the carrots, sweet potatoes, crushed tomatoes, potatoes and cooked lentils then pour veggie broth. Turn down the heat and let it simmer for about 40 minutes until the veggies become soft.

Nutrition Information

- Calories: 360 calories;
- Sodium: 475
- Total Carbohydrate: 61.8
- Cholesterol: 0
- Protein: 12.5
- Total Fat: 8.6

723. Mumze's Sticky Chicken

Serving: 4 | Prep: 15mins | Cook: 1hours | Ready in:

Ingredients

- 2 pounds chicken drumettes
- 1/4 cup light corn syrup
- 1/2 cup soy sauce
- 1/2 cup white sugar
- 1/4 cup white wine
- 1 pinch garlic powder, or to taste

Direction

- Preheat oven to 400° F (200° C).
- In a baking dish, position chicken in a single layer.
- In a medium bowl, stir the wine, sugar, soy sauce, and corn syrup together. Spread over chicken and dust with garlic powder.
- In the preheated oven, bake until sauce is bubbly and hot.
- Lower temperature to 350° F (175° C), then bake while repeatedly basting, until sticky and thick.

Nutrition Information

- Calories: 689 calories;
- Sodium: 1983
- Total Carbohydrate: 43.8
- Cholesterol: 175
- Protein: 43.7
- Total Fat: 36.3

724. Mushroom Slow Cooker Roast Beef

Serving: 8 | Prep: 5mins | Cook: 9hours | Ready in:

Ingredients

- 1 pound sliced fresh mushrooms
- 1 (4 pound) standing beef rib roast
- 1 (1.25 ounce) envelope onion soup mix
- 1 (12 fluid ounce) bottle beer
- ground black pepper

Direction

- In the bottom of a slow cooker, put the mushrooms, then put the roast on top of the mushrooms. Sprinkle the onion soup mix on top of the beef and pour the beer all over, then sprinkle black pepper to season. Set the slow cooker to Low and let it cook for 9-10 hours, until the meat easily pulls apart using a fork.

Nutrition Information

- Calories: 388 calories;
- Total Carbohydrate: 6.2
- Cholesterol: 82
- Protein: 24.4
- Total Fat: 28.1
- Sodium: 453

725. My Amish Friend's Caramel Corn

Serving: 28 | Prep: 15mins | Cook: 1hours | Ready in:

Ingredients

- 7 quarts plain popped popcorn
- 2 cups dry roasted peanuts (optional)
- 2 cups brown sugar
- 1/2 cup light corn syrup
- 1 teaspoon salt
- 1 cup margarine
- 1/2 teaspoon baking soda
- 1 teaspoon vanilla extract

Direction

- Put popped popcorn into 2 shallow baking pans that are greased. Feel free to use disposable roasting pans, roasting pans, or jelly roll pans. Add peanuts to the popped corn if using and set aside.
- Preheat an oven to 120 degrees C (250 degrees F). In a saucepan, mix the salt, brown sugar, margarine and corn syrup. Heat to boil on medium heat and stir well to blend. After the mixture starts to boil, let to boil while stirring continuously for five minutes.
- Take out from heat and mix in vanilla and baking soda. Mixture should be foamy and light. Immediately spread on top of popcorn in pans and mix to coat. You should not worry about having all corn coated at this point.
- Bake for one hour, taking out the pans and stirring each well after every 15 minutes. Line waxed paper onto the counter top. Then dump out the corn on the waxed paper and divide the pieces. Leave to cool completely, and then keep bags that are sealable or in airtight containers.

Nutrition Information

- Calories: 238 calories;
- Sodium: 388
- Total Carbohydrate: 21.9
- Cholesterol: 0
- Protein: 3.4
- Total Fat: 16.3

726. My Own Famous Stuffed Grape Leaves

Serving: 12 | Prep: 40mins | Cook: 1hours | Ready in:

Ingredients

- 2 cups uncooked long-grain white rice
- 1 large onion, chopped
- 1/2 cup chopped fresh dill
- 1/2 cup chopped fresh mint leaves
- 2 quarts chicken broth
- 3/4 cup fresh lemon juice, divided
- 60 grape leaves, drained and rinsed
- hot water as needed
- 1 cup olive oil

Direction

- Sauté mint, dill, onion and rice in a big saucepan on medium high heat until onion is softened, for 5 minutes. Add in 1-qt. broth and lower heat to low, then simmer for another 10-15 minutes, until rice is nearly cooked. Stir in half of the lemon juice and take away from the heat.
- Take one leaf with shiny side down and put 1 tsp. rice mixture at the bottom (stem) end of the leaf. Fold both sides of the leaf towards the center and roll up from the broad bottom to the top, then put into a 4-qt. pot. Repeat the process with all leaves, leaving no gaps as leaves are put in pot (to avoid opening while cooking). Sprinkle over with olive oil and leftover lemon juice.
- Pour over all with chicken broth to cover grape leaves. Cover pot and simmer for an hour without boiling to avoid making the stuffing burst out of the leaves. Take away from the heat, then remove cover and allow to cool about a half hour. Turn to a serving dish and serve.

Nutrition Information

- Calories: 303 calories;
- Total Fat: 18.7
- Sodium: 573
- Total Carbohydrate: 30.9
- Cholesterol: 0
- Protein: 3.6

727. Night Before Oatmeal In A Jar

Serving: 1 | Prep: 10mins | Cook: | Ready in:

Ingredients

- 1/2 cup quick-cooking oats
- 2 tablespoons coconut sugar
- 1 tablespoon almond butter
- 3/4 cup hot water

Direction

- In a small jar with a tight-fitting lid, mix almond butter, coconut sugar, and oats; cover and refrigerate for 8 hours to overnight.
- Pour hot water into the oat mixture, cover with the lid, and let sit for 3-5 minutes. Stir well and serve.

Nutrition Information

- Calories: 358 calories;
- Sodium: 87
- Total Carbohydrate: 57.4
- Cholesterol: 0
- Protein: 7.8
- Total Fat: 12.1

728. No Bake Coconut Fruit Tarts

Serving: 6 | Prep: 15mins | Cook: | Ready in:

Ingredients

- 1/4 cup almonds
- 12 Medjool dates, pitted
- 1 (11 ounce) bottle So Delicious® Dairy Free Culinary Coconut Milk
- 1/2 cup fresh raspberries
- 1/2 cup sliced fresh strawberries

Direction

- In a food processor, chop almonds and put medjool dates. Process until smooth.
- Save about 1/8 cup of date mixture and put aside.
- Line two individual-sized tart pans with parchment or grease with oil to prepare. Split the date mixture into the two pans and press along the sides and bottom.
- In a mixing bowl, use a hand mixer to whip the culinary Coconut milk for a minute or so

then add about 5 berries and the reserved date mixture. Stir to incorporate.
- Scoop the coconut mixture into the tart crusts and freeze for at least 2 hours.
- Take the frozen tarts out of the pans. Top with sliced strawberries and raspberries to garnish.

Nutrition Information

- Calories: 183 calories;
- Total Fat: 12.4
- Sodium: 7
- Total Carbohydrate: 19.2
- Cholesterol: 0
- Protein: 2.5

729. No Bake Quinoa Bars

Serving: 12 | Prep: 10mins | Cook: 20mins | Ready in:

Ingredients

- 1 1/2 cups water
- 3/4 cup quinoa
- 1 cup pitted dates
- 1 cup old-fashioned oats
- 2/3 cup dried cranberries
- 1/2 cup maple syrup
- 1 tablespoon ground cinnamon

Direction

- In a saucepan, boil quinoa and water. Lower heat to moderately-low, place cover, and allow to simmer for 15 to 20 minutes till quinoa is soft. Remove cover, fluff using fork, and allow to cool fully for half an hour.
- In food processor, mix maple syrup, cranberries, oats and dates. Process into a sticky paste.
- In a bowl, combine cinnamon, date mixture and 2 cups cooled quinoa together.

- Line parchment paper on small baking pan. Force the mixture rigidly into pan. Slice into bars.

Nutrition Information

- Calories: 155 calories;
- Total Carbohydrate: 35.3
- Cholesterol: 0
- Total Fat: 1.2
- Protein: 2.7
- Sodium: 3

730. Nutty Granola II

Serving: 17 | Prep: 5mins | Cook: 25mins | Ready in:

Ingredients

- 1/2 cup canola oil
- 1/3 cup hot water
- 2/3 cup honey
- 6 cups rolled oats
- 3/4 cup sliced almonds
- 3/4 cup chopped pecans
- 3/4 cup chopped walnuts
- 1 cup raisins
- 1 1/2 cups golden raisins
- 1/2 cup dried cherries

Direction

- Preheat an oven to 165°C/325°F.
- Whisk honey, hot water and oil in medium bowl. Mix walnuts, pecans, almonds and oats in big bowl. Put honey mixture in oat mixture; mix till nuts and oats are coated evenly. Spread granola on 2 baking sheets.
- Bake for 10 minutes; mix. Bake till toasted for 10 more minutes. Completely cool granola; then mix dried cherries, golden raisins and raisins in. While it cools, granola hardens. Break apart any big lumps; keep at room temperature in an airtight container.

Nutrition Information

- Calories: 398 calories;
- Total Carbohydrate: 55.3
- Cholesterol: 0
- Protein: 7.4
- Total Fat: 18.6
- Sodium: 6

731. Oatmeal Peanut Butter Cookies

Serving: 48 | Prep: 15mins | Cook: 15mins | Ready in:

Ingredients

- 1/2 cup shortening
- 1/2 cup margarine, softened
- 1 cup packed brown sugar
- 3/4 cup white sugar
- 1 cup peanut butter
- 2 eggs
- 1 1/2 cups all-purpose flour
- 2 teaspoons baking soda
- 1 teaspoon salt
- 1 cup quick-cooking oats

Direction

- Preheat the oven to 350°F (175°C).
- Cream together the peanut butter, white sugar, brown sugar, margarine and shortening in a large bowl until mixture is smooth. Beat in one egg at a time until well combined.
- Mix together the salt, baking soda and flour; stir into the creamed mixture. Stir in oats until just mixed. Drop onto ungreased cookie sheets by teaspoonfuls.
- Bake in the preheated oven for 10 to 15 minutes or until cookies are just light browned. Remember not to over bake. Allow to cool and then keep in an airtight container to store.

Nutrition Information

- Calories: 120 calories;
- Cholesterol: 8
- Protein: 2.3
- Total Fat: 7.1
- Sodium: 152
- Total Carbohydrate: 12.8

732. Okra And Tomatoes

Serving: 6 | Prep: 10mins | Cook: 20mins | Ready in:

Ingredients

- 2 slices bacon
- 1 pound frozen okra, thawed and sliced
- 1 small onion, chopped
- 1/2 green bell pepper, chopped
- 2 celery, chopped
- 1 (14.5 ounce) can stewed tomatoes
- salt and pepper to taste

Direction

- In a big, deep skillet, put the bacon in. Over medium-high heat, cook until it turns brown evenly. Once done, drain and crumble the bacon. Set aside.
- Remove the bacon from the pan. In the same pan, sauté the celery, pepper, onion and the okra until tender. Put the pepper, salt and tomatoes. Cook until the tomatoes are heated through.
- If desired, garnish with the crumbled bacon.

Nutrition Information

- Calories: 94 calories;
- Cholesterol: 6
- Protein: 3.8
- Total Fat: 4.7
- Sodium: 250

- Total Carbohydrate: 11.5

733. Old Fashioned Fruit Soup

Serving: 6 | Prep: 15mins | Cook: 30mins | Ready in:

Ingredients

- 3/4 cup chopped dried apricots
- 3/4 cup chopped prunes
- 6 cups cold water
- 1 cinnamon stick
- 2 slices lemon
- 3 tablespoons instant tapioca
- 1 cup white sugar
- 2 tablespoons raisins
- 1 tablespoon dried currants
- 1 tart apple - peeled, cored and chopped

Direction

- Combine water, prunes and apricots together in a large pot; allow to rest for 30 minutes.
- Mix in sugar, tapioca, lemon slices and cinnamon stick; boil over medium-high heat. Turn the heat down; simmer with a cover for 10 minutes. Mix in apple, currants and raisins; simmer till the apples become tender, 5 minutes longer. Take away from the heat; allow to cool completely. Take the cinnamon stick away; place in the refrigerator till cold.

Nutrition Information

- Calories: 236 calories;
- Protein: 1
- Total Fat: 0.2
- Sodium: 3
- Total Carbohydrate: 61.3
- Cholesterol: 0

734. One Bowl Rice

Serving: 8 | Prep: 15mins | Cook: 45mins | Ready in:

Ingredients

- 2 cups uncooked long-grain rice
- 1 (4.5 ounce) can mushrooms, with liquid
- 2 stalks celery, finely chopped
- 1 red bell pepper, finely chopped
- 1 (1 ounce) package dry onion soup mix
- 1 (10.5 ounce) can beef broth
- 1/2 cup vegetable oil
- 1 cup water
- 3 tablespoons soy sauce

Direction

- Set the oven to 175°C or 350°F.
- Mix together soy sauce, water, oil, beef broth, onion soup mix, red bell pepper, celery, mushrooms and rice in a 9"x13" baking dish.
- In the preheated oven, bake with a cover until rice is cooked and liquid is absorbed, or for about 45 minutes.

Nutrition Information

- Calories: 325 calories;
- Total Carbohydrate: 43.8
- Cholesterol: 0
- Protein: 5.3
- Total Fat: 14.3
- Sodium: 845

735. One Skillet Corned Beef Hash

Serving: 6 | Prep: 15mins | Cook: 20mins | Ready in:

Ingredients

- 2 tablespoons vegetable oil
- 2 onions, chopped

- 4 potatoes, peeled and chopped
- 2 (12 ounce) cans corned beef
- 1 tablespoon ground black pepper
- 5 tablespoons cider vinegar

Direction

- Heat oil in big skillet on medium high heat then sauté potatoes and onions till slightly browned; mix corned beef in. Season using pepper; 1 tbsp. at a time, add vinegar. Cook in between each addition for 3-5 minutes. Cover skillet partially; lower heat to medium low. Cook, occasionally mixing till potatoes are tender for 20 minutes.

Nutrition Information

- Calories: 450 calories;
- Sodium: 1135
- Total Carbohydrate: 29.5
- Cholesterol: 96
- Protein: 33.1
- Total Fat: 21.6

736. Onions In Raisin Sauce

Serving: 8 | Prep: 5mins | Cook: 30mins | Ready in:

Ingredients

- 1 1/2 teaspoons olive oil
- 3/4 pound pearl onions, peeled
- 2 cloves garlic, minced
- 1/3 cup dry white wine
- 1 cup beef broth
- 2 tablespoons tomato paste
- 2 tablespoons raisins
- 1/2 teaspoon grated orange zest
- 1/4 teaspoon dried thyme, crushed
- 1/8 teaspoon ground black pepper
- 1 tablespoon minced fresh parsley

Direction

- In a medium saucepan, heat the oil on medium heat, then sauté the onions for about 7 minutes until it becomes golden.
- Stir in parsley, black pepper, thyme, orange zest, raisins, tomato paste, broth, wine and garlic. Let it simmer for 20 minutes without a cover, mixing frequently. Turn up the heat to high once the onion becomes tender and let it cook for about 3 minutes, stirring continuously, until the sauce becomes thick.

Nutrition Information

- Calories: 54 calories;
- Protein: 1.1
- Total Fat: 1
- Sodium: 139
- Total Carbohydrate: 8.9
- Cholesterol: 0

737. Orange, Mango, And Ginger Sorbet

Serving: 8 | Prep: 10mins | Cook: 10mins | Ready in:

Ingredients

- 1 1/2 cups water
- 1 1/2 cups white sugar
- 1 (2 inch) piece fresh ginger, peeled and thinly sliced
- 1 pinch sea salt
- 1 teaspoon lime zest
- 2 cups orange juice
- 1 cup mango juice
- 1/3 cup lemon juice

Direction

- In a saucepan, mix the lime zest, salt, ginger, sugar and water together and bring it to a boil. Adjust the heat to low and let it simmer for 5 minutes. Let the mixture cool down then strain it and stir in the lemon juice, mango juice and orange juice. Cover it up and leave it to chill for 3 hours. Transfer the mixture into an ice cream maker and follow the manufacturer's directions to freeze.

Nutrition Information

- Calories: 195 calories;
- Cholesterol: 0
- Protein: 0.6
- Total Fat: 0.2
- Sodium: 43
- Total Carbohydrate: 49.8

738. Oriental Style Halibut

Serving: 4 | Prep: 15mins | Cook: 6mins | Ready in:

Ingredients

- 3/4 pound halibut
- 2 strips celery, thinly sliced
- 1 carrot, thinly sliced
- 2/3 cup fresh orange juice
- 1/4 teaspoon ground ginger
- 1 (15 ounce) can pineapple tidbits, drained
- 1 tablespoon cornstarch
- 2 tablespoons reduced-sodium soy sauce
- 1 tablespoon vinegar
- 1 tablespoon honey

Direction

- Cut halibut to 1-in. cubes with a very sharp knife; put aside. Mix ginger, orange juice, carrots and celery in a medium saucepan; boil. Mix halibut in.
- Cook on medium heat, covered, till fish easily flakes with a fork for 4-6 minutes and is opaque completely through. Transfer halibut onto a plate carefully with a slotted spoon; put aside.
- Meanwhile, strain can of pineapple tidbits. Keep 2 tbsp. juice. Mix honey, vinegar, soy sauce, cornstarch and 2 tbsp. pineapple juice in a small bowl. Mix it into veggie mixture in the saucepan.
- Stir and cook till it starts to gently boil and mixture thickens. Stir and cook for 2 more minutes.
- Put halibut into pan. Add fruit. Cook, covered, till heated through for 1 minute.

Nutrition Information

- Calories: 211 calories;
- Cholesterol: 27
- Protein: 19
- Total Fat: 2.2
- Sodium: 326
- Total Carbohydrate: 29.4

739. Orzo With Mushrooms And Walnuts

Serving: 8 | Prep: 10mins | Cook: 25mins | Ready in:

Ingredients

- 1/3 cup chopped walnuts
- 3 tablespoons olive oil
- 2 onions, chopped
- 1 pound fresh mushrooms, sliced
- 4 cups chicken broth
- 2 cups uncooked orzo pasta
- salt and pepper to taste

Direction

- Preheat the oven to 175°C or 350°F. Spread the walnuts on a baking sheet, then bake for 8-10mins in the preheated oven, until it becomes fragrant. Mix them 1-2 times to toast evenly.
- On medium-high heat, heat the oil in a big heavy pot; add mushrooms and onion. Sauté until golden brown and tender.
- Add broth then boil; mix in orzo. Turn to low heat, then cover. Let it simmer for about

15mins, until the liquid is absorbed, and the orzo is tender. If there's still liquid after 15mins, uncover and cook until it evaporates. Take off from heat, then mix in walnuts. Sprinkle pepper and salt to taste.

Nutrition Information

- Calories: 290 calories;
- Cholesterol: 3
- Protein: 9.5
- Total Fat: 9.5
- Sodium: 485
- Total Carbohydrate: 43.2

740. Oven Baked Vegetables

Serving: 6 | Prep: 10mins | Cook: 25mins | Ready in:

Ingredients

- 1 vegetable cooking spray
- 2 potatoes, cubed
- 1 carrot, sliced
- 2 onions, sliced
- 1 green bell pepper, chopped
- 1/3 cup fat free Italian-style dressing
- 1/8 teaspoon garlic salt
- 1/4 teaspoon cayenne pepper
- 1/8 teaspoon onion salt

Direction

- Set an oven to preheat to 175°C (350°F). Use cooking spray to spray a 9x13-inch baking pan.
- Mix together the bell pepper, onions, carrots and potatoes in the prepped pan.
- Mix together the onion salt, cayenne pepper, garlic salt and Italian dressing in a small bowl, then pour it on top of the vegetables.
- Let it bake for 15 minutes with a cover. Take off the cover, then mix and bake for another 10 minutes.

Nutrition Information

- Calories: 98 calories;
- Total Carbohydrate: 22.5
- Cholesterol: 0
- Protein: 2.1
- Total Fat: 0.2
- Sodium: 224

741. Oven Fried Potatoes II

Serving: 2 | Prep: 10mins | Cook: 30mins | Ready in:

Ingredients

- 1 tablespoon vegetable oil
- 1 tablespoon lemon juice
- 2 large baking potatoes, cut into wedges
- salt and pepper to taste

Direction

- Preheat oven to 425°F (220°C). Use an aluminum foil to line a baking sheet and spray with vegetable cooking spray.
- Combine lemon juice and oil in a shallow bowl. Dip potatoes in the oil-lemon mixture and season with pepper and salt. Transfer potatoes to the baking sheet.
- Bake for 20 minutes. Remove baking sheet from oven and flip the wedges over. Put back into the oven and bake until brown and crispy on both sides, about 10 minutes more.

Nutrition Information

- Calories: 172 calories;
- Total Fat: 6.9
- Sodium: 12
- Total Carbohydrate: 26.1
- Cholesterol: 0
- Protein: 2.4

742. Oven Fried Sesame Potatoes

Serving: 4 | Prep: 10mins | Cook: 55mins | Ready in:

Ingredients

- 4 medium potatoes, cut into wedges
- 2 teaspoons canola oil
- 1 teaspoon seasoning salt
- 1 teaspoon ground paprika
- 1 tablespoon sesame seeds
- 1 teaspoon chili powder, or to taste
- freshly ground black pepper to taste

Direction

- Preheat an oven to 400°F or 200°C. Line an aluminum foil on a big baking sheet.
- In a bowl with a lid or plastic bag, put the potato wedges. Put in oil, coat by tossing. Spice the potatoes with pepper, chili powder, paprika and seasoning salt and add the sesame seeds. Close bag or put lid on and shake to coat equally. On the prepped baking sheet, scatter the potato wedges in 1 layer.
- Bake till potatoes are golden and tender, about 50- 60 minutes, mixing every 15 minutes or so.

Nutrition Information

- Calories: 203 calories;
- Total Fat: 3.9
- Sodium: 249
- Total Carbohydrate: 38.8
- Cholesterol: 0
- Protein: 4.9

743. Oven Roasted Potatoes

Serving: 4 | Prep: 15mins | Cook: 30mins | Ready in:

Ingredients

- 1/8 cup olive oil
- 1 tablespoon minced garlic
- 1/2 teaspoon dried basil
- 1/2 teaspoon dried marjoram
- 1/2 teaspoon dried dill weed
- 1/2 teaspoon dried thyme
- 1/2 teaspoon dried oregano
- 1/2 teaspoon dried parsley
- 1/2 teaspoon crushed red pepper flakes
- 1/2 teaspoon salt
- 4 large potatoes, peeled and cubed

Direction

- Set oven to 475 degrees F or 245 degrees C.
- In a big bowl, combine salt, red pepper flakes, parsley, oregano, thyme, dill weed, marjoram, basil, garlic, and oil. Stir in the potatoes until coated evenly, then place them in one layer onto a baking sheet or roasting pan.
- Roast in the preheated oven for 20-30 minutes, occasionally turning, until all sides are brown.

Nutrition Information

- Calories: 289 calories;
- Total Carbohydrate: 53.1
- Cholesterol: 0
- Protein: 5
- Total Fat: 7.1
- Sodium: 304

744. Paleo Spaghetti Pie (Grain, Gluten, And Dairy Free)

Serving: 6 | Prep: 15mins | Cook: 1hours30mins | Ready in:

Ingredients

- 1 large spaghetti squash, halved lengthwise and seeded

- 1 pound ground turkey sausage
- 1/2 cup diced onion
- 1 cup pizza sauce
- 1 cup coarsely chopped baby spinach leaves
- 1/2 cup diced red bell pepper
- 1/4 cup unsweetened applesauce
- 1 teaspoon dried basil
- 1/2 teaspoon garlic powder
- 1/2 teaspoon dried oregano
- 1/4 teaspoon ground black pepper
- 3 eggs, beaten

Direction

- Preheat an oven to 200 °C or 400 °F. On a baking sheet, set spaghetti squash cut-side facing down.
- In the prepped oven, allow the squash to bake for 25 minutes till cooked completely. Once cool enough to touch, using a spoon, scrape out squash strands and put in a square 8-inch baking dish.
- Lower oven temperature to 175 °C or 350 °F.
- In a big skillet over medium-high heat, let cook and mix onion and turkey sausage for 4 to 6 minutes till turkey is browned. Take off from heat and into the turkey mixture, mix black pepper, oregano, garlic powder, basil, applesauce, red bell pepper, spinach and pizza sauce. In baking dish, scatter mixture on top of squash.
- Put eggs on top of turkey mixture and combine squash, turkey mixture and egg together till egg is just incorporated.
- In the prepped oven, let bake for an hour till eggs are firm and mixture is bubbling.

Nutrition Information

- Calories: 295 calories;
- Total Fat: 13
- Sodium: 775
- Total Carbohydrate: 29.8
- Cholesterol: 152
- Protein: 19.2

745. Paleo Tropical Ice Cream

Serving: 6 | Prep: 15mins | Cook: |Ready in:

Ingredients

- 4 cups frozen banana slices
- 1 cup frozen pineapple chunks
- 1 (14 ounce) can coconut milk
- 1 lime, juiced
- 1 pinch kosher salt

Direction

- Let pineapple chunks and banana slices thaw for 5 minutes at room temperature.
- Process coconut milk, pineapple and bananas in a food processor for about 60 seconds until smooth; put in kosher salt, lime juice and pulse more until mixed.
- Prepare a plastic-wrap-lined 8x11" baking dish. Bring banana mixture into the baking dish. Leave in the freezer for 30-45 minutes until the 'ice cream' is soft enough to serve.

Nutrition Information

- Calories: 246 calories;
- Sodium: 77
- Total Carbohydrate: 32.4
- Cholesterol: 0
- Protein: 2.7
- Total Fat: 14.3

746. Party Pancit

Serving: 8 | Prep: 15mins | Cook: 15mins |Ready in:

Ingredients

- 1/2 tablespoon sesame oil
- 2 cloves garlic, minced
- 2 teaspoons minced fresh ginger root

- 1 bunch green onions, chopped into 1 inch pieces
- 2 hot chile peppers, minced
- 1 (8 ounce) package fresh mushrooms, sliced
- 1 cup chopped cooked chicken breast
- 1 cup peeled, chopped shrimp
- 3 links spicy pork sausage, sliced
- 1/2 cup sake
- 1/4 cup soy sauce
- 7 cups chicken broth
- 1 (12 ounce) package rice noodles
- 1/2 pound fresh bean sprouts
- 1/2 pound snow peas

Direction

- Sauté sausage, shrimp, chicken, mushrooms, chile peppers, green onion, ginger, and garlic in the hot oil in a large Dutch oven or wok until the sausage is lightly browned and shrimp turns pink. Mix in the soy sauce and sake and simmer for 2-3 minutes. Cover and reserve.
- Add chicken broth in a large saucepan then make it to a rolling boil. Put in the noodles then cook for 2 minutes over high heat. Drain instantly and rinse with cold water.
- Put the shrimp mixture over medium heat and put the bean sprouts; stir-fry for 2 minutes. Mix in the snow pear and stir-fry for 2 minutes. Mix in noodles and toss until well combined. Serve right away.

Nutrition Information

- Calories: 261 calories;
- Sodium: 568
- Total Carbohydrate: 35.9
- Cholesterol: 41
- Protein: 13.6
- Total Fat: 5.2

747. Passover Chocolate Chip Cookies

Serving: 60 | Prep: 15mins | Cook: 10mins | Ready in:

Ingredients

- 3/4 cup chopped walnuts (optional)
- 1 cup matzo cake meal
- 1/4 teaspoon salt
- 1/2 cup potato starch
- 3 eggs
- 1/2 cup margarine, softened
- 1 1/4 cups white sugar
- 1 (12 ounce) bag chocolate chips

Direction

- Set oven to preheat at 275°F (135°C).
- On a baking sheet, spread the walnuts out, and toast until the nuts become fragrant and begin to turn golden brown, for about 45 minutes. Keep an eye on the nuts as they bake because they burn quickly. After being toasted, let the walnuts cool aside to room temperature.
- Turn up the oven temperature to 175°C (350°F). Use parchment paper to line baking sheets. Whisk together the potato starch, salt, and matzo cake meal in a bowl.
- In a large bowl, beat together the sugar, margarine, and eggs until smooth and well combined. Mix the meal mixture into the wet ingredients till thoroughly mixed and mix the chocolate chips into the mixture. On the baking sheets lined with parchment, drop spoonfuls of the dough.
- In the preheated oven, bake until lightly golden brown, for 10 to 15 minutes. Take the cookies out of the baking sheets straight out of the oven; allow to cool on baking racks.

Nutrition Information

- Calories: 79 calories;
- Total Fat: 4.4
- Sodium: 31

- Total Carbohydrate: 10
- Cholesterol: 9
- Protein: 1

748. Pasta With Tuna Sauce

Serving: 6 | Prep: 15mins | Cook: 25mins | Ready in:

Ingredients

- 1 tablespoon olive oil
- 1 onion, chopped
- 2 cloves crushed garlic
- 1 tablespoon capers
- 1 (14.5 ounce) can crushed tomatoes
- 1 tablespoon lemon juice
- 1 tablespoon chopped fresh parsley
- 1/4 teaspoon red pepper flakes
- 2 (5 ounce) cans tuna, drained
- 1 (16 ounce) package dry pasta

Direction

- Heat oil in a large sauté pan over low heat. Sauté garlic and onion until onion is tender. Mix in parsley, lemon juice, tomatoes and capers. Sprinkle mixture with red pepper flakes to season to taste. Let simmer gently until sauce is thickened, for 3 minutes. Mix in tuna; cook until thoroughly heated.
- Meanwhile, cook pasta in a large pot of rapidly boiling water until al dente. Drain pasta well.
- Toss pasta with sauce and serve.

Nutrition Information

- Calories: 384 calories;
- Total Fat: 6.2
- Sodium: 174
- Total Carbohydrate: 59.6
- Cholesterol: 102
- Protein: 23

749. Pat's Baked Beans

Serving: 10 | Prep: 15mins | Cook: 1hours15mins | Ready in:

Ingredients

- 6 slices bacon
- 1 cup chopped onion
- 1 clove garlic, minced
- 1 (16 ounce) can pinto beans
- 1 (16 ounce) can great Northern beans, drained
- 1 (16 ounce) can baked beans
- 1 (16 ounce) can red kidney beans, drained
- 1 (15 ounce) can garbanzo beans, drained
- 3/4 cup ketchup
- 1/2 cup molasses
- 1/4 cup packed brown sugar
- 2 tablespoons Worcestershire sauce
- 1 tablespoon yellow mustard
- 1/2 teaspoon pepper

Direction

- Set the oven to 190°C or 375°F to preheat.
- In a big, deep skillet, add bacon, then cook on moderately high heat until browned evenly. Drain and save 2 tbsp. of bacon drippings, then crumble it and set aside in a big bowl. Cook in the reserved drippings the garlic and onion until onion is tender, then drain excess grease and turn to the bowl with bacon.
- Put garbanzo beans, kidney beans, baked beans, northern beans and pinto beans into the bowl with bacon and onions. Stir in black pepper, mustard, Worcestershire sauce, brown sugar, molasses and ketchup, then blend well together and turn to a 9"x12" casserole dish.
- Cover and bake in the preheated oven about an hour.

Nutrition Information

- Calories: 399 calories;
- Sodium: 950

- Total Carbohydrate: 68
- Cholesterol: 12
- Protein: 14.1
- Total Fat: 9.1

750. Pea Shoots And Chicken In Garlic Sauce

Serving: 4 | Prep: 10mins | Cook: 15mins | Ready in:

Ingredients

- 2 skinless, boneless chicken breast halves - cut into thin strips
- 1 tablespoon cornstarch
- 1 1/2 teaspoons sesame oil
- 2 tablespoons vegetable oil
- 4 cloves garlic, minced
- 1 bunch pea shoots, trimmed
- 3/4 cup chicken broth
- salt and black pepper to taste

Direction

- In a mixing bowl, toss the chicken breast strips with the cornstarch. Drizzle with sesame oil then toss again until it's mixed evenly.
- In a wok or big cooking pan, heat the vegetable oil on high heat. Cook the chicken in the oil for 5 minutes while stirring until it's lightly browned. Mix in the garlic and continue to cook until fragrant. Add the pea shoots while stirring and cook just until they're wilted. Add the chicken broth in and simmer. Cook for a few minutes more while stirring until the broth has thickened. Add salt and pepper to season to taste.

Nutrition Information

- Calories: 171 calories;
- Sodium: 212
- Total Carbohydrate: 6.4
- Cholesterol: 33

- Protein: 13.9
- Total Fat: 10.2

751. Peach And Strawberry Sorbet

Serving: 4 | Prep: 15mins | Cook: | Ready in:

Ingredients

- 2 cups sliced fresh peaches
- 1 cup fresh strawberries, hulled
- 1 cup fresh orange juice
- 1/4 cup brown sugar

Direction

- In a food processor, combine the strawberries, peaches, brown sugar, and orange juice. Process unto a smooth puree.
- Transfer mixture into ice cream maker and, following manufacturer's direction, freeze until it sets.

Nutrition Information

- Calories: 90 calories;
- Total Fat: 0.2
- Sodium: 6
- Total Carbohydrate: 22
- Cholesterol: 0
- Protein: 0.7

752. Peanut Butter Bliss Cookies Vegan, Gluten Free, No Sugar Added

Serving: 24 | Prep: 20mins | Cook: 8mins | Ready in:

Ingredients

- 1 1/4 cups finely chopped pitted dates

- 1 cup natural peanut butter
- 1/4 cup almond milk
- 2 teaspoons vanilla extract
- 1/2 cup oat flour, or more as needed
- 1 teaspoon baking soda
- 1/2 teaspoon salt (optional)
- 2 tablespoons raisins, or to taste

Direction

- Preheat an oven to 190°C/375°F; line parchment paper on 2 baking sheets.
- Process peanut butter and dates in 15-sec intervals on high in food processor; add almond milk slowly while processing till mixture is smooth then add vanilla extract. Stir well.
- Mix salt, baking soda and oat flour in bowl; stir date mixture into flour mixture, if needed add more oat flour till dough holds together. Shape dough, 1-2 tbsp. each, to balls; put on prepped baking sheets. Press fork in every dough ball; dip fork into water after every press; press few raisins gently into each one.
- In preheated oven, bake for 8-12 minutes till edges just begin to be golden; fully cool before eating.

Nutrition Information

- Calories: 104 calories;
- Sodium: 131
- Total Carbohydrate: 11.5
- Cholesterol: 0
- Protein: 3.2
- Total Fat: 5.9

753. Peanut Butter Stuffed Jalapenos

Serving: 7 | Prep: 10mins | Cook: 20mins | Ready in:

Ingredients

- 7 fresh jalapeno peppers, stems removed and seeded
- 1/2 cup peanut butter

Direction

- Set an oven to preheat to 175°C (350°F).
- Fill peanut butter in the cavities of the peppers. On a sheet of aluminum foil, line up the peppers side by side and wrap tightly.
- Let it bake for about 20 minutes in the preheated oven.

Nutrition Information

- Calories: 113 calories;
- Sodium: 85
- Total Carbohydrate: 4.4
- Cholesterol: 0
- Protein: 4.8
- Total Fat: 9.4

754. Pear Hedgehog

Serving: 4 | Prep: 10mins | Cook: | Ready in:

Ingredients

- 1/4 cup slivered almonds
- 1/2 (15 ounce) can pear halves, drained
- 12 raisins

Direction

- Stick flaked almonds all over the pear halves so that they look like spikes. Leave the pointy side of the pear empty for face. On the face side, put two raisins for the eyes and another one on front for nose.

Nutrition Information

- Calories: 72 calories;
- Total Fat: 3.5

- Sodium: 3
- Total Carbohydrate: 9.3
- Cholesterol: 0
- Protein: 1.6

- Sodium: 102
- Total Carbohydrate: 24
- Cholesterol: 23
- Protein: 5.6

755. Pear And Almond Tart (Dairy And Gluten Free)

Serving: 8 | Prep: 15mins | Cook: 22mins | Ready in:

Ingredients

- 1 1/4 cups almond meal
- 1/4 cup gluten-free oat flour
- 1/2 teaspoon gluten-free baking powder
- 1 egg, beaten
- 1/4 cup maple syrup
- 2 tablespoons coconut oil, melted
- 1 teaspoon vanilla extract
- 1/4 teaspoon sea salt
- 1/4 teaspoon almond extract
- 1 1/2 (16 ounce) cans pear halves, drained and patted dry

Direction

- Set an oven to 175°C (350°F) to preheat. Grease the bottom of a tart pan with removable bottom and line it with parchment paper.
- In a bowl, mix together the baking powder, oat flour and almond meal.
- In a separate bowl, whisk together the almond extract, salt, vanilla extract, coconut oil, maple syrup and egg. Fold in the almond meal mixture to create a sticky dough.
- Press the dough into the prepped tart pan, then lay the pears on top.
- Bake for 22-25 minutes in the preheated oven until it turns golden brown in color.

Nutrition Information

- Calories: 234 calories;
- Total Fat: 14

756. Pecan Pie Bars I

Serving: 48 | Prep: | Cook: | Ready in:

Ingredients

- 3 cups all-purpose flour
- 1/2 cup white sugar
- 1 cup butter
- 1/2 teaspoon salt
- 4 eggs
- 1 1/2 cups light corn syrup
- 1 1/2 cups white sugar
- 3 tablespoons margarine, melted
- 1 1/2 teaspoons vanilla extract
- 2 1/2 cups chopped pecans

Direction

- Set an oven to 175°C (350°F) and start preheating. Coat the bottom and sides of a 15x10-inch pan with cooking spray.
- Mix salt, butter or margarine, 1/2 cup of sugar, and flour in a large bowl until the mixture looks like coarse crumbs. Press in the prepared pan firmly.
- Bake at 175°C (350°F) for 20 minutes.
- Stir vanilla, melted margarine, 1 1/2 cups of white sugar, corn syrup, and eggs in a large bowl until combined. Add in the chopped pecans and stir.
- Add the filling onto the hot crust evenly. Bake at 175°C (350°F) until set, 25 minutes. Before cutting, allow to cool.

Nutrition Information

- Calories: 175 calories;
- Cholesterol: 26

- Protein: 1.9
- Total Fat: 9.1
- Sodium: 72
- Total Carbohydrate: 23

757. Peppered Elk Skillet

Serving: 4 | Prep: 30mins | Cook: 15mins | Ready in:

Ingredients

- 1 tablespoon vegetable oil
- 1 pound elk steak, cut into thin strips
- 1 clove minced garlic
- salt and pepper to taste
- 1 tablespoon vegetable oil
- 2 green bell peppers, cut into strips
- 1 medium onion, chopped
- 1 cup beef broth
- 1 tablespoon soy sauce
- 1 (14.5 ounce) can diced tomatoes
- 1 (8 ounce) package sliced mushrooms
- 1 (15 ounce) can baby corn, drained
- 1 1/2 tablespoons cornstarch
- 1/4 cup water

Direction

- In a big skillet, heat 1 tbsp. of oil on medium-high heat, then add garlic and elk strips. Let it cook and stir for about 4 minutes until the elk turns brown. Season pepper and salt to taste once it is done and take out the elk from the skillet.
- Pour the leftover tablespoon of oil into the skillet and mix in the onion and bell pepper. Let it cook and stir for about 5 minutes, until the vegetables become soft, add the corn, mushrooms, tomatoes, soy sauce and beef broth, then boil. Dissolve the cornstarch in water and mix into the boiling vegetables. Mix for about 30 seconds until it becomes thick. Mix in the browned elk until heated through, then serve.

Nutrition Information

- Calories: 258 calories;
- Protein: 25.8
- Total Fat: 8.6
- Sodium: 669
- Total Carbohydrate: 17.6
- Cholesterol: 52

758. Pepperoncini Beef

Serving: 8 | Prep: 10mins | Cook: 8hours | Ready in:

Ingredients

- 1 (3 pound) beef chuck roast
- 4 cloves garlic, sliced
- 1 (16 ounce) jar pepperoncini
- 8 hoagie rolls, split lengthwise
- 16 slices provolone cheese

Direction

- Make small cuts in the roast and fill it with garlic slices. Arrange roast in a slow cooker and pour over the meat all the contents of the jar of pepperoncini including the liquid. Under low heat, cover and cook for 6 to 8 hours.
- In preparing the sandwiches, arrange meat in rolls with cheese on top; microwave for a few seconds. Ensure to use pepperoncini in the sandwiches.

Nutrition Information

- Calories: 998 calories;
- Total Carbohydrate: 71.5
- Cholesterol: 160
- Protein: 55.9
- Total Fat: 52.7
- Sodium: 2550

759. Perfect Pita Chips

Serving: 8 | Prep: 15mins | Cook: 15mins | Ready in:

Ingredients

- 1 package pita pockets
- 2 tablespoons olive oil
- 1 tablespoon garlic powder
- 1 teaspoon kosher salt
- 1 teaspoon garlic salt

Direction

- Prepare oven by heating it to 175° or 350° F.
- Brush a side of every pita pocket using olive oil. Dust with garlic salt, salt, and garlic powder on pita pockets. Cut every pocket to 4 equal triangles.
- Bake in oven for 15-20 minutes until the triangles become light brown.

Nutrition Information

- Calories: 130 calories;
- Sodium: 654
- Total Carbohydrate: 20.3
- Cholesterol: 0
- Protein: 3.4
- Total Fat: 3.8

760. Perfect Sushi Rice

Serving: 15 | Prep: 5mins | Cook: 20mins | Ready in:

Ingredients

- 2 cups uncooked glutinous white rice (sushi rice)
- 3 cups water
- 1/2 cup rice vinegar
- 1 tablespoon vegetable oil
- 1/4 cup white sugar
- 1 teaspoon salt

Direction

- Rinse rice in a colander or strainer until water runs clear. Then mix with water in a medium saucepan and heat to boil. Decrease heat to low, then cover and let to cook for 20 minutes. The rice will be tender and the water will be absorbed. Let cool until cooled enough to work with.
- Mix salt, sugar, oil, and rice vinegar in a small saucepan. Let cook on medium heat until sugar is dissolved. Let cool, and mix into the cooked rice. Once you add this to rice, it will look very wet. Continue stirring and rice should dry while it cools.

Nutrition Information

- Calories: 112 calories;
- Total Fat: 1
- Sodium: 158
- Total Carbohydrate: 23.5
- Cholesterol: 0
- Protein: 1.7

761. Persian Sabzi Polo (Herb Rice With Fava Beans)

Serving: 16 | Prep: 20mins | Cook: 55mins | Ready in:

Ingredients

- 6 cups water
- 4 cups uncooked long-grain white rice
- 3 tablespoons vegetable oil
- 1/2 cup water
- 1 bunch fresh dill, chopped
- 1 bunch fresh parsley, chopped
- 1 bunch fresh cilantro, chopped
- 2 cups fresh or frozen fava beans
- ground turmeric to taste
- ground cinnamon to taste
- 1 teaspoon salt
- 1 teaspoon pepper

Direction

- Boil water in a large saucepan. Wash the rice first before placing it into the boiling water. Continue to boil until the rice reaches the surface of the water. Drain the rice and bring it back into the saucepan. Pour in water and oil. Stir in pepper, turmeric, fava beans, salt, dill, cilantro, cinnamon, and parsley.
- Set the heat to medium and allow the rice to cook for 5 minutes.
- Adjust the heat to the lowest. Cover the pan and let it simmer for 40-45 minutes. Take note that it is normal to come up with crispy rice or also called as Tadig on the bottom of the pan after cooking, it's delicious.

Nutrition Information

- Calories: 234 calories;
- Total Fat: 3.1
- Sodium: 214
- Total Carbohydrate: 44.7
- Cholesterol: 0
- Protein: 5.5

762. Pineapple Angel Food Cake I

Serving: 24 | Prep: | Cook: |Ready in:

Ingredients

- 1 (16 ounce) package angel food cake mix
- 1 (20 ounce) can crushed pineapple with juice
- 1 (12 ounce) container frozen whipped topping, thawed

Direction

- Preheat the oven to 175 ° C or 350 ° F. Use a vegetable oil spray to coat a pan, 9x13 inch in size.
- Mix pineapple including the juice and cake mix in a big bowl. Combine till thoroughly incorporated.
- Put the batter to prepped pan. Bake for 25 minutes at 175 ° C or 350 ° F or till golden brown in color. Cool down.
- Serve along with whipped topping.

Nutrition Information

- Calories: 127 calories;
- Total Carbohydrate: 22.1
- Cholesterol: 0
- Protein: 1.7
- Total Fat: 3.6
- Sodium: 166

763. Pineapple Chicken

Serving: 5 | Prep: 10mins | Cook: 30mins |Ready in:

Ingredients

- 5 skinless, boneless chicken breast halves
- 1 1/2 (1 ounce) packages dry onion soup mix
- 2 cups water
- 1 (15 ounce) can pineapple, drained
- 1 large orange, sliced in rounds
- 1 tablespoon vegetable oil

Direction

- Use vegetable spray to coat a big frying pan or electric skillet. Add chicken breasts in pan, with the meat side down, until brown.
- Flip chicken over; place in water, onion soup, and pineapple chunks.
- Then cover, lower heat. Simmer for 30 minutes. Decorate with fresh orange slices and cooked pineapple chunks.

Nutrition Information

- Calories: 245 calories;

- Sodium: 802
- Total Carbohydrate: 22.8
- Cholesterol: 67
- Protein: 25.8
- Total Fat: 5.8

764. Pineapple Chicken Tenders

Serving: 10 | Prep: 30mins | Cook: 10mins | Ready in:

Ingredients

- 1 cup pineapple juice
- 1/2 cup packed brown sugar
- 1/3 cup light soy sauce
- 2 pounds chicken breast tenderloins or strips
- skewers

Direction

- Stir pineapple juice, soy sauce, and brown sugar in a small saucepan over medium heat. Take it off the heat just before boiling.
- In a medium bowl, cover the chicken tenders with the pineapple marinade. Refrigerate for at least half an hour.
- Set grill on medium to pre-heat. Thread the chicken on the long side onto wooden skewers.
- Grease the grates lightly. Grill the chicken tenders for 5 minutes each side, or until juices come out clear. Do not overcook!

Nutrition Information

- Calories: 160 calories;
- Total Fat: 2.2
- Sodium: 332
- Total Carbohydrate: 14.7
- Cholesterol: 52
- Protein: 19.4

765. Pineapple Orange Sorbet

Serving: 10 | Prep: 20mins | Cook: 10mins | Ready in:

Ingredients

- 1/2 cup water
- 1/2 cup granulated sugar
- 2 cups orange juice
- 1 tablespoon lemon juice
- 1 (20 ounce) can crushed pineapple
- 2 teaspoons freshly grated orange zest

Direction

- Combine sugar and water in a medium saucepan. Heat on medium high heat and let it simmer until sugar dissolves.
- Mix together pineapple and the juice in a food processor and puree until smooth. Pour pineapple puree into a metal bowl, and add in orange zest, orange juice, lemon juice and syrup. Put in the freezer until slightly firm, but not frozen.
- Transfer mixture in the food processor and process it again or use an electric mixer to beat it until smooth. Move to a freezer container and keep tin the freezer for 2 hours until slightly solid.

Nutrition Information

- Calories: 95 calories;
- Protein: 0.6
- Total Fat: 0.1
- Sodium: 1
- Total Carbohydrate: 24.2
- Cholesterol: 0

766. Pineapple Salsa

Serving: 8 | Prep: 20mins | Cook: | Ready in:

Ingredients

- 1 cup finely chopped fresh pineapple
- 1/2 cup diced red bell pepper
- 1/2 cup diced green bell pepper
- 1 cup frozen corn kernels, thawed
- 1 (15 ounce) can black beans, drained and rinsed
- 1/4 cup chopped onions
- 2 green chile peppers, chopped
- 1/4 cup orange juice
- 1/4 cup chopped fresh cilantro
- 1/2 teaspoon ground cumin
- salt and pepper to taste

Direction

- Toss cilantro, orange juice, green Chile peppers, onions, black beans, corn, green bell pepper, red bell pepper and pineapple together in a big bowl. Season to taste with pepper, salt and cumin. Chill, covered, in the fridge until ready to serve.

Nutrition Information

- Calories: 92 calories;
- Total Fat: 0.5
- Sodium: 207
- Total Carbohydrate: 19.3
- Cholesterol: 0
- Protein: 4.5

767. Pineapple And Mango Skewers With Coconut Dip

Serving: 12 | Prep: 15mins | Cook: 5mins | Ready in:

Ingredients

- 1/2 cup unsalted raw cashews
- 3/4 cup coconut milk
- 2 tablespoons honey
- 1 tablespoon coconut oil
- 1 1/2 cups flaked coconut
- 1 fresh pineapple, peeled and cut into cubes
- 1 fresh mango, peeled and cut into cubes
- skewers

Direction

- In a bowl, soak the cashews for 1-2 hours, then drain.
- In a blender, blend the coconut oil, honey, coconut milk and soaked cashews until the dip becomes smooth. Move the dip to a bowl, put cover and chill in fridge.
- Place an oven rack approximately 6 inches from the heat source and set the oven's broiler to preheat. Spread the flaked coconut on the baking tray.
- Broil the coconut for 10 seconds to 1 minute in the preheated oven, watching it the entire time, until the coconut becomes toasted. Take out the baking tray from the oven and let the coconut cool.
- Set an outdoor grill to medium-high heat and oil the grate lightly. Thread the mango and pineapple onto the skewers.
- Put the skewers on the preheated grill and let it cook for around 1 minute on each side, flipping once.
- Sprinkle toasted coconut on top of the dip and serve it on the side of the skewers.

Nutrition Information

- Calories: 184 calories;
- Total Fat: 14.2
- Sodium: 8
- Total Carbohydrate: 15
- Cholesterol: 0
- Protein: 2.4

768. Pipirrana (Spanish Potato Salad)

Serving: 6 | Prep: 30mins | Cook: 20mins | Ready in:

Ingredients

- 6 eggs
- 6 potatoes, peeled and cubed
- 1 green bell pepper, seeded and diced
- 1 red bell pepper, seeded and diced
- 1/2 onion, chopped
- 1 large fresh tomato, chopped
- 1 (5 ounce) can tuna, drained
- 1/2 cup green olives with pimento or anchovy, halved
- 1/4 cup extra virgin olive oil
- 2 tablespoons distilled white vinegar
- 1 teaspoon salt, or to taste

Direction

- In a saucepan, put in egg and pour in cold water to cover; boil. Take off heat and cover. Let the eggs soak in hot water for 10-12 minutes. Take the eggs out of hot water and let it cool. Peel and slice eggs into quarters. Let it stand.
- Boil a bit pot of salted water; put in potatoes. Cook for 15 minutes until the potatoes are tender but still a bit firm; drain. Move potatoes in a big bowl.
- Mix together potatoes, vinegar, eggs, olive oil, bell peppers, green olives, onion, tuna, and tomato; sprinkle salt to season. Let it chill in the refrigerator before serving.

Nutrition Information

- Calories: 377 calories;
- Protein: 16.8
- Total Fat: 16.3
- Sodium: 764
- Total Carbohydrate: 41.9
- Cholesterol: 192

769. Pistachio Coconut Ice Cream

Serving: 14 | Prep: 35mins | Cook: | Ready in:

Ingredients

- 3/4 cup roasted pistachios
- 1/4 cup roasted flax seeds
- 2 (14 ounce) cans full-fat coconut milk, chilled
- 2 teaspoons vanilla extract
- 1 teaspoon stevia powder
- 1 teaspoon xanthan gum (optional)
- 1 teaspoon coconut oil (optional)
- 1/2 teaspoon almond extract
- 1/4 teaspoon Himalayan black salt
- 1/2 cup coarsely chopped roasted pistachios

Direction

- In a coffee grinder, pulse 3/4 cup of pistachios till finely ground. Move into a blender.
- In a coffee grinder, pulse flax seeds till finely ground. Put into the blender.
- Transfer coconut milk into the blender. Put in black salt, almond extract, coconut oil, xanthan gum, stevia powder and vanilla extract; blend for around 2 minutes or till very smooth.
- Move the blender container to the freezer; briefly chill for around 15 minutes.
- Transfer the mixture into an ice cream maker; following the manufacturer's directions, churn properly; put in 1/2 cup of chopped pistachios during the last few minutes of churning. Before serving, move to a lidded container.

Nutrition Information

- Calories: 196 calories;
- Total Carbohydrate: 6.1
- Cholesterol: 0
- Protein: 4
- Total Fat: 18.6
- Sodium: 59

770. Platski

Serving: 4 | Prep: 10mins | Cook: 20mins | Ready in:

Ingredients

- 4 large potatoes, grated
- 1 teaspoon onion powder
- 1/2 teaspoon garlic powder
- 1 teaspoon salt, or to taste
- 1/2 teaspoon paprika
- 1 tablespoon all-purpose flour
- ground black pepper to taste
- 2 tablespoons vegetable oil

Direction

- Mix the pepper, flour, paprika, salt, garlic powder, onion powder and potatoes in a medium bowl and stir it very well.
- Heat a medium pan coated with oil on medium-high heat. Over the entire bottom of the pan, quickly spread a thin layer of potato mixture with a fork or a spoon. Make sure to make the pancake as thin as possible without holes or gaps. Fry it until it turns golden brown or for 2 minutes. Turn it over using a spatula to cook the other side.
- Redo the process with the rest of the potato mixture.

Nutrition Information

- Calories: 346 calories;
- Protein: 7.7
- Total Fat: 7.3
- Sodium: 1302
- Total Carbohydrate: 64.8
- Cholesterol: 0

771. Playgroup Granola Bars

Serving: 24 | Prep: 15mins | Cook: 35mins | Ready in:

Ingredients

- 2 cups rolled oats
- 3/4 cup packed brown sugar
- 1/2 cup wheat germ
- 3/4 teaspoon ground cinnamon
- 1 cup all-purpose flour
- 3/4 cup raisins (optional)
- 3/4 teaspoon salt
- 1/2 cup honey
- 1 egg, beaten
- 1/2 cup vegetable oil
- 2 teaspoons vanilla extract

Direction

- Turn the oven to 175°C (350° F). Grease generously a 9-inch x 13-inch baking tray.
- In a big bowl, combine the brown sugar, wheat germ, raisins cinnamon, flour, salt and oats. Make a crater in the middle, and put in the oil, egg, vanilla and honey. Combine well with your hands. Dab the mixture evenly in the prepared tray.
- Bake for 30-35 minutes in the oven, until the bars start to become golden around edges. Let it cool 5 minutes, and then slice the bars while still hot. Don't let the bars cool completely before slicing, or they will be too firm to slice.

Nutrition Information

- Calories: 161 calories;
- Sodium: 79
- Total Carbohydrate: 26.6
- Cholesterol: 8
- Protein: 2.4
- Total Fat: 5.5

772. Porcupine Meatballs II

Serving: 6 | Prep: 25mins | Cook: 20mins | Ready in:

Ingredients

- 1 (10.75 ounce) can condensed tomato soup
- 1/2 cup water
- 1 1/2 pounds ground beef
- 1 cup uncooked instant rice
- 1 tablespoon minced onion
- 1 teaspoon salt
- 1 dash ground black pepper

Direction

- Mix together the water and tomato soup in a medium mixing bowl, then stir thoroughly and put aside.
- Mix together 1/2 cup of the soup mixture, pepper, salt, onion, instant rice and ground beef in a big mixing bowl. Stir thoroughly and form into 1-inch balls.
- In a big skillet, put the meatballs on medium heat and pour in the leftover soup mixture, then boil. Let it simmer for 15-20 minutes or until the rice is cooked and the meatballs become thoroughly browned.

Nutrition Information

- Calories: 462 calories;
- Protein: 22.9
- Total Fat: 17.2
- Sodium: 721
- Total Carbohydrate: 52.3
- Cholesterol: 68

773. Pork Chops And Sauerkraut

Serving: 4 | Prep: 15mins | Cook: 30mins | Ready in:

Ingredients

- 2 tablespoons vegetable oil
- 4 (3/4 inch) thick pork chops
- 2 cloves garlic, minced
- 1 onion, thinly sliced
- 16 ounces sauerkraut
- 1 teaspoon caraway seed
- 2 tablespoons apple juice
- salt and pepper to taste

Direction

- In a big skillet, heat oil on medium heat. Brown all sides of chops. Take out of pan.
- In hot skillet, add apple juice, caraway seed, sauerkraut, onion, garlic and pepper and salt to taste. Sauté it for 3-4 minutes. On sauerkraut mixture, lay browned pork chops. Cover. Lower heat to low then cook, occasionally mixing, for 20 minutes.

Nutrition Information

- Calories: 245 calories;
- Sodium: 806
- Total Carbohydrate: 9
- Cholesterol: 59
- Protein: 24.6
- Total Fat: 12.2

774. Pork Medallions With Port And Dried Cranberry Sauce

Serving: 4 | Prep: 15mins | Cook: 10mins | Ready in:

Ingredients

- 1/2 cup dried cranberries
- 1 cup water
- 1 teaspoon vegetable oil
- 1 pound pork medallions
- salt and pepper to taste
- 2 tablespoons minced shallots
- 1/2 cup tawny port wine
- 1/4 cup distilled white vinegar
- 1 cup chicken broth
- 1/2 teaspoon dried thyme
- 1 teaspoon cornstarch
- 1 tablespoon water

Direction

- Put cranberries over medium low heat in a small saucepan. Add water; stir together. Bring to a simmer; allow to simmer for 3 minutes. Drain, saving both cooking liquid and cranberries. Put aside.
- Heat oil over medium heat in a large skillet. Season pork medallions with pepper and salt; add to skillet. Sauté on both sides, about 3 minutes each, until browned and not pink inside anymore. Place on a platter, loosely cover and keep warm.
- Add chopped shallot and cook for half a minute in the same skillet. Pour in vinegar and port; bring to boiling; stir to scrape up brown bits on the bottom of the skillet. Boil for 3-5 minutes until liquid reduces by 1/2. Add reserved cranberry liquid, thyme and chicken stock; boil all together for 5-7 minutes until it reduces by 1/2.
- Dissolve cornstarch in a tablespoon of water in a small bowl; combine. Beat the mixture into the saucepan; let it simmer while stirring until sauce is glossy and slightly thickened. Stir in reserved cranberries; sprinkle with pepper and salt as preferred. Scoop the sauce over pork; serve.

Nutrition Information

- Calories: 245 calories;
- Total Fat: 5.2
- Sodium: 62
- Total Carbohydrate: 17.9
- Cholesterol: 74
- Protein: 23.6

775. Pot Sticker Dumplings

Serving: 12 | Prep: 20mins | Cook: 20mins | Ready in:

Ingredients

- 1 1/2 cups all-purpose flour
- 1/2 teaspoon salt
- 3 tablespoons vegetable oil
- boiling water
- 4 ounces ground chicken
- 4 water chestnuts, drained and finely chopped
- 3 green onions, finely chopped
- 1/2 teaspoon Chinese five-spice powder
- 1 tablespoon reduced-sodium soy sauce
- 1 teaspoon white sugar
- 1 teaspoon sesame oil
- 1/2 cup oil for frying

Direction

- Into a big bowl, sift salt and flour. Create a well in the middle and add about 4 tablespoons of boiling water and vegetable oil. Mix using a wooden spoon till smooth, putting in additional boiling water as needed. Knead approximately 5 minutes, till elastic. Place on the cover and let it rest for half an hour.
- Split dough to make a dozen of even pieces. Roll every portion into circles, 6-inch in size each.
- Let ground chicken breast cook in a medium saucepan over medium high heat till evenly brown.
- Allow chicken to drain and put in medium bowl together with sesame oil, white sugar, reduced-sodium soy sauce, Chinese five-spice powder, green onions and water chestnuts. Stir well.
- In a big skillet, heat the oil. In the middle of each dough circle, put about a tablespoon of the chicken mixture. Fold over the mixture and press edges together to seal. In hot oil, cook in small batches till bottoms turn golden brown. In pan, put about 1/3 cup of water. Place on the cover and keep cooking for about 5 minutes, till dumpling tops of are steamed thoroughly. Serve right away.

Nutrition Information

- Calories: 115 calories;
- Cholesterol: 6

- Protein: 3.9
- Total Fat: 5.2
- Sodium: 147
- Total Carbohydrate: 13.1

776. Pot Stickers Traditional

Serving: 15 | Prep: 1hours | Cook: 10mins | Ready in:

Ingredients

- 1/2 pound ground pork
- 1/2 medium head cabbage, finely chopped
- 1 green onion, finely chopped
- 2 slices fresh ginger root, finely chopped
- 2 water chestnuts, drained and finely chopped
- 1 teaspoon salt
- 1/2 teaspoon white sugar
- 1 teaspoon sesame oil
- 1 (14 ounce) package wonton wrappers
- 5 tablespoons vegetable oil
- 3/4 cup water
- 1 tablespoon chili oil
- 1 tablespoon soy sauce
- 1 teaspoon rice vinegar

Direction

- On medium-high heat, crumble and cook pork in a big deep pan until brown; drain. Put aside.
- Stir sesame oil, pork, sugar, cabbage, salt, green onion, water chestnuts, and ginger together in a bowl. Refrigerate for 6-8 hrs or overnight.
- Scoop 1 tbsp. pork mixture in every wonton wrapper; fold and seal corners using a moist fork.
- On medium-high heat, pour 3 tbsp. vegetable oil in a big, deep pan; heat. Put the pot stickers in the skillet with their seams up; cook for half to a full minute. Pour in water and boil until it begins to sizzle, 7-8 minutes. Pour in left oil. Take the pot stickers out of pan once the bottoms start to brown.
- Combine vinegar, chili oil, and soy sauce in a serving bowl. Modify the quantity depending on your tastes.

Nutrition Information

- Calories: 166 calories;
- Sodium: 378
- Total Carbohydrate: 17.3
- Cholesterol: 12
- Protein: 5.7
- Total Fat: 8.2

777. Potato Chip Cookies VI

Serving: 36 | Prep: 15mins | Cook: 10mins | Ready in:

Ingredients

- 1 cup shortening
- 1 cup white sugar
- 1 cup brown sugar
- 2 eggs
- 1 teaspoon vanilla extract
- 2 cups all-purpose flour
- 1 teaspoon baking soda
- 1/2 teaspoon salt
- 2 cups crushed potato chips
- 1 cup chopped walnuts (optional)

Direction

- Set the oven to 175°C or 350°F to preheat.
- Cream brown sugar, white sugar and shortening together in a big bowl until fluffy and light. Put in 1 egg at a time while beating well between additions, then stir in vanilla. Mix together salt, baking soda and flour, then stir into the creamed mixture slowly. Lastly, stir in walnuts and potato chips. Drop on unprepared cookie sheet with rounded spoonfuls of the dough.
- In the preheated oven, bake for about 8-10 minutes. Let cookies cool on baking sheet for

about 5 minutes prior to transferring to a wire rack to cool thoroughly.

Nutrition Information

- Calories: 162 calories;
- Sodium: 94
- Total Carbohydrate: 17.4
- Cholesterol: 14
- Protein: 1.9
- Total Fat: 9.8

778. Potato Medley

Serving: 6 | Prep: 10mins | Cook: 20mins | Ready in:

Ingredients

- 5 large potatoes, chopped
- 3 carrots, peeled and sliced
- 1 onion, chopped
- 1 green bell pepper, chopped
- 1 (15.25 ounce) can whole kernel corn
- 3 cups water
- 3 cubes vegetable bouillon

Direction

- Mix together the water, corn, green bell pepper, onion, carrots and potatoes in a big pot on high heat, then boil until it becomes tender. Add the bouillon.
- Lower the heat to medium and let it simmer for 10 minutes.

Nutrition Information

- Calories: 323 calories;
- Total Fat: 1.1
- Sodium: 247
- Total Carbohydrate: 74.8
- Cholesterol: 0
- Protein: 7.7

779. Potato Squash Cakes

Serving: 12 | Prep: 15mins | Cook: 15mins | Ready in:

Ingredients

- 2 cups shredded potatoes
- 1 cup shredded yellow squash
- 1/2 cup chopped onion
- 1 egg
- 4 tablespoons self-rising flour
- 1/4 teaspoon garlic salt
- salt and pepper to taste
- 1/4 cup cooking oil

Direction

- Mix pepper, salt, garlic salt, flour, egg, onion, squash and potatoes in big bowl. Add extra flour if batter is very thin and milk if very thick. Shape batter to 3-in. patties.
- Use enough oil to cover bottom of big skillet; heat on medium high heat. Put patties into hot oil; cook till each side is golden brown. Drain on paper towels.

Nutrition Information

- Calories: 80 calories;
- Sodium: 78
- Total Carbohydrate: 7.7
- Cholesterol: 16
- Protein: 1.4
- Total Fat: 5

780. Potatoes And Onions

Serving: 2 | Prep: | Cook: | Ready in:

Ingredients

- 3 potatoes, cubed
- 1/4 cup fat free Italian-style dressing

- 2 cups fresh sliced mushrooms
- 1 onion, finely diced
- 2 stalks celery, chopped

Direction

- In a pot with boiling water, add potatoes and cook until softened, then drain well.
- Spray non-stick cooking spray to a frying pan and add in dressing. Fry celery, onions and mushrooms on moderate heat. Once cooked to your wanted texture, drizzle the mixture over the potatoes and serve hot.

Nutrition Information

- Calories: 337 calories;
- Total Carbohydrate: 75.7
- Cholesterol: 0
- Protein: 9.5
- Total Fat: 0.6
- Sodium: 367

781. Potatoes And Peppers

Serving: 4 | Prep: 10mins | Cook: 20mins | Ready in:

Ingredients

- 1/3 cup olive oil
- 6 potatoes, sliced
- 2 large red bell peppers, sliced into rings
- 1 large sweet onion, peeled and chopped
- salt and pepper to taste

Direction

- In a big frying pan, heat oil on medium high heat. Fry the potatoes for 5 minutes then put in onions and peppers. Season with pepper and salt. Cook for a minimum of 15 minutes while turning the potatoes often, or until the potatoes begin to look mushy.

Nutrition Information

- Calories: 389 calories;
- Sodium: 14
- Total Carbohydrate: 53.5
- Cholesterol: 0
- Protein: 5.2
- Total Fat: 18.4

782. Presto Vegan Pesto

Serving: 4 | Prep: 5mins | Cook: | Ready in:

Ingredients

- 1 bunch fresh basil
- 1/3 cup pine nuts
- 5 cloves garlic
- 1/2 cup olive oil
- 1 tablespoon lemon juice
- 2 tablespoons water
- 1/4 cup Parmesan flavor grated soy topping

Direction

- In a blender, puree soy topping, water, lemon juice, olive oil, garlic, pine nuts and basil, covered, until smooth.

Nutrition Information

- Calories: 337 calories;
- Protein: 6.6
- Total Fat: 32.9
- Sodium: 100
- Total Carbohydrate: 5.2
- Cholesterol: 0

783. Prize Winning Baby Back Ribs

Serving: 6 | Prep: 30mins | Cook: 1hours5mins | Ready in:

Ingredients

- 1 tablespoon ground cumin
- 1 tablespoon chili powder
- 1 tablespoon paprika
- salt and pepper to taste
- 3 pounds baby back pork ribs
- 1 cup barbeque sauce

Direction

- Preheat gas grill on high heat or place charcoal briquettes on one side of the barbeque. Oil grate lightly.
- Mix pepper, salt, paprika, chili powder, and cumin in a small jar. Close lid then mix by shaking.
- Trim membrane sheath from each rack's back. Run a sharp, small knife between every rib and membrane then snip membrane off as much as you possible. Sprinkle on as much rub as you like on both sides of the ribs. Don't rub the spices thoroughly in the ribs if you don't want it too spicy and dark. Keep leftover spice mix for another use.
- Put aluminum foil on the lower rack to get drippings and avoid flare-ups. Lay ribs on the top rack of the grill, away from coals if you chose briquettes. Bring heat to low, close the lid, then leave for 1 hour without disturbing. Don't lift the lid.
- Brush barbecue sauce on ribs and grill for another 5 minutes. Serve cut between every rib bone, piled individually on platters or as a whole rack.

Nutrition Information

- Calories: 441 calories;
- Total Fat: 30
- Sodium: 582
- Total Carbohydrate: 16.9
- Cholesterol: 117
- Protein: 24.6

784. Pumpkin Cake I

Serving: 12 | Prep: 15mins | Cook: 1hours | Ready in:

Ingredients

- 1 cup vegetable oil
- 3 eggs
- 1 (15 ounce) can pumpkin puree
- 1 teaspoon vanilla extract
- 2 1/2 cups white sugar
- 2 1/2 cups all-purpose flour
- 1 teaspoon baking soda
- 1 teaspoon ground nutmeg
- 1 teaspoon ground allspice
- 1 teaspoon ground cinnamon
- 1 teaspoon ground cloves
- 1/4 teaspoon salt
- 1 cup chopped walnuts (optional)

Direction

- Preheat an oven to 175°C/350°F; grease 1 10-in. tube/Bundt pan.
- Blend vanilla, pumpkin, beaten eggs and oil together.
- Sift salt, ground cloves, ground cinnamon, ground allspice, ground nutmeg, baking soda, sugar and flour. Put flour mixture into the pumpkin mixture; mix just till combined. Mix in some chopped nuts if desired; put batter into the prepped pan.
- In the preheated oven, bake for 1 hour till an inserted toothpick in the center exits clean; cool cake for 5 minutes in pan. Turn onto a plate; sprinkle with confectioners' sugar.

Nutrition Information

- Calories: 517 calories;

- Sodium: 258
- Total Carbohydrate: 66.4
- Cholesterol: 46
- Protein: 6.2
- Total Fat: 26.6

785. Pumpkin Chai Pie (Dairy Free)

Serving: 8 | Prep: 10mins | Cook: 45mins | Ready in:

Ingredients

- 1 cup almond milk
- 2 spiced chai tea bags
- 1 1/2 (16 ounce) cans pumpkin puree
- 3/4 cup white sugar
- 1 tablespoon ground flax seeds
- 2 teaspoons ground cinnamon
- 1 teaspoon vegetable oil
- 1/2 teaspoon salt
- 1 prepared deep-dish pie shell

Direction

- Preheat an oven to 200°C or 400°F.
- In a small saucepan, boil almond milk. Take off from heat; put chai tea bags. Let the tea steep for a minimum of 5 minutes.
- In a big bowl, combine salt, vegetable oil, cinnamon, ground flax seeds, sugar and pumpkin puree till fully smooth. Put in chai-flavored almond milk; mix once more till smooth. Put filling into pie shell.
- In the preheated oven, bake for about 40 minutes till an inserted knife into the middle comes out clean.

Nutrition Information

- Calories: 235 calories;
- Cholesterol: 0
- Protein: 2.6
- Total Fat: 9

- Sodium: 488
- Total Carbohydrate: 37.8

786. Pumpkin Chocolate Coconut Oil Bars

Serving: 16 | Prep: 10mins | Cook: 30mins | Ready in:

Ingredients

- cooking spray
- 1 cup almond flour
- 1 cup coconut sugar
- 3/4 cup pumpkin puree
- 1/2 cup coconut oil
- 1/2 cup dairy-free mini chocolate chips
- 1/4 cup tapioca flour
- 1 egg white
- 1 1/2 teaspoons pumpkin pie spice
- 1 1/2 teaspoons ground cinnamon
- 1 teaspoon almond extract

Direction

- Preheat an oven to 175°C/350°F. Grease cooking spray on 9x9-in. baking pan/glass dish.
- In a bowl, mix almond extract, cinnamon, pumpkin pie spice, egg white, tapioca flour, dairy-free chocolate chips, coconut oil, pumpkin puree, coconut sugar and almond flour till mixed well. Put into prepped pan.
- In preheated oven, bake for 30 minutes till top is golden brown and chocolate chips are melted. Cool for 15 minutes till set. Cut to bars.

Nutrition Information

- Calories: 153 calories;
- Total Fat: 10.7
- Sodium: 34
- Total Carbohydrate: 13.6
- Cholesterol: 0

- Protein: 2

787. Pumpkin Pie (Dairy, Egg, And Gluten Free)

Serving: 8 | Prep: 10mins | Cook: 55mins | Ready in:

Ingredients

- 1 (15 ounce) can pumpkin puree
- 1 (8 ounce) package silken tofu
- 3/4 cup baker's sugar
- 2 tablespoons cornstarch
- 1 teaspoon ground cinnamon
- 1/2 teaspoon salt
- 1/2 teaspoon pure vanilla extract
- 1/2 teaspoon ground ginger
- 1/4 teaspoon ground cloves
- 1 gluten-free graham cracker crust (such as Mi-Del®)

Direction

- Preheat the oven to 220°C or 425°F.
- In a blender, mix cloves, ginger, vanilla extract, salt, cinnamon, cornstarch, sugar, tofu and pumpkin puree. Mix till silky smooth, scraping down sides of blender as necessary. Put mixture into the pie crust.
- In the preheated oven, bake for about 15 minutes till browned lightly. Lower oven temperature to 175°C or 350°F; let bake for 40 to 50 minutes till an inserted knife in the middle comes out clean.
- Put pie in refrigerator for 8 hours to overnight till set and chilled.

Nutrition Information

- Calories: 227 calories;
- Total Fat: 6
- Sodium: 460
- Total Carbohydrate: 42.7
- Cholesterol: 0

- Protein: 3.4

788. Pumpkin Pie (Wheat Free, Egg Free, And Dairy Free)

Serving: 8 | Prep: 20mins | Cook: 1hours15mins | Ready in:

Ingredients

- Crust:
- 1 1/2 cups gluten-free all purpose baking flour
- 1 teaspoon salt
- 1/2 cup vegetable oil
- 2 tablespoons french vanilla soy creamer
- Pie Filling:
- 2 cups canned pumpkin
- 1 cup french vanilla soy creamer
- 3/4 cup brown sugar
- 1/4 cup cornstarch
- 1 tablespoon dark corn syrup
- 1 teaspoon ground cinnamon
- 1/2 teaspoon ground ginger
- 1/2 teaspoon ground nutmeg
- 1/2 teaspoon salt
- 1/8 teaspoon ground cloves

Direction

- Preheat the oven to 220°C or 425°F.
- Mix together 1 teaspoon salt and all-purpose gluten-free flour. Beat together the soy creamer and vegetable oil till creamy in another bowl. Into the flour mixture put oil mixture, mix using fork till incorporated. Press crust into the base and sides of a pie pan, 9-inch in size. In preheated oven, let bake for 15 minutes. Take off and reserve.
- Reduce oven to 175°C or 350°F. In a blender, put cloves, salt, nutmeg, ginger, cinnamon, corn syrup, cornstarch, brown sugar, soy creamer and pumpkin. Mix till incorporated. Put into the prebaked pie crust. Put foil surrounding the edges of pie crust and allow to bake for an hour or till an inserted knife, an

inch from crust, comes out clean. Let pie cool for 2 hours on counter then chill overnight prior to serving.

Nutrition Information

- Calories: 264 calories;
- Total Fat: 16.3
- Sodium: 615
- Total Carbohydrate: 31.1
- Cholesterol: 0
- Protein: 0.7

789. Pumpkin Puree

Serving: 5 | Prep: 30mins | Cook: 1hours | Ready in:

Ingredients

- 1 sugar pumpkin

Direction

- Set an oven to 165°C (325°F) to preheat.
- Halve the pumpkin, from stem to base. Take out the pulp and seeds. Use foil to cover each half.
- Bake for 1 hour in the preheated oven, foil side up, or until it becomes tender.
- Scrape out the pumpkin meat from the shell halves and puree it using a blender. Strain to take out any leftover stringy pieces. Put it in the freezer safe bags and store in the freezer.

Nutrition Information

- Calories: 189 calories;
- Total Carbohydrate: 47.2
- Cholesterol: 0
- Total Fat: 0.7
- Protein: 7.3
- Sodium: 7

790. Pumpkin Tart With Pecan Crust

Serving: 8 | Prep: | Cook: | Ready in:

Ingredients

- 3/4 cup pecan halves
- 3/4 cup rolled oats
- 3/4 cup whole wheat pastry flour
- 1/2 teaspoon ground cinnamon
- 1 pinch salt
- 1/4 cup vegetable oil
- 3 tablespoons real maple syrup
- 1 cup soy milk
- 1/4 cup arrowroot powder
- 1 (15 ounce) can pumpkin puree
- 1/2 cup real maple syrup
- 1 tablespoon grated fresh ginger
- 1 1/2 teaspoons ground cinnamon
- 1/2 teaspoon salt
- 1/4 teaspoon freshly grated nutmeg
- 1/8 teaspoon ground cloves

Direction

- Place the rack in the center of the oven then preheat to 190°C or 375°F. Grease a 9-in pie plate lightly; set aside.
- Scatter nuts all over a baking pan then toast for 7-10 minutes or until aromatic. Reserve 16 pecan halves for later use.
- In a food processor bowl, pulse a pinch of salt, oats, half teaspoon cinnamon, the rest of the pecans, and flour until it turns to a coarse meal; move to a mixing bowl. Stir 3 tbsp. maple syrup and oil together; combine into the dry ingredients until a soft dough forms. Push the mixture in the greased pie plate; flute the edges and bake for 10 minutes then let it rest to cool.
- In a food processor, combine arrowroot and soymilk for 15 seconds until the mixture is smooth and the arrowroot dissolves completely. Blend in cloves, pumpkin,

nutmeg, half cup maple syrup, half teaspoon salt, 1 1/2 tsp. cinnamon, and ginger until well combined; smooth over the baked crust using a spatula.
- Bake for 35 minutes or until the exterior inch of the filling sets and the crust is pale brown. The soft center will firm up as it cools. Move to a wire rack. In two concentric circles, push the toasted pecan halves in the hot filling. Cool the pie to room temperature then refrigerate for 3 hours until set. Serve the pie at room temperature or chilled.

Nutrition Information

- Calories: 313 calories;
- Cholesterol: 0
- Protein: 4.7
- Total Fat: 15.6
- Sodium: 312
- Total Carbohydrate: 41.8

791. Puttanesca I

Serving: 4 | Prep: 25mins | Cook: 15mins | Ready in:

Ingredients

- 8 ounces pasta
- 1/2 cup olive oil
- 3 cloves garlic, minced
- 2 cups chopped tomatoes, pushed through a sieve
- 4 anchovy filets, rinsed and chopped
- 2 tablespoons tomato paste
- 3 tablespoons capers
- 20 Greek olives, pitted and coarsely chopped
- 1/2 teaspoon crushed red pepper flakes

Direction

- Boil the lightly salted water in a large pot. In the boiling water, cook pasta until al dente, about for 8-10 minutes; then drain.
- In a skillet, heat oil over low heat. In oil, cook garlic until golden. Put in the sieved tomatoes. Cook for 5 minutes. Stir in red pepper flakes, olives, capers, tomato paste and anchovies. Cook, stirring occasionally, for 10 minutes.
- Toss the pasta with the sauce. Enjoy!

Nutrition Information

- Calories: 490 calories;
- Total Carbohydrate: 38.7
- Cholesterol: 44
- Protein: 9.3
- Total Fat: 34
- Sodium: 728

792. Quick Black Beans And Rice

Serving: 4 | Prep: 5mins | Cook: 15mins | Ready in:

Ingredients

- 1 tablespoon vegetable oil
- 1 onion, chopped
- 1 (15 ounce) can black beans, undrained
- 1 (14.5 ounce) can stewed tomatoes
- 1 teaspoon dried oregano
- 1/2 teaspoon garlic powder
- 1 1/2 cups uncooked instant brown rice

Direction

- On medium-high heat, place a large saucepan and heat oil. Pour in onion, cook and stir until soft. Put in garlic powder, oregano, tomatoes, and beans. Bring it to a boil; mix in rice. Put the lid on; turn the heat down and simmer for 5 minutes. Take it away from heat; allow to rest for 5 minutes before serving.

Nutrition Information

- Calories: 271 calories;

- Total Fat: 5.3
- Sodium: 552
- Total Carbohydrate: 47.8
- Cholesterol: 0
- Protein: 10

793. Quick And Easy Chicken

Serving: 4 | Prep: | Cook: | Ready in:

Ingredients

- 2 tablespoons olive oil
- 1 onion, chopped
- 4 skinless, boneless chicken breast halves
- 3 tablespoons ketchup
- 2 tablespoons soy sauce
- 3 tablespoons white sugar
- 2 tablespoons lemon juice
- 1 teaspoon ground black pepper

Direction

- In oil, sauté onion until translucent.
- Put in chicken, then lightly brown.
- Combine pepper, lemon juice, sugar, soy sauce and ketchup; mix well. Then add over the chicken. Boil. Lower the heat, simmer, covered, for 25-35 minutes.

Nutrition Information

- Calories: 255 calories;
- Protein: 28.3
- Total Fat: 8.3
- Sodium: 655
- Total Carbohydrate: 16.4
- Cholesterol: 68

794. Quinoa And Black Beans

Serving: 10 | Prep: 15mins | Cook: 35mins | Ready in:

Ingredients

- 1 teaspoon vegetable oil
- 1 onion, chopped
- 3 cloves garlic, chopped
- 3/4 cup quinoa
- 1 1/2 cups vegetable broth
- 1 teaspoon ground cumin
- 1/4 teaspoon cayenne pepper
- salt and ground black pepper to taste
- 1 cup frozen corn kernels
- 2 (15 ounce) cans black beans, rinsed and drained
- 1/2 cup chopped fresh cilantro

Direction

- In a pan, heat oil over medium heat and cook the garlic and onion, stirring, for 10 minutes until browned lightly.
- Mix in the quinoa and cover with vegetable broth, then season with pepper, salt, cayenne pepper, and cumin. Allow to boil, then cover and turn down the heat. Let the mixture simmer for 20 minutes, or until the broth is absorbed and the quinoa is tender.
- Stir in the frozen corn and continue simmering for 5 minutes until it is heated through. Mix in the cilantro and black beans.

Nutrition Information

- Calories: 153 calories;
- Cholesterol: 0
- Protein: 7.7
- Total Fat: 1.7
- Sodium: 517
- Total Carbohydrate: 27.8

795. Raspberry Salsa

Serving: 20 | Prep: 10mins | Cook: | Ready in:

Ingredients

- 2 cups fresh raspberries
- 1/4 cup chopped sweet onion
- 3 teaspoons finely chopped jalapeno chile peppers
- 1 clove minced garlic
- 1/4 cup chopped fresh cilantro
- 1/2 teaspoon white sugar
- 3 tablespoons fresh lime juice

Direction

- Combine the lime juice, white sugar, cilantro, garlic, jalapeno chile peppers, sweet onion and raspberries in a medium bowl. Put cover on and chill in the fridge for a minimum of 1 hour prior to serving.

Nutrition Information

- Calories: 8 calories;
- Total Fat: 0.1
- Sodium: < 1
- Total Carbohydrate: 2
- Cholesterol: 0
- Protein: 0.2

796. Raw Candy

Serving: 40 | Prep: 20mins | Cook: | Ready in:

Ingredients

- 1 cup raisins
- 1 cup walnuts
- 1 tablespoon vegetable oil
- 1 cup sliced almonds

Direction

- Mix walnuts and raisins in a food processor and then process until you have a sticky ball.
- Grease your hands with oil and then roll the mixture into balls similar to the size of large marbles. Coat with chopped almonds.
- Cover and chill for a maximum of three days.

Nutrition Information

- Calories: 45 calories;
- Total Fat: 3.5
- Sodium: < 1
- Total Carbohydrate: 3.2
- Cholesterol: 0
- Protein: 1

797. Raw Chia 'Porridge'

Serving: 1 | Prep: 10mins | Cook: | Ready in:

Ingredients

- 1/4 cup chia seeds
- 1 banana
- 2 dates, pitted
- 1 cup almond milk
- 1/4 teaspoon ground cinnamon
- salt to taste
- 1/4 cup fresh blueberries, or more to taste

Direction

- Put chia seeds in a bowl.
- In a blender, add in layers banana and dates. Put in almond milk, salt and cinnamon. Puree until smooth then dump onto chia seeds; stir well. Set aside for at least 15 minutes until thickened.
- Mix chia porridge and add blueberries on top.

Nutrition Information

- Calories: 385 calories;
- Total Fat: 12.5
- Sodium: 323
- Total Carbohydrate: 66.8
- Cholesterol: 0
- Protein: 7.7

798. Raw Chocolate Mousse

Serving: 2 | Prep: 10mins | Cook: | Ready in:

Ingredients

- 3/4 cup cashews
- 3 tablespoons agave syrup, or to taste
- 2 tablespoons cocoa powder, or to taste
- 2 tablespoons coconut cream

Direction

- In a blender, blend cashews for 2 minutes until it reaches consistency of smooth butter. Add coconut cream, cocoa powder, and agave syrup, blending until creamy and smooth.

Nutrition Information

- Calories: 465 calories;
- Total Fat: 27.6
- Sodium: 337
- Total Carbohydrate: 53.9
- Cholesterol: 0
- Protein: 9.1

799. Raw Vegan Gingerbread Balls

Serving: 20 | Prep: 10mins | Cook: | Ready in:

Ingredients

- 3/4 cup gluten-free rolled oats
- 1/2 cup almond flour
- 1 tablespoon ground cinnamon
- 1 teaspoon ground ginger
- 1/2 teaspoon ground nutmeg
- 1/2 teaspoon vanilla extract
- 1 1/4 cups dates, pitted and chopped
- 3 tablespoons coconut sugar

Direction

- Blend almond flour, nutmeg, ginger, vanilla extract, cinnamon, and rolled oats in a blender until smooth. Blend in dates, little by little, until it forms a soft dough. Shape the dough into 1-inch balls and roll the balls in coconut sugar.

Nutrition Information

- Calories: 71 calories;
- Sodium: 1
- Total Carbohydrate: 13.5
- Cholesterol: 0
- Protein: 1.4
- Total Fat: 1.8

800. Real Food Orange Cream Ice Pops

Serving: 6 | Prep: 15mins | Cook: | Ready in:

Ingredients

- 1 cup freshly squeezed orange juice
- 1 cup canned coconut milk
- 3 tablespoons raw honey
- 1/2 teaspoon pure vanilla extract
- 6 wooden pop sticks

Direction

- Whisk vanilla extract, honey, coconut milk and orange juice in bowl with spout/big measuring cup. Put mixture in small paper cups/ice pop molds. Add wooden pop sticks.
- Put in freezer for 8 hours to overnight till solid.

Nutrition Information

- Calories: 126 calories;
- Sodium: 6

- Total Carbohydrate: 14.1
- Cholesterol: 0
- Protein: 1.1
- Total Fat: 8.1

801. Refried Beans Without The Refry

Serving: 15 | Prep: 15mins | Cook: 8hours | Ready in:

Ingredients

- 1 onion, peeled and halved
- 3 cups dry pinto beans, rinsed
- 1/2 fresh jalapeno pepper, seeded and chopped
- 2 tablespoons minced garlic
- 5 teaspoons salt
- 1 3/4 teaspoons fresh ground black pepper
- 1/8 teaspoon ground cumin, optional
- 9 cups water

Direction

- In a slow cooker, put cumin, pepper, salt, garlic, jalapeño, rinsed beans and onion. Put in water and mix to combine. Cook for 8 hours on High and put in more water if needed. The temperature is too high if more than 1 cup of water has evaporated while cooking.
- Strain the beans when they are cooked but set aside the liquid. Use a potato masher to mash the beans. To attain desired consistency, put in more reserved water as needed while mashing.

Nutrition Information

- Calories: 139 calories;
- Protein: 8.5
- Total Fat: 0.5
- Sodium: 785
- Total Carbohydrate: 25.4
- Cholesterol: 0

802. Rich Vegan Kheer (Indian Rice Pudding)

Serving: 6 | Prep: 5mins | Cook: 40mins | Ready in:

Ingredients

- 1 1/2 cups water
- 1 cup basmati rice
- 1 cup rice milk
- 3/4 cup coconut milk
- 1/2 cup soy creamer
- 1/4 cup white sugar
- 1/4 teaspoon ground cardamom
- 1/3 cup raisins
- 1/3 cup sliced pistachios, toasted

Direction

- In a saucepan, boil the rice and water. Lower the heat to medium-low, put on cover and let it simmer for 20-25 minutes, until their water was absorbed, and the rice becomes tender.
- Pour the rice milk on top of the rice, then boil. Lower the heat to low and let it simmer for about 5 minutes until the mixture becomes a bit thick.
- Turn up the heat to medium and add cardamom, sugar, soy creamer and coconut milk, then return to a boil. Lower the heat to low once again and let it simmer for 5-10 minutes until it becomes thick.
- Take it out of the heat and mix in pistachios and raisins. Modify the sugar and flavoring to your preferred strength and serve it either cold or hot.

Nutrition Information

- Calories: 309 calories;
- Total Fat: 11.3
- Sodium: 57
- Total Carbohydrate: 48.8

- Cholesterol: 0
- Protein: 5.2

803. Roast Beef With Coffee

Serving: 5 | Prep: 20mins | Cook: 3hours | Ready in:

Ingredients

- 4 pounds chuck roast
- 5 cloves garlic, minced
- 1 1/2 cups prepared strong coffee
- 2 tablespoons cornstarch
- 1/2 cup water

Direction

- Start preheating the oven to 350°F (175°C) OR start preheating a slow cooker to low setting.
- Create 5-6 deep slits around top and side of roast with a sharp knife. Push down into slits with whole cloves of the garlic. Put the meat into a 10x15 inch roasting pan OR a slow cooker. Add coffee over meat.
- Bake at 350°F (175°C) for 2-3 hours OR cook in slow cooker on low setting for 6-8 hours.
- Discard from the oven OR slow cooker when the roast is done. Add drippings into the small saucepan over medium low heat. Combine water and cornstarch in the separate small bowl. Mix well and slowly put into the drippings, stirring constantly. Simmer until it is thickened.

Nutrition Information

- Calories: 754 calories;
- Total Fat: 48.7
- Sodium: 282
- Total Carbohydrate: 3.9
- Cholesterol: 236
- Protein: 70.1

804. Roast Pork With Maple And Mustard Glaze

Serving: 8 | Prep: 15mins | Cook: 1hours | Ready in:

Ingredients

- 2 1/2 pounds boneless pork loin roast
- 1 cup real maple syrup
- 4 tablespoons prepared Dijon-style mustard
- 2 1/2 tablespoons cider vinegar
- 2 1/2 tablespoons soy sauce
- salt to taste
- ground black pepper to taste

Direction

- Set oven to 175°C (or 350°F) and start preheating.
- In a small bowl, combine pepper, salt, soy sauce, vinegar, mustard and maple syrup. Put pork roast into a shallow roasting pan. Evenly spread glaze onto the pork roast.
- Roast pork for 60 minutes in the prepared oven without a cover, until the internal temperature of the meat registers 63°C (or 145°F). Take out of the oven, then let it stand for about 10 minutes; cut to serve.

Nutrition Information

- Calories: 290 calories;
- Sodium: 522
- Total Carbohydrate: 28.4
- Cholesterol: 68
- Protein: 24.4
- Total Fat: 8.2

805. Roasted Brussels Sprouts

Serving: 6 | Prep: 15mins | Cook: 45mins | Ready in:

Ingredients

- 1 1/2 pounds Brussels sprouts, ends trimmed and yellow leaves removed
- 3 tablespoons olive oil
- 1 teaspoon kosher salt
- 1/2 teaspoon freshly ground black pepper

Direction

- Set the oven to 400 deg F.
- In a large air-tight plastic container, add olive oil, kosher salt, and pepper together with trimmed Brussels sprouts. Cover tight and shake to mix thoroughly. Place on a baking sheet and set on the center oven rack.
- Cook for 30 to 45 minutes inside the oven, In 5 to 7 minute intervals, shake the pan to brown the sides evenly and adjust the heat as needed to avoid burning. If the Brussels sprouts appear dark brown to almost black, they are done. Remove from oven and add salt to taste. Serve right away.

Nutrition Information

- Calories: 104 calories;
- Sodium: 344
- Total Carbohydrate: 10
- Cholesterol: 0
- Protein: 2.9
- Total Fat: 7.3

806. Roasted Fall Vegetables

Serving: 2 | Prep: 15mins | Cook: 1hours | Ready in:

Ingredients

- 3 medium beets, peeled and cut into 1 inch cubes
- 1 large turnip, peeled and cubed
- 1 cup pearl onions, peeled
- 1/4 cup olive oil
- 1/2 teaspoon dried rosemary
- salt to taste

Direction

- Preheat an oven to 220°C/425°F.
- Put turnip and beets in 9x9-in. baking dish; slice X in root end of onions. Put into dish. Drizzle olive oil on veggies; add salt and rosemary. Mix to coat veggies with oil.
- In preheated oven, bake till veggies are tender and golden brown or for 1 hour then serve hot.

Nutrition Information

- Calories: 368 calories;
- Total Fat: 27.3
- Sodium: 119
- Total Carbohydrate: 30.2
- Cholesterol: 0
- Protein: 3.7

807. Roasted Garlic

Serving: 15 | Prep: 5mins | Cook: 1hours | Ready in:

Ingredients

- 10 medium heads garlic
- 3 tablespoons olive oil

Direction

- Preheat an oven to 200 degrees C (400 degrees F).
- Spread heads of garlic onto a baking sheet. Drizzle olive oil onto garlic. Bake for about 40 minutes to 1 hour. The garlic is done when it's soft and squeezable. Take out, cool and then serve.

Nutrition Information

- Calories: 79 calories;
- Total Fat: 2.9

- Sodium: 6
- Total Carbohydrate: 12.3
- Cholesterol: 0
- Protein: 2.4

808. Roasted Lemon Herb Chicken

Serving: 8 | Prep: 15mins | Cook: 1hours30mins | Ready in:

Ingredients

- 2 teaspoons Italian seasoning
- 1/2 teaspoon seasoning salt
- 1/2 teaspoon mustard powder
- 1 teaspoon garlic powder
- 1/2 teaspoon ground black pepper
- 1 (3 pound) whole chicken
- 2 lemons
- 2 tablespoons olive oil

Direction

- Start preheating the oven at 350°F (175°C).
- Mix black pepper, garlic powder, mustard powder, salt, and seasoning; put aside. Wash the chicken thoroughly, then remove the giblets. In a 9x13-inch baking dish, place the chicken. Scatter 1 1/2 teaspoons of the spice mixture inside the chicken. Rub the leftover mixture on the outside of the chicken.
- Squeeze the juice from 2 lemons into a small bowl or cup and combine with olive oil. Sprinkle the oil-juice mixture over the chicken.
- Bake in the prepared oven for 1 1/2 hours until juices run clear, basting several times with the remaining oil mixture.

Nutrition Information

- Calories: 405 calories;
- Total Carbohydrate: 3.6
- Cholesterol: 128

- Protein: 32.2
- Total Fat: 29.2
- Sodium: 178

809. Roasted Potatoes And Apples

Serving: 4 | Prep: 20mins | Cook: 30mins | Ready in:

Ingredients

- 1/4 cup apple cider vinegar
- 1 teaspoon soy sauce
- 3 tablespoons brown sugar
- 1 1/2 teaspoons yellow mustard
- 1 tablespoon paprika
- 1 teaspoon salt
- 1/4 cup olive oil
- 1 pound potatoes, scrubbed and cubed with skin
- 1 pound apples, cored and cut into wedges

Direction

- Set the oven for preheating to 400°F (200°C). Prepare and grease a 9x13 inch baking dish lightly.
- Combine together the soy sauce, vinegar, mustard, paprika, salt and brown sugar and whisk in a big bowl until well blended. Add in the olive oil and whisk until the consistency turns smooth, then add the apples and potatoes, and toss to coat. Pour over the mixture in the baking dish.
- Let it bake inside the oven for 30 to 35 minutes just until the potatoes turns golden brown and have softened.

Nutrition Information

- Calories: 313 calories;
- Sodium: 668
- Total Carbohydrate: 46.7
- Cholesterol: 0

- Protein: 2.9
- Total Fat: 14

810. Rocky Road Cake

Serving: 8 | Prep: 15mins | Cook: 35mins | Ready in:

Ingredients

- 1 1/2 cups all-purpose flour
- 1 cup white sugar
- 1/2 cup unsweetened cocoa powder
- 1 teaspoon baking soda
- 1/2 teaspoon salt
- 5 tablespoons vegetable oil
- 1 teaspoon vinegar
- 1 teaspoon vanilla extract
- 1 cup water
- 2 (1 ounce) squares unsweetened chocolate, chopped
- 1/4 cup margarine
- 1/4 cup water
- 1 teaspoon vanilla extract
- 2 cups confectioners' sugar
- 1 cup miniature marshmallows

Direction

- Set the oven to 175°C to 350°F to preheat. Sift together salt, baking soda, cocoa, sugar and flour, then sift one more time. Sift again into a 9-in. square pan.
- Create in the center a well, then measure in vanilla, vinegar and oil. Pour over all with water and use a fork to mix until the mixture is smooth.
- In the preheated oven, bake until a toothpick stuck in the center of cake exits clean, about 30-35 minutes. Let cake cool.
- For frosting: Mix together water, margarine and chocolate in a saucepan. Cook on low heat until smooth and melted. Take away from the heat and stir in confectioners' sugar and vanilla. Fold in miniature marshmallows and spread over cake.

Nutrition Information

- Calories: 502 calories;
- Total Carbohydrate: 84.4
- Cholesterol: 0
- Protein: 4.4
- Total Fat: 18.8
- Sodium: 380

811. Ronaldo's Beef Carnitas

Serving: 12 | Prep: 10mins | Cook: 4hours | Ready in:

Ingredients

- 4 pounds chuck roast
- 1 (4 ounce) can green chile peppers, chopped
- 2 tablespoons chili powder
- 1/2 teaspoon dried oregano
- 1/2 teaspoon ground cumin
- 2 cloves garlic, minced
- salt to taste

Direction

- Set the oven to 150°C or 300°F to preheat.
- On a heavy foil that is big enough to enclose the meat, position the roast. Mix together garlic, salt to taste, cumin, oregano, chili powder and green chile peppers in a small bowl. Mix well and rub the spice mixture over the meat.
- Wrap the meat entirely in foil and put in a roasting pan.
- Bake at 150°C or 300°F until the roast just falls apart using a fork, about 3 1/2-4 hours. Take out of the oven and use 2 forks to shred the meat.

Nutrition Information

- Calories: 218 calories;
- Total Fat: 13.8

- Sodium: 170
- Total Carbohydrate: 1.4
- Cholesterol: 70
- Protein: 20.8

812. Ruth's Grandma's Pie Crust

Serving: 32 | Prep: 10mins | Cook: |Ready in:

Ingredients

- 4 cups all-purpose flour
- 1 3/4 cups shortening
- 3 tablespoons white sugar
- 2 teaspoons salt
- 1 egg
- 1/2 cup water

Direction

- Mix salt, sugar, shortening and all-purpose flour in a large mixing bowl. Use a pastry cutter to blend together until crumbly.
- Mix egg with water in a small bowl. Mix into flour mixture. Chill in the fridge till ready to use.

Nutrition Information

- Calories: 163 calories;
- Protein: 1.8
- Total Fat: 11.5
- Sodium: 148
- Total Carbohydrate: 13.1
- Cholesterol: 6

813. Salmon Croquettes

Serving: 2 | Prep: 10mins | Cook: 10mins |Ready in:

Ingredients

- 1 (6 ounce) can salmon, drained and flaked
- 1 egg
- 1/4 cup finely chopped celery
- 1/4 cup sliced green onion
- 1 tablespoon chopped fresh dill weed
- 1/2 teaspoon garlic powder
- 1/3 cup wheat germ
- 3 tablespoons olive oil

Direction

- Combine the salmon, egg, green onion, celery, dill, and garlic powder in a medium bowl. Take each portion of the mixture and shape into balls the size of golf balls. Roll them to coat with wheat germ.
- Set the heat to medium and use a large skillet to heat the oil. Slightly flatten the balls, then let it fry for another 10 minutes to a golden brown color, turning if necessary.

Nutrition Information

- Calories: 435 calories;
- Protein: 27.9
- Total Fat: 30.9
- Sodium: 360
- Total Carbohydrate: 12.2
- Cholesterol: 130

814. Salsa II

Serving: 96 | Prep: 30mins | Cook: 20mins |Ready in:

Ingredients

- 6 pounds roma (plum) tomatoes
- 1/4 pound roma (plum) tomatoes, chopped
- 2 tablespoons garlic powder
- 1/4 cup lemon juice
- 1 1/2 tablespoons salt
- 1 tablespoon ground cayenne pepper
- 1 1/2 teaspoons ground cumin
- 1 red onion, chopped

- 1 white onion, chopped
- 1 yellow onion, chopped
- 1 pound jalapeno peppers, chopped
- 1/3 bunch fresh cilantro, chopped

Direction

- Boil a big saucepan of water, then briefly put 6 pounds of tomatoes into the water to loosen the skins and set the color. Strain, peel and crush.
- Mix the cumin, cayenne pepper, salt, lemon juice, garlic powder and chopped tomatoes into the saucepan with the crushed tomatoes; whip to the preferred thickness, then boil. Mix in cilantro, jalapeno peppers, yellow onion, white onion and red onion. Keep on boiling until the mixture reaches the preferred consistency and the vegetables become tender. Take out of the heat and chill in the fridge until ready to serve.

Nutrition Information

- Calories: 9 calories;
- Total Carbohydrate: 2
- Cholesterol: 0
- Protein: 0.4
- Total Fat: 0.1
- Sodium: 111

815.   Salsa Steak For One

Serving: 1 | Prep: 15mins | Cook: 40mins | Ready in:

Ingredients

- 1 (6 ounce) boneless beef top sirloin steak, cut 1 1/2 inches thick
- seasoned salt to taste
- 3 tablespoons water
- 1 cup prepared salsa
- 1 large potato, peeled and diced
- 1 carrot, peeled and chopped
- 1 small white onion, diced

Direction

- Set an oven to 175°C (350°F) and start preheating.
- Scatter the seasoned salt on both sides of steak. Arrange with 3 tablespoons of water in a foil-lined baking dish. Pour salsa on the steak and spread all around the pan with the chopped vegetables. Put a cover on and use foil to seal.
- In the prepared oven, bake until reaching the desired doneness, or for 1 hour. Serve right away.

Nutrition Information

- Calories: 613 calories;
- Total Fat: 16.5
- Sodium: 2142
- Total Carbohydrate: 81.8
- Cholesterol: 91
- Protein: 38.2

816.   Sarah's Applesauce

Serving: 4 | Prep: 10mins | Cook: 20mins | Ready in:

Ingredients

- 4 apples - peeled, cored and chopped
- 3/4 cup water
- 1/4 cup white sugar
- 1/2 teaspoon ground cinnamon

Direction

- In a pan, combine water, apples, sugar, and cinnamon. Cover, let it cook until apples are soft over medium heat, 15 to 20 minutes. Wait for it to cool, then mash using a fork or potato masher.

Nutrition Information

- Calories: 121 calories;
- Sodium: 3
- Total Carbohydrate: 31.8
- Cholesterol: 0
- Protein: 0.4
- Total Fat: 0.2

817. Sauteed Napa Cabbage

Serving: 2 | Prep: 5mins | Cook: 20mins | Ready in:

Ingredients

- 1 tablespoon olive oil
- 1 small onion, chopped
- 1 shredded napa cabbage
- 1 teaspoon white sugar
- 1 teaspoon ground ginger
- 1 teaspoon ground cumin
- salt and freshly ground black pepper to taste
- 1/2 cup sake
- 1/2 cup vegetable broth
- 1 tablespoon white balsamic vinegar, or to taste
- 2 tablespoons chopped fresh parsley

Direction

- In a big skillet, heat olive oil on medium low heat and cook onion for approximately 5 minutes, until translucent and softened. Put in napa cabbage and sprinkle with sugar, then blend well. Cook and stir on low heat for 3-5 minutes. Season with pepper, salt, cumin and ginger then cook for 1 minute longer.
- Add broth and sake into the skillet with cabbage and bring all to a boil. Lower the heat, cover and simmer for 10 minutes. Add balsamic vinegar and adjust seasoning to taste. Combine in parsley.

Nutrition Information

- Calories: 219 calories;
- Protein: 4.1
- Sodium: 221
- Total Carbohydrate: 19.4
- Cholesterol: 0
- Total Fat: 7.7

818. Sauteed Sugar Snap Peas With Mushrooms

Serving: 2 | Prep: 5mins | Cook: 10mins | Ready in:

Ingredients

- 2 tablespoons olive oil
- 4 fresh mushrooms, or more to taste, sliced
- salt to taste
- 20 sugar snap peas, or more to taste

Direction

- Prepare a sauté pan, heat over medium heat. Add olive oil. Use salt for seasoning mushrooms and sauté with olive oil for approximately 5 minutes till tender.
- During the time mushrooms are cooking, add water into a small pot and bring to a boil. Put sugar snap peas in; allow to cook for 1-2 minutes till bright green. Using a slotted spoon, remove sugar snap peas out of water and toss snap peas with mushrooms for 1-2 minutes in the pan. Use salt for seasoning and serve right away.

Nutrition Information

- Calories: 537 calories;
- Sodium: 80
- Total Carbohydrate: 72.9
- Cholesterol: 0
- Protein: 21.6
- Total Fat: 13.6

819. Scampi Style Scallops Over Linguine

Serving: 4 | Prep: 15mins | Cook: 25mins | Ready in:

Ingredients

- 1 (16 ounce) package linguine
- 1 (2 ounce) can anchovy fillets with oil
- 1/2 onion, minced
- 3/4 cup chicken stock
- 1/4 cup white wine
- 1 teaspoon minced garlic
- 1/2 teaspoon dried parsley
- 1/8 teaspoon seafood seasoning (such as Old Bay®)
- 12 ounces bay scallops
- salt and pepper to taste

Direction

- Add lightly salted water to a large pot and bring to a rolling boil over high heat. When the water is boiling, mix in the linguine, and bring back to a boil. Cook the pasta without a cover, stirring sometimes, until the pasta has heated through, but is still firm to the bite, approximately 11 minutes. In a colander set in the sink, drain the pasta well.
- Heat a large skillet over medium heat; cook while stirring the anchovies together with the oil in the skillet for about 2 minutes until the anchovies melt into the oil. Put in the onion and cook for 3 to 5 minutes until translucent. Mix in the seafood seasoning, parsley, garlic, wine and chicken stock; put the scallops into the liquid and use pepper and salt to season. Bring the mixture to a boil and cook for about 7 minutes until the scallops are opaque. Serve the scallops over the cooked linguine.

Nutrition Information

- Calories: 556 calories;
- Total Carbohydrate: 87.6
- Cholesterol: 60
- Protein: 39.5
- Total Fat: 4.6
- Sodium: 807

820. Schweinebraten Pork Roast

Serving: 12 | Prep: 10mins | Cook: 2hours30mins | Ready in:

Ingredients

- 1 1/2 teaspoons salt
- 1 pinch dried marjoram
- 1 pinch dried basil
- 1 teaspoon ground black pepper
- 1/2 teaspoon garlic powder
- 1 (5 pound) boneless pork loin roast
- 2 onions, coarsely chopped
- 1 1/2 cups light beer

Direction

- Set the oven to 175°C or 350°F to preheat.
- In a small bowl, mix together garlic powder, pepper, basil, marjoram and salt, then rub over all the pork roast with the spice mixture. Put roast into roasting pan and place onions around the roast. Add to pan with beer and place a cover on.
- In the preheated oven, roast the pork for half an hour. Take off the cover and turn over the meat. Keep on roasting while checking for its doneness after each half an hour. Put in more liquid in case the pan runs dry. Roast for about 2 hours, until the meat's internal temperature registers 180°.

Nutrition Information

- Calories: 176 calories;
- Sodium: 331
- Total Carbohydrate: 2.5
- Cholesterol: 66
- Protein: 22.2

- Total Fat: 7.3

821. Seasoned Rice

Serving: 5 | Prep: 5mins | Cook: 25mins | Ready in:

Ingredients

- 1 cup Basmati rice
- 3 2/3 cups water, divided
- 2 tablespoons soy margarine
- 2 tablespoons nutritional yeast
- 1/2 teaspoon garlic powder
- 1 1/2 teaspoons dried basil
- salt to taste

Direction

- Bring 3 cups of water in a saucepan to a boil. Put in rice and stir. Lower the heat, then cover and simmer until rice is cooked and liquid is entirely absorbed, or for 20 minutes.
- In a big saucepan, melt margarine on medium heat. Stir in salt, basil, garlic powder, nutritional yeast and the remaining 2/3 cup of water, then heat for 5 minutes. Stir in cooked rice and cook for around 2 minutes, until heated through.

Nutrition Information

- Calories: 185 calories;
- Total Fat: 5.1
- Sodium: 54
- Total Carbohydrate: 30.8
- Cholesterol: 0
- Protein: 4.6

822. Serbian Cevapcici

Serving: 4 | Prep: 10mins | Cook: 30mins | Ready in:

Ingredients

- 1 1/2 pounds ground pork
- 1 pound lean ground beef
- 1/2 pound ground lamb
- 1 egg white
- 4 cloves garlic, minced
- 1 teaspoon salt
- 1 teaspoon baking soda
- 2 teaspoons ground black pepper
- 1 teaspoon cayenne pepper
- 1/2 teaspoon paprika

Direction

- Prepare the grill by preheating at medium-low heat.
- Mix the ground beef, egg white, ground pork, and the ground lamb in a big bowl. Toss in salt, baking soda, cayenne pepper, paprika, garlic, and black pepper. Use your hands to blend mixture well. Mold mixture into a sausage shapes the length of a finger and 3/4 inch thick.
- On grilling surface, lightly oil. For 30 minutes, grill sausages while flipping as necessary until cooked completely.

Nutrition Information

- Calories: 690 calories;
- Total Fat: 46.1
- Sodium: 1097
- Total Carbohydrate: 2.1
- Cholesterol: 223
- Protein: 62.8

823. Sesame Green Beans

Serving: 4 | Prep: 5mins | Cook: 25mins | Ready in:

Ingredients

- 1 tablespoon olive oil
- 1 tablespoon sesame seeds

- 1 pound fresh green beans, cut into 2 inch pieces
- 1/4 cup chicken broth
- 1/4 teaspoon salt
- freshly ground black pepper to taste

Direction

- In a big skillet or wok, heat oil on medium heat. Put in sesame seeds. Once seeds begin to darken, stir in green beans. Cook and stir until the beans have bright green color.
- Add pepper, salt and chicken broth. Cover and cook for around 10 minutes, until beans are crisp-tender. Uncover and cook until liquid evaporates.

Nutrition Information

- Calories: 78 calories;
- Total Fat: 4.6
- Sodium: 152
- Total Carbohydrate: 8.6
- Cholesterol: 0
- Protein: 2.5

824. Sesame Noodles

Serving: 8 | Prep: 15mins | Cook: 15mins | Ready in:

Ingredients

- 1 (16 ounce) package linguine pasta
- 6 cloves garlic, minced
- 6 tablespoons sugar
- 6 tablespoons safflower oil
- 6 tablespoons rice vinegar
- 6 tablespoons soy sauce
- 2 tablespoons sesame oil
- 2 teaspoons chili sauce
- 6 green onions, sliced
- 1 teaspoon sesame seeds, toasted

Direction

- Boil a pot of lightly salted water. Add pasta; cook for 8-10 minutes till al dente. Drain; put in a serving bowl.
- Meanwhile, put a saucepan on medium high heat. Mix in chili sauce, sesame oil, soy sauce, vinegar, oil, sugar and garlic; boil till sugar melts, constantly mixing. Put sauce on linguine; toss till coated. Garnish with sesame seeds and green onions.

Nutrition Information

- Calories: 371 calories;
- Cholesterol: 0
- Protein: 7.9
- Total Fat: 14.8
- Sodium: 699
- Total Carbohydrate: 52

825. Sesame Raisin Cookies

Serving: 8 | Prep: | Cook: | Ready in:

Ingredients

- 3/4 cup water
- 1/2 cup raisins
- 1/2 cup sesame seeds
- 1 cup brown rice flour
- 1 1/4 cups rolled oats
- 1/4 teaspoon salt
- 1 1/8 cups unsweetened apple juice
- 2 tablespoons vegetable oil
- 1 teaspoon vanilla extract

Direction

- Preheat the oven to 175 degrees C (350 degrees F).
- Boil three-quarter cup of the water and put in raisins. Once water is back to a boil, switch off heat. Allow raisins to plump for no less than 10 minutes. Drain raisins well, and then cut them coarsely.

- Toast sesame seeds by whisking them using a wooden spoon in a heavy sauté pan on medium heat. Sauté for roughly 10 minutes till seeds start to crackle, pop and smells toasted.
- Mix the toasted sesame seeds, salt, oats and rice flour. Whisk the vanilla, oil, and apple-juice into flour mixture.
- Shape the dough into 8 big balls. Arrange each ball onto the greased cookie sheets or parchment paper. Moisten the fingers and flatten each of the balls till reaching half an inch in thickness.
- Bake till turning golden-brown or for 25 minutes. Allow it to cool down on the pans prior to taking out.

Nutrition Information

- Calories: 238 calories;
- Total Carbohydrate: 35.2
- Cholesterol: 0
- Protein: 4.8
- Total Fat: 9.3
- Sodium: 77

826. Shakshooka

Serving: 6 | Prep: 30mins | Cook: 25mins | Ready in:

Ingredients

- 2 tablespoons olive oil
- 4 cloves garlic, thinly sliced
- 1 onion, chopped
- 1 jalapeno pepper, sliced
- 1 large red bell pepper, chopped
- 2 tomatoes, coarsely chopped
- 2 tablespoons sweet paprika
- 2 tablespoons hot paprika
- salt and pepper to taste
- 1 (6 ounce) can tomato paste
- 3/4 cup water
- 1/4 teaspoon saffron
- 1/4 cup chopped fresh parsley
- 6 eggs

Direction

- Heat olive oil on medium heat in a skillet. Mix in jalapeno, onion and garlic; mix and cook for 5 minutes till onion is translucent and soft. Add tomatoes and bell pepper.
- Cook veggies for 10 minutes till tomatoes release their juices and break down; mix in pepper, salt, hot paprika and sweet paprika. Simmer for 3 minutes then add water and tomato paste; stir well.
- Add parsley and saffron when veggies get a sauce-like consistency. Crack eggs over sauce like prepping sunny side up eggs; cover pan. Cook eggs till yolks reach preferred consistency for 10-15 minutes.

Nutrition Information

- Calories: 176 calories;
- Cholesterol: 164
- Protein: 8.8
- Total Fat: 9.9
- Sodium: 295
- Total Carbohydrate: 16.3

827. Shiitake Mushroom Ceviche

Serving: 2 | Prep: 15mins | Cook: 5mins | Ready in:

Ingredients

- 1 (8 ounce) package fresh shiitake mushrooms
- 1 tomato, chopped
- 1/2 onion, chopped
- 9 pitted green olives, chopped
- 1/2 teaspoon dried oregano
- 1/2 orange, juiced
- 1 lime, juiced
- 1 tablespoon Mexican-style hot sauce (such as Cholula®), or to taste

- 1 1/2 teaspoons apple cider vinegar
- salt to taste

Direction

- Bring salted water in a pot to a boil. Put in shiitake mushrooms and boil for a minute, then take away from the heat and drain. Rinse under cold water and allow to cool about 10 minutes.
- Chop the mushrooms as though they were fish for ceviche and put them into a glass bowl. Put in dried oregano, olives, onion and tomato.
- In a separate bowl, combine together vinegar, Mexican hot sauce, ketchup, lime juice and orange juice, then drizzle over the mushrooms. Put in salt and blend carefully. Chill for 20 minutes to let the flavors blend.

Nutrition Information

- Calories: 133 calories;
- Total Fat: 2.6
- Sodium: 715
- Total Carbohydrate: 23.5
- Cholesterol: 0
- Protein: 4.7

828. Short Cut Mexican Fideo (Vermicelli)

Serving: 4 | Prep: 10mins | Cook: 15mins | Ready in:

Ingredients

- 1 tablespoon canola oil
- 2 tablespoons minced onion
- 7 ounces vermicelli pasta
- 4 cups chicken stock
- 2 cubes tomato-flavored bouillon

Direction

- In a big saucepan, heat the oil on medium high heat. Cook and stir the onion in the hot oil for a minute. Stir in the vermicelli and cook for about 3 minutes, until turn golden brown. Put in bouillon cubes and stock then cover. Simmer for 10 to 11 minutes, until the vermicelli in softened.

Nutrition Information

- Calories: 219 calories;
- Sodium: 693
- Total Carbohydrate: 37.2
- Cholesterol: < 1
- Protein: 7.2
- Total Fat: 5.3

829. Shrimp Creole IV

Serving: 6 | Prep: 1hours10mins | Cook: 1hours5mins | Ready in:

Ingredients

- 3 pounds medium shrimp - peeled, deveined and shells reserved
- 1/2 onion, chopped
- 1 carrot, finely chopped
- 2 strips celery, chopped
- 4 cups water
- 1/3 cup bacon grease
- 2 onions, chopped
- 2 strips celery, chopped
- 1 tablespoon minced garlic
- 1 large chopped green bell pepper
- 2 bay leaves
- salt to taste
- 1 1/2 teaspoons freshly ground black pepper
- 2 teaspoons brown sugar
- 1 teaspoon cayenne pepper
- 1 teaspoon hot pepper sauce (e.g. Tabasco™), or to taste
- 1 teaspoon dried rosemary
- 1 teaspoon dried thyme
- 1 teaspoon dried basil
- 4 tomatoes, chopped

- 2 cups canned tomato sauce
- 1 cup chopped green onion

Direction

- In a medium stockpot, mix 4 cups of water, 2 strips celery, 1 carrot, 1/2 onion, and the reserved shrimp shells. Simmer for 1 hour, without covering; stirring from time to time. In a smaller saucepan, strain the stock, boil and reduce to 2 cups. Turn off the heat.
- Heat grease in a heavy skillet over medium heat. Add green bell pepper, garlic, celery, and onions; sauté until tender and starts to caramelize around the edges.
- Add 2 cups of reduced shrimp stock, hot sauce, cayenne pepper, brown sugar, black pepper, salt, and bay leaves. Heat to a boil and add tomato sauce, tomatoes, crushed basil, crushed thyme, and crushed rosemary.
- Simmer, covered, on low/medium heat for 1 hour, stirring from time to time.
- Put in the cleaned and deveined shrimp. Stir, cover and turn off the heat. Allow the shrimp to sit for 15 to 20 minutes until pink throughout. Top with green onions.

Nutrition Information

- Calories: 428 calories;
- Cholesterol: 358
- Protein: 41.3
- Total Fat: 17.7
- Sodium: 1234
- Total Carbohydrate: 26.7

830. Shrimp Marinaders

Serving: 8 | Prep: 10mins | Cook: 12hours | Ready in:

Ingredients

- 3/4 cup vegetable oil
- 2/3 cup vinegar
- 2 teaspoons hot pepper sauce
- 3 teaspoons celery seed
- 1 teaspoon salt
- 2 large onions, chopped
- 1 1/2 pounds cooked shrimp, peeled and deveined without tail

Direction

- Mix together salt, celery seed, hot sauce, vinegar and oil in a big glass or stainless steel mixing bowl. Combine well. Bring in shrimp and chopped onion into the oil mixture. Toss to incorporate thoroughly. Make sure to not use an aluminum mixing bowl because high acid content in vinegar reacts with aluminum and can possibly intoxicate the food.
- Refrigerate overnight.

Nutrition Information

- Calories: 285 calories;
- Protein: 18.5
- Total Fat: 21.6
- Sodium: 515
- Total Carbohydrate: 4.2
- Cholesterol: 166

831. Shrimp And Garlic

Serving: 10 | Prep: 20mins | Cook: | Ready in:

Ingredients

- 2 pounds cooked medium shrimp, peeled and deveined without tail
- 1 green bell pepper, finely chopped
- 1 red bell pepper, finely chopped
- 5 cloves garlic, minced
- 1 sweet onion, diced
- chopped fresh cilantro
- 1 avocado - peeled, pitted and diced
- salt and pepper to taste
- 1/2 cup olive oil

- chili pepper flakes

Direction

- Bring shrimp into a large mixing bowl, along with avocado, cilantro, onion, garlic, green and red bell peppers. Stream olive oil on top, and add pepper and salt to season. Refrigerate, covered, for at least 60 minutes until flavors develop. Serve chilled.

Nutrition Information

- Calories: 231 calories;
- Sodium: 323
- Total Carbohydrate: 4.7
- Cholesterol: 177
- Protein: 19.9
- Total Fat: 14.9

832. Simple Lemon Herb Chicken

Serving: 2 | Prep: 10mins | Cook: 15mins | Ready in:

Ingredients

- 2 skinless, boneless chicken breast halves
- 1 lemon
- salt and pepper to taste
- 1 tablespoon olive oil
- 1 pinch dried oregano
- 2 sprigs fresh parsley, for garnish

Direction

- Cut the lemon in half, and squeeze out juice from 1/2 lemon onto the chicken. Add in salt for seasoning. Allow to stand. Meanwhile, in a small skillet heat oil over medium low heat.
- Once the oil is hot, place in chicken. While sautéing the chicken, add juice from the other 1/2 lemon, oregano and pepper to taste. Sauté until juices run clear, about 5 - 10 minutes per side. Garnish with parsley and serve.

Nutrition Information

- Calories: 212 calories;
- Total Fat: 8.6
- Sodium: 94
- Total Carbohydrate: 7.9
- Cholesterol: 68
- Protein: 28.8

833. Simple Parsnip Pancakes

Serving: 2 | Prep: 10mins | Cook: 15mins | Ready in:

Ingredients

- 1 cup grated peeled parsnips
- 2 small eggs
- 1/4 cup finely chopped onion
- 1 tablespoon olive oil
- 1/2 teaspoon salt
- 1/2 teaspoon dried rosemary
- ground black pepper to taste (optional)
- 1 teaspoon sunflower oil, or more as needed

Direction

- In a bowl, mix together black pepper, rosemary, salt, olive oil, onion, eggs and parsnips till batter is blended and lumpy.
- In a heavy frying pan, heat the sunflower oil over medium heat. Into oil, scoop the batter and fry for 6 to 7 minutes each side till pancakes turn brown and the edges are crispy.

Nutrition Information

- Calories: 194 calories;
- Total Fat: 13
- Sodium: 641
- Total Carbohydrate: 14.7
- Cholesterol: 138
- Protein: 5.8

834. Simply Guacamole

Serving: 20 | Prep: 25mins | Cook: | Ready in:

Ingredients

- 5 avocados - peeled, pitted, and mashed
- 2 tablespoons fresh lemon juice
- 3/4 cup minced green onion
- 1/2 cup minced fresh cilantro
- salt and pepper, to taste

Direction

- Get a serving bowl then mix together the lemon juice and avocado in it; stir in the cilantro and green onion; blend well. Add pepper and salt to taste. Cover the bowl using a plastic wrap then place inside the refrigerator with avocado seeds in the bowl to prevent browning or you can serve it right away.

Nutrition Information

- Calories: 82 calories;
- Total Fat: 7.4
- Sodium: 5
- Total Carbohydrate: 4.7
- Cholesterol: 0
- Protein: 1.1

835. Simply Delicious Tamari Almond Green Beans

Serving: 4 | Prep: 5mins | Cook: 10mins | Ready in:

Ingredients

- 1 (16 ounce) package frozen French-cut green beans
- 1/3 cup almonds
- 1/4 cup tamari

Direction

- Use the cooking spray to spray one skillet slightly and place on medium heat. Add green beans into skillet; cook and whisk for roughly 8 minutes till thoroughly cooked. Put in tamari and almonds. Keep cooking and whisking till green beans turn brown slightly.

Nutrition Information

- Calories: 93 calories;
- Total Fat: 4
- Sodium: 997
- Total Carbohydrate: 9.8
- Cholesterol: 0
- Protein: 5

836. Slow Cooked Corned Beef For Sandwiches

Serving: 15 | Prep: 15mins | Cook: 4hours | Ready in:

Ingredients

- 2 (3 pound) corned beef briskets with spice packets
- 2 (12 fluid ounce) bottles beer
- 2 bay leaves
- 1/4 cup peppercorns
- 1 bulb garlic cloves, separated and peeled

Direction

- In a large pot, put the corned beef briskets. Add in one of spice packets, keep for future use or discard the other one. Add in the beer, then pour water in the pot, sufficient to cover the briskets by an inch. Put garlic cloves, peppercorns and bay leaves. Put cover, boil.
- When liquid boils, lower heat to medium-low, let simmer, checking hourly, for 4 to 5 hours, to keep the meat covered, add extra water if needed.

- Gently take meat out of the pot, as it will be extremely tender. Place on a cutting board, and let it rest for 10 minutes till it firms up a little. Shred or cut, then serve. Cooking liquid can be kept and use to cook other vegetables like cabbage or thrown away.

Nutrition Information

- Calories: 229 calories;
- Total Carbohydrate: 4.2
- Cholesterol: 78
- Protein: 15
- Total Fat: 15.1
- Sodium: 904

837. Slow Cooked Pork Barbeque

Serving: 4 | Prep: 10mins | Cook: 8hours | Ready in:

Ingredients

- 4 pork chops
- 1 (18 ounce) bottle barbeque sauce
- salt and pepper to taste

Direction

- In the slow cooker, put the chops and pour a bottle of your preferred barbeque sauce on top. Mix the sauce all over the chops using your hands and make sure that they are very well coated. Put cover on and cook for 8 hours on low.

Nutrition Information

- Calories: 304 calories;
- Total Fat: 6.6
- Sodium: 1431
- Total Carbohydrate: 45.7
- Cholesterol: 37
- Protein: 13.8

838. Slow Cooker Adobo Chicken

Serving: 6 | Prep: 30mins | Cook: 8hours | Ready in:

Ingredients

- 1 small sweet onion, sliced
- 8 cloves garlic, crushed
- 3/4 cup low sodium soy sauce
- 1/2 cup vinegar
- 1 (3 pound) whole chicken, cut into pieces

Direction

- In a slow cooker, put the chicken. Combine vinegar, soy sauce, garlic, and onion in a small bowl, and add to the chicken. Cook for 6-8 hours on low.

Nutrition Information

- Calories: 254 calories;
- Sodium: 1121
- Total Carbohydrate: 5.3
- Cholesterol: 61
- Protein: 23
- Total Fat: 14.7

839. Slow Cooker Barbecue Beans

Serving: 8 | Prep: 15mins | Cook: 6hours | Ready in:

Ingredients

- 1 pound lean ground beef
- 3/4 cup chopped raw bacon
- 1 small onion, finely chopped
- 2 (16 ounce) cans baked beans with pork

- 1 (15.25 ounce) can red kidney beans, with liquid
- 1 (15 ounce) can lima beans, partially drained
- 1 cup ketchup
- 1 tablespoon liquid smoke flavoring
- 1 tablespoon salt
- 1 tablespoon hot sauce
- 1/4 tablespoon garlic powder

Direction

- In a big and deep skillet, cook beef over medium-high heat until completely brown. Discard then put aside. In a big and deep skillet, cook bacon over medium-high heat until completely brown, Discard then put aside. Mix onion, salt, ketchup, kidney beans, lima beans, baked beans, hot sauce, liquid smoke, garlic powder, bacon and ground beef. Let it cook in low fire for 4 to 6 hours,

Nutrition Information

- Calories: 472 calories;
- Total Fat: 18.4
- Sodium: 2150
- Total Carbohydrate: 53.2
- Cholesterol: 60
- Protein: 25

840. Slow Cooker Chicken Curry With Coconut Milk

Serving: 3 | Prep: 10mins | Cook: 4hours10mins | Ready in:

Ingredients

- 2 boneless chicken breasts, cubed
- 1 (14.5 ounce) can diced tomatoes
- 1/2 (14 ounce) can coconut milk
- 2 medium carrots, sliced
- 1 onion, finely chopped
- 1 clove garlic, minced
- 2 tablespoons mild curry paste
- 1 tablespoon finely ground almonds
- 1 small bunch chopped fresh cilantro
- 1 tablespoon cornstarch
- 1 tablespoon water, or as needed
- 1/4 cup sliced almonds
- 1 1/2 cups uncooked white rice

Direction

- Mix together 4/5 of the cilantro, ground almonds, curry paste, garlic, onion, carrots, coconut milk, tomatoes and chicken in a slow cooker and close the lid.
- Cook on high for about 4 hours, until chicken is cooked through. If sauce is too thin, in a small bowl, stir cornstarch with water and blend into the sauce. Cook for 10 minutes more.
- In the meantime, bring 3 cups water and rice to a boil in a saucepan. Lower the heat to medium-low, cover up, and let it simmer for 20 to 25 minutes until the rice gets tender and water has been absorbed.
- Serve the curry over rice, use the rest of cilantro and sliced almonds to sprinkle.

Nutrition Information

- Calories: 707 calories;
- Total Fat: 21.9
- Sodium: 584
- Total Carbohydrate: 97.6
- Cholesterol: 43
- Protein: 28.4

841. Slow Cooker Chile Verde

Serving: 8 | Prep: 20mins | Cook: 8hours | Ready in:

Ingredients

- 3 tablespoons olive oil
- 1/2 cup onion, chopped

- 2 cloves garlic, minced
- 3 pounds boneless pork shoulder, cubed
- 5 (7 ounce) cans green salsa
- 1 (4 ounce) can diced jalapeno peppers
- 1 (14.5 ounce) can diced tomatoes

Direction

- Heat the oil over medium heat in a big skillet or Dutch oven. Put in the garlic and onion; cook and mix until fragrant. Put in cubed pork then cook until the outside is browned. Move the garlic, onions, and pork to a slow cooker and mix in the tomatoes, jalapeno peppers, and green salsa.
- Cover and cook for 3 hours on High. Lower setting to low then cook for another 4 to 5 hours.

Nutrition Information

- Calories: 265 calories;
- Total Fat: 12.4
- Sodium: 765
- Total Carbohydrate: 12.1
- Cholesterol: 64
- Protein: 22.5

842. Slow Cooker Cider Pork Roast

Serving: 8 | Prep: 30mins | Cook: 7hours | Ready in:

Ingredients

- 1 large onion, roughly chopped
- 1 apple, peeled and roughly chopped
- 3 cloves garlic
- 2 cups apple cider
- 1 1/2 cups water
- salt, or to taste
- 1/2 teaspoon ground black pepper, or to taste
- 1/2 teaspoon ground ginger
- 1/4 cup all-purpose flour
- 1 (3 pound) pork loin roast
- 2 teaspoons vegetable oil
- 1 stalk celery, roughly chopped
- 4 large carrots, roughly chopped

Direction

- In a food processor bowl, mix garlic with 1/2 of the apple and 1/4 of the onion. Process until it's smooth. Put into a slow cooker along with water and apple cider.
- Season roast with pepper and salt. In a shallow container, mix the flour and ginger. Press the roast gently on the flour blend to coat all sides. Brush off any extra flour. In a big heavy skillet, heat the oil. Brown the pork in hot oil, flipping until golden on all sides. In the slow cooker, put the browned roast and scatter the leftover apple, leftover onion and celery on top. Cook for 4 hours on low; add in the carrots. Cook for another 3 hours.
- Place carrots and cooked roast to a heated plate. Thicken cooking juices from the slow cooker to make a gravy, if desired.

Nutrition Information

- Calories: 235 calories;
- Total Fat: 7.9
- Sodium: 509
- Total Carbohydrate: 19.5
- Cholesterol: 60
- Protein: 20.9

843. Slow Cooker German Style Pork Roast With Sauerkraut And Potatoes

Serving: 8 | Prep: 20mins | Cook: 8hours | Ready in:

Ingredients

- 6 white potatoes, peeled and quartered
- 1 tablespoon minced garlic

- salt and pepper to taste
- 1 (3 pound) boneless pork loin roast
- 1 (32 ounce) jar sauerkraut with liquid
- 2 teaspoons caraway seeds

Direction

- In a slow cooker, put pepper, salt, garlic and potatoes; mix to coat. Use pepper and salt to season the pork roast; put on top of the potatoes. Pour over the roast with the sauerkraut, sprinkle caraway seeds over.
- Cook in the slow cooker for 8-10 hours on Low.

Nutrition Information

- Calories: 385 calories;
- Total Fat: 15.2
- Sodium: 810
- Total Carbohydrate: 30.5
- Cholesterol: 83
- Protein: 31.3

844. Slow Cooker Kielbasa And Beer

Serving: 8 | Prep: 10mins | Cook: 6hours | Ready in:

Ingredients

- 2 pounds kielbasa sausage, cut into 1 inch pieces
- 1 (12 fluid ounce) can or bottle beer
- 1 (20 ounce) can sauerkraut, drained

Direction

- Mix the beer, sauerkraut and sausage together in a slow cooker. Allow the mixture to cook for 5-6 hours on low setting until the sausage has softened and bulged.

Nutrition Information

- Calories: 383 calories;
- Cholesterol: 75
- Protein: 14.7
- Total Fat: 31.1
- Sodium: 1491
- Total Carbohydrate: 7.8

845. Slow Cooker Roast Beef

Serving: 6 | Prep: 5mins | Cook: 22hours | Ready in:

Ingredients

- 1/3 cup soy sauce
- 1 (1 ounce) package dry onion soup mix
- 3 pounds beef chuck roast
- 2 teaspoons freshly ground black pepper

Direction

- Pour the dry onion soup mix and soy sauce into the slow cooker, then stir well. Put the chuck toast into the slow cooker, then pour water until the top 1/2-inch of the roast is not covered. Sprinkle with ground pepper.
- Put on cover and let it cook for 22 hours on low.

Nutrition Information

- Calories: 555 calories;
- Total Carbohydrate: 4.4
- Cholesterol: 161
- Protein: 40.4
- Total Fat: 40.8
- Sodium: 1369

846. Slow Cooker Spicy Black Eyed Peas

Serving: 10 | Prep: 30mins | Cook: 6hours | Ready in:

Ingredients

- 6 cups water
- 1 cube chicken bouillon
- 1 pound dried black-eyed peas, sorted and rinsed
- 1 onion, diced
- 2 cloves garlic, diced
- 1 red bell pepper, stemmed, seeded, and diced
- 1 jalapeno chile, seeded and minced
- 8 ounces diced ham
- 4 slices bacon, chopped
- 1/2 teaspoon cayenne pepper
- 1 1/2 teaspoons cumin
- salt, to taste
- 1 teaspoon ground black pepper

Direction

- In a slow cooker, pour the water then add the bouillon cube and mix until it dissolves. Mix together the pepper, salt, cumin, cayenne pepper, bacon, ham, jalapeno pepper, bell pepper, garlic, onion and black-eyed peas and mix to combine. Cover the slow cooker and let it cook for 6-8 hours on Low, until the beans become tender.

Nutrition Information

- Calories: 199 calories;
- Total Fat: 2.9
- Sodium: 341
- Total Carbohydrate: 30.2
- Cholesterol: 10
- Protein: 14.1

847. Slow Cooker Wieners In Wiener BBQ Sauce

Serving: 7 | Prep: 10mins | Cook: 1hours | Ready in:

Ingredients

- 2 pounds hot dogs
- 1 (18 ounce) jar grape jelly
- 1 (8 ounce) jar prepared mustard
- 1 tablespoon brown sugar
- 1 tablespoon apple cider vinegar

Direction

- In a slow cooker, add the wieners. Mix together cider vinegar, brown sugar, mustard and grape jelly in a medium bowl. Blend well and drizzle over the wieners.
- On low setting, cook wieners for a minimum of an hour prior to serving.

Nutrition Information

- Calories: 633 calories;
- Cholesterol: 67
- Protein: 16.8
- Total Fat: 39.6
- Sodium: 1813
- Total Carbohydrate: 53.9

848. Smoked Salmon Deviled Eggs

Serving: 12 | Prep: 15mins | Cook: 15mins | Ready in:

Ingredients

- 6 eggs
- 1 ounce smoked salmon, finely chopped
- 1 tablespoon mayonnaise
- 1 1/2 teaspoons fresh lemon juice
- 1 1/2 teaspoons prepared yellow mustard
- 1 teaspoon dried dill weed
- 1/2 teaspoon salt
- 1 pinch ground black pepper
- 1/4 teaspoon dried dill weed, for garnish
- 1 pinch paprika, for garnish

Direction

- In a saucepan, lay eggs in a single layer and add water to cover by 1 inch. Cover the saucepan and bring to a boil over high heat. As soon as the water is boiling, remove from the heat and allow the eggs to sit for 15 minutes in the hot water. Pour hot water out, then run cold water over eggs in the sink to cool. Once cold, remove eggshells.
- Slice eggs in half lengthways and scoop yolks out of eggs. In a small mixing bowl, place yolks and use a fork to mash. Stir pepper, salt, a teaspoon of dried dill, yellow mustard, lemon juice, mayonnaise, and smoked salmon in, mix well.
- Fill the egg whites with yolk mixture and use a bit of extra dried dill and paprika to dredge on.
- Carefully use plastic wrap to cover and let sit in the refrigerator until ready to serve.

Nutrition Information

- Calories: 47 calories;
- Total Fat: 3.5
- Sodium: 196
- Total Carbohydrate: 0.4
- Cholesterol: 93
- Protein: 3.6

849. Smoked Turkey

Serving: 18 | Prep: 30mins | Cook: 6hours | Ready in:

Ingredients

- 1 (12 pound) whole turkey, neck and giblets removed
- 1 (20 pound) bag high quality charcoal briquettes
- hickory chips or chunks

Direction

- Brush the grate lightly with oil. Light the coals on the bottom pan of the smoker. Wait till the temperature to reach 240 degrees F (115 degrees C).
- Under cold water, rinse the turkey thoroughly, then pat dry with paper towels. Soak hickory chips in a pan with water.
- Put the turkey on the oiled grate. Toss 2 handfuls of soaked hickory chips before cooking and add a handful every 2 hours throughout the cooking process. DO NOT let the heat out by checking the turkey every now and then. You can cook the turkey till the coals die out or check the internal temperature of the turkey. It should be 165 degrees F (74 degrees C).

Nutrition Information

- Calories: 447 calories;
- Sodium: 146
- Total Carbohydrate: 0
- Cholesterol: 176
- Protein: 60.4
- Total Fat: 20.9

850. Snappy Green Beans

Serving: 4 | Prep: 5mins | Cook: 25mins | Ready in:

Ingredients

- 6 slices bacon
- 1 cup chopped onions
- 3 tablespoons distilled white vinegar
- 1 (15 ounce) can cut green beans, drained

Direction

- In a deep, big skillet, put the bacon, then cook on medium-high heat until it turns brown evenly. Let it drain, crumble and put aside.
- Sauté the onions in the bacon grease, then add the vinegar and sauté until the onions become tender. Add the green beans and let it cook until heated through, then crumble the bacon on top.

Nutrition Information

- Calories: 225 calories;
- Total Fat: 19
- Sodium: 649
- Total Carbohydrate: 7.2
- Cholesterol: 29
- Protein: 6.2

851. Snickerdoodles I

Serving: 36 | Prep: 15mins | Cook: 10mins | Ready in:

Ingredients

- 1 cup shortening
- 1 1/2 cups white sugar
- 2 eggs
- 2 3/4 cups all-purpose flour
- 1 teaspoon baking soda
- 2 teaspoons cream of tartar
- 1/2 teaspoon salt
- 2 tablespoons white sugar
- 2 teaspoons ground cinnamon

Direction

- Preheat an oven to 190°C/375°F.
- Cream 1 1/2 cups sugar and shortening in a medium bowl; mix in eggs. Sift salt, cream of tartar, baking soda and flour together; mix into creamed mixture till blended well. Mix cinnamon and 2 tbsp. sugar in a small bowl. Roll dough to walnut-size balls; roll balls in cinnamon-sugar. Put onto unprepped cookie sheet, 2-in. apart.
- In the preheated oven, bake till edges are slightly browned for 8-10 minutes; transfer to wire racks. Cool.

Nutrition Information

- Calories: 125 calories;
- Cholesterol: 10
- Protein: 1.3
- Total Fat: 6.1
- Sodium: 71
- Total Carbohydrate: 16.5

852. Snow Cone Topping

Serving: 6 | Prep: 3mins | Cook: | Ready in:

Ingredients

- 1 (4 ounce) packet sweetened tropical punch flavored drink mix powder
- 3/4 cup water

Direction

- In squeeze bottle, mix together water and drink mix, then seal bottle and shake well to mix. Squeeze over shaved ice.

Nutrition Information

- Calories: 70 calories;
- Sodium: 2
- Total Carbohydrate: 17.8
- Cholesterol: 0
- Protein: 0
- Total Fat: 0

853. Soft Peanut Butter Cookies

Serving: 12 | Prep: | Cook: | Ready in:

Ingredients

- 1/2 cup margarine, softened
- 1/2 cup peanut butter
- 1/2 cup white sugar
- 1/2 cup packed brown sugar

- 1 egg
- 1/2 teaspoon vanilla extract
- 3/4 teaspoon baking soda
- 1/4 teaspoon salt
- 1 3/4 cups all-purpose flour

Direction

- Combine vanilla, egg, sugars, peanut butter and margarine. Blend very well together.
- Put in salt, baking soda and flour with mixer. Let the dough chill in the refrigerator for 15 mins. Using hand to roll into balls.
- Place on the sprayed cookie sheet. Bake for 7-10 mins in a preheated 350°F (175°C) oven until the edges are very lightly brown. Do not overcook. Keep in plastic storage containers, they will stay soft!

Nutrition Information

- Calories: 270 calories;
- Sodium: 273
- Total Carbohydrate: 33.5
- Cholesterol: 16
- Protein: 5.2
- Total Fat: 13.5

854. Southern Burgers

Serving: 7 | Prep: 5mins | Cook: 15mins | Ready in:

Ingredients

- 1 pound ground beef
- 1 slice bread, crumbled
- 1 egg
- 2 tablespoons prepared mustard
- 3 tablespoons Worcestershire sauce
- garlic salt to taste
- salt and pepper to taste

Direction

- Mix beef, Worcestershire sauce, mustard, egg, and bread together in a large bowl until combined. Shape beef mixture into 6 to 8 patties; sprinkle with pepper, salt, and garlic salt to season.
- Sauté patties over in a large skillet over medium heat until burgers are cooked through and reach desired doneness, about 10 to 15 minutes.

Nutrition Information

- Calories: 229 calories;
- Total Fat: 18.2
- Sodium: 247
- Total Carbohydrate: 3.5
- Cholesterol: 82
- Protein: 12.1

855. Southern Dirty Rice

Serving: 8 | Prep: 15mins | Cook: 30mins | Ready in:

Ingredients

- 1/4 pound chicken gizzards, rinsed
- 1/2 pound chicken livers, rinsed and trimmed
- 1 tablespoon vegetable oil
- 1 onion, finely chopped
- 3 cloves garlic, minced
- 2 cups uncooked white rice
- 4 cups chicken broth
- salt to taste
- 1/2 teaspoon ground black pepper
- 1/4 teaspoon cayenne pepper
- 1 cup thinly sliced green onions

Direction

- In a food processor, pulse gizzards, then pulse livers.
- In a big saucepan, heat oil, then sauté gizzards and onion on medium heat while stirring continuously for approximately 5 minutes,

until the meat starts to brown. Put in garlic and livers, then cook for around 3 minutes until brown, while stirring continuously.
- Put in rice and stir until coated well with oil. Put in cayenne pepper, pepper, salt and broth. Bring the mixture to a boil then lower the heat to simmer. Cook with a cover until rice has absorbed liquid, for about 20 minutes. Sprinkle over with green onion and serve.

Nutrition Information

- Calories: 252 calories;
- Sodium: 29
- Total Carbohydrate: 41.7
- Cholesterol: 127
- Protein: 11.5
- Total Fat: 3.7

856. Southern As You Can Get Collard Greens

Serving: 8 | Prep: 15mins | Cook: 1hours | Ready in:

Ingredients

- 1 bunch collard greens - rinsed, trimmed and chopped
- 2 smoked ham hocks
- 2 (10.5 ounce) cans condensed chicken broth
- 21 fluid ounces water
- 1 tablespoon distilled white vinegar
- salt and pepper to taste

Direction

- In a big pot, mix vinegar, water and chicken broth in ham hocks and collard greens. Season with pepper and salt. Boil, lower heat to low, then simmer for an hour.

Nutrition Information

- Calories: 165 calories;
- Sodium: 502
- Total Carbohydrate: 2.6
- Cholesterol: 35
- Protein: 12.7
- Total Fat: 11.4

857. Southwest Chicken

Serving: 4 | Prep: | Cook: | Ready in:

Ingredients

- 1 tablespoon vegetable oil
- 4 skinless, boneless chicken breast halves
- 1 (10 ounce) can diced tomatoes with green chile peppers
- 1 (15 ounce) can black beans, rinsed and drained
- 1 (8.75 ounce) can whole kernel corn, drained
- 1 pinch ground cumin

Direction

- Heat oil over medium high in a big pan. Cook chicken breasts and brown on both sides. Place tomatoes with green chili peppers, corn and beans. Lower heat. For 25 to 30 minutes, let it simmer or until chicken is cooked through. Top with a dash of cumin. Serve.

Nutrition Information

- Calories: 310 calories;
- Sodium: 863
- Total Carbohydrate: 27.9
- Cholesterol: 68
- Protein: 35
- Total Fat: 6.4

858. Spaetzle And Chicken Soup

Serving: 8 | Prep: 20mins | Cook: 2hours | Ready in:

Ingredients

- 1 (2 to 3 pound) whole chicken
- 2 (14.5 ounce) cans chicken broth
- 2 medium yellow onions, quartered
- 1 bunch celery with leaves, cut into pieces
- 1 (16 ounce) package baby carrots
- salt and ground black pepper to taste
- 1/2 teaspoon garlic salt, or to taste
- 5 eggs
- 1/2 cup water
- 1 teaspoon salt
- 3 cups all-purpose flour
- 1/2 teaspoon parsley flakes

Direction

- In a stockpot, arrange chicken, pour enough amount of water to cover. Add chicken broth, then onions and celery. Use garlic salt, pepper, and salt to season. Boil and cook until nicely done, around an hour.
- Once the chicken gets tender and is cooked through, transfer to a platter and allow to cool enough to handle. Then strain the broth, throw onions and celery away. Place the broth back into the stockpot. Debone the chicken, tear or chop the meat into pieces, then place back into the pot. Boil the broth and pour carrots in.
- Stir salt, water, and eggs together in a medium bowl. Pour in flour gradually until firm enough to shape into a ball. Less or more flour may be needed. On a flat plate, pat the dough. Cut slices of dough off the edge of the plate with a butter knife to get around 2-3 inches long slices. Pour directly into the boiling broth.
- When the carrots get tender, the soup is done. Use parsley flakes to dust, then serve.

Nutrition Information

- Calories: 562 calories;
- Total Fat: 25.2
- Sodium: 648
- Total Carbohydrate: 45.3
- Cholesterol: 223
- Protein: 36.3

859. Spaghetti Squash Pie (Gluten Free And Dairy Free)

Serving: 10 | Prep: 20mins | Cook: 1hours40mins | Ready in:

Ingredients

- 1 spaghetti squash, cut in half lengthwise and seeded
- olive oil cooking spray
- 1 pound lean ground beef
- 1/2 cup diced red onion
- 1 (10 ounce) can diced tomatoes and green chiles (such as RO*TEL® Mild)
- 1 (10 ounce) can diced tomatoes with green chiles (such as RO*TEL® Original), drained
- 1 cup chopped baby spinach
- 1/2 cup unsweetened applesauce
- 1/2 cup diced red bell pepper
- 2 tablespoons tomato paste
- 1 teaspoon garlic salt
- 1 teaspoon dried basil
- 1 teaspoon dried oregano
- 1/2 teaspoon ground black pepper
- 3 eggs, beaten

Direction

- Preheat an oven to 200 °C or 400 °F. With olive oil cooking spray, coat lightly squash and a baking dish, 9x13-inch in size. In baking dish, put the squash cut-side facing down.
- In the prepped oven, bake the squash for half an hour till easily pricked using a knife. Take off from oven and allow to cool till easily touched.
- Lower temperature of oven to 175 °C or 350 °F.

- In a big skillet, allow the onion and ground beef to cook over medium heat for 5 minutes till meat is cooked completely and not pink anymore. Let drain. Mix in both tomatoes diced cans with black pepper, oregano, basil, garlic salt, tomato paste, red bell pepper, applesauce, spinach and green chiles; combine thoroughly. Take off from heat.
- Scrape inner of squash with a fork into spaghetti strands. Slightly oil baking dish once more and put strands of squash on base. Add beef mixture on top of squash. Mix beaten eggs over and combine thoroughly to incorporate.
- In the prepped oven, allow to bake without cover for an hour, till golden on top and firm.

Nutrition Information

- Calories: 157 calories;
- Total Fat: 8.3
- Sodium: 493
- Total Carbohydrate: 10.6
- Cholesterol: 83
- Protein: 11.1

860. Spaghetti With Tomato And Sausage Sauce

Serving: 16 | Prep: 15mins | Cook: 3hours30mins | Ready in:

Ingredients

- 1 pound beef sausage
- 1 onion, minced
- 2 cups fresh sliced mushrooms
- 1/4 cup olive oil
- 2 (6 ounce) cans tomato paste
- 1 (46 fluid ounce) can tomato juice
- 1 (16 ounce) can crushed tomatoes
- 1 cup Burgundy wine
- 1 1/2 tablespoons dried oregano
- 1 tablespoon dried basil
- 2 tablespoons dried parsley
- 1 tablespoon minced garlic
- 2 tablespoons garlic salt
- 1/2 cup white sugar
- 2 pounds spaghetti

Direction

- Start preheating the oven at 350°F (175°C). Cook sausage about 30 minutes. Slice into bite-sized pieces, and put aside.
- In a Dutch oven, sauté mushrooms and onion in olive oil until soft. Use a slotted spoon to transfer, and put aside. Blend wine, Italian tomatoes, tomato juice, tomato paste into Dutch oven. Stir until become smooth. Combine in sugar, garlic salt, garlic, parsley, basil and oregano. Bring mushroom and onion with sausage back to the sauce. Heat to a boil. Lower the heat, and simmer for a minimum of 3 hours. Cover the pot if the sauce looks too thick.
- Based on the package directions, cook pasta. Drain. Pour sauce over pasta and then enjoy.

Nutrition Information

- Calories: 415 calories;
- Total Fat: 12.2
- Sodium: 1428
- Total Carbohydrate: 61.1
- Cholesterol: 19
- Protein: 14

861. Spam Musubi

Serving: 10 | Prep: 25mins | Cook: 30mins | Ready in:

Ingredients

- 2 cups uncooked short-grain white rice
- 2 cups water
- 6 tablespoons rice vinegar
- 1/4 cup soy sauce

- 1/4 cup oyster sauce
- 1/2 cup white sugar
- 1 (12 ounce) container fully cooked luncheon meat (e.g. Spam)
- 5 sheets sushi nori (dry seaweed)
- 2 tablespoons vegetable oil

Direction

- Soak rice that is not cooked for 4 hours; stain and wash.
- Place 2 cups water in a saucepan and make it boil. Stir in rice. Lower heat, cover, and simmer for 20 minutes. Mix in rice vinegar then reserve to cool.
- Mix sugar, oyster sauce, and soy sauce in another bowl until the sugar is fully melted. Cut luncheon meat into 10 slices, lengthwise, or to a thickness that you want, then marinate in the sauce for 5 minutes.
- Add oil in a big skillet set on medium-high heat. Then cook slices for 2 minutes each side, or until browned lightly. Slice nori sheets in half then place on a flat work surface. Put a slice of luncheon meat on top, then discard press. Cover nori around the rice mold, securing edges with a bit of water. (You may also form the rice using your hand in the shape of meat slices, 1-inch thick. You may eat musubi chilled or warm.

Nutrition Information

- Calories: 276 calories;
- Protein: 6.8
- Total Fat: 12
- Sodium: 866
- Total Carbohydrate: 34.7
- Cholesterol: 24

862. Spanish Rice I

Serving: 4 | Prep: 5mins | Cook: 15mins | Ready in:

Ingredients

- 1 tablespoon vegetable oil
- 1 1/2 cups instant rice
- 1 onion, chopped
- 1 red bell pepper, chopped
- 1/2 green bell pepper, chopped
- 1 teaspoon prepared mustard
- 1/2 teaspoon salt
- 1 1/2 (14.5 ounce) cans whole peeled tomatoes
- 1 cup tomato juice

Direction

- Mix green bell pepper, red bell pepper, onion, rice and oil on a big saucepan over medium heat. Sauté until onions become translucent. Mix in tomato juice, tomatoes, salt and mustard. Allow to simmer for 5 minutes.

Nutrition Information

- Calories: 509 calories;
- Total Carbohydrate: 108.4
- Cholesterol: 0
- Protein: 10.8
- Total Fat: 3.8
- Sodium: 684

863. Spanish Rice II

Serving: 4 | Prep: 10mins | Cook: 30mins | Ready in:

Ingredients

- 2 tablespoons vegetable oil
- 1 cup uncooked white rice
- 1 onion, chopped
- 1/2 green bell pepper, chopped
- 2 cups water
- 1 (10 ounce) can diced tomatoes and green chiles
- 2 teaspoons chili powder, or to taste
- 1 teaspoon salt

Direction

- In a deep skillet, heat oil over medium heat. Sauté bell pepper, onion and rice until onions become tender and rice turn brown.
- Mix in tomatoes and water. Use salt and chili powder to season. Cover and simmer until liquid is absorbed and rice is cooked, about 30 minutes.

Nutrition Information

- Calories: 270 calories;
- Protein: 4.8
- Total Fat: 7.6
- Sodium: 882
- Total Carbohydrate: 45.7
- Cholesterol: 0

864. Spanish Rice In The Pressure Cooker

Serving: 4 | Prep: 10mins | Cook: 20mins | Ready in:

Ingredients

- 2 cups uncooked instant long-grain rice (such as Uncle Ben's®)
- 1 (14.5 ounce) can diced tomatoes with green chilies (such as RO*TEL®)
- 1 3/4 cups water, or more as needed
- 1 large onion, chopped
- 1 small green bell pepper, chopped
- 1/4 cup salsa
- 1 1/2 teaspoons garlic powder
- 1/2 teaspoon chili powder, or to taste
- salt and pepper to taste

Direction

- In a multi-functional pressure cooker, mix together the pepper, salt, chili powder, garlic powder, salsa, green bell pepper, onion, water, diced tomatoes and rice. Close and lock the lid, then select the Rice function following the manufacturer's directions. Cook for about 10 minutes until the flavors blend and the rice becomes tender. Allow 10-15 minutes for the pressure to build.
- Release the pressure using the natural release method following the manufacturer's directions for 10-40 minutes.

Nutrition Information

- Calories: 225 calories;
- Total Carbohydrate: 49.5
- Cholesterol: 0
- Protein: 5.5
- Total Fat: 0.7
- Sodium: 295

865. Spiced Air Fried Chickpeas

Serving: 4 | Prep: 5mins | Cook: 20mins | Ready in:

Ingredients

- 1 (15 ounce) can chickpeas, rinsed and drained
- 1 tablespoon nutritional yeast
- 1 tablespoon olive oil
- 1 teaspoon smoked paprika
- 1 teaspoon granulated garlic
- 1/2 teaspoon salt
- 1 pinch cumin

Direction

- On a double layer of paper towels, spread the chickpeas, then cover with another layer of paper towels, and allow to dry for 30 minutes.
- Set an air fryer to 180°C (355°F) to preheat.
- In a bowl, mix together the cumin, salt, garlic, smoked paprika, olive oil, nutritional yeast and dry chickpeas, then toss until coated.

- Add the chickpeas to the air fryer and cook for 20-22 minutes, shaking them every four minutes, until becoming crispy.

Nutrition Information

- Calories: 124 calories;
- Total Fat: 4.4
- Sodium: 501
- Total Carbohydrate: 17.4
- Cholesterol: 0
- Protein: 4.7

866. Spiced Nuts II

Serving: 8 | Prep: 10mins | Cook: 20mins | Ready in:

Ingredients

- 1 egg white, beaten
- 2 cups mixed nuts
- 6 tablespoons granulated sugar
- 1 tablespoon ground cinnamon
- 1/8 teaspoon ground nutmeg
- 1/8 teaspoon ground cloves
- 1 cup raisins
- 1/2 teaspoon salt (optional)

Direction

- Set the oven for preheating to 325°F (165°C).
- Whisk the egg white until its smooth and add nuts. Mix nutmeg, cinnamon, cloves and sugar in a bowl and add it into the nut mixture. Transfer and spread on a baking pan. Bake it for about 20 minutes in the oven while stirring occasionally.
- Take it out from the oven and mix in raisins and salt. Let it cool before serving or before storing in a completely sealed container.

Nutrition Information

- Calories: 298 calories;
- Total Carbohydrate: 33.2
- Cholesterol: 0
- Protein: 7
- Total Fat: 17.7
- Sodium: 384

867. Spiced Pecans

Serving: 6 | Prep: 10mins | Cook: 30mins | Ready in:

Ingredients

- 1 egg white, lightly beaten
- 1 tablespoon water
- 3 cups pecan halves
- 1/2 cup white sugar
- 1/2 teaspoon salt
- 1 teaspoon ground cinnamon
- 1/2 teaspoon ground cloves
- 1/2 teaspoon ground nutmeg

Direction

- Set the oven to 350°F (175°C) for preheating. Use an aluminum foil to line the baking sheet.
- Whisk egg white and water in a small bowl. Mix in pecans until well-moistened.
- Combine cloves, salt, sugar, nutmeg, and cinnamon in a small bowl. Sprinkle with moistened nuts. Transfer the nuts into the prepared pan.
- Let them bake inside the preheated oven for 30 minutes, stirring only once or twice. Make sure that the nuts are not burned or overcooked.

Nutrition Information

- Calories: 443 calories;
- Total Fat: 39
- Sodium: 204
- Total Carbohydrate: 24.7
- Cholesterol: 0
- Protein: 5.6

868. Spicy Avocado Chocolate Pudding

Serving: 6 | Prep: 10mins | Cook: | Ready in:

Ingredients

- 2 avocados - peeled, pitted, and diced
- 3/4 cup sweetened cream of coconut
- 5 tablespoons cocoa powder
- 1/2 teaspoon ground cinnamon
- 1/4 teaspoon cayenne pepper

Direction

- Blend cayenne pepper, cinnamon, cocoa powder, cream of coconut and avocados till smooth in blender. Put in bowl; refrigerate for at least 2 hours.

Nutrition Information

- Calories: 261 calories;
- Cholesterol: 0
- Protein: 2.2
- Total Fat: 17
- Sodium: 25
- Total Carbohydrate: 30.6

869. Spicy Chicken Breasts

Serving: 4 | Prep: 15mins | Cook: 15mins | Ready in:

Ingredients

- 2 1/2 tablespoons paprika
- 2 tablespoons garlic powder
- 1 tablespoon salt
- 1 tablespoon onion powder
- 1 tablespoon dried thyme
- 1 tablespoon ground cayenne pepper
- 1 tablespoon ground black pepper
- 4 skinless, boneless chicken breast halves

Direction

- Combine the ground black pepper, cayenne pepper, thyme, onion powder, salt, garlic powder and paprika in a medium bowl. Reserve around 3 tbsp. of this seasoning mixture to use for the chicken. Store the leftover in an airtight container to use later (for seasoning the vegetables, meats or fish).
- Set the grill to preheat to medium-high heat. Rub some of the reserved 3 tbsp. of seasoning on both sides of the chicken breasts.
- Oil the grill grate lightly. Put the chicken on the grill and let it cook for 6-8 minutes per side, until the juices run clear.

Nutrition Information

- Calories: 173 calories;
- Protein: 29.2
- Total Fat: 2.4
- Sodium: 1826
- Total Carbohydrate: 9.2
- Cholesterol: 68

870. Spicy Roasted Edamame

Serving: 4 | Prep: 5mins | Cook: 15mins | Ready in:

Ingredients

- 1 1/4 cups frozen shelled edamame (green soybeans), thawed
- 2 teaspoons olive oil
- 1/2 teaspoon chili powder
- 1/4 teaspoon dried basil
- 1/4 teaspoon onion powder
- 1/4 teaspoon ground cumin
- 1/8 teaspoon paprika
- 1/8 teaspoon ground black pepper

Direction

- Preheat the oven to 190 degrees C (375 degrees F).
- Into a mixing bowl, put thawed edamame, then trickle with olive oil, and sprinkle with pepper, paprika, cumin, chili powder, basil and onion powder. Mix until edamame is coated evenly with the spices and oil. Put in a single layer into a 9x13 inch glass baking dish, then spread.
- Bake while uncovered for 12 to 15 minutes in the oven until the beans start to brown. Mix once when halfway through the cooking.

Nutrition Information

- Calories: 141 calories;
- Protein: 10.5
- Total Fat: 7.9
- Sodium: 16
- Total Carbohydrate: 9.3
- Cholesterol: 0

871. Spinach Chickpea Curry

Serving: 4 | Prep: 5mins | Cook: 15mins | Ready in:

Ingredients

- 1 tablespoon vegetable oil
- 1 onion, chopped
- 1 (14.75 ounce) can creamed corn
- 1 tablespoon curry paste
- salt to taste
- ground black pepper to taste
- 1/2 teaspoon garlic powder, or to taste
- 1 (15 ounce) can garbanzo beans (chickpeas), drained and rinsed
- 1 (12 ounce) package firm tofu, cubed
- 1 bunch fresh spinach, stems removed
- 1 teaspoon dried basil or to taste

Direction

- Heat oil in a big skillet or a big wok over medium heat; sauté onions until turning translucent. Mix in curry paste and creamed corn. Cook for 5 minutes, tossing often. While stirring, add garlic, pepper, and salt.
- Mix in garbanzo beans and lightly fold in tofu. Add spinach and put a cover on. Once the spinach is soft, take away from heat and mix in basil.

Nutrition Information

- Calories: 346 calories;
- Protein: 21.7
- Total Fat: 12.3
- Sodium: 849
- Total Carbohydrate: 44.7
- Cholesterol: 0

872. Spinach And Bean Casserole

Serving: 4 | Prep: 5mins | Cook: 45mins | Ready in:

Ingredients

- 1 cup dry black-eyed peas
- 1/4 cup olive oil
- 1 onion, chopped
- 3 cups fresh spinach
- 1 (28 ounce) can peeled and diced tomatoes
- 2 teaspoons salt
- 1 teaspoon fennel seed, ground

Direction

- Preheat an oven to 175°C/350°F.
- In pressure cooker, cook black-eye peas for 12 minutes.
- Heat oil in big saucepan on medium-high heat; sauté fennel, salt, tomatoes, spinach and onion for 15 minutes.
- Mix spinach mixture and beans in a 2-qt. casserole dish.

- In preheated oven, bake for 15 minutes.

Nutrition Information

- Calories: 282 calories;
- Total Fat: 14.2
- Sodium: 1707
- Total Carbohydrate: 28.7
- Cholesterol: 0
- Protein: 9.7

873. Spinach And Pasta Shells

Serving: 8 | Prep: | Cook: |Ready in:

Ingredients

- 1 pound seashell pasta
- 1 (10 ounce) package frozen chopped spinach
- 2 tablespoons olive oil
- 7 cloves garlic, minced
- 1 teaspoon dried red pepper flakes (optional)
- salt to taste

Direction

- Boil a big pot of slightly salted water. Put in the spinach and pasta and cook till pasta is al dente, about 8 to 10 minutes; drain and set aside.
- In a big skillet, heat oil over moderate heat. Put in the red pepper flakes and garlic; sauté till garlic becomes pale gold, about 5 minutes. In the skillet, put the spinach and cooked pasta and combine thoroughly. Add salt to season and toss; serve.

Nutrition Information

- Calories: 248 calories;
- Total Fat: 4.9
- Sodium: 30
- Total Carbohydrate: 43.8
- Cholesterol: 0
- Protein: 9

874. Spring Pea Medley With Edible Bowl

Serving: 4 | Prep: 15mins | Cook: 5mins |Ready in:

Ingredients

- 2 tablespoons butter
- 1 small sweet onion, diced
- 1 cup fresh shelled green peas
- 1/2 cup low sodium, low fat vegetable broth
- 1/2 pound sugar snap peas, trimmed
- 1/2 pound snow peas, trimmed
- 1 tablespoon chopped fresh parsley
- salt and pepper to taste
- 1 medium head radicchio

Direction

- Melt butter over medium-low heat in a medium skillet. Add in the onion and sauté until translucent, for 5 minutes. Blend in the broth and green peas, and cook for 3 minutes. Put in parsley, snow peas, and snap peas, and flavor to taste with salt and pepper. Cover and cook, about 3 minutes longer.
- Take the inner leaves away from the radicchio and spread the outer leaves out to make a bowl. Pour the pea mixture in the hollow and top with additional Italian parsley to garnish.

Nutrition Information

- Calories: 151 calories;
- Total Fat: 6.1
- Sodium: 102
- Total Carbohydrate: 18.5
- Cholesterol: 15
- Protein: 5.4

875. Steak, Onion, And Pepper Fajitas

Serving: 6 | Prep: 25mins | Cook: 25mins | Ready in:

Ingredients

- 1 1/2 pounds beef round steak
- 1/4 cup tequila
- 1/2 cup fresh lime juice
- 1/2 cup cooking oil
- 2 tablespoons liquid smoke
- 1 teaspoon Worcestershire sauce
- 1/4 teaspoon ground black pepper
- 1/2 teaspoon salt
- 3/4 teaspoon paprika
- 1/2 cup sliced onion
- 3/4 cup bell peppers, sliced into thin strips

Direction

- In a plastic bag, combine lime juice, tequila, and steak, then marinate inside the refrigerator for 2 hours; throw away the marinade.
- Heat up the outdoor grill to high heat and oil the grate lightly.
- Grill the steak until the insides are no longer pink, roughly 8 minutes on each side. Take them off the grill and slice them into 1/4-inch strips, then arrange them onto a serving plate.
- Heat up a skillet with oil on medium heat. Add in the paprika, salt, pepper, Worcestershire sauce, and liquid smoke, then stir. Once the mixture becomes hot, add in the peppers and onions and cook until the peppers become tender. Pour the mixture over the strips of steak and serve right away.

Nutrition Information

- Calories: 357 calories;
- Cholesterol: 39
- Protein: 14.1
- Total Fat: 29.2
- Sodium: 235
- Total Carbohydrate: 4.6

876. Steamed Vegan Rice Cakes (Banh Bo Hap)

Serving: 12 | Prep: 10mins | Cook: 15mins | Ready in:

Ingredients

- 4 cups rice flour
- 2 cups lukewarm water
- 1 (14 ounce) can coconut milk
- 1 cup white sugar
- 4 teaspoons tapioca starch
- 1 1/2 teaspoons active dry yeast
- 1/2 teaspoon vanilla extract
- 1/4 teaspoon salt
- 2 teaspoons oil, or as needed

Direction

- Combine salt, rice flour, yeast, coconut milk, tapioca starch, vanilla extract, water and sugar together in a bowl and whisk until it turns smooth. Cover with a lid and allow the batter to rest for about 2 hours until the bubbles rise on top. Stir the mixture well.
- Grease cake molds using an oil. Put a steamer insert in a saucepan and put water just below the bottom of a steamer. Position the cake molds on top of the steamer and spoon the batter into each molds, leaving 1 3/4-inch space at the top to give a space once the batter risen. Bring water to a boil. Cover and steam for about 10 minutes. It should be done once a toothpick inserted into a cake comes out clean.

Nutrition Information

- Calories: 334 calories;
- Sodium: 54
- Total Carbohydrate: 60.8
- Cholesterol: 0
- Protein: 4
- Total Fat: 8.5

877. Steve's Bodacious Barbecue Ribs

Serving: 10 | Prep: 15mins | Cook: 8hours | Ready in:

Ingredients

- 2 tablespoons paprika
- 1 teaspoon cayenne pepper
- 1 teaspoon garlic powder
- 1 teaspoon onion powder
- 1 tablespoon salt
- 1 teaspoon ground black pepper
- 2 teaspoons ground cumin
- 1 1/2 tablespoons brown sugar
- 1/4 teaspoon ground cinnamon
- 1/8 teaspoon ground cloves
- 1/8 teaspoon ground nutmeg
- 5 pounds pork spareribs
- 2 pounds hickory wood chips, soaked

Direction

- Mix together nutmeg, cloves, cinnamon, brown sugar, cumin, ground black pepper, salt, onion powder, garlic powder, cayenne pepper and paprika in a medium bowl. Apply generously to the ribs. In a big roasting pan, put the ribs, place cover, and chill for overnight. Take ribs off the refrigerator an hour prior to smoking.
- Have an outdoor smoker ready, setting temperature to 95 to 110 °C or 200 to 225 °F.
- Let the ribs smoke for 6 to 8 hours, putting wood chips to keep a consistent smoke, about a handful after every 30 to 45 minutes. Ribs are set once crispy on the outside and soft on the inside. Take out of smoker, and reserve for 15 to 20 minutes prior to serving.

Nutrition Information

- Calories: 383 calories;
- Total Carbohydrate: 3.6
- Cholesterol: 117
- Protein: 24.5
- Total Fat: 29.7
- Sodium: 800

878. Stir Fried Kale And Broccoli Florets

Serving: 6 | Prep: 5mins | Cook: 5mins | Ready in:

Ingredients

- 1/8 cup extra virgin olive oil
- 7 cloves garlic, sliced
- 1 chile pepper, chopped (optional)
- 1 head fresh broccoli, chopped
- 1 bunch kale, stems removed and chopped
- 1/4 cup sun-dried tomatoes, cut in thin strips
- juice of 2 limes
- salt

Direction

- In a big wok or frying pan, heat the olive oil on high heat, then stir in chile pepper and garlic and let it cook for 2 minutes, mixing often. Mix in broccoli and let it cook for a minute. Add kale and let it cook for 2 minutes, mixing often. Mix in sun-dried tomatoes. Pour in lime juice and sprinkle salt to taste, then toss it well.

Nutrition Information

- Calories: 114 calories;
- Sodium: 97
- Total Carbohydrate: 15
- Cholesterol: 0
- Protein: 4.6
- Total Fat: 5.5

879. Strawberry Tapioca

Serving: 4 | Prep: 10mins | Cook: 20mins | Ready in:

Ingredients

- 1/2 cup fresh strawberries, hulled and halved
- 1 1/2 cups water
- 1/4 cup quick-cooking tapioca

Direction

- In food processor or blender, put water and strawberries, and process till smooth. Put in one small saucepan. Mix tapioca in, and rest for 10 minutes till softened. Boil on moderate heat, mixing often to avoid adhering. Once thick, take off from heat, and add to serving dishes.

Nutrition Information

- Calories: 41 calories;
- Total Fat: 0.1
- Sodium: 3
- Total Carbohydrate: 9.5
- Cholesterol: 0
- Protein: 1.1

880. Stuffed Boneless Quail With Wild Rice And Sage Stuffing

Serving: 6 | Prep: 20mins | Cook: 2hours | Ready in:

Ingredients

- 6 boneless quail
- salt to taste
- 2 teaspoons grated orange zest, divided
- 2 1/2 cups vegetable broth
- 1/2 cup uncooked wild rice
- 1 bay leaf
- 1 tablespoon vegetable oil
- 1 cup diced onion
- 3/4 cup diced celery
- 1/2 cup fresh sage, minced
- 1 egg white
- 1/3 cup toasted walnuts
- 1/2 teaspoon freshly ground black pepper
- 1/4 cup fresh parsley, minced
- 1/2 cup chicken broth

Direction

- Prepare the oven by preheating to 375°F (190°C). Prepare a roasting pan that is lightly greased.
- Rinse quail and use salt and 1 teaspoon orange zest to rub inside cavities.
- Place vegetable broth in a medium saucepan then make it boil. Put the bay leaf then lower the heat; simmer for 35-40 minutes, covered, or until the liquid is soaked up.
- In the meantime, in a medium skillet set on medium heat, add oil. Stir-fry onions until translucent; add sage and celery then stir-fry for 2 minutes. Place in a medium bowl. Mix in the parsley, cooked rice, black pepper, walnuts, the rest of the orange zest, and egg white; blend well. Fill the rice mixture into the cavities of the quail. Then season lightly the skins with cracked black pepper and salt. Place in preheated oven and bake for 35-40 minutes, or until cooked well. Take the quail from the pan then deglaze with chicken broth. Drain and scoop on the quail.

Nutrition Information

- Calories: 339 calories;
- Total Fat: 20.3
- Sodium: 273
- Total Carbohydrate: 13.8
- Cholesterol: 83
- Protein: 25.4

881. Stuffed Peppers

Serving: 6 | Prep: 20mins | Cook: 1hours | Ready in:

Ingredients

- 1 pound ground beef
- 1/2 cup uncooked long grain white rice
- 1 cup water
- 6 green bell peppers
- 2 (8 ounce) cans tomato sauce
- 1 tablespoon Worcestershire sauce
- 1/4 teaspoon garlic powder
- 1/4 teaspoon onion powder
- salt and pepper to taste
- 1 teaspoon Italian seasoning

Direction

- Preheat the oven to 175°C or 350°Fahrenheit.
- Boil water and rice together in a saucepan. Lower heat and cook rice for 20mins while covered. On medium heat, cook beef in a pan until evenly brown.
- Remove the membranes, seeds, and tops of the bell pepper; place with the pepper's hollowed side up in a baking dish. If needed, cut the base of the peppers to help them stay upright.
- Stir pepper, browned beef, salt, cooked rice, onion powder, a can of tomato sauce, garlic powder, and Worcestershire sauce together. Evenly scoop in mixture into each pepper. In a bowl, combine Italian seasoning and remaining tomato sauce together; drizzle on top of the stuffed peppers.
- Bake peppers in the 350°Fahrenheit oven for an hour until tender. Every 15mins, baste peppers with sauce.

Nutrition Information

- Calories: 248 calories;
- Total Fat: 9.4
- Sodium: 564
- Total Carbohydrate: 25.6
- Cholesterol: 46
- Protein: 16

882. Stuffed Zucchini II

Serving: 6 | Prep: 30mins | Cook: 40mins | Ready in:

Ingredients

- 2 large tomatoes - peeled, seeded and chopped
- 5 tablespoons chopped fresh basil
- 3 tablespoons olive oil
- 4 tablespoons chopped fresh parsley
- 1 teaspoon grated orange zest
- 1 teaspoon grated lemon zest
- 2 cloves garlic, minced
- salt and pepper to taste
- 6 small zucchini
- 2 tablespoons olive oil
- 1 1/2 cups soft bread crumbs
- 1 egg, beaten
- 1/2 cup chicken broth

Direction

- Mix pepper, salt, 1/2 of the garlic, lemon peel, orange peel, 1 tablespoon of parsley, 3 tablespoons of basil, and tomatoes together in a small bowl to taste. Stir thoroughly and put aside at room temperature, about 60 minutes.
- Turn the oven to 350°F (175°C) to preheat. Lightly coat a 9x13-in. baking dish with oil.
- Remove the stem ends from zucchini and cut lengthwise a thin layer off the tops. If needed, trim the bottoms to balance the zucchini; keep the trimmings. Remove the flesh, leaving shells with a 1/4-in. thickness. Coarsely chop the flesh and the saved trimmings. In a big saucepan, cook the shells with boiling salted water for 2 minutes. Strain and wash in cold water; put on paper towels to strain.
- In a medium-sized frying pan, heat oil over medium heat; sauté the chopped zucchini until soft, about 5 minutes. Mix in garlic, basil, and the leftover parsley; cook for 1 minute. Bring to a medium-sized bowl and mix in egg and bread crumbs. Use pepper and salt to season

to taste. In the shells, put in the mixture with the spoon and put in the prepared baking dish. Pour over the zucchini with chicken stock.
- Put a cover on and bake for 25-30 minutes in the preheated oven until soft. Enjoy with the tomato salsa.

Nutrition Information

- Calories: 251 calories;
- Sodium: 226
- Total Carbohydrate: 26.5
- Cholesterol: 31
- Protein: 6.8
- Total Fat: 13.9

883. Sugar Free Cake

Serving: 12 | Prep: | Cook: | Ready in:

Ingredients

- 2 cups raisins
- 3 cups water
- 2 eggs
- 3 tablespoons liquid sweetener
- 3/4 cup vegetable oil
- 1 teaspoon vanilla extract
- 1 teaspoon baking soda
- 1/2 teaspoon salt
- 1 1/2 teaspoons ground cinnamon
- 1/2 teaspoon ground nutmeg
- 2 cups all-purpose flour
- 1 cup chopped walnuts
- 1 cup unsweetened applesauce

Direction

- Set oven to 175°C (350°F) and start preheating. Grease a 10-in. tube or Bundt pan and dust with flour.
- Mix together water and raisins in a saucepan, cook until the raisins absorb the water; allow to cool.
- Whisk together liquid sweetener, vanilla, vegetable oil, applesauce and eggs. Stir thoroughly. Sift ground nutmeg, ground cinnamon, salt, baking soda and flour into the wet mixture. Mix just until incorporated. Stir in chopped nuts and raisins. Transfer to the cake pan.
- Bake at 175°C (350°F) oven for 60 minutes.

Nutrition Information

- Calories: 373 calories;
- Cholesterol: 31
- Protein: 5.5
- Total Fat: 21.3
- Sodium: 219
- Total Carbohydrate: 43.1

884. Sugar Snap Peas

Serving: 4 | Prep: 10mins | Cook: 8mins | Ready in:

Ingredients

- 1/2 pound sugar snap peas
- 1 tablespoon olive oil
- 1 tablespoon chopped shallots
- 1 teaspoon chopped fresh thyme
- kosher salt to taste

Direction

- Preheat the oven to 230 degrees C (450 degrees F).
- Spread a single layer of sugar snap peas onto a medium baking sheet and then brush with olive oil. Sprinkle with kosher salt, shallots and thyme.
- Bake for 6 to 8 minutes in the oven until tender but firm.

Nutrition Information

- Calories: 59 calories;
- Cholesterol: 0
- Protein: 1.4
- Total Fat: 3.4
- Sodium: 100
- Total Carbohydrate: 5.3

885. Sugar Snap Peas With Mint

Serving: 4 | Prep: 6mins | Cook: 4mins | Ready in:

Ingredients

- 2 teaspoons olive oil
- 3/4 pound sugar snap peas, trimmed
- 3 green onions, chopped
- 1 clove garlic, chopped
- 1/8 teaspoon salt
- 1/8 teaspoon pepper
- 1 tablespoon chopped fresh mint

Direction

- In a big pan, heat oil over medium heat and add garlic, green onion, and sugar snap peas, seasoning with pepper and salt. Stir fry the mixture for 4 minutes, then take off the heat and stir in mint leaves.

Nutrition Information

- Calories: 67 calories;
- Total Carbohydrate: 8.3
- Cholesterol: 0
- Protein: 2.3
- Total Fat: 2.4
- Sodium: 75

886. Sugar Free And Dairy Free Slow Cooker Steel Cut Oatmeal

Serving: 6 | Prep: 10mins | Cook: 3hours | Ready in:

Ingredients

- 2 bananas, mashed
- 5 cups water, divided
- 1 cup steel cut oats
- 1/4 cup raisins (optional)
- 1 teaspoon cinnamon
- 1 teaspoon vanilla extract

Direction

- In a blender, pour 1 cup water over bananas; puree bananas and transfer into a slow cooker. Add vanilla extract, cinnamon, raisins, oats, and remaining water.
- Cook mixture on medium heat setting for 3 hours, stirring every 30 minutes.

Nutrition Information

- Calories: 159 calories;
- Total Fat: 1.8
- Sodium: 7
- Total Carbohydrate: 32.8
- Cholesterol: 0
- Protein: 4

887. Sugar Free And Keto Fat Bombs

Serving: 16 | Prep: 10mins | Cook: | Ready in:

Ingredients

- 1 1/2 cups unsweetened coconut flakes
- 1/2 cup melted coconut oil
- 1/2 cup melted cocoa butter
- 1/4 cup hemp seed hearts

Direction

- In a food processor, blend cocoa butter, coconut oil and coconut flakes for approximately 2 minutes till creamy. Form mixture into balls of 1-inch in size; roll in hemp hearts. Place in the refrigerator to chill for nearly 30 minutes till set.

Nutrition Information

- Calories: 190 calories;
- Total Fat: 20.4
- Sodium: 3
- Total Carbohydrate: 2.4
- Cholesterol: 0
- Protein: 1.4

888. Sukhothai Pad Thai

Serving: 8 | Prep: 20mins | Cook: 10mins | Ready in:

Ingredients

- 1/2 cup white sugar
- 1/2 cup distilled white vinegar
- 1/4 cup soy sauce
- 2 tablespoons tamarind pulp
- 1 (12 ounce) package dried rice noodles
- 1/2 cup vegetable oil
- 1 1/2 teaspoons minced garlic
- 4 eggs
- 1 (12 ounce) package firm tofu, cut into 1/2 inch strips
- 1 1/2 tablespoons white sugar
- 1 1/2 teaspoons salt
- 1 1/2 cups ground peanuts
- 1 1/2 teaspoons ground, dried oriental radish
- 1/2 cup chopped fresh chives
- 1 tablespoon paprika
- 2 cups fresh bean sprouts
- 1 lime, cut into wedges

Direction

- Pad Thai sauce: Mix tamarind pulp, soy sauce, vinegar, and sugar on medium heat in a medium saucepan.
- Pad Thai: In cold water, soak rice noodles until soft then drain. On medium heat, warm oil in a wok or big skillet. Add eggs and garlic, scrambling the eggs. Stir in tofu until well combined. Add noodles and mix until cooked.
- Mix in 1 1/2 teaspoons salt, 1 1/2 tablespoon sugar, and Pad Thai sauce. Mix in ground radish and peanuts. Take off from heat then add paprika and chives.
- Serve with bean sprouts and lime on the side.

Nutrition Information

- Calories: 619 calories;
- Cholesterol: 93
- Protein: 19.5
- Total Fat: 34
- Sodium: 1010
- Total Carbohydrate: 64.1

889. Superb Sausage Casserole

Serving: 3 | Prep: 10mins | Cook: 1hours | Ready in:

Ingredients

- 6 links pork sausage
- 1 large red bell pepper, chopped
- 1 large orange bell pepper, chopped
- 1 large yellow bell pepper, chopped
- 1 large onion, diced
- 1/2 cup ketchup
- 3/4 cup hot water
- salt and pepper to taste

Direction

- Brown the sausage in a big skillet on medium heat. Take it out of the heat and slice it into thirds.

- Mix together the hot water, ketchup, onion, yellow bell pepper, orange bell pepper, red bell pepper and sausages in a 2-qt. casserole dish. Mix it together until well blended and sprinkle ground black pepper and salt to season.
- Let it bake for 1 hour at 175°C (350°F), mixing every 15 minutes.

Nutrition Information

- Calories: 237 calories;
- Total Fat: 11
- Sodium: 736
- Total Carbohydrate: 25.4
- Cholesterol: 41
- Protein: 11.3

890. Sushi Roll

Serving: 8 | Prep: 45mins | Cook: | Ready in:

Ingredients

- 2/3 cup uncooked short-grain white rice
- 3 tablespoons rice vinegar
- 3 tablespoons white sugar
- 1 1/2 teaspoons salt
- 4 sheets nori seaweed sheets
- 1/2 cucumber, peeled, cut into small strips
- 2 tablespoons pickled ginger
- 1 avocado
- 1/2 pound imitation crabmeat, flaked

Direction

- Boil 1 1/3 cups water in a medium pot; stir in rice. Lower heat; let it simmer for 20 mins while covered. Combine salt, sugar, and rice vinegar in a small bowl; mix into the rice.
- Preheat the oven to 150°C or 300°Fahrenheit. Heat nori in a medium baking sheet for 1-2 mins in the preheated oven, or until warm.
- On a bamboo sushi mat, put one nori sheet in the center. Slather a thin layer of rice on the nori sheet using damp hands, and then press the rice. Put a quarter of the cucumber, imitation crabmeat, avocado, and ginger down in the middle of the rice. Lift and roll the end of the mat gently over the contents then gently press. Complete the roll by rolling forward. Repeat with the rest of the ingredients.
- Use a wet and sharp knife to slice each roll into 4-6 portions.

Nutrition Information

- Calories: 152 calories;
- Cholesterol: 6
- Protein: 3.9
- Total Fat: 3.9
- Sodium: 703
- Total Carbohydrate: 25.8

891. Sweet Polish Sausage

Serving: 4 | Prep: 1hours | Cook: 1hours | Ready in:

Ingredients

- 2 pounds kielbasa sausage, cut into 1 inch pieces
- 1/3 cup Worcestershire sauce
- 1 tablespoon fresh lemon juice
- 1 onion, chopped
- 1/2 cup brown sugar
- 2 dashes hot pepper sauce
- 2/3 cup water

Direction

- In a big pan, put the sausage. Pour water to cover and let it simmer for 1 hour on low heat. Drain the water and take out the sausage; put aside.
- Set an oven to preheat at 175°C (350°F).

- Mix the water, hot pepper sauce, sugar, onion, lemon juice and Worcestershire sauce in the same pan. Boil then stir. In a 9x13-inch baking dish, put the reserved sausage and use the sauce mixture to cover it.
- Bake for 1 hour at 175°C (350°F).

Nutrition Information

- Calories: 837 calories;
- Total Fat: 62
- Sodium: 2296
- Total Carbohydrate: 40.9
- Cholesterol: 150
- Protein: 28.2

892. Sweet Potato And Prune Casserole

Serving: 8 | Prep: | Cook: | Ready in:

Ingredients

- 6 sweet potatoes
- 1 (16 ounce) jar stewed prunes
- 3/4 cup honey
- 3/4 teaspoon ground cinnamon
- 1 teaspoon salt
- 1 fluid ounce prune juice
- 2 tablespoons lemon juice
- 1/4 cup pareve margarine, melted

Direction

- Prick the sweet potatoes then arrange on a baking sheet; bake for an hour in a preheated 220°C or 425°Fahrenheit oven or until tender. Set the sweet potatoes aside until cool enough to touch; skin then slice into quarter-inch thick portions.
- Mix melted margarine, honey, prune and lemon juice, salt, and cinnamon together in a small bowl.
- Halve then pit the prunes. Put the potatoes and prunes in alternating layers in a casserole dish. Scoop honey mixture on top of each layer.
- Bake for 45 minutes in a 175°C or 350°Fahrenheit oven. Use the liquid in the casserole dish to baste from time to time.

Nutrition Information

- Calories: 296 calories;
- Cholesterol: 0
- Protein: 2.3
- Total Fat: 5.8
- Sodium: 412
- Total Carbohydrate: 63

893. Sweet And Gooey Chicken Wings

Serving: 4 | Prep: 4hours5mins | Cook: 1hours35mins | Ready in:

Ingredients

- 1/2 cup soy sauce
- 1/4 cup packed brown sugar
- 1/2 tablespoon vegetable oil
- 1/2 teaspoon minced fresh ginger root
- 1/2 teaspoon garlic powder
- 1 1/2 pounds chicken wings

Direction

- Mix together the garlic powder, ginger, oil, brown sugar and soy sauce in a 9x13-inch casserole. Stir until the brown sugar is fully dissolved into the mixture. In the dish, put the chicken wings and flip them over until all are coated well. Cover the dish and let it chill in the fridge for a minimum of 4 hours. After 2 hours, flip the chicken again.
- Set an oven to preheat to 175°C (350°F).

- Let the chicken bake for 45 minutes at 175°C (350°F) with a cover. Flip the chicken wings and scoop the sauce from the bottom of the pan on the tops of the wings, then cook for 50 minutes more without a cover.

Nutrition Information

- Calories: 464 calories;
- Cholesterol: 131
- Protein: 33.3
- Total Fat: 28.9
- Sodium: 1932
- Total Carbohydrate: 16.2

894. Sweet And Sour Meatballs I

Serving: 7 | Prep: 10mins | Cook: 5hours | Ready in:

Ingredients

- 2 pounds ground beef
- 1 egg
- 1 onion, chopped
- 1 pinch salt
- 1 (12 fluid ounce) can or bottle chili sauce
- 2 teaspoons lemon juice
- 1 cup grape jelly

Direction

- Place the salt, onion, egg, and beef in a large bowl. Combine them together, form into little balls.
- Blend the grape jelly, lemon juice, and chili sauce in a slow cooker. Add in the meatballs and stir, cook for 4-5 hours on high.

Nutrition Information

- Calories: 562 calories;
- Sodium: 99
- Total Carbohydrate: 37.5

- Cholesterol: 137
- Protein: 24
- Total Fat: 35.2

895. Sweet And Sour Onions

Serving: 8 | Prep: | Cook: | Ready in:

Ingredients

- 4 large onions, peeled and halved
- 2 tablespoons distilled white vinegar
- 2 teaspoons white sugar
- 1 cup dried bread crumbs
- 1/2 cup olive oil
- 1/4 teaspoon dried sage
- 1 teaspoon dried rosemary
- 1/4 cup chopped fresh parsley
- salt and pepper to taste

Direction

- Set the oven to 190°C or 375°F to preheat.
- In a 9"x13" baking pan, place the onions. Arrange onions so that the flat side of the onion is facing the ceiling.
- Combine together sugar and vinegar in a small mixing bowl, then scoop the mixture onto the flat surface of the onions.
- Mix together parsley, rosemary, sage, 1/4 cup oil and breadcrumbs in a separate mixing bowl. Blend the mixture until well mixed, then pat the mixture onto the flat side of the onions evenly.
- Pour over the onions with the leftover 1/4 cup oil and bake until onions are softened when pierced, or for about 45 minutes. Allow the onions to cool at room temperature and serve with pepper and salt to taste.

Nutrition Information

- Calories: 208 calories;
- Sodium: 103

- Total Carbohydrate: 18
- Cholesterol: 0
- Protein: 2.7
- Total Fat: 14.3

896. Sweet And Sour Sauce II

Serving: 48 | Prep: 5mins | Cook: 15mins | Ready in:

Ingredients

- 2 cups water
- 2/3 cup distilled white vinegar
- 1 1/2 cups white sugar
- 1 (6 ounce) can tomato paste
- 1 (8 ounce) can pineapple tidbits, drained
- 3 tablespoons cornstarch

Direction

- Combine the cornstarch, pineapple tidbits, tomato paste, white sugar, distilled white vinegar and water in a medium saucepan on medium heat. Let it cook for 15 minutes, stirring occasionally, or until the mixture achieves the preferred consistency and color.

Nutrition Information

- Calories: 32 calories;
- Sodium: 28
- Total Carbohydrate: 8.1
- Cholesterol: 0
- Protein: 0.2
- Total Fat: 0

897. Swiss Chard With Garbanzo Beans And Fresh Tomatoes

Serving: 4 | Prep: 10mins | Cook: 15mins | Ready in:

Ingredients

- 2 tablespoons olive oil
- 1 shallot, chopped
- 2 green onions, chopped
- 1/2 cup garbanzo beans, drained
- salt and pepper to taste
- 1 bunch red Swiss chard, rinsed and chopped
- 1 tomato, sliced
- 1/2 lemon, juiced

Direction

- In a big pan, heat olive oil then mix in green onions and shallot. Cook and stir for 3-5mins until aromatic and soft. Mix in garbanzo beans then sprinkle pepper and salt; heat completely then add chard. Cook until the chard wilts; put in tomato slices. Squeeze lemon juice on top of the greens then heat completely. Arrange on a plate then sprinkle pepper and salt to taste.

Nutrition Information

- Calories: 122 calories;
- Total Carbohydrate: 13.3
- Cholesterol: 0
- Protein: 3.2
- Total Fat: 7.3
- Sodium: 253

898. Syrian Spaghetti

Serving: 8 | Prep: 15mins | Cook: 1hours | Ready in:

Ingredients

- 1 (16 ounce) package spaghetti
- 1 (8 ounce) can tomato sauce
- 1 (6 ounce) can tomato paste
- 1 teaspoon ground cinnamon
- 1/4 cup vegetable oil
- salt and pepper to taste

Direction

- Start preheating the oven to 350°F (175°C). Grease 9x13 inches baking dish.
- Boil the lightly salted water in a large pot. Put in spaghetti. Cook until al dente or 8-10 mins. Drain, then stir in the pepper, salt, oil, cinnamon, tomato paste and tomato sauce. Place into the prepared dish.
- Bake for 60 mins in the preheated oven, or until the top becomes crunchy.

Nutrition Information

- Calories: 293 calories;
- Sodium: 318
- Total Carbohydrate: 47.6
- Cholesterol: 0
- Protein: 8.6
- Total Fat: 7.8

899. Tangy Chicken Breasts

Serving: 4 | Prep: 10mins | Cook: 20mins | Ready in:

Ingredients

- 4 skinless, boneless chicken breast halves
- 1 cup Worcestershire sauce
- 1 cup vegetable oil
- 1 cup lemon juice
- 1 teaspoon garlic powder

Direction

- In a bowl or pan, arrange chicken in a single layer. Combine garlic, lemon juice, oil, and Worcestershire sauce; spread over chicken. Cover. Put in the refrigerator for at least 6 hours.
- Transfer the chicken out of the marinade and into a broiler pan or grill. Broil for about 7 minutes per side until done.

Nutrition Information

- Calories: 676 calories;
- Total Fat: 57.4
- Sodium: 717
- Total Carbohydrate: 19
- Cholesterol: 61
- Protein: 23.3

900. Tangy Chicken Fajitas

Serving: 6 | Prep: 10mins | Cook: 20mins | Ready in:

Ingredients

- 1/2 cup olive oil
- 1/2 cup distilled white vinegar
- 1/2 cup fresh lime juice
- 2 (.7 ounce) packages dry Italian-style salad dressing mix
- 3 whole boneless, skinless chicken breast, cubed
- 1 onion, sliced
- 1 green bell pepper, sliced

Direction

- Combine dry salad dressing mix, lime juice, vinegar and oil in large glass bowl. Mix together. Put in bell pepper, onion and chicken strips. Refrigerate, cover the dish. Marinate them for 3-6 hours.
- Heat oil in a large pan. Take out bell pepper, onion and chicken from the marinade. In oil, sauté until onion becomes translucent, juices run clear and chicken has been cooked through.

Nutrition Information

- Calories: 257 calories;
- Total Fat: 18.8
- Sodium: 1101
- Total Carbohydrate: 7.7
- Cholesterol: 34
- Protein: 14.1

901. Tart Meyer Lemon Sorbet

Serving: 6 | Prep: 10mins | Cook: 1mins | Ready in:

Ingredients

- 1 3/4 cups water
- 3/4 cup honey
- 2 cups Meyer lemon juice
- 1 tablespoon lemon zest

Direction

- In a microwaveable bowl, combine honey and water then microwave for 30 seconds. Mix together to completely dissolve honey in water.
- Add lemon zest and lemon juice to honey water. Transfer mixture to an ice cream machine and process for 25 minutes following the manufacturer's directions.
- Spoon sorbet in a chilled loaf dish and store in the freezer.

Nutrition Information

- Calories: 150 calories;
- Sodium: 5
- Total Carbohydrate: 42.1
- Cholesterol: 0
- Protein: 0.5
- Total Fat: 0

902. Tempeh Fajitas

Serving: 4 | Prep: 10mins | Cook: 15mins | Ready in:

Ingredients

- 2 tablespoons corn oil
- 1 (8 ounce) package tempeh, broken into bite-sized pieces
- 2 tablespoons soy sauce
- 1 tablespoon lime juice
- 1 1/2 cups chopped green bell pepper
- 1 (4.5 ounce) can sliced mushrooms, drained
- 1/2 cup frozen chopped spinach, thawed and drained
- 1 tablespoon chopped green chile peppers
- 1 tablespoon chopped fresh cilantro
- 1 tablespoon dried minced onion

Direction

- In a big skillet, heat oil on moderate heat. Sauté together tempeh, lime juice and soy sauce until tempeh is browned. Stir in dried onion, cilantro, chile peppers, spinach, mushrooms and bell peppers.
- Upper heat to moderately high and cook while stirring sometimes, until fluids are reduced.

Nutrition Information

- Calories: 207 calories;
- Cholesterol: 0
- Protein: 12.8
- Total Fat: 13.3
- Sodium: 606
- Total Carbohydrate: 13.2

903. Tequila Lime Shrimp

Serving: 6 | Prep: 10mins | Cook: 15mins | Ready in:

Ingredients

- 2 1/2 cups olive oil
- 3/4 cup tequila
- 1/2 cup chopped fresh cilantro
- 1/2 cup fresh lime juice
- 1/2 cup pineapple juice
- 1/4 cup white vinegar
- 1/4 cup garlic salt

- 1/4 cup ground black pepper
- 1 tablespoon chopped fresh oregano
- 1 teaspoon seasoned salt
- 30 medium shrimp - peeled and deveined

Direction

- In a blender, mix together seasoned salt, oregano, pepper, garlic salt, vinegar, pineapple juice, lime juice, cilantro, tequila and the olive oil; blend until smooth.
- Place the shrimp in a bowl, drizzle with the olive oil mixture; mix to combine. Cover and let marinate in the refrigerator for 2 hours.
- Heat a skillet over medium heat. Cook while stirring the shrimp for about 15 minutes in the skillet until heated through.

Nutrition Information

- Calories: 949 calories;
- Total Fat: 91.1
- Sodium: 3858
- Total Carbohydrate: 9.2
- Cholesterol: 76
- Protein: 11.2

904. Tequila Steak

Serving: 1 | Prep: 5mins | Cook: 15mins | Ready in:

Ingredients

- 1/3 cup tequila
- 2 tablespoons Worcestershire sauce
- 1 tablespoon cayenne pepper
- 2 cloves garlic
- 8 ounces London broil steak

Direction

- In a blender, add the garlic, cayenne pepper, Worcestershire sauce and tequila; blend until smooth. Lay the steak on a dish, add the marinade over. Put in the fridge to marinate for at least 8 hours or overnight.
- Set an outdoor grill to high heat and brush oil lightly over the grate.
- Transfer the steak to the preheated grill and grill for 7 to 8 minutes each side to get medium steak, or until it reaches your preferred doneness.

Nutrition Information

- Calories: 428 calories;
- Total Carbohydrate: 11.7
- Cholesterol: 51
- Protein: 28.4
- Total Fat: 10.2
- Sodium: 389

905. Teriyaki Tofu With Pineapple

Serving: 4 | Prep: 10mins | Cook: 20mins | Ready in:

Ingredients

- 1 (12 ounce) package firm tofu
- 1 cup chopped fresh pineapple
- 2 cups teriyaki sauce

Direction

- Slice tofu into bite-sized pieces and put the tofu pieces in a deep baking dish; add pineapple. Pour in teriyaki sauce. Chill for at least 60 minutes.
- Turn the oven to 350°F (175°C) to preheat.
- Put in the preheated oven and bake until bubbling and hot, about 20 minutes.

Nutrition Information

- Calories: 272 calories;
- Total Carbohydrate: 31.5
- Cholesterol: 0

- Protein: 22.2
- Total Fat: 7.5
- Sodium: 5532

906. Teriyaki Wraps

Serving: 4 | Prep: 10mins | Cook: 15mins | Ready in:

Ingredients

- 1 cup uncooked long grain white rice
- 2 cups water
- 2 tablespoons olive oil
- 1 onion, chopped
- 1 red bell pepper, chopped
- 1 small zucchini, chopped
- 1 small yellow squash, chopped
- 1 1/4 cups teriyaki sauce
- 3 tablespoons soy sauce
- 2 teaspoons garlic powder
- 1/2 teaspoon salt
- 1 teaspoon ground black pepper
- 4 (10 inch) whole wheat tortillas

Direction

- Bring 2 cups of water in a saucepan to a boil and put in rice. Lower heat and simmer with a cover about 20 minutes.
- In a big skillet, heat olive oil over moderate heat. Sauté together yellow squash, zucchini, bell pepper and onion until onions are soft then stir in teriyaki sauce. Once vegetables are softened, stir in pepper, salt, garlic powder, soy sauce and cooked rice, then simmer the mixture about 3-5 minutes.
- In each tortilla, put a quarter of rice and vegetables, then roll it up.

Nutrition Information

- Calories: 540 calories;
- Sodium: 4426
- Total Carbohydrate: 100.6

- Cholesterol: 0
- Protein: 15
- Total Fat: 7.8

907. Texas Caviar I

Serving: 16 | Prep: 15mins | Cook: | Ready in:

Ingredients

- 1/2 onion, chopped
- 1 green bell pepper, chopped
- 1 bunch green onions, chopped
- 2 jalapeno peppers, chopped
- 1 tablespoon minced garlic
- 1 pint cherry tomatoes, quartered
- 1 (8 ounce) bottle zesty Italian dressing
- 1 (15 ounce) can black beans, drained
- 1 (15 ounce) can black-eyed peas, drained
- 1/2 teaspoon ground coriander
- 1 bunch chopped fresh cilantro

Direction

- Mix coriander, black-eyed peas, black beans, zesty Italian dressing, cherry tomatoes, garlic, jalapeno peppers, green onions, green bell pepper and onion in a big bowl. Cover; chill for 2 hours in the fridge. Toss with preferred amount of fresh cilantro; serve.

Nutrition Information

- Calories: 107 calories;
- Sodium: 415
- Total Carbohydrate: 11.8
- Cholesterol: 0
- Protein: 3.5
- Total Fat: 5.4

908. Thai Basil Rolls With Hoisin Peanut Sauce

Serving: 12 | Prep: 20mins | Cook: 30mins | Ready in:

Ingredients

- Rolls
- 1/2 pound medium shrimp
- 1/2 pound pork loin
- 1 (8 ounce) package rice noodles
- 12 round rice wrapper sheets
- 1 bunch fresh Thai basil - leaves picked from stems
- 1 cup chopped fresh cilantro
- 1 cup chopped fresh mint
- 2 cups bean sprouts
- Sauce
- 1 cup hoisin sauce
- 1 tablespoon creamy peanut butter
- 1 tablespoon water
- chopped roasted peanuts

Direction

- Put a medium sized stockpot of lightly salted water on a low boil. Cook shrimp until opaque for 2-3 minutes. Drain then let slightly cool. Pat dry using a paper towel. Peel shrimp, devein, then cut in half.
- Boil another stockpot of lightly salted water. Cook pork for approximately 10 minutes on a low boil until the internal temperature is 63 degrees C/145 degrees F. Let cool then cut to thin strips.
- Boil another stockpot of water. Cook noodles for approximately 7-8 minutes, occasionally stirring, until tender. Drain then rinse to avoid sticking.
- Fill warm water in a medium bowl. Dip every wrapper in water for about 30 seconds until flexible and soft. Put wrapper on a surface that's flat. Put 2 basil leaves in the middle next to each other, about 2 inches away from the wrapper's edge. Put 4-5 shrimp halves on the basil then a bit of pork and a bit of noodles. Drizzle with mint and cilantro. Place bean sprouts on top. Roll wrapper over one time, starting at one end. Fold both of the sides in towards the middle, keep tightly rolling without tearing. It should be approximately 1 – 1 1/2 inches thick.
- Warm water, peanut butter, and hoisin sauce in a saucepan on medium-high heat. Boil then take off heat immediately. Top sauce with chopped peanuts if you want, then serve alongside rolls as a dip.

Nutrition Information

- Calories: 195 calories;
- Total Carbohydrate: 29.2
- Cholesterol: 38
- Protein: 9.6
- Total Fat: 4.3
- Sodium: 448

909. Thai Spicy Basil Chicken Fried Rice

Serving: 6 | Prep: 30mins | Cook: 10mins | Ready in:

Ingredients

- 3 tablespoons oyster sauce
- 2 tablespoons fish sauce
- 1 teaspoon white sugar
- 1/2 cup peanut oil for frying
- 4 cups cooked jasmine rice, chilled
- 6 large cloves garlic clove, crushed
- 2 serrano peppers, crushed
- 1 pound boneless, skinless chicken breast, cut into thin strips
- 1 red pepper, seeded and thinly sliced
- 1 onion, thinly sliced
- 2 cups sweet Thai basil
- 1 cucumber, sliced (optional)
- 1/2 cup cilantro sprigs (optional)

Direction

- In a bowl, mix fish sauce, sugar and oyster sauce.
- Heat a wok with oil over medium-high heat until the oil is starting to smoke. Put in the serrano peppers and garlic and stir quickly. Add in the onion, oyster sauce mixture, bell pepper and chicken. Cook until the chicken is no longer pink inside. Increase the heat setting to high and put in the chilled rice then quickly stir-fry until the rice is well coated with sauce. Break chunks of rice that stick together using the back of a spoon.
- Remove the wok from heat and put in the basil leaves. Top it with cilantro and sliced cucumber as desired.

Nutrition Information

- Calories: 794 calories;
- Protein: 29.1
- Total Fat: 22.1
- Sodium: 469
- Total Carbohydrate: 116.4
- Cholesterol: 46

910. The Best Sweet And Sour Meatballs

Serving: 4 | Prep: 20mins | Cook: 30mins | Ready in:

Ingredients

- 1 pound ground beef
- 1 egg
- 1/4 cup dry bread crumbs
- 1 onion, diced
- 1 cup packed brown sugar
- 3 tablespoons all-purpose flour
- 1 1/2 cups water
- 1/4 cup distilled white vinegar
- 3 tablespoons soy sauce

Direction

- Combine onion, bread crumbs, egg, and ground beef in a medium bowl. Thoroughly mix and roll into golf ball-sized balls.
- Over medium heat, gently brown the meatballs in a large skillet, then put aside.
- Combine soy sauce, white vinegar, water, flour, and brown sugar in a large saucepan. Mix thoroughly. Place in the meatballs and bring to a boil. Lower the heat and simmer for 30 minutes, stirring regularly.

Nutrition Information

- Calories: 516 calories;
- Total Carbohydrate: 67.1
- Cholesterol: 122
- Protein: 24.5
- Total Fat: 16.8
- Sodium: 815

911. The Sarge's Goetta German Breakfast Treat

Serving: 20 | Prep: 5hours | Cook: 10mins | Ready in:

Ingredients

- 3 quarts water
- 2 tablespoons salt
- 2 teaspoons ground black pepper
- 5 cups steel cut oats
- 2 pounds ground beef
- 2 pounds ground pork sausage
- 2 large onions, finely chopped
- 1/4 cup cooking oil

Direction

- Bring to boil water, pepper, and salt in a slow cooker that is set to High. Mix in the steel cut oats, cover the cooker and let to cook for 90 minutes.
- Combine onions, mix beef, and pork in a large bowl. Mix into the oat mixture and decrease

the heat to Low. Cover and continue to cook while stirring time to time for 3 hours.
- Pour the mixture into a medium baking pan and let to cool until semi-solid. Roll out on top of a wax paper and then refrigerate for 1 hour or until firm.
- Over medium high heat, heat oil in a large, heavy skillet. Chop the chilled mixture into thin slices and then cook the slices one by one in the hot oil until brown evenly.

Nutrition Information

- Calories: 511 calories;
- Total Fat: 35.6
- Sodium: 1036
- Total Carbohydrate: 29
- Cholesterol: 69
- Protein: 18

912. Thit Bo Xao Dau

Serving: 4 | Prep: 10mins | Cook: 20mins | Ready in:

Ingredients

- 1 clove garlic, minced
- 1/4 teaspoon ground black pepper
- 1 teaspoon cornstarch
- 1 teaspoon vegetable oil
- 1 pound sirloin tips, thinly sliced
- 3 tablespoons vegetable oil
- 1/2 onion, thinly sliced
- 2 cups fresh green beans, washed and trimmed
- 1/4 cup chicken broth
- 1 teaspoon soy sauce

Direction

- Combine a teaspoon vegetable oil, garlic, cornstarch and black pepper in a large mixing bowl. Add the beef, and mix thoroughly.
- Heat 2 tablespoons of oil in a big wok over high heat for a minute. Add the meat; cook while stirring for about 2 minutes, or until it starts to brown. Place the beef in a large bowl, and put aside.
- Heat the remaining tablespoon oil in wok. Stir in onion and cook until softened. Add in green beans and mix; add the broth. Adjust the heat to medium. Simmer with cover for about 4 to 5 minutes, or until beans are tender crisp. Mix in soy sauce and beef. Cook while stirring from time to time, for a minute or 2, or until heated completely.

Nutrition Information

- Calories: 376 calories;
- Protein: 23.1
- Total Fat: 28.6
- Sodium: 199
- Total Carbohydrate: 6.3
- Cholesterol: 76

913. Three Berry Pie

Serving: 8 | Prep: 45mins | Cook: 45mins | Ready in:

Ingredients

- Pastry for a Double-Crust Pie:
- 2 cups all-purpose flour
- 1/2 teaspoon salt
- 2/3 cup shortening, chilled
- 6 tablespoons cold water
- Three-Berry Filling:
- 1 cup fresh strawberries, halved
- 2 cups fresh raspberries
- 1 1/2 cups fresh blueberries
- 1/2 cup white sugar
- 3 tablespoons cornstarch

Direction

- Mix the salt and flour. Mash in the shortening with a pastry blender until small pea-sized pieces form. Scatter a tablespoon of the water on part of the mixture, then toss with a fork gently. Press moistened part to the side of the bowl. Repeat with a tablespoon of water at a time, until all is moist. Spit the dough in half. Roll each half into a ball and flatten slightly. Encase in plastic and chill for no less than 30 minutes.
- Put one piece of dough onto a lightly floured surface. Stretch the dough from the center to the edges to form a 12-inch circle. Roll the crust around the rolling pin. Roll out on a 9-inch pie pan. Ease the shell into the pie pan, be sure not to stretch it. Cut off the bottom crust evenly with the rim of the pie pan, and put the pastry-lined-pie-pan back to the fridge.
- Mix the sugar with cornstarch in a big mixing bowl. Put in the blueberries, raspberries, and strawberries; toss gently until berries are covered. Let fruit mixture sit for about 15 minutes.
- Set the oven to 375°F (190°C) to preheat. Put a baking tray in the oven to preheat.
- Unroll the leftover pastry for the top crust. Mix the berry mixture and add the filling to the pastry-lined pie pan. Put the top crust on top of the pie and cut off the edges, leaving a 1/2-inch overhang. Fold the top shell under the bottom shell, lightly pinch to seal. Crimp the edges of the shell and score vents in the top to let steam escape. To avoid over-browning, cover the edge of the pie using foil.
- Bake for 25 minutes in the prepared oven on the baking sheet. Take off the foil.
- Bake for 20 to 30 minutes more, or until the crust is golden and the filling is bubbling. Let cool on a wire rack.

Nutrition Information

- Calories: 361 calories;
- Total Fat: 17.7
- Sodium: 147
- Total Carbohydrate: 48
- Cholesterol: 0
- Protein: 3.8

914. Three Ingredient Peanut Butter Cookies

Serving: 6 | Prep: | Cook: | Ready in:

Ingredients

- 1 cup peanut butter
- 1 cup white sugar
- 1 egg

Direction

- Preheat an oven to 175°C/350°F; line parchment paper on baking sheets.
- Mix egg, white sugar and peanut butter till smooth.
- Drop dough spoonfuls on prepped baking sheet; bake for 6-8 minutes at 175°C/350°F, don't overbake. Best when barely brown on bottom and still soft.

Nutrition Information

- Calories: 394 calories;
- Total Fat: 22.5
- Sodium: 209
- Total Carbohydrate: 41.8
- Cholesterol: 31
- Protein: 11.8

915. Tofu Fudge Mocha Bars

Serving: 24 | Prep: 5mins | Cook: 10mins | Ready in:

Ingredients

- 1 (12 ounce) package silken tofu, undrained
- 2 tablespoons safflower oil

- 1 pinch salt
- 2 1/3 cups turbinado sugar
- 1 cup cocoa powder
- 1/3 cup instant decaffeinated coffee powder
- 1 teaspoon vanilla extract
- 1 cup whole wheat flour

Direction

- Set the oven at 325°F (165°C) and start preheating.
- Blend tofu with an electric mixer till creamy. Include vanilla, coffee, cocoa, sugar, salt and oil; blend properly.
- Once the sugar is dissolved into the tofu mixture; take the bowl away from the electric mixer and whisk in flour.
- Transfer the batter into a 9x13-in. baking pan coated with grease.
- Bake till the cake pulls away from the side of the pan, 25-30 minutes. The bars will appear almost underdone and glossy. Allow to cool in the pan; use a clean and wet knife to cut into bars once cool.

Nutrition Information

- Calories: 117 calories;
- Total Fat: 2.1
- Sodium: 14
- Total Carbohydrate: 24.6
- Cholesterol: 0
- Protein: 2.4

916. Tofu Hummus

Serving: 8 | Prep: 10mins | Cook: | Ready in:

Ingredients

- 1/2 cup diced silken tofu
- 1/4 cup lemon juice
- 2 tablespoons creamy peanut butter
- 2 tablespoons olive oil
- 3 cloves garlic
- 1 (19 ounce) can garbanzo beans, drained

Direction

- In a food processor or blender, stir in garbanzo beans, garlic, olive oil, peanut butter, lemon juice and tofu, then process until the mixture becomes smooth. Refrigerate until serving time.

Nutrition Information

- Calories: 296 calories;
- Sodium: 364
- Total Carbohydrate: 40.5
- Cholesterol: 0
- Protein: 14.6
- Total Fat: 9.5

917. Tofu Pumpkin Pie

Serving: 8 | Prep: 5mins | Cook: 55mins | Ready in:

Ingredients

- 1 (10.5 ounce) package silken tofu, drained
- 1 (16 ounce) can pumpkin puree
- 3/4 cup white sugar
- 1/2 teaspoon salt
- 1 teaspoon ground cinnamon
- 1/2 teaspoon ground ginger
- 1/4 teaspoon ground cloves
- 1 (9 inch) unbaked pie crust

Direction

- Preheat the oven to 230°C or 450°F.
- Into a blender, put clove, ginger, cinnamon, salt, sugar, pumpkin and tofu. Puree till smooth. Put into pie crust.
- In the preheated oven, bake for 15 minutes, then lower heat to 175°C or 350°F, and keep baking for about 40 minutes longer till an

inserted knife into the mixture comes out clean. Let cool prior to serving.

Nutrition Information

- Calories: 230 calories;
- Sodium: 413
- Total Carbohydrate: 34.9
- Cholesterol: 0
- Protein: 4.6
- Total Fat: 8.7

918. Tofu And Artichoke Risotto

Serving: 8 | Prep: 20mins | Cook: 30mins | Ready in:

Ingredients

- 2 tablespoons olive oil
- 1 tablespoon unsalted margarine
- 1 small onion, chopped
- 2 cups uncooked carnaroli rice
- 1/4 cup soy milk
- 1/4 cup apple juice
- 6 cups vegetable stock
- 1 (8 ounce) container firm tofu, cubed
- 1 (6.5 ounce) jar marinated artichoke hearts, drained, liquid reserved
- 2 cloves garlic, minced
- 1 (8.75 ounce) can low salt yellow corn
- cayenne pepper to taste

Direction

- Heat margarine and oil in a big saucepan on moderate heat. Mix in half of the onion and sauté till soft. Mix in rice and cook till slightly browned.
- Into the rice, put apple juice and soy milk. Once rice has soaked in the liquids, slowly add the vegetable stock, approximately half cup at a time, till soaked in. Set aside approximately a quarter cup of stock. Put on a cover and cook till rice is soft for 20 minutes.
- In the reserved marinated artichoke heart liquid, slightly brown the rest of onion and the tofu in medium-sized saucepan on moderate heat. Mix in garlic.
- Take rice off the heat and mix in cayenne pepper, corn, artichoke hearts, tofu mixture and the rest of the vegetable stock; stir well.

Nutrition Information

- Calories: 347 calories;
- Total Carbohydrate: 57.3
- Cholesterol: 0
- Protein: 10.4
- Total Fat: 9.2
- Sodium: 303

919. Tofu And Vegetables Stir Fry With Couscous

Serving: 4 | Prep: 15mins | Cook: 30mins | Ready in:

Ingredients

- 10 ounces tofu, cubed
- 2 tablespoons olive oil, divided, or as needed
- 1 teaspoon curry powder, or to taste
- salt and ground pepper to taste
- 1 head broccoli, cut into florets
- 1 carrot, sliced
- 8 cups fresh spinach
- 1 onion, diced
- 1/2 cucumber, sliced
- 1 radish, sliced
- 1 pinch ground nutmeg, or to taste
- 2 tablespoons soy sauce, divided, or to taste
- 1 tablespoon honey, or to taste
- 1 tablespoon peanut butter
- 1 pinch ground ginger, or to taste
- 1 pinch ground black pepper to taste (optional)

- 1 cup water
- 1 cup couscous
- 1 tablespoon vegan margarine, or to taste
- 1 clove garlic, minced
- 1 tablespoon pistachio nuts, or to taste

Direction

- Mix together pepper, salt, curry powder, 1 tbsp. oil and tofu in a bowl; stand for 30 minutes.
- Put carrot, 1 pinch of salt, 1 tbsp. water and broccoli in a microwave-safe bowl as tofu is marinating; cover. Cook for 2 1/2 minutes in microwave.
- Heat 1 tbsp. oil in a wok on high heat; sauté 1 pinch of salt, nutmeg, radish, cucumber, onion and spinach for approximately 1 minute till spinach wilts. Add black pepper, ginger, peanut butter, honey and 1 tbsp. soy sauce; add cooked carrot and broccoli. Lower the heat to low; cover the wok.
- Transfer marinated tofu in a pan on medium heat then add 1 tbsp. soy sauce; cook for about 3 minutes till heated through. Add to veggie mixture in the wok.
- Boil water in a saucepan. Add garlic, margarine and couscous. Stir well; cover saucepan. Rest for approximately 10 minutes till water is absorbed.
- Serve couscous in a bowl with pistachios and tofu mixture on top.

Nutrition Information

- Calories: 431 calories;
- Total Fat: 16.8
- Sodium: 640
- Total Carbohydrate: 56.6
- Cholesterol: 0
- Protein: 18.1

920. Tofu And Veggies In Peanut Sauce

Serving: 4 | Prep: 10mins | Cook: 10mins | Ready in:

Ingredients

- 1 tablespoon peanut oil
- 1 small head broccoli, chopped
- 1 small red bell pepper, chopped
- 5 fresh mushrooms, sliced
- 1 pound firm tofu, cubed
- 1/2 cup peanut butter
- 1/2 cup hot water
- 2 tablespoons vinegar
- 2 tablespoons soy sauce
- 1 1/2 tablespoons molasses
- ground cayenne pepper to taste

Direction

- In a wok or large skillet over medium-high heat, heat oil. Sauté tofu, mushrooms, red bell pepper, and broccoli for 5 minutes.
- Combine cayenne pepper, molasses, soy sauce, vinegar, hot water, and peanut butter in a small bowl. Pour the mixture over tofu and vegetables. Simmer until veggies are soft but crisp, about 3-5 minutes.

Nutrition Information

- Calories: 443 calories;
- Total Fat: 29.9
- Sodium: 642
- Total Carbohydrate: 24
- Cholesterol: 0
- Protein: 29

921. Tomato, Corn And Avocado Salsa

Serving: 16 | Prep: 30mins | Cook: | Ready in:

Ingredients

- 1 (11 ounce) can whole kernel corn, drained
- 1 (4 ounce) can sliced black olives, drained
- 1 1/2 cups diced roma tomatoes
- 3/4 cup diced red onion
- 1 red bell pepper, seeded and diced
- 1 1/2 teaspoons minced jalapeno pepper
- 1 avocados - peeled, pitted and diced
- 2 tablespoons olive oil
- 2 tablespoons fresh lime juice
- 1 teaspoon salt

Direction

- In a large bowl, combine jalapeno pepper, red pepper, onion, tomatoes, olives and corn. Then gently fold in salt, lime juice, olive oil and diced avocado.

Nutrition Information

- Calories: 68 calories;
- Total Fat: 4.5
- Sodium: 266
- Total Carbohydrate: 7.1
- Cholesterol: 0
- Protein: 1.1

922. Tropical Tuna Hash

Serving: 3 | Prep: 10mins | Cook: 15mins | Ready in:

Ingredients

- 3/4 cup almond flour
- 1/2 cup coconut flour
- 1 (5 ounce) can tuna, drained
- 1/4 cup orange juice
- 1/4 cup almond milk
- 1 tablespoon baking powder
- 3 pineapple rings, chopped
- 1 large egg
- 2 tablespoons olive oil

Direction

- Mix egg, pineapple, baking powder, almond milk, orange juice, tuna, coconut flour and almond flour till incorporated into batter in bowl.
- Heat olive oil in big skillet on medium heat; put batter into skillet. Cook for 3 minutes, don't mix. Every 3 minutes for 15 minutes, flip batter using spatula till it's an even mixture of light tuna color and golden and crispy batter on both sides.

Nutrition Information

- Calories: 279 calories;
- Total Fat: 11.8
- Sodium: 552
- Total Carbohydrate: 21.7
- Cholesterol: 75
- Protein: 24.2

923. Tuna Tartare

Serving: 6 | Prep: 10mins | Cook: | Ready in:

Ingredients

- 1 pound sushi grade tuna, finely diced
- 3 tablespoons olive oil
- 1/4 teaspoon wasabi powder
- 1 tablespoon sesame seeds
- 1/8 teaspoon cracked black pepper
- sliced French bread

Direction

- Stir together the cracked black pepper, sesame seeds, wasabi powder and olive oil in a bowl. Toss the tuna into the mixture until coated evenly. Modify the seasoning as preferred with more black pepper or wasabi powder. Serve it on a slice of French bread.

Nutrition Information

- Calories: 366 calories;
- Sodium: 514
- Total Carbohydrate: 42.6
- Cholesterol: 34
- Protein: 26.7
- Total Fat: 9.6

924. Twice Cooked Coconut Shrimp

Serving: 6 | Prep: 30mins | Cook: 15mins | Ready in:

Ingredients

- 1 1/2 pounds large shrimp - peeled and deveined
- 1/2 cup all-purpose flour
- 1/2 cup cornstarch
- 1 tablespoon salt
- 1/2 tablespoon ground white pepper
- 2 tablespoons vegetable oil
- 1 cup ice water
- 2 cups shredded coconut
- 1 quart vegetable oil for frying
- 1/2 cup orange marmalade
- 1/4 cup Dijon-style prepared mustard
- 1/4 cup honey
- 1/4 teaspoon hot pepper sauce

Direction

- Remove the shell and the vein of the shrimp. Wash and dry with paper towels. Mix together white pepper, salt, cornstarch, and flour. Add ice water and 2 tablespoons of vegetable oil. Mix well to blend.
- In a shallow pan, pour the coconut. Dip the shrimp into the batter one by one. Roll the shrimp in the coconut. Fry the coated shrimps in a frying pan with the oil heated to 350°F (175°C). Cook the shrimp in hot oil for about 4 minutes until it browns lightly. Bake the fried shrimp in an oven preheated to 300°F (150°C) for 5 minutes.
- In a small bowl, mix together hot sauce, honey, mustard, and marmalade to make the dipping sauce. Mix well. Serve the shrimp with the dipping sauce.

Nutrition Information

- Calories: 602 calories;
- Total Fat: 28.2
- Sodium: 1673
- Total Carbohydrate: 63.3
- Cholesterol: 173
- Protein: 25.1

925. Ultimate Maple Snickerdoodles

Serving: 36 | Prep: 15mins | Cook: 10mins | Ready in:

Ingredients

- 2 cups all-purpose flour
- 1 1/2 teaspoons baking powder
- 1/4 teaspoon baking soda
- 1 1/2 teaspoons ground cinnamon
- 1/2 cup margarine, softened
- 1 cup white sugar
- 3 tablespoons real maple syrup
- 1 egg
- 1/2 cup white sugar
- 1/4 cup maple sugar

Direction

- Preheat an oven to 175°C/350°F. Mix cinnamon, baking soda, baking powder and flour together; put aside.
- Cream 1 cup white sugar and margarine till fluffy and light in a big bowl; beat in maple syrup and egg. Blend in the dry ingredients slowly till just mixed. Mix maple sugar and leftover 1/2 cup white sugar together in a

small dish. Roll dough into 1-in. balls; roll balls in sugar mixture. Put cookies on ungreased cookie sheets, 2-in. apart.
- In the preheated oven, bake for 8-10 minutes; cookies will appear wet in the center and crackly on top. Transfer from cookie sheets onto wire racks; cool.

Nutrition Information

- Calories: 91 calories;
- Total Fat: 2.7
- Sodium: 61
- Total Carbohydrate: 16.2
- Cholesterol: 5
- Protein: 0.9

926. Unbelievable Chicken

Serving: 6 | Prep: 15mins | Cook: 20mins | Ready in:

Ingredients

- 1/4 cup cider vinegar
- 3 tablespoons prepared coarse-ground mustard
- 3 cloves garlic, peeled and minced
- 1 lime, juiced
- 1/2 lemon, juiced
- 1/2 cup brown sugar
- 1 1/2 teaspoons salt
- ground black pepper to taste
- 6 tablespoons olive oil
- 6 skinless, boneless chicken breast halves

Direction

- In a big glass bowl, combine pepper, salt, brown sugar, lemon juice, lime juice, garlic, mustard and cider vinegar, then whisk in the olive oil. Put chicken into the mixture. Cover and let chicken marinate for 8 hours to overnight.
- Preheat an outdoor grill for high heat.
- Coat the grate lightly with oil and arrange chicken on the prepped grill. Cook until juices run clear, about 6-8 minutes on each side. Get rid of marinade.

Nutrition Information

- Calories: 337 calories;
- Sodium: 736
- Total Carbohydrate: 22.4
- Cholesterol: 67
- Protein: 24.8
- Total Fat: 16.4

927. Unbelievable Vegan Mashed Potatoes

Serving: 4 | Prep: 10mins | Cook: 16mins | Ready in:

Ingredients

- 3 russet potatoes, peeled and cut into chunks
- 1 bay leaf
- 1/2 cup soy milk (such as Silk®)
- 2 tablespoons vegan mayonnaise (such as Vegenaise®)
- 2 tablespoons vegan margarine (such as Earth Balance®)
- 1 tablespoon vegan grated Parmesan-style topping (such as Go Veggie®
- salt and ground black pepper to taste

Direction

- In a big pot, place bay leaf and potato chunks; pour in water to cover. Heat to a boil. Decrease to medium-low heat, let simmer 10-15 minutes until tender. Drain and remove to a big bowl.
- In a microwave-safe bowl, combine pepper, salt, Parmesan-style topping, vegan margarine, vegan mayonnaise, and soy milk. Heat in 30-second intervals for 1-2 minutes until margarine melts.

- In the bowl of potatoes, add soy milk mixture; use a potato masher to mash until smooth.

Nutrition Information

- Calories: 232 calories;
- Total Fat: 9.9
- Sodium: 167
- Total Carbohydrate: 31.9
- Cholesterol: 0
- Protein: 5.2

928. Unsloppy Joes

Serving: 8 | Prep: 15mins | Cook: 15mins | Ready in:

Ingredients

- 1 tablespoon olive oil
- 1/2 cup chopped onion
- 1/2 cup chopped celery
- 1/2 cup chopped carrots
- 1/2 cup chopped green bell pepper
- 1 clove garlic, minced
- 1 (14.5 ounce) can diced tomatoes
- 1 1/2 tablespoons chili powder
- 1 tablespoon tomato paste
- 1 tablespoon distilled white vinegar
- 1 teaspoon ground black pepper
- 1 (15 ounce) can kidney beans, drained and rinsed
- 8 kaiser rolls

Direction

- Heat olive oil in a huge skillet and place it over medium heat. Stir in celery, garlic, green pepper, carrot, and onion, and cook it until tender. Add chili powder, tomatoes, vinegar, pepper, and tomato paste into the mixture. Cover the skillet and adjust its heat to low. Simmer for 10 minutes.
- Add kidney beans, and then let it cook for 5 more minutes.
- Slice 1/4 inch size from the top of each Kaiser roll. Set aside for a while. Leave the center of each roll vacant and make sure that only half-sized thick shells remain. Leave the inside of the rolls empty for other uses.
- Add bean mixture evenly into the rolls and replace its tops. Serve immediately.

Nutrition Information

- Calories: 204 calories;
- Total Fat: 3.9
- Sodium: 489
- Total Carbohydrate: 34.6
- Cholesterol: 0
- Protein: 7.8

929. Vegan Almond Snack

Serving: 10 | Prep: 10mins | Cook: | Ready in:

Ingredients

- 10 dates, pitted
- 8 tablespoons almond butter
- 6 tablespoons almonds
- 6 tablespoons brown rice syrup
- 4 tablespoons sunflower seeds
- 6 tablespoons roasted sesame seeds

Direction

- Mix sunflower seeds, rice syrup, almonds, almond butter, and dates in the bowl of a food processor; process until forming a thick paste. Put in a bit more rice syrup if paste gets too thick.
- In a small soup bowl, put sesame seeds. Form paste into 1/2-inch balls and place on sesame seeds and roll to coat.

Nutrition Information

- Calories: 279 calories;

- Sodium: 64
- Total Carbohydrate: 36.9
- Cholesterol: 0
- Total Fat: 14
- Protein: 6

930. Vegan Almond Truffles

Serving: 24 | Prep: 30mins | Cook: | Ready in:

Ingredients

- 1 cup raw almonds
- 5 Medjool dates, pitted and chopped
- 2 teaspoons coconut oil
- 1 cup raw cocoa powder
- 1/4 cup water
- 3 tablespoons agave nectar, or more to taste
- 2 teaspoons chia seeds
- 2 teaspoons flax seeds
- 2 tablespoons raw cocoa powder, or as needed
- Himalayan pink salt to taste

Direction

- Grind almonds finely in the bowl of a food processor. Add dates and pulse until well combined.
- Place coconut oil in a large microwaveable bowl and microwave for about 10 seconds until melted. Add flax seeds, chia seeds, agave nectar, water, 1 cup cocoa powder, and date and almond mixture; mix with a spatula or wooden spoon until a stiff dough is formed.
- Place salt and 2 tablespoons cocoa powder in shallow bowls. Line parchment paper onto a baking sheet.
- Roll dough into tablespoon-sized balls using your hands. Cover balls with cocoa powder, lightly dip in salt then place on the prepared baking sheet. Refrigerate or freeze until firm before storing them.

Nutrition Information

- Calories: 62 calories;
- Total Fat: 4.1
- Sodium: 3
- Total Carbohydrate: 6.8
- Cholesterol: 0
- Protein: 2.2

931. Vegan Apple Pie

Serving: 8 | Prep: 30mins | Cook: 48mins | Ready in:

Ingredients

- Crust:
- 2 1/3 cups all-purpose flour
- 1 cup vegan margarine (such as Earth Balance®)
- 1 tablespoon white sugar
- 1 teaspoon salt
- 1/4 cup ice water
- Filling:
- 1 cup brown sugar
- 1/2 cup vegan margarine (such as Earth Balance®)
- 1/4 cup white sugar
- 1/4 cup rice milk
- 3 tablespoons all-purpose flour
- 2 teaspoons ground cinnamon
- 1/2 teaspoon ground nutmeg
- 7 Granny Smith apples - peeled, cored, and sliced

Direction

- Mix together salt, 1 tbsp. white sugar, 1 cup vegan margarine and 2 1/3 cups of all-purpose flour and pulse till it clumps together in a food processor. Add water slowly; pulse several times till a dough forms.
- Place dough onto a flat work surface; knead it for 30 seconds. Form into a disk; wrap in plastic wrap. Refrigerate for approximately 30 minutes till firm.
- Preheat an oven to 165°C/325°F.

- Dust flour on a flat work surface; roll out dough into two 10-in. crusts. Gently press 1 crust into a 9-in. pie plate.
- Mix together nutmeg, cinnamon, 3 tbsp. flour, rice milk, 1/4 cup white sugar, 1/2 cup vegan margarine and brown sugar in a saucepan and cook while stirring on medium heat for 3-5 minutes till brown sugar dissolves and margarine melts.
- Put apples slices in a big bowl. Put brown sugar mixture over; mix till apples are coated evenly. Pile apples into the bottom crust; use 2nd crust to cover. Use a sharp knife to cut slits in the top crust.
- In preheated oven, bake for 45-60 minutes till apples are semi translucent and crust is golden brown.

Nutrition Information

- Calories: 642 calories;
- Sodium: 637
- Total Carbohydrate: 81.2
- Cholesterol: 0
- Protein: 4.6
- Total Fat: 33.9

932. Vegan Apple Yogurt Parfait With Maca Powder

Serving: 4 | Prep: 20mins | Cook: | Ready in:

Ingredients

- For the Chocolate-Hazelnut Layer:
- 2 tablespoons carob powder
- 2 teaspoons cacao powder
- 1/4 cup coconut milk
- For the Applesauce Layer:
- 1/4 cup unsweetened applesauce
- 1 teaspoon maca powder (optional)
- 2 teaspoons raisins
- 1 teaspoon maple syrup
- For the Maple Coconut Flake Layer:
- 1/4 cup shredded coconut
- 2 teaspoons maple syrup
- For the Coconut Yogurt Layer:
- 1/4 cup coconut yogurt
- For the Toppings:
- 2 dried figs, thinly sliced
- 2 fresh strawberries, sliced
- 1/3 (1 ounce) square unsweetened chocolate, shaved

Direction

- In a small bowl, mix cacao powder and carob powder. Mix in coconut milk little by little, whisking well until free from lumps.
- In a bowl, combine maca powder and applesauce. Put in 1 teaspoon maple syrup and raisins.
- Combine in a bowl the 2 teaspoons maple syrup and shredded coconut.
- Into 4 small wine glasses or digestif glasses, scoop layers of 1 tablespoon each carob mixture, maple coconut flakes, maca applesauce and coconut yogurt, in that order.
- Keep the parfaits in the refrigerator for at least 4 hours, covered, until very cold.
- Garnish parfaits with shaved chocolate, strawberries, and figs.

Nutrition Information

- Calories: 160 calories;
- Total Fat: 9.2
- Sodium: 9
- Total Carbohydrate: 22.3
- Cholesterol: 0
- Protein: 2

933. Vegan Avocado Brownies

Serving: 16 | Prep: 15mins | Cook: 30mins | Ready in:

Ingredients

- 1 avocado, peeled and pitted
- 1/2 cup coconut oil, melted
- 2 cups all-purpose flour
- 1 1/2 cups coconut sugar
- 1 1/2 cups almond milk
- 1 cup cacao powder
- 2 teaspoons baking soda
- 1 teaspoon salt

Direction

- Set oven to 350 degrees F or 175 degrees C then grease a baking dish that is 9x13 inches in size.
- In a blender or food processor, place avocado and blend until it becomes smooth. In a bowl, whisk together coconut oil with the avocado until smooth.
- Whisk salt, baking soda, cacao powder, almond milk, coconut sugar, and flour into the avocado mixture until combined thoroughly, then spread onto the greased baking dish.
- Bake in preheated oven for 30 minutes until the middle is set and brownies start to pull away from the sides.

Nutrition Information

- Calories: 203 calories;
- Sodium: 322
- Total Carbohydrate: 28.1
- Cholesterol: 0
- Protein: 2.5
- Total Fat: 9.3

934. Vegan Baked Oatmeal Patties

Serving: 18 | Prep: 30mins | Cook: 40mins | Ready in:

Ingredients

- 4 cups water
- 4 cups quick cooking oats
- 1/2 onion, chopped
- 1/3 cup vegetable oil
- 1/2 cup spaghetti sauce
- 1/2 cup chopped pecans
- 1/4 cup nutritional yeast
- 2 teaspoons garlic powder
- 1 teaspoon dried basil
- 2 teaspoons onion powder
- 1 teaspoon ground coriander
- 1 teaspoon sage
- 1 teaspoon active dry yeast

Direction

- Set the oven to 350°F (175°C) and start preheating. Grease a baking sheet.
- Bring water to boiling; stir in oatmeal. Cover and lower the heat to low. Cook until the oats are cooked and water are all absorbed or for 5-10 minutes. Take out of the heat; allow to stand for 5 minutes.
- Add active yeast, sage, coriander, onion powder, basil, garlic powder, nutritional yeast, pecans, spaghetti sauce, oil and onion to the oatmeal. Combine well; shape into patties. Transfer to the greased baking sheet.
- Bake 15 minutes. Turn patties over; bake for 15 more minutes.

Nutrition Information

- Calories: 141 calories;
- Protein: 3.9
- Total Fat: 7.7
- Sodium: 31
- Total Carbohydrate: 15
- Cholesterol: < 1

935. Vegan Banana Ice Cream

Serving: 2 | Prep: 10mins | Cook: | Ready in:

Ingredients

- 2 large frozen bananas, cut into small chunks
- 1 cup unsweetened almond milk
- 1 tablespoon chopped pecans
- 1 pinch ground cinnamon, or to taste

Direction

- In a food processor or blender, blend together cinnamon, pecans, almond milk and bananas until creamy and smooth.

Nutrition Information

- Calories: 180 calories;
- Sodium: 81
- Total Carbohydrate: 36.2
- Cholesterol: 0
- Protein: 2.4
- Total Fat: 4.4

936. Vegan Bean Taco Filling

Serving: 8 | Prep: 15mins | Cook: 15mins | Ready in:

Ingredients

- 1 tablespoon olive oil
- 1 onion, diced
- 2 cloves garlic, minced
- 1 bell pepper, chopped
- 2 (14.5 ounce) cans black beans, rinsed, drained, and mashed
- 2 tablespoons yellow cornmeal
- 1 1/2 tablespoons cumin
- 1 teaspoon paprika
- 1 teaspoon cayenne pepper
- 1 teaspoon chili powder
- 1 cup salsa

Direction

- Over medium heat, heat olive oil in a medium skillet. Stir bell pepper, garlic and onion in and cook until tender. Stir the mashed bean in, then, put the cornmeal. Mix salsa, chili powder, cayenne, paprika and cumin in and cover. Cook for 5 minutes.

Nutrition Information

- Calories: 142 calories;
- Total Carbohydrate: 24
- Cholesterol: 0
- Protein: 7.5
- Total Fat: 2.5
- Sodium: 596

937. Vegan Blueberry Coconut Ice Cream

Serving: 14 | Prep: 35mins | Cook: | Ready in:

Ingredients

- 2 tablespoons roasted flax seeds
- 2 (15 ounce) cans full-fat coconut milk, chilled
- 2 cups blueberries
- 1 tablespoon lemon juice
- 1 teaspoon vanilla extract
- 1 teaspoon coconut oil (optional)
- 1 teaspoon stevia powder
- 1/2 teaspoon xanthan gum, or more as desired (optional)
- 1/4 teaspoon Himalayan black salt (optional)

Direction

- In a coffee grinder, pulse flax seeds until finely ground.
- In a blender, mix together lemon juice, blueberries and 1 can coconut milk; puree until blueberry skins completely break down. Put in ground flax seeds, the rest of coconut milk, vanilla extract, salt, coconut oil, stevia and xanthan gum; puree until very smooth.
- Place blender container into the freezer to chill mixture quickly, about 15 minutes.
- Pour the mixture into an ice cream maker and churn following manufacturer's instructions

for about 20 minutes. Move to a lidded container before serving.

Nutrition Information

- Calories: 142 calories;
- Total Carbohydrate: 5.5
- Cholesterol: 0
- Protein: 1.6
- Total Fat: 13.8
- Sodium: 54

938. Vegan Brownies

Serving: 16 | Prep: 15mins | Cook: 25mins | Ready in:

Ingredients

- 2 cups unbleached all-purpose flour
- 2 cups white sugar
- 3/4 cup unsweetened cocoa powder
- 1 teaspoon baking powder
- 1 teaspoon salt
- 1 cup water
- 1 cup vegetable oil
- 1 teaspoon vanilla extract

Direction

- Set the oven to 175°C or 350°F to preheat.
- Stir together salt, baking powder, cocoa powder, sugar and flour in a big bowl. Add in vanilla, vegetable oil and water, then mix until well-combined. Spread in a 13"x9" baking pan evenly.
- In the preheated oven, bake until the top is not shiny anymore, about 25-30 minutes. Allow to cool for a minimum of 10 minutes prior to cutting into squares.

Nutrition Information

- Calories: 284 calories;
- Total Carbohydrate: 39.2
- Cholesterol: 0
- Protein: 2.4
- Total Fat: 14.3
- Sodium: 169

939. Vegan Butternut Squash And Chickpea Curry

Serving: 4 | Prep: 20mins | Cook: 1hours | Ready in:

Ingredients

- 1 cup dry chickpeas (garbanzo beans)
- 2 tablespoons vegetable oil
- 2 onions, chopped
- 4 cloves garlic, minced
- 6 pods green cardamom
- 2 dried red chile peppers, stemmed and seeded
- 2 teaspoons coriander seeds
- 2 teaspoons ground turmeric
- 1 teaspoon black mustard seeds
- 1 tablespoon tomato paste, or more to taste
- 1 large butternut squash, peeled and cut into 1-inch cubes
- 3 carrots, chopped
- 1 1/2 cups water, or as needed
- 1/2 bunch fresh cilantro, chopped

Direction

- Add chickpeas into a big bowl and cover using cold water. Allow to steep, 8 hours to overnight.
- Drain and wash chickpeas in the running cold water. Add into a big pot, cover it with several in. of water, and boil. Lower the heat and let it simmer for 60-75 minutes or till chickpeas become soft. Drain.
- Once chickpeas are halfway cooked, heat oil in a big pot and cook onions for roughly 5 minutes or till becoming soft and translucent. Mix in garlic and cook for roughly half a minute or till becoming fragrant. Put in mustard seeds, turmeric, coriander seeds, chile

peppers, and cardamom pods and toast for 60 seconds. Whisk in the tomato paste.
- Mix carrots and butternut squash into the pot. Pour in enough water to cover the vegetables halfway. Let it simmer on low heat, while covered partly, for 25-35 minutes or till all the vegetables become tender. Pour in extra water if curry gets too dry.
- Stir in cooked chickpeas briefly prior to serving and heat till warm. Serve sprinkled with cilantro.

Nutrition Information

- Calories: 468 calories;
- Sodium: 84
- Total Carbohydrate: 86.3
- Cholesterol: 0
- Protein: 15.4
- Total Fat: 10.9

940. Vegan Cashew Ricotta

Serving: 8 | Prep: 10mins | Cook: | Ready in:

Ingredients

- 2 cups raw cashews
- 4 tablespoons lemon juice
- 2 tablespoons olive oil
- 2 tablespoons nutritional yeast
- 3 cloves garlic
- 1/4 teaspoon salt
- 2 leaves fresh basil

Direction

- Cover cashews in few inches of cool water in big container; soak for 3-4 hours.
- Drain cashews; put into food processor. Add basil leaves, salt, garlic, nutritional yeast, olive oil and lemon juice; process for 3-4 minutes till smooth and thick. Stop to occasionally scrape down sides.

- Put cashew mixture into airtight container and refrigerate for 1-2 hours.

Nutrition Information

- Calories: 228 calories;
- Cholesterol: 0
- Total Fat: 18.4
- Protein: 7.3
- Sodium: 78
- Total Carbohydrate: 11.9

941. Vegan Cheesecake

Serving: 6 | Prep: 20mins | Cook: 30mins | Ready in:

Ingredients

- 1 (12 ounce) package soft tofu
- 1/2 cup soy milk
- 1/2 cup white sugar
- 1 tablespoon vanilla extract
- 1/4 cup maple syrup
- 1 (9 inch) prepared graham cracker crust

Direction

- Set an oven to 175°C (350°F) to preheat.
- Mixed together the maple syrup, vanilla extract, sugar, soy milk and tofu in a blender. Blend until it has a smooth consistency and pour into the pie crust.
- Bake for 30 minutes at 175°C (350°F). Take out of the oven and let cool, then chill it in the fridge.

Nutrition Information

- Calories: 323 calories;
- Sodium: 216
- Total Carbohydrate: 50.8
- Cholesterol: 0
- Protein: 5.8
- Total Fat: 11.2

942. Vegan Chickpea Curry Without Coconut Milk

Serving: 4 | Prep: 10mins | Cook: 30mins |Ready in:

Ingredients

- 2 (15 ounce) cans chickpeas
- 1 tablespoon baking soda
- 1 tablespoon vegetable oil
- 1 onion, finely chopped
- 1 teaspoon ginger-garlic paste
- 1/2 teaspoon cayenne pepper
- 1/2 teaspoon salt
- 1/2 teaspoon ground turmeric
- 1/2 teaspoon garam masala
- 1 (14.5 ounce) can diced tomatoes
- 2 (10 ounce) packages frozen chopped spinach, thawed and drained

Direction

- Drain off and wash the chickpeas in the cold running water. Add into the bowl, cover with the cold water, and whisk in the baking soda. Steep it for 10 minutes. Drain off and wash thoroughly.
- Heat the oil in the pot and cook the onion for roughly 5 minutes or till tender and translucent. Whisk in the garam masala, turmeric, salt, cayenne, and ginger-garlic paste. Cook and whisk for roughly 2 minutes or till the spices have been absorbed well by onion.
- Put in the frozen spinach and tomatoes; mix by whisking. Put in the chickpeas and whisk lightly. Let simmer for roughly 20 minutes or till the flavors have been well-mixed. Pour in small amount of the water if the sauce is too thick.

Nutrition Information

- Calories: 286 calories;
- Cholesterol: 0
- Protein: 13.6
- Total Fat: 6
- Sodium: 1970
- Total Carbohydrate: 46.6

943. Vegan Chocolate Cake

Serving: 8 | Prep: 15mins | Cook: 45mins |Ready in:

Ingredients

- 1 1/2 cups all-purpose flour
- 1 cup white sugar
- 1/4 cup cocoa powder
- 1 teaspoon baking soda
- 1/2 teaspoon salt
- 1/3 cup vegetable oil
- 1 teaspoon vanilla extract
- 1 teaspoon distilled white vinegar
- 1 cup water

Direction

- Set the oven to 175°C or 350°F to preheat. Coat a 5"x9" loaf pan slightly with grease.
- Sift salt, baking soda, cocoa, sugar and flour together, then put in water, vinegar, vanilla and oil. Combine together until smooth.
- Transfer into prepped pan and bake for 45 minutes at 175°C or 350°F. Take out of the oven and allow to cool.

Nutrition Information

- Calories: 275 calories;
- Sodium: 304
- Total Carbohydrate: 44.6
- Cholesterol: 0
- Protein: 3
- Total Fat: 9.7

944. Vegan Chocolate Ice Cream

Serving: 3 | Prep: 5mins | Cook: | Ready in:

Ingredients

- 1 1/2 cups ice cubes
- 3 frozen bananas
- 1/2 cup cashew milk
- 1 tablespoon cacao powder, or more to taste
- 1 1/2 tablespoons rice whipped topping, or to taste
- 1 tablespoon vegan chocolate shavings, or to taste

Direction

- Mix together cacao powder, cashew milk, bananas and ice in a blender; pulse till creamy.
- Put ice cream into a serving bowl; top with chocolate shavings and rice whipped topping.

Nutrition Information

- Calories: 232 calories;
- Total Carbohydrate: 37
- Cholesterol: 0
- Protein: 2.3
- Total Fat: 10.3
- Sodium: 126

945. Vegan Coconut Brownies

Serving: 16 | Prep: 15mins | Cook: 26mins | Ready in:

Ingredients

- 1 cup virgin coconut oil
- 1 cup unsweetened almond-coconut milk blend
- 1 teaspoon vanilla extract
- 2 cups raw sugar
- 2 cups all-purpose flour
- 3/4 cup unsweetened cocoa powder
- 1 teaspoon baking powder
- 1 teaspoon sea salt
- 1/3 cup shredded coconut

Direction

- Set oven to 350 0 F (175 0 C) and preheat.
- Pour coconut oil in a microwave-safe bowl; heat the oil for about 1 minute in the microwave until melted. Mix in milk blend and vanilla extract until well mixed.
- In a large bowl, combine sea salt, baking powder, cocoa powder, flour and sugar. Pour in coconut oil mixture; stir until batter is thick and blended. Fold in shredded coconut.
- Spread the batter evenly into a 9x13-inch baking dish.
- Put in the prepared oven and bake for 25 to 30 minutes until when you insert a toothpick into the center, it should come out clean. Let it cool for 15 minutes before slicing into squares.

Nutrition Information

- Calories: 286 calories;
- Total Fat: 15
- Sodium: 166
- Total Carbohydrate: 38.8
- Cholesterol: 0
- Protein: 2.5

946. Vegan Coconut Rice Pudding

Serving: 4 | Prep: 5mins | Cook: 25mins | Ready in:

Ingredients

- 4 cups water
- 2 cups long-grain white rice
- 1/2 cup cashew milk
- 1/2 cup full-fat coconut milk

- 1/4 cup coconut flakes
- 2 tablespoons maple syrup
- 1 teaspoon chia seeds
- 1 teaspoon ground cinnamon
- 1/2 teaspoon vanilla extract

Direction

- Combine rice and water in a saucepan, bring to a boil. Lower the heat to medium-low and simmer, covered, for 20 to 25 minutes until water is fully absorbed and rice is softened.
- In a bowl, combine vanilla extract, cinnamon, chia seeds, maple syrup, coconut flakes, coconut milk, cashew milk and cooked rice; mix until well incorporated. Keep pudding in refrigerator, covered, for 8 hours to overnight till firm.

Nutrition Information

- Calories: 501 calories;
- Sodium: 109
- Total Carbohydrate: 84.7
- Cholesterol: 0
- Protein: 7.7
- Total Fat: 14.3

947. Vegan Curry With Tomatoes, Cauliflower, And Lentils

Serving: 4 | Prep: 10mins | Cook: 40mins | Ready in:

Ingredients

- 2 tablespoons olive oil
- 1 small onion, diced
- 1 fresh red chile pepper, finely chopped
- 1 clove garlic, finely chopped
- 1 teaspoon ground cumin
- 1 teaspoon curry powder
- 1 teaspoon ground coriander
- 1 teaspoon ground turmeric
- 12 cherry tomatoes, chopped
- 1/4 cup dried red lentils
- 1/2 cup water
- salt to taste
- 1 head cauliflower, separated into large florets
- 2 cups fresh spinach leaves, or to taste
- 2 tablespoons chopped cilantro, or to taste

Direction

- In a large skillet, over medium heat, heat olive oil; cook garlic, onion and chile pepper while stirring frequently for about 5 minutes. Stir in turmeric, ground coriander, curry powder and cumin; cook for 1-2 minutes until heated through.
- Stir water, lentils and cherry tomatoes into the pot. Season with salt; stir well; simmer for about 20 minutes until lentils are almost cooked through. Stir in spinach leaves and cauliflower; cook with a cover for about 10-15 minutes until spinach is wilted and cauliflower becomes soft. Serve with freshly chopped cilantro.

Nutrition Information

- Calories: 174 calories;
- Sodium: 104
- Total Carbohydrate: 22.1
- Cholesterol: 0
- Protein: 7.7
- Total Fat: 7.7

948. Vegan Edamame

Serving: 2 | Prep: 5mins | Cook: 10mins | Ready in:

Ingredients

- 2 tablespoons soy sauce
- 2 tablespoons rice vinegar
- 1 teaspoon finely grated ginger root
- 2 1/2 cups frozen edamame in the pod

Direction

- In a bowl, mix ginger, rice vinegar and soy sauce together; reserve dipping sauce.
- Boil a big saucepan of water. Put the edamame and let boil for 5 minutes till soft. Allow to drain and wash under cold water.
- Serve the pods along with sauce as dipping.

Nutrition Information

- Calories: 235 calories;
- Total Fat: 9.4
- Sodium: 921
- Total Carbohydrate: 18.3
- Cholesterol: 0
- Protein: 19.8

949. Vegan Fajitas

Serving: 6 | Prep: 20mins | Cook: 20mins | Ready in:

Ingredients

- 1/4 cup olive oil
- 1/4 cup red wine vinegar
- 1 teaspoon dried oregano
- 1 teaspoon chili powder
- garlic salt to taste
- salt and pepper to taste
- 1 teaspoon white sugar
- 2 small zucchini, julienned
- 2 medium small yellow squash, julienned
- 1 large onion, sliced
- 1 green bell pepper, cut into thin strips
- 1 red bell pepper, cut into thin strips
- 2 tablespoons olive oil
- 1 (8.75 ounce) can whole kernel corn, drained
- 1 (15 ounce) can black beans, drained

Direction

- Mix sugar, pepper, salt, garlic salt, chili powder, oregano, vinegar, and olive oil together in a large bowl. Add red pepper, green pepper, onion, yellow squash, and zucchini to the marinade. Allow vegetables to marinate in the fridge for at least half an hour but not more than 24 hours. Heat oil over medium-high heat in a large skillet. Drain vegetables; sauté drained vegetables in heated oil for about 10 to 15 minutes until softened. Mix in beans and corn; turn heat to high; cook over high heat for 5 minutes until vegetables are evenly browned.

Nutrition Information

- Calories: 198 calories;
- Total Fat: 14.4
- Sodium: 130
- Total Carbohydrate: 17.9
- Cholesterol: 0
- Protein: 3

950. Vegan Homemade Plain Cream Cheese

Serving: 32 | Prep: 10mins | Cook: | Ready in:

Ingredients

- 2 cups unsalted raw cashews
- 1/2 teaspoon Himalayan pink salt
- 3 tablespoons plain non-dairy yogurt

Direction

- In a bowl of water, soak the cashews for 8 hours up to overnight.
- Drain the cashews and throw away the water. In a food processor bowl, combine salt and cashews, then pulse until creamy and smooth, 10-15 minutes. Stir in the yogurt, mixing well to combine. Allow to sit at room temperature for an hour before placing in the refrigerator.

Nutrition Information

- Calories: 48 calories;
- Total Fat: 3.8
- Sodium: 37
- Total Carbohydrate: 2.7
- Cholesterol: 0
- Protein: 1.5

951. Vegan Indian Curry With Cauliflower And Lentils

Serving: 4 | Prep: 15mins | Cook: 40mins | Ready in:

Ingredients

- 3 tablespoons vegetable oil, divided
- 1 onion, finely chopped
- 1 (4 inch) piece fresh ginger, peeled and grated
- 1 large clove garlic, minced
- 2 teaspoons ground coriander
- 2 teaspoons ground cumin
- 1/2 teaspoon ground turmeric
- 1/2 cup red lentils
- 3/4 cup hot vegetable stock
- 1 head cauliflower, cut into small florets
- 1 (14 ounce) can coconut milk
- 1 large carrot, peeled and diced
- 1/2 cup frozen green beans, thawed
- 3 tablespoons chopped fresh cilantro
- 1 tablespoon lemon juice
- 1 pinch salt and freshly ground black pepper to taste
- 1 sprig fresh cilantro

Direction

- Over low heat, heat two tablespoons of oil in a large saucepan and add onion. Cook while stirring often for about 10 minutes until translucent and soft. Add turmeric, cumin, coriander, garlic and ginger. Cook while stirring constantly for two minutes. Mix in the lentils and add vegetable stock. Heat to a boil, decrease the heat, then cover and let it simmer gently for ten minutes.
- In the meantime, over medium heat, heat remaining one tablespoon of oil in a skillet and then cook the cauliflower for 2 to 3 minutes until browned lightly.
- Mix carrot, coconut milk and cauliflower into lentil mixture. Return the curry to a gentle simmer and let it cook for about 10 minutes until the veggies become tender. Mix in the green beans and let it cook for 3 to 4 more minutes.
- Mix lemon juice and three tablespoons of cilantro into the curry. Add pepper and salt to taste. Scoop onto a warmed serving dish and garnish with cilantro sprig.

Nutrition Information

- Calories: 448 calories;
- Total Fat: 32.5
- Sodium: 201
- Total Carbohydrate: 33
- Cholesterol: 0
- Protein: 12.5

952. Vegan Key Lime Pie

Serving: 8 | Prep: 15mins | Cook: | Ready in:

Ingredients

- Crust:
- 1 cup almond flour
- 1 cup pitted Medjool dates
- 1 tablespoon agave nectar
- 1 teaspoon vanilla extract
- 1/2 teaspoon salt
- 1/8 teaspoon ground nutmeg
- Filling:
- 5 avocados, peeled and pitted
- 1/2 cup melted coconut oil
- 6 tablespoons lime juice
- 1/4 cup agave nectar

Direction

- In food processor, process nutmeg, salt, vanilla extract, 1 tablespoon agave, dates and almond flour till crust adheres together once pinched. Force the crust evenly into springform pan base.
- In a food processor, blend quarter cup agave nectar, lime juice, coconut oil and avocados till filling is really smooth; put on top of crust, leveling using spatula or back of spoon.
- Put pie in freezer for a minimum of 4 hours till firm. Allow to stand for 10 minutes at room temperature prior to serving.

Nutrition Information

- Calories: 415 calories;
- Protein: 3
- Total Fat: 32.5
- Sodium: 155
- Total Carbohydrate: 35.6
- Cholesterol: 0

953. Vegan Mashed Potatoes

Serving: 4 | Prep: 10mins | Cook: 35mins | Ready in:

Ingredients

- 2 pounds russet potatoes
- 8 cloves garlic, peeled and smashed
- 1 sprig fresh rosemary
- 1 sprig fresh thyme
- 1/4 cup olive oil
- 1 pinch salt and ground black pepper to taste

Direction

- In a big pot filled with salted water, add thyme, rosemary, garlic and potatoes, then bring to a boil. Cook with a cover for a half hour, until potatoes are easily pierced with a knife. Drain and save 1 cup of cooking water.
- Turn to a bowl with garlic and boiled potatoes, then get rid of the thyme and rosemary. Put in pepper, salt and olive oil, then use a potato masher to mash the mixture while putting in more cooking water to get wanted consistency.

Nutrition Information

- Calories: 303 calories;
- Total Fat: 13.7
- Sodium: 54
- Total Carbohydrate: 41.7
- Cholesterol: 0
- Protein: 5

954. Vegan Mashed Potatoes (Low Fat)

Serving: 4 | Prep: 10mins | Cook: 20mins | Ready in:

Ingredients

- 6 baby red potatoes, halved, or more to taste
- 1/4 cup unsweetened almond milk, or more to taste
- 1/2 lemon, juiced, or more to taste
- 1 tablespoon soy-free buttery spread (such as Earth Balance®), melted, or more to taste
- 1 teaspoon minced garlic, or more to taste
- 1/2 teaspoon salt, or to taste

Direction

- Bring water in a big pot to a boil, then put in potatoes. Lower the heat to medium low and simmer for around 15 minutes, until potatoes fall apart with pierced with a fork. Drain.
- In a deep bowl, add potatoes and stir lightly. Put in salt, garlic, buttery spread, lemon juice and almond milk, then mash to wanted consistency.

Nutrition Information

- Calories: 68 calories;
- Sodium: 327
- Total Carbohydrate: 11.3
- Cholesterol: 0
- Protein: 1.4
- Total Fat: 2.5

955. Vegan Mug Cake With Pineapple And Mint

Serving: 2 | Prep: 5mins | Cook: 3mins | Ready in:

Ingredients

- 2 slices fresh pineapple
- 1 ripe banana
- 2 tablespoons cream of coconut
- 1 tablespoon rolled oats
- 1 tablespoon quick-cooking oats
- 1/4 teaspoon baking powder
- 3 leaves fresh mint
- 1 teaspoon chia seeds
- 1 teaspoon poppy seeds

Direction

- In a blender, mix together banana, cream of coconut, pineapple, quick-cooking oats, rolled oats, mint, baking powder, poppy seeds and chia seeds until smooth. Transfer the mixture into 2 mugs.
- Microwave mug cakes on high temperature until set and risen well for about 3 minutes. Set aside for a few minutes to cool. Serve.

Nutrition Information

- Calories: 196 calories;
- Cholesterol: 0
- Protein: 2.4
- Total Fat: 4.7
- Sodium: 70
- Total Carbohydrate: 39.1

956. Vegan Oat Salted Caramel Cookies

Serving: 20 | Prep: 10mins | Cook: 20mins | Ready in:

Ingredients

- Salted Caramel:
- 1 cup dates, pitted and chopped
- 1/4 cup almond milk
- 1/4 teaspoon sea salt
- Cookies:
- 2 cups gluten-free oats
- 1/3 cup chopped pecans
- 2 bananas, mashed

Direction

- Set oven at 175°C (350°F) and start preheating. Use parchment paper to line a baking tray.
- Add almond milk and dates to a blender, puree for about 2 minutes to get creamy paste. Add sea salt.
- Add pecans and oats to a food processor's bowl, pulse until they turn into rough flour. Add swirl salted caramel and mashed bananas into the dough and combine them together. Drop big spoonfuls 2 inches away from another on the lined baking trays.
- Take them to the preheated oven and bake for about 20 minutes until golden.

Nutrition Information

- Calories: 83 calories;
- Total Fat: 2
- Sodium: 25
- Total Carbohydrate: 15.3
- Cholesterol: 0
- Protein: 1.6

957. Vegan Potato Leek Gratin

Serving: 8 | Prep: 30mins | Cook: 40mins |Ready in:

Ingredients

- 2 medium leeks, chopped
- 1 tablespoon vegan margarine
- 3 cloves garlic, crushed
- 3 teaspoons chopped fresh oregano, divided
- 3 teaspoons chopped fresh rosemary, divided
- 1 teaspoon salt
- 2 teaspoons ground black pepper
- 2 pounds Yukon gold potatoes, peeled and thinly sliced
- 2 (5.6 ounce) cans coconut milk
- 1 1/2 cups almond milk, or as needed
- 2 tablespoons all-purpose flour
- 1 cup shredded vegan cheese

Direction

- In a big saucepan, mix together pepper, salt, 2 tsp. rosemary, 2 tsp. oregano, garlic, margarine and leeks on moderate heat. Cook for 7-8 minutes until leeks are softened. Put in flour, almond milk, coconut milk and potatoes then bring to a simmer. Cover and simmer about 10-15 minutes, until potatoes are nearly cooked. Put in more liquid if the mixture begins to stick.
- Set the oven to 200°C or 400°F to preheat and grease a casserole dish.
- Scoop into the prepared casserole dish with potato mixture and sprinkle over with shredded cheese. Decorate with leftover oregano and rosemary.
- In the preheated oven, bake for 20 to 30 minutes, until the top turns golden brown and potatoes are cooked thoroughly.

Nutrition Information

- Calories: 204 calories;
- Total Fat: 7.3
- Sodium: 562
- Total Carbohydrate: 29.2
- Cholesterol: 0
- Protein: 4.9

958. Vegan Protein Chocolate Overnight Oats

Serving: 1 | Prep: 10mins | Cook: |Ready in:

Ingredients

- 1 banana
- 1 1/4 cups rolled oats
- 2 tablespoons pea protein powder
- 1 tablespoon unsweetened cocoa powder
- 1 cup soy milk
- 1/3 cup water
- 1 1/2 tablespoons flax seeds
- 1/2 cup fresh mixed berries

Direction

- Use a fork to mash banana into puree in a mixing bowl. Add berries, flax seeds, water, soy milk, cocoa powder, protein powder, and oats; mix thoroughly and pour into a mason jar.
- Chill, covered overnight.

Nutrition Information

- Calories: 826 calories;
- Total Fat: 20.5
- Sodium: 263
- Total Carbohydrate: 130.1
- Cholesterol: 0
- Protein: 37.9

959. Vegan Pumpkin Brownie

Serving: 8 | Prep: 30mins | Cook: 50mins |Ready in:

Ingredients

- Pumpkin Swirl:
- 3/4 cup pumpkin puree
- 1 1/2 tablespoons coconut oil
- 3 tablespoons orange juice
- 1 pinch ground nutmeg
- 1 pinch ground cinnamon
- Brownie:
- 5 tablespoons hot water
- 3 tablespoons flaxseed meal
- 1 cup almond flour
- 6 tablespoons white sugar
- 3 tablespoons orange juice
- 1 1/2 tablespoons coconut oil
- 1 tablespoon vanilla extract
- 2/3 cup dark chocolate, melted
- 1/3 cup chopped pecans
- 1 teaspoon baking powder
- 1 pinch salt
- 1 pinch ground black pepper

Direction

- Start preheating the oven to 350°F (175°C). Oil a 9-inch square baking pan.
- In a bowl, blend together cinnamon, nutmeg, 3 tablespoons of the orange juice, 1 1/2 tablespoons of coconut oil and pumpkin puree. Put the pumpkin swirl in refrigerator until needed.
- In a small bowl, mix the flaxseed meal and hot water. Stir and allow to soak about 5 minutes.
- In a blender, mix vanilla extract, 1 1/2 tablespoons of the coconut oil, sugar, 3 tablespoons of the orange juice, almond flour, and flaxseed mixture and process. Place into a bowl. Mix pepper, salt, baking powder, pecans and melted chocolate into the brownie mixture.
- Spread the brownie mixture into preheated baking pan. Add the pumpkin swirl on top and spread. Create a pretty marbled look by running a knife through mixture.
- Bake for half an hour in the prepared oven. Return the baking pan covered with aluminum foil to hot oven. Bake for 20 minutes longer until the brownies are set. Cool completely for half an hour. Then slice and serve. Refrigerate to store.

Nutrition Information

- Calories: 303 calories;
- Total Fat: 21.5
- Sodium: 139
- Total Carbohydrate: 26.6
- Cholesterol: 0
- Protein: 5.1

960. Vegan Pumpkin Macaroni And Cheese

Serving: 3 | Prep: 15mins | Cook: 15mins | Ready in:

Ingredients

- 8 ounces penne pasta
- 2 tablespoons flour
- 1 tablespoon extra virgin olive oil
- 1/2 cup oat milk
- 8 ounces pumpkin puree
- 2 teaspoons garlic salt
- 5 ounces shredded vegan Cheddar-style cheese, divided (such as Daiya®)

Direction

- Boil lightly salted water in a big pot. Put in penne and cook for 11 minutes, whisking occasionally until it's tender but firm to chew. Strain pasta and put back in the pot.
- Mix oil and flour in the same pot and whisk until it firms a smooth paste. Gradually mix in oat milk. Stir in pumpkin, stirring well until incorporated. Mix in 4 ounces of vegan cheese and garlic salt. Blend until smooth.
- Place an oven rack 6 inches away from the heat source and prepare the oven's broiler by preheating.

- Fill up 3 separate oval gratin casserole dishes with pasta mixture. Equally place leftover vegan cheese on top.
- Place in the broiler and broil for 1-3 minutes until cheese is dissolved. Then serve warm.

Nutrition Information

- Calories: 547 calories;
- Total Carbohydrate: 74.1
- Cholesterol: 0
- Total Fat: 19
- Protein: 16.5
- Sodium: 2117

961. Vegan Pumpkin Pie

Serving: 8 | Prep: 15mins | Cook: 40mins | Ready in:

Ingredients

- 1 cup vanilla-flavored almond milk
- 1/2 cup raw sugar
- 2 tablespoons arrowroot powder
- 1 (15 ounce) can pumpkin puree
- 2 teaspoons pumpkin pie spice
- 1/2 teaspoon salt
- 1 (9 inch) vegan pie shell (such as Wholly Wholesome®)

Direction

- Preheat the oven to 190°C or 375°F.
- In a blender, mix arrowroot powder, sugar and almond milk; blend till arrowroot and sugar are dissolved fully. Put in salt, pumpkin pie spice and pumpkin puree; blend till smooth. Put into pie shell. Using aluminum foil, cover the edges of pie shell.
- In the prepped oven, bake for 40 minutes till middle is set.
- Cool down pie for an hour to room temperature. Chill for 8 hours to overnight till firm.

Nutrition Information

- Calories: 202 calories;
- Total Fat: 8.3
- Sodium: 419
- Total Carbohydrate: 30.8
- Cholesterol: 0
- Protein: 2.2

962. Vegan Pumpkin Spice Cake

Serving: 12 | Prep: 15mins | Cook: 30mins | Ready in:

Ingredients

- 1 cup water
- 1 tablespoon instant coffee, or as needed
- 1 teaspoon oil for greasing
- 2 3/4 cups all-purpose flour
- 1 pinch white sugar
- 2 1/2 teaspoons pumpkin pie spice
- 1 1/2 teaspoons baking powder
- 1 teaspoon salt
- 1/2 teaspoon ground cinnamon
- 1/2 teaspoon nutmeg
- 1/2 teaspoon ground ginger
- 3/4 cup vegetable oil
- 3/4 cup water
- 3 tablespoons pumpkin puree
- 1 teaspoon vanilla extract

Direction

- Let a cup of water boil and in a mug or measuring cup, stir with instant coffee. Reserve to cool.
- Preheat an oven to 175 °C or 350 °F. With margarine, grease a 9x13 inches rectangular baking pan.
- In a bowl, mix ginger, nutmeg, cinnamon, salt, baking powder, mixed spice, demarara sugar and flour and combine thoroughly. Put the

3/4 cup water, oil and cooled coffee, and stir till blended thoroughly. Fold in the vanilla extract and pumpkin puree; stir well. Into prepped baking pan, evenly put the batter.
- In prepped oven, bake for half an hour till a toothpick pricked into the middle gets out clean or nearly clean, as the cake may be quite sticky.
- Cool for 5 minutes on wire rack. To loosen, trace a table knife surrounding edges. Cautiously flip cake over on cooling rack or serving plate. Cool for a minimum of 15 minutes longer prior to slicing.

Nutrition Information

- Calories: 320 calories;
- Cholesterol: 0
- Total Fat: 14.3
- Protein: 3.1
- Sodium: 273
- Total Carbohydrate: 45.3

963. Vegan Raspberry Chocolate Tarts

Serving: 12 | Prep: 40mins | Cook: 5mins | Ready in:

Ingredients

- Crust:
- 1 cup firmly packed pitted dates
- 1/2 cup walnuts
- Ganache:
- 1 1/2 cups vegan chocolate chips
- 1 tablespoon coconut oil
- 1/2 cup coconut cream (mix solid and liquid creams together before measuring)
- 3 tablespoons unsweetened cocoa powder
- Raspberry Filling:
- 6 ounces fresh raspberries

Direction

- In the bowl of a food processor, mix walnuts and dates and then blend about 2 minutes until combined well. Into the bottom of 12 mini tart pans, press approximately two tablespoons of the mixture. Transfer into the freezer as you prepare ganache.
- Put coconut oil and chocolate chips at the top of a double boiler on simmering water. To prevent scorching, mix often while scraping down the sides using a rubber spatula for about 5 minutes until the chocolate has melted. Pour the melted chocolate into the bowl of food processor. Pour in cocoa powder and coconut cream and blend for about 1 minutes on high until smooth.
- Take out the crusts from freezer. Scoop approximately 1 1/2 teaspoons of ganache over each crust and spread to the edges. Pour in enough to reach halfway up the side of tart cup. Return the tarts into freezer for about 10 minutes until firm.
- Use a fork to mash the raspberries in a bowl until you get consistency of a sauce. Onto the hardened ganache layer, layer mashed raspberries and do not go all the way to the edges. Place in a freezer for about 20 minutes until the sauce becomes firm and doesn't collapse after topping with ganache.
- Take out the tarts from the freezer. Pour the rest of the ganache on top and spread all the way to the edges. Ensure you seal in raspberry sauce as much as you can. Place back in the freezer to firm up. Store the tarts in the fridge in case you're serving them within two hours.

Nutrition Information

- Calories: 173 calories;
- Sodium: < 1
- Total Carbohydrate: 14.2
- Cholesterol: 0
- Protein: 1.5
- Total Fat: 13.8

964. Vegan Refried Beans

Serving: 6 | Prep: 5mins | Cook: 10mins | Ready in:

Ingredients

- 1 tablespoon olive oil
- 1 onion, diced
- 1 (15 ounce) can pinto beans, drained
- 3 tablespoons tomato paste
- chili powder to taste
- 1 cup vegetable broth

Direction

- In a medium skillet, heat oil over medium heat. Sauté the onions till soft. Mix in vegetable broth, chili powder, tomato paste and beans. Let cook for 5 minutes, or till stock has reduced. Crush using potato masher.

Nutrition Information

- Calories: 202 calories;
- Total Fat: 3.1
- Sodium: 143
- Total Carbohydrate: 33.9
- Cholesterol: 0
- Protein: 11

965. Vegan Roasted Vegetable Hummus

Serving: 8 | Prep: 15mins | Cook: 30mins | Ready in:

Ingredients

- 1 carrot, chopped (optional)
- 1 tomato
- 1 red bell pepper, cut lengthwise in half, seeded
- 1 onion, chopped
- 1 (15 ounce) can chickpeas, drained and 1/3 cup liquid reserved
- 2 tablespoons lemon juice
- 1 teaspoon salt
- 1 clove garlic, smashed and chopped
- 1 teaspoon paprika
- 1 teaspoon ground black pepper
- 1 teaspoon ground cumin
- 1 teaspoon ground coriander
- 1 teaspoon dried parsley

Direction

- Set the oven to 400°F (200°C) and start preheating.
- On a baking dish, arrange carrot pieces.
- Bake for 20 minutes in the preheated oven. Put in red bell pepper and tomato. Roast for about 10 more minutes or to your desired brownness.
- Place a pot on medium-high heat; heat oil. Sauté onion for 5 minutes till translucent.
- In a food processor, blend parsley, coriander, cumin, black pepper, paprika, garlic, salt, lemon juice, chickpeas with the reserved liquid, red bell pepper, tomato, the roasted carrot and the onion until smooth. Spoon into a bowl.

Nutrition Information

- Calories: 70 calories;
- Total Fat: 0.7
- Sodium: 405
- Total Carbohydrate: 14.1
- Cholesterol: 0
- Protein: 2.6

966. Vegan Seitan Curry With Rice

Serving: 1 | Prep: 10mins | Cook: 50mins | Ready in:

Ingredients

- 1/3 cup basmati rice
- 1 small zucchini, cubed

- 1/2 onion, cubed
- 4 1/2 ounces seitan beef, sliced
- 1 teaspoon pure coconut oil
- 1 tablespoon cumin
- 1 tablespoon ground coriander
- 1 teaspoon curry powder
- 1/2 teaspoon salt
- 1/2 teaspoon ground turmeric
- 1 pinch ground black pepper
- 1 pinch garlic powder
- 2/3 cup water

Direction

- In 1/2 cup cold water, soak basmati rice for 30 minutes. Drain.
- In a pot, mix together onion and zucchini in water. Boil it for 20 minutes. Drain. Add to a blender and process until smooth.
- Pour the pureed zucchini mixture to a pot over medium heat. Add garlic powder, pepper, turmeric, salt, curry powder, coriander, cumin, coconut oil, and seitan. Simmer for 30 minutes until the sauce has thickened, adding 1 tablespoon of water occasionally to avoid burning.
- In the meantime, in a saucepan, mix together soaked rice and 2/3 cup water and boil. Lower the heat to medium-low, put a cover on and simmer for 20-25 minutes until the rice is soft and the water has been absorbed.
- Enjoy the rice with seitan.

Nutrition Information

- Calories: 547 calories;
- Cholesterol: 0
- Protein: 36.3
- Total Fat: 10.8
- Sodium: 1600
- Total Carbohydrate: 80.8

967. Vegan Spanish Rice Dinner

Serving: 6 | Prep: 25mins | Cook: 15mins | Ready in:

Ingredients

- 1 large red bell pepper, diced
- 1/2 large onion, diced
- olive oil
- 1 Asian eggplant, diced
- 1 yellow summer squash, diced
- 1 (16 ounce) can pinto beans, drained and rinsed
- 3 tablespoons capers
- 3 cups cooked rice
- 1/4 teaspoon whole mustard seeds, or to taste
- 1/4 teaspoon dehydrated minced garlic, or to taste
- 1/4 teaspoon red pepper flakes, or to taste
- 1/4 teaspoon ground cumin, or to taste
- 1/4 teaspoon dried cilantro, or to taste
- salt to taste

Direction

- In a big frying pan, add onion and red bell pepper on moderate heat. Put in olive oil, then cook and stir for 5 minutes, until onion is translucent. Put in squash and eggplant, then cover and cook for 5 minutes longer, until softened. Put in capers and pinto beans, then cook for 5 minutes, until heated through. Put in rice and stir well, then put in salt, cilantro, cumin, pepper flakes, garlic and mustard seeds.

Nutrition Information

- Calories: 232 calories;
- Protein: 7.6
- Total Fat: 3.6
- Sodium: 381
- Total Carbohydrate: 43.6
- Cholesterol: 0

968. Vegan Sweet And Sour Meatballs

Serving: 4 | Prep: 25mins | Cook: 35mins | Ready in:

Ingredients

- 1/2 cup warm water
- 2 tablespoons egg replacer
- 1 cup shredded vegan cheese
- 1/2 cup grated tofu
- 1/4 cup nutritional yeast
- 1 teaspoon salt
- 1/2 teaspoon garlic powder
- 1/2 cup finely chopped onion
- 1/2 cup finely chopped pecans
- 1 tablespoon Italian seasoning
- 1 teaspoon dried basil
- 1/2 teaspoon dried sage
- 1 cup dry bread crumbs, or more as needed
- Sauce:
- 3/4 cup grape jelly
- 1/2 cup ketchup
- 1/4 cup olive oil
- 1/4 cup white vinegar
- 1 tablespoon chopped garlic
- 1 teaspoon dried oregano

Direction

- Set an oven to preheat to 175°C (350°F).
- In a big bowl, mix together the egg replacer and warm water. Stir in the garlic powder, salt, nutritional yeast, tofu and vegan cheese, then add the sage, basil, Italian seasoning, pecans and onion and stir until well blended. Mix in enough bread crumbs to achieve a crumbly and moist texture.
- Shape the mixture into 1 1/2-inch balls and put it in an 8-inch baking pan.
- In another bowl, combine the oregano, garlic, vinegar, olive oil, ketchup and grape jelly, then pour it on top of the meatballs.
- Let it bake in the preheated oven for 35-40 minutes, until the meatballs become firm.

Nutrition Information

- Calories: 703 calories;
- Total Fat: 35.1
- Sodium: 1555
- Total Carbohydrate: 84.5
- Cholesterol: 0
- Protein: 15.6

969. Vegan Thai Pumpkin Curry

Serving: 4 | Prep: 10mins | Cook: 30mins | Ready in:

Ingredients

- 1 tablespoon rapeseed oil
- 2 tablespoons sesame seeds
- 1 small onion, finely chopped
- 4 1/2 cups peeled, chopped pumpkin
- 1 1/2 teaspoons red curry paste, or to taste
- 1 (14 ounce) can coconut milk
- 1 cube vegetable bouillon
- salt and freshly ground black pepper
- 1/4 cup chopped green onion, or to taste

Direction

- In a pot, heat rapeseed oil over medium heat; put in sesame seeds, toast for about 3 minutes or until golden brown. Add chopped onion; continue to cook and stir for around 5 minutes or until soft and transparent.
- Stir pumpkin cubes into the pot; cook for about 5 minutes, stirring constantly. Put in the curry paste, stir and mix well with the pumpkin. Add coconut milk and dissolve the vegetable bouillon. Then, cover and boil. Lower the heat and cook for 15-20 minutes until the pumpkin is soft. Season with pepper and salt. Dust with green onions and serve.

Nutrition Information

- Calories: 293 calories;
- Sodium: 93
- Total Carbohydrate: 14.7
- Cholesterol: 0
- Protein: 4.4
- Total Fat: 26.7

970. Vegan Tofu Quiche

Serving: 8 | Prep: 30mins | Cook: 55mins | Ready in:

Ingredients

- 1/8 cup vegetable oil
- 1 medium sweet onion (such as Vidalia®), chopped
- 1 (8 ounce) package sliced fresh mushrooms
- 1 clove garlic, minced
- 1 (8 ounce) package fresh spinach, cut into strips
- 1/4 cup red wine
- 2 tablespoons balsamic vinegar
- 1 teaspoon liquid smoke
- 1 (9 inch) vegan pie crust
- 1 1/2 pounds extra-firm tofu, cubed, or more to taste
- 1/4 cup arrowroot
- 1/4 cup nutritional yeast
- 1/4 cup olive oil
- 1/4 cup Dijon mustard
- 2 teaspoons agar-agar powder

Direction

- In a big pot at medium heat, heat vegetable oil then fry onion for 5 minutes. Put in garlic and mushrooms, cook for 5 more minutes, stirring regularly. Between stirs, cover the pot. Add in balsamic vinegar, red wine, spinach and liquid smoke. Briefly stir then close the lid, take away from the heat. Let it cool down.
- Preheat the oven at 175°C (or 350°F). Place pie crust in a 9 or 10 inch pie plate.
- In a food processor, add tofu, arrowroot, nutritional yeast, olive oil, mustard and agar powder then mix until the mixture form a thick paste. Transfer to mushroom mixture to make a more liquid paste. Pour then scrape them into the pie crust.
- Bake for about 45 minutes in the prepared oven, until the center is set and the crust is golden. Allow the quiche to completely cool before cutting

Nutrition Information

- Calories: 349 calories;
- Total Carbohydrate: 22.7
- Cholesterol: 0
- Protein: 13.7
- Total Fat: 23.5
- Sodium: 338

971. Vegan Ube Blueberry Ice Cream

Serving: 6 | Prep: 5mins | Cook: | Ready in:

Ingredients

- 1 (14 ounce) can coconut cream, chilled
- 1 (14.5 ounce) package frozen ube (purple yam)
- 1 1/2 cups frozen blueberries
- 1 tablespoon light agave syrup

Direction

- In high-speed blender like Vitamix(R), put the coconut cream. Put the agave syrup, blueberries and ube. Place cover and process for a minute, beginning at Variable 1 and gently raising to maximum speed. Force ingredients on the blades with tamper.
- For soft-serve consistency, serve right away. Keep in freezer for a tougher consistency.

Nutrition Information

- Calories: 294 calories;
- Total Fat: 23.2
- Sodium: 12
- Total Carbohydrate: 23
- Cholesterol: 0
- Protein: 3.5

972. Vegan Or Lactose Intolerant Ice Cream

Serving: 6 | Prep: 30mins | Cook: | Ready in:

Ingredients

- 1 pound silken tofu
- 1 cup white sugar
- 1/2 teaspoon salt
- 2 cups almond milk
- 3 tablespoons matcha green tea powder

Direction

- In a blender, mix salt, sugar and silken tofu; blend till the tofu reaches the consistency of thick cream. Include matcha powder and almond milk; using a spoon, stir till well-blended.
- Transfer the mixture into your ice cream maker; following the manufacturer's instructions, churn for 15-20 minutes. Remove into a lidded container.
- Before serving, freeze for at least 30 minutes.

Nutrition Information

- Calories: 196 calories;
- Total Fat: 3
- Sodium: 252
- Total Carbohydrate: 39
- Cholesterol: 0
- Protein: 4.4

973. Vegetable Lo Mein

Serving: 4 | Prep: 10mins | Cook: 25mins | Ready in:

Ingredients

- 8 ounces uncooked spaghetti
- 1/4 cup vegetable oil
- 2 cups fresh sliced mushrooms
- 1 cup shredded carrots
- 1/2 cup sliced red bell peppers
- 1 onion, chopped
- 2 cloves garlic, minced
- 2 cups fresh bean sprouts
- 1/2 cup chopped green onions
- 1 tablespoon cornstarch
- 1 cup chicken broth
- 1/4 cup hoisin sauce
- 2 tablespoons honey
- 1 tablespoon soy sauce
- 1 teaspoon grated fresh ginger
- 1/4 teaspoon cayenne pepper
- 1/4 teaspoon curry powder

Direction

- Fill a large pot with lightly salted water and bring to a boil. Cook pasta until al dente or for about 8 to 10 minutes; drain. In a large pan or wok, heat oil and cook carrots, onion, peppers, garlic, and mushrooms until tender. Add in green onions and bean sprouts, and cook for about a minute. In a small bowl, make a slurry with chicken broth and cornstarch. Pour the mixture into the stir fry. Add in curry powder, hoisin sauce, ginger, cayenne pepper, honey and soy sauce. Stir and cook until the mixture becomes bubbly and thick. Mix in the spaghetti and coat with sauce. Serve immediately.

Nutrition Information

- Calories: 452 calories;
- Total Fat: 15.6

- Sodium: 512
- Total Carbohydrate: 69.2
- Cholesterol: < 1
- Protein: 11.2

974. Vegetable Medley II

Serving: 4 | Prep: 20mins | Cook: 15mins | Ready in:

Ingredients

- cooking spray
- 1 tomato, diced
- 1 pinch garlic pepper seasoning
- 2 cups fresh mushrooms, sliced
- 2 yellow squash, cubed
- 2 zucchini, cubed

Direction

- Use cooking spray to spray a big skillet, then add the tomatoes. Let it cook for 5 minutes on medium heat and add the garlic pepper. Stir in the zucchini, squash and mushrooms and let it simmer for 10-15 minutes, until the vegetables become tender-crisp.

Nutrition Information

- Calories: 66 calories;
- Total Fat: 1.5
- Sodium: 202
- Total Carbohydrate: 12.6
- Cholesterol: 0
- Protein: 3.3

975. Vegetable Paella

Serving: 4 | Prep: 15mins | Cook: 30mins | Ready in:

Ingredients

- 2 cups water
- 1 cup long grain rice, rinsed and drained
- vegetable oil
- 1 cup frozen corn and peas
- 1 cup frozen broccoli
- 1 cup sliced mushrooms
- 1 (12 ounce) package texturized vegetable protein (TVP)
- 1/4 teaspoon garlic salt
- 1/4 teaspoon paprika
- 1 pinch black pepper

Direction

- Boil water in medium saucepan. Add rice; mix. Lower heat; cover and simmer for 20 minutes. Put aside.
- Heat oil in deep-frying pan/wok on medium high heat. Cook broccoli, peas and frozen corn till thawed. Mix in veggie ground beef and sliced mushrooms; cook for 5 minutes, occasionally mixing. Mix in paprika and garlic salt in when veggie protein is brown and veggies are tender. Lower heat to low; cook for 3 minutes more. Serve while warm over rice.

Nutrition Information

- Calories: 535 calories;
- Cholesterol: 0
- Protein: 74.6
- Total Fat: 6.9
- Sodium: 984
- Total Carbohydrate: 53.5

976. Vegetarian Garden Stir Fry

Serving: 3 | Prep: 15mins | Cook: 10mins | Ready in:

Ingredients

- 1 serving cooking spray
- 1/2 cup sugar snap peas

- 1/4 cup cherry tomatoes, halved
- 1/2 cup dried fruit and nut mix, such as cranberries, almonds, and cashews
- 1/4 cup chopped mushrooms
- 1/4 cup bell pepper, thinly sliced
- 2 tablespoons chia seeds
- 2 teaspoons cayenne pepper, or to taste
- 1 tablespoon garlic, minced
- salt to taste
- 3 tablespoons egg whites
- 2 tablespoons shredded Cheddar cheese, or as desired

Direction

- Use cooking spray to grease a large skillet and heat over medium-low heat. Add in chia seeds, bell pepper, mushrooms, nut and fruit mix, cherry tomatoes, and sugar snap peas. Stir-fry for approximately 2 minutes. Use salt, garlic, and cayenne for seasoning. Keep cooking and stirring for approximately 2 more minutes.
- Slowly stir in egg whites, mix till they are thoroughly cooked, yet not crusty, for 3-5 minutes. Remove stir-fry to a large bowl and use Cheddar cheese to dredge on. Allow cheese to melt and it is ready to serve.

Nutrition Information

- Calories: 158 calories;
- Total Fat: 4.5
- Sodium: 120
- Total Carbohydrate: 25.6
- Cholesterol: 6
- Protein: 6.3

977. Vegetarian Nori Rolls

Serving: 5 | Prep: 30mins | Cook: 30mins | Ready in:

Ingredients

- 2 cups uncooked short-grain white rice
- 2 1/4 cups water
- 1/4 cup soy sauce
- 2 teaspoons honey
- 1 teaspoon minced garlic
- 3 ounces firm tofu, cut into 1/2 inch strips
- 2 tablespoons rice vinegar
- 4 sheets nori seaweed sheets
- 1/2 cucumber, julienned
- 1/2 avocado, julienned
- 1 small carrot, julienned

Direction

- Cover rice with water in a large saucepan and leave it to sit for half an hour.
- Mix garlic, honey and soy sauce in a shallow dish. Marinate tofu for a minimum of half an hour in this mixture.
- Bring to boil the water and rice and then decrease the heat. Leave it to simmer for approximately twenty minutes or until sticky and thick. Mix rice vinegar with the cooked rice in a large glass bowl.
- Onto a bamboo mat, put a sheet of nori. Onto the nori, spread 1/4 of rice evenly with wet hands leaving approximately half inch at the top edge of nori. Put two strips of the marinated tofu end to end around one inch from bottom. Next to the tofu, put two strips of cuke, then avocado and carrot.
- Using the mat to help, fold the nori tightly from bottom to make a tight roll. Half inch at the top, seal by moistening with water. Repeat this with the ingredients remaining. Use a serrated knife to cut into slices of one inch thick.

Nutrition Information

- Calories: 289 calories;
- Total Fat: 4.8
- Sodium: 734
- Total Carbohydrate: 53.6
- Cholesterol: 0
- Protein: 8.1

978. Vegetarian Shepherd's Pie II

Serving: 8 | Prep: 15mins | Cook: 1hours | Ready in:

Ingredients

- 2 cups vegetable broth, divided
- 1 teaspoon yeast extract spread, e.g. Marmite/Vegemite
- 1/2 cup dry lentils
- 1/4 cup pearl barley
- 1 large carrot, diced
- 1/2 onion, finely chopped
- 1/2 cup walnuts, coarsely chopped
- 3 potatoes, chopped
- 1 teaspoon all-purpose flour
- 1/2 teaspoon water
- salt and pepper to taste

Direction

- Set oven to 175° C (350° F) and start preheating.
- In a big saucepan on medium-low heat, combine barley, lentils, yeast extract, and 1 1/4 cups broth. Allow to simmer 30 minutes.
- At the same time, combine walnuts, onion, carrot and the remaining 3/4 cup broth in a medium saucepan; cook for 15 minutes until tender.
- Meanwhile, heat a big pot filled with salted water to a boil. Place in potatoes; cook for 15 minutes until tender yet still firm. Drain potatoes then mash.
- Mix water and flour together; blend into the carrot mixture then allow to simmer until thickened. Mix together lentil mixture and carrot mixture, season with pepper and salt. Transfer the mixture into a 2-qt. casserole dish. Using a spoon to arrange mashed potatoes atop lentil mixture.
- Put into the preheated oven and bake for 30 minutes until slightly browned on top.

Nutrition Information

- Calories: 184 calories;
- Total Carbohydrate: 29.8
- Cholesterol: 0
- Protein: 6.2
- Total Fat: 5.2
- Sodium: 147

979. Vegetarian Spanish Rice

Serving: 4 | Prep: 10mins | Cook: 45mins | Ready in:

Ingredients

- 1 (16 ounce) can stewed tomatoes
- 1 1/2 cups water
- 1 cup uncooked brown rice
- 1/2 large orange bell pepper, diced
- 1/2 yellow onion
- 1/4 cup vegetable oil
- 2 tablespoons ancho chile powder
- 1 cube vegetable bouillon (such as The Organic Gourmet™)

Direction

- In a saucepan, combine vegetable bouillon, ancho chile powder, oil, onion, orange bell pepper, brown rice, water, and stewed tomatoes over low heat. Put on cover, mixing from time to time. Allow to simmer 45 minutes until liquid is almost absorbed and rice is cooked.

Nutrition Information

- Calories: 344 calories;
- Cholesterol: 0
- Protein: 5.4
- Total Fat: 15.5
- Sodium: 257
- Total Carbohydrate: 47.7

980. Veggie Pate

Serving: 16 | Prep: 15mins | Cook: 1hours |Ready in:

Ingredients

- 1 cup sunflower seeds
- 1/2 cup whole wheat flour
- 1/2 cup nutritional yeast
- 1/2 teaspoon salt
- 1/2 cup vegetable oil
- 2 tablespoons lemon juice
- 1 potato, peeled and chopped
- 1 large carrot, peeled and sliced
- 1 onion, chopped
- 1 stalk celery, chopped
- 1 clove garlic, peeled
- 1 1/2 cups water
- 1/2 teaspoon dried thyme
- 1/2 teaspoon dried basil leaves
- 1/2 teaspoon dried sage
- 1/2 teaspoon dried savory
- 1/2 teaspoon ground black pepper
- 1/2 teaspoon ground dry mustard

Direction

- Prepare the oven by preheating to 350 degrees F (175 degrees C). Get an 8x8 inch baking and light grease,
- Blend together the dry mustard, pepper, savory, sage, basil, thyme, water, garlic, celery, onion, carrot, potato, lemon juice, vegetable oil, salt, nutritional yeast, whole wheat flour and sunflower seeds in a food processor. Mix well until becomes smooth.
- The send the mixture to a baking dish. Place inside the preheated oven for 1 hour or until lightly browned and bubble holes appear.

Nutrition Information

- Calories: 102 calories;
- Total Fat: 7.1
- Sodium: 80
- Total Carbohydrate: 7.8
- Cholesterol: 0
- Protein: 3

981. Veggie Quinoa

Serving: 2 | Prep: 10mins | Cook: 25mins |Ready in:

Ingredients

- 1 cup vegetable broth
- 1/2 cup uncooked quinoa
- 2 teaspoons olive oil
- 2 teaspoons minced garlic
- 1/2 cup broccoli florets
- 1/2 cup diced firm tofu
- 1/4 cup vegetable broth
- 1/4 cup sliced mushrooms
- 1 cup chopped fresh spinach

Direction

- Boil 1 cup of vegetable stock in a medium saucepan, then mix in the quinoa and lower the heat to low. Put cover and let it simmer for 20 minutes.
- In a frying pan, heat olive oil on medium heat while the quinoa cooks. Add the tofu, broccoli florets and garlic, then stir for 1 minute. Put cover and let it steam for 2 minutes on low heat. Stir in spinach, mushrooms and 1/4 cup of the vegetable broth. Put cover and let it cook for about 3 minutes on medium heat until the spinach wilts and the mushrooms become soft.
- Mix the vegetable-tofu mixture into the cooked quinoa. Put cover and let it sit for 10 minutes prior to serving.

Nutrition Information

- Calories: 282 calories;

- Sodium: 315
- Total Carbohydrate: 34.9
- Cholesterol: 0
- Protein: 13.3
- Total Fat: 10.8

982. Veneto Chicken

Serving: 8 | Prep: 15mins | Cook: 50mins | Ready in:

Ingredients

- 3 large tomatoes - peeled, seeded and chopped
- 1 (3 pound) whole chicken, cut into pieces
- 4 tablespoons olive oil
- 1 onion, chopped
- 1 stalk celery, chopped
- 1/2 cup dry white wine
- 1/4 teaspoon dried oregano
- 1 pinch salt
- 1 pinch ground black pepper
- 2 tablespoons balsamic vinegar
- 1/4 pound fresh mushrooms, sliced

Direction

- Coat chicken lightly in flour. Over medium-high heat, heat oil. Briefly fry chicken pieces; turn to brown evenly. Add celery and onion; cook for 1-2 minutes. Stir in chopped tomatoes and wine. Season with ground pepper, salt and oregano as preferred. Cover, lower the heat; simmer gently for half an hour, turn pieces once.
- Pour in mushrooms and balsamic vinegar; cook for 5-10 more minutes.

Nutrition Information

- Calories: 463 calories;
- Total Fat: 32.6
- Sodium: 130
- Total Carbohydrate: 5.7
- Cholesterol: 128
- Protein: 32.9

983. Very Berry And Soy Delicious Ice Pops

Serving: 12 | Prep: 15mins | Cook: | Ready in:

Ingredients

- 1 pint blueberries
- 1 pint strawberries, hulled
- 1/2 cup brown sugar
- 2 1/2 cups vanilla soy milk

Direction

- In batches, puree strawberries and blueberries in food processor/blender. Strain into medium bowl through a cheesecloth-lined sieve.
- Mix brown sugar into berries. Mix soymilk in till blended well. Put mixture in small paper cups to 2/3 full. Freeze till it starts to firm. Insert wooden sticks. Freeze for 2-3 hours till firm.

Nutrition Information

- Calories: 83 calories;
- Total Carbohydrate: 17.8
- Cholesterol: 0
- Protein: 1.8
- Total Fat: 1
- Sodium: 26

984. Vietnamese Spring Rolls

Serving: 4 | Prep: 10mins | Cook: 15mins | Ready in:

Ingredients

- 1/2 (6.75 ounce) package dried rice noodles
- 8 rice wrappers (8.5 inch diameter)

- 8 fresh mint leaves
- 8 cooked medium shrimp, sliced in half lengthwise
- 1 1/2 cups bean sprouts
- 3 tablespoons fish sauce, or to taste
- 1/2 cup cilantro leaves

Direction

- In a big bowl with hot water, put rice noodles in and soak for about 15 minutes until cooked. Drain then rinse using cold water. Fill hot water in a big bowl then soak rice wrapper sheets, one by one, for about 20 seconds until soft yet rather firm. Put sheets on a big dish cloth, then separate from each other. Put a mint leaf in the middle of every wrapper. Put two halves of shrimp on mint leaf, then top with a small handful of noodles, then add 5-6 bean sprouts. Season with fish sauce to taste then top with cilantro leaves.
- Roll, burrito style, by folding the wrapper's bottom on the filling in the middle. Fold in right and left sides, then roll the whole thing tightly away from you.

Nutrition Information

- Calories: 145 calories;
- Cholesterol: 20
- Protein: 5.2
- Total Fat: 0.4
- Sodium: 890
- Total Carbohydrate: 29.7

985. Wacky Cake VIII

Serving: 10 | Prep: | Cook: | Ready in:

Ingredients

- 1 1/2 cups all-purpose flour
- 1 cup white sugar
- 4 tablespoons unsweetened cocoa powder
- 1 teaspoon baking soda
- 1/2 teaspoon salt
- 1 teaspoon vanilla extract
- 1 tablespoon cider vinegar
- 6 tablespoons vegetable oil
- 1 cup water

Direction

- Set oven to 3500F (1750C) and preheat.
- In an 8x8-inch ungreased cake pan, sift together cocoa, soda, salt, sugar and flour. Create three depressions. In the first well, add oil, add vinegar into second, and add vanilla into third well. Pour water over all, and use fork to mix well.
- Put in the prepared oven and bake at 350°F (1750C) until a toothpick inserted comes out clean, about 30 to 40 minutes. Use your favorite icing to frost the cake.

Nutrition Information

- Calories: 225 calories;
- Sodium: 243
- Total Carbohydrate: 35.5
- Cholesterol: 0
- Protein: 2.4
- Total Fat: 8.7

986. War Cake

Serving: 18 | Prep: | Cook: | Ready in:

Ingredients

- 1 cup packed brown sugar
- 1 1/4 cups water
- 1 cup raisins
- 1 cup chopped walnuts
- 1/2 cup chopped candied citron
- 1/3 cup shortening
- 1/2 teaspoon salt
- 1 teaspoon ground nutmeg

- 1 teaspoon ground cinnamon
- 2 cups all-purpose flour
- 5 teaspoons baking powder

Direction

- Set oven to 350°F (175°C) and start preheating. Grease a 9x13-inch baking pan.
- Mix water and brown sugar over medium heat, in a large saucepan. Add cinnamon, nutmeg, salt, shortening, candied citron, nuts and raisins; boil the mixture for 3 minutes. Take out of the heat; cool.
- Sift in baking powder and flour; stir until blended well. Place in greased pan.
- Bake for 45 minutes at 350°F (175°C) or until the inserted toothpick in the center is clean when coming out. Take out of the oven; place on wire rack to cool. Leave in pan; cut into squares.

Nutrition Information

- Calories: 220 calories;
- Sodium: 224
- Total Carbohydrate: 35.7
- Cholesterol: 0
- Protein: 2.7
- Total Fat: 8.3

987. Watermelon Fruit Bowl

Serving: 20 | Prep: 30mins | Cook: 5mins | Ready in:

Ingredients

- 1 large watermelon
- 1 cantaloupe, halved and seeded
- 1 honeydew melon, halved and seeded
- 2 (15 ounce) cans mandarin oranges, drained
- 2 (20 ounce) cans pineapple chunks, drained
- 2 cups halved fresh strawberries
- 2 cups seedless grapes
- 1/2 cup water
- 1/4 cup white sugar
- 2 tablespoons grated lemon zest

Direction

- Cut off the top 1/4 section of the watermelon, using a big, sharp knife. Take out the flesh from inside of watermelon, using a melon baller and remove as many seeds as you can. Leave inside the shell of watermelon with 1/2" of flesh. Scoop honeydew and cantaloupe in the same manner, removing as much flesh as you can and get rid of the rinds. Chill the fruits independently until assembly.
- Bring water and sugar in a small saucepan to a boil on moderately high heat. Take away from the heat and keep on stirring until sugar has dissolved thoroughly. Put in lemon zest and set aside to cool.
- To serve, in a big mixing bowl, add grapes, strawberries, pineapple, oranges, honeydew, cantaloupe and watermelon balls. Drizzle over with syrup and toss carefully. Turn the mixture to the watermelon bowl and serve. Set aside any unfitted fruit mixture. There will be enough fruit to refill the bowl.

Nutrition Information

- Calories: 179 calories;
- Sodium: 23
- Total Carbohydrate: 45.4
- Cholesterol: 0
- Protein: 2.8
- Total Fat: 0.7

988. Western Style Baked Beans

Serving: 32 | Prep: 15mins | Cook: 3hours10mins | Ready in:

Ingredients

- 1 pound ground beef
- 2 (28 ounce) cans baked beans with pork
- 1 pound bacon, cooked and crumbled
- 1/2 pound cooked ham, chopped
- 2 tablespoons minced onion
- 1 tablespoon chili powder
- 1/4 cup ketchup
- 1/4 cup packed brown sugar
- 1 tablespoon molasses
- 1/4 cup water (optional)

Direction

- In a big skillet, crumble the ground beef on medium-high heat and let it cook and stir for 5-10 minutes, until it has no visible pink color. Drain off the grease and place the beef into a 4-qt. or bigger slow cooker. Stir in the molasses, brown sugar, ketchup, chili powder, onion, ham, bacon and baked beans. Mix in water if it seems thick. Put on cover and let it cook for 6-8 hours on Low or 3 hours on High.

Nutrition Information

- Calories: 186 calories;
- Protein: 11.6
- Total Fat: 9.7
- Sodium: 617
- Total Carbohydrate: 13.5
- Cholesterol: 32

989. Whipped Banana "Ice Cream"

Serving: 1 | Prep: 5mins | Cook: |Ready in:

Ingredients

- 2 bananas, peeled and sliced

Direction

- In an airtight container, add sliced bananas and freeze for 1 1/2 hours, until solid.
- In a blender, process frozen bananas until smooth and whipped.

Nutrition Information

- Calories: 210 calories;
- Total Fat: 0.8
- Protein: 2.6
- Sodium: 2
- Total Carbohydrate: 53.9
- Cholesterol: 0

990. Whipped Raspberry Instant Pudding

Serving: 2 | Prep: 5mins | Cook: |Ready in:

Ingredients

- 2 cups fresh raspberries
- 3 tablespoons white sugar

Direction

- Use back of spoon to mash raspberries till jelly-like layer appears on top in a bowl. Freeze for 5 minutes.
- Mix sugar in mashed raspberries. Spoon bottom raspberries layer on top and mix. Repeat 5-6 times till incorporated well. Freeze for 15 minutes then serve chilled.

Nutrition Information

- Calories: 133 calories;
- Cholesterol: 0
- Protein: 1.1
- Total Fat: 0.7
- Sodium: 0
- Total Carbohydrate: 33

991. White Chocolate Nut Free Keto And Vegan Fat Bombs

Serving: 16 | Prep: 5mins | Cook: | Ready in:

Ingredients

- 1/2 cup melted coconut oil
- 1/2 cup melted white cocoa butter
- 1/2 teaspoon low-calorie natural sweetener (such as Swerve®)

Direction

- In a food processor, blend the sweetener, cocoa butter and coconut oil for about 2 minutes until creamy. Fill the mini muffin cups with the mixture and let it chill in the fridge for about 30 minutes until set.

Nutrition Information

- Calories: 119 calories;
- Total Carbohydrate: 0
- Cholesterol: 0
- Protein: 0
- Total Fat: 13.6
- Sodium: 0

992. Wild Rice Pilaf

Serving: 5 | Prep: 5mins | Cook: 25mins | Ready in:

Ingredients

- 1/2 pound sausage
- 1 (6 ounce) package uncooked long grain and wild rice
- 1 (4.5 ounce) can sliced mushrooms

Direction

- In a medium skillet over medium high heat, cook sausage until evenly brown. Drain and put aside.
- In the meantime, in a saucepan, bring water to a boil. Add rice and mix in sausage and mushrooms. Lower heat, cover and simmer for 20 minutes.

Nutrition Information

- Calories: 307 calories;
- Total Carbohydrate: 28.8
- Cholesterol: 32
- Protein: 9.9
- Total Fat: 16.8
- Sodium: 971

993. Wild Rice And Asparagus Chicken Breasts

Serving: 2 | Prep: 20mins | Cook: 10mins | Ready in:

Ingredients

- 1 whole boneless, skinless chicken breast, cubed
- 2 cups wild rice, cooked
- 1/2 pound fresh asparagus
- 3 tablespoons hoisin sauce
- 4 tablespoons peanut oil
- 1 tablespoon brown sugar

Direction

- Cut asparagus to 3/4-in.-1-in. pieces; discard spear's tough bottoms. Mix brown sugar and hoisin sauce in small bowl; put aside. Reheat cooked rice/prep rice then keep warm.
- Heat wok on medium high heat. Dribble 1 tbsp. oil around rim when hot; stir fry asparagus for 2 about minutes. Take out of wok; keep warm then heat wok on high heat.
- Heat the wok for high heat; add chicken pieces and 2 tbsp. oil. Stir fry till chicken isn't pink.

Add hoisin/sugar sauce and reserved asparagus; stir fry together till pieces get coated in sauce. Serve on hot rice.

Nutrition Information

- Calories: 635 calories;
- Sodium: 473
- Total Carbohydrate: 56.6
- Cholesterol: 69
- Protein: 37.1
- Total Fat: 30

994. Williamsburg Pork Cake

Serving: 14 | Prep: 1hours | Cook: 1hours30mins | Ready in:

Ingredients

- 1/2 cup brandy
- 2 1/2 cups raisins
- 1 1/2 cups dried currants
- 1/2 pound finely ground salt pork
- 1 cup boiling water
- 1 cup molasses
- 1/2 cup brown sugar
- 3 1/2 cups all-purpose flour
- 1 teaspoon baking powder
- 1 tablespoon ground allspice
- 1 tablespoon ground cinnamon
- 1/2 teaspoon ground nutmeg
- 1/2 teaspoon ground cloves

Direction

- Mix currants, raisins and brandy in a medium saucepan. Boil the mixture; take out of the heat. Put aside until all liquid is absorbed and mixture is cooled.
- Set the oven to 275°F (135°C) and start preheating. Grease and flour a 10 inch tube pan. Sift together cloves, nutmeg, cinnamon, allspice, baking powder and flour. Put aside.
- Mix sugar, molasses, boiling water and ground salt pork in a large bowl. Whisk well. Add flour mixture; whisk until incorporated. Stir in raisin mixture. Place batter into floured pan.
- Bake for 90 minutes in the prepared oven or until the inserted toothpick in the cake's center is clean when coming out. Cool in the pan for 15 minutes. Take out of the pan; completely cool.

Nutrition Information

- Calories: 458 calories;
- Total Carbohydrate: 75.4
- Cholesterol: 14
- Protein: 5.2
- Total Fat: 13.6
- Sodium: 272

995. World's Best Oatmeal Cookies

Serving: 24 | Prep: 15mins | Cook: 12mins | Ready in:

Ingredients

- 1/2 cup shortening
- 1/4 cup white sugar
- 1/2 cup packed brown sugar
- 1 egg
- 1/2 teaspoon vanilla extract
- 3/4 cup all-purpose flour
- 1/2 teaspoon baking soda
- 1/2 teaspoon salt
- 1 cup rolled oats
- 1/2 cup chopped walnuts

Direction

- Set oven to preheat to 375 degrees F (190 degrees C)
- Combine brown sugar, white sugar and shortening in a big bowl until smooth. Mix in

vanilla and egg. Mix together salt, baking soda and flour; mix into the batter until combined. Stir in walnuts and oats. On the greased cookie sheet, drop by teaspoonful, keep 1 inch apart.
- Let it bake until browned a bit, for 12 minutes. Remove cookies to the wire racks right away to cool down.

Nutrition Information

- Calories: 109 calories;
- Protein: 1.5
- Total Fat: 6.3
- Sodium: 79
- Total Carbohydrate: 12.2
- Cholesterol: 8

996. Yellow Squash And Zucchini Delight

Serving: 4 | Prep: 15mins | Cook: 25mins | Ready in:

Ingredients

- 1 zucchini, sliced
- 1 yellow squash, sliced
- 1/2 small head cabbage, sliced
- 1 large onion, sliced
- 1 (14.5 ounce) can fat-free chicken broth

Direction

- In big pot, put onion, cabbage, yellow squash and zucchini. Put broth on veggies; boil on medium heat. Lower heat to low and cover; simmer for 20-30 minutes.

Nutrition Information

- Calories: 63 calories;
- Total Fat: 0.3
- Sodium: 174
- Total Carbohydrate: 12.3
- Cholesterol: 0

- Protein: 4.8

997. Yummy Vegan Chocolate Pudding

Serving: 4 | Prep: 5mins | Cook: 25mins | Ready in:

Ingredients

- 2 tablespoons cornstarch
- 1 cup soy milk
- 1 cup soy creamer
- 1/2 cup white sugar
- 3 tablespoons egg replacer (dry)
- 3 ounces semisweet chocolate, chopped
- 2 teaspoons vanilla extract

Direction

- Mix together soy creamer, soy milk and cornstarch in a medium saucepan, then stir to dissolve the cornstarch. Put on moderate heat and stir in sugar, then cook until the mixture comes to a low boil while whisking often. Take away from the heat.
- Whisk together 1/4 cup of hot milk mixture and egg replacer in a small bowl, then turn back to the pan along with leftover milk mixture. Cook on moderate heat until thick but not boiling, about 3-4 minutes.
- In a medium bowl, add chocolate and put in hot milk mixture. Allow to stand about half minute then stir the mixture until smooth and melted. Allow to cool about 10-15 minutes then stir in vanilla.
- Transfer into custard cups or ramekins, then use plastic wrap to cover and allow to cool at room temperature. Chill about 3 hours to overnight prior to serving.

Nutrition Information

- Calories: 594 calories;
- Sodium: 144

- Total Carbohydrate: 87.8
- Cholesterol: < 1
- Protein: 5.7
- Total Fat: 25.8

- Protein: 20.6
- Total Fat: 21.6
- Sodium: 1250
- Total Carbohydrate: 32.4

998. Zesty Porcupine Meatballs

Serving: 5 | Prep: 20mins | Cook: 20mins | Ready in:

Ingredients

- 1 egg
- 2 (10.75 ounce) cans condensed tomato soup
- 1/4 cup instant rice
- 1/4 cup chopped onion
- 1 tablespoon chopped fresh parsley
- 1 teaspoon onion salt
- 1/4 teaspoon ground black pepper
- 1 pound lean ground beef
- 1/4 cup Worcestershire sauce

Direction

- Use a fork, lightly beat the egg, then put in a heaping tablespoon of the soup and lightly mix. Mix in rice, pepper, onion salt, parsley, and onion. Stir in the ground beef, mix well with hands. Form the mixture into 1 1/2 inch round meatballs.
- Use cooking spray to coat a large skillet over medium heat. Cook the meatballs and brown on all sides.
- Mix Worcestershire and the remaining soup (decrease or increase the Worcestershire to your desire), stir until smooth, then scoop over the meatballs. Use a lid to cover and simmer for around 20-30 minutes, stirring every few minutes.

Nutrition Information

- Calories: 408 calories;
- Cholesterol: 105

999. Zesty Zucchini And Squash

Serving: 6 | Prep: 15mins | Cook: 25mins | Ready in:

Ingredients

- 3 medium small yellow squash, cubed
- 3 small zucchini, cubed
- 1 (10 ounce) can diced tomatoes with green chile peppers
- 1/2 onion, chopped
- salt to taste
- garlic powder to taste

Direction

- Mix together garlic powder, salt, onion, chiles, tomatoes, zucchini and squash in a big saucepan. Bring to a boil on moderately high heat.
- Reduce heat to low and cook until crisp-tender.

Nutrition Information

- Calories: 43 calories;
- Sodium: 328
- Total Carbohydrate: 9.7
- Cholesterol: 0
- Protein: 1.8
- Total Fat: 0.4

1000. Zucchini Galore

Serving: 3 | Prep: 5mins | Cook: 5mins | Ready in:

Ingredients

- 3 zucchini
- 1 sweet onion
- 2 tablespoons olive oil
- salt to taste

Direction

- Halve the zucchini lengthways, then slice crosswise into thin half-moons. Dice onion into big pieces. Heat a big skillet on moderately high heat, then add in olive oil. Sauté onion in the hot oil until browned slightly. Stir in zucchini and keep on sautéing until zucchini is lightly browned and tender. Season to taste with salt.

Nutrition Information

- Calories: 122 calories;
- Protein: 2.7
- Total Fat: 9.3
- Sodium: 8
- Total Carbohydrate: 9.1
- Cholesterol: 0

1001. Zucchini Saute

Serving: 6 | Prep: 20mins | Cook: 25mins | Ready in:

Ingredients

- 1 tablespoon vegetable oil
- 1 onion, sliced
- 2 tomatoes, chopped
- 2 pounds zucchini, peeled and cut into 1 inch thick slices
- 1 green bell pepper, chopped
- salt to taste
- ground black pepper to taste
- 1/4 cup uncooked white rice
- 1/2 cup water

Direction

- In a sauté pan, heat oil over medium heat. Put in onion then cook and stir for 3mins. Put in green pepper, zucchini and tomatoes then mix. Use black pepper and salt to season. Decrease heat then cover. Allow it to simmer for 5 minutes.
- Mix in water and rice then cover. Cook for 20 minutes over low heat.

Nutrition Information

- Calories: 94 calories;
- Protein: 3.2
- Total Fat: 2.8
- Sodium: 19
- Total Carbohydrate: 16.1
- Cholesterol: 0

Index

A

Almond 6,8,9,10,11,12,13,171,172,233,243,268,289,335,376,412,455,456

Apple 3,6,8,9,10,12,13,16,37,55,175,176,234,244,285,315,324,400,403,456,457

Apricot 6,176

Arborio rice 261

Artichoke 6,13,177,450

Asafoetida 73,74

Asparagus 6,9,14,179,298,486

Avocado 6,7,9,13,86,181,182,287,427,451,457

B

Bacon 5,6,7,9,10,134,135,139,153,156,184,185,203,279,294,295,339

Banana 6,7,9,10,14,171,191,192,193,289,310,315,458,485

Basil 8,9,13,243,263,445

Basmati rice 46,237,406

Beans 3,4,6,7,8,9,10,11,12,13,14,40,54,63,84,85,94,174,180,183,185,186,193,202,203,206,246,255,257,258,269,271,294,295,304,325,335,354,358,373,378,393,394,397,406,412,413,418,440,473,484

Beef 3,4,5,6,7,8,9,10,11,12,23,35,38,41,77,100,178,194,198,215,220,240,241,247,258,286,304,320,336,357,361,366,377,398,401,412,416

Beer 4,7,12,67,196,416

Beetroot 7,197

Berry 13,14,447,482

Biscotti 7,8,9,200,243,244,286

Blueberry 7,14,204,205,459,476

Bread 3,8,10,16,220,259,331

Brie 41,44,254,476,482

Broccoli 7,13,209,210,431

Broth 7,188,284

Brussels sprouts 102,212,399

Buckwheat 3,26

Burger 3,4,5,7,9,10,13,24,72,98,106,217,276,284,306,420

Butter 3,5,6,7,8,9,10,11,13,14,28,102,171,175,199,213,223,231,267,272,275,310,325,327,365,374,375,419,448,460

C

Cabbage 3,4,5,7,8,9,12,35,89,102,214,241,279,404

Cake 3,6,7,8,9,10,11,12,13,14,52,174,175,191,192,198,205,231,240,248,255,266,267,271,274,277,285,287,289,310,313,324,347,355,360,379,387,389,401,430,434,462,468,471,483,487

Caramel 5,7,11,14,135,221,353,362,468

Carrot 7,8,216,217,218,254

Cashew 7,9,14,192,219,287,461

Cauliflower 3,14,42,464,466

Caviar 13,444

Celery 11,346

Chard 13,440

Cheddar 113,114,220,470,479

Cheese 5,8,10,14,113,260,285,313,340,461,465,470

Cherry 8,222

Chicken 3,4,5,6,7,8,9,10,11,12,13,14,16,20,21,23,25,26,29,30,31,32,43,48,49,51,59,60,61,63,68,74,78,81,84,93,94,95,99,101,104,107,125,126,136,173,176,186,206,212,213,222,224,225,2

26,227,228,247,261,276,282,283,284,285,291,297,299,302,311,321,322,324,330,334,337,342,344,346,349,357,361,374,379,380,394,400,411,413,414,421,422,427,438,441,445,454,482,486

Chickpea 5,7,8,13,14,116,121,127,206,228,425,428,460,462

Chips 7,11,187,378

Chocolate 7,8,9,10,11,12,13,14,192,198,230,231,232,233,236,238,250,260,274,310,350,372,390,396,427,457,462,463,469,472,486,488

Cider 12,415

Cinnamon 3,8,10,37,234,248,315

Cocktail 8,234,235

Coconut 5,7,8,9,10,11,12,13,14,103,206,224,230,233,236,237,238,245,264,293,327,331,354,363,381,382,390,414,453,457,459,462,463

Cod 3,4,7,15,65,80,187

Coffee 8,12,248,398

Cola 3,34

Collar 13,421

Couscous 4,5,8,10,13,57,99,242,341,450

Crab 6,8,145,243

Crackers 9,288

Cranberry 3,4,8,9,12,37,93,243,244,288,384

Cream 3,7,8,9,10,11,12,14,37,38,192,193,200,223,230,232,245,260,261,267,269,272,285,291,293,313,352,354,365,371,382,386,396,419,453,458,459,463,465,476,477,485

Crisps 9,288

Crumble 111,139,295,340

Cucumber 5,9,139,296

Curry 3,4,5,8,11,12,13,14,49,83,101,112,116,118,119,228,345,357,414,428,460,462,464,466,473,475

D

Dab 383

Dal 4,73

Date 5,7,8,99,185,252

Dijon mustard 87,88,142,146,150,154,166,167,243,314,476

Dill 5,6,8,131,138,163,255

Duck 3,4,42,81

Dumplings 8,12,227,385

E

Edam 13,14,427,464

Egg 3,4,5,9,10,12,45,46,86,101,105,127,266,267,268,341,391,417

F

Fat 6,8,9,10,13,14,15,16,17,18,19,20,21,22,23,24,25,26,27,28,29,30,31,32,33,34,35,36,37,38,39,40,41,42,43,44,45,46,47,48,49,50,51,52,53,54,55,56,57,58,59,60,61,62,63,64,65,66,67,68,69,70,71,72,73,74,75,76,77,78,79,80,81,82,83,84,85,86,87,88,89,90,91,92,93,94,95,96,97,98,99,100,101,102,103,104,105,106,107,108,109,110,111,112,113,114,115,116,117,118,119,120,121,122,123,124,125,126,127,128,129,130,131,132,133,134,135,136,137,138,139,140,141,142,143,144,145,146,147,148,149,150,151,152,153,154,155,156,157,158,159,160,161,162,163,164,165,166,167,168,169,170,171,172,173,174,175,176,177,178,179,180,181,182,183,184,185,186,187,188,189,190,191,192,193,194,195,196,197,198,199,200,201,202,203,204,205,206,207,208,209,210,211,212,213,214,215,216,217,218,219,220,221,222,223,224,225,226,227,228,229,230,231,232,233,234,235,236,237,238,239,240,241,242,243,244,245,246,247,248,249,250,251,252,253,254,255,256,257,258,259,260,261,262,263,264,265,266,267,268,269,270,271,272,273,274,275,276,277,278,279,280,281,282,283,284,285,286,287,288,289,290,291,292,293,294,2

95,296,297,298,299,300,301,302,303,304,305,306,307,308,309,310,311,312,313,314,315,316,317,318,319,320,321,322,323,324,325,326,327,328,329,330,331,332,333,334,335,336,337,338,339,340,341,342,343,344,345,346,347,348,349,350,351,352,353,354,355,356,357,358,359,360,361,362,363,364,365,366,367,368,369,370,371,372,373,374,375,376,377,378,379,380,381,382,383,384,385,386,387,388,389,390,391,392,393,394,395,396,397,398,399,400,401,402,403,404,405,406,407,408,409,410,411,412,413,414,415,416,417,418,419,420,421,422,423,424,425,426,427,428,429,430,431,432,433,434,435,436,437,438,439,440,441,442,443,444,445,446,447,448,449,450,451,452,453,454,455,456,457,458,459,460,461,462,463,464,465,466,467,468,469,470,471,472,473,474,475,476,477,478,479,480,481,482,483,484,485,486,487,488,489,490

Fennel 3,48

Fish 3,4,6,9,49,54,65,74,78,80,180,274

Flank 3,23

Flour 6,9,172,274,275,287

French bread 452

Fruit 4,7,11,14,60,66,216,363,366,484

Fudge 10,13,327,448

G

Game 3,36

Garlic 3,4,5,6,9,10,11,12,20,23,36,43,51,94,105,114,158,282,283,284,313,321,360,374,399,410

Gin 3,4,7,9,10,11,12,49,52,56,191,200,267,269,285,286,292,298,310,334,358,367,396

Gnocchi 4,8,9,82,254,290

Grain 11,370

Grapes 9,282

Gratin 14,469

Gravy 4,57,81

Guacamole 7,8,9,10,12,195,199,252,262,270,296,305,307,412

H

Halibut 4,10,11,56,306,368

Ham 3,4,7,10,34,57,94,204,308

Hazelnut 9,295,457

Heart 10,83,108,311

Herbs 9,299

Honey 3,4,5,8,10,20,60,65,94,123,126,225,313,314,328

Hummus 7,9,10,13,14,195,197,201,264,270,316,317,320,449,473

I

Icing 307

J

Jam 4,10,63,84,322

K

Kale 7,10,13,187,196,325,431

Ketchup 4,57

L

Lamb 4,10,65,85,87,331,332,333,336

Leek 4,9,14,86,270,469

Lemon 4,9,10,11,12,13,65,276,285,295,299,321,334,335,336,344,349,400,411,442

Lentils 3,4,14,31,66,95,464,466

Lettuce 6,8,178,222

Lime 3,5,8,10,13,14,24,106,228,327,442,466

Ling 10,12,337,405

Lobster 3,4,55,67

M

Macaroni 6,8,14,143,260,470

Mandarin 10,341

Mango 3,6,8,10,11,25,159,247,302,303,306,342,367,381

Marsala wine 46

Marshmallow 10,313

Marzipan 11,345

Mayonnaise 11,145,347,360

Meat 4,5,7,8,10,11,12,13,14,69,104,115,122,222,234,235,326,340,348,383,439,446,475,489

Melon 5,110

Milk 7,8,9,11,12,14,206,219,224,236,245,266,267,291,327,328,354,363,414,462

Mint 8,11,13,14,230,354,435,468

Molasses 11,356,357

Monkfish 9,270

Mushroom 3,5,7,8,10,11,12,38,114,127,213,229,242,261,301,312,343,361,368,404,408

Mussels 4,75

Mustard 3,5,6,7,10,12,20,48,134,142,166,212,314,328,398

N

Noodles 4,7,8,12,84,221,229,237,407

Nori 14,479

Nut 4,5,7,8,9,11,13,14,15,16,17,18,19,20,21,22,23,24,25,26,27,28,29,30,31,32,33,34,35,36,37,38,39,40,41,42,43,44,45,46,47,48,49,50,51,52,53,54,55,56,57,58,59,60,61,62,63,64,65,66,67,68,69,70,71,72,73,74,75,76,77,78,79,80,81,82,83,84,85,86,87,88,89,90,91,92,93,94,95,96,97,98,99,100,101,102,103,104,105,106,107,108,109,110,111,112,113,114,115,116,117,118,119,120,121,122,123,124,125,126,127,128,129,130,131,132,133,134,135,136,137,138,139,140,141,142,143,144,145,146,147,148,149,150,151,152,153,154,155,156,157,158,159,160,161,162,163,164,165,166,167,168,169,170,171,172,173,174,175,176,177,178,179,180,181,182,183,184,185,186,187,188,189,190,191,192,193,194,195,196,197,198,199,200,201,202,203,204,205,206,207,208,209,210,211,212,213,214,215,216,217,218,219,220,221,222,223,224,225,226,227,228,229,230,231,232,233,234,235,236,237,238,239,240,241,242,243,244,245,246,247,248,249,250,251,252,253,254,255,256,257,258,259,260,261,262,263,264,265,266,267,268,269,270,271,272,273,274,275,276,277,278,279,280,281,282,283,284,285,286,287,288,289,290,291,292,293,294,295,296,297,298,299,300,301,302,303,304,305,306,307,308,309,310,311,312,313,314,315,316,317,318,319,320,321,322,323,324,325,326,327,328,329,330,331,332,333,334,335,336,337,338,339,340,341,342,343,344,345,346,347,348,349,350,351,352,353,354,355,356,357,358,359,360,361,362,363,364,365,366,367,368,369,370,371,372,373,374,375,376,377,378,379,380,381,382,383,384,385,386,387,388,389,390,391,392,393,394,395,396,397,398,399,400,401,402,403,404,405,406,407,408,409,410,411,412,413,414,415,416,417,418,419,420,421,422,423,424,425,426,427,428,429,430,431,432,433,434,435,436,437,438,439,440,441,442,443,444,445,446,447,448,449,450,451,452,453,454,455,456,457,458,459,460,461,462,463,464,465,466,467,468,469,470,471,472,473,474,475,476,477,478,479,480,481,482,483,484,485,486,487,488,489,490

O

Oatmeal 3,5,6,7,9,10,11,13,14,37,103,119,171,173,192,238,266,293,311,329,363,365,435,458,487

Oats 3,5,8,14,45,114,115,230,469

Oil 3,8,9,12,18,20,24,51,54,63,64,184,231,249,263,271,285,297,299,300,304,314,324,334,337,344,389,390,427,470

Okra 9,11,280,365

Olive 3,6,8,9,20,153,231,263,271

Onion 5,7,11,12,13,135,196,221,367,387,430,439

Orange 4,10,11,12,56,267,341,367,380,396

Oyster 8,253

P

Paella 14,478

Pancakes 8,12,241,411

Papaya 11,342

Parfait 13,457

Parmesan 388,454

Parsnip 12,411

Pasta 3,4,5,9,10,11,13,17,38,43,47,59,72,77,78,100,114,263,309,335,347,373,429

Pastry 447

Peach 7,11,186,374

Pear 9,11,277,375,376

Peas 6,7,8,12,13,178,204,248,404,416,434,435

Pecan 8,11,12,13,250,342,376,392,426

Peel 103,129,130,131,136,137,139,140,141,145,149,151,153,154,160,161,162,164,290,337,382,445

Penne 3,7,38,210

Pepper 3,4,5,9,10,11,12,13,46,65,115,220,264,285,296,299,335,343,348,377,388,430,433

Perry 1,2

Pesto 4,12,78,388

Pickle 4,78

Pie 5,7,8,10,11,12,13,14,23,111,122,199,244,246,260,300,327,329,370,376,390,391,402,422,447,449,456,466,471,480

Pineapple 9,10,11,13,14,278,308,379,380,381,443,468

Pistachio 8,12,244,382

Pizza 3,5,26,120,123

Polenta 7,209

Popcorn 11,353

Pork 3,4,5,7,9,10,11,12,14,21,44,51,53,71,75,79,92,93,95,106,183,184,262,273,297,298,314,344,384,398,405,413,415,487

Port 4,7,10,12,80,220,301,384

Potato 3,4,5,6,7,8,9,10,11,12,13,14,33,80,116,118,128,129,130,131,132,133,134,135,136,137,138,139,140,141,142,143,144,145,146,147,148,149,150,151,152,153,154,155,156,157,158,159,160,161,162,163,164,165,166,167,189,214,241,242,284,294,296,312,346,359,369,370,381,386,387,388,400,415,438,454,467,469

Prawn 3,5,24,105

Prosciutto 6,179

Prune 13,438

Pulse 124,218,288,294

Pumpkin 3,5,7,8,9,10,12,13,14,38,115,188,251,289,311,329,389,390,391,392,449,469,470,471,475

Q

Quail 13,432

Quinoa 7,8,11,12,14,218,248,364,394,481

R

Radish 3,6,16,153,154

Raspberry 12,14,394,472,485

Rice 3,4,5,6,7,8,9,10,11,12,13,14,23,32,41,46,50,63,78,84,85,115,120,174,188,195,203,208,209,210,217,234,237,246,253,256,263,281,284,304,316,318,324,338,343,348,351,352,366,378,393,397,406,420,424,425,430,432,445,463,473,474,480,486

Ricotta 14,461

Risotto 8,13,261,450

Roast pork 398

Rosemary 3,4,9,11,31,36,43,85,87,288,344

S

Sage 13,432

Salad 5,6,12,125,128,129,130,131,132,133,134,135,136,137,138,139,140,141,142,143,144,145,146,147,148,149,150,151,15

2,153,154,155,156,157,158,159,160,161,162,163,164,165,166,167,381

Salmon 3,4,5,6,8,9,10,11,12,18,35,40,52,55,76,88,103,160,171,257,274,300,301,319,360,402,417

Salsa 3,4,5,6,7,9,10,11,12,13,25,60,110,170,177,202,278,303,315,342,380,394,402,403,451

Salt 14,133,135,220,243,468

Sausage 3,4,5,7,10,13,32,95,96,111,209,304,423,436,437

Savoy cabbage 108

Scallop 4,12,80,405

Seasoning 243

Sirloin 3,4,51,91

Sorbet 11,13,367,374,380,442

Soup 5,11,13,124,366,422

Spaghetti 4,10,11,13,84,97,321,370,422,423,440

Spinach 4,5,7,9,13,66,114,118,218,269,428,429

Squash 3,5,7,10,12,13,14,28,102,213,310,387,422,460,488,489

Steak 3,4,5,6,7,8,11,12,13,23,25,54,62,88,90,110,166,177,183,215,224,344,403,430,443

Stew 3,10,33,46,322

Stock 51

Strawberry 7,11,13,199,374,432

Stuffing 5,9,13,127,265,432

Sugar 4,7,8,9,11,12,13,88,218,223,238,252,298,352,355,356,374,404,434,435

Swiss chard 440

Syrup 10,307

T

Tabasco 409

Taco 3,7,14,41,182,459

Tamari 3,12,49,412

Tapioca 13,432

Tea 6,172,188

Tequila 5,10,13,105,106,321,442,443

Teriyaki 7,8,13,184,261,443,444

Thai basil 445

Thyme 10,327,328,336

Tilapia 3,7,10,20,44,190,303

Tofu 3,4,5,6,7,8,13,14,54,71,109,117,118,170,189,260,443,448,449,450,451,476

Tomato 3,6,7,8,9,10,11,13,14,15,180,206,218,242,263,278,279,280,296,322,341,365,423,440,451,464

Tongue 3,10,41,336

Trout 10,303

Truffle 13,456

Turkey 3,5,9,12,43,109,111,284,418

V

Veal 5,111

Vegan 3,4,5,6,7,8,9,10,11,12,13,14,38,39,45,62,83,107,112,113,114,115,116,117,118,119,120,173,198,230,232,233,250,254,260,261,271,307,313,340,350,355,360,374,388,396,397,430,454,455,456,457,458,459,460,461,462,463,464,465,466,467,468,469,470,471,472,473,474,475,476,477,486,488

Vegetables 4,7,10,11,12,13,56,188,190,337,353,369,399,450

Vegetarian 5,10,14,121,308,478,479,480

Vinegar 5,7,132,191

W

Walnut 9,11,271,368

Watermelon 14,484

Whisky 4,89

Wine 4,10,65,312,334

Worcestershire sauce

16,22,24,48,69,70,88,89,90,92,106,122,136,137,142,185,186,194,207,215,235,284,294,314,315,323,334,340,344,348,373,420,430,433,437,438,441,443,489

Wraps 6,8,13,178,222,226,444

Z

Zest 3,14,23,489

L

lasagna 118

Conclusion

Thank you again for downloading this book!

I hope you enjoyed reading about my book!

If you enjoyed this book, please take the time to share your thoughts and post a review on Amazon. It'd be greatly appreciated!

Write me an honest review about the book – I truly value your opinion and thoughts and I will incorporate them into my next book, which is already underway.

Thank you!

If you have any questions, **feel free to contact at:** _author@polentarecipes.com_

Lisa Perry

polentarecipes.com

Printed in Great Britain
by Amazon